ECOLOGY, EVOLUTION, AND POPULATION BIOLOGY

Readings from

**SCIENTIFIC
AMERICAN**

ECOLOGY, EVOLUTION, AND POPULATION BIOLOGY

With Introductions by

Edward O. Wilson

Harvard University

W. H. Freeman and Company
San Francisco

Library of Congress Cataloging in Publication Data

Wilson, Edward Osborne, 1929– comp.
  Ecology, Evolution, and population biology.

  Bibliography: p.
  1. Ecology—Addresses, essays, lectures.   2. Evolution—
Addresses, essays, lectures.   3. Biotic communities—
Addresses, essays, lectures.   I. Scientific American.

II. Title.   [DNLM: 1. Biology—Collected works.
2. Ecology—Collected works.   3. Evolution—Collected
works.   QH366.2 W747e 1974]
QH541.145.W54   574.5'08   73–17448
ISBN 0–7167–0888–4
ISBN 0–7167–0887–6 (pbk.)

Most of the SCIENTIFIC AMERICAN articles in
ECOLOGY, EVOLUTION, AND POPULATION
BIOLOGY are available as separate Offprints. For a
complete list of more than 950 articles now available
as Offprints, write to W. H. Freeman and Company,
660 Market Street, San Francisco, California 94104.

Printed in the United States of America

9 8 7 6 5 4 3 2 1

PREFACE

The selection of articles for *Ecology, Evolution, and Population Biology* was motivated by the recognition that modern biology consists of essentially two enterprises. One, molecular and cellular biology, elucidates the machinery of life. Its goal is to explain the ways in which cells, tissues, and organs are constructed out of molecular building blocks and run on chemical reactions. The other discipline, evolutionary biology, is the subject of the present book. Viewing life at the level of whole organisms and populations, it interprets the functions of the machinery used in adapting organisms to the natural environment, and it attempts to trace the history of life from the beginning four billion years ago as giant replicating molecules to the eventual origin of living species.

Ecology and evolutionary theory are the major components of this higher level of biology. Ecology cannot fully explain the relation of organisms to their environment without substantial recourse to evolutionary history and population dynamics. Conversely, evolutionary theory would be mostly nonsense without ecology. The purpose of the present selection of *Scientific American* articles, then, is to clarify the relation between these two disciplines and to direct the reader as truthfully as possible through the series of logical steps that ecologists and other evolutionary biologists follow when considering their subject in its broadest possible terms. By this means it becomes possible to recognize a strong thread of common thought running through the study of even such disparate topics as the evolution of hemoglobin, the nature of plant toxins, and the cycle of energy through the biosphere.

August 1973   Edward O. Wilson

CONTENTS

IV ECOSYSTEMS

Note on cross-references: References to articles included in this book are noted by the title of the article and the page on which it begins; references to articles that are available as Offprints, but are not included here, are noted by the article's title and Offprint number; references to articles published by SCIENTIFIC AMERICAN, but which are not available as Offprints, are noted by the title of the article and the month and year of its publication.

ECOLOGY, EVOLUTION, AND POPULATION BIOLOGY

Two great unifying ideas form the underpinning of modern biology. The first is the well-substantiated belief that every aspect of the functioning of organisms is based on molecular events that are subject to the conventional laws of physics and chemistry. The second idea, compatible with but curiously independent of the first, is the theory of organic evolution. Starting with Charles Darwin's *The Origin of Species* in 1859, evolutionary biology has proliferated into a major discipline that embraces the study of life at all the levels of organization—from molecules and organelles to ecosystems and societies. Complete evolutionary explanations are dual in nature. On the one hand, they provide straightforward historical accounts of lineages—for example, the hypothetical steps in the origin of life from abiotic giant molecules, the origin of mammals from reptiles and their subsequent diversification, the origin of man from ape-like ancestors, and so on. Simultaneously, the explanations illuminate the basic process of evolutionary change itself. This process, as Darwin was the first to realize clearly, is a statistical change that takes place over entire populations. It is not, as Lamarck proposed in the chief rival theory of the nineteenth century, a stepwise modification within single lineages of individuals. Stated in the modern language of genetics, evolution is a *shift in the frequency of genes within total populations*. Darwin theorized, and a century of investigation has confirmed, that most such shifts of a sustained nature are due to natural selection—the capacity of some genotypes to gain more representation in subsequent generations than other genotypes. Evolution by natural selection is simply another phrase for biological adaptation. Biologists, desiring to add the historical dimension to their analysis, study adaptation in this, its deeper meaning. They interpret each phenomenon as a precise genetic response to particular qualities in the natural environment of individual species.

Thus, it is in the study of adaptation that evolutionary theory and ecology are joined. One discipline no longer makes much sense without recourse to the other. In the collection of articles to follow, we will trace the entire line of this reasoning all the way from the gene to the ecosystem. The articles, including both reports of personal research and general reviews, are grouped into four sections briefly summarized as follows:

I. *The Evolutionary Process.* Genes change by mutations, which are primarily alterations of base pairs of DNA that find their initial phenotypic expression as amino acid substitutions in proteins. Mutations are the raw material of evolution. Some survive and reproduce better than others and hence gain in relative frequency; this is, by definition, the process of evolution by natural selection. Natural selection is never perfect in its operation. Many unfavorable genes are always being either phased out or renewed by mutation. Some genes are selected against in the homozygous state but favored when heterozygous or in combination with genes on other loci. These elements of imperfection, insofar as they can be realistically measured, constitute the "genetic load." While reducing the immediate adaptiveness of organisms, they increase the adaptability of future generations by providing genetic flexibility to cope with changes in the environment. Some evolution also occurs by random fluctuations in the gene frequency at least temporarily outside the influence of natural selection.

II. *The multiplication and dispersal of species.* In spite of the irregularities of the evolutionary process, natural selection always tends to make the populations fit more precisely to the existing environment. But the environment is constantly shifting, and populations are consequently forced to track it. They are always a little behind; if they fall too far behind, they become extinct. *Species* are populations that diverge enough from each other during evolution to become reproductively isolated. At this critical juncture in their history, they are freed to evolve along their own paths and to disperse to new distributions that are different from those of all other genetically similar populations.

III. *The growth and interaction of populations.* The multiplication of species sets the stage for the next act in the ecological drama. A newly formed species, instead of breeding with genetically similar populations, can specialize in such a way as to displace these other populations as competitors, eat them as prey, cooperate with them as symbionts, or simply avoid them altogether. Further adjustments are made in evolution to perfect the efficiency of these interactions, some leading to extremely complex physiological and behavioral mechanisms.

IV. *Ecosystems.* The total ensemble of species in a given place, together with all their interactions and the physical environment, comprise the *ecosystem*. An ecosystem is not a random phenomenon. Because the amount of available radiant energy is rigidly limited, allowing only so many plants, herbivores, predators, and other specialists to exist in each unit of area, the number of species soon reaches equilibrium. When the ecosystem is studied as a whole and its species counted out, rules emerge that could not have been predicted from a knowledge of single organisms or species alone. Chemical elements can be seen to cycle in regular and distinctive ways; energy is observed to dissipate during predation at rapid and roughly predictable rates; food chains are found to be limited to five links or less; and so on. The ecosystem is fragile, as the ecology movement of the past ten years has made us all aware. Why it is fragile, and precisely what must be done to hold it together in the face of the human onslaught, is a set of scientific problems of the first magnitude. These problems can be expected to yield only through close study of the evolutionary process by which species have been fitted together to create the observed orderliness of the ecosystem.

I

THE EVOLUTIONARY PROCESS

I
THE EVOLUTIONARY
PROCESS

The success of a species is most accurately measured not by its abundance, the width of its range, or the spectacular qualities of its organisms— but by the length of time it endures before going extinct. The species around us are the temporary winners in this existential game. Dinosaurs were ultimately losers, but the other Mesozoic reptiles that gave rise to birds and mammals are still winning. In order to endure, a species must be both adaptive and adaptable. To be adaptive, its genes must generate phenotypes that fit the environment well enough for immediate survival and reproduction. Adaptability means that as the environment changes—and it is always changing, every generation—new genes and combinations of genes are assembled in offspring that fit the altered conditions well enough for the species to keep going. Whereas completely new genes are created only by mutations, the formation of new combinations of existing genes is speeded by meiosis in the production of sex cells and by the joining of the sex cells in fertilization. Indeed, sexual reproduction has evidently evolved as a device to permit organisms to assemble a variety of genotypes among their offspring. They spread their bets, so to speak, against a capricious and unyielding environment.

The adaptability of populations and of the organisms that comprise them increases with the number of kinds of genes present. In the face of continuing environmental change, this amount of genetic diversity determines the rate at which populations can evolve. It follows that one of the principal tasks of population geneticists is to measure genetic diversity in natural populations. The techniques employed are outlined by Christopher Wills in the first article of this series; they range from ingenious genetic crosses that reveal hidden recessive alleles to the electrophoretic separation of minor hereditary variants of the same enzyme. Electrophoresis, which has been employed extensively in population genetics only since the late 1960s, has provided the technical breakthrough needed to detect minor genes at a rapid pace. The total amount of genetic diversity revealed has been astonishing: in some species 40 or more percent of the loci contain multiple alleles, while 20 percent or more of the loci in individual organisms are heterozygous. As a consequence the classical concept of the "normal" genotype has begun to crumble; it is being replaced by a view of the population as a kaleidoscopically changing ensemble of genotypes fitted loosely to the environment.

But we really do not know what most of this genetic variation means. Some of it consists of new, raw mutations of such low survival value that they are encountered only for a short time after originating. Many genes are present as declining residues, once favored by natural selection but now in the process of being replaced by better adapted genes. Some may be neutral, in other words unaffected by selection, their numbers drifting randomly up and down. Still others occur at intermediate frequencies because they are suspended there by balanced polymorphism. Like the sickle-cell trait described by Anthony C. Allison in his article "Sickle Cells and Evolution," the balanced morphs enjoy superior fitness when they occur in combination with other genes on the same locus, but they survive and reproduce less well when in the pure, homozygous state. The sickle-cell trait protects its carriers from falciparum malaria in both a single dose (heterozygous condition) and double dose (homozygous condition); but in the case of a double dose, it causes severe anemia which is usually fatal during childhood. As a result the sickle-cell heterozygote is superior to both the sickle-cell and "normal" homozygotes in malarious regions, and both kinds of genes are kept in balance within the population as a whole.

The significance of only a minute fraction of the known genetic variation has been accounted for by one or another of the available explanations. A stimulating debate is now in progress within population genetics: the "selectionists," on the one hand, postulate that most or perhaps all of the variation is under the control of selection. The "neutralists," on the other hand, believe that a large fraction of the genes are not influenced by selection and represent just so much noise, their frequencies being tossed about by random fluctuation from generation to generation. The neutralists' position rests on theoretical calculations which show that the observed variation could be based on random fluctuation of genes originating at known mutation rates. However, the potential adequacy of genetic drift does not prove its prevalence in nature. The selectionists can point to many examples of seemingly meaningless variation which on deeper analysis prove to have a sound basis in natural selection. A great deal more empirical research lies ahead before the selectionist-versus-neutralist controversy can be resolved. By simply striving toward that goal, geneticists will undoubtedly, in the best tradition of science, stumble upon unexpected phenomena and gain a new depth of understanding of the evolutionary process.

Two of the articles in this series illustrate the probable direction in which population genetics will travel. Luigi L. Cavalli-Sforza reviews the painstaking work he and his associates have conducted on genetic differences among village populations in the Parma Valley of Italy. Genetic drift is a prominent factor because the populations were founded by small groups of people and have remained small and partially isolated, permitting the random fluctuation of numbers to come into play. But drift is in competition with the two other major evolutionary factors: selection, which tends to hold the gene frequencies at steady values, and the migration of people (along with their genes) from one village to another. Unless the populations are extremely small, the effects of drift are nearly obliterated by these other two factors. As Cavalli-Sforza demonstrates, gene frequencies are determined by complex interactions of drift, selection, and migration. A wholly different approach to this problem is taken, in a fine display of serendipity, by Richard E. Dickerson in his article on protein evolution. We know that the primary phenotypes, determining all other phenotypes, lie in the structure of the proteins and particularly of the enzymes. By working out the complete structure of these key molecules, biochemists are beginning to understand the potential adaptive value of each amino acid substitution. Rather like the comparative anatomists of the nineteenth century, the molecular evolutionists are defining form and function—only now at the ultimate level—and they are supplying one of the essential pieces for the complete explanation of genetic variation.

The reader may be surprised at first to see an article on the social behavior of turkeys in this section ("The Social Order of Turkeys," by C. R. Watts and A. W. Stokes). Its purpose is to introduce group selection, another fundamental, though controversial, subject in evolutionary theory. Group selection is the differential survival and reproduction of sets of individuals—parents and their offspring, brothers and sisters, entire breeding populations, and so forth. When gene frequencies are affected by one such unit gaining better representation in subsequent generations over equivalent units, the process is referred to as *group selection*. An excellent example is the evolution of ants and other social insects. The unit of survival and reproduction is the entire colony, not its separate members, so that much of the evolution shapes the behavior and properties of the colony as a whole. Group selection can reinforce individual selection, thereby accelerating the rate of evolution, but a much more interesting possibility is that selection on the two levels can be opposed. In other words, what is good for the group in terms of genetic fitness may be bad for the individual. If such counteracting selection at the group level is strong enough, it can overwhelm the selection at the individual level and allow altruistic traits to evolve. A special case of group selection is *kin selection*, in which groups of relatives are affected as a unit. Individuals can afford to sacrifice their own personal genetic fitness if they make up for the loss by increasing the fitness of their relatives. Since many of their own genes are shared with the relatives by common descent, helping the relatives actually multiplies part of their own genetic structure. Altruism which evolves at the personal level by such a process is not really altruism in evolutionary terms. Watts and Stokes raise just such a possibility in their account of the strange social behavior of wild turkeys. Brothers from the same brood remain together for life, with one assuming a dominant position and sole access to hens on the breeding grounds. The subordinate brothers assist their sibling in contests against other brotherhoods for access to the females. An obvious question arises: why don't they strike out on their own, or at least struggle to gain partial access to the hens in the presence of the brother? We cannot be sure of the answer, but it is entirely plausible that the tight sibling bonds insure a more than adequate reproduction of the genes shared with the dominant brother, despite the fact that their personal genetic fitness is reduced to zero. This example is typical in that the data suggest, but cannot prove, the evolutionary origin of altruistic behavior by group selection.

The articles in Section I accurately reflect the tantalizing nature of modern population genetics. They make clear that, as a science, the field is very young; it is capable of providing us with a general view of the process of adaptation but unable to predict the course of evolution in particular cases over even a short period of time. Nonetheless, population genetics must be employed to its maximum potential as the foundation stone of most of the remainder of evolutionary biology, including speciation and biogeography, the topics to be covered in Section II.

SUGGESTED
FURTHER READING

The following list is recommended for students and other readers who have had a beginning course in biology or the equivalent and wish to go directly into more scholarly reading. It proceeds stepwise from elementary to more advanced levels.

Wilson, Edward O., and Bossert, William H. *A primer of population biology.* Stamford, Connecticut: Sinauer Associates, 1971. 192 pp. Designed to be self-teaching, this short textbook supplements explanations of basic population genetics and evolutionary theory with sets of problems and answers.

Dobzhansky, Theodosius. *Genetics of the evolutionary process.* New York: Columbia University Press, 1970. 505 pp. An authoritative account by one of the founders of experimental population genetics. It is strong on case histories from laboratory and field studies and touches on many of the implications of genetics for the study of man.

Mayr, Ernst. *Populations, species, and evolution.* Cambridge, Mass.: Belknap Press, 1970. 453 pp. A wide-ranging and clearly written account of the origin and genetic structure of animal species. Since Mayr writes from the viewpoint of a systematist, his book forms an excellent bridge to speciation, the subject of Section II in the present collection.

Wallace, Bruce. *Topics in population genetics.* New York: W. W. Norton and Company, 1968. 481 pp. A clear review of a large part of both theoretical and experimental population genetics by one of the principal current investigators.

Crow, James F. and Kimura, Motoo. *An introduction to population genetics theory.* New York: Harper and Row, 1970. 519 pp. A largely mathematical but concise, authoritative account of most of the topics of modern theoretical population genetics.

1

GENETIC LOAD

CHRISTOPHER WILLS
March 1970

The term refers to the accumulated mutations in the gene pool of an entire species. Part of the load reduces the viability of the species; the rest may be a priceless genetic resource

Every human being has tens of thousands (possibly hundreds of thousands) of genes, each a small part of the long chains of deoxyribonucleic acid in his cells. When this DNA is duplicated and passed on to the next generation through the reproductive cells, there is a certain probability that one or more genes have mutated. That is, they have changed in such a way that the enzyme or other protein they specify is also changed. Over a period of time, as each generation gives rise to the next, such mutations accumulate in the pool of genes of all members of the species living at a particular moment. Since the process of evolution consists of changes in the quality and quantity of the genetic variability stored in the gene pool, it is a matter of some importance to consider the role of mutations, which provide this variability.

Some mutations are "beneficial," that is, the individual in whom they are expressed is better able to adapt to a given set of environmental circumstances. The large majority of mutations, however, are harmful or even lethal to the individual in whom they are expressed. Such mutations can be regarded as introducing a "load," or genetic burden, into the pool. The term "genetic load" was first used by the late H. J. Muller, who recognized that the rate of mutations is increased by numerous agents man has introduced into his environment, notably ionizing radiation and mutagenic chemicals. We now know that this mutational load is not the only kind of genetic load. We must ask the question: What is the overall load on the gene pool, and how does it affect living populations? The answer is currently being sought in genetic studies of many different organisms from man to yeasts.

One might suppose that harmful or lethal genes could not survive for very long in the gene pool because the individuals who carry them are less likely to reproduce than other individuals. The fact is, however, that such genes can survive in spite of the strong negative pressures of natural selection. The reason is that the genetic material of man, like that of all other sexually reproducing organisms, is diploid: human body cells (as distinct from human reproductive cells) have a double set of genes. As is well known, each individual receives a complete set of chromosomes from each parent. Hence every individual has two genes for every genetic function, one from his mother and one from his father. (The sex chromosomes, two of the 46 chromosomes in man, are a complication that need not concern us here.)

For each maternal chromosome, then, there is a corresponding chromosome in the paternal set. If each of these chromosomes has the same gene at exactly the same locus, the individual is said to be homozygous for that gene. If the gene happens to be a lethal mutant, the individual will of course die, by definition without being able to reproduce. If the gene is "subvital" (harmful without being lethal), the homozygous individual will often survive to transmit it to the next generation.

An individual who has two different genes at the same locus is said to be heterozygous. He might be heterozygous for (1) a mutant gene and a "normal" one, (2) two different "normal" genes or (3) two different mutant genes. The effect of the mutant genes in the heterozygote can vary from complete recessiveness (their effect is completely masked by a normal gene) to complete dominance (the normal gene is masked). Partial dominance is not uncommon; what it means is that the effect of the mutant

gene is not completely masked but leaks through to a greater or lesser degree. Because of the masking effect a heterozygote can carry either lethal or subvital genes and transmit them to the next generation. All that is required is that the individual have a normally functioning gene that compensates for the mutant one.

Considering the complexity of the genetic material, mutations are remarkably rare. Nonetheless, they do arise con-

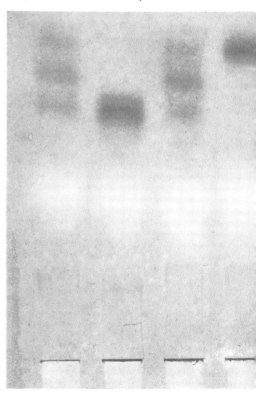

HIDDEN DIFFERENCES in the genetic material of fruit flies are revealed by this electrophoretic pattern on a slab of polyacrylamide gel. Such genetic variation, originally caused by mutation, can form a part of the genetic load. Each slot at the bottom of the slab was filled with juice from an instantly; indeed, they are occurring in the reader as he reads this article. Fortunately most of them take place in cells that are not involved in reproduction, and hence they are not conveyed to the next generation. Any influence that increases the rate of mutation of those genes that are passed on to the next generation will also increase the chance of homozygosity for recessive genes. If the mutation rate remains constant for some time, there will be an equilibrium in the population between the rate at which new recessive lethals appear at a particular locus, and the rate at which they are removed by premature death as two of them turn up by chance in the same individual. If a harmful gene is dominant or partially dominant, its effects will appear right away in the heterozygote, and it will not be as common in a population at equilibrium as a completely recessive lethal with the same mutation rate would be.

From studies of marriages between close relatives Muller, Newton E. Morton and James F. Crow estimated that between 6 and 15 percent of human egg and sperm cells carry new recessive lethal mutations or mutations that are so harmful that they are "lethal equiva-

lents." These workers calculated that the average individual is heterozygous for three to five lethals or lethal equivalents. Will such a gene leak through a masking gene? In order to find out Terumi Mukai and his co-workers at the National Institute of Genetics in Japan and later at North Carolina State University conducted a Herculean set of experiments with the fruit fly *Drosophila*. Mukai patterned his experiments on a technique developed by Muller that has become standard in modern genetics.

The consequences of a given level of genetic load can be examined experimentally by causing mutations in the gene pool of the experimental population through exposure to X rays or a chemical mutagen. There is, however, a difficulty in this simple strategy. The effects of such agents may not be easy to detect because the mutations they cause are mostly recessive. In fact, Muller worked for a decade before he was able to show in 1927 that X rays actually do produce mutations in *Drosophila*. Muller and later workers solved the problem by taking advantage of certain genetic peculiarities of *Drosophila* that allowed an entire chromosome to be passed from one generation to the next as a unit. This

made it possible to produce flies that were, for example, completely homozygous for one or more chromosomes, so that new mutations would be revealed. Once the effects of a chromosome have been demonstrated in this way, new crosses can be made to pair it with other chromosomes of known effects in order to form heterozygous combinations. The results of these crosses reveal what consequences the genes have when they are heterozygous [*see illustration on pages 14 and 15*].

Mukai and his colleagues examined millions of flies that had been made either homozygous or heterozygous for chromosomes that had a known effect on the flies' survival. They discovered (among other interesting facts) that recessive lethals were hardly expressed at all in the heterozygote but that subvital genes leaked through the masking gene to a startling extent: about 40 percent of the homozygous effect.

Why should a subvital gene be expressed while a lethal one is almost completely concealed? There may be a good biochemical reason. If the product of a recessive lethal gene is so changed that it no longer functions, then in the hetero-

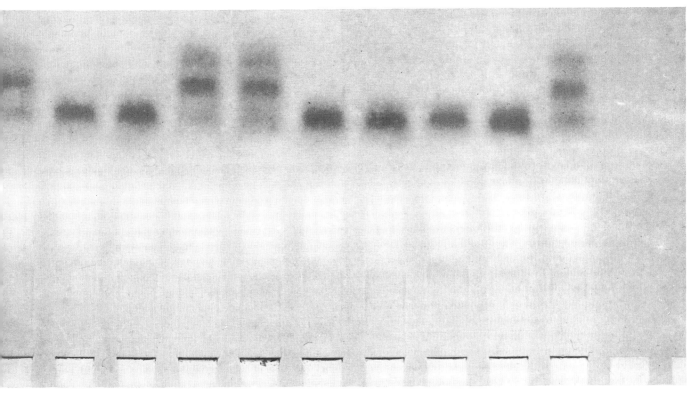

dividual fly containing the enzyme octanol dehydrogenase (among many others). When an electric current was passed through the gel, each enzyme was carried toward the top at a characteristic speed determined by minute charge differences among enzyme molecules. After current was stopped, staining of the product of the octanol dehydrogenase revealed three types (*visible as purple bands*). Fly second from left has two genes, each of which produces a slow-

moving form of the enzyme. Fly fourth from left carries two genes for a fast-moving form of the enzyme. Some flies, such as the one at left and the one third from left, have genes for "fast" and "slow" enzymes and therefore also produce an intermediate form (*middle band*) made up of fast and slow subunits. Subunits produced by genes are polypeptide chains that are not yet functional. Such subunits must combine to form a normal enzyme or other protein.

zygote the normal gene for that function could take over completely without too much harm to the organism. The product of a subvital gene may be partially functional (as is suggested by the fact that some of the homozygotes survive), and it may interfere in some way with the "good" product from the other gene in the heterozygote so that its effect is felt. For example, many genes give rise to protein subunits rather than complete gene products, and these subunits are put together in the cell. Subunits from normal and subvital genes could combine to yield an abnormal product [*see bottom illustration on opposite page*].

In order to test this assumption my colleagues and I at Wesleyan University turned to the common one-celled brewer's yeast *Saccharomyces*, which has the advantage over *Drosophila* that millions of cells can quickly be screened for mutants. Yeast also has the interesting property that during its life cycle it exists in both a diploid phase and a haploid phase. In the haploid phase the yeast cells have only one set of chromosomes instead of two. Both of these phases can be maintained and studied at leisure. The effect of mutations can be observed in the haploid phase, when they are fully expressed, and then in the heterozygous diploid phase, when they are masked. The system thus resembles the *Drosophila* one, but the experiments are much easier to do. It is impractical to follow individual yeast cells to see if they die or exhibit defects, and so we used as a measure of genetic effect the rate of increase in the size of a small yeast colony viewed under the microscope.

The yeast cells were exposed to two types of chemical mutagen. One kind of agent apparently inserts or deletes bits of genetic code, so that the sense of that particular gene is usually destroyed. Agents of this type produced large numbers of recessive genes that were completely masked in the heterozygote, and these colonies grew at normal rates. The other kind of agent produces small mistakes in the genes that do not destroy sense completely; these genes did show through in the heterozygote by diminishing the growth of the experimental colonies. In outline, then, the theory seems to be correct, but we are now working on individual genes in an effort to determine the actual mechanisms involved in this partial dominance.

A start has thus been made on classifying the genes that constitute the mutational load. There is, however, a different kind of burden that is also a part of the genetic load. This burden primarily consists not of harmful mutations that are masked in the heterozygote but strangely enough of apparently normal homozygotes. In order for the load to appear the gene pool must contain two or more functioning genes at a locus, and circumstances must be such that organisms heterozygous for these genes have an apparent selective advantage, that is, they can leave more offspring than the homozygotes can. There is thus a load associated with being homozygous, even for normal genes. Such circumstances might include environmental conditions that favor a heterozygote over a homozygote or conditions that select against the homozygote but do not affect the heterozygote. This kind of load is called a balanced load because, as we shall see, a balance in the population is struck between the heterozygotes and the homozygotes.

The term "balanced load" encompasses many phenomena, but the most important is hybrid vigor, a remarkable effect observable in many organisms that was first put to work by geneticists when they crossed different inbred lines of corn to produce vigorous strains with greatly increased yield. A number of mechanisms have been proposed for hybrid vigor, but regardless of the mechanism the end result is the same: an organism heterozygous at a large number of loci is "fitter" in some sense than one that is heterozygous at fewer loci. There must accordingly be a load attached to being homozygous, because the homozygous organism often leaves fewer and less vigorous offspring than the heterozygous one.

The balanced load is different from the mutational load in another respect. The frequency of a recessive gene in the mutational load depends directly on the mutation rate. An altered gene that gives an advantage to the heterozygote, however, might appear only once and then

MASKING of a harmful or a lethal gene by a normal gene is demonstrated in a hypothetical population. Nine out of every 10 of the sperm and the eggs that produced this population carried gene *A*; the rest carried gene *a*. When sperm fertilized the eggs at random, 100 individuals were produced. Eighty-one are homozygous, that is, they carry two identical genes, *A* and *A*, for the same function. Eighteen individuals are heterozygous (*shading*); they carry two different genes for the same function, *A* and *a*. The *a* gene is lethal, but because each heterozygote carries a normal *A* gene that masks the *a* gene, none displays a defect. One individual, however, carries two lethal genes (*solid color*). It dies because it has no normal gene to compensate for the lethal one. Two individuals within diagram are mutants (*color*); they carry an *A* gene that was changed into an *a* gene. An average of two mutations must arise in each generation in order to maintain the ratio of *A* to *a* as *aa* homozygotes die.

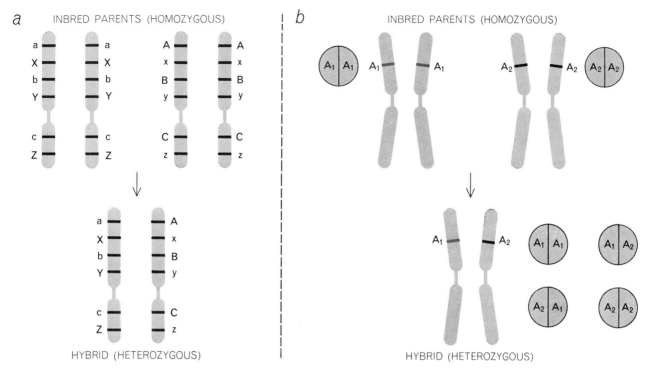

a INBRED PARENTS (HOMOZYGOUS)

HYBRID (HETEROZYGOUS)

b INBRED PARENTS (HOMOZYGOUS)

HYBRID (HETEROZYGOUS)

HYBRID VIGOR may be explained as a masking of harmful genes by normal genes in the heterozygote. In *a* one homozygous parent plant is crossed with another. Both parents carry homozygous harmful genes and homozygous normal genes. The offspring produced is heterozygous (*bottom*). In this hybrid the genes on each parental chromosome are paired so that the harmful genes (*small letters*) are masked by normal genes (*capital letters*). Another ex-

planation of hybrid vigor that does not exclude the first is shown in *b*. Here the *A* genes of homozygous parents at top are each capable of producing only one kind of subunit of the functioning gene product, A_1 or A_2, and one product, A_1A_1 or A_2A_2. The hybrid offspring, however, can produce both kinds of subunit (a nonfunctioning polypeptide chain) and three kinds of gene product (an enzyme or functioning protein) because it has both kinds of *A* gene.

automatically build up to a high level in the population as the number of heterozygotes increases. It is important to realize that no matter how strong the heterozygote appears to be, the homozygotes never disappear; they continue to occur in each generation by the normal mechanisms of the production and the subse-

quent fusion of haploid reproductive cells. In other words, when two heterozygotes mate and reproduce, a certain number of their offspring will inevitably be homozygotes. Eventually, therefore, a balance is struck between the heterozygotes and the homozygotes at that locus [*see illustration on page 16*].

The dependence of the balanced load on environmental conditions has been conclusively demonstrated by Theodosius Dobzhansky and his colleagues at Columbia University and at Rockefeller University. The demonstration has been achieved by experiments with inversions in the chromosomes of *Drosophila*. Such

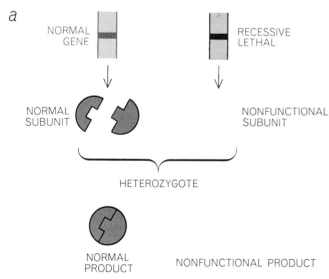

a

NORMAL GENE

RECESSIVE LETHAL

NORMAL SUBUNIT

NONFUNCTIONAL SUBUNIT

HETEROZYGOTE

NORMAL PRODUCT

NONFUNCTIONAL PRODUCT

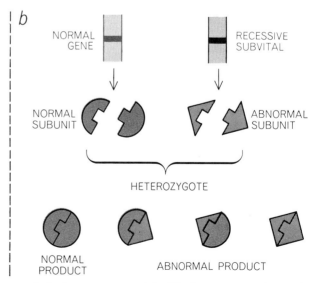

b

NORMAL GENE

RECESSIVE SUBVITAL

NORMAL SUBUNIT

ABNORMAL SUBUNIT

HETEROZYGOTE

NORMAL PRODUCT

ABNORMAL PRODUCT

LEAKAGE of a subvital gene through a masking gene is shown schematically. In heterozygote at left (*a*) normal gene (*color*) is paired with a recessive lethal that produces nonfunctional subunits. Because the normal gene produces a normal subunit and normal product, however, the individual carrying the genes appears

normal. In heterozygote at right (*b*) the same normal gene is paired with a subvital gene. The subunit of the subvital is partly functional and therefore can combine randomly with a normal subunit to form an abnormal but functioning product. Only a quarter of the product of this heterozygote is normal and a defect is obvious.

inversions are reversed segments of chromosomes, and they are themselves under genetic control; they have been found in wild populations of many *Drosophila* species. The normal mechanism of crossing-over, which exchanges individual genes between maternal and paternal chromosomes in each generation, is disrupted in flies that are heterozygous for these inversions. Specifically the genes within the inversion are "locked in" and pass from one generation to the next in a group that Kenneth Mather has called a supergene, with inheritance just like that for a single gene. These supergenes are visible in the giant chromosomes of *Drosophila* larvae. In a heterozygous larva one can see corresponding maternal and paternal chromosomes paired so that the normal and the inverted segments form a loop [*see illustration on page 17*]. Because inversions are so easily recognizable their frequencies can be followed in either laboratory populations or wild ones.

One of Dobzhansky's experimental populations consisted of flies carrying a normal chromosome and an inverted chromosome from a particular wild population, maintained in the laboratory at 25 degrees Celsius. The population included three kinds of flies: flies homozygous for the normal chromosome, flies homozygous for the inverted chromosome and heterozygous flies, that is, flies that carried both the inverted chromosome and the normal one. If the conditions of the experiment are such as to give a selective advantage to the heterozygotes, one would predict that, whatever the initial ratios in the population, the proportions of the three types of flies would reach some specific equilibrium value.

Such was the case. Regardless of the number of each type of fly present in the original population, the population reached an equilibrium after a certain number of generations. In this equilibrium state 49 percent of the flies were homozygous for the normal chromosome, 9 percent were homozygous for the inverted chromosome and the remainder (42 percent) were heterozygous. The unequal numbers of the two types of homozygote in the equilibrium population can be explained if the normal homozygote is fitter than the homozygote for the inverted chromosome. Subsequent experiments showed that this was true, and also showed that the heterozygotes clearly had an advantage over the two kinds of homozygote in many factors that together make up genetic fitness: ability to survive to adulthood, number of eggs

laid and so on. This explained the stability of the frequencies, which were governed not by mutation rate but by the relative genetic fitness of the two kinds of homozygote and the heterozygotes. The two kinds of homozygote carried a balanced load, since they were at a disadvantage compared with the heterozygotes.

When the temperature was lowered to 16.5 degrees C., however, the advantage of the heterozygotes—and the balanced load—disappeared. The frequencies of normal and inverted chromosomes now stayed at about the frequencies in the starting populations. In other words, the homozygote disadvantage was conditional on temperature. One explanation (there are others) might be that certain mutant genes on both the normal and the inverted chromosomes worked well at 16.5 degrees but poorly at 25 degrees. These genes were matched with normal ones in the heterozygote, which would therefore be fitter than the homozygotes at 25 degrees. At the lower temperature, however, the balanced load had disappeared, and all three kinds of flies were equally fit.

Flies homozygous for either of these chromosomes do perfectly well by themselves in the laboratory, producing large, healthy populations that look perfectly normal. Dobzhansky's experiments, and those of many other workers, have repeatedly demonstrated the now-you-see-it, now-you-don't quality of the balanced load, with its extreme dependence on the environment. The heterozygote is often fitter, but not under all conditions.

Could the heterozygous advantage that Dobzhansky observed arise at any locus, or were the supergenes unique in some way? Much indirect evidence had accumulated that they were not, but an elegant experiment performed by Edwin Vann at Cornell University provided a direct answer. If such heterozygosity were common, Vann reasoned, it might be observed at many loci on the chromosomes. The problem was finding a way of detecting the heterozygous loci. Vann solved this problem by creating inversions of varying lengths in the chromosomes of a population of highly homozygous *Drosophila*. Next he mated carriers of the newly created supergenes with members of the same population without the inversion, or with members of other populations. The gene pools of these populations were also homozygous; some were related to the original population and some were not. The offspring of these last matings, because of the diverse genetic background of the parents,

could be expected to be heterozygous at a great many of the loci covered by an inversion. Equally important, the fate of this group of loci could be followed by using the inversion as a marker.

If heterozygous advantage had actually been produced by such matings, the inversions would probably remain in the population and increase in frequency, since heterozygotes for the inversion would also always be heterozygous for the genes within the inversion. After several generations had passed Vann observed that in fact the longer inversions (containing more genes and therefore preserving more heterozygosity) were much less likely to be lost than the shorter ones. He also found that the longer inversions often tended to achieve high frequencies. Finally, because Vann's supergenes covered varying lengths of all the chromosomes, it could be concluded that heterozygote advantage existed up and down the chromosomes and needed only to be revealed by a suitable genetic marker.

One proposition remained to be disproved. It seemed possible that an inversion at any point on a chromosome might have some selective advantage per se that had nothing to do with heterozygosity at all. The reader will recall that Vann also introduced his inversions back into the populations from which the inversions had been derived in the first place. In these crosses the genes on the inverted and the uninverted chromosomes were the same, and little if any heterozygosity was present in these flies. After several generations had passed Vann found that the inversions had completely disappeared. It seemed, then, that the mere production of an inversion, rather than providing an advantage, actually constituted a genetic liability that caused the individuals carrying them to

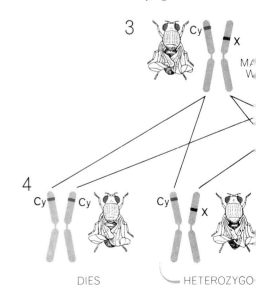

DIES   HETEROZYGO

be eliminated from the population after a few generations.

V ann had proved that heterozygous advantage could exist at many places on a chromosome, but there was no way of directly determining what functions, if any, these genes performed. Clearly they could not be lethals or subvitals. A fly heterozygous for more than a few severe subvitals would be very sick indeed, and if it were heterozygous for too many lethals, there would be a good chance it would be homozygous for at least one. In order to prove that these genes were normal it was necessary to develop a method for identifying the function of an individual gene.

Until recently population geneticists investigating such problems were in the position of early oceanographers, who tried to reconstruct the bottom of the ocean from a few soundings and samples of sand and mud taken at random over thousands of square miles. If one made a *Drosophila* chromosome homozygous and discovered a lethal gene on it, for example, one had to ignore the thousands of other genes on the same chromosome. There were no markers with which to detect these genes, which were lumped together under the term "wild type." Most mutant genes are nonfunctional or do something very different from wild-type genes, so that they can be

easily distinguished. How can one distinguish one wild-type gene from another when all appear to be perfectly functional? In actuality different wild-type genes with similar functions at the same locus could be detected in a few instances. In man there are three genes at the same locus controlling the ABO blood-type system, and a person may be homozygous or heterozygous for any combination of these genes. He is not distinguishable from his fellows, however, except by immunological tests of himself and in some cases of his parents or children.

Some population geneticists felt that this was only the tip of the iceberg. A few years ago Bruce Wallace at Cornell suggested that a fruit fly from a wild population might be heterozygous at 50 percent of its paired genes, a suggestion that was met with consternation and disbelief. Wallace may have overestimated

the proportion, but it turns out that he was not too far off. The technique of electrophoresis, long used by chemists and adapted to biological systems by Oliver Smithies of the University of Wisconsin, has provided population geneticists with a method for examining the gene pool that is as useful as sonar has been to the mapping of the ocean bottom. Harry Harris of the University of London and Richard C. Lewontin and John L. Hubby of the University of Chicago have used it to examine the wild-type genes of man and *Drosophila*.

The technique is a simple one. A tiny sample of serum from a man or the juice from the body of a single fly is inserted into a strip of a supporting medium such as a slab of starch soaked with an electrolyte, or conducting liquid. When a direct current is passed through the medium, molecules that are very much alike but that differ slightly in size or electric

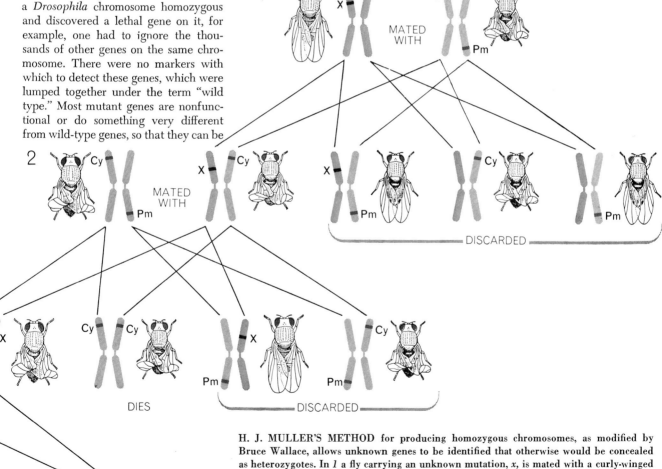

H. J. MULLER'S METHOD for producing homozygous chromosomes, as modified by Bruce Wallace, allows unknown genes to be identified that otherwise would be concealed as heterozygotes. In *1* a fly carrying an unknown mutation, *x*, is mated with a curly-winged (*Cy*), plum-eyed (*Pm*) fly whose chromosomes (*color*) carry dominant genes specifying these marks, which allow gene types to be followed through many generations. *Cy* and *Pm* chromosomes are modified so that they are inherited as single units. In a homozygote these genes are lethal. In *2* one *Cy* fly is mated with a *Cy-Pm* fly. If it is a *Cy-x* fly (*fourth from right*), all *Cy* flies in the next generation carry the *x* gene on their chromosomes. An *x* chromosome cannot recombine with a *Cy* chromosome, so that it must also be inherited as a single unit. In *3 Cy-x* flies are mated with one another. In *4* a quarter are *Cy-Cy* homozygotes, half are heterozygotes and a quarter are *xx* homozygotes. If the *x* gene is lethal, all *xx* flies die. If it is subvital (harmful but not lethal), some may die or be unable to reproduce.

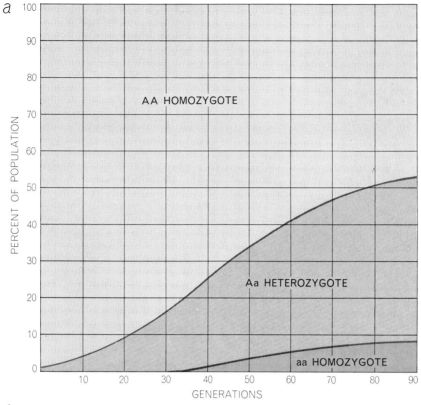

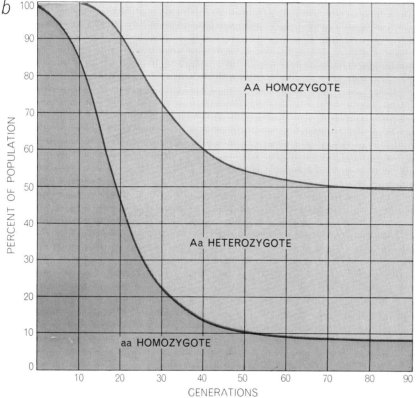

BALANCED LOAD appears in a population when heterozygotes seem to have a selective advantage over homozygotes, so that a load is borne by the normal genes. In this idealized case (a) Aa heterozygotes have a fitness of 100 percent, AA homozygotes are 92 percent as fit as the heterozygotes, and aa homozygotes are 80 percent as fit. In first generation 98 percent of the population consist of AA homozygotes and about 2 percent are Aa heterozygotes. By the 90th generation 42 percent are the favored Aa heterozygotes, whereas 9 percent are aa homozygotes that have merged through recombination. In the reverse situation (b), where aa homozygotes form 98 percent of the first generation and 2 percent are Aa heterozygotes, the latter still increase to 42 percent. The percentage of Aa heterozygotes cannot increase further in this case because the three kinds of gene type balance one another.

charge migrate at different rates in the electric field. When the current is turned off, the protein products of different genes will have migrated to different places in the gel, where each forms a band. The products of two wild-type genes differing by as little as one amino acid can be separated in this way. They can then be made visible in the starch by staining them [*see illustration on pages 10 and 11*].

Not all gene products can be examined by electrophoresis, but from those that can it is possible to make an estimate of the hidden differences between paired wild-type genes. Lewontin and Hubby calculated that their flies were heterozygous at 10 to 14 percent of their gene pairs. They emphasized that, since not all the differences can be detected by electrophoresis, this was a minimum estimate. Harris' results for man, although they were obtained from smaller numbers of genes, agreed. Other workers have found similar differences between the paired genes of organisms as diverse as butterflies and mice.

These slightly different forms of the same gene that perform the same function are called isoalleles. They are, of course, produced by mutation from other forms of the same gene, but mutations to functionally useful isoalleles must occur very rarely. One can take two extreme positions with regard to isoallelic differences. The first is that they are entirely accidental, and that the homozygosity or heterozygosity of the isoalleles makes no difference whatsoever to the fitness of the organism. The second is that the differences (or most of them) are held in the population by heterozygous advantage, and that the homozygotes for the isoalleles contribute to the balanced load. Ingenious mathematical arguments have been advanced in favor of the first view, but strong experimental evidence has now appeared against it.

Satya Prakash, working with Lewontin and Hubby, used electrophoresis to examine populations of *Drosophila* separated from one another by hundreds or thousands of miles. Many of the isoalleles the investigators detected had the same frequencies in these far-flung populations, and those that did not varied in a regular way depending on the geographic location of the sample. Other evidence of strong selection of isoalleles in wild populations of mice has been provided by Robert K. Selander and his co-workers at the University of Texas. Selection must be holding most of these genes in the population, because if they were selectively neutral, their frequency from place to place would vary greatly. It is almost certainly these functional isoalleles, rather than the harmful genes of the mutational load, that provide the variability on which natural selection acts. Isoalleles in the gene pool make a species far more responsive to natural selection than it would be if there were simply one kind of gene at each locus and every organism in the species were homozygous for that gene.

If we can extrapolate from the few genes sampled to the entire gene pool, there would appear to be thousands of isoalleles held in the population by some form of heterozygous advantage, and homozygotes for these isoalleles must be contributing to the balanced load. Therefore either there is a very large load or the selection against any particular gene must be very slight. The former possibility can be ruled out; the balanced load is simply not very large. If it were, most of the offspring of an organism would die from its effects. If we accept the latter possibility, however, we are faced with a difficulty. In any sexually reproducing population (small ones in particular) there is a random effect, known as genetic drift, that causes isoalleles at a locus to be lost simply by chance. Selection pressures have to be large enough to overcome such random forces if these genes are to be retained. The difficulty can be overcome if one assumes that genes, even on chromosomes free of inversions, have a tendency to hold together in groups. Within these groups selection pressures that are individually very small might be large enough in the aggregate to overcome the random drift forces.

Recently John W. Crenshaw of the University of Rhode Island, Joseph N. Vitale of the Yale Computer Center and I collaborated in an attempt to test this assumption by following a population of sexually reproducing organisms simulated by means of a computer program. We gave this "population" a balanced load but left out the mutational one, since it is relatively well understood. In addition we tried to make the balanced load as realistic as possible. It may be recalled that the flies homozygous for chromosomal inversions in Dobzhansky's experiment could fend perfectly well for themselves. In competition and under certain environmental conditions, however, the heterozygotes had a slight advantage. Similarly, the isoalleles discovered by electrophoresis are apparently perfectly functional and do no detectable harm to an organism homozygous for them, but such an or-

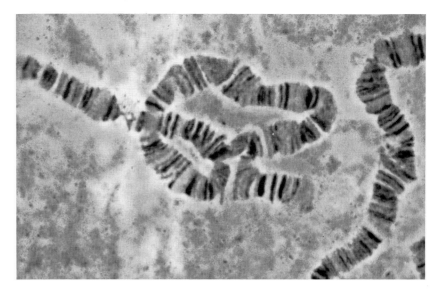

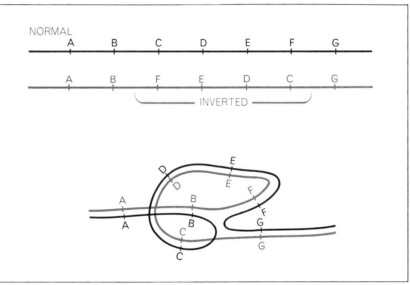

INVERSION in salivary-gland chromosome of a fruit fly (*top*) was produced with X rays by Edwin Vann. The inversion, similar to those found in wild populations, upsets the order of genes (*bottom*). One chromosome must therefore form loop so that genes at the same locus can be paired. A locus is a place on a chromosome for a gene with a specific function.

ganism might not do quite so well in competition as a heterozygote would. This conditional kind of selection has been considered theoretically by a number of workers, notably Wallace, who has called selection against the mutational type of load "hard" selection (since it occurs under almost all conditions) and selection against the balanced type of load "soft" selection.

Our computer organisms consisted of strings of digits. Each organism was a pair of such strings, one representing a maternal chromosome and one a paternal. These "chromosomes" could be manipulated to mimic sexual reproduction and recombination. Genes along the string were represented by a 1 or a 0, so that if an organism had a 1 or a 0 at a particular locus on both of its chromo-

somes, it was homozygous at that locus. If it had a 1 on one chromosome and a 0 on the other, it was heterozygous. At the beginning of each computer run the population contained a mixture of 1's and 0's, so that each organism was heterozygous at many loci. During many generations of simulated sexual reproduction we monitored the population to see how much of this variability would be retained.

Some of our populations were subjected to soft selection, by surveying them each generation and removing a few of the organisms homozygous at the largest number of loci, regardless of which loci. The places of these organisms in the population were then filled with duplicates of those organisms that were heterozygous at the largest number of loci. We found that by doing this we could maintain a surprising amount of variability in the population, even by removing as few as 5 percent of the organisms each generation. As time went on the genes actually did become organized into blocks along the chromosomes, and the patterns that appeared helped to preserve the variability [*see upper illustration below*]. It will be most interesting to see if such patterns are eventually detected in nature as well as in the computer.

We are learning more about the gene pool and genetic load, but many questions remain unanswered. We know very little about the biochemical reasons for heterozygote advantage, or about the relative proportions of balanced and mutational load produced by the common mutagenic agents. In our laboratory we are able to classify the genetic variability of yeast as "rigid" (expressed in a similar way in many different environments) or "flexible" (expressed in different ways in different environments). Most of the variability we have produced with our mutagenic agents is rigid, and we suspect that this is mutational load. The flexible variability is therefore presumably the same as the balanced load, but this relation has not been proved.

We must seek a better understanding of the size and nature of the human mutational load. Certain genetic diseases are clear-cut members of the mutational load, and until such time as genetic repair work can be done on the chromosomes themselves carriers of these diseases should be informed about the probability of their having defective

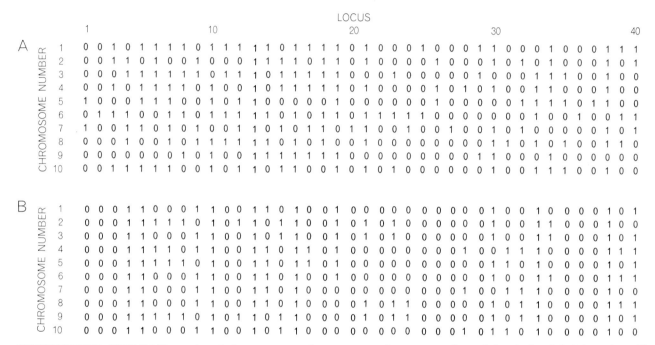

COMPUTERIZED GENE POOL consists of chromosomes made up of genes (represented by 1 or 0) that are simulated in a program and subjected to "natural selection." (Only short sections of a few chromosomes are shown.) The experiment, conducted by the author, John W. Crenshaw and Joseph N. Vitale, consisted of following chromosomes through many generations. Without selective pressure the pronounced variability (*colored digits*) in *A* would have been eradicated by random forces. Column of black digits represents a locus occupied by a "fixed" gene, one for which every "organism" (that is, pair of chromosomes) is homozygous. In *B*, generations later, selection has helped to retain variability (*color*), although homozygosity (*black digits*) has advanced markedly.

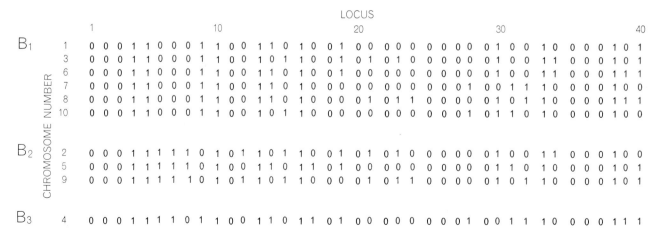

HOW HETEROZYGOSITY IS MAXIMIZED by selection is demonstrated with chromosomes of *B* in upper illustration. Chromosomes with genes 0001 at loci 6 through 9 are in B_1; those with genes 1110 at those loci are in B_2. Any organism in the next generation getting one chromosome from B_2 and the other from B_1 will therefore be heterozygous at these loci. Recombination breaks up these groups so that new ones form such as loci 6 through 9 in B_3, a pairing of loci 6 and 7 from B_2 and loci 8 and 9 from B_1. Such chromosomes are selected against because they cannot pair with other chromosomes to give maximum heterozygosity.

children. A small start has been made on this reasonable form of negative eugenics. Genetic counseling services associated with many of our larger hospitals and universities are providing such information, and they are being aided by the fact that an increasing number of genetic diseases can be detected when they are heterozygous. The most important actions that need to be taken, however, are in the area of minimizing the addition of new mutagens to those already present in the environment. Any increase in the mutational load is harmful, if not immediately, then certainly to future generations.

What of positive eugenics? The human gene pool is made up of a complex array of isoalleles, the product of a long and largely unknown genetic history. In most cases there is no way of telling which isoalleles of particular genes are outmoded relics of our past that no longer have a function. We have some examples of such genetic relics, which are detectable because of their striking effects. Populations inhabiting certain malarial regions carry a gene for sickle-cell anemia that kills homozygotes but helps to protect heterozygotes against malaria. In these regions this gene is part (in fact a large part) of the balanced load. It changes to mutational load, however, when malaria is eradicated and the heterozygote advantage disappears. How many less drastic genes of this kind do we still carry that once gave us protection against the plague or smallpox but now serve no useful function? Even if we were to discover many such genes, we dare not select against them. Whatever the optimum gene pool is for technological man, it should enable him to survive if circumstances suddenly change.

Conceivably a changed social climate and increased knowledge will make it possible for positive eugenics to be practiced on man. I suspect that the only rational course would be to select for genetic diversity. Such selection would have to favor isoalleles that pair to produce balanced heterozygosity but are not detectably harmful as homozygotes. This approach would have at least two advantages: actually or potentially valuable isoalleles would not be lost, and the balanced load would not increase directly with added heterozygosity as the mutational load does. No one knows if a more heterozygous human population would in fact be "better" in some sense, but any other kind of selection would literally paint us into an evolutionary corner. Our mutational load is a true burden, but it appears that our balanced load may be a priceless resource.

2

SICKLE CELLS AND EVOLUTION

ANTHONY C. ALLISON

August 1956

Why has the hereditary trait in which the red blood cells are sickle-shaped persisted for so many generations? The surprising answer is that under some conditions it is actually beneficial

Persevering study of small and seemingly insignificant phenomena sometimes yields surprising harvests of understanding. This article is an account of what has been learned from an oddly shaped red blood cell.

Forty-six years ago a Chicago physician named James B. Herrick, examining a Negro boy with a mysterious disease, found that many of his red blood cells were distorted into a crescent or sickle shape. After Herrick's report, doctors soon recognized many other cases of the same disease. They learned that it was hereditary and common in Negroes [see "Sickle-Cell Anemia," by George W. Gray; SCIENTIFIC AMERICAN, August, 1951]. The curious trait of the sickled blood cells gradually attracted the in-

terest of physiologists, biochemists, physical chemists, geneticists, anthropologists and others. And their varied investigations of this quirk of nature led to enlightenment on many unexpected subjects: the behavior of the blood's hemoglobin, inherited resistance to disease, the movements of populations over the world and the nature of some of the agencies that influence human evolution.

Let us review first what has been learned about the sickle cell phenomenon itself. As every student of biology knows, the principal active molecule in the red blood cells is hemoglobin, which serves as the carrier of oxygen. It appears that an unusual form of hemoglobin, pro-

duced under the influence of an abnormal gene, is responsible for the sickling of red cells. This hemoglobin molecule differs only slightly from the normal variety, and when there is an ample supply of oxygen it behaves normally: *i.e.*, it takes on oxygen and preserves its usual form in the red cells. But when the sickle cell hemoglobin (known as hemoglobin S)- loses oxygen, as in the capillaries where oxygen is delivered to the tissues, it becomes susceptible to a peculiar kind of reaction. It can attach itself to other hemoglobin S molecules, and they form long rods, which in turn attract one another and line up in parallel. These formations are rigid enough to distort the red cells from their normal disk shape into the shape

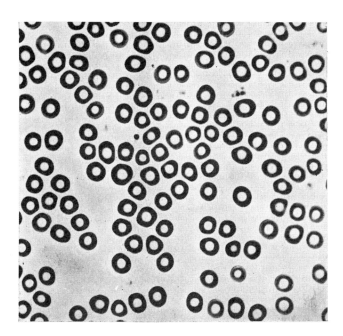

RED BLOOD CELLS of an individual with sickle cell trait, *i.e.*, a sickle cell gene from only one parent, are examined under the microscope. At the left are oxygenated red cells; they are disk-shaped. At the right are the same cells deoxygenated; they are sickle-shaped.

of a sickle [see *photomicrographs on page 21*]. Now the sickled cells may clog blood vessels; and they are soon destroyed by the body, so that the patient becomes anemic. The destruction of the hemoglobin converts it into bilirubin—the yellow pigment responsible for the jaundiced appearance often characteristic of anemic patients.

Most sufferers from sickle cell anemia die in childhood. Those who survive have a chronic disease punctuated by painful crises when blood supply is cut off from various body organs. There is no effective treatment for the disease.

From the first, a great deal of interest focused on the genetic aspects of this peculiarity. It was soon found that some Negroes carried a sickling tendency without showing symptoms of the disease. This was eventually discovered to mean that the carrier inherits the sickle cell gene from only one parent. A child who receives sickle cell genes from both parents produces only hemoglobin S and therefore is prone to sickling and anemia. On the other hand, in a person who has a normal hemoglobin gene from one parent and a hemoglobin S from the other sickling is much less likely; such persons, known as carriers of the "sickle cell trait," become ill only under exceptional conditions—for example, at high altitudes, when their blood does not receive enough oxygen.

The sickle cell trait is, of course, much more common than the disease. Among Negroes in the U. S. some 9 per cent carry the trait, but less than one fourth of 1 per cent show sickle cell anemia. In some Negro tribes in Africa the trait is present in as much as 40 per cent of the population, while 4 per cent have sickle cell genes from both parents and are subject to the disease.

The high incidence of the sickle cell gene in these tribes raised a most interesting question. Why does the harmful gene persist? A child who inherits two sickle cell genes (*i.e.*, is homozygous for this gene) has only about one fifth as much chance as other children of surviving to reproductive age. Because of this mortality, about 16 per cent of the sickle cell genes must be removed from the population in every generation. And yet the general level remains high without any sign of declining. What can be the explanation? Carriers of the sickle cell trait do not produce more children than those who lack it, and natural mutation could not possibly replace the lost sickle cell genes at any such rate.

The laws of evolution suggested a possible answer. Carriers of the sickle cell trait (a sickle cell gene from one parent and a normal one from the other) might have some advantage in survival over those who lacked the trait. If people with the trait had a lower mortality rate, counterbalancing the high mortality of sufferers from sickle cell anemia, then the frequency of sickle cell genes in the population would remain at a constant level.

What advantage could the sickle cell trait confer? Perhaps it protected its carriers against some other fatal disease—say malaria. The writer looked into the situation in malarious areas of Africa and found that children with the sickle cell trait were indeed relatively resistant to malarial infection. In some places they had as much as a 25 per cent better chance of survival than children without the trait. Children in most of Central Africa are exposed to malaria nearly all year round and have repeated infections during their early years. If they survive, they build up a considerable immunity to the disease. In some unknown way the sickle cell trait apparently protects young children against the malaria parasite during the dangerous years until they acquire an immunity to malaria.

On the African continent the sickle cell gene has a high frequency among people along the central belt, near the Equator, where malaria is common and is transmitted by mosquitoes through most

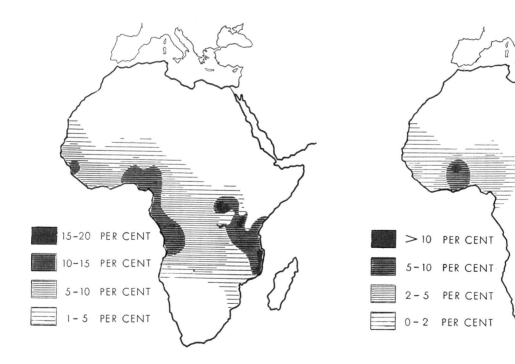

15–20 PER CENT
10–15 PER CENT
5–10 PER CENT
1–5 PER CENT

> 10 PER CENT
5–10 PER CENT
2–5 PER CENT
0–2 PER CENT

FREQUENCY OF THE SICKLE CELL GENE is plotted in per cent on the map of Africa. High frequencies are confined to a broad belt in which malignant tertian malaria is an important cause of death.

FREQUENCY OF THE HEMOGLOBIN C GENE is similarly plotted. Unlike the sickle cell gene, which has a widespread distribution, this gene is confined to a single focus in West Africa.

of the year. North and south of this belt, where malaria is less common and usually of the benign variety, the sickle cell gene is rare or absent. Moreover, even within the central belt, tribes in nonmalarious areas have few sickle cell genes.

Extension of the studies showed that similar situations exist in other areas of the world. In malarious parts of southern Italy and Sicily, Greece, Turkey and India, the sickle cell trait occurs in up to 30 per cent of the population. There is no reason to suppose that the peoples of all these areas have transmitted the gene to one another during recent times. The sickle cell gene may have originated independently in the several populations or may trace back to a few such genes passed along among them a thousand years ago. The high frequency of the gene in these populations today can be attributed mainly to the selective effect of malaria.

On the other hand, we should expect that when a population moves from a malarious region to one free of this disease, the frequency of the sickle cell gene will fall. The Negro population of the U. S. exemplifies such a development. When Negro slaves were first brought to North America from West Africa some 250 to 300 years ago, the frequency of the sickle cell trait among them was probably not less than 22 per cent. By mixed mating with Indian and white people this figure was probably reduced to about 15 per cent. In the absence of any appreciable mortality from malaria, the loss of sickle cell genes through deaths from anemia in 12 generations should have reduced the frequency of the sickle cell trait in the Negro population to about 9 per cent. This is, in fact, precisely the frequency found today.

Thus the Negroes of the U. S. show a clear case of evolutionary change. Within the space of a few hundred years this population, because of its transfer from Africa to North America, has undergone a definite alteration in genetic structure. This indicates how rapidly human evolution can take place under favorable circumstances.

Since the discovery of sickle cell hemoglobin (hemoglobin S), many other abnormal types of human hemoglobin have been found. (They are usually distinguished by electrophoresis, a separation method which depends on differences in the amount of the negative charge on the molecule.) One of the most

HEMOGLOBIN MOLECULES are represented as ellipsoids in these drawings. At the top are normal hemoglobin molecules, which are arranged almost at random in the red blood cell. Second and third from the top are sickle cell hemoglobin molecules, which form long helixes when they lose oxygen. Fourth is an aggregate of normal (*white*) and sickle cell molecules (*black*), in which every fourth molecule of the helix is normal. Fifth is an aggregate of hemoglobin C (*gray*) and sickle cell molecules; every other molecule is hemoglobin C.

common of these other varieties is called hemoglobin C. It, too, causes anemia in persons who have inherited the hemoglobin C gene from both parents. Moreover, the combination of hemoglobin S and hemoglobin C (one inherited from each parent) likewise leads to anemia. These two hemoglobins combine to form the rodlike structures that cause sickling of the red blood cells [*see drawings on page 23*].

The hemoglobin C gene is largely confined to West Africa, notably among people in the northern section of the Gold Coast, where the frequency of the trait runs as high as 27 per cent. Whether hemoglobin C, like hemoglobin S, protects against malaria is not known. But the C gene must give some advantage, else it would not persist. Obviously inheritance of both C and S is a disadvantage, since it leads to anemia. As a consequence we should expect to find that where the C gene is present, the spread of the S gene is retarded. This does seem to be the case: in the northern Gold Coast the frequency of the S gene goes no higher than 5 per cent.

Another gene producing abnormal hemoglobin, known as the thalassemia gene, is common in Greece, Italy, Cyprus, Turkey and Thailand. The trait is most prevalent in certain areas (*e.g.*, lowlands of Sardinia) where malaria used to be serious, but there have not yet been any direct observations as to whether its carriers are resistant to malaria. The trait almost certainly has some compensating advantage, for it persists in spite of the fact that even persons who have inherited the gene from only one parent have a tendency to anemia. The same is probably true of another deviant gene, known as the hemoglobin E gene, which is common in Thailand, Burma and among some populations in Ceylon and Indonesia.

By now the identified hemoglobin types form a considerable alphabet: besides S, C, thalassemia and E there are D, G, H, I, J, K and M. But the latter are relatively rare, from which it can be inferred that they provide little or no advantage.

For anyone interested in population genetics and human evolution, the sickle cell story presents a remarkably clear demonstration of some of the principles at play. It affords, for one thing, a simple illustration of the principle of hybrid vigor. Hybrid vigor has been investigated by many breeding experiments with fruit flies and plants, but in most cases the crossbreeding involves so many genes that it is impossible to say what gene combinations are responsible for the advantages of the hybrid. Here we can see a human cross involving only a single gene, and we can give a convincing explanation of just how the hybridization provides an advantage. In a population exposed to malaria the heterozygote (hybrid) possessing one normal hemoglobin gene and one sickle cell hemoglobin gene has an advantage over either homozygote (two normal genes or two sickle cell genes). And this selective advantage, as we can observe, maintains a high frequency of a gene which is deleterious in double dose but advantageous in single dose.

Secondly, we see a simple example of inherited resistance to disease. Resistance to infection (to say nothing of disorders such as cancer or heart disease) is generally complex and unexplainable, but in this case it is possible to identify a single gene (the sickle cell gene) which controls resistance to a specific disease (malaria). It is an unusually di-

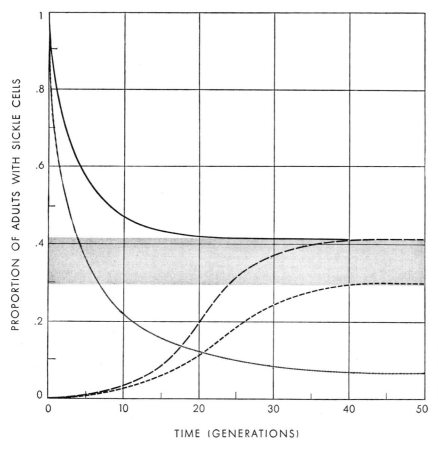

TIME (GENERATIONS)

RATE OF CHANGE IN FREQUENCY of adults with sickle cells under different conditions is shown in this chart. The horizontal gray band represents the equilibrium frequency in a region where individuals with the sickle cell trait have an evolutionary advantage of about 25 per cent over individuals without the sickle cell trait. If a population of individuals with a low sickle cell frequency enters the region, the frequency will increase to an equilibrium value (*long dashes*). If hemoglobin C is already established in the same population, the frequency will increase to a lower value (*short dashes*). If a population of individuals with a high sickle cell frequency enters the region, the frequency will decrease (*solid line*). If this population enters a nonmalarious region, the frequency will fall to a low value (*gray line*).

rect manifestation of the fact, now universally recognized but difficult to demonstrate, that inheritance plays a large role in controlling susceptibility or resistance to disease.

Thirdly, the sickle cell situation shows that mutation is not an unmixed bane to the human species. Most mutations are certainly disadvantageous, for our genetic constitution is so carefully balanced that any change is likely to be for the worse. To adapt an aphorism, all is best in this best of all possible bodies. Nonetheless, the sickle cell mutation, which at first sight looks altogether harmful, turns out to be a definite advantage in a malarious environment. Similarly other mutant genes that are bad in one situation may prove beneficial in another. Variability and mutation permit the human species, like other organisms, to adapt rapidly to new situations.

Finally, the sickle cell findings offer a cheering thought on the genetic future of civilized man. Eugenists often express alarm about the fact that civilized societies, through medical protection of the ill and weak, are accumulating harmful genes: *e.g.*, those responsible for diabetes and other hereditary diseases. The sickle cell history brings out the other side of the story: improving standards of hygiene may also *eliminate* harmful genes—not only the sickle cell but also others of which we are not yet aware.

PHENOTYPE	GENOTYPE	ELECTROPHORETIC PATTERN	HEMOGLOBIN TYPES
NORMAL	Hb^A ⊢⊣ Hb^A		A
SICKLE CELL TRAIT	Hb^S ⊢⊣ Hb^A		SA
SICKLE CELL ANEMIA	Hb^S ⊢⊣ Hb^S		SS
HEMOGLOBIN C SICKLE CELL ANEMIA	Hb^C ⊢⊣ Hb^S		CS
HEMOGLOBIN C DISEASE	Hb^C ⊢⊣ Hb^C		CC

HEMOGLOBIN SPECIMENS from various individuals are analyzed by electrophoresis. The phenotype is the outward expression of the genotype, which refers to the hereditary make-up of the individual. The H-shaped symbols in the genotype column are schematic representations of sections of human chromosomes, one from each parent. The horizontal line of the H represents a gene for hemoglobin type. Hb^A is normal hemoglobin; Hb^S, sickle cell hemoglobin; Hb^C, hemoglobin C. This kind of electrophoretic pattern is made on a strip of wet paper between a positive and a negative electrode. The specimen of hemoglobin is placed on the line at the left side of each strip. In this experiment hemoglobin A migrates faster toward the positive electrode than sickle cell hemoglobin, which migrates faster than hemoglobin C. Thus the pattern for individuals with two types of hemoglobin is double.

3

"GENETIC DRIFT" IN AN ITALIAN POPULATION

LUIGI LUCA CAVALLI-SFORZA
August 1969

*Studies of blood-group frequencies and consanguineous
marriages among the people of the Parma Valley indicate
that this random change in hereditary type distinctly
influences human evolution*

The variety of hereditary types in a human population originates with mutations in the genetic material. The survival and preferential multiplication of types better adapted to the environment (natural selection) is the basis of evolution. Into this process, however, enters another kind of variation that is so completely independent of natural selection that it can even promote the predominance of genes that oppose adaptation rather than favoring it. Called genetic drift, this type of variation is a random, statistical fluctuation in the frequency of a gene as it appears in a population from one generation to the next. Sometimes genetic drift seems to exert only a moderate influence, causing the frequency of a gene to fluctuate by 5 or 10 percent. At other times it may result in one gene overwhelming other genes responsible for the same characteristic.

How strong is the influence of genetic drift in evolution, and what factors control it? Together with my colleagues Franco Conterio and Antonio Moroni of the University of Parma, Italo Barrai and Gianna Zei of the University of Pavia and our collaborators at other institutions, I have for the past 15 years been investigating genetic drift in the populations of the cities and villages in the Parma Valley in Italy. We have examined parish books, studied marriage records in the Vatican archives, made surveys of blood types, developed mathematical theories and finally simulated some of the region's populations on a computer. We have found that genetic drift can affect evolution significantly, and we have been successful in identifying factors that control it.

Hypothetically genetic drift can happen in the following way. Suppose a small group of Europeans, perhaps 10 people, colonized an island (as the mu-

tinous sailors of the *Bounty* and their Tahitian women did). Among 10 such randomly chosen people there might well be no one with blood of Type B or Type AB, because the genes for these blood types are respectively carried by only 15 percent and 5 percent of Europeans. Forty percent of Europeans have blood of Type O, and the same percentage have blood of Type A. In this small group, then, the frequency of the Type B gene might be zero rather than 15 percent because, in the nature of statistical processes, it is absent and cannot reappear unless a rare mutation takes place. The gene may also be extinguished if only one or a few members of the group

carry the Type B gene and they produce no descendants. Conversely, the frequency of a rare gene may sometimes increase until it becomes "fixed," or predominant. In remote valleys of the Alps, for instance, there is a relatively high frequency of such traits as albinism, mental deficiency and deaf-mutism, which are normally subject to negative selection.

This view of genetic drift suggests that two factors determine its strength: population size and migration. In the population of an alpine village, or among our hypothetical island colonists, a gene might vanish or become fixed in relatively few generations because the popula-

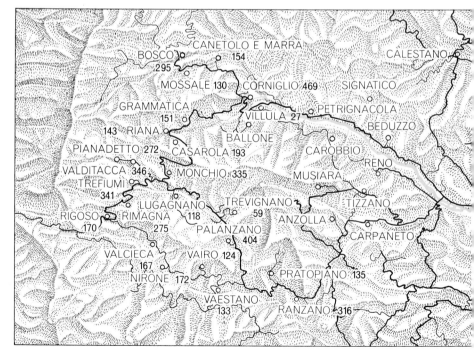

THE PARMA VALLEY stretches from the ridges behind the village of Rigoso at left to the plains of the Po River, 90 kilometers to the north. Because the settlement patterns of the Parma Valley include isolated villages in its steep-sided upper reaches, hill towns at lower

tion is so small that even a slight change in the actual number of people carrying a gene causes a large change in the percentage of the population endowed with that trait. In a larger population a change in gene frequency would affect a smaller percentage of the people, and thus drift would be less pronounced. Migration can offset the movement of a gene toward predominance or extinction by increasing the frequency of rival genes. Like migration, natural selection may also restore equilibrium, by promoting adaptive combinations of genes, even after the situation has been profoundly disturbed by genetic drift.

Isolated observations, however, offer only glimpses of the significance of genetic drift, and speculating on such observations cannot provide us with a basis for measuring the phenomenon or identifying the factors that control it. Accordingly my colleagues and I began to search for an experimental group in which we could conduct tests that would clarify these issues. We decided that the Parma Valley, which stretches for 90 kilometers to the south of the city of Parma, would provide an ideal population.

The Parma Valley, located in north-central Italy, is named after a stream that flows through it into the Po from the Apennines. The river has carved out what in its upper reaches is a steep-sided, inhospitable valley that gradually opens out into gentle hills and finally into a broad plain on which lies the city of Parma. The very geology of the valley creates an almost complete spectrum of the patterns of human habitation. In the highlands the steep countryside encourages people to gather in small villages of about 200 to 300 inhabitants. Farther downstream the rural villages become bigger as the hills give way to the plain, and where the stream flows into the Po stands the city of Parma [*see illustration below*].

People have lived in the Parma Valley since prehistoric times. Because there have been no major immigrations since the seventh century B.C. a certain demographic and genetic equilibrium has been reached. The effect of natural factors such as migration, natural selection and genetic drift can therefore be studied under the simplest conditions: when they are, or can be reasonably believed to be, in equilibrium. On the plain and in the hills, however, immigration and migratory exchanges are more frequent than in the mountains. Important demographic information is supplied by the parish books of marriages, births and deaths in the area since the end of the 16th century. Accordingly the valley offers excellent opportunities for measuring the effects of population size and migration on drift.

One of the first hypotheses we decided to test was the one that drift should be more pronounced in a small, isolated population than in a large one, since a large population has a wide variety of gene types and is more susceptible to migration. If this proposition were true, we could expect to detect the strongest drift in small, isolated mountain villages in the uplands of the Parma Valley, less drift in the hill communities farther down the valley and the least drift on the plain.

The most convenient way to measure drift is suggested by the nature of the phenomenon itself. Under the influence of drift village populations will tend to become more and more different, even if at the beginning they were homogeneous in their composition of hereditary types. Taking a particular hereditary characteristic, say blood of Type A, individuals with blood of this type may become more frequent in one village and rare in other villages. What is needed is a measure of this kind of variation among villages. If we had only two villages, we could take the percentage of individuals with blood of Type A in one village and the percentage in the other village and compute the difference between the two percentages as a measure of the variation between the two villages. In examining many villages we might consider the differences between all possible pairs of villages and average them out. In actuality we use a somewhat different way

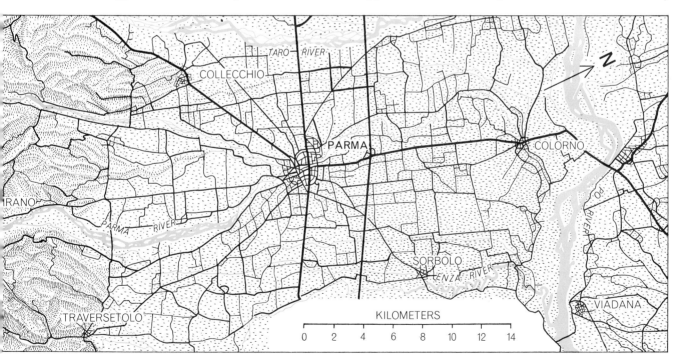

altitudes and the city of Parma on the plain south of the Po, the valley constitutes an excellent natural laboratory for studying how genetic drift affects human evolution. In order to study genetic drift, blood samples were taken throughout the cities and towns of the valley, and those upland villages whose population sizes are indicated by numbers were simulated in a computer experiment.

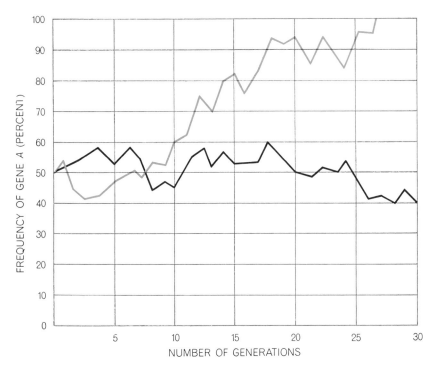

GENETIC DRIFT can cause the frequency of a gene to vary markedly from one population to another. In this calculation performed with random numbers Gene *A* appears in '50 percent of the members of two populations. Only 27 generations later Gene *A* has become "fixed" in one (*color*) and in the other its frequency fluctuates from 40 to 60 percent.

of measuring the variation, but the principle is much the same. Here let us simply call the result "measure of genetic variation between villages." Estimates of the variation were obtained after we had grouped villages in somewhat larger local areas, from the highlands down through the hill towns to the city of Parma. The measure we used excludes the effects due to sampling because we used a fraction of the total population.

As predicted, the variation between villages declined as population size increased, from .03 in the high valley, where the population density was well under 50 people per square kilometer, to less than .01 in the hill country, where there are about 100 people per square kilometer, to almost nothing on the plain, where the density reaches 200 people per square kilometer [*see bottom illustration on page 30*].

It is possible that the variation between villages could be caused by adaptation to different environments rather than by genetic drift. As unlikely as it may seem, it is possible that the environmental conditions differ from village to village so that different genes are favored in each place. It may also be that people of diverse origins and therefore of diverse blood groups have settled in the more populous regions, and that because of these historical accidents there

has not yet been time to reach an equilibrium.

If natural selection or historical accidents were responsible, the percentage of individuals possessing a certain gene would vary from village to village. The percentage would not necessarily vary in the same way for all genes, since there is no reason why the selective factors or historical accidents should operate with equal force on all genes. It would, in fact, be a strange coincidence if they did. If the variations in genes were caused by genetic drift, however, they would be the same, on the average, for any gene. The reason is that genetic drift, being a property of the population rather than of the gene, should affect all genes in the same way. Our evidence shows that the variations between villages are indeed the same for any gene.

This first test of our ideas about genetic drift was convincing, but in order to test our analysis more severely we wanted to make exact forecasts of the amount of genetic variation caused by drift. Such an exercise would require a precise quantitative prediction rather than a simple qualitative statement. Unfortunately the classical mathematical theories of population genetics (put forward by Sewall Wright, Motoo Kimura and Gustave Malécot) require that vil-

lages be of equal size, and that migrations between them follow a highly homogeneous pattern, simplifications that are rather far from reality.

To avoid this difficulty we developed other methods of predicting variations in the frequency of a gene on the basis of population size and migration. With the help of Walter Bodmer of Stanford University it was possible to devise a new theory that takes account of the actual observed migration pattern from village to village, however complex it may be. The model removes many of the oversimplifications of the classical theories but not all of them. We have therefore also developed a more general method that makes it possible on the basis of simple demographic information to predict the expected amount of drift with unlimited adherence to reality. This method consists in the use of artificial populations generated in a computer. Before I describe it, however, I should mention an apparently independent but in fact closely related approach, using a substantially different body of data, that we have followed in parallel with the study of genes.

This alternative approach we have followed is the study of relationships between individuals, which can be obtained from pedigrees or similar sources. One intuitively understands that the relationship between people must be associated with the similarities (or the differences) between the genes they carry. Both depend on common ancestry. Greater isolation between villages implies a lesser degree of common ancestry between the people of the villages, and therefore both a lesser degree of relationship between them and more differences between their genes. Thus the study of pedigrees, making it possible to estimate common ancestry, or degrees of relationship, should yield almost the same information as an analysis of the frequency of genes in the various villages. It has been shown that even data as simple as the identity of surnames can, in indicating common ancestry, supply information similar to what can be obtained from the direct study of genes.

It is the availability of parish books in the Parma Valley that makes it possible to carry on this investigation in parallel with the study of genes. Unfortunately the reconstruction of pedigrees from parish books is a laborious task, and it has not yet been completed. We do, however, have data on relationships from another source: records of consanguineous marriages. We found it particularly interesting to test the validity of this method as an alternative to the direct study of the effects of drift on genes. In the Parma Valley we could compare all these approaches. We could see, for instance, if we could predict drift from consanguinity or vice versa, or better still, predict both from a common source: simple demographic data.

Consanguineous marriages and genetic drift are similarly affected by common factors: population size and migration. A small population encourages consanguineous marriage because after a few generations most marriage partners would also be relatives. Migration, on the other hand, tends to decrease the frequency of consanguineous marriage by introducing new partners who are not relatives, or, if the flow is outward, by removing relatives who would otherwise be available.

The mathematical model with which the frequency of consanguineous marriage can be predicted is relatively simple. It is based on the idea that the population whose size critically affects the frequency of consanguineous marriage and genetic drift is somewhat diffuse, ge-

ographically speaking. As the Swedish geneticist Gunnar Dahlberg pointed out in 1938, this population basically consists of a group of people who are potential marriage partners for one another. This population is therefore not identical with the marriageable population because there are social barriers that reduce marriage choice. A village or a town might also be so large that not all the available partners would know one another. Such factors tend to make the population of eligible partners smaller than it is in a smaller village. The group can, however, extend across political boundaries, so that marriages are made between people living in different villages.

Since a simple census will not yield the size of the population of marriageable individuals, the population must be determined mathematically. By definition the population consists of a circle of N people available to one another for marriage. Assume now that an individual is not prohibited from marrying a blood relative (provided they are not so closely related that the marriage is forbidden by law). In this case the probability that he (or she) will marry a relative will be equal to the ratio between the number of eligible blood relatives, c, and the number of candidates who are not relatives. The probability of consanguineous marriage, m, will therefore equal c/N. This probability is also identical with the overall frequency of consanguineous marriage; all other factors being excluded, the frequency of consanguineous marriage would depend only on the number of available partners who are also kinsmen. Thus if there were 40 available partners and 20 of them were blood relatives, the frequency of consanguineous marriage would be one in two, or 50 percent. Knowing the number of blood relatives from simple calculations, and the frequency m of consanguineous marriages from ecclesiastical records, we can determine the size N of the population of eligible mates because it is a function of m and c. In other words, if $m = c/N$, then $N = c/m$.

Having determined the population size, it would be convenient at this point if we could simply complete our

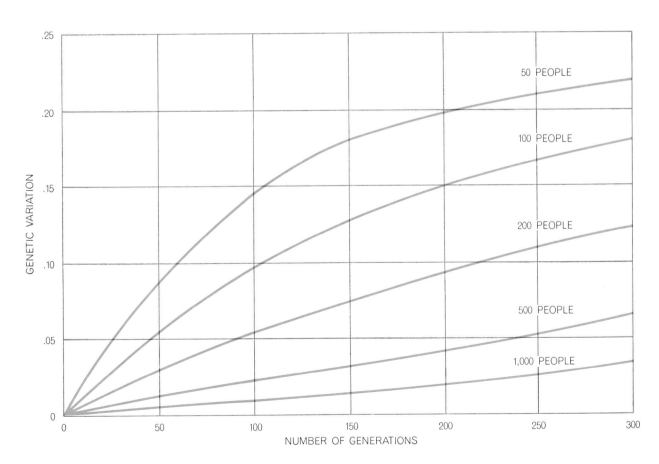

POPULATION AND DRIFT are closely related. The frequency of a particular gene in each population begins in the first generation at 50 percent, equivalent to zero on the vertical scale marked according to a measure of genetic drift called variance. After 300 generations the variation of the gene in the smallest population has increased to .22, almost as far as it can go, whereas in the largest population it has reached only .03. Genetic drift, then, is strongest in smaller populations and weakens as the population size increases.

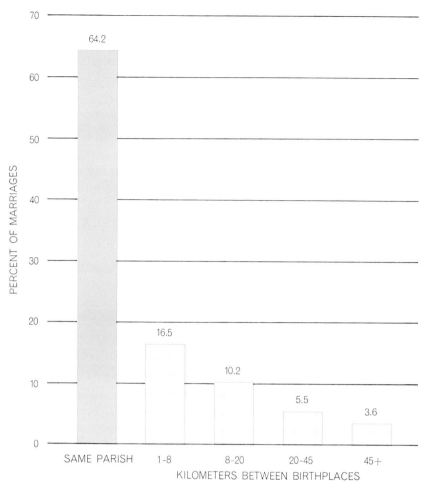

MIGRATION in upper Parma Valley has been infrequent, a conclusion drawn from the fact that most marriages recorded from 1650 to 1950 in parish books unite men and women who are from the same village. The number falls as the distance separating birthplaces increases.

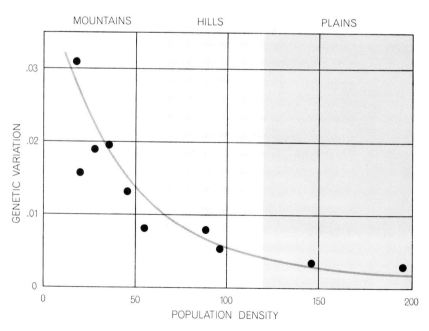

VARIATION in the frequency of a blood type between one village and another was greatest, as predicted, in the isolated upland hamlets, and declined as population density increased farther down the valley in the hill towns, on the plain and in the city of Parma.

model by taking into account the effect of migration on the available supply of marriage partners. We could then predict the frequency of consanguineous marriage and therefore estimate the amount of genetic drift. Reality, however, forces us to make a circuitous detour. It appears that there are certain factors (such as the tendency of people to marry people of a similar age, biases for or against certain kinds of consanguineous marriage and the fact that degrees of kinship too remote are recorded incompletely or not at all) that would distort the prediction of genetic drift because they affect only the frequency of consanguineous marriage without influencing the rate of variation for a gene. In order to calculate genetic drift on the basis of consanguineous marriage we must identify and compensate for such factors.

These factors can be inferred from the study of consanguineous marriages. The Vatican archives contain records of 590,-000 dispensations for consanguineous marriages granted from 1911 to 1964, the year in which our gathering of data temporarily ended. Only the dispensations for the more distantly consanguineous marriages that were granted directly by the bishops in certain areas such as Sicily and Sardinia and a few other remote dioceses are excluded. This material provided our investigators (led by Moroni, who had been a student of mine at the University of Parma) with a mass of valuable information. The records provide, among other data, the given name and the family name of the parents of the couple and the degree to which the marriage is consanguineous.

These records exist because the Roman custom and religious belief that prohibited marriage between blood relatives was inherited and diffused by the Catholic church. During the Middle Ages only the Pope could grant dispensations from the prohibition, and the dispensations (at least those known to us) were not numerous. The degree of consanguinity eligible for dispensation, however, has varied through the centuries, and a progressively more liberal trend can be detected. In the 16th century the Council of Trent recommended that a special dispensation be required for marriages up to "the fourth degree" (third cousins). Since 1917 dispensation has been required only for marriages between second cousins. The Vatican Council has recently pushed the liberalization one degree further, so that today only a marriage between first cousins, or between uncle and niece, require dispen-

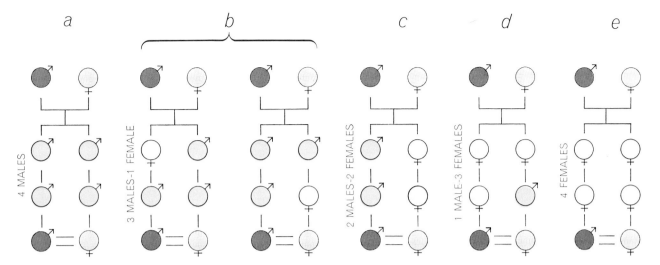

FAMILY TREES affect the frequency of consanguineous marriage. Different family trees associated with second-cousin marriages show that when spouses share only male ancestors (*a*), the number of consanguineous marriages reaches 774. As the number of female ancestors rises the number of marriages falls. Trees such as *b* (two varieties are shown) have produced 652 marriages, *c* 325 marriages, *d* 262 marriages and *e* 252 marriages, according to diocesan records from 1850 to 1950. Since land passes from father to son, men do not usually emigrate and marriages among relatives are therefore much more likely. There are 10 other trees for second-cousin marriages.

sation. Marriages between closer relatives are not and never have been eligible for dispensation.

The dispensation must be requested by the parish priest from the Curia before the marriage can be celebrated. In some cases the bishop can grant dispensations, but customarily he must forward a copy of the request to Rome (or, in other countries, to the representative of the Pope in that country). The Vatican will then reply to the bishop, and he will reply to the priest. The Vatican practically always grants dispensations in allowed cases, and therefore the dispensation request has constituted, or at least constitutes today, only a formal obstacle.

Of the factors that seem to alter the frequency of consanguineous marriage, one is the very closeness of the blood relationship. Apart from legal and religious restrictions, there is the widespread knowledge that consanguineous marriages may result in hereditary handicaps for the offspring.

Age can also have an important effect. As the archives show, marriages in which the consanguineous mates are a generation apart, such as those between uncle and niece and between first cousins once removed, are rarer than those between first cousins and between second cousins. We can explain this fact if we assume that in both consanguineous marriages and nonconsanguineous marriages age affects the choice of mates in the same way. In Italy, for instance, there is a mean age difference between husband and wife of about five years; the differ-

ence is smaller for young spouses and larger and more variable for older spouses. Therefore by considering the age differences among children of the same family, between parents and children and between normal spouses we can predict that marriages between uncle and niece will be only 3 percent of what would be expected on the basis of the frequency of this relationship, and marriages between aunt and nephew will be still rarer. By the same token one could expect a higher frequency of marriage between first cousins, because they tend to be of a similar age.

Migration also tends to reduce the frequency of consanguineous marriage. In places where the population is small and migration is low, blood relatives remain in contact. Hence we are not surprised to find most of the consanguineous marriages in rural areas whose populations have been rooted in the same soil for many generations. In industrial areas migration tends to disperse blood relatives so that they may not even meet, much less marry. Therefore consanguineous marriage tends to be diluted in frequency, or even to vanish, just as genetic drift does.

The effects of migration become more complex when we study specific types of genealogical trees. From data gathered in northern Emilia, a broad region including the Parma Valley, it appears that in the past century the number of consanguineous marriages diminishes when among the immediate ancestors of husband and wife there are more females

than males. The reason is that men and women migrate in different patterns. In a largely rural area such as the one we were examining, where land is inherited by the male child, fewer sons emigrate than daughters. Moreover, a woman who marries someone from another village will emigrate in the process, and the distance between the villages will make her descendants a little less available for marriage with descendants remaining in the original place. The more women there are in the genealogical tree, the more significant this pattern is [*see illustration above*].

We have also isolated a factor of a sociological nature. It is scarcely important enough on the statistical level to merit consideration, but I shall cite it as a curiosity. It is the tendency of children of consanguineous mothers to intermarry. Probably this is because the mothers, when related, have a greater tendency to conserve bonds that favor marriage among the children.

With the help of Kimura (who is with the National Institute of Genetics in Japan) and Barrai, we incorporated these inhibiting factors and the effects of migration into a mathematical model that predicts the incidence of consanguineous marriage with some accuracy.

Even this carefully derived mathematical theory suffers, as all applications of mathematics in biology do, from the necessity of simplifying reality in order to make results calculable. The difficulty lies not only in solving complicated mathematical problems but also in successfully simplifying the terms of the problem to allow the use of appropriate mathematical instruments without losing essential features of the problem. Computers, however, make possible another technique for attacking these problems. If we have enough data available on the population under examination, we can reconstruct it in the computer and see what happens in experiments. The repetition of these experiments a sufficient number of times gives us a view of what we can expect in reality. In this way we can, without the use of higher mathematics and with the employment of real data, forecast the complicated effects of the genetic structure of a population on phenomena such as the frequency of consanguineous marriages or genetic drift.

Naturally we simplify the artificial population that we reconstruct in a computer as much as we can. Our computer "men" and "women" do not have hands and brains, only a number (0 or 1) that indicates sex, a number of several digits representing a name, and other numbers that identify the father and the mother of each individual, his distant ancestors and his descendants. If we study the effects of age, we must give our artificial subjects an age, and by the same token we can characterize their geographic location and social class [*see illustration below*].

An artificial population so constructed marries, reproduces and dies according to certain probability tables drawn from reality. For reasons of economy we make the time advance crudely, in steps of 10 years. Thus if we have a 30-year-old person, we ask the probability of his dying before 40, and on the basis of tables of the real population we make him die according to a random procedure that has a probability equal to the real one. To determine whether a 30-year-old man dies before 40, for example, we calculate from the program a random number between 00 and 99. Such a number has equal probability of being one of the 100 numbers from 00 to 99. Since the probability of a man of this age dying is 12 percent, the individual dies if the chosen number lies between 00 and 11 and survives if it falls between 12 and 99. In the same way, using a random-number table that gives real probabilities, we decide if he marries and whom he marries by making the choice based on age, social class and geographical location. Finally, computer-generated marriages can be analyzed to determine the degree of consanguinity.

The results obtained by simulating the population of the Parma Valley confirm the impressions we had gained from our mathematical analysis of the actual population. That is, taking into account age, migration and the number of blood relatives of a given degree, the frequency of consanguineous marriages is about the same as what one would expect it to be if such marriages happened randomly. This is particularly true for the more remote degrees of consanguinity. Among first cousins, however, it seems that the frequency of consanguineous marriages is only half what it would have been if such marriages had been random.

Our final experiment consisted in sim-

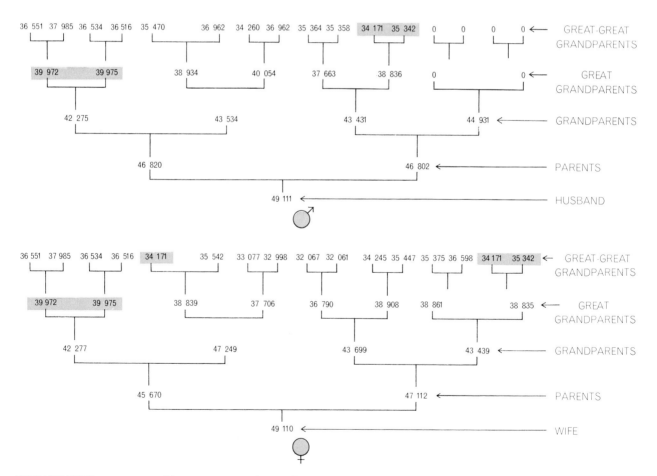

MAN AND WIFE are programmed for a computer run that simulates populations in order to determine the rate of genetic drift through the frequency of consanguineous marriage. The male's name is encoded in the digits 49 111. Other numbers (not shown) can be programmed that indicate the person's sex, age, social class and genetic endowment. Shading indicates ancestors shared by man and wife.

ulating the populations of 22 villages in order to test our hypotheses of genetic drift. The 5,000 individuals in the test population were given genes of the three blood-group systems: ABO (governed by the gene types A_1, A_2, B and O), Rh (seven gene types) and MN (two gene types). At the beginning of the simulation the frequencies of these genes in each simulated village were the same as the average of the frequencies in the actual villages. With the passage of each simulated generation, however, the frequencies began to change by a factor that was approximately the same for each blood-group system. They finally leveled off when the number of people belonging to a blood group was two or three times the original value. This equilibrium was reached fairly soon (after about 15 generations) as a consequence of the establishment of a balance between drift, which tends to make villages different, and migration, which tends to make them more nearly the same.

We found that the variations among the simulated villages quite closely matched the variations predicted by Bodmer's theory, thus confirming its capacity to represent real data. We also found that the variations among the simulated villages matched, although less closely, the variations observed among the real villages. In both the simulated and the real villages no single gene type either vanished or became predominant; the drift was not strong enough to achieve this result. Fairly divergent proportions of genes could be found in the different villages. Which gene increased in which particular village was of course a matter of chance. We did not expect a real village to show the same proportion of a given gene as its artificial counterpart [*see illustration on this page*].

It is clear that since the observed variation corresponds—within limits that we are now investigating—to the expected one it is not necessary to invoke explanations other than the action of genetic drift. The methods we have used in our study of the Parma Valley have now been applied to other populations as diverse as African pygmies, New Guinea tribesmen and the descendants of the Maya Indians. The results so far have confirmed the concept that genetic drift is the principal agent responsible for the variations among villages, tribes or clans. In fact, at the microgeographical and microevolutionary levels on which we worked the differences attributable to natural selection were not large (apart

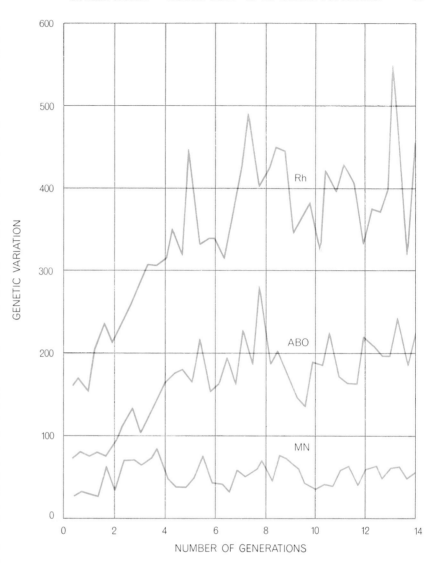

GENE FREQUENCIES for the ABO, Rh and MN blood-group systems in the populations of the villages from the upper part of the Parma Valley vary with the passing of each generation. Differences in gene frequency between villages simulated in a computer program and measured by "chi square" were similar to the differences in the real villages. Therefore migration, population size and other demographic influences that control the simulated genetic drift are probably equivalent to the forces at work in the real villages.

from some minor ones we intend to reexamine). Furthermore, there is evidence that drift can operate on a macroevolutionary scale extending over millions of years. Recent comparisons of the sequences of amino acids in the proteins of separate species show differences that are at least in part caused by drift, although the evidence is still controversial.

In seeking to extend these conclusions one could study populations distributed over large areas. In that case, however, it would be easier to encounter disturbing factors. For example, in a large enough region one might encounter selective pressures whose diversifying effects would be added to the effects of

drift on certain genes, whereas in another area or in the case of another gene natural selection might oppose drift and reduce the variations.

In any case, the discovery that genetic drift can affect evolution on a small scale over a short period of time gives the phenomenon a more important role in evolution than was once thought. It would be an error to assume, however, that evolution is almost entirely random. Only natural selection can bring about adaptation to the environment, and its importance must not be underestimated. The relative importance of drift and natural selection in determining the course of evolution remains to be assessed.

4

THE STRUCTURE AND HISTORY OF AN ANCIENT PROTEIN

RICHARD E. DICKERSON

April 1972

To oxidize food molecules all organisms from yeasts to man require a variant of cytochrome c. *Differences in this protein from species to species provide a 1.2-billion-year record of molecular evolution*

Between 1.5 and two billion years ago a profound change took place in some of the single-celled organisms then populating our planet, a change that in time would contribute to the rise of many-celled organisms. The machinery evolved for extracting far more energy from foods than before by combining food molecules with oxygen. One of the central components of the new metabolic machinery was cytochrome *c*, a protein whose descendants can be found today in every living cell that has a nucleus. By studying the cytochrome *c* extracted from various organisms it has been possible to determine how fast the protein has evolved since plants and animals diverged into two distinct kingdoms and in fact to provide an approximate date of 1.2 billion years ago for the event. For example, the cytochrome *c* molecules in men and chimpanzees are exactly the same: in the cells of both the molecule consists of 104 amino acid units strung together in exactly the same order and folded into the same three-dimensional structure. On the other hand, the cytochrome *c* in man has diverged from the cytochrome *c* in the red bread mold *Neurospora crassa* in 44 out of 104 places, yet the three-dimensional structures of the two cytochrome *c* molecules are essentially alike. We think we can now explain how it is that so many of the 104 amino acid units in cytochrome *c* are interchangeable and also why certain units cannot be changed at all without destroying the protein's activity.

Let us try to visualize the earth before cytochrome *c* first appeared. The first living organisms on the planet were little more than scavengers, extracting energy-rich organic compounds (includ-

ing their neighbors) from the water around them and releasing low-energy breakdown products. We still have the "fossils" of this life-style in the universal process of anaerobic (oxygenless) fermentation, as when a yeast extracts energy from sugar and releases ethyl alcohol, or when an athlete who exercises too rapidly converts glucose to lactic acid and gets muscle cramps. Anaerobic fermentation is part of the common biochemical heritage of all living things.

The upper limit on how much life the planet could support with only fermentation as an energy source was determined by the rate at which high-energy compounds were synthesized by nonbiological agencies: ultraviolet radiation, lightning discharges, radioactivity or heat. When some organisms developed the ability to tap sunlight for energy, photosynthesis was born and the life-carrying capacity of the earth increased enormously. This was the age of the bac-

SKELETON OF CYTOCHROME *c* MOLECULE is depicted in the illustration by Irving Geis on the opposite page. A variant of this protein molecule is found in the cells of every living organism that utilizes oxygen for respiration. The illustration shows in simplified form how 104 amino acid units are linked in a continuous chain that grips and surrounds a heme group, a complex rosette with an atom of iron (*Fe*) at its center. The picture is color-coded to indicate how much variation has been tolerated by evolution at each of the 104 amino acid sites in the molecule. Some species lack the 104th amino acid, and all species except vertebrates have as many as eight extra amino acids at the beginning of the chain (*see table on pages 36 and 37*). The amino acids that are most invariant throughout evolution, and presumably the most important, are shown in red and orange; the more variable sites appear in yellow-green, blue-green, blue and purple. The indispensable heme group is crimson. Each amino acid is represented only by its "alpha" carbon atom: the atom that carries a side chain unique for each of the 20 amino acids. The upper drawing at left below shows how two amino acids link up through an amide group (*colored panel*); the side chains connected to the alpha carbons (*color*) are represented by the balls labeled *R*. The lower drawing at left below shows the scheme used in the cytochrome *c* skeleton on the opposite page; all amide linkages (—CO—NH—) are omitted and the only side groups shown are those that are attached to the heme. The amino acids at the 35 invariant sites of the cytochrome *c* molecule (*red*) are designated in abbreviated form (*see key at right below*).

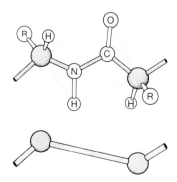

Ala	Alanine	Leu	Leucine
Asp	Aspartic acid	Lys	Lysine
Asn	Asparagine	Met	Methionine
Arg	Arginine	Phe	Phenylalanine
Cys	Cysteine	Pro	Proline
Gly	Glycine	Ser	Serine
Glu	Glutamic acid	Thr	Threonine
Gln	Glutamine	Trp	Tryptophan
His	Histidine	Tyr	Tyrosine
Ile	Isoleucine	Val	Valine

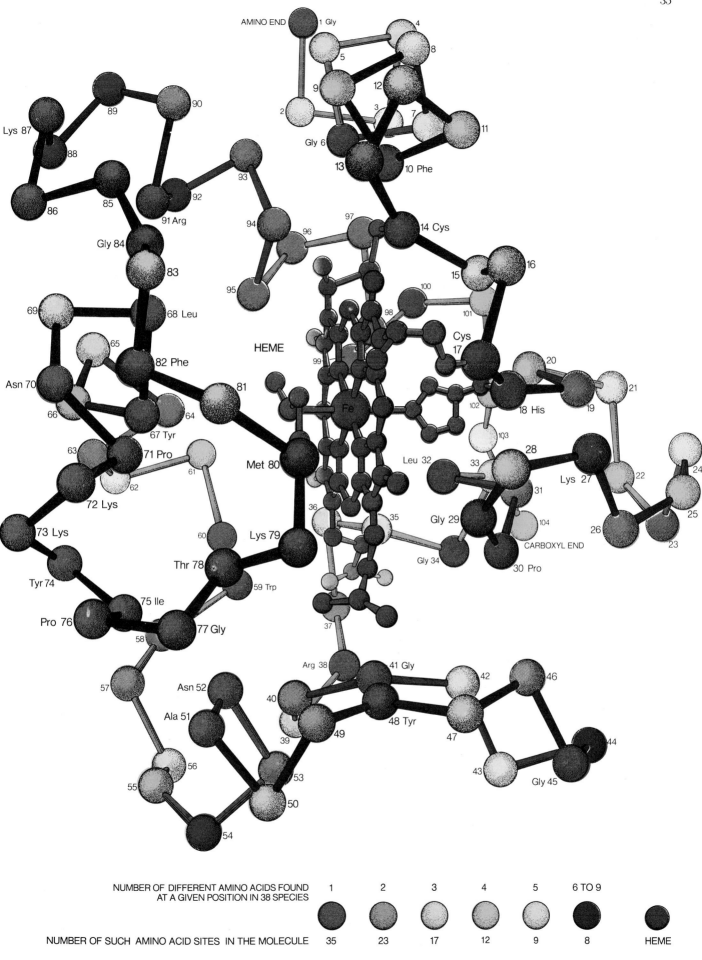

NUMBER OF DIFFERENT AMINO ACIDS FOUND
AT A GIVEN POSITION IN 38 SPECIES

1 2 3 4 5 6 TO 9

NUMBER OF SUCH AMINO ACID SITES IN THE MOLECULE

35 23 17 12 9 8 HEME

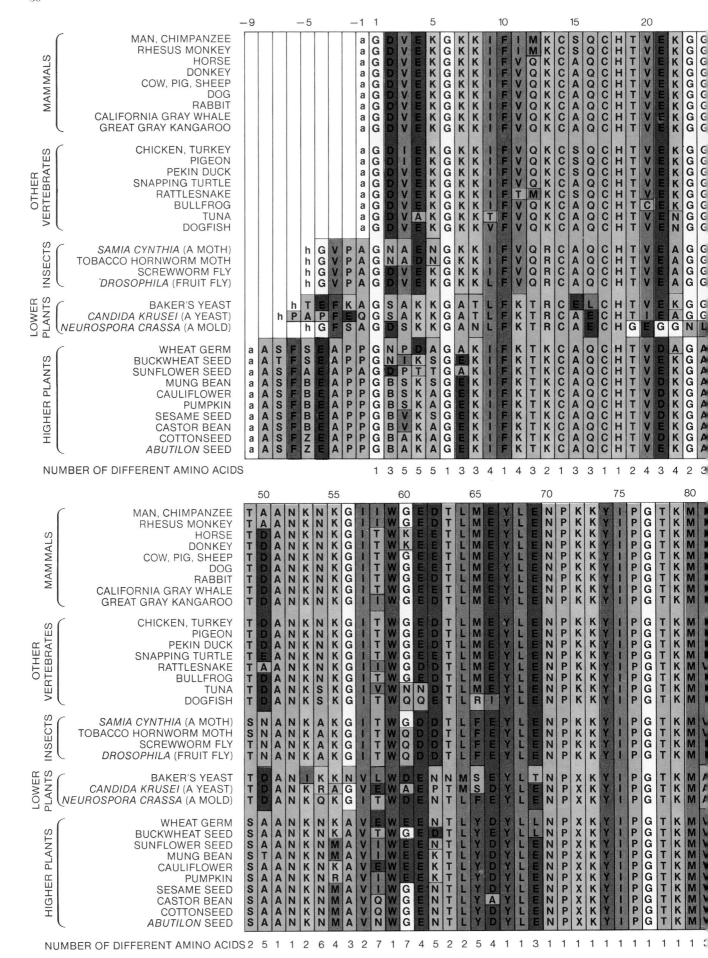

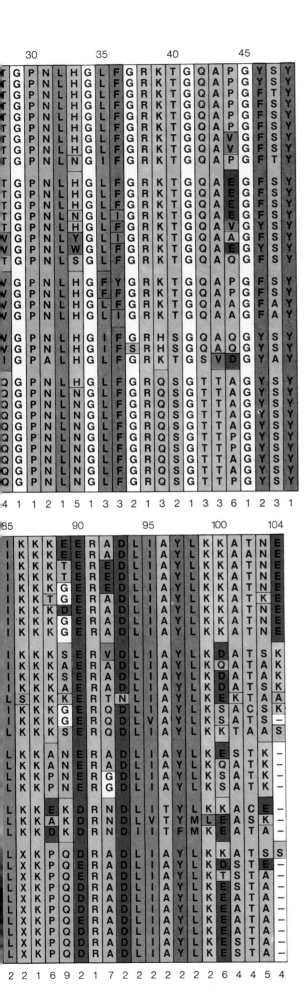

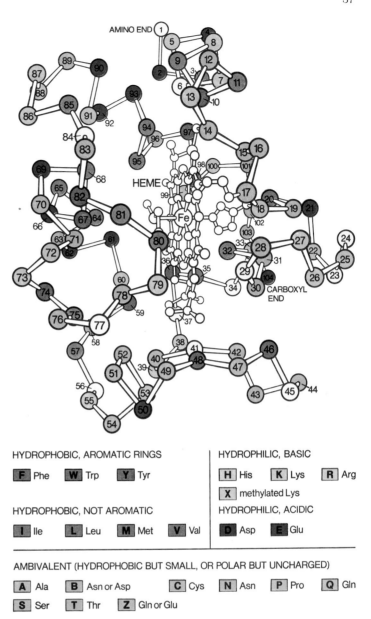

AMINO END

HEME

Fe

CARBOXYL END

HYDROPHOBIC, AROMATIC RINGS

| F | Phe | W | Trp | Y | Tyr |

HYDROPHOBIC, NOT AROMATIC

| I | Ile | L | Leu | M | Met | V | Val |

HYDROPHILIC, BASIC

| H | His | K | Lys | R | Arg |
| X | methylated Lys |

HYDROPHILIC, ACIDIC

| D | Asp | E | Glu |

AMBIVALENT (HYDROPHOBIC BUT SMALL, OR POLAR BUT UNCHARGED)

| A | Ala | B | Asn or Asp | C | Cys | N | Asn | P | Pro | Q | Gln |
| S | Ser | T | Thr | Z | Gln or Glu |

NO SIDE CHAIN (HYDROGEN ATOM) | G | Gly |

COMPOSITION OF CYTOCHROME c IN 38 SPECIES is presented in the table at left. No other protein has been so fully analyzed for so many different organisms. The color code used here differs from the one used in the molecular skeleton on page 35. On these two pages color is employed to classify amino acids according to their chemical properties (*see key directly above*). Thus the three "oily" (hydrophobic) amino acids with aromatic benzene rings in their side chains (phenylalanine, tryptophan and tyrosine) are shown in red. Four other amino acids that are hydrophobic but nonaromatic are shown in orange. At the other extreme, amino acids that are hydrophilic, or water-loving, are shown in blue or violet. Amino acids that can be found in either aqueous or nonaqueous environments (and hence are ambivalent) are green or yellow. Polar amino acids can have asymmetric distributions of positive and negative charge. The detailed structure of the side chains of the amino acids can be found on page 39. It is easy to pick out from the table at left the amino acid sites where evolution has allowed no change or has allowed substitution only by chemically similar amino acids; these sites are identified by vertical bands of a single color. A letter *a* at the beginning of the chain indicates that a methyl group (CH₃) is attached to the amino end of the molecular chain. A letter *h* indicates that the methyl group is absent.

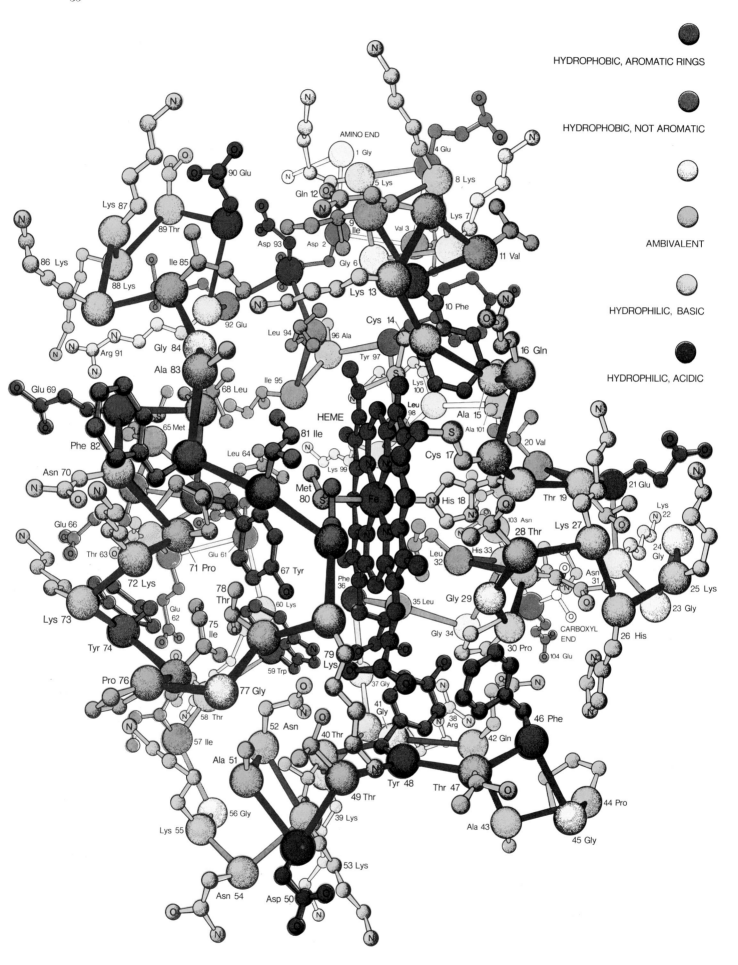

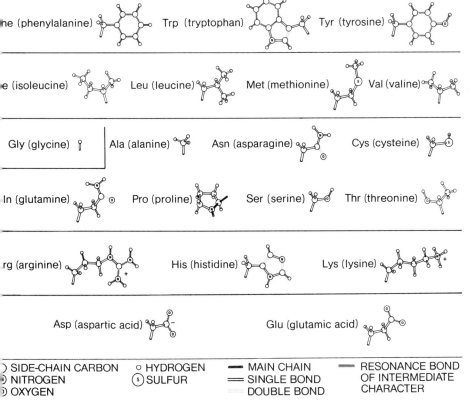

SIDE-CHAIN CARBON o **HYDROGEN**   ▬ **MAIN CHAIN**   ▬▬ **RESONANCE BOND**
NITROGEN   (s) **SULFUR**   ═ **SINGLE BOND**   **OF INTERMEDIATE**
OXYGEN   ═ **DOUBLE BOND**   **CHARACTER**

CYTOCHROME c MOLECULE WITH SIDE CHAINS appears in the illustration on the opposite page. The picture shows the structure of horse-heart cytochrome c in the oxidized state as determined through X-ray crystallography by the author and his colleagues at the California Institute of Technology. Alpha-carbon atoms are numbered and the amide groups (—CO—NH—) connecting the alpha carbons are represented only by a solid bond, as in the preceding drawings. For clarity three side chains at the "back" of the molecule have been left out: leucine 35, phenylalanine 36 and leucine 98. The color coding follows the coding in the illustration on pages 36 and 37. One can see from the three-dimensional structure that side chains in the interior of the molecule, around the heme group (*crimson*), tend to be hydrophobic (*red and orange*), whereas amino acids with hydrophilic side chains (*blue and violet*) are found on the outside, where they are ordinarily in contact with water. A major exception to this rule is the hydrophobic side chain of phenylalanine 82, which sits on the surface of the molecule at the left of the heme. The region between the hydrophilic chains, and above isoleucine 81, is a cavity that is apparently open to solvent molecules. Lysine 13, above this cavity, is known to interact with a large oxidase complex when cytochrome c is oxidized. The structures of the side chains of 20 amino acids appear above.

teria and the blue-green algae [see "The Oldest Fossils," by Elso S. Barghoorn; SCIENTIFIC AMERICAN Offprint 895].

The more advanced forms of photosynthesis released a corrosive and poisonous gas into the atmosphere: oxygen. Some bacteria responded by retreating to oxygen-free corners of the planet, where their descendants are found today. Other bacteria and blue-green algae developed ways to neutralize gaseous oxygen by combining it with their own waste products. The next step was to harness the energy released by oxidation of these waste compounds. (If you are going to burn your garbage, you might as well keep warm by the fire.) This was the beginning of oxidation, or respiration, the second big breakthrough in increasing the supply of energy available to life on the earth.

When a yeast cell oxidizes sugars all the way to carbon dioxide and water instead of stopping short at ethyl alcohol, it gets 19 times as much energy per gram of fuel. When oxygen combines with lactic acid in the athlete's muscles and the cramps are dissipated, he receives a correspondingly greater energy return from his glucose. Any improvement in metabolism that multiplies the supply of energy available by such a large factor would be expected to have a revolutionary effect on the development of life. We now believe the specialization of cells and the appearance of multicelled plants and animals could only have come about in the presence of such a large new supply of energy.

Bacteria and blue-green algae are prokaryotes (prenuclear cells); their genetic material, DNA, is not confined

within an organized nucleus, and their respiratory and photosynthetic machinery (if it is present) is similarly dispersed. Green algae and all the higher plants and animals are eukaryotes (cells with "good" nuclei); their DNA is organized within a nucleus, and their respiration is carried out in the organelles called mitochondria. In eukaryote plants photosynthesis is conducted in still other organelles called chloroplasts. Mitochondria are the powerhouse of all eukaryote cells. Their role is to break down the energy-rich molecules obtained from foods, combine them with oxygen and store the energy produced by harnessing it to synthesize molecules of adenosine triphosphate (ATP). The mitochondria of all eukaryotes are alike in their chemistry, as if once the optimum chemical mechanism had been arrived at it was never changed.

Biological oxidation involves at least a score of special enzymes that act first as acceptors and then as donors of the electrons or hydrogen atoms removed from food molecules. In the last part of the process one finds a series of cytochrome molecules (identified by various subscript letters), all of which incorporate a heme group containing iron, the same heme group found in hemoglobin. Electrons are passed down a chain of cytochrome molecules: from cytochrome b to cytochrome c_1, from cytochrome c_1 to cytochrome c, to cytochromes a and a_3 and finally to oxygen atoms, where they are combined with hydrogen ions to produce water. This is a stepwise process designed to release energy in small parcels rather than all at once. In the transfer of electrons from cytochrome b to cytochrome c_1 and again in the transfer between the cytochromes a, a_3 and oxygen, energy is channeled off to synthesize ATP, which acts as a general-purpose energy source for cell metabolism.

Most of the cytochromes are bound tightly to the mitochondrial membrane, but one of them, cytochrome c, can easily be solubilized in aqueous mediums and can be isolated in pure form. The other components can be isolated as multienzyme complexes: b and c_1 as a cytochrome reductase complex, and a and a_3 as a cytochrome oxidase. The reductase donates electrons to cytochrome c; the oxidase accepts them again. To illustrate how similar all eukaryotes really are to one another, it has been found that cytochrome c from any species of plant, animal or eukaryotic microorganism can react in the test tube with the cytochrome oxidase from any other species. Worm or primate, whale or wheat are all alike under the mitochondrial membrane.

The Evolution of Cytochrome *c*

Since cytochrome *c* is so ancient and at the same time so small and easily purified, it has received much attention from protein chemists interested in the evolutionary process. The complete amino acid sequence of cytochrome *c* has been determined for more than 40 species of eukaryotic life. Thirty-eight of these sequences are compared in the illustration on pages 36 and 37. We have more information on the evolution of this molecule than on the evolution of any other protein.

Emanuel Margoliash of Northwestern University and Emil Smith of the University of California at Los Angeles were among the first to notice that the amino acid sequences from various species are different and that the degree of difference corresponds quite well with the distance that separates the two species on the evolutionary tree. Detailed computer analyses of these differences by Margoliash, by Walter Fitch of the University of Wisconsin and by others have led to the construction of elaborate family trees of living organisms entirely without recourse to the traditional anatomical data. The family trees agree remarkably well with those obtained from classical morphology; it is obvious that

comparison of amino acid sequence is a powerful tool for studying the process of evolution.

Another result may at first be surprising. Cytochrome *c* is still evolving slowly and is doing so at a rate that is approximately constant for all species, when the rate is averaged over geological time periods. This kind of analysis of molecular evolution was first carried out on hemoglobin a decade ago by Linus Pauling and Emile Zuckerkandl at the California Institute of Technology. If we compare hemoglobin and cytochrome *c*, we find that cytochrome *c* is changing much more slowly. Why should this be? The protein chains are synthesized from instructions that are embodied in DNA, and it is in the DNA that mutations take place. Do mutations occur more often in the DNA that makes hemoglobin than in the DNA that makes cytochrome *c*? There is no reason to think so. The explanation therefore must lie in the natural-selection, or screening, process that tests whether or not mutant molecules can do their job.

Before discussing the various "formulas" that have passed the test of making a successful cytochrome *c*, I shall describe briefly the structure of proteins. All protein molecules are built up by linking amino acids end to end. Each of the 20 different amino acids has a carboxyl group (–COOH) at one end and an amino group (–NH$_2$) at the other. To link the carboxyl group of one amino acid with the amino group of another amino acid a molecule of water must be removed, producing an amide linkage (–CO–NH–). Because only a part (although, to be sure, the distinctive part) of an amino acid enters a protein chain, the chemist refers to it as a "residue." Thus he speaks of a glycine residue or a phenylalanine residue at such-and-such a position in a protein chain.

The carbon adjacent to the amide linkage is called the alpha carbon. It is important because each amino acid has a distinctive side chain at this position. The side chain may be nothing more than a single atom of hydrogen (as it is in the case of the amino acid glycine) or it may consist of a number of atoms, including a six-carbon "aromatic" ring (as it does in the case of phenylalanine, tryptophan and tyrosine).

The 20 amino acids can be grouped into three broad classes, depending on the character of their side chains [see illustration on preceding page]. Five are hydrophilic, or water-loving, and tend to acquire either a positive or a negative charge when placed in aqueous solution; three of the five are basic in character

PLOT OF DISTRIBUTION OF ELECTRIC CHARGES on the back of horse-heart cytochrome *c* reveals that most of the 19 hydrophilic lysines (*color*), which carry positive charges (and hence are basic), are distributed on the two flanks of the molecule. Nine of 12 negatively charged (acidic) side chains (*gray*) are clustered in one zone in the upper center of the molecule. The electrically negative character of this zone has been maintained throughout evolution, although the specific locations of the acidic side groups vary. No organism, from wheat germ to man, has a cytochrome *c* with fewer than six acidic amino acids in this zone and no organism has more than five acidic amino acids everywhere else on the molecule. Furthermore, these extreme values are not found in the same species. It is highly likely that these charged zones participate in binding cytochrome *c* to other large molecules.

(arginine, histidine and lysine) and the other two are acidic (aspartic acid and glutamic acid). Seven are not readily soluble in water and hence are termed hydrophobic; they include the three amino acids mentioned above that have rings in their side chains plus leucine, isoleucine, methionine and valine. The remaining eight amino acids react ambivalently to water: alanine, asparagine, cysteine, glutamine, glycine, proline, serine and threonine.

Now let us see how much the successful formulas for cytochrome c differ from species to species. The cytochrome c molecules of men and horses differ by 12 out of 104 amino acids. The cytochrome c's of the higher vertebrates—mammals, birds and reptiles—differ from the cytochrome c's of fishes by an average of 19 amino acids. The cytochrome c's of vertebrates and insects differ by an average of 27 amino acids; moreover, the cytochrome c molecules of insects and plants have a few more amino acid residues at the beginning of the chain than the equivalent molecules of vertebrates. The greatest disparity between two cytochrome c's is the one between man and the bread mold *Neurospora;* they differ at more than 40 percent of their amino acid positions. How can two molecules with such large differences in amino acid composition perform identical chemical functions?

We begin to see an answer when we look at where these changes are. Some parts of the amino acid sequence, as indicated on pages 36 and 37, never vary. Thirty-five of the 104 amino acid positions in cytochrome c are completely invariant in all known species, including a long sequence from residue 70 through residue 80. The 35 invariant sites are occupied by 15 different amino acids; they are shown in red in the structural drawing on page 35. Another 23 sites are occupied by only one of two different but closely similar amino acids. There are 18 different sets of interchangeable pairs at these 23 sites; they are shown in orange in the illustration. At 17 sites natural selection has evidently accepted only sets of three different amino acids; these 17 interchangeable triplets are colored yellow-green.

It was already known from sequence studies, before the X-ray structural analysis, that where such substitutions are allowed the interchangeable amino acids almost always have the same chemical character. In general all must be either hydrophilic or hydrophobic or else neutral with respect to water. Such interchanges are called conservative substitutions because they conserve the

overall chemical nature of that part of the protein molecule.

In only a few places along the chain can radical changes be tolerated. Residue 89, for example, can be acidic (aspartic acid or glutamic acid), basic (lysine), polar but uncharged (serine, threonine, asparagine and glutamine), weakly hydrophobic (alanine) or devoid of a side chain (glycine). Almost the only type of side chain that appears to be forbidden at this point in the molecule is a large hydrophobic one. Such "indifferent" regions are rare, however, and cytochrome c overall is an evolutionarily conservative molecule.

We have no reason to think the gene for cytochrome c mutates more slowly than the gene for hemoglobin, or that the invariant, conservative and radical regions of the sequence reflect any difference in mutational rate within the cytochrome c gene. The mutations are presumably random, and what we see in these species comparisons are the molecules that are left after the rigid test of survivability has been applied. Invariant regions evidently are invariant because any mutational changes there are lethal and are weeded out. Conservative changes can be tolerated elsewhere as long as they preserve the essential chemical properties of the molecule at that point. Radical changes presumably indicate portions of the molecule that do not matter for the operation of the protein.

This is as far as we can go from sequence comparisons alone. The explanation of variability in terms of the essential or nonessential character of different parts of the molecule is plausible, yet science has always been plagued by plausible but incorrect hypotheses. To progress any further we need to know how the amino acid sequence is folded to make an operating molecule. In short, we need the three-dimensional structure of the protein.

The Molecule in Three Dimensions

With the active collaboration of Margoliash, who was then working at the Abbott Laboratories in North Chicago, I began the X-ray-crystallographic analysis of horse-heart cytochrome c at Cal Tech in 1963, with the sponsorship of the National Science Foundation and the National Institutes of Health. As cytochrome c transfers electrons in the mitochondrion, it oscillates between an oxidized form (ferricytochrome) and a reduced form (ferrocytochrome); the iron atom in the heme group is alternately in the +3 and +2 oxidation state.

We decided to begin our analysis with the oxidized form, a decision that was largely tactical since both oxidation states would ultimately be needed if we were to try to decipher the electron-transfer process.

In X-ray crystallography one directs a beam of X rays at a purified crystal of the substance under study and records the diffraction pattern produced as the beam strikes the sample from different angles. X rays entering the sample are themselves deflected at various angles by the distribution of electron charges within the crystal. Highly sophisticated computer programs have been devised for deducing from tens of thousands of items of X-ray-diffraction data the three-dimensional distribution of electronic charge. From this distribution one can infer, in turn, the distribution of the amino acid side chains in the protein molecule.

We obtained our first low-resolution map of the oxidized form of horse-heart cytochrome c five years ago and the first high-resolution map three years ago. These maps have been used to construct detailed three-dimensional models of the protein. One can also feed the three-dimensional coordinates into a computer and obtain simple ball-and-stick drawings that can be viewed stereoptically, enabling one to visualize the folded chain of the protein in three dimensions [*see illustrations on next two pages*]. Just a year ago we calculated the first high-resolution map for the reduced form of cytochrome c. We are now improving this model and comparing the two oxidation states.

Several striking features of the amino acid sequences of cytochrome c were in the back of our minds as we worked out the first high-resolution structure. We knew that the most strongly conserved sites throughout evolution were those occupied by three distinctive types of residue: the positively charged (basic) residues of lysine; the three hydrophobic and aromatic residues of phenylalanine, tryptophan and tyrosine, and the four hydrophobic but nonaromatic residues of leucine, isoleucine, methionine and valine. These sites can now be located with the help of the illustration on page 38, whose color coding differs from the coding of the illustration on page 35. Here hydrophobic residues are shown in warm colors (red and orange) whereas neutral residues and hydrophilic residues, both basic and acidic, are shown in cool colors (green, yellow, blue and violet).

It had been known from the chemical analysis of the molecule's amino acid se-

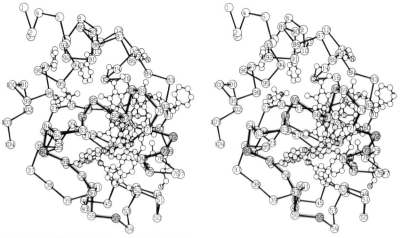

STEREOSCOPIC PAIR OF LEFT SIDE of oxidized cytochrome c molecule, drawn by computer, shows only a few key side chains for clarity. The main chain (*color*) from sites 55 to 75 defines a loop, the "left channel," which is filled with strongly hydrophobic side chains; their alpha carbons are in light color. Three of these side chains include aromatic rings: tryptophan 59, tyrosine 67 and tyrosine 74, also shown in light color. Alpha carbons with hydrophilic, positively charged side chains around the left channel are shown in dark color. This pair and one on opposite page can be viewed with standard stereoscopic viewer.

quence that the basic and hydrophobic groups tend to appear in clusters along the chain. For example, basic residues are found in the regions of sites 22 through 27, sites 38 and 39, sites 53 through 55 and sites 86 through 91. Hydrophobic residues are found in regions 9 through 11, 32 through 37, 80 through 85 and 94 through 98. The residues at sites 14 and 17 (cysteine) and site 18 (histidine) are invariant, which is understandable since they form bonds to the heme group. Less understandably, the long stretch from site 70 to site 80 is equally invariant. Before the structural evidence was available it had been suspected that methionine, at site 80, might be bonded to the iron atom on the other side of the heme from the histidine at site 18, but it was impossible to be sure from chemical evidence alone.

It was also known from chemical analysis that horse cytochrome c incorporates 12 glycines (the residues with only hydrogen as a side chain) and that these glycines were either invariant or else conserved in the great majority of species. It was known too that of the eight phenylalanines or tyrosines (with aromatic rings in their side chains) seven are either invariant in all species or replaceable only by one another. In the case of residue 36, phenylalanine or tyrosine is replaced in three species by isoleucine, whose side chain, although it is nonaromatic, is at least as large and hydrophobic as the side chains it replaces.

All these similarities and conservatisms were known before the X-ray analysis, but none could be explained in terms of structure. It was assumed that every residue had been placed where it was by natural selection and that it contained potentially important information about the working parts of the cytochrome molecule. Natural selection, however, does not act on an amino acid sequence but rather on the folded and operating molecule in its association with other biological molecules. Having a sequence without the folding instructions is like having a list of parts without a blueprint of the entire machine.

Cytochrome c and Evolution

Now that the blueprint for cytochrome c is revealed, let us look more closely at its representation on page 35. To keep the illustration simple no side chains have been included except for those that are bonded to the heme group. Moreover, along the main chain the illustration depicts only the alpha-carbon atoms from which side chains would, if they were shown, branch off. The amide groups (–CO–NH–) that connect alpha carbons are represented simply by straight lines. The picture is therefore a simplified folding diagram of the cytochrome molecule.

We see that the flat heme group, a symmetrical rosette of carbon and nitrogen atoms with an atom of iron at its center, sits in a crevice with only one edge exposed to the outside world. If the heme participates directly in shuttling electrons in and out of the molecule, the transfer probably takes place along this edge. Cysteines 14 and 17 and histidine 18 hold the heme in place

from the right as depicted, and the other heme-binding group on the left is indeed methionine 80, as had been suspected.

It was known from earlier X-ray studies of proteins that sequences of amino acids frequently fold themselves into the helical configuration known as the alpha helix; in other cases the amino acids tend to assume a rippled or corrugated configuration called a beta sheet. Cytochrome c has no beta sheets and only two stretches of alpha helix, formed by residues 1 through 11 and 89 through 101. For the most part the protein chain is wrapped tightly around the heme group, leaving little room for the alpha and beta configurations that are prominent in other proteins.

Just as one can use cytochrome c to learn about evolution, one can also use evolution to learn about cytochrome c. As I have noted, the illustration on page 35 is color-coded to indicate the amount of variability in the kind of amino acid tolerated at each site. The structure is "hot" (red and orange) in the functionally important places in the molecule when differences among species are absent or rare, and it is "cool" (green blue and violet) in regions that vary widely from one species to another and thus are presumably less important to a viable molecule of cytochrome c.

The heme crevice is hot, indicating that strong selection pressures tend to keep the environment of the heme group constant throughout evolution. The invariant residues 70 through 80 are also hot, and we now see that they are folded to make the left side of the molecule and the pocket in which the heme sits. The right side of the molecule is warm, consisting of sites where only one, two or three different amino acids are tolerated. The back of the molecule is its cool side; residues 58 and 60 and four more residues on the back of the alpha helix are each occupied by six or more different amino acids in various species. These are powerful clues to the important parts of the molecule, whether for electron transfer or for interaction with two large molecular complexes, the reductase and the oxidase.

How the Molecule Folds Itself

If we now turn to the illustration on page 38, which shows all the side chains of horse-heart cytochrome c, many of the evolutionary conservatisms become understandable. (As before, amide groups are still shown only as straight lines; their atomic positions are known but are not particularly relevant to this article.) In this illustration the colors are selected to classify the various sites according to the character of the amino acid tolerated (hydrophilic, hydrophobic or ambivalent); the same color coding applies in the illustration on pages 36 and 37 showing the amino acid sequences in the cytochrome *c*'s of 38 different species.

Nonpolar, hydrophobic groups are found predominantly on the inside of the molecule, away from the external aqueous world, whereas charged groups, acidic or basic, are always on the outside. This arrangement is a good example of the "oil drop" model of a folded protein. According to this model, when an amino acid chain is synthesized inside a cell, it is helped to fold in the proper way by the natural tendency of hydrophobic, or "oily," side chains to retreat as far as possible from the aqueous environment and cluster in the center of the molecule. An even stronger statement can be made: If it is necessary for the successful operation of a protein molecule that certain portions of the polypeptide chain be folded into the interior, then natural selection will favor the retention of hydrophobic side chains at that point so that the proper folding is achieved. A charged, or hydrophilic, side chain can be pushed into the interior of a protein molecule, but a considerable price must be paid in terms of energy. Thus in most cases the presence of a charged group at a given site helps to ensure that the chain at that point will be on the outside of the folded molecule. (Charged groups inside a protein are known only in one or two cases where they play a role in the catalytic mechanism of the protein.)

We can now see the reason for the evolutionary conservatism of hydrophobic side chains, and one of the reasons for the conservatism of the hydrophilic residue lysine: they help to make the molecule fold properly. Radical changes of side chain that prevent proper folding are lethal. No folding, no cytochrome; no cytochrome, no respiration; no respiration, no life. It is seldom that cause and effect in evolution are quite so clear-cut.

There is still more to the lysine story. The lysines are not only on the outside; they are clustered in two positively charged regions of the molecular surface, separated by another zone of negative charge. This segregation of charge has not been found in any other protein structure and, as we shall see, probably occurs because cytochrome *c* interacts with two molecular complexes (the reductase and the oxidase) rather than with small substrate molecules as an en-

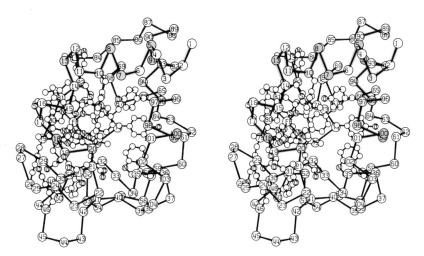

STEREOSCOPIC PAIR OF RIGHT SIDE of oxidized cytochrome *c* shows two sequences forming alpha helixes: the sequence from 1 through 11 and the sequence from 89 through 101. The two alpha helixes and the chain from 12 through 20 outline the right channel. Like the left channel it is lined with hydrophobic side groups, but it apparently contains a slot large enough to receive a hydrophobic side chain from another molecule. As in the stereoscopic drawing on the opposite page, alpha carbons with positively charged side chains around this channel are indicated in dark color; alpha carbons with strongly hydrophobic side chains are indicated in light color. The computer program for preparing the stereoscopic pictures was written by Carroll Johnson of the Oak Ridge National Laboratory.

zyme does. The charge arrangements are believed to be part of the process by which large molecules recognize each other.

Most of the 19 lysines are found on the left and right sides of the molecule viewed from the back on page 40. The left and right sides of the molecule can be examined separately in the two stereoscopic pairs on these two pages. On the left side eight lysines surround a loop of chain from sites 55 through 75 that is tightly packed with hydrophobic groups, including the invariant tyrosine 74, tryptophan 59 and tyrosine 67 farther inside. Although we do not yet know the electron-transfer mechanism, it has been suggested that the aromatic rings of the three invariant residues could provide an inward path for the electron when cytochrome *c* is reduced. Another eight lysines are found on the right side, on the periphery of what appears to be a true channel large enough to hold a hydrophobic side chain of another large molecule. This right-side channel is bounded by the two alpha helixes and by the continuation from the first alpha helix through residues 12 to 20. Within this channel are found two large aromatic side chains: phenylalanine 10 (which cannot change) and tyrosine 97 (which can also be phenylalanine but nothing else). In summary, on the right side is a channel lined with hydrophobic groups (including two aromatic rings) and surrounded by an outer circle of positive charges. As someone in our laboratory remarked on looking at the

model, it resembles a docking ring for a spaceship.

This remark may not be entirely frivolous. It is known from chemical work that the attraction between cytochrome *c* and the cytochrome oxidase complex is largely electrostatic, involving negatively charged groups on the oxidase and positively charged basic groups on cytochrome *c*. Either the left or the right cluster of lysines must be involved in this binding. Moreover, Kazuo Okunuki of the University of Osaka has shown that if just one positive charge, lysine 13, is blocked with a bulky aromatic chemical group, the reactivity of cytochrome with its oxidase is cut in half. Chemically blocking lysine 13 means physically blocking the upper part of the heme crevice. Lysine 13 is closer to the right cluster of positive charges than to the left; thus it would appear more likely that the heme crevice and the right channel together are the portions of the molecular surface that "see" the oxidase complex.

What, then, are the roles of the positive zone on the left side and the negative patch at the rear? The positive zone, with its three aromatic rings, may be the binding site to the reductase; we know virtually nothing about the chemical nature of this binding. The negative patch may be a "trash dump," an unimportant part of the molecule's surface where there are enough negative charges to prevent an excessively positive overall charge. The fact that the six most variable amino acid sites are in this part

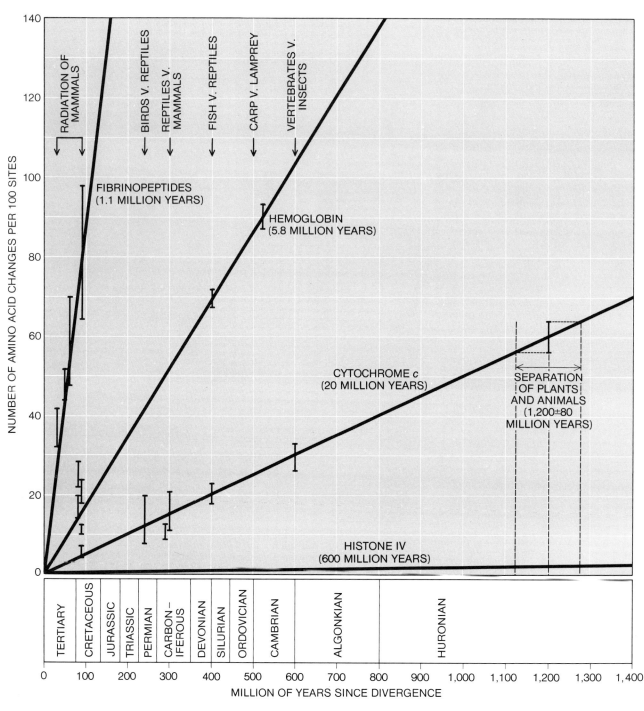

NUMBER OF AMINO ACID CHANGES PER 100 SITES

RADIATION OF MAMMALS

BIRDS V. REPTILES

REPTILES V. MAMMALS

FISH V. REPTILES

CARP V. LAMPREY

VERTEBRATES V. INSECTS

FIBRINOPEPTIDES (1.1 MILLION YEARS)

HEMOGLOBIN (5.8 MILLION YEARS)

CYTOCHROME c (20 MILLION YEARS)

SEPARATION OF PLANTS AND ANIMALS (1,200±80 MILLION YEARS)

HISTONE IV (600 MILLION YEARS)

TERTIARY | CRETACEOUS | JURASSIC | TRIASSIC | PERMIAN | CARBON-IFEROUS | DEVONIAN | SILURIAN | ORDOVICIAN | CAMBRIAN | ALGONKIAN | HURONIAN

MILLION OF YEARS SINCE DIVERGENCE

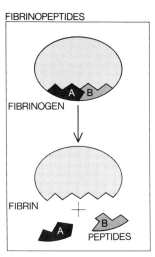

FIBRINOPEPTIDES

FIBRINOGEN

FIBRIN

A
B PEPTIDES

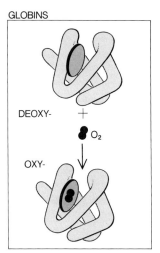

GLOBINS

DEOXY- + O₂

OXY-

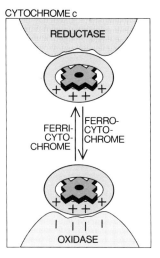

CYTOCHROME c

REDUCTASE

FERRI-CYTO-CHROME

FERRO-CYTO-CHROME

OXIDASE

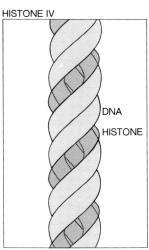

HISTONE IV

DNA

HISTONE

of the molecule would support such an idea.

On the other hand, it is equally possible that this collection of negative charges has a function. Acidic amino acids are actually conserved throughout the various species, although in a subtle way that was overlooked in the earlier sequence comparisons. Selection pressures have kept this zone of the molecular surface negative, even though the individual residues that carry the negative charges differ from one species to another. Because several sections of the protein chain bend into and out of this acidic region, the conservation of negative charge is not immediately obvious if one looks only at the stretched-out sequence. This is a good illustration of the principle of molecular evolution that natural selection acts on the folded, functioning protein and not on its amino acid sequence alone.

If we look carefully at where the glycine residues are, we can appreciate why such a large number are evolutionarily invariant. The heme group is so large that 104 amino acids are barely enough to wrap around it. There are many places where a chain comes too close to the heme or to another chain for a side chain to fit in. It is just at these points that we find the glycines with their single hydrogen atom as a side chain.

The last type of conservatism, the conservatism of the aromatic side chains, is more difficult to explain. Tyrosines and phenylalanines tend to occur in nearby pairs in the folded cytochrome c molecule: residues 10 and 97 in the right channel, 46 and 48 below the heme crevice, 67 and 74 along with tryptophan 59 in the hydrophobic left channel. Only residue 36, which can be tyrosine, phenylalanine or isoleucine, seems to have merely a space-filling role on the back of the molecule; it is an "oily brick."

The three aromatic rings in the left channel may be involved in electron transfer during reduction. The two rings in the right channel could also be employed in electron transfer, or might only help to define the hydrophobic slot in the middle of that channel. Tyrosine 48 at the bottom of the molecule helps to hold the heme in place by making a hydrogen bond to one of the heme's propionic acid side chains. In cytochrome c from the tuna and the bonito, where residue 46 is tyrosine, electron-density maps have shown that this residue also holds the heme by a hydrogen bond to its other propionic acid group. These two tyrosines, along with cysteines 14 and 17, help to lock the heme in place in a way not seen in hemoglobin or myoglobin.

Phenylalanine 82 is the enigma. Never tyrosine or anything else, it extends its oily side chain out into the aqueous world on the left side of the heme crevice, where it has no visible role. A price must be paid in energy for its being there. Why should such a large hydrophobic group be on the outside of the molecule, and why should it be absolutely unchanging through the entire course of evolution? Viewing the oxidized molecule alone, it is impossible to say, but when at the end of this article we look briefly at the recently revealed structure of reduced cytochrome, we shall see the answer fall into place at once.

The structural reasons for the evolutionary conservatism in cytochrome c throughout the history of eukaryotic life can now largely be explained. Cytochrome c is unique among the structurally analyzed proteins in that it has segregated regions of charge on its surface. The roles assigned to these regions in the foregoing discussions have been speculative and may be quite wrong. What we can be sure of is that these regions do have roles in the operation of the molecule. Chance alone, or even common ancestry, could not maintain these positive and negative regions, along with paired and exposed aromatic groups, in all species through more than a billion years of molecular evolution. The conservative sequences are shouting to us, "Look!" Now we have to be clever enough to know what to look for.

Rates of Protein Evolution

With this background we are equipped to return to a question raised earlier: What determines the rates of evolution of different proteins? We begin by making a graph where the vertical axis represents the average difference in amino acid sequence between two species of organism on two sides of an evolutionary branch point, for example the branch point between fish and reptiles or between reptiles and mammals. The horizontal axis represents the time elapsed since the divergence of the two lines as determined by the geological record. If such a graph is plotted for cytochrome c, one finds that all the branch points fall close to a straight line, indicating a constant average rate of evolutionary change [*see illustration on opposite page*].

How can this be? How can cytochrome c change at so nearly a constant rate during the long period in which the external morphology of the organism was diversifying toward the present-day cotton plant, bread mold, fruit fly, rattlesnake and chimpanzee? This is an illustration of a fundamental advantage of proteins as tools in studying evolution. Natural selection ultimately operates on populations of whole living organisms, the only criterion of success being the ability of the population to survive, reproduce and leave behind a new generation. The farther down toward the molecular level one goes in examining living organisms, the more similar they become and the less important the morphological differences are that separate a clam from a horse. One kind of chemical machinery can serve many diverse organisms. Conversely, one external change in an organism that can be acted on by natural selection is usually the effect not of a single enzyme molecule but of an entire set of metabolic pathways.

The observed uniform rate of change in cytochrome c simply means that the biochemistry of the respiratory package, the mitochondrion, is so well adjusted, and the mitochondrion is so well insulated from natural selection, that the selection pressures become smoothed out at the molecular level over time spans of millions of years. A factory can convert

RATES OF EVOLUTION OF PROTEINS (*opposite page*) can be inferred by plotting average differences in amino acid sequences between species on two sides of an evolutionary branch point that can be dated, for example the branch point between fish and reptiles or between reptiles and mammals. The average differences (*vertical axis*) have been corrected to allow for the occurrence of more than one mutation at a given amino acid site. The length of the vertical data bars indicates the experimental scatter. Times since the divergence of two lines of organisms from a common branch point (*horizontal axis*) have been obtained from the geological record. The drawings below the graph show schematically the function (described in the text) of the molecules whose evolutionary rate of change is plotted. The rate of change is proportional to the steepness of the curve. It can be represented by a number called the unit evolutionary period, which is the time required for the amino acid sequence of a protein to change by 1 percent after two evolutionary lines have diverged. For fibrinopeptides this period is about 1.1 million years, whereas for histone IV it is 600 million years. The probable reasons for these differences are discussed in the text.

from making military tanks to making sports cars and keep the same machine tools and power source. Similarly, a primitive eukaryote cell line can lead to such diverse organisms as sunflowers and mammals and still retain a common metabolic chemistry, including the respiratory package that comprises cytochrome c. One of the advantages of proteins in studying the process of evolution is just this relative insulation from the immediate effects of external selection. Protein structure is farther removed from selection pressures and closer to the sources of genetic variation in DNA than gross anatomical features or inherited behavior patterns are.

The only other proteins for which enough sequence information is available to allow this kind of analysis are hemoglobin and the fibrinopeptides: the short amino acid chains left over when fibrinogen is converted to fibrin in the process of blood clotting. One hemoglobin chain consists of approximately 140 amino acids. Fibrinopeptides A and B, on the other hand, consist of only about 20 amino acids, which are cut out of fibrinogen and discarded during the clotting process. The hemoglobins and the fibrinopeptides also appear to be evolving individually at a uniform average rate, but their rates are quite different. Whereas 20 million years are required to produce a change of 1 percent in the amino acid sequence of two diverging lines of cytochrome c, the same amount of change takes a little less than six million years in hemoglobins and just over one million years in the fibrinopeptides, as indicated on page 44. The approximate time required for a 1 percent change in sequence to appear between diverging lines of the same protein is defined as the unit evolutionary period. That period has been roughly estimated for a number of proteins for which only two or three sequences from different species are known. Most simple enzymes evolve approximately as fast as hemoglobin and much more rapidly than cytochrome c. Does all of this mean that the genes for these proteins are mutating at different rates? Are we looking at differences in variation or in selection?

Since there is no evidence to suggest variable rates of mutation, one asks what case can be made for differences in selection pressure among the different proteins. The case appears to be quite convincing [see inset figures in illustration on page 44]. The fibrinopeptides are "spacers" that prevent fibrinogen from adopting the fibrin configuration before the clotting mechanism is trig-

gered. As long as they can be cut out by an enzyme when the time comes for the blood to clot, they would seem to have few other requirements. Thus one would expect a fibrinogen molecule to tolerate many random changes in the fibrinopeptide spacers. If the unit evolutionary period measures not the rate of appearance of mutations but the rate of appearance of harmless mutations, then it is not surprising that a 1 percent change can occur in the sequence of fibrinopeptides in just over a million years.

A successful hemoglobin molecule has more constraints. Each hemoglobin molecule embodies four heme groups that not only bind oxygen but, also cooperate in such a way that the oxygen is released more rapidly into the cell when the local acidity, created by the presence of carbon dioxide, builds up. The structural basis for this "breathing" mechanism has only recently been explained with the help of X-ray crystallography by M. F. Perutz and his co-workers at the Medical Research Council Laboratory of Molecular Biology in England. If a random mutation is five times as likely to be harmful in hemoglobin as in the fibrinopeptides, one can account for hemoglobin's having a unit evolutionary period that is five times as long.

The chances of randomly damaging cytochrome c are evidently three to four times greater than they are for hemoglobin. Why should this be, and why should the unit evolutionary period for cytochrome c be greater than the period for enzymes of comparable size? The X-ray structure has given us a clue to the answer. Cytochrome c is a small protein that interacts over a large portion of its surface with molecular complexes that are larger than itself. It is virtually a "substrate" for the reductase and oxidase complexes. A large fraction of its surface is subject to strong conservative selection pressures because of the requirement that it mate properly with other large molecules, each with its own genetic blueprint. This evidently explains why the patches of positive and negative charge are preserved so faithfully throughout the history of eukaryotic life. Hemoglobin and most enzymes, in contrast, interact principally with smaller molecules: with oxygen in the case of hemoglobin or with small substrate molecules at the active sites of enzymes. As long as these restricted regions of the molecule are preserved the rest of the molecular surface is relatively free to change. Mutations are weeded out less rigorously and sequences diverge faster.

A satisfying confirmation of these

ideas comes from the amino acid sequences of histone IV, one of the basic proteins that binds to DNA in the chromosomes and that may play a role in expressing or suppressing genetic information. When molecules of histone IV from pea seedlings and calf thymus are compared, one finds that they differ in only two of their 102 amino acids. If we adopt an approximate date of 1.2 billion years ago from the cytochrome study for the divergence of plants and animals, we find that histone IV has a unit evolutionary period of 600 million years. Clearly the conservative selection pressure on histone IV must be intense. Since histone IV participates in the control processes that are at the heart of the genetic mechanism, its sensitivity to random changes is hardly surprising.

The date of 1.2 billion years ago for the divergence of plants and animals is based on the cytochrome-sequence comparisons, assuming that the observed linear rate of evolution of cytochrome c in more recent times can be extrapolated back to that remote epoch. Is this a fair extrapolation? It probably is for cytochrome c because the biochemistry of the mitochondrion evolved still earlier; the great similarity in respiratory reactions among all eukaryotes argues that there has not been much innovation in cytochrome systems since. The respiratory chain had probably "settled down" by 1.2 billion years ago. It is reassuring that the cytochrome figure of 1.2 billion years is in harmony with the relatively scarce fossil record of Precambrian life.

If one accepts the provocative suggestion that eukaryotes developed from a symbiotic association of several prokaryotes, one of which was a respiring bacterium that became the ancestor of present-day mitochondria, one is obliged to conclude that the respiratory machinery had stabilized in essentially its present form before or during this symbiosis. The same thing cannot be said for hemoglobin and its probable ancestor, myoglobin. They can provide no clue to the date when animals and plants diverged, since the globins were evolving to play several different roles during and after this period, as multicelled organisms arose. In no sense had the globins settled down 1.2 million years ago. Nevertheless, if the right proteins are selected, and if the data are not overextended, it should be possible to use the rates of protein evolution to assign times to events in the evolution of life that have left only faint traces in the geological record.

So far we have mentioned the electron-transfer mechanism of cytochrome *c* only in passing, virtually ignoring the structure of the reduced molecule. The mechanism is another story in itself, and one that cannot yet be written. One hopes that the clues supplied by X-ray analysis will suggest the best chemical experiments to try next, in order to learn the mechanism of the oxidation-reduction process. The reduced cytochrome structure has been obtained so recently that it would be premature to base many deductions on it.

A Glimpse of Molecular Dynamics

One obvious structural feature, which undoubtedly has great physiological significance, is that in the reduced molecule the top of the heme crevice is closed. The chain from residues 80 to 83 swings to the right (as the molecule is depicted on page 38), the exposed phenylalanine 82 slips into the heme crevice to the left of the heme and nearly parallel to it, and the heme becomes less accessible to the outside world. The absolute preservation of this phenylalanine side chain throughout evolution, in an environment that is energetically unfavorable in the oxidized molecule, argues that closing of the heme crevice in the reduced molecule is important for its biological activity.

Several explanations might be offered. The aromatic ring of phenylalanine 82 may be part of the electron-transfer mechanism, or its removal from the heme crevice may be necessary to permit an electron-transferring group to enter beside the heme or just to approach the edge of the heme. At a minimum the refolding of the chain from residues 80 to 83 may be a "convulsive" motion that pushes the oxidase complex away from the protein after electron transfer is achieved by some other pathway.

This article has been speculative enough without making a choice between these or other alternatives. At this stage, as both oxidized and reduced cytochrome analyses are being extended to higher resolution, it is enough to say that we can see more refolding of the protein chain in passing between the two states than has been observed in any other protein. Phenylalanine 82 swings to an entirely new position and several other aromatic rings change orientation, including the three in the left channel. As the molecule is reduced, the right channel apparently is partly blocked by residues 20 and 21. We now have pictures of both strokes of a very ancient two-stroke molecular engine. We hope in time to be able to figure out how it operates.

5

THE SOCIAL ORDER OF TURKEYS

C. ROBERT WATTS AND ALLEN W. STOKES
June 1971

*The society of the wild turkeys that live in the semiarid
grasslands of southeastern Texas is so rigidly stratified that
most of the males never have an opportunity to mate*

Social hierarchies existed in the animal world long before man crowned his first king. Investigating the structure and behavior of animal societies, one is increasingly impressed by how frequently their communities fall into a stratified pattern, with the members divided inexorably into dominant leaders and subordinates. Apparently this form of organization has high survival value, contributing in one way or another to the stability of a population or a species.

We made a detailed study of a population of wild turkeys living in and around the Welder Wildlife Refuge in Texas and found it to be characterized by an astonishing degree of social stratification, greater than had previously been seen in any society of vertebrates short of man. The status of each individual in this turkey society is determined during the first year of life, and it usually remains fixed for the animal's lifetime. One of the consequences is that most of the males never have an opportunity to mate! Presumably this phenomenon carries some benefits for the society, which presents an interesting subject for speculation.

The Welder Refuge is an area of 8,000 acres near Corpus Christi, Tex. Among its denizens are several hundred wild turkeys (*Meleagris gallopavo*) of the subspecies known as the Rio Grande turkey. By banding young turkeys in the Welder population with distinctive identification tags we were able to follow their subsequent career and behavior. We observed the social interactions of the tagged individuals and groups over a period of two years. As background for our findings let us first outline the yearly cycle of events in the life of the Welder turkeys as we observed it.

In March or sometimes as early as February, depending on the weather, the hens nest and begin to lay eggs, generally producing a clutch of 14 over a period of 15 or 16 days. The eggs hatch in 28 days. The resulting family of poults is subject to a high rate of attrition, owing to predators, vagaries of the weather and desertion. During the first six weeks it is not uncommon for a poult to leave its mother and join another family, particularly if it is the only survivor in the clutch. The mother of the switching offspring may also join the other family if she is compatible with the new mother. During the spring and summer the families combine in brood flocks; those hens that have lost their clutch of eggs or their poults and are left alone form broodless flocks.

The brood flock remains together until late fall, when the youngsters are six to seven months old. The young males of each family then break away as a sibling group. This group continues to be an inseparable unit for life. Even if it has been reduced to a single member, the survivor does not try to join another sibling group or form a group with other loners; he maintains an independent sibling identity.

After the male sibling unit breaks off from the brood flock it flocks with other males for the winter. Usually it attempts to join an established flock of adult males; the adult flocks, however, generally reject juveniles, so that the juvenile groups are relegated to joining together in flocks of their own.

It is at this stage in the life of the young male that his status is decided. In the exclusively male winter flock he is forced into two contests: one to establish his position within his own group of siblings, the other to determine the status of his sibling group with respect to other groups. Each sibling engages in physical combat with his brothers. The battle consists in wrestling, spurring in the fighting-cock style, striking with the wings and pecking at the head and neck. The fight often lasts more than two hours and ends when one or both of the contestants are too exhausted to continue. The strongest fighter in the group becomes the dominant bird, and the order of rank established among the siblings is seldom challenged thereafter as long as the dominant bird lives.

Meanwhile the sibling groups are testing one another and determining their relative ranking as units. Generally in a juvenile male flock the sibling group with the largest number of members wins the dominant status. When one flock encounters another, they also fight each other as units, again to determine which will be dominant. As in the case of individual contests, the group battles end in clear-cut decisions that create a remarkably stable society. The vanquished contestants accept their subordinate rank and rarely seek to renegotiate the result unless there is an important change in circumstances such as the death of a leader.

The society's stability is fortified by similar contests among the females, although in their case individual status appears to be less important than it is for the males when it comes to mating, as we shall see. While the juvenile males are still with the hens in the brood flocks, fighting occurs only between flocks, with victory generally going to the flock containing more males. After the males have left to form their own flocks for the winter the hens combine into large, all-female aggregations, and they then proceed to battle for individual rank among themselves. Each hen is on her own; there are no contests between sibling

WRESTLING MATCH between juvenile wild turkeys, members of the same sibling group, is one of several forms of combat that eventually determine which male will dominate the other members of the group. The birds usually fight until exhausted. Dominant males at the Welder Wildlife Refuge in Texas act as sires in the great majority of annual matings among the turkeys resident there.

PRELUDE TO MATING on the display grounds at the Welder Refuge is stereotyped male strutting, with tail fanned and wings drooping. Two sibling pairs are shown strutting; the movements of each pair are almost perfectly synchronized. The female (*left*), the object of the males' display, stands in the characteristic pre-mating posture, awaiting the dominant male of the senior pair.

groups or families. In these fights adult hens usually prevail over juvenile females. Significantly, however, females that have been members of winning brood flocks often win over older hens that have not been thus "conditioned" to winning. This kind of conditioning was demonstrated in chickens during the 1930's by the Chinese biologist Z. Y. Kuo. He "trained" birds to win by never allowing them to lose.

We found that the turkey hens in and around the Welder Refuge congregated for the winter in two roosts within the refuge. The male flocks also had two winter roosts in the refuge, and in the

area around the refuge there were six additional male roosts, spaced about a mile to a mile and a half apart. This tended to minimize encounters between flocks, as the males rarely ventured more than six-tenths of a mile from their roost during the winter.

By the end of February the wintering flocks, both male and female, left their roosts to visit mating grounds. The signal for the breakup of winter roosting came when the hens set out at daybreak for certain display grounds. As the males left their winter quarters their tendency to flock together waned and their flocks gradually disintegrated. The sib-

ling groups, however, remained tightly knit.

At each display ground a band of females numbering 50 or more hens became available for courting. This group would receive the attention of 10 to 15 sibling groups totaling about 30 males in all. The sibling group that had gained dominance over all the others moved about within the ranks of the females, and the subordinate groups followed along at the periphery, taking what opportunities they could to display to females there. The display consisted in strutting before the hens. The members of each sibling group usually strut-

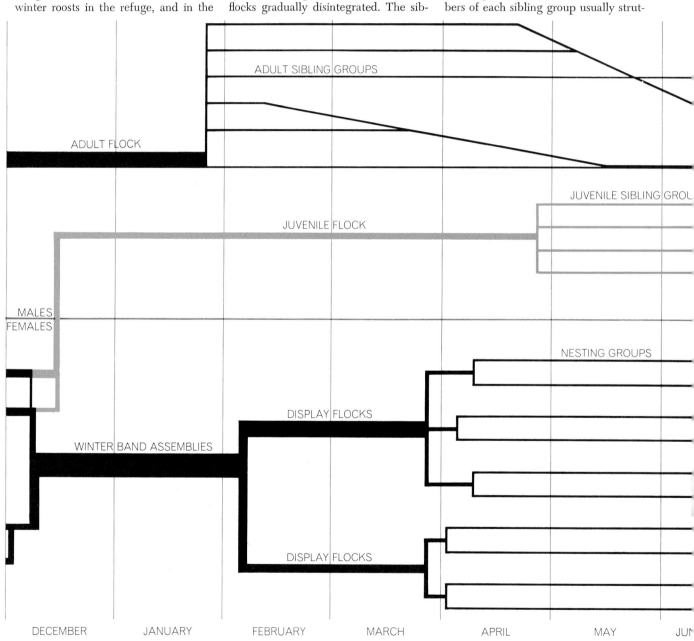

MALE AND FEMALE TURKEYS gather in flocks, divide into smaller units and flock together again in the course of a year. An idealized sequence appears in this chart. Two flocks of males (*top*) exist in late December. One (*color*) is made up of juvenile sibling groups newly departed from the summertime brood flocks. The other (*black*) is made up of adult sibling groups and remains aloof

from the juveniles. At this time the females (*bottom*) are gathered in a single large winter band. By February the adult male flock has divided into its component sibling groups. The juvenile males, however, continue to flock until near the end of the breeding season. The female band divides in February; smaller groups, numbering about 50 birds, appear on the display grounds. By April

ted in unison, more or less synchronously and close together. Occasionally more than one sibling group would strut to the same hen.

Notwithstanding the general participation in strutting, only the dominant male of the dominant group actually had the privilege of mating with hens at the height of the breeding season. We had tagged all the 170 males that used the four display grounds in the refuge and hence were able to identify them individually. In close observation of three of the display grounds we found that at two grounds just one male in each did all the mating, and at the third ground only two males were involved in mating. At the fourth ground, which was lightly used by the turkeys that year, we were not able to keep a close watch, but it could reasonably be assumed that only one or two males dominated the mating there. Overall, then, of the 170 males using the four grounds no more than six males accounted for all the mating with the hens. We observed 59 copulations during this period.

The dominant leader's ability to monopolize the mating prerogative is aided by the circumstance that a complete copulation generally takes four minutes or longer. A subordinate male presuming to couple with a hen does not have time to fulfill the mating attempt before the dominant male detects it. The dominant one, after driving off the presumptuous subordinate, proceeds to mate the prepared hen. Only once in two mating seasons did we see a member of a subordinate sibling group (the dominant member) succeed in achieving a mating on the display grounds; in that case two widely separated females in the area were ready to mate at the same time, and the leader of the subordinate group mated one while the flock leader was occupied with the other. There were also

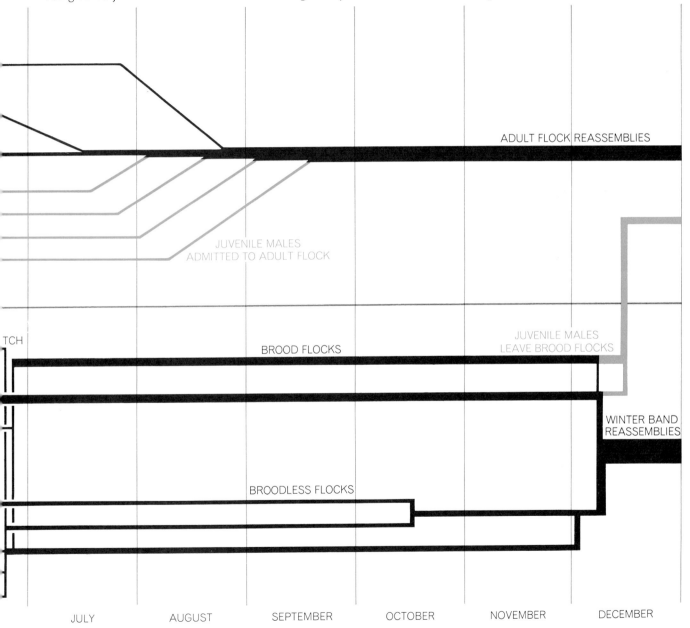

most breeding is over; the females have further divided into groups of two to five and are nesting. Some adult male sibling groups begin to recombine. Now the juvenile male flock splits into its sibling groups; these court any unattended females. By mid-June the year's hatch reaches a peak. Soon thereafter females with young collect in small brood flocks, and those without young form in broodless flocks. Meanwhile juvenile males are gradually allowed to enter the recombining flock of adult males, filling out ranks that have been thinned by the high mortality rate among adults. Finally, by December, the next generation of young males leaves the brood flock and forms a new juvenile flock. Adult and young females then join broodless females to reestablish winter band.

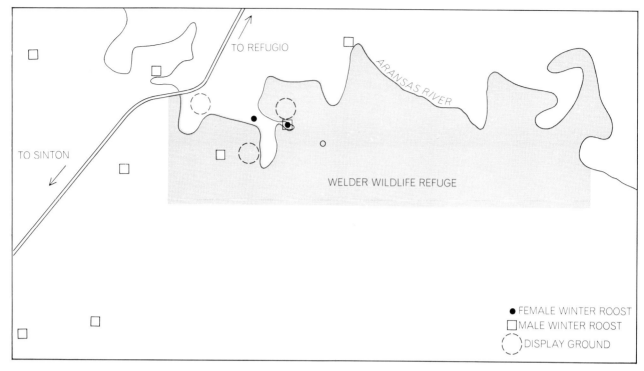

WELDER WILDLIFE REFUGE occupies a 12-square-mile strip of land (*colored area*) along the Aransas River near Corpus Christi. In winter the female turkeys in the area, gathered into two large seasonal flocks, occupy roosts less than a mile apart inside the refuge (*black*). The small winter flocks of males occupy roosts that are well separated; only two of the eight overlap female ranges.

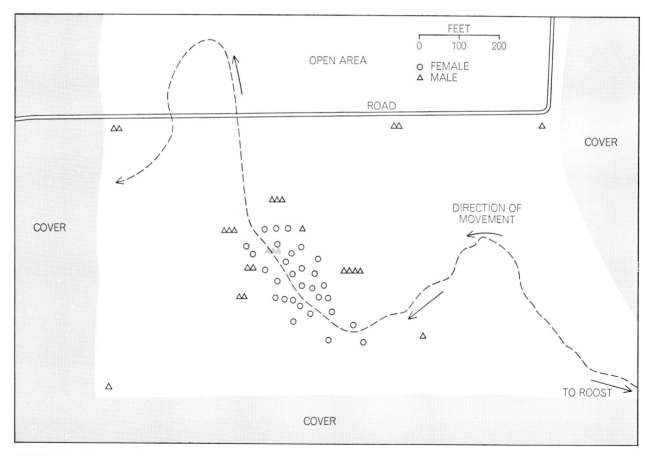

DISPLAY-GROUND ACTIVITY during a morning in mid-March, before the female flock breaks into nesting groups, is presented diagrammatically. Shortly after daylight 30 females began a slow passage across a display area, starting at lower right (*arrows*). A senior male sibling group, numbering three birds, soon moved into the midst of the females (*color*). Six junior male sibling groups, including a solitary male, have followed closely along the periphery of the band, displaying when they can but seldom managing to mate.

two instances in which a previously subordinate male of the dominant sibling group was able to mate after the dominant member of the group died during the display-ground period.

Although subordinate males had no chance to mate with hens at the display grounds, they did perform mock matings, often just before or after a mating by the dominant male. Mounting a pile of dry cow manure or a log or simply squatting on the ground, they would go through the stereotype of mating actions: treading the object, fluttering their wings, lowering their tail and even in some cases ejaculating. Some males that were not allowed to mate with hens at the display grounds did have opportunities to mate later. The hens left the display grounds within four weeks and went in groups of two to five (not as sibling groups) to a common nesting ground. During the nesting period male sibling groups roved about from one nesting area to another seeking receptive hens. Thus a sibling group that had had only subordinate status at the display grounds might have an uncontested meeting with a nesting group of hens. In that event the dominant member of the male group could mate with the hens unless he was interrupted by the arrival of a dominant sibling group. Our observations indicated, however, that the few dominant males that were engaged in all the mating at the display grounds probably accounted also for 75 percent of the later matings achieved during the hens' nesting period.

By May or June the adult males cease courting the females and go off in their own flocks, to which they now admit most of the year-old males that hang about the flock. Late in the season some sibling groups composed of year-old males, left alone either with females that are late nesters or with females nesting for a second time, can be seen strutting to the hens and performing other courtship acts, but they do not consummate mating. In this respect the behavior of the Rio Grande turkeys parallels that of other bird species such as the Canada goose and jungle fowl; the year-old males of those species also go through the courting ritual without actually breeding.

Such is the life style of the Welder turkeys. How are we to explain its unique features? Nowhere else in the world of birds has any investigator observed so rigidly structured a society: the permanent division of its members into dominant and subordinate classes, the lifelong cohesion of male sibling groups,

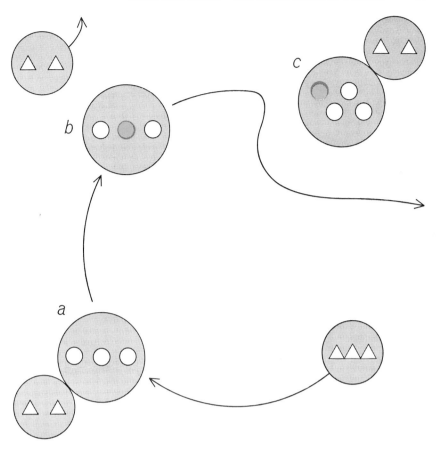

ROLE OF DOMINANCE in breeding activity is evident in this diagram of the encounters between three roaming males of a sibling group and female turkeys in various nesting groups. Each nesting group is attended by a group of males that is dominant over or subordinate to the roaming group. In the initial encounter (a) the roamers outranked the attendants but the females did not respond to their display and the roamers moved on. In the second encounter (b) the roamers were also senior to the attendants, and one of the nesting group (color) was responsive. The dominant male among the three roamers mated with the responsive female. In the final encounter (c), although a responsive female was present, the attendants outranked the roamers. The three therefore moved on to another nesting area.

the monopolization of mating by a few dominant males. The Welder turkeys' social pattern is not duplicated even by their close relative of the same species, the Eastern wild turkey inhabiting the Atlantic coastal states.

In seeking an explanation one factor to consider is the extent to which the Welder turkeys' life style may be dictated by the nature of their habitat. The Welder Refuge and its environs is an area of grassland and brush. Studies of the social weaverbirds in Africa by the British investigator John Crook have shown that weavers living in woodlands tend to form small social units; in contrast, those inhabiting open grasslands are inclined to form large flocks. In explanation Crook pointed out that the widely dispersed, year-round supply of food in a tropical forest can be exploited most efficiently by small groups of roving birds, whereas in a grassland, with a seasonally abundant, concentrated food supply and relatively few available nesting sites, the birds can make the most of the environment by flocking together in large social units. This interpretation is borne out by the habits of game birds in North America: woodland species such as the ruffed grouse and the spruce grouse typically are widely dispersed and tend to be loners except during the mating season; on the other hand, species with a habitat of grassland and brush such as the prairie chicken, the sharp-tailed grouse and the sage grouse live in large flocks. The Welder turkeys exhibit the same influence of habitat. They follow the grassland pattern of social organization, whereas the Eastern wild turkey, living in woodlands, favors small social units.

The nature of the habitat and food supply also influences the mating systems of birds. Where food is not easy to find and the young need parental help, the birds favor monogamy. This is particularly well illustrated by the quail and the partridge. Polygamy, on the other hand, tends to be the rule when food is readily available and the rearing of the young does not require help from the male parent. In some cases the polygamy system takes the form of the creation of harems; a male acquires several hens that stay with him until they are bred. The Eastern wild turkey uses this system. In contrast, the Welder turkeys have adopted the "lek" mode of polygamy, in which most of the mating is done in a common arena (called the lek). A number of ground-dwelling birds (including the prairie chicken, the sharp-tailed grouse and the sage grouse) practice the lek system; the Welder turkeys, however, have developed their own unique version. On a prairie-chicken or grouse lek each male forms a small territory and stays within it, waiting for a sexually ready female to seek him out. The hens in those societies do show a definite preference for relatively dominant males. However, the Welder modification of the system, with the males pursuing the females on the courting ground, applies a more positive control; there the males determine rigorously which of them will mate.

How can we account for the fact that the Texas wild turkeys use the lek mating system rather than the harem sys-

tem favored by their Eastern relatives of the same species? The Texas climate suggests an answer. In the Welder Refuge area rainfall is comparatively infrequent, and when it occurs, it brings on a quick but short-lived growth of vegetation and insects. In order to take advantage of this ephemeral food supply it is important that the females be brought quickly into readiness for breeding. The displays and courtship by groups of males on a lek presumably have that effect. (It is interesting to note that in a part of Oklahoma that is less drought-ridden than the Welder Refuge region the turkeys of the Rio Grande subspecies display on leks but do not usually mate until afterward, when they go off to form harems. Their combination of the two systems apparently adds a string to their bow, enabling them to cope with whatever weather conditions may befall during the breeding season.) In addition to the rapid preparation of the females for breeding there is another obvious advantage in the lek system: it guards the birds against surprise attacks by predators, to which the turkeys are particularly vulnerable in the grasslands.

We are still left with a most puzzling question: How does one explain the remarkable restriction of mating to just a few males and the close lifelong bond that holds a sibling group together? We suggest a hypothesis that relates the two phenomena. A hen may be stimulated

more strongly by the compact, synchronized strutting of a male sibling group than she would be by the display of an individual suitor. Hence the probability of eventual mating may be enhanced even for the subordinate members of the group in the event that the dominant bird dies. (The average annual mortality of adult male turkeys at Welder is 40 percent.) Sibling unity also provides protection for the member that does the mating: during the four minutes or more that he is coupled with the female his brothers stand by to fight off intruders or predators.

Perhaps most significant, the collaboration of the sibling members in assisting mating by one of their group helps to ensure the propagation of the family genes, since on the average between brothers 50 percent of the genes are exact duplicates. The dominant member thus acts as a representative of his brothers in passing on their genes; the British geneticist W. D. Hamilton calls natural selection of this kind "kin selection."

Such an arrangement may seem less than ideal with respect to those deprived of the opportunity to mate. In genetic and evolutionary terms, however, it may be advantageous to the community as a whole. Perhaps the Welder turkeys offer a moral for human conduct, suggesting that people might often benefit, even as individuals, by giving less attention to self-gratification and more to group effectiveness.

II

THE MULTIPLICATION
AND DISPERSAL OF SPECIES

The species is the pivotal unit in the great majority of studies of evolution and ecology. The species is also, unfortunately, one of the less objective concepts of biology. When we view local faunas and floras—say, for example, the birds of Pennsylvania or the butterflies of Jamaica—the species is reasonably sound currency. It is defined as a population that does not interbreed freely under natural conditions with coexisting populations. While birdwatching in Pennsylvania, one has no trouble distinguishing such entities as the song sparrow, *Melospiza melodia,* or the broad-winged hawk, *Buteo platypterus.* Each consists of a population of organisms, or a closely bunched series of populations, which interbreed freely with each other but only rarely, or not at all, with other species living in the same area. The local species are kept apart by hereditary differences in the habitats they occupy, the seasons and times they breed, the signals they pass back and forth during courtship, and other traits crucial for the coordination of breeding. Species can be viewed as closed gene pools which are forever evolving away from each other. The longer they remain reproductively isolated, the stronger become the hereditary barriers that isolate them.

When increasingly broader geographic areas are examined, the species concept steadily declines in value. The bird species of all of North America are much more difficult to delineate than just those of Pennsylvania. The reason is that populations classified within the same species but breeding in different parts of the range—the song sparrows of Florida and Quebec, for example—show various degrees of divergence from each other. Some geographic populations are identical, at least in outward appearance; many are different enough to be distinguished as geographical races, or subspecies as they are more technically labeled; and still others are so distinct that they can be justifiably ranked as full species. The problem is that the populations do not occur in the same places, so we have no easy way of telling whether they are also potentially isolated by hereditary differences. The rank of such geographically separated populations must consequently be chosen by arbitrary criteria. The limits of the populations themselves are also hard to define; often one grades imperceptibly into another. Finally, the traits by which they differ show discordant patterns of variation. One characteristic may change along a north-south gradient, whereas another changes from east to west. Hence, the break from one race to another depends on the choice of the trait.

The very chaos of the species concept contains the key to the process of the multiplication of species. When populations belonging to the same species are isolated from each other by geographical barriers such as rivers, mountain ranges, sea straits, or dry land (in the case of aquatic and marine species), they tend to diverge in evolution. Given enough time, in fact, divergence will *always* occur. This first step in speciation is inevitable for no other reason than that the environments occupied by geographically separated populations differ in many details and hence subject their organisms to different kinds of natural selection. Given still more time, the populations will pass through the subspecies stage and eventually acquire enough genetic differences to reach the rank of species. After becoming reproductively isolated, and providing that the geographic barriers can somehow be breached, the newly formed species are in a position to invade one another's ranges and mingle. In so doing, they are free to divide the exploitable environment among themselves by specializing into different niches. This process, which is of great importance in the evolution of ecosystems, is called *adaptive radiation.* An alternate mode of speciation, especially common in plants, is *polyploidy,* the multiplication of sets of chromosomes. The organisms containing such duplicated sets find it difficult to breed with the ancestral strains. The process is especially effective if accompanied by hybridization, in which case the new species contains two or more sets of chromosomes from each parental strain. Speciation by polyploidy can also lead to adaptive radiation.

In his article on Darwin's finches, David Lack presents one of the classic examples of geographic speciation and adaptive radiation. The finches are a group of 14 species believed to have descended from a single species that colonized the Galápagos Islands. Because of the remoteness of the landfall, few other bird species were established on the islands, and Darwin's finches had an unusual opportunity to expand into unfilled niches. As a result, their ecological diversification has been unusually broad and presents in microcosm some of the major features of evolution ordinarily discernible only in much larger assemblages of species. One of the species behaves like a rather inept woodpecker, picking insects out of tree crevices with the aid of a broken-off cactus spine. Others catch insects in a warbler-like manner, while still others dine mostly on seeds. One minor correction must be made to Lack's article, written in 1953: among the seed-eaters, larger bill size is an adaptation to handle *harder* seeds, not larger ones as supposed by Lack. In his account of the desert pupfish, James H. Brown shows how the same principles of geographic speciation operate in organisms that live in a radically different environment. Here, the isolated environments are tiny fresh-water springs all but lost in the deserts of California and Nevada. The pupfish populations display varying degrees of genetic divergence in response to the particular environments created by the individual springs.

Species are born; they expand and contract their ranges; and they go extinct. Because the vast majority have a finite life and are restricted in dispersal by the specialized nature of their adaptations, almost no species ever attain a worldwide distribution. The species found together on a group of islands, such as the Galápagos, or even on a continent, are much more likely to be descended from common ancestors than are species selected at random from different parts of the world. As Carl Welty shows in his article, this is true to a striking degree even of birds, which are among the most wide-ranging of all organisms. As a result it is possible to divide the world into major regions and lesser biogeographic units according to the catalogs of living species that live in them. When this classification is undertaken, a remarkable corollary of adaptive radiation becomes apparent: adaptive radiations that occur in different parts of the world tend to be similar. Just as the Galápagos finches produced a woodpecker-like form in the absence of a real woodpecker to compete with it, the mammals of the isolated continents of Australia and South America have produced forms resembling wolves, cats, rabbits, and other adaptive categories that are familiar to most people in the world. This phenomenon of evolutionary convergence, which is an inevitable complement to adaptive radiation, occurs in many other groups of organisms and in various parts of the earth.

Only when data are taken from mammals, birds, or some other "youthful" group of organisms that has radiated principally during the past 70 million years, do the biogeographic regions fit the existing continents reasonably well. For such groups no major difficulty is encountered in reconstructing the routes of dispersal of the evolving species. However, when the organisms are more ancient, such as dinosaurs or the more primitive frogs that have histories going back to the Mesozoic Era or beyond, the correlations fail. As A. Hallam and Björn Kurtén show in their separate but complementary articles, the needed correction is supplied by continental drift. In early Paleozoic times virtually all of the land mass of the world was joined into a single supercontinent. It then began to break up and the pieces have moved steadily farther apart. In steady succession, India broke away from Africa and began the long journey toward the southern rim of Asia; the land of the present northern hemisphere parted from that of the southern hemisphere; and Africa and South America were separated by the newly created Atlantic Ocean. When the timing of these and other events is added to the analysis, the biogeography of ancient faunas begins to make more sense. It also helps to explain, as Kurtén suggests, why the Paleozoic and Mesozoic faunas contained fewer major groups: because a smaller number of well-isolated continents existed, fewer opportunities for principal adaptive radiations were offered.

Speciation, with its concomitants of adaptive radiation and convergence, provides the basic machinery for the evolution of entire ecosystems. Given that species are generated in a way that promotes repeated radiations, the next subject of interest is their interaction. The ways in which they can interact are limited in number and constrained by certain rules that ecologists are now defining with increasing rigor. This subject will form the theme of Section III.

SUGGESTED

FURTHER READING

Carlquist, Sherwin. *Island life: a natural history of the islands of the world.* Garden City, New York: Natural History Press, 1965. 451 pp. A popular but highly informative account of species multiplication and adaptive radiation on island systems around the world, among both plants and animals. Carlquist's book also contains an excellent account of the mammals of Australia.

Mayr, Ernst. *Populations, species, and evolution.* Cambridge, Mass.: Belknap Press, 1970. 453 pp. A systematic and easily understood account of the genetic basis of species formation in animals.

Grant, Verne. *Plant speciation.* New York: Columbia University Press, 1971. 435 pp. An account of species formation in plants that is complementary to the preceding zoological book by Mayr.

MacArthur, Robert H. *Geographical ecology.* New York: Harper and Row. 1972. 269 pp. A definitive account of the ecological principles underlying the distribution of plants and animals. MacArthur's book is concerned less with species formation than with the modes of interaction of organisms that permit particular species to live in certain places but not in others.

6

DARWIN'S FINCHES

DAVID LACK

April 1953

*These drab but famous little birds of the Galapagos Islands
are a living case study in evolution. Isolated in the South
Pacific, they have developed 14 species from a common
ancestor*

ON THE Galapagos Islands in the Pacific Charles Darwin in 1835 saw a group of small, drab, finch-like birds which were to change the course of human history, for they provided a powerful stimulus to his speculations on the origin of species—speculations that led to the theory of evolution by natural selection. In the study of evolution the animals of remote islands have played a role out of all proportion to their small numbers. Life on such an island approaches the conditions of an experiment in which we can see the results of thousands of years of evolutionary development without outside intervention. The Galapagos finches are an admirable case study.

These volcanic islands lie on the Equator in the Pacific Ocean some 600 miles west of South America and 3,000 miles east of Polynesia. It is now generally agreed that they were pushed up out of the sea by volcanoes more than one million years ago and have never been connected with the mainland. Whatever land animals they harbor must have come over the sea, and very few species have established themselves there: just two kinds of mammals, five reptiles, six songbirds and five other land birds.

Some of these animals are indistinguishable from the same species on the mainland; some are slightly different; a few, such as the giant land-tortoises and the mockingbirds, are very different. The latter presumably reached the Galapagos a long time ago. In addition, there are variations from island to island among the local species themselves, indicating that the colonists diverged into variant forms after their arrival. Darwin's finches go further than this: not only do they vary from island to island but up to 10 different species of them can be found on a single island.

The birds themselves are less dramatic than their story. They are dull in color, unmusical in song and, with one exception, undistinguished in habits. This dullness is in no way mitigated by their dreary surroundings. Darwin in his diary succinctly described the islands: "The country was compared to what we might imagine the cultivated parts of the Infernal regions to be." This diary, it is interesting to note, makes no mention of the finches, and the birds received only a brief mention in the first edition of his book on the voyage of the *Beagle*. Specimens which Darwin brought home, however, were recognized by the English systematist and bird artist, John Gould, as an entirely new group of birds. By the time the book reached its second edition, the ferment had begun to work, and Darwin added that "one might really fancy that from an original paucity of birds in this archipelago, one species had been taken and modified for different ends." Thus obscurely, as an afterthought in a travel book, man received a first intimation that he might once have been an ape.

THERE ARE 13 species of Darwin's finches in the Galapagos, plus one on Cocos Island to the northwest. A self-contained group with no obvious relations elsewhere, these finches are usually placed in a subfamily of birds named the *Geospizinae*. How did this remarkable group evolve? I am convinced, from my observations in the islands in 1938-39 and from subsequent studies of museum specimens, that the group evolved in much the same way as other birds. Consequently the relatively simple story of their evolution can throw valuable light on the way in which birds, and other animals, have evolved in general. Darwin's finches form a little world of their own, but a world which differs from the one we know only in being younger, so that here, as Darwin wrote, we are brought nearer than usual "to that great fact—that mystery of mysteries—the first appearance of new beings on this earth."

The 14 species of Darwin's finches fall into four main genera. First, there are the ground-finches, embracing six species, nearly all of which feed on seeds on the ground and live in the arid coastal regions. Secondly, there are the tree-finches, likewise including six species, nearly all of which feed on insects in trees and live in the moist forests. Thirdly, there is the warbler-like finch (only one species) which feeds on small insects in bushes in both arid and humid regions. Finally, there is the isolated Cocos Island species which lives on insects in a tropical forest.

Among the ground-finches, four species live together on most of the islands: three of them eat seeds and differ from each other mainly in the size of their beaks, adapted to different sizes of seeds; the fourth species feeds largely on prickly pear and has a much longer

THE 14 SPECIES of Darwin's finches are arranged at the left to suggest the evolutionary tree of their development. Grayish brown to black, all belong to the subfamily *Geospizinae*, divided broadly into ground finches (*Geospiza*), closest to the primitive form, and tree finches (mainly *Camarhynchus*), which evolved later. Of the tree species, 1 is a woodpecker-like finch (*C. pallidus*), 2 inhabits mangrove swamps (*C. heliobates*), 3, 4 and 5 are large, medium and small insect-eating birds (*C. psittacula, pauper* and *parvulus*), 6 is a vegetarian (*C. crassirostris*), 7 is a single species of warbler-finch (*Certhidea*) and 8 an isolated species of Cocos Island finch (*Pinaroloxias*). The ground-finches, mainly seed-eaters, run thus: 9, 10 and 11 are large, medium and small in size (*G. magnirostris, fortis* and *fuliginosa*), 12 is sharp-beaked (*G. difficilis*), 13 and 14 are cactus eaters (*G. conirostris* and *scandens*). All of the species in the drawing are shown about half-size.

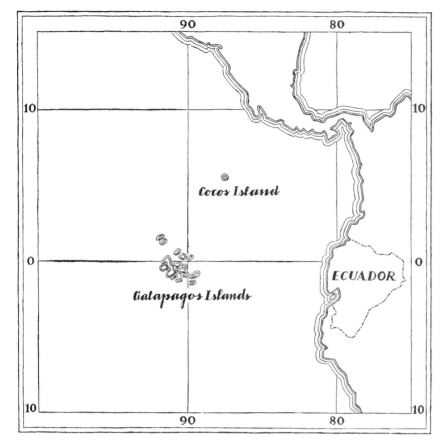

THE GALAPAGOS are shown some 600 miles west of Ecuador, above, and close up below. Cocos Island is not in the group, but it has developed one species of finch, presumed to have come originally from the mainland.

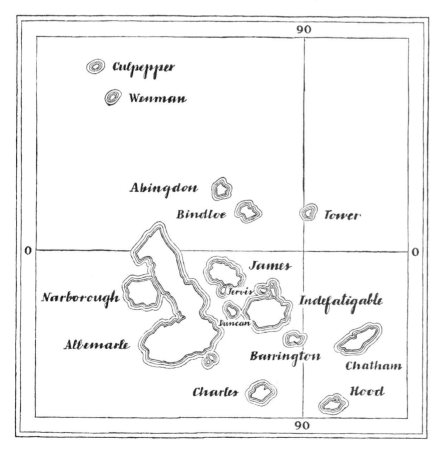

and more pointed beak. The two remaining species of ground-finches, one large and one small, live chiefly on the outlying islands, where some supplement their seed diet with cactus, their beaks being appropriately modified.

Of the tree-finches, one species is vegetarian, with a parrot-like beak seemingly fitted to its diet of buds and fruits. The next three species are closely alike, differing primarily in body size and in the size of their beaks, presumably scaled to the size of the insects they take. A fifth species eats insects in mangrove swamps. The sixth species of tree-finch is one of the most remarkable birds in the world. Like a woodpecker, it climbs tree trunks in search of insects, which it excavates from the bark with its chisel-shaped beak. While its beak approaches a woodpecker's in shape, it has not evolved the long tongue with which a woodpecker probes insects from crannies. Instead, this tree-finch solves the problem in another way: it carries about a cactus spine or small twig which it pokes into cracks, dropping the stick to seize any insect that emerges. This astonishing practice is one of the few recorded cases of the use of tools by any animal other than man or the apes.

The warbler-like finch is in its own way as remarkable as the Galapagos attempt at a woodpecker. It has no such wonderful habit, but in its appearance and character it has evolved much closer to a warbler than the other finch has to a woodpecker. Thus its beak is thin and pointed like that of a warbler; its feeding methods and actions are similar, and it even has the warbler-like habit of flicking its wings partly open as it hunts for food. For nearly a century it was classified as a warbler, but its internal anatomy, the color of its eggs, the shape of its nest and other characteristics clearly place it among the finches.

The close resemblance among Darwin's finches in plumage, calls, nests, eggs and display suggests that they have not yet had time to diverge far from one another. The only big difference is in their beaks, adapted to their different diets. It is reasonably certain that all the Galapagos finches evolved from one original colonizing form. What is unusual about them is the existence of several distinct species on the same island. In this we may have an indirect clue to how separate species establish themselves.

LET US consider first how new forms of an animal may originate from a common ancestor. When a member of the original species moves into a new environment, it is likely to evolve new features adapted to the new local conditions. Such geographical variations among animals are commonly found; in the Galapagos, for instance, the land birds other than finches vary from island to island, with only one form on each island. These forms are not distinct species but subspecies, or geographical races. Their differences, however, are hereditary and not trivial or accidental. There are several examples of such geographical variation among Darwin's finches. Three common species of the ground-finch, for instance, are found on most of the islands; they are large, medium and small, feeding on large, medium and small seeds respectively. Now on two southern islands the large species is missing, and here the medium species has a rather larger beak than elsewhere, presumably an adaptation to the large seeds available to it in the absence of the large species. Again, on another islet the small ground-finch is absent, and the medium species fills the gap by being rather smaller than elsewhere. On still other islets the medium species is missing and the small species is rather larger than elsewhere.

It seems clear that the beak differences among the subspecies of Darwin's finches are adaptive. Further, some of these differences are as great as those distinguishing true species.

What is likely to happen if a subspecies evolved in isolation on one island later spreads to an island occupied by another race of the same species? If the two populations have not been isolated for long and differ in only minor ways, they may interbreed freely and so merge with each other. But evidence from the study of insects suggests that if two populations have been isolated for a long time, so many hereditary differences will have accumulated that their genes will not combine well. Any hybrid offspring will not survive as well as the parent types. Hence natural selection will tend to intensify the gap between the two forms, and they will continue to evolve into two distinct species.

DARWIN'S finches provide circumstantial evidence for the origin of a new species by means of geographical isolation. Consider three different forms of the large insectivorous tree-finch. On the most southerly Galapagos island is a small dark form with a comparatively small beak. On another island to the northwest is a rather larger and less barred form. On the central islands is a yet larger and paler type with a larger, more parrot-like beak. Evidently these three forms had a common ancestor and evolved their differences in geographical isolation. The differences among them do not seem great enough to set them apart as separate species, and they would be classed as subspecies but for one curious circumstance: on the southernmost island the two extremes—the small dark form and the largest pale form—live side by side without merging.

Clearly these must be truly separate species. It seems likely that the large pale form spread from the central islands to the southern island in comparatively recent times, after both it and the small dark form had evolved into distinct species.

If differentiated forms are to persist alongside each other as separate species, two conditions must be met. First, they must avoid interbreeding. In birds this is usually taken care of by differences in appearance (generally in the color pattern) and in the song. It is no accident that bird-watchers find male birds so easy to recognize: correct identification is even more important for the female bird! Darwin's finches recognize each other chiefly by the beak. We have often seen a bird start to chase another from behind and quickly lose interest when a front view shows that the beak is that of a species other than its own.

The second requirement for the existence of two species together is that they must not compete for the same food. If they tend to eat similar food, the one that is better adapted to obtain that food will usually eliminate the other. In those cases where two closely related species live side by side, investigation shows that they have in fact evolved differences in diet. Thus the beak differences among

the various Galapagos finches are not just an insular curiosity but are adapted to differences in diet and are an essential factor in their persistence together. It used to be supposed that related species of birds overlapped considerably in their feeding habits. A walk through a wood in summer may suggest that many of the birds have similar habits. But having established the principle of food differentiation in Darwin's finches, I studied many other examples of closely related species and found that most, if not all, differ from one another in the places where they feed, in their feeding methods or in the size of the food items they can take. The appearance of overlap was due simply to inadequate knowledge.

NOW the key to differentiation is geographical isolation. Probably one form can establish itself alongside another only after the two have already evolved some differences in separate places. Evolutionists used to believe that new species evolved by becoming adapted to different habitats in the same area. But there is no positive evidence for that once popular theory, and it is now thought that geographical isolation is the only method by which new species originate, at least among birds. One of

THE WOODPECKER-FINCH is the most remarkable of Darwin's finches. It has evolved the beak but not the long tongue of a woodpecker, hence carries a twig or cactus spine to dislodge insects from bark crevices.

Darwin's species of finches provides an interesting illustration of this. The species on Cocos Island is so different from the rest that it must have been isolated there for a long time. Yet despite this long isolation, along with a great variety of foods and habitats and a scarcity of other bird competitors, the Cocos finch has remained a single species. This is because Cocos is an isolated island, and so does not provide the proper opportunities for differentiation. In the Galapagos, differentiation was possible because the original species could scatter and establish separate homes on the various islands of the archipelago. It is significant that the only other group of birds which has evolved in a similar way, the sicklebills of Hawaii, are likewise found in an archipelago.

Why is it that this type of evolution has been found only in the Galapagos and Hawaii? There are other archipelagoes in the world, and geographical isolation is also possible on the continents. The ancestor of Darwin's finches, for instance, must formerly have lived on the American mainland, but it has not there given rise to a group of species similar to those in the Galapagos. The answer is, probably, that on the mainland the available niches in the environment were already occupied by efficient species of other birds. Consider the woodpecker-like finch on the Galapagos, for example. It would be almost impossible for this type to evolve in a land which already possessed true woodpeckers, as the latter would compete with it and eliminate it. In a similar way the warbler-like finch would, at least in its intermediate stages, have been less efficient than a true warbler.

Darwin's finches may well have been the first land birds to arrive on the Galapagos. The islands would have provided an unusual number of diverse, and vacant, environmental niches in which the birds could settle and differentiate. The same may have been true of Hawaii. In my opinion, however, the type of evolution that has occurred in those two groups of islands is not unique. Similar developments could have taken place very long ago on the continents; thus our own finches, warblers and woodpeckers may have evolved from a common ancestor on the mainland. What is unique about the Galapagos and Hawaii is that the birds' evolution there occurred so recently that we can still see the evidence of the differentiations.

MUCH MORE is still to be learned from the finches. Unfortunately the wonderful opportunities they offer may not long remain available. Already one of the finches Darwin found in the Galapagos is extinct, and so are several other animals peculiar to the islands. With man have come hunters, rats, dogs and other predators. On some islands men and goats are destroying the native vegetation. This last is the most serious threat of all to Darwin's finches. Unless we take care, our descendants will lose a treasure which is irreplaceable.

7

THE DESERT PUPFISH

JAMES H. BROWN
November 1971

More than 20 populations of these hardy fish are found in tiny aquatic "islands" in the vicinity of Death Valley. Isolated for thousands of years, they have evolved into four distinct species

The theory of evolution can fairly be dated from Charles Darwin's visit to the Galápagos Islands aboard H.M.S. *Beagle* in 1835, where he observed varieties of finches and other animals he had never seen before. Reflecting on the voyage, he wrote to a friend nine years later: "At last gleams of light have come, and I am almost convinced (quite contrary to the opinion I started with) that species are not (it is like confessing a murder) immutable." Darwin recognized that finches and other organisms that had been isolated on the various islands of the remote Galápagos Archipelago for thousands of generations had gradually evolved in distinctive ways, producing in the case of finches a "perfect gradation in the size of the beaks in the different species."

The isolation provided by remote islands has its counterpart in small springs and small streams that dot the Death Valley region of southern California and adjacent Nevada, one of the bleakest and most arid deserts in the world. These small aquatic "islands," some not much larger than a bathtub, are populated by four species of a tiny fish of the genus *Cyprinodon*. About 1½ inches long when full-grown, they are known as desert pupfish. More than 20 distinct populations of pupfish have been identified in an area of about 3,000 square miles.

Each population is confined to a single, isolated desert oasis, which may be either a warm spring or a small stream. Like other organisms that have been isolated in islands, desert pupfish can tell much about evolution and the response of living things to the selective pressures exerted by various environments. Pupfish can tolerate an unusually wide range of temperatures and salinities. Some populations have evidently survived for thousands of years in small, restricted habitats where their numbers have never exceeded a few hundred individuals.

The present populations of *Cyprinodon* are the descendants of an ancestral pupfish that once had a broader and continuous distribution. At intervals during the ice ages of 10,000 to 30,000 years ago, when glaciers covered the northern part of the continent, the climate of southwestern North America was much cooler and wetter than it is today. Death Valley then contained a large body of fresh water, Lake Manly, fed by several rivers and numerous streams. The ancestral pupfish lived in Lake Manly and were undoubtedly distributed throughout most of its large drainage system. As the climate became hotter and drier most of the watercourses disappeared, leaving small populations of *Cyprinodon* to survive to the present time in isolated oases where the supply of water has never failed.

Thus isolated, the populations have gradually evolved into four distinct species and several subspecies. The classification has been done principally by Robert R. Miller of the University of Michigan. As a result of evolutionary divergence the species have distinctive shapes and markings [*see illustration on page 67*]. The four species and their habitats are as follows. *Cyprinodon radiosus* is found in Owens Valley, which lies to the northwest of Death Valley. *C. salinus* inhabits Salt Creek and Cottonball Marsh at the northern end of Death Valley. *C. diabolis,* the smallest and most distinctive species, is found only in Devil's Hole, a long-isolated spring to the east of Death Valley. *C. nevadensis* inhabits a number of springs and streams in the Amargosa River basin to the south and east of Death Valley.

The most differentiated and longest-isolated populations of *C. nevadensis* have been recognized as subspecies, and nearly all populations of this species have some distinctive characteristics. The species and perhaps some of the subspecies have been isolated for at least 10,000 to 30,000 years. The less differentiated populations are still only partly isolated; aquatic connections are available to them at times of heavy flooding [*see illustrations on page 68*].

Desert pupfish survive in radically different kinds of environment. In fact, about the only requirement for their existence seems to be an unfailing supply of water. Their habitats can be divided into three basic types. The first consists of shallow streams and marshes fed by ground-water springs. The temperature and the amount of water in these habitats fluctuate drastically with the season; the salinity ranges from the equivalent of seawater to about a fourth of that value. The second type of habitat is represented chiefly by thermal springs, which are fed by water from depths where it has been heated by layers of warm rock. Some of these springs have no outflow; in others most of the pupfish are confined to the source pool where the salinity is low and the temperature is warm and virtually constant throughout the year. The third basic type of habitat consists of hot artesian wells that have been dug by man. Water emerges from these wells at temperatures above 105 degrees Fahrenheit and discharges into shallow streams, where it gradually cools to the ambient air temperature. Two such wells were dug near the town of Tecopa, Calif., in the 1960's. Their outflow streams reached the Amargosa, and they were colonized by the natural population of pupfish that inhabited the river.

My experience with desert pupfish began in early 1969 when C. Robert

Feldmeth and I visited a number of the oases and began a comparative study of thermal tolerances in *Cyprinodon*. We wanted to define the limits of temperature that can be tolerated by the populations of pupfish inhabiting the thermally variable streams and marshes and the outflows of hot artesian wells. We also wanted to find out if these populations are more tolerant of extreme temperatures than those populations that live in the constant-temperature environments of thermal springs. We reasoned that populations that have evolved for thousands of years in springs of constant temperature might have lost some of their ability to tolerate extreme temperatures, in the same way that cave fishes living in absolute darkness have lost their "useless" eyes and skin pigment.

We learned that pupfish in their natural habitats readily survive at temperatures as low as 38 degrees F. and as high as 108 degrees. Such extreme temperatures, however, are always separated either in time or in space, so that an individual fish would never experience the entire 70-degree range within a period of a few hours or even a few days. Thus shallow desert streams and marshes are often covered with ice on cold winter nights and the temperatures in parts of these same habitats can rise to 100 degrees F. on hot summer days. Even during the winter, however, some fish may be swimming in water of 108 degrees near the outflow of a hot artesian well while others just a few hundred yards downstream are swimming under ice. Of course, the fish are free to move up and down in the outflows of the artesian wells, and they tend to regulate their movements so as to remain at a relatively constant temperature.

By testing in the laboratory the thermal tolerances of fish from habitats where the temperature varies, we found that at any given time an individual pupfish can withstand temperatures over the full range of approximately 70 degrees [*see lower illustration on page 69*]. The actual temperatures the fish can tolerate depended on the temperatures the fish had recently experienced. Thus if a fish had just come from a cold environment in the field or had been kept at a low temperature in the laboratory, it might be able to tolerate temperatures ranging from 32 to 102 degrees F. If it had just come from a warm environment, its range of thermal tolerance would be shifted upward, so that it might be able to survive temperatures between 40 and 109 degrees F. From these results it can be seen that the ability of pupfish to endure extreme temperatures in their natural environments depends on a combination of two phenomena. On the one hand there is an inherent, genetic capacity to withstand a wide range of temperatures; on the other there is the process, usually called thermal acclimation, that enables the fish to shift its tolerance to higher or lower absolute temperatures depending on its recent thermal history. The combination of these phenomena enables the pupfish to occupy environments where thermal variation is extreme as long as the temperature changes do not come too rapidly.

A thermal tolerance involving both a genetic component and an acclimation component is typical of nearly all organisms. What is unusual about pupfish is that their temperature tolerance is exceptionally broad for an aquatic organism, particularly for a fish. Many freshwater fishes, such as some species of trout, can tolerate a thermal range of only about 40 degrees F., and some ma-

HABITAT OF DESERT PUPFISH is one of about 20 along the southern reach of the California-Nevada border. The photograph shows a portion of the Amargosa River that contains water and pupfish in the winter and spring but dries up completely in summer. In the dry season the population of desert pupfish (*Cyprinodon nevadensis*) retreats to a number of headwater springs.

rine and tropical fishes are much less tolerant than that. The wide thermal tolerances of desert pupfish have enabled them to persist in the shallow desert streams and marshes where temperature variation approaches the extreme for any aquatic habitat. The pupfish share these habitats with only a few equally hardy kinds of plants and invertebrates.

Quite to our surprise we found that pupfish inhabiting thermal springs of constant temperature are just as tolerant of extreme temperatures as their relatives that occupy habitats where the temperature varies tremendously. Even *C. diabolis*, which has lived at 92 degrees F. in Devil's Hole for at least 30,000 years and has evolved consider-

ably in other respects, is capable of tolerating a 66-degree range in temperature (from 43 to 109 degrees) when just removed from water of 92 degrees in its native spring. Pupfish from thermal springs also have the same capacity for thermal acclimation as fish from environments where there is great variation in temperature.

These unexpected results are difficult to interpret. Why should so many organisms gradually lose characteristics that no longer have a function, yet pupfish retain the ability to tolerate extremes of temperatures they have not experienced for thousands of years? Perhaps part of the answer is that the ability to tolerate extreme temperatures is differ-

ent from those "useless" characteristics that are generally lost during evolution. It is easy to see how organs such as the eye, once they are completely unable to function in the absolute darkness of caves, might actually become disadvantageous. Since they would be subject to injury and infection, it would be beneficial to the organism if they were eventually eliminated by natural selection. There appears to be no corresponding disadvantage for the pupfish to retain the ability to tolerate a wide range of temperatures even though it is living securely at some constant temperature. Part of the explanation may be that the genetic or biochemical basis of thermal tolerance in desert pupfish makes this at-

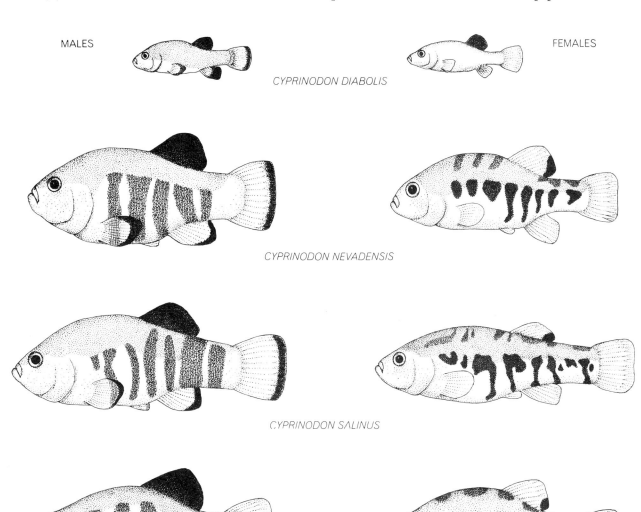

MALES   CYPRINODON DIABOLIS   FEMALES

CYPRINODON NEVADENSIS

CYPRINODON SALINUS

CYPRINODON RADIOSUS

FOUR SPECIES OF PUPFISH have evolved in the streams and thermal springs of the Death Valley region. The smallest, *Cyprinodon diabolis*, is found only in Devil's Hole, a thermal spring in a rocky mountainside (*see maps on opposite page*). *C. nevadensis* populates a number of springs and streams in southwestern Nevada and eastern California. *C. salinus* is found in Salt Creek, a marshy desert stream that is sometimes as salty as seawater. *C. radiosus* inhabits warm springs in Owens Valley. The species can be distinguished by their size and markings. Males are a bright, iridescent blue; females are greenish with black markings.

⊙ *CYPRINODON RADIOSUS*   ● *CYPRINODON SALINUS*   ○ *CYPRINODON NEVADENSIS*

POPULATIONS OF DESERT PUPFISH are sparsely scattered throughout an area of about 3,000 square miles straddling the California-Nevada border. During the ice ages of some 30,000 years ago there were aquatic connections among the various habitats. As the climate became drier, isolating the habitats, the pupfish evolved into four separate species.

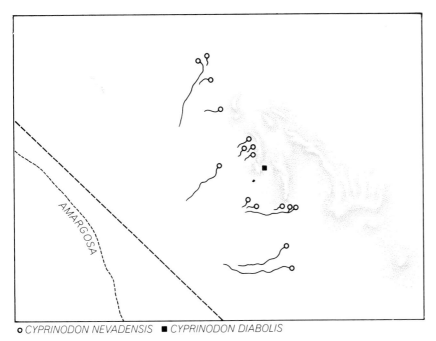

○ *CYPRINODON NEVADENSIS*   ■ *CYPRINODON DIABOLIS*

ENLARGEMENT OF AREA designated by colored rectangle on the map at top of page shows Devil's Hole, home of *C. diabolis*, and a number of spring-fed streams populated by *C. nevadensis*. Mexican Spring, hardly bigger than a bathtub, holds about 30 *C. nevadensis*.

tribute resistant to evolutionary change.

Granted that the pupfish has an unusually broad thermal tolerance, one would also like to know if it has thermal preferences and if it is able to avoid stressfully high temperatures. I have investigated the matter by studying the behavior of pupfish in the outflows of hot artesian wells. In one of the wells the water is 117 degrees F. at the source and gradually cools as it moves down the outflow stream [*see illustration on page 70*]. Fish are found in all parts of the stream where the temperature is less than 108 degrees, but they rarely enter water that is hotter than that even though they can tolerate temperatures up to 111 degrees for several minutes. Moreover, a sizable portion of the population can always be found where the temperature is between 107 and 108 degrees. As the outflow stream cools at different rates (depending on ambient wind and temperature conditions) these fish move up and down the stream and stay within the 107-to-108-degree temperature range. In this habitat one of the main foods of the pupfish is a blue-green alga that can grow at higher temperatures than the fish can withstand. Every time the outflow cools more rapidly and the 107-to-108-degree band retreats upstream, the fish encounter large mats of algae that have been growing unmolested.

The pupfish are able to sense the critical temperature of 108 degrees F. with remarkable precision in both steep and gradual thermal gradients. In the main part of the stream the temperature changes only one degree in several yards, yet it is possible to identify the place where the temperature is 108 degrees by finding the greatest upstream aggregation of pupfish. A quite different state of affairs is observed in small shallow pools to the side of the main channel. Sometimes fish get trapped in these pools when the outflow cools more slowly and intolerably hot water moves downstream. The temperature in such a pool often remains below 108 degrees (largely because of the high rate of evaporation from its surface), but the temperature increases abruptly at the edge bordering the main stream where hotter water is flowing past. In a distance of an inch or less the temperature may go from 105 degrees to more than 112 degrees. The fish dart about the pools to within a fraction of an inch of lethal temperatures but normally never enter them. If the fish get a bad scare, one may occasionally dart out into the hot stream; there it dies within seconds. The ability of pupfish to detect and avoid critically high temperatures enables them to live for weeks and even to reproduce in these pools where they are literally inches from instant death.

The ability of pupfish to inhabit waters of varying salinity is almost as impressive as their thermal tolerance. In the Death Valley region the salinity in pupfish habitats varies from very low in the thermal springs to near the concentration of seawater in parts of some streams and marshes. A related *Cyprinodon* that inhabits the Gulf coast of Texas can tolerate salinities several times the concentration of seawater. Populations from both freshwater and saline habitats can survive for long periods in a wide range of salinities.

Other attributes of desert pupfish are just as interesting as the adaptations that enable them to live in pools and streams with extreme temperatures and salinities. The size and constancy of the pupfish habitats vary greatly, and so do the size and constancy of the various populations of *Cyprinodon*. Populations that occupy streams and marshes fed by ground-water springs usually fluctuate greatly in numbers in response to seasonal changes in temperature, salinity and amount of water available. The Death Valley region receives most of its scanty rain in winter and early spring. In the rainy seasons the marshes fill with

HABITAT	GENERAL DESCRIPTION	SIZE	TEMPERATURE	SALINITY
Salt Creek	Marshes and stream fed by ground-water springs.	Stream varies in length from at least five miles in spring to one mile in summer.	Fluctuates from freezing to at least 100 degrees F.	Varies from concentration of seawater to half that value.
Big Spring	Large thermal spring; discharges water at 1,500 gallons per minute.	Source pool 50 feet in diameter and 30 feet deep. Outlet stream runs about two miles.	Constant 81 degrees F.	Fresh
Devil's Hole	Thermal spring in deep cleft in rocky mountainside; no outlet.	Rectangular pool eight by 60 feet; more than 200 feet deep.	Constant 92 degrees F.	Fresh
Mexican Spring	Tiny spring; discharges a trickle of water that flows only a few feet.	Pool 12 feet long, 18 inches wide and one or two inches deep.	Fluctuates from 40 to 95 degrees F.	Fresh
Tecopa Bore	Hot artesian well; dug in 1967 and colonized by pupfish from nearby marsh.	Outlet stream runs about 3/4 mile to marsh.	Gradient: 117 degrees F. at source; marsh may freeze in winter.	Fresh

REPRESENTATIVE HABITATS OF PUPFISH are small streams and pools, mostly fed by springs. Pupfish have also found their way into the outlet streams of recently dug hot artesian wells. More commonly populations are being destroyed by human activities.

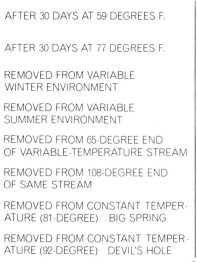
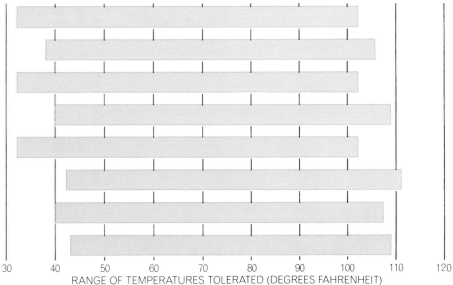

AFTER 30 DAYS AT 59 DEGREES F.

AFTER 30 DAYS AT 77 DEGREES F.

REMOVED FROM VARIABLE WINTER ENVIRONMENT

REMOVED FROM VARIABLE SUMMER ENVIRONMENT

REMOVED FROM 65-DEGREE END OF VARIABLE-TEMPERATURE STREAM

REMOVED FROM 108-DEGREE END OF SAME STREAM

REMOVED FROM CONSTANT TEMPERATURE (81-DEGREE) BIG SPRING

REMOVED FROM CONSTANT TEMPERATURE (92-DEGREE) DEVIL'S HOLE

30   40   50   60   70   80   90   100   110   120
RANGE OF TEMPERATURES TOLERATED (DEGREES FAHRENHEIT)

THERMAL TOLERANCE OF PUPFISH is approximately 70 degrees Fahrenheit. The tolerance range is shifted up or down several degrees depending on the temperature the fish had most recently experienced. The two top bars show the result of acclimation in the laboratory; the other bars show the temperature tolerance of fish that had recently been exposed to the conditions shown.

water and the streams flow far out onto the desert floor. Then as the temperatures rise in late spring the pupfish population increases explosively. The fish become so numerous that the Shoshoni Indians used to travel to the marshes to harvest the inch-long fish. The population reaches a maximum in midsummer just before large areas of the habitat begin to dry up.

In July, August and September hundreds of thousands of fish become stranded in shallow pools and perish as the temperature and salinity increase

and the remaining water rapidly disappears. A fraction of the maximum population survive in the permanent waters of the source springs. The survivors are often further decimated by the scouring action of winter floods, but with the coming of spring the remnants begin reproducing to repeat the cycle. Some of these populations, such as the one inhabiting Salt Creek, probably fluctuate more than a hundredfold each year, and literally millions of pupfish perish each summer.

In contrast with the streams and

marshes, the source pools of the thermal springs provide one of the most constant environments to be found in the Temperate Zone. There is essentially no variation in temperature, salinity or size of habitat. There is, however, some fluctuation in the growth of algae, the principal food of the pupfish, as a result of seasonal variations in the number of daylight hours. Even in these habitats the populations of *Cyprinodon* fluctuate, apparently in response to the availability of food, but the changes are small compared with those that regularly take

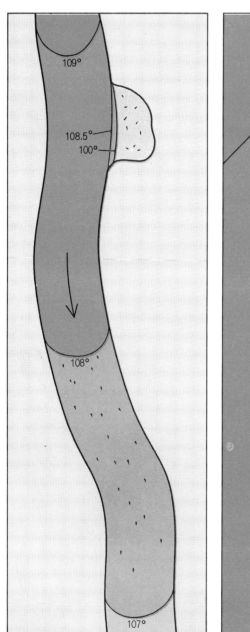
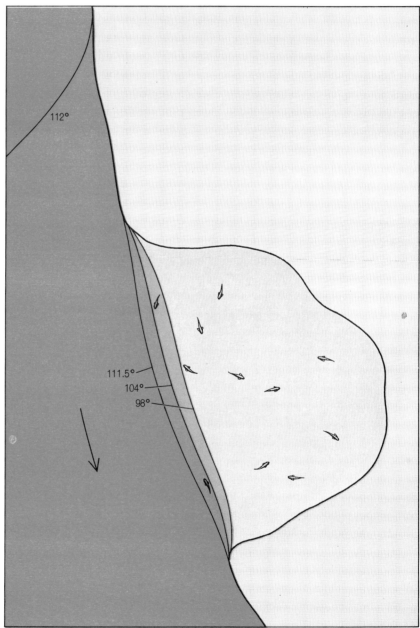

ACUTE TEMPERATURE SENSITIVITY is exhibited by desert pupfish in the main outflow of an artesian well (*left*), where they concentrate in regions below 108 degrees F. By swimming as close as possible to the 108-degree boundary they improve their access to

blue-green algae, which can grow at a higher temperature than the fish can stand. Pupfish are sometimes trapped in small, shallow side pools (*right*), where one can see them swimming within a fraction of an inch of temperatures that could kill them in seconds.

place in streams and marshes. Variations in population size of more than a few fold are rare; the source pools of the larger springs, such as Big Spring, always contain a few thousand fish. The smaller springs support smaller populations. Devil's Hole, which is located in a deep fissure in the side of a mountain, receives only a few hours of sunlight a day. The limited supply of algae supports a population of only 200 to 800 pupfish.

The ultimate in small population size is attained in Mexican Spring, a long narrow pool that is only one or two inches deep in most places. The entire spring contains an estimated 80 gallons of water, barely enough to fill a bathtub. The spring is separated from the nearest other pupfish habitat by hundreds of yards of desert. Its inhabitants have been isolated for many generations, perhaps for hundreds or thousands of years. No more than 20 to 40 fish constitute the entire population of the spring. Of these only four or five are mature males, five to 15 are mature females and the remainder are young. This must certainly approach the minimum size for any self-maintaining population of organisms. Only the constancy of the spring environment and the reproductive capacity of the pupfish have enabled the tiny fish to survive.

The desert pupfish of Death Valley offer manifold opportunities for studies whose results should be every bit as interesting as those reported here. Some of the work is in progress but most of it remains to be done. Unfortunately the pupfish habitats are extremely vulnerable to the activities of man. Since the 1940's at least eight populations of desert pupfish have been exterminated, at least half of them since I began working in the Death Valley area in 1969. These extinctions can be attributed directly to the introduction of predatory fishes, to the construction of bathhouses over the sources of thermal springs and to the filling or draining of springs for agricultural purposes. As this article is written, pumping of water from the natural underground reservoirs is lowering the water level in several springs and threatening the extinction of several additional populations, including the C. diabolis of Devil's Hole. Each population of pupfish is the unique product of a long period of evolutionary history, and the creation of thousands of years of natural selection is now threatened by a single generation of human activity. Both man and the pupfish require water to survive in the desert; unfortunately the absence of water is one environmental condition to which this amazing little fish has not become adapted.

8

THE GEOGRAPHY OF BIRDS

CARL WELTY
July 1957

*Although they are free to fly wherever they please, few birds
are cosmopolitan. After 150 million years of evolution in a
constantly changing environment, most species are confined
to provincial abodes*

When birds took to the air, some 150 million years before the Wright brothers, they had a highway to every possible habitat on the earth's surface. Today they are at home in the polar regions and the tropics, in forest and desert, on mountain and prairie and on the ocean and its islands. Yet when one considers the superb mobility of birds and the eons of time they have had to populate the globe, it is surprising how few cosmopolitan species there are. Some shore and sea birds—sandpipers and plovers, petrels and gulls—are fairly world-wide in distribution. The barn owls, kingfishers, hawks and acrobatic swallows are at home on every continent. Ravens have inherited the earth except, for some obscure reason, South America. But what we mostly see, especially in land

BROWN PELICAN is restricted in range by its feeding habits. It must be able to see the swimming fish it seizes in plunging dives. The turbidity of the Atlantic at the mouth of the Amazon [*see map on page 76*] bars it from that region and the waters farther to the south. This and all the other photographs that accompany this article were provided by the National Audubon Society.

birds, is a picture of curiously limited and seemingly haphazard distribution.

Why are the birds of England and Japan more alike, though 7,000 miles apart, than the birds of Africa and Madagascar, separated by a mere 250 miles? Why does South America have more than 400 species of hummingbird and Africa, with quite similar habitats, not a single one? Why have the finches, found on even the most isolated oceanic islands, not found their way to Australia? Why does the North American turkey, Benjamin Franklin's nominee for our national bird, occur nowhere else in the world? How explain the even more circumscribed range of the wirebird plover, unique to the little island of Saint Helena; or the confinement of a species of Ecuadorian hummingbird to the slopes of the volcano Chimborazo at an elevation of 16,000 feet; or the perilous distinction of the 161 remaining Laysan teal that inhabit the tiniest range of all, the shores of a marshy lagoon, one square mile in area, on the tiny Hawaiian island of Laysan?

The main scheme of the world distribution of birds was laid out by Alfred Russel Wallace in his monumental *Geographic Distribution of Animals,* published in 1876. His six great zoogeographic regions today provide a useful way to sort out the distribution of species, as shown in the map on the next two pages. But this still does not explain how the birds came to be distributed as they are. As a Darwinian intensely aware of the dynamic nature of evolution, Wallace could have told us that we must seek our answer in the interplay of two great dynamic agents: the perpetually changing environment and the unending evolution of the birds.

A restless world of heaving earthquakes, wandering shorelines, shifting climate and changing coats of vegetation can scarcely be expected to have sedentary tenants. A species' range is not likely to stand firm before the chilling, grinding advance of a glacier. We dig up the bones of large ostrich-like birds in the U.S.S.R. and the U. S. The fossils around Paris tell us this was once the home of now pan-tropical trogons and parrots. Ancient guano deposits in Peru show how the native pelican shifted from place to place during prehistoric times.

But birds are not mere passive creatures of these forces. The very geological and climatic changes that move and isolate existing species provide the mechanism of natural selection through which new species evolve. The families

PIGMENTATION AND SIZE of bird species are correlated with climate. British chickadee (*upper right*) is more heavily pigmented than Siberian chickadee (*upper left*). Hairy woodpecker of Canada (*lower left*) is larger than the same species in Costa Rica (*lower right*).

of modern birds, though established as late as the Miocene, have still had enough time to undergo many profound genetic changes. These in interaction with the changing environment have played their part, too, in distributing species around the globe. The migratory birds that summer in the temperate latitudes and winter in the tropics must have evolved during the comparatively recent millennia in which the world developed its present climatic system. But evolution does not always provide for maintenance and extension of range. The Ascension man-of-war bird, for instance, is a splendid sea-flyer, yet cannot venture far from land. Its oil-producing preen gland has become so small that it cannot alight on the ocean without becoming waterlogged, and it is endangered if caught too far from shore by a heavy rain.

Wallace's map, then, is a single frame from a motion picture, a moment arrested in a long history. To understand how it came about requires the accounting of many factors. Principal among these are the arrangement of the earth's land and sea masses, the circulation systems of the oceans and of the atmosphere, climate, the availability of plant life and the competition of animal life. By considering what éach element contributes to the picture alone and in concert with others we can begin to reconstruct the history that lies behind the present geography of birds.

Let us consider first the accidents of geography. It is obvious that land masses are barriers to the spread of sea birds and that the seas are barriers to land birds. This leads straight to the explanation of why South American birds are so different from those of North America: It is because the two continents were so long separated by a sea before the Isthmus of Panama was thrust up. Conversely the fact that many North American birds are closely related to Asiatic species clearly means that their ancestors must have come over "from the old country" when the Bering Strait was a land bridge.

We can see the same processes going on today. As Ernst Mayr of Harvard University has observed, the geologically active regions are also regions of active species-making. The tributaries of the Amazon have cut the forest bordering the river into great "islands," each of which has isolated its distinct but related species of birds. The geologically recent building of the Andes split apart numerous populations of tropi-

cal birds in Colombia and Ecuador. They have evolved into new species, with those on the Pacific side of the range having their nearest relatives across the peaks in the Amazon basin. Just as mountains may isolate species, so mountain passes can provide bridges to join them. The ornithologist Frank Chapman described one pass where the tropical zone reaches nearly up to the saddle. Here we can actually see a large reservoir of species ready to spill over into a new and enlarged range the moment a saddle sinks, or the life zones rise, a few hundred feet.

Once a species surmounts a barrier, it may invade and colonize an enormously larger range with explosive speed, as did the starlings here or the skylarks in New Zealand. About 20 years ago the Old World cattle egret somehow made its way to South America, where it prospered mightily. Now it has reached the United States and is already consolidating its invasion by breeding.

The winds set up by the circulation system of the atmosphere have played the decisive part in distributing some species. For birds as for planes the flight west across the Atlantic in the teeth of the prevailing westerlies is more difficult than the reverse trip. Only five species of wild European land birds have been taken alive in North America; in Great Britain, with but one tenth the coastline, there have been recorded 14 American land species, not to mention 25 aquatic. On the island of South Georgia in the Antarctic are two endemic species, a pipit and a teal, whose nearest relatives live 1,000 miles due west to windward, on the tip of Tierra del Fuego. The islands of the Caribbean are to the leeward of the late summer cyclones of the north equatorial Atlantic; hence they have received as guests from the eastern Atlantic one species each of the tropic bird, frigate bird and booby.

The circulation system of the oceans is important in the distribution of birds not only because it helps or hinders their locomotion but for its effects on climate and food resources. The royal tern, a warm-water species, is bottled up in the Pacific within 30 degrees of latitude, between the cool south-flowing California Current and the chilly north-flowing Peru Current. But in the Atlantic, thanks to the warm Gulf Stream and Brazil Current, its range covers 70 degrees of latitude, from Florida to Argentina. The shoemaker petrel, on the other hand, is tied to cold surface waters and is sand-

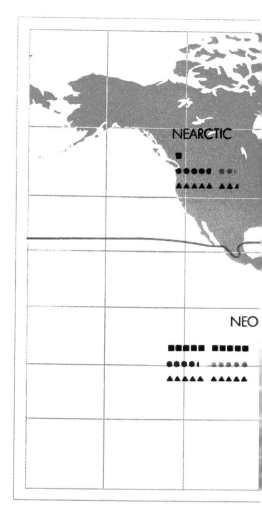

■   1 PECULIAR FAMILY

●   25 GENERA (◉ PECULIAR GENERA)

▲   100 SPECIES

wiched in between the Antarctic pack ice and the Equatorial and Brazil currents. The 12-degree surface-water isotherm marks the northern limit of both the snow petrel and its chief food, the opossum shrimp.

Sea birds in general, unlike land birds, are more abundant in the cooler latitudes because the circumpolar waters are more fertile than the equatorial. Where cool upwelling currents bring nitrates, phosphates and other essential minerals upward into the sunlight, marine plants and consequently fish life abound. Hence the flying multitudes that follow the cold Peru Current, while the warm Sargasso Sea remains a silent watery desert.

The dependence of certain birds on the prevailing ocean currents is dramatically demonstrated on those occasions when nature experiments with the circulation of the oceans. Once about every

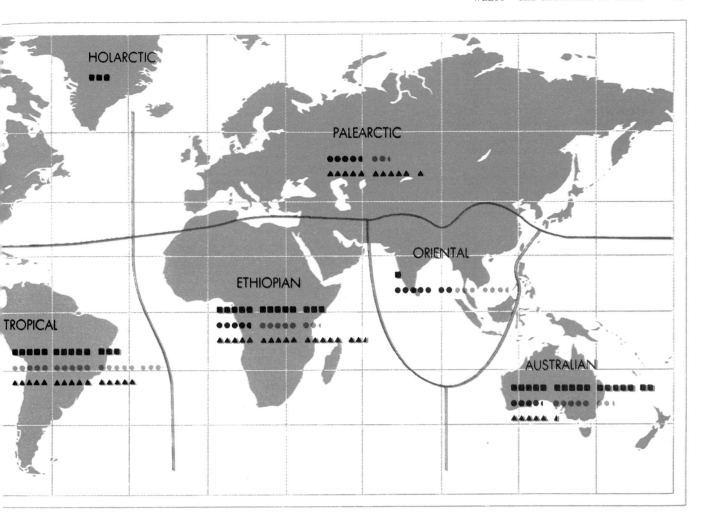

DISTRIBUTION OF BIRDS is mapped in the six zoogeographic regions proposed by Alfred Russel Wallace in 1876. The black squares tally the families "peculiar" to each region, but not all of the families in it. The black and gray circles together tally all the genera in each region; the black triangles, all the species. The Holarctic, comprising the two northern regions, has only three families peculiar to it. The contrast with tropical regions indicates that the latter have been the principal recent evolutionary center for birds.

seven years "*El Niño*," the warm equatorial countercurrent off Colombia and Ecuador, swings south, head-on into the Peru Current. In 1925 *El Niño* shifted its course so strongly that it warmed the littoral waters as far south as Arica, Chile, with these catastrophic effects: the Peru Current plankton died; the normal fish population died or fled and was replaced by warm-water species; hundreds of thousands of cormorants, boobies and pelicans perished or succumbed to disease; tropical sea birds moved down the coast, supplanting the sick and dying guano birds.

The distribution of sea birds, as has been indicated, runs counter to the major pattern of land-bird distribution. Some 85 per cent of all living species occur in the tropics, becoming progressively less abundant toward the poles. The major factor in these statistics is undoubtedly climate. Birds have special physiological problems of high body-temperature, rapid breathing and water conservation; all of these, to say nothing of food needs, are more readily solved in a warm, moist climate. This reflects the fact that more of the earth was tropical, humid and perpetually verdant in the Miocene and early Pliocene, when the birds were evolving. So today we find 1,780 species of birds breeding in Ecuador, 195 in New York State, 56 in Greenland and 3 in Antarctica.

The intimate and long-standing relationship between climate and bird distribution is reflected in the contrasting anatomy and physiology of warm- and cold-climate birds. The response of bird evolution to change of environment is so direct and systematic that it can be expressed in a series of biological rules. For example, species of birds living in colder climates will be larger than related species in warmer climates. This rule, which also holds for mammals, clearly results from natural selection in favor of the physiological advantage involved. Birds with larger bodies have relatively less surface through which to lose heat, a large bird being in essence the same as two or three small birds huddled together to keep warm. Birds in colder regions also have relatively shorter beaks, legs and wings from which to radiate body heat. According to another rule, the birds in the cooler part of a species' range will lay more eggs per clutch than those in the warmer. Egg counts by David Lack, the British ornithologist, show the European robin laying an average of 6.2 eggs per clutch in Scandinavia, 4.9 in Spain and 3.5 in the Canary Islands. Despite the short Scandinavian summer, birds can raise large broods of young because of the abundance of insect food and the long daylight hours. For less obviously adap-

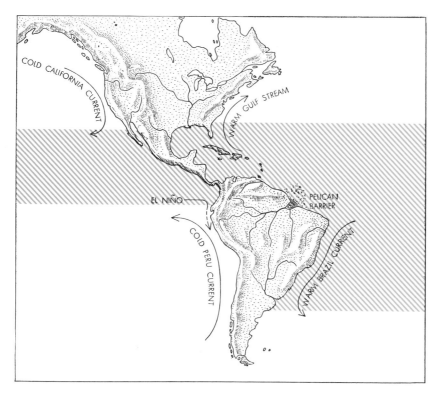

OCEAN TEMPERATURE is important in the distribution of oceanic birds. The warm-water zone (*colored area*) of the Atlantic is wider than that of the Pacific; the currents in the two oceans account for the contrast. Caption on page 72 explains "pelican barrier."

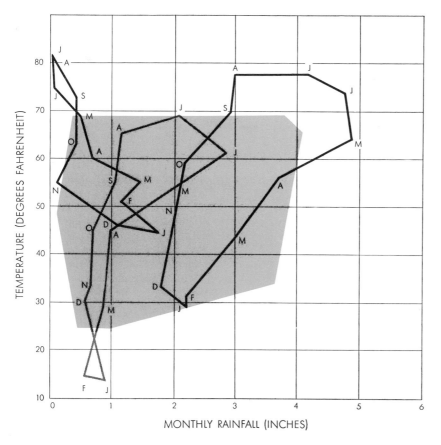

CLIMOGRAPH charts monthly rainfall and temperature. The colored area is the optimum climograph for the European partridge. The black lines give the data for California (*left*) and Missouri, where this bird fails; the gray line describes Montana, where it succeeds.

tive reasons, birds and mammals in the tropics have more of the dark pigment melanin than their relatives in cooler climates. Where tropical birds have brighter and more metallic hues, those in the polar regions tend toward white.

The high correlation of range and climate in some species is clearly demonstrated when the climate changes. As is well known, the mean annual temperature of the Northern Hemisphere has been gradually rising during recent decades. It is equally common knowledge that many southern birds, like the cardinal, egret and mockingbird, have been slowly coming northward. In Sweden 50 years ago the hooded crow was a harbinger of spring; today it is a common winter resident. In Finland 262 bird species were known before 1885; now there are 298, the new ones coming mostly from southern Europe and the Mediterranean.

The principle of climatic distribution has been put to practical use in game management. Before a game species is transplanted to a new habitat a climograph, a chart combining temperature and humidity factors [*see illustration at bottom of this page*], is drawn up for its natural range and compared with that of its proposed home. Where the two match fairly closely, there is at least a chance that the transplant will take hold.

The concentration of bird species in the tropics is correlated with food supply as well as with climate. Since green plants supply the first step in the animal food chain, it follows that the verdure of the tropics offers more of all kinds of sustenance than other regions. Conversely it is clear that insect-eating birds must migrate southward from freezing temperatures when winter comes.

The connection between food supply and range is clearly indicated in cases of adaptation to special diets. Woodpeckers will scarcely seek wood-boring insects on steppes or prairies. Nectar-feeding hummingbirds must have long-season flower resources; some species are bound by the shape of their bills to particular flowering plants. The beaks of crossbills are peculiarly adapted to secure a diet of conifer seeds. The white booby specializes in the catching of flying fish; its breeding islands must accordingly lie in waters where they abound. Such narrow dependency is, of course, an invitation to extinction. When a natural catastrophe all but wiped out the eelgrass along the Atlantic coast of the U. S. in 1931-33, one of the many casualties was the sea brant that fed upon it; the numbers of this goose were reduced by 80 per cent. Such a fate is not likely to overtake the wide-ranging South American kelp gull. Its diet includes fish, marine invertebrates and shellfish, the eggs and young of other birds, carrion, offal—in fact, almost anything.

The ranges of some species are fixed by adaptations to other aspects of their environment that may seem less compelling than food. For nesting sites Scott's oriole in the American Southwest is apparently dependent on the drooping dead leaves of the yucca; the European reed warbler, on beds of freshwater reeds; the palm swift, on the hanging fronds of the fan palm. The Tristan Island penguins depend upon the indigenous tussock grass to protect them from the elements and predatory gulls, and they reciprocally fertilize it with their droppings. The Bigua cormorant of Tierra del Fuego and the redfooted booby of Little Cayman in the Caribbean present a contrasting picture. They are tree-top nesters; sometimes they nest in such dense colonies that their guano kills the trees, compelling them to move on to new ones.

A force that seems always to promote the expansion of range and the wider dispersal of a species is the competition of other birds of the same species. Overpopulation—or the shortage of food, which is the other side of the same coin—gives a dramatic demonstration of its power in the occasional mass movements of a species, known as "invasions" or "irruptions." The snowy owl's repeated southward irruptions into the U. S. are known to coincide with the ebb years in the population cycle of the Canadian lemming. Siberian nutcrackers have invaded Germany 15 times between 1896 and 1933, each time when the pine-seed crop failed at home. Pallas's sand grouse has many times in years of drought burst out of its native steppes northeast of the Caspian Sea and swept in enormous numbers across Europe as far as Britain and Ireland. In the great invasion of 1888 the British Parliament, hoping to naturalize the bird, passed a special act for its protection, but four years later there was not a single grouse to be seen in all England. In these irruptions we see a momentary surmounting of normal barriers through the build-up of dispersal pressure from behind. They provide a mechanism for sampling new ranges, though they rarely succeed in establishing permanent new homes for the species.

Competition within a species promotes the extension of range more com-

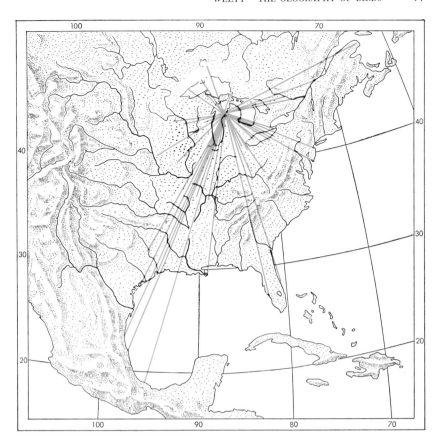

DISTANCES FLOWN by herring gulls, banded and released in the Great Lakes region, are charted here. Most of the birds recaptured at the most distant points were found to be yearlings. Dispersal tendency in young birds relieves population pressure on natal areas.

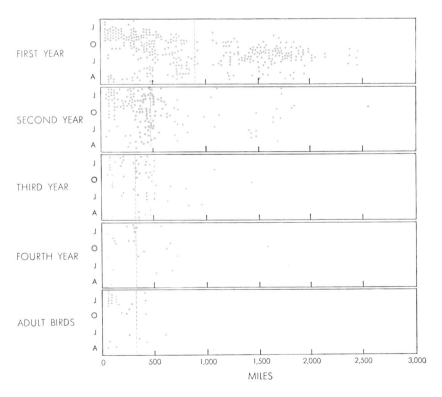

DISPERSAL TENDENCY of yearling herring gulls is indicated by this chart based upon recapture of 773 out of 23,434 nestlings banded in New Brunswick. The chart shows the age, the season of the year and the distance from home to the place of recapture of each bird. The mean distance traveled by the birds in each age group is indicated by the broken line.

SKYLARK, the common, field-nesting bird celebrated in Shelley's ode, was transplanted from Europe to New Zealand and has prospered there.

RING-NECKED PHEASANT, familiar to U. S. sportsmen, is an import, a hybrid of British and Chinese species.

CALIFORNIA CONDOR is nearly extinct. A carrion eater, it requires a wide range of undisturbed wilderness to sustain its life.

TURKEY is a genus peculiar to North America. Domesticated varieties now abound, but the wild bird is very nearly extinct.

monly through what seems to be an inborn tendency in the young of all species to strike out and explore the world in all directions. Every new generation puts some added strain on the traditional habitat for food, territory and nesting sites, and the younger birds find themselves in unequal competition with the entrenched older ones. The wanderlust of first-year birds is the adaptive device by which natural selection has met this contingency. In Switzerland the banding of young barn owls showed that in years

of high nestling productivity 57 to 68 per cent of them dispersed 50 kilometers or more from their natal nests; in years of normal productivity the percentage was only 37. Similar results were found by Alfred Gross in the banding of 23,434 herring gulls on Kent Island in the Canadian province of New Brunswick between 1934 and 1938. Of the 3 per cent recovered at points distant from Kent Island more than half were less than a year old and the great majority of these were captured

hundreds of miles from their birthplace.

Seasonal migration is quite a different thing, but it also undoubtedly encourages the extension of range. Long-distance migrants are in a better position to discover new habitats, and they are naturally more tolerant of diversity in the environment. In the mountains of Colombia such winter visitors from North America as the yellow-billed cuckoo, the rose-breasted grosbeak and the yellow, blackburnian and mourning

CATTLE EGRET, from Africa, is established in South America and is invading U. S.

WHOOPING CRANE is another nearly extinct American genus; some 30 survive.

warbler have been observed ranging freely throughout the temperate, subtropical and tropical life-zones, whereas the permanent residents are more rigidly confined within zonal boundaries.

Competition between species, in contrast to the dispersal force of intraspecific competition, tends to confine species to narrower ranges. Lack observes that if two species of the same genus have the same diet, they rarely live in the same habitat. Competition be-

tween related species thus promotes the concentration of each in a slightly different locality. In this country the black-capped chickadee is without close relatives and ranges widely over forests and marshes. But in Europe this same bird must compete with eight other titmouse species and so breeds only in swampy thickets, leaving all its other possible habitats for relatives to enjoy.

The same sort of mutual accommodation is found even among unrelated species. The amateur naturalist T. E. Musselman tells of a late-spring freeze that killed several thousand bluebird eggs in the nesting boxes he had set up around Quincy, Ill. The birds laid substitute clutches, but this caused their incubation to coincide with the arrival of the house wrens from the south. In the ensuing competition for nesting sites the wrens destroyed many bluebird eggs. It may have been precisely to avoid such disastrous competition that natural selection had advanced the first nesting of the bluebird, thus permitting both species to occupy the same range.

Sometimes interspecific relations are even more accommodating. In Germany the stock dove depends upon the black woodpecker to furnish it with nest holes. Small, defenseless birds have been known to build their nests in the margins of hawk and eagle nests, thereby securing the protection of their landlords against other predators.

On the other hand, it must be conceded that birds are not always so cooperative with one another. On Muskeget Island, off the coast of Maine, there used to be great colonies of terns. These were supplanted around 1940 by colonies of laughing gulls. Now the laughing gulls are being displaced by the more aggressive herring gulls. In rural areas of the U. S. the aggressive English sparrow has driven the cliff swallow from its former haunts under the eaves of barns and farmhouses.

Predators may close a habitat to a species, especially if they prevent it from breeding. In tropical forests many open-nesting species, like the pigeons, have been virtually eliminated by nest-robbing monkeys. Nesting ducks suffer heavy losses of eggs and young wherever there is an abundance of crows. Such predation may not be an unmixed curse; if the marauding crows did not force the ducks to stagger their egg-laying, their usually synchronized nesting would expose them to wholesale calamity in late-spring freezes.

The biological force that has had the harshest impact and most far-reaching effect on the geography of birds is man.

In a few cases his cultural interference with the natural environment has encouraged the spread of a species, like the robin, barn swallow or chimney swift. The spread of the barn owl through the state of New York has been attributed to mechanical refrigeration and the resulting abandonment of old icehouses. But in the main man has been a force for restriction and extermination. The classic instruments of his predation have been the ax, the plow, the cow, fire and the gun. To which the modern era has added water pollution, insecticides and herbicides. Cats and rats have been known to depopulate oceanic islands of their birds, completely extinguishing a half-dozen species at a time. That byword for an extinct species, the flightless, ground-nesting dodo, was sent on its way by the pigs introduced onto the island of Mauritius.

Occasionally civilized man has tried to atone for his ecological misdeeds by importing foreign species. Alas, as with the English sparrow and the starling, only the less desirable species seem to take hold. The worst failures have been his experiments with the bird life of oceanic islands. There used to be about 40 passerine (perching) species on the Hawaiian Islands; more than half have been driven out by the hundred or more foreign species that have been imported there. Mayr says that more kinds of birds have become extinct on the islands of the Pacific than in all the rest of the world put together.

HERRING GULL, shown here in adult plumage, is a wide-ranging bird, familiar in inland regions as well as on coasts of U. S.

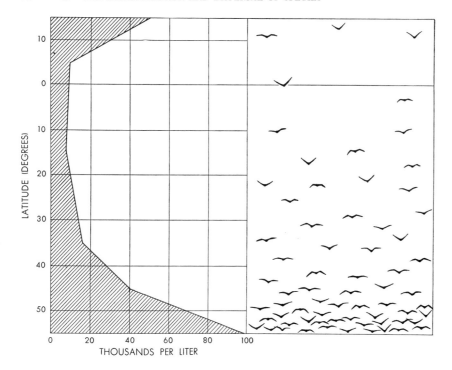

DISTRIBUTION OF SEA BIRDS in Southern Hemisphere, roughly indicated at right, shows significant correlation with the concentration of plankton in ocean waters, indicated by the crosshatched area at left. Plankton provides food for fish on which the birds depend.

Even without man, of course, the bright tapestry of bird geography will continue to be alternately torn and mended by the wearing and restorative forces of nature. But since man has willy-nilly taken a hand in the process, we must hope he will acquire the wisdom to provide refuge for the most threatened species before they too go the way of the dodo.

9

CONTINENTAL DRIFT AND THE FOSSIL RECORD

A. HALLAM

November 1972

Similarities between the fossils found in widely separated areas led to the first of continental drift. Today's advocates of plate-tectonic theory are also supported by the fossil record

In the past 10 years geologists have been widely converted to plate tectonics, a concept that implies the lateral migration of the continents. If Alfred Wegener, who put forward the hypothesis of continental drift around the turn of the century, were alive today, he might be wryly amused. The workers who revitalized his conception paid comparatively little attention to the evidence in its favor provided by fossils. Yet by Wegener's own account he began to take the idea of drifting continents seriously only after learning of the fossil evidence for a former land connection between Brazil and Africa. The fossil record, rather than the much noted physical "fit" between the opposing coastlines, was what inspired him.

The fossil record is no less important to students of continental drift today. The similarities and differences between fossils in various parts of the world from Cambrian times onward are now helping paleontologists both to support the drift concept and to provide a reasonably precise timetable for a number of the key events before and after the breakup of the ancestral continent of Pangaea.

In Wegener's day there was nothing particularly novel about the idea that the various continents had been connected in various ways off and on in the distant past. Biologists and paleontologists in the 19th century and in the early 20th readily invoked such land connections to explain the strong resemblances between plants and animals on different continents. It was generally agreed that links had existed between Australia and other regions bordering the Indian Ocean until early in the Jurassic period, some 180 million years ago. The same was held to be true of a link between Africa and Brazil until early in the Cretaceous period, some 140 million years

ago, and a link between Madagascar and India up to the start of the Cenozoic era, only 65 million years ago.

At the same time the orthodox explanation of these connections was that the position of the continents was fixed but that "land bridges" had spanned the considerable distances of open ocean between them. In the orthodox view these extensive bridges had later sunk without a trace [*see upper illustration on page 83*]. Wegener dismissed such explanations in trenchant terms. The earth's crust, he pointed out, is composed of rocks that are far less dense than the material of the earth's interior. If the floors of the oceans were paved with vast sunken bridges composed of the same thickness of light crustal material as the continental areas that lie above sea level, then gravity measurements made at sea should reveal that fact. The gravity measurements indicate the exact opposite: the underlying rock of the ocean floor is much denser than the crustal material of the continents.

The essential improbability of sunken land bridges can also be stated in terms of isostatic balance. If the low-density crustal rocks of the vanished bridges had indeed been somehow forced downward into the denser sea bottom, the bridges would tend to rise again. None of the hypothetical land bridges, however, has reemerged. This makes it necessary to assume the existence of some colossal unspecified force that continues to hold the bridges submerged. The existence of such a force seems improbable in the extreme. Unless one chose to dismiss the fossil evidence out of hand, Wegener concluded, the only feasible means of explaining intercontinental plant and animal resemblances was by the drifting of the continents themselves.

It is odd that neither paleontologists

nor geophysicists paid much heed to Wegener's cogent argument. The paleontologists were almost unanimous in rejecting the notion, perhaps because they did not fully appreciate the force of Wegener's geophysical proposals. The main effect of his hypothesis on this group was that quite narrow land bridges became more popular than the embarrassingly broad avenues that had been favored at the turn of the century [*see lower illustration on page 83*]. Of course even when the bridges were pared down in this fashion, serious isostatic problems remained. As for the geophysicists, they largely ignored the considerable body of fossil evidence for continental drift that Wegener had assembled. Perhaps they failed to appreciate its significance or perhaps they mistrusted data of a merely qualitative kind and were suspicious of the seemingly subjective character of taxonomic assessments.

The Zoogeography of the Past

In recent years there has been a major resurgence of interest in the zoogeography of the past. This is no doubt due in part to the prospect that fossil evidence will enable paleontologists to test independently the conclusions that have been reached on purely geological and geophysical grounds about plate tectonics. Here I shall describe how some of this evidence, in particular the remains of higher animals on land and of simpler bottom-dwelling marine organisms offshore, can shed light on the making and breaking of connections between continents in the past and can help to determine how long some of these continental linkages and separations endured.

Two principal factors control the geo-

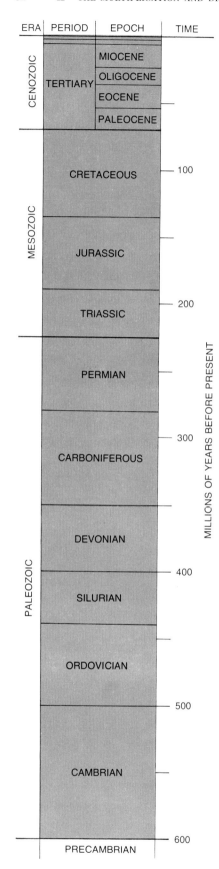

ERA	PERIOD	EPOCH	TIME
CENOZOIC	TERTIARY	MIOCENE	
		OLIGOCENE	
		EOCENE	
		PALEOCENE	
MESOZOIC	CRETACEOUS		100
	JURASSIC		200
	TRIASSIC		
PALEOZOIC	PERMIAN		
	CARBONIFEROUS		300
	DEVONIAN		400
	SILURIAN		
	ORDOVICIAN		500
	CAMBRIAN		
	PRECAMBRIAN		600

MILLIONS OF YEARS BEFORE PRESENT

THREE SUCCESSIVE ERAS occupy the 600-million-year span seen in this geological time scale. Patterns of distribution found in the fossil record of each era throw light on plate-tectonic theory of continental drift.

graphical distribution of land animals. They are on the one hand the climate and on the other various water barriers and in particular wide stretches of sea. The effectiveness of climate as a barrier is nicely illustrated by the fact that the animals that live near the poles are far less diverse than those that live in the Tropics. Polar ice, however, is not a permanent feature of the planet. In times of a more equable world climate such as prevailed during the Mesozoic era far and away the most significant deterrents to movement must have been ocean barriers.

An animal need not be exclusively terrestrial to be confined by an ocean barrier. For example, a large number of fishes cannot survive except in fresh water. Amphibians are also severely circumscribed by the sea, although frogs are better able to colonize islands by swimming across the sea than newts or salamanders. As for the probability that reptiles or mammals might successfully move across the sea by accidental rafting, the chances are obviously best for the small and the rapidly reproducing. By the same token, however, the small animals are the very ones that would first die of starvation if the rafting were prolonged. Hence even fairly narrow marine straits can be highly effective barriers to terrestrial animals.

The paleontologist George Gaylord Simpson has made a useful distinction between three kinds of dispersal route. The first, which he calls "corridors," are land connections that allow free migration of animals in both directions. The second, called "filter bridges," combine a land connection with some additional factor, such as climate, in a way that bars some prospective migrants. As an example, it seems doubtful that warm-weather-loving animals crossed the Bering Strait bridge between Asia and North America during the Pleistocene. The passage was open only when the sea level was low during the colder phases of that glacial epoch.

Simpson's third category, "sweepstakes routes," takes its name from the small proportion of winners compared with losers. The rare winners are those that survive chance rafting and succeed in colonizing isolated areas. Unlike corridors (or even filter bridges), which favor the eventual homogeneity of the faunas at both ends of the passage, sweepstakes routes lead to the development of populations that are low in diversity and ecologically unbalanced. The reason is that, in addition to the high mortality rate, chance rafting can only be possible for a

very small fraction of any continental fauna. One result of this double selectivity is that islands are often a refuge for a comparatively primitive group of animals. The tuataras of New Zealand, the sole surviving representatives of one major order of reptiles, are one example; the lemurs of Madagascar are another.

The three routes Simpson defines are the ones that are available to land animals in general and to the higher vertebrates in particular. It is obvious, however, that the same kinds of connection would also influence the dispersal of marine organisms such as bottom-dwelling invertebrates. Of course, the effects would be exactly reversed. For example, the establishment of a corridor between two landmasses would simultaneously raise a barrier between two segments of a previously homogeneous marine fauna. The disappearance of a land connection, in turn, would result in the establishment of a corridor as far as marine organisms were concerned. Analogous to the filter bridge for land animals would be the marine "filter barrier." Here a bottom-dweller on one side of an ocean basin might migrate freely to the other side as long as it could drift in tropical waters, but it would be unable to survive the rigors of such a journey in the cooler waters of the temperate zones.

Isolation and Homogenization

Bearing these considerations in mind, what does evolutionary theory predict with respect to continental drift? Clearly when a formerly unified landmass splits up, the result is genetic isolation (and hence morphological divergence) among the separated segments of a formerly homogeneous land fauna. Conversely, the suturing of two continental areas is followed by the homogenization of the corresponding faunas as there is cross-migration. The process will quite probably be accompanied by the extinction of any less well-adapted groups that may now face stronger competition.

In land areas that are unconnected two factors, parallel evolution and convergence, may produce animal species that develop a similar morphology because they occupy identical ecological niches. A well-known instance is provided by the ant bear of South America, the aardvark of Africa and the cosmopolitan pangolin. Forces of this kind are unlikely, however, to affect entire faunas.

So much for the land animals. What are the effects of continental drift on the invertebrates that inhabit the shallow ocean floor? It is obvious that a stretch of land that separates two oceans acts as a barrier to marine migration. It is less well appreciated that a wide stretch of deep ocean may be almost as effective as a land barrier in preserving the genetic isolation of the marine shelf dwellers on opposite shores. This isolation is due to the fact that such animals disperse at only one time in their life cycle: when they are newly hatched larvae that join the plankton commu-

nity at the ocean surface or close to it. A bottom dweller's larval stage is normally not long enough to enable the animal to survive a slow ocean crossing.

This matter was quantified some time ago by the Danish biologist Gunnar Thorson. He studied the larval stages of no fewer than 200 species of marine invertebrates, and he concluded that only 5 percent could survive in the plankton for more than three months. That length of time is too short to allow transoceanic

colonization except by an occasional "transport miracle." More recently Thorson has been criticized for confining his attention to organisms that inhabit cool temperate waters. New data gathered by towing fine nets through the plankton indicate that a significant number of larvae of tropical species can survive an Atlantic crossing in either direction; they drift with the equatorial surface current one way and with the subsurface countercurrent the other way. It is also true

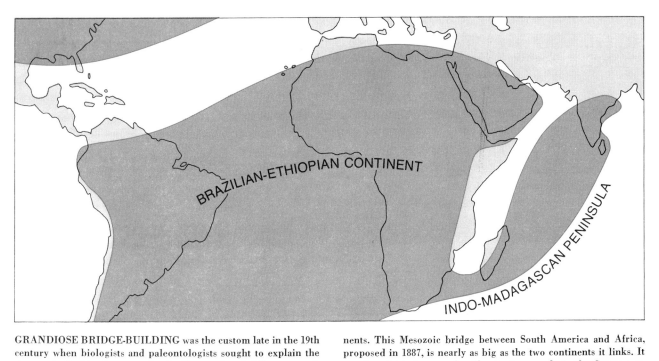

GRANDIOSE BRIDGE-BUILDING was the custom late in the 19th century when biologists and paleontologists sought to explain the strong similarities between the fossil records of different conti-

nents. This Mesozoic bridge between South America and Africa, proposed in 1887, is nearly as big as the two continents it links. It was thought to have sunk without a trace early in the Cretaceous.

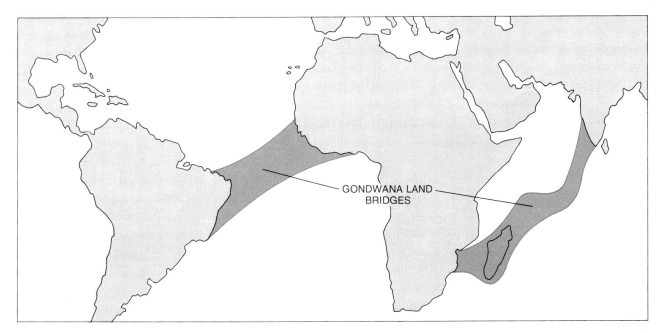

MORE MODEST BRIDGES were proposed in the 20th century as geophysical studies found no evidence in support of vast drowned intercontinental connections. This pared-down link between Brazil

and West Africa and another (supposedly in existence until the end of Cretaceous times) between East Africa and India represent an effort to satisfy those who were critical of the broader bridges.

that some mollusks and some corals are found everywhere in the Tropics, a fact that gives added support to the notion that transoceanic migration is possible for long-lived larvae. At the same time it is possible that organisms with prolonged larval stages represent a late evolutionary development that has taken place only since the present Atlantic and Indian oceans began to open up.

Be this as it may, it is evident that, although Thorson's conclusions must be somewhat amended, an ocean barrier is effective in restricting the migration of a majority of the shelf-dwelling marine invertebrates. Moreover, the capacity for migration being in direct proportion to the length of the larval stage, it follows that the wider the deep-ocean barrier is, the more the faunas of the opposing shelves should differ. That is true today. There are fewer species in common among the faunas on opposite sides of the Pacific than there are on opposite sides of the Atlantic. Therefore among marine fossil faunas the degrees of similarity or difference between two coastal assemblages should allow an estimate of the amount of deep-ocean separation between the two coasts.

Given the present state of knowledge, it would be futile to seek any absolute measure of similarity between fossil faunas. If, however, one adopts a dynamic approach and deals with changes in the degree of resemblance during successive intervals of geologic time, a fair amount of progress can be made. Such an approach has several advantages. For one, animals belonging to widely separated phyla can be grouped together. For another, the specific factors that control a particular species' migration potential need not be precisely understood. Further, one can use the work of many different taxonomists, without regard to whether they are "lumpers" or "splitters" in their method of classification, as long as the work is self-consistent. Best of all, the approach takes fully into account the factor that is all-important to the geologist: the factor of time.

The Distribution of Fossils

There are four principal patterns revealed by the distribution of fossils. They are closely interrelated and I shall define them in order, accompanying

each definition with one or more examples. All the examples will concern the making or breaking of land or sea connections, but not all will be the result of continental drift.

The first pattern is "convergence." The term describes an increase, as time passes, in the degree of resemblance between faunas of different regions. An example unrelated to continental drift is provided by the history of South America during the Cenozoic era, beginning some 65 million years ago. Throughout most of the era South America had a highly distinctive land fauna [see illustration below]. The fossil mammals from Cenozoic formations in Argentina were among the most spectacular finds of Darwin's voyage aboard H.M.S. Beagle. The strongly endemic nature of this fauna, comparable in this respect to the fauna of Australia today, is clear evidence that the continent was isolated for many millions of years.

At about the end of the Pliocene epoch, two million or so years ago, a drastic change took place. A land connection—the Isthmus of Panama—was established between North and South America and many New World animals

DIVERGENCE OF MAMMALS in the New World occurred during a period of millions of years when North and South America were unconnected. Mammals then unknown in the south included mastodons, tapirs, primitive camels and various carnivores. The mammals of the south included many that are now extinct. Illustrated here are (a) *Mylodon*, a giant sloth, (b) *Paedotherium*, a notoungulate, (c) *Prodolichotis*, a rodent, (d) *Macrauchenia*, an ungulate, and (e) *Plaina*, an early relative of the more successful armadillo.

that had been unable to move south now crossed the bridge. Among them were the mastodon, the tapir, primitive camels and a number of carnivores. Simultaneously many of the indigenous South American faunas became extinct; the losers included all but two genera of the many primitive marsupials that had been sheltered there and were evidently incapable of competing with the better-adapted migrants from North America. The traffic was not, however, entirely one-way. Armadillos soon extended their range northward throughout Central America and into the southern U.S. [see illustration below].

Simpson has estimated that before North America and South America were united perhaps 29 families of mammals lived in the area south of the Isthmus of Panama and perhaps 27 entirely different families of mammals lived to the north. After the union the faunas of both continents had 22 families of mammals in common. This is a particularly dramatic example of convergence, even though the establishment of the Panama bridge seems to have owed nothing to continental drift.

The mammalian fauna of Africa dur-ing the Cenozoic era provides another example of convergence. Up to some 25 million years ago the African fauna had a strong endemic element. The animals ancestral to the living elephants, the manatees and the hyrax were found only there. This suggests that the continent had been isolated for a substantial period.

Early in the Miocene epoch a number of mammals from Eurasia entered Africa by means of one or more land connections. The migration led to the reduction and even the extinction of some of the indigenous African fauna. At the same time the ancestral elephants crossed over to Eurasia and had soon spread around the world. Less than 25 million years later mastodons were waiting at the emerging Isthmus of Panama to enter the last major continental area in the world still barred to the proboscoids. The Miocene bridge-building that allowed a substantial degree of convergence between the faunas of Africa and Eurasia can be attributed to continental drift, specifically a northward movement of the Africa-Arabia plate.

A third example of convergence takes us all the way back to the Cambrian and early Ordovician periods, some 500 to 600 million years ago. The most spectacular marine organisms of the Cambrian, the early anthropods known as trilobites, turn out to be sharply separated into two distinct faunas; the line that divides the two faunal provinces runs through eastern North America and through the British Isles and Scandinavia [see illustration on page 89]. Over the next 75 million years or so, during late Ordovician and Silurian times, the two trilobite faunas tend to lose their regional distinctiveness. So do a number of other early marine invertebrates: corals, brachiopods, graptolites and conodonts. So do two groups of early freshwater fishes: primitive jawless ostracoderms belonging to the orders Anaspida and Thelodonti. Freshwater fishes are, of course, prisoners of the continental streams they inhabit. By late Silurian or early Devonian times, some 400 million years ago, only one faunal province existed in the North Atlantic region.

The paleontologist A. W. Grabau noted the difference between the trilobites of adjacent areas many years ago, and he suggested that the sharp delineation might be attributable to the former

CONVERGENCE OF MAMMALS began about the end of the Pliocene epoch, after a land bridge was established between North and South America. One mammal native to South America, the armadillo, migrated northward. So many mammals formerly unknown south of Panama moved to South America, however, that the two continents soon came to have 22 families of mammals in common. At the same time many South American mammals were unable to compete with the immigrants from the north and became extinct.

existence of a deep-ocean barrier. More recently J. Tuzo Wilson of the University of Toronto followed up Grabau's suggestion and proposed that the border between the two faunal provinces marked the closure of a proto-Atlantic ocean that was eliminated by continental drift in Paleozoic times. Since then John F. Dewey of the State University of New York at Albany has developed this concept with considerable success in terms of plate tectonics and subduction: the process in which the leading edge of a drifting plate is destroyed by plunging under another plate [see "Plate Tectonics," by John F. Dewey; SCIENTIFIC AMERICAN, May 1972].

Dewey's view, which is based primarily on geological grounds, envisions the loss of an ancient segment of ocean down one or more zones of subduction as an American and a European plate drifted together. Compression and subsequent uplift in the region of subduction formed the Caledonian mountain belt in northwestern Europe and the

"old" Appalachian Mountains in eastern North America. The record of faunal convergence in the interval between Cambrian and Devonian times evidently reflects the steady narrowing of the proto-Atlantic, a process that continued for tens of millions of years until most of the ancient ocean was swallowed up. Here we have an example of the fossil record supporting a reconstruction of a drift episode that has been independently inferred from geological data.

The Case of the Urals

The Caledonian belt is not the only ancient mountain range that hints of a collision between two drifting plates. The Urals, the mountains that separate the European and Asiatic parts of the U.S.S.R., have also been interpreted as a collision feature on geological grounds. Let us see whether the fossil record supports this interpretation.

In Devonian times an order of jawless freshwater fishes, cousins to the orders

that once flourished on opposite sides of the proto-Atlantic, inhabited the streams of the region that is now the European and Asiatic flanks of the Urals. These fishes are the Heterostraci. Specimens of the order from fossil formations on the European side of the Urals clearly belong to a faunal province that is distinct from the province on the Asiatic slope. It follows that, at least during the 50 million years of Devonian times, a marine barrier separated the two landmasses that now meet in the Urals.

There is negative evidence to suggest that the same barrier persisted during the succeeding interval: the Carboniferous period. Fossil deposits of Carboniferous age in the European U.S.S.R. contain the remains of amphibians and reptiles. In spite of more than a century of prospecting, however, no Carboniferous amphibians or reptiles have been found in the Asiatic U.S.S.R. Yet 50 million years later, at the beginning of the Mesozoic era, the amphibians and reptiles of Asia closely resemble those found elsewhere in the world. Evidently by that time land connections between the two regions were firmly established.

Does this array of fossil evidence, which seems very much like the evidence for a proto-Atlantic, show that the Urals are indeed the products of continental drift? Not necessarily. A further example will show why. Early in the Cenozoic era the mammals of Europe comprised a fauna that was different in many respects from the mammalian fauna of Asia. This was not, however, because two continental plates had drifted apart. Instead the regions were separated at that time by the intrusion of a long arm of shallow sea. As far as land animals are concerned, a shallow sea is quite as effective a barrier as a true deep-ocean basin. How do we know that the separation of the two regions in Paleozoic times was not a similar shallow sea?

Examination of another fossil group, the bottom-dwelling marine invertebrates, should enable us to resolve this question. If a deep-ocean basin separated the European and Asiatic parts of the U.S.S.R. in Paleozoic times, then the wider that ocean was, the more divergent the invertebrate fossils on opposite sides of the Urals should be. Unfortunately, when we apply this test, the existing data prove to be somewhat indecisive. Still, the weight of evidence seems to suggest that the Paleozoic marine gap between Europe and Asia was not very large. This fossil finding suggests that, if continental drift formed the

THREE PAIRS OF MOLLUSKS, each pair belonging to the same genus but to different species, exemplify the divergence that marine animals undergo when a barrier divides a once uniform fauna. The cowries (*top*) are of the genus *Cypraea;* the Caribbean species, *C. zebra* (*left*), has diverged from the Pacific species, *C. cervinetta* (*right*). The same is true of a second gastropod pair (*middle*), both of the genus *Strombus,* and the bivalve pair (*bottom*), both of the genus *Arca.* Divergence began when the Isthmus of Panama arose.

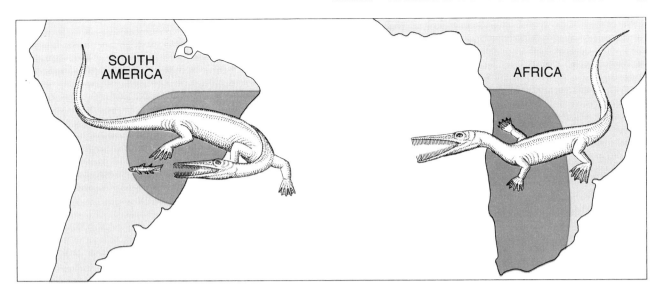

FOSSILS OF MESOSAURUS, a late Paleozoic reptile seen in a restoration here, are found on both sides of the South Atlantic and nowhere else in the world. If *Mesosaurus* was able to swim well enough to cross the ocean, it should have diffused far more widely. Since it did not, this example of "disjunct endemism" suggests that South America and Africa must have been joined at that time.

Urals, the ocean that disappeared as a consequence was a narrow one.

The Pattern of Divergence

We can now consider the second principal pattern of fossil distribution. This is "divergence," which is simply the reverse of convergence. To illustrate the pattern I shall use three examples drawn from the Cenozoic fossil record and one from the Mesozoic. The first is the late Cenozoic rise of the Isthmus of Panama that, as we have seen, allowed the convergence of the land faunas of North America and South America. Simultaneously the rise cut in two a marine region that until then had been inhabited by a homogeneous population of bottom-dwelling invertebrates. The consequence of this genetic isolation was divergence; during the Pleistocene epoch a number of "twin" species, the descendants of identical but isolated genera of marine invertebrates, have evolved independently on opposite sides of the isthmus.

The second example concerns the invertebrate faunas of the Tethys seaway, an ancient span of ocean that in early Cenozoic times reached all the way from the Caribbean, by way of the Mediterranean basin, to the western shores of Indonesia. Throughout this vast region in early Cenozoic times the invertebrate faunas were markedly homogeneous. Beginning about 25 million years ago, however, during the Miocene period, the homogeneity of the Tethys faunas was abruptly disturbed. Thereafter the ma-

rine invertebrates of the Indian Ocean differed sharply from those of the Mediterranean. And whereas the faunas of the Mediterranean continued in general to resemble the faunas of the Atlantic, there are indications that some groups, in particular bottom-dwelling foraminifera, also began to show divergence.

The land animals of the Cenozoic era provide the third example. During that era the fossil faunas of the various continents, the mammals in particular, differ in many respects. The most obvious differences are evident in Australia, South America and Africa—the continents of the Southern Hemisphere. During the preceding Mesozoic era, in contrast to this Cenozoic pattern of divergence, the land-dwelling animals (most of them reptiles) were quite homogeneous irrespective of their continued residence. The Cenozoic pattern of divergence is the inevitable consequence of the breakup of Pangaea in late Mesozoic times.

Two groups of late Mesozoic marine invertebrates yield a fourth example of divergence. They flourished during the Cretaceous period, when the breakup of Pangaea was well under way. When one compares certain species of bivalves and foraminifera from fossil strata of the lower Cretaceous in the Caribbean with similar organisms in the Mediterranean region, the two faunas prove to be very much alike. By late Cretaceous times, however, new genera of bivalves and foraminifera have appeared that are unique to one or the other of the formerly homogeneous regions.

This late Cretaceous divergence con-

forms with the inference, drawn from geological and geophysical data, that the final period of the Mesozoic era witnessed a progressive enlargement of the deep-ocean separation between the Mediterranean and the Caribbean. To the north of the Tropics in the newborn Atlantic a sea-shelf connection between the Old World and the New persisted, but there is little doubt that the diverging marine faunas (including the rudists, a peculiar group of reef-building bivalves) were unable to migrate in any but warm waters and were thus inhibited from crossing from one side of the Atlantic to the other through the cool shelf sea.

The Pattern of Complementarity

I term the third of the patterns of fossil distribution "complementarity" because the faunas in adjacent areas of shore and ocean shelf react to alterations of the environment in a complementary way. For example, when a land connection forms, the newly united land faunas tend to converge and the newly divided marine faunas tend to diverge, whereas the breaking of a land connection gives rise to the opposite effect. The pattern of complementarity is significant because it provides a cross-check on interpretations of the fossil record that depend exclusively on either the marine faunas or the terrestrial ones.

One additional example will suffice to define complementarity. As we have already noted, there is evidence from the Miocene of divergence among the

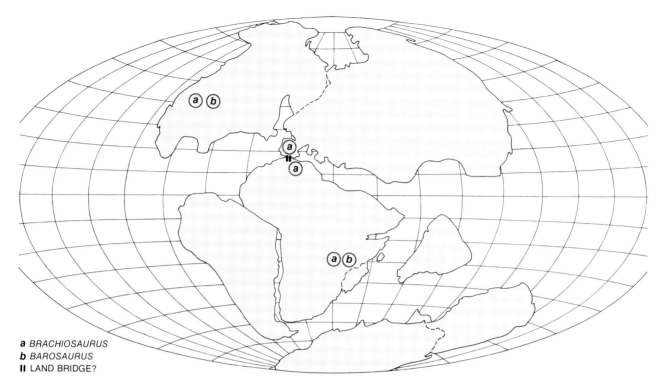

a BRACHIOSAURUS
b BAROSAURUS
II LAND BRIDGE?

FOSSIL-RICH STRATA that contain the remains of two genera of late Jurassic dinosaurs are located in western North America and in East Africa respectively. Fossils of one genus (a) are also found in Portugal and Algeria. At that time the ancient world continent, Pangaea, had broken apart; its components are shown here at the positions calculated by Robert S. Dietz and John C. Holden of the National Oceanic and Atmospheric Administration. Unless a land bridge existed in the late Jurassic where North Africa and Spain nearly touch, the presence of identical fossils on separate continents is another example of disjunct endemism. But where the bridge should be there are oceanic rocks of Jurassic age instead, making the existence of a land connection at that time improbable.

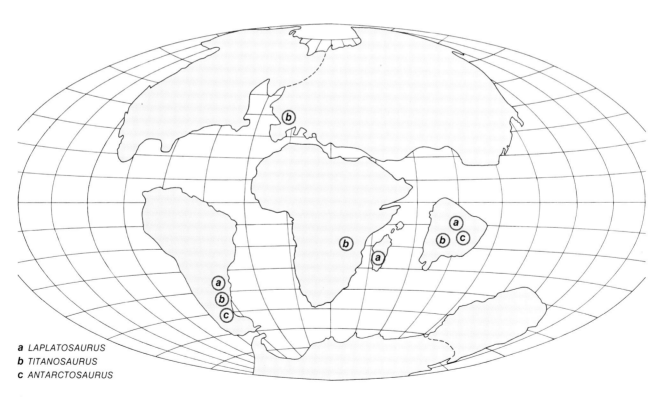

a LAPLATOSAURUS
b TITANOSAURUS
c ANTARCTOSAURUS

SIMILAR DILEMMA is posed by the disjunct endemism of three genera of late Cretaceous dinosaurs. All three genera are present in fossil formations in South America and in India. One genus (b) is also present in both Europe and Africa and another (a) is also found in Madagascar. The map shows the various continents in the positions calculated for the late Cretaceous by Dietz and Holden. By that time, students of continental drift generally agree, India had moved well away from the Africa-Arabia plate, continuing a trend that supposedly first isolated the drifting subcontinent some 100 million years earlier. Unless the dinosaur fossil identifications are mistaken, however, the land connection between India and South America could scarcely have been severed at so early a date.

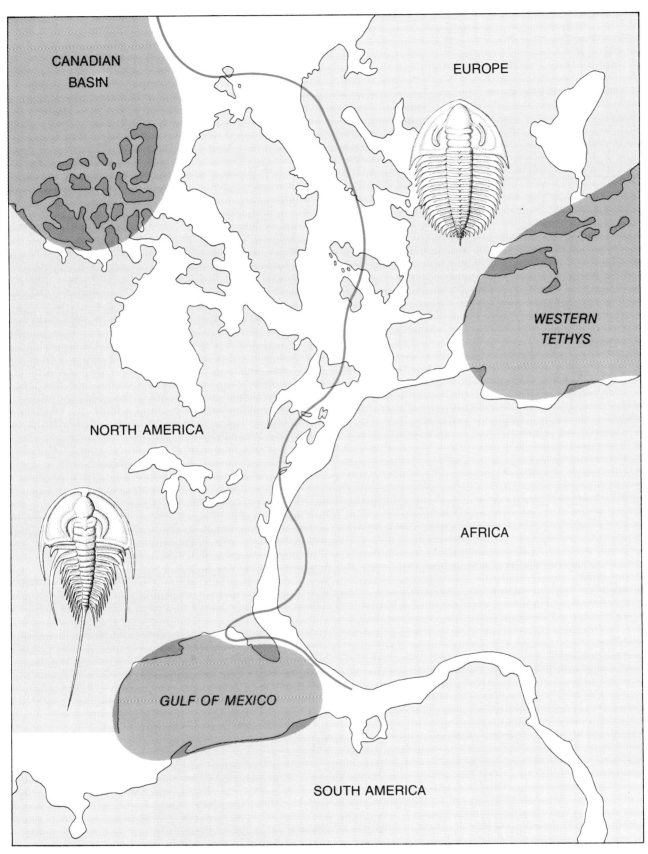

DISAPPEARING ATLANTIC of some 400 million years ago may have been reduced to two comparatively minor bodies of water: the Canadian basin and the Gulf of Mexico. The broad colored line divides regions that are connected today, such as the Scandinavian peninsula, the British Isles and parts of eastern North America. It marks the boundary between faunal realms that were distinctly different in Cambrian and early Ordovician times. A fossil typical of each realm is illustrated. The American form is the trilobite *Paedeumias transitans*; the European form is the trilobite *Holmia kjerulfi*. The difference between the two realms grew progressively less, and by the middle of the Paleozoic era it had vanished. Convergence of the two faunas suggests that what had once been a wide, deep proto-Atlantic was swallowed up along zones of subduction as American and European continental plates came together.

marine invertebrates along the length of the Tethys seaway on the one hand and of convergence among the land mammals of Africa and Eurasia on the other. It appears that this pattern of complementarity in the Miocene fossil record signals the withdrawal of the Tethys seaway from the region of the Near East and Middle East. From the viewpoint of plate tectonics the withdrawal of the Tethys must have been a consequence of the Africa-Arabia plate impinging on Eurasia. The fossil evidence is thus in accord with the geological evidence of compressive, generally north-south earth movements and mountain uplift in southern Spain, Turkey and Iran in Miocene times.

There is also geological evidence of compressive tectonic activity in the Near East and Middle East in late Cretaceous times, some 50 million years earlier. This episode could not, however, have eliminated the Tethys seaway; the fossil record shows no matching record of complementarity in the late Cretaceous. When the story of the faunal migrations between Europe and Africa is finally known in detail, it will surely prove to be a complex narrative. It will probably not call, however, for any fundamental modification of the general picture I have presented here.

Disjunct Endemism

We come now to the fourth and last of the fossil-distribution patterns, which I call "disjunct endemism." The term describes the following situation. A group of fossil organisms is limited in its geographical distribution but nonetheless appears in two or more parts of the world that are now separated by major geographical barriers such as zones of deep ocean. The classic case in point is *Mesosaurus*, a small, snaggle-toothed reptile that lived in late Paleozoic times, some 270 million years ago. Strata that contain fossils of *Mesosaurus* are found only in Brazil and in South Africa [*see illustration on page* 87]. This animal, measuring some 18 inches from snout to tip of tail, was evidently aquatic. It could hardly have been able to swim very far, however, without having diffused into many parts of the world other than Brazil and South Africa. The application of Occam's razor suggests that in late Paleozoic times Brazil and South Africa were contiguous; this bit of fossil evidence in favor of continental drift was first noted many years ago.

In at least two instances that involve the ruling reptiles of the Mesozoic era, the dinosaurs, the fossil evidence seems

to require sharp revisions of the drift timetable. The dinosaurs involved are five genera of sauropods, the line that gave rise to such museum favorites as *Brontosaurus* and *Diplodocus*. Two of the genera flourished in late Jurassic times and three in the late Cretaceous, some 70 million years afterward.

The Jurassic dinosaur genera are *Brachiosaurus*, the biggest of all the sauropods, and *Barosaurus*. The remains of dinosaurs of both genera are found in the Morrison Formation of the western U.S. and in the Tendaguru fossil beds of Tanzania; *Brachiosaurus* fossils have also been found in Portugal and in Algeria. These huge herbivores seem to have occupied an ecological niche comparable to an elephant's. Although they might possibly have negotiated swamps, they would have had trouble swimming across a wide river, let alone an ocean. Their presence in both Africa and North America thus points to the existence of a land connection between these areas in late Jurassic times. The necessity for this connection in turn imposes a constraint on the timing of the oceanic separation of the northern and southern halves of Pangaea.

Now, one popular reconstruction of the continental array in Jurassic times, prepared by Robert S. Dietz and John C. Holden of the National Oceanic and Atmospheric Administration, shows a possible place of crossing between Eurasia (which was then linked to North America) and Africa. That is where Spain and North Africa nearly touch; a Jurassic land bridge here would solve the problem of the seemingly disjunct endemism of the two sauropods [*see top illustration on page* 88]. The existence of marine deposits of Jurassic age in the parts of Spain and North Africa that might have been joined, however, seems to rule out any such land bridge.

Another way to be rid of this supposed example of disjunct endemism is to attack the biological classifications involved. One could assert that the African species of these two dinosaur genera are actually quite different from the North American species and attribute this divergence to a break in the land connection between the two regions. By and large, however, the dinosaurs are a group that has been excessively split by taxonomists. An admitted resemblance even at the genus level is likely to signify a close genetic affinity if not an actual ability to interbreed. On balance, then, close similarities between the late Jurassic dinosaur faunas of the Tendaguru beds and of the Morrison Formation pose a problem for the continental-

drift timetable that has not yet been satisfactorily resolved.

The disjunct endemism of the three late Cretaceous sauropods—*Titanosaurus*, *Laplatosaurus* and *Antarctosaurus*—presents an even more clear-cut contradiction between the fossil record and the accepted timetable for continental drift. These three dinosaurs are known from fossil formations both in South America and in India. Yet the Indian subcontinent had supposedly become isolated by surrounding ocean some 100 million years before late Cretaceous times, toward the close of the Triassic [*see bottom illustration on page* 88]. Unless the fossil identifications are in error, such an early date for the severance of India from the rest of Gondwanaland is clearly inadmissible. Several similar arguments from the fossil record, which I need not give in detail, can be used to support the persistence of land connections (if only intermittent ones) between the Africa–South America landmass and the Australia-Antarctic landmass until quite late in the Mesozoic period.

I have tried to show here how the fossil record can contribute to plate-tectonic theory by helping to establish a more refined timetable for continental drift. Critics may say that the fossil data are often imprecise and are in addition subject to ambiguous interpretation. That is undoubtedly true in some instances. Moreover, we must beware of oversimplification and of overinterpretation of patchy evidence. We should also acknowledge that endemism cannot be explained in every instance on the basis of continental movements. Nonetheless, the general level of agreement between paleontology and the other earth sciences is sufficiently high to warrant some confidence in our fossil-based conclusions.

As time passes and the reconstruction of past plate movements becomes more precise, I believe interest in several biological questions that arise from the new view of earth history will increase. For one thing, we shall be in a better position to learn more about the rates of evolution among isolated organisms. For another, we shall be able to make findings about the relative ease of migration and colonization under different geographical circumstances. The disjunct distribution of many living animals—for example the lungfishes, the marsupials and the giant flightless birds—will be better understood. Perhaps most intriguing of all, we may acquire new insights into why many groups of plants and animals have become extinct.

10

CONTINENTAL DRIFT AND EVOLUTION

BJÖRN KURTÉN

March 1969

The breakup of ancient supercontinents would have had major effects on the evolution of living organisms. Does it explain the difference in the diversification of reptiles and mammals?

The history of life on the earth, as it is revealed in the fossil record, is characterized by intervals in which organisms of one type multiplied and diversified with extraordinary exuberance. One such interval is the age of reptiles, which lasted 200 million years and gave rise to some 20 reptilian orders, or major groups of reptiles. The age of reptiles was followed by our own age of mammals, which has lasted for 65 million years and has given rise to some 30 mammalian orders.

The difference between the number of reptilian orders and the number of mammalian ones is intriguing. How is it that the mammals diversified into half again as many orders as the reptiles in a third of the time? The answer may lie in the concept of continental drift, which has recently attracted so much attention from geologists and geophysicists [see "The Confirmation of Continental Drift," by Patrick M. Hurley; SCIENTIFIC AMERICAN Offprint 874]. It now seems that for most of the age of reptiles the continents were collected in two supercontinents, one in the Northern Hemisphere and one in the Southern. Early in the age of mammals the two supercontinents had apparently broken up into the continents of today but the present connections between some of the continents had not yet formed. Clearly such events would have had a profound effect on the evolution of living organisms.

The world of living organisms is a world of specialists. Each animal or plant has its special ecological role. Among the mammals of North America, for instance, there are grass-eating prairie animals such as the pronghorn antelope, browsing woodland animals such as the deer, flesh-eating animals specializing in large game, such as the mountain lion, or in small game, such as the fox, and so on. Each order of mammals comprises a number of species related to one another by common descent, sharing the same broad kind of specialization and having a certain physical resemblance to one another. The order Carnivora, for example, consists of a number of related forms (weasels, bears, dogs, cats, hyenas and so on), most of which are flesh-eaters. There are a few exceptions (the aardwolf is an insect-eating hyena and the giant panda lives on bamboo shoots), but these are recognized as late specializations.

Radiation and Convergence

In spite of being highly diverse, all the orders of mammals have a common origin. They arose from a single ancestral species that lived at some unknown time in the Mesozoic era, which is roughly synonymous with the age of reptiles. The American paleontologist Henry Fairfield Osborn named the evolution of such a diversified host from a single ancestral type "adaptive radiation." By adapting to different ways of life—walking, climbing, swimming, flying, plant-eating, flesh-eating and so on—the descendant forms come to diverge more and more from one another. Adaptive radiation is not restricted to mammals; in fact we can trace the process within every major division of the plant and animal kingdoms.

The opposite phenomenon, in which stocks that were originally very different gradually come to resemble one another through adaptation to the same kind of life, is termed convergence. This too seems to be quite common among mammals. There is a tendency to duplication—indeed multiplication—of orders performing the same function. Perhaps the most remarkable instance is found among the mammals that have specialized in large-scale predation on termites

and ants in the Tropics. This ecological niche is filled in South America by the ant bear *Myrmecophaga* and its related forms, all belonging to the order Edentata. In Asia and Africa the same role is played by mammals of the order Pholidota: the pangolins, or scaly anteaters. In Africa a third order has established itself in this business: the Tubulidentata, or aardvarks. Finally, in Australia there is the spiny anteater, which is in the order Monotremata. Thus we have members of four different orders living the same kind of life.

One can cite many other examples. There are, for instance, several living and extinct orders of hoofed herbivores. There are two living orders (the Rodentia, or rodents, and the Lagomorpha, or rabbits and hares) whose chisel-like incisor teeth are specialized for gnawing. Some extinct orders specialized in the same way, and an early primate, an ice-age ungulate and a living marsupial have also intruded into the "rodent niche" [*see top illustration on page 97*]. This kind of duplication, or near-duplication, is an essential ingredient in the richness of the mammalian life that unfolded during the Cenozoic era, or the age of mammals. Of the 30 or so orders of land-dwelling mammals that appeared during this period almost two-thirds are still extant.

The Reptiles of the Cretaceous

The 65 million years of the Cenozoic are divided into two periods: the long Tertiary and the brief Quaternary, which includes the present [*see illustration on page 92*]. The 200-million-year age of reptiles embraces the three periods of the Mesozoic era (the Triassic, the Jurassic and the Cretaceous) and the final period (the Permian) of the preceding era. It is instructive to compare the number

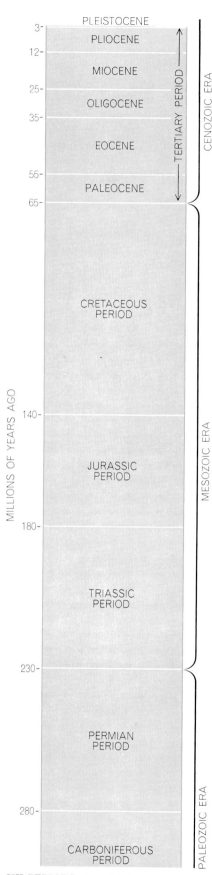

SIX PERIODS of earth history were occupied by the age of reptiles and the age of mammals. The reptiles' rise began 280 million years ago, in the final period of the Paleozoic era. Mammals replaced reptiles as dominant land animals 65 million years ago.

of reptilian orders that flourished during some Mesozoic interval about as long as the Cenozoic era with the number of mammalian orders in the Cenozoic. The Cretaceous period is a good candidate. Some 75 million years in duration, it is only slightly longer than the age of mammals. Moreover, the Cretaceous was the culmination of reptilian life and its fossil record on most continents is good. In the Cretaceous the following orders of land reptiles were extant:

Order Crocodilia: crocodiles, alligators and the like. Their ecological role was amphibious predation; their size, medium to large.

Order Saurischia: saurischian dinosaurs. These were of two basic types: bipedal upland predators (Theropoda) and very large amphibious herbivores (Sauropoda).

Order Ornithischia: ornithischian dinosaurs. Here there were three basic types: bipedal herbivores (Ornithopoda), heavily armored quadrupedal herbivores (Stegosauria and Ankylosauria) and horned herbivores (Ceratopsia).

Order Pterosauria: flying reptiles.

Order Chelonia: turtles and tortoises.

Order Squamata: The two basic types were lizards (Lacertilia) and snakes (Serpentes). Both had the same principal ecological role: small to medium-sized predator.

Order Choristodera (or suborder in the order Eosuchia): champsosaurs. These were amphibious predators.

One or two other reptilian orders may be represented by rare forms. Even if we include them, we get only eight or nine orders of land reptiles in Cretaceous times. One could maintain that an order of reptiles ranks somewhat higher than an order of mammals; some reptilian orders include two or even three basic adaptive types. Even if these types are kept separate, however, the total rises only to 12 or 13. Furthermore, there seems to be only one clear-cut case of ecological duplication: both the crocodilians and the champsosaurs are sizable amphibious predators. (The turtles cannot be considered duplicates of the armored dinosaurs. For one thing, they were very much smaller.) A total of somewhere between seven and 13 orders over a period of 75 million years seems a sluggish record compared with the mammalian achievement of perhaps 30 orders in 65 million years. What light can paleogeography shed on this matter?

The Mesozoic Continents

The two supercontinents of the age of reptiles have been named Laurasia (after

Laurentian and Eurasia) and Gondwanaland (after a characteristic geological formation, the Gondwana). Between them lay the Tethys Sea (named for the wife of Oceanus in Greek myth, who was mother of the seas). Laurasia, the northern supercontinent, consisted of what would later be North America, Greenland and Eurasia north of the Alps and the Himalayas. Gondwanaland, the southern one, consisted of the future South America, Africa, India, Australia and Antarctica. The supercontinents may have begun to split up as early as the Triassic period, but the rifts between them did not become effective barriers to the movement of land animals until well into the Cretaceous, when the age of reptiles was nearing its end.

When the mammals began to diversify in the late Cretaceous and early Tertiary, the separation of the continents appears to have been at an extreme. The old ties were sundered and no new ones had formed. The land areas were further fragmented by a high sea level; the waters flooded the continental margins and formed great inland seas, some of which completely partitioned the continents. For example, South America was cut in two by water in the region that later became the Amazon basin, and Eurasia was split by the joining of the Tethys Sea and the Arctic Ocean. In these circumstances each chip of former supercontinent became the nucleus for an adaptive radiation of its own, each fostering a local version of a balanced fauna. There were at least eight such nuclei at the beginning of the age of mammals. Obviously such a situation is quite different from the one in the age of reptiles, when there were only two separate land masses.

Where the Reptiles Originated

The fossil record contains certain clues to some of the reptilian orders' probable areas of origin. The immense distance in time and the utterly different geography, however, make definite inferences hazardous. Let us see what can be said about the orders of Cretaceous reptiles (most of which, of course, arose long before the Cretaceous):

Crocodilia. The earliest fossil crocodilians appear in Middle Triassic formations in a Gondwanaland continent (South America). The first crocodilians in Laurasia are found in Upper Triassic formations. Thus a Gondwanaland origin is suggested.

Saurischia. The first of these dinosaurs appear on both supercontinents in the Middle Triassic, but they are more

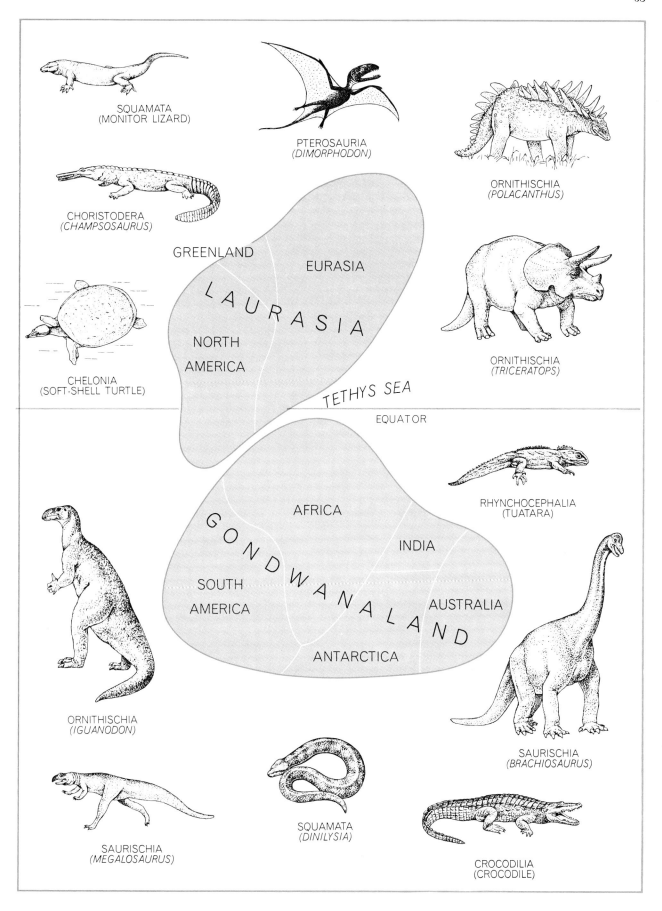

SQUAMATA
(MONITOR LIZARD)

PTEROSAURIA
(*DIMORPHODON*)

ORNITHISCHIA
(*POLACANTHUS*)

CHORISTODERA
(*CHAMPSOSAURUS*)

GREENLAND

EURASIA

L A U R A S I A

NORTH
AMERICA

ORNITHISCHIA
(*TRICERATOPS*)

CHELONIA
(SOFT-SHELL TURTLE)

TETHYS SEA

EQUATOR

RHYNCHOCEPHALIA
(TUATARA)

AFRICA

G O N D W A N A L A N D

INDIA

SOUTH
AMERICA

AUSTRALIA

ANTARCTICA

ORNITHISCHIA
(*IGUANODON*)

SAURISCHIA
(*BRACHIOSAURUS*)

SAURISCHIA
(*MEGALOSAURUS*)

SQUAMATA
(*DINILYSIA*)

CROCODILIA
(CROCODILE)

TWO SUPERCONTINENTS of the Mesozoic era were Laurasia in the north and Gondwanaland in the south. The 12 major types of reptiles, represented by typical species, are those whose fossil remains are found in Cretaceous formations. Most of the orders inhabited both supercontinents; migrations were probably by way of a land bridge in the west, where the Tethys Sea was narrowest.

varied in the south. A Gondwanaland origin is very tentatively suggested.

Ornithischia. These dinosaurs appear in the Upper Triassic of South Africa (Gondwanaland) and invade Laurasia somewhat later. A Gondwanaland origin is indicated.

Pterosauria. The oldest fossils of flying reptiles come from the early Jurassic of Europe. They represent highly specialized forms, however, and their antecedents are unknown. No conclusion seems possible.

Chelonia. Turtles are found in Triassic formations in Laurasia. None are found in Gondwanaland before Cretaceous times. This suggests a Laurasian origin. On the other hand, a possible forerunner of turtles appears in the Permian of South Africa. If the Permian form was in fact ancestral, a Gondwanaland origin would be indicated. In any case, the order's main center of evolution certainly lay in the northern supercontinent.

Squamata. Early lizards are found in the late Triassic of the north, which may suggest a Laurasian origin. Unfortunately the lizards in question are aberrant gliding animals. They must have had a long history, of which we know nothing at present.

Choristodera. The crocodile-like champsosaurs are found only in North America and Europe, and so presumably originated in Laurasia.

The indications are, then, that three orders of reptiles—the crocodilians and the two orders of dinosaurs—may have originated in Gondwanaland. Three others—the turtles, the lizards and snakes and the champsosaurs—may have originated in Laurasia. The total number of basic adaptive types in the Gondwanaland group is six; the Laurasia group has four. The Gondwanaland radiation may well have been slightly richer than the Laurasian because it seems that the southern supercontinent was somewhat larger and had a slightly more varied climate. Laurasian climates seem to have been tropical to temperate. Southern parts of Gondwanaland were heavily glaciated late in the era preceding the Mesozoic, and its northern shores (facing the Tethys Sea) had a fully tropical climate.

Although some groups of reptiles, such as the champsosaurs, were con-fined to one or another of the supercontinents, most of the reptilian orders sooner or later spread into both of them. This means that there must have been ways for land animals to cross the Tethys Sea. The Tethys was narrow in the west and wide to the east. Presumably whatever land connection there was—a true land bridge or island stepping-stones—was located in the western part of the sea. In any case, migration along such routes meant that there was little local differentiation among the reptiles of the Mesozoic era. It was over an essentially uniform reptilian world that the sun finally set at the end of the age of reptiles.

Early Mammals of Laurasia

The conditions of mammalian evolution were radically different. In early and middle Cretaceous times the connections between continents were evidently close enough for primitive mammals to spread into all corners of the habitable world. As the continents drifted farther apart, however, populations of these primitive forms were gradually isolated from one another. This was par-

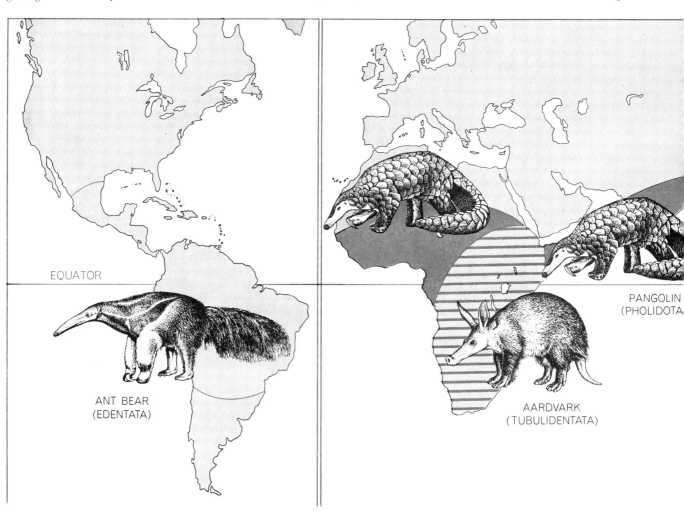

EQUATOR

ANT BEAR
(EDENTATA)

AARDVARK
(TUBULIDENTATA)

PANGOLIN
(PHOLIDOTA)

ticularly the case, as we shall see, with the mammals that inhabited the daughter continents of Gondwanaland. Among the Laurasian continents North America was drifting away from Europe, but at the beginning of the age of mammals the distance was not great and there is good evidence that some land connection remained well into the early Tertiary. North American and European mammals were practically identical as late as early Eocene times. Furthermore, throughout the Cenozoic era there was a connection between Alaska and Siberia, at least intermittently, across the Bering Strait. On the other hand, the inland sea extending from the Tethys to the Arctic Ocean formed a complete barrier to direct migration between Europe and Asia in the early Tertiary. Migrations could take place only by way of North America.

In this way the three daughter continents of ancient Laurasia formed three semi-isolated nuclear areas. Many orders of mammals arose in these Laurasian nuclei, among them seven orders that are now extinct but that covered a wide spectrum of specialized types, including

primitive hoofed herbivores, carnivores, insectivores and gnawers. The orders of mammals that seem to have arisen in the northern daughter continents and that are extant today are:

Insectivora: moles, hedgehogs, shrews and the like. The earliest fossil insectivores are found in the late Cretaceous of North America and Asia.

Chiroptera: bats. The earliest-known bat comes from the early Eocene of North America. At a slightly later date bats were also common in Europe.

Primates: prosimians (for example, tarsiers and lemurs), monkeys, apes, man. Early primates have recently been found in the late Cretaceous of North America. In the early Tertiary they are common in Europe as well.

Carnivora: cats, dogs, bears, weasels and the like. The first true carnivores appear in the Paleocene of North America.

Perissodactyla: horses, tapirs and other odd-toed ungulates. The earliest forms appear at the beginning of the Eocene in the Northern Hemisphere.

Artiodactyla: cattle, deer, pigs and other even-toed ungulates. Like the odd-toed ungulates, they appear in the early Eocene of the Northern Hemisphere.

Rodentia: rats, mice, squirrels, beavers and the like. The first rodents appear in the Paleocene of North America.

Lagomorpha: hares and rabbits. This order makes its first appearance in the Eocene of the Northern Hemisphere.

Pholidota: pangolins. The earliest come from Europe in the middle Tertiary.

The fact that a given order of mammals is found in older fossil deposits in North America than in Europe or Asia does not necessarily mean that the order arose in the New World. It may simply reflect the fact that we know much more about the early mammals of North America than we do about those of Eurasia. All we can really say is that a total of 16 extant or extinct orders of mammals probably arose in the Northern Hemisphere.

Early Mammals of South America

The fragmentation of Gondwanaland seems to have started earlier than that

of Laurasia. The rifting certainly had a much more radical effect. Looking at South America first, we note that at the beginning of the Tertiary this continent was tenuously connected to North America but that for the rest of the period it was completely isolated. The evidence for the tenuous early linkage is the presence in the early Tertiary beds of North America of mammalian fossils representing two predominantly South American orders: the Edentata (the order that includes today's ant bears, sloths and armadillos) and the Notoungulata (an order of extinct hoofed herbivores).

Four other orders of mammals are exclusively South American: the Paucituberculata (opossum rats and other small South American marsupials), the Pyrotheria (extinct elephant-like animals), the Litopterna (extinct hoofed herbivores, including some forms resembling horses and camels) and the Astrapotheria (extinct large hoofed herbivores of very peculiar appearance). Thus a total of six orders, extinct or extant, probably originated in South America. Still another order, perhaps of even more ancient origin, is the Marsupicarnivora. The order is so widely distributed, with species found in South America, North America, Europe and Australia, that its place of origin is quite uncertain. It includes, in addition to the extinct marsupial carnivores of South America, the opossums of the New World and the native "cats" and "wolves" of the Australian area.

The most important barrier isolating South America from North America in the Tertiary period was the Bolívar Trench. This arm of the sea cut across the extreme northwest corner of the continent. In the late Tertiary the bottom of the Bolívar Trench was lifted above sea level and became a mountainous land area. A similar arm of sea, to which I have already referred, extended across the continent in the region that is now the Amazon basin. This further enhanced the isolation of the southern part of South America.

Africa's role as a center of adaptive radiation is problematical because practically nothing is known of its native mammals before the end of the Eocene.

SPINY ANTEATER
(MONOTREMATA)

FOUR ANT-EATING MAMMALS have become adapted to the same kind of life although each is a member of a different mammalian order. Their similar appearance provides an example of an evolutionary process known as convergence. The ant bears of the New World Tropics are in the order Edentata. The aardvark of Africa is the only species in the order Tubulidentata. Pangolins, found both in Asia and in Africa, are members of the order Pholidota. The spiny anteater of Australia, a very primitive mammal, is in the order Monotremata.

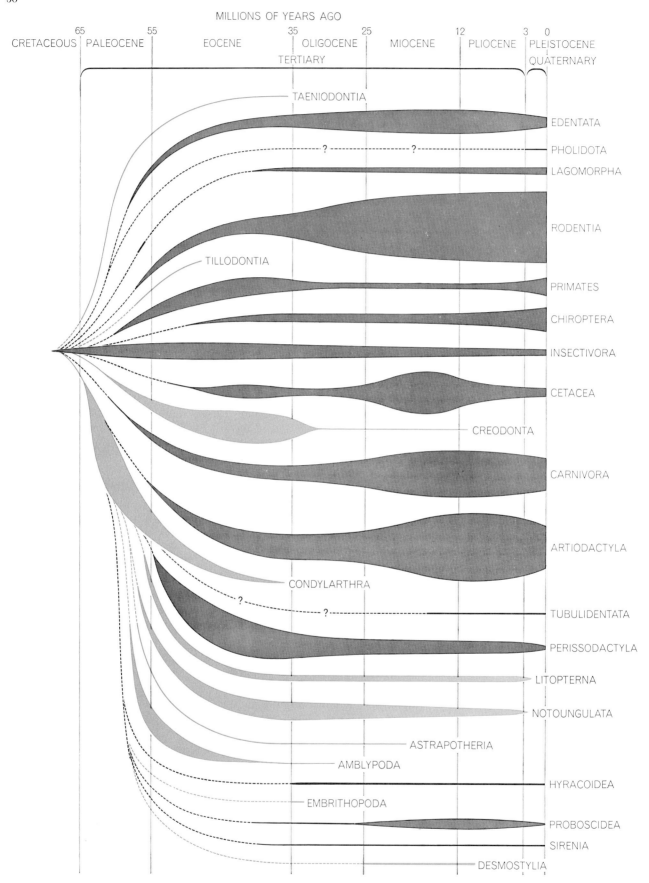

MILLIONS OF YEARS AGO

CRETACEOUS	PALEOCENE	EOCENE	OLIGOCENE	MIOCENE	PLIOCENE	PLEISTOCENE

65   55   35   25   12   3   0

TERTIARY

QUATERNARY

TAENIODONTIA

EDENTATA

PHOLIDOTA

LAGOMORPHA

RODENTIA

TILLODONTIA

PRIMATES

CHIROPTERA

INSECTIVORA

CETACEA

CREODONTA

CARNIVORA

ARTIODACTYLA

CONDYLARTHRA

TUBULIDENTATA

PERISSODACTYLA

LITOPTERNA

NOTOUNGULATA

ASTRAPOTHERIA

AMBLYPODA

HYRACOIDEA

EMBRITHOPODA

PROBOSCIDEA

SIRENIA

DESMOSTYLIA

ADAPTIVE RADIATION of the mammals has been traced from its starting point late in the Mesozoic era by Alfred S. Romer of Harvard University. Records for 25 extinct and extant orders of placental mammals are shown here. The lines increase and decrease in width in proportion to the abundance of each order. Extinct orders are shown in color; broken lines mean that no fossil record exists during the indicated interval and question marks imply doubt about the suggested ancestral relation between some orders.

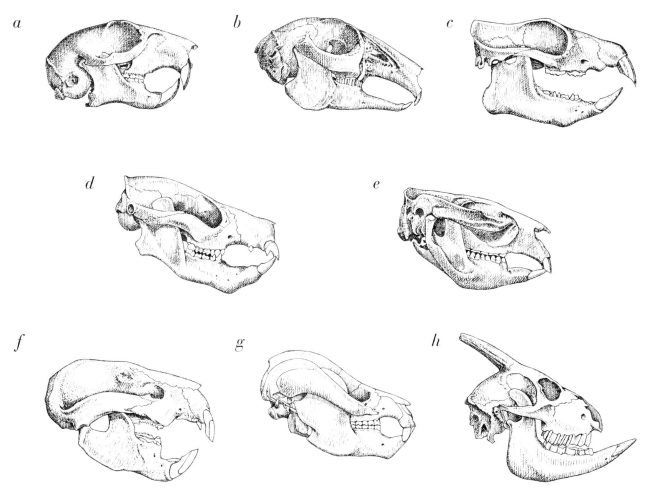

CHISEL-LIKE INCISORS, specialized for gnawing, appear in animals belonging to several extinct and extant orders in addition to the rodents, represented by a squirrel (*a*), and the lagomorphs, represented by a hare (*b*), which are today's main specialists in this ecological role. Representatives of other orders with chisel-like incisor teeth are an early tillodont, *Trogosus* (*c*), an early primate, *Plesiadapis* (*d*), a living marsupial, the wombat (*e*), one of the extinct multituberculate mammals, *Taeniolabis* (*f*), a mammal-like reptile of the Triassic, *Bienotherium* (*g*), and a Pleistocene cave goat, *Myotragus* (*h*), whose incisor teeth are in the lower jaw only.

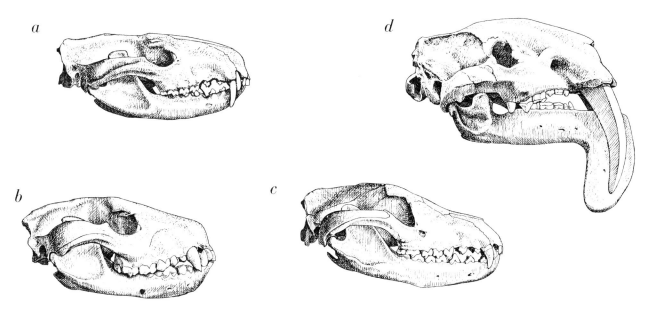

CARNIVOROUS MARSUPIALS, living and extinct, fill an ecological niche more commonly occupied by the placental carnivores today. Illustrated are the skulls of two living forms, the Australian "cat," *Dasyurus* (*a*), and the Tasmanian devil, *Sarcophilus* (*b*). The Tasmanian "wolf," *Thylacinus* (*c*), has not been seen for many years and may be extinct. A tiger-sized predator of South America, *Thylacosmilus* (*d*) became extinct in Pliocene times, long before the placental sabertooth of the Pleistocene, *Smilodon*, appeared.

98

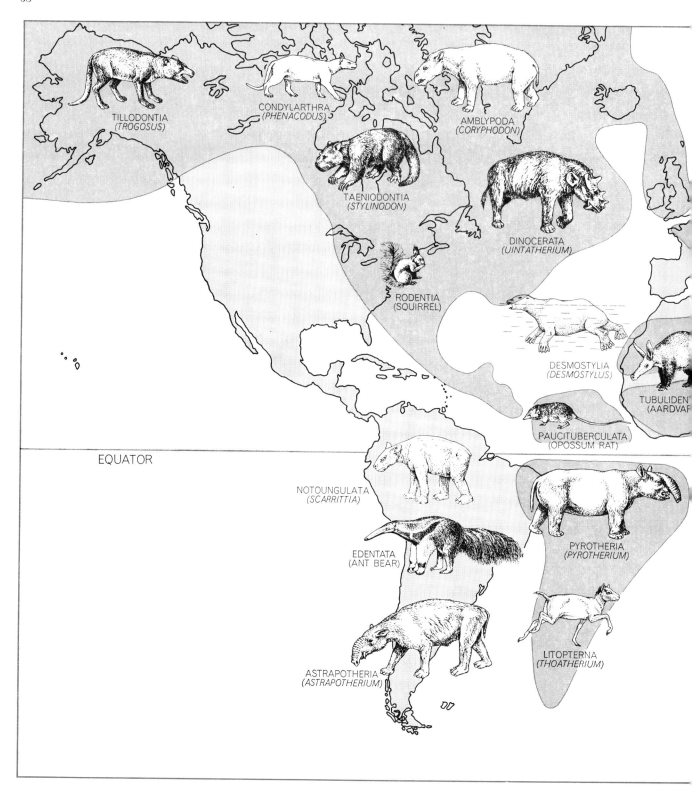

EQUATOR

TILLODONTIA
(TROGOSUS)

CONDYLARTHRA
(PHENACODUS)

AMBLYPODA
(CORYPHODON)

TAENIODONTIA
(STYLINODON)

DINOCERATA
(UINTATHERIUM)

RODENTIA
(SQUIRREL)

DESMOSTYLIA
(DESMOSTYLUS)

PAUCITUBERCULATA
(OPOSSUM RAT)

TUBULIDEN
(AARDVA

NOTOUNGULATA
(SCARRITTIA)

PYROTHERIA
(PYROTHERIUM)

EDENTATA
(ANT BEAR)

LITOPTERNA
(THOATHERIUM)

ASTRAPOTHERIA
(ASTRAPOTHERIUM)

CONTINENTAL DRIFT affected the evolution of the mammals by fragmenting the two supercontinents early in the Cenozoic era. In the north, Europe and Asia, although separated by a sea, remained connected with North America during part of the era. The

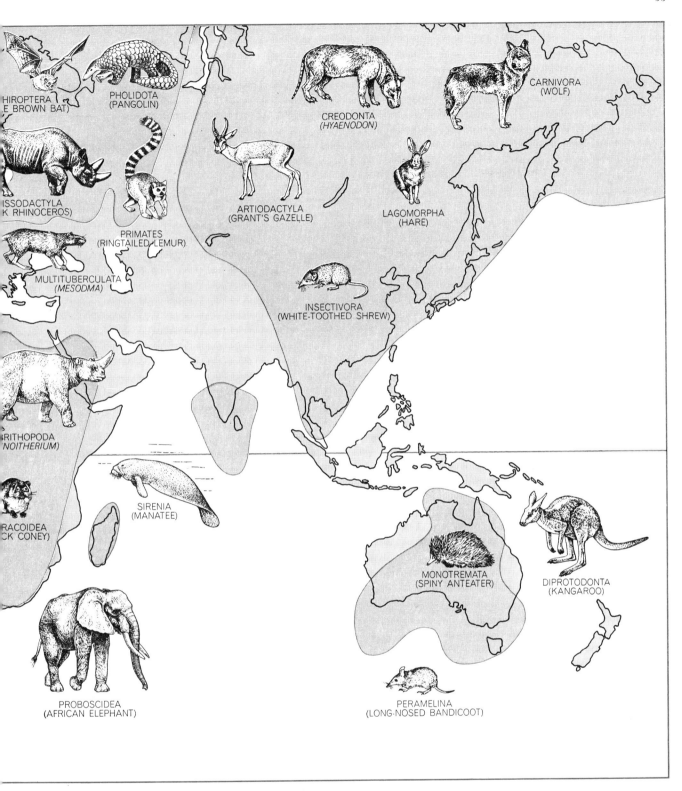

HIROPTERA
E BROWN BAT)

PHOLIDOTA
(PANGOLIN)

CREODONTA
(HYAENODON)

CARNIVORA
(WOLF)

ISSODACTYLA
K RHINOCEROS)

PRIMATES
(RINGTAILED LEMUR)

ARTIODACTYLA
(GRANT'S GAZELLE)

LAGOMORPHA
(HARE)

MULTITUBERCULATA
(MESODMA)

INSECTIVORA
(WHITE-TOOTHED SHREW)

RITHOPODA
NOITHERIUM)

SIRENIA
(MANATEE)

RACOIDEA
CK CONEY)

MONOTREMATA
(SPINY ANTEATER)

DIPROTODONTA
(KANGAROO)

PROBOSCIDEA
(AFRICAN ELEPHANT)

PERAMELINA
(LONG-NOSED BANDICOOT)

free migration that resulted prevents certainty regarding the place of origin of many orders of mammals that evolved in the north. The far wider rifting of Gondwanaland allowed the evolution of unique groups of mammals in South America, Africa and Australia.

We do know, however, that much of the continent was flooded by marginal seas, and that in the early Tertiary, Africa was cut up into two or three large islands. Still, there must have been a land route to Eurasia even in the Eocene; some of the African mammals of the following epoch (the Oligocene) are clearly immigrants from the north or northeast. Nonetheless, the majority of African mammals are of local origin. They include the following orders:

Proboscidea: the mastodons and elephants.

Hyracoidea: the conies and their extinct relatives.

Embrithopoda: an extinct order of very large mammals.

Tubulidentata: the aardvarks.

In addition the order Sirenia, consisting of the aquatic dugongs and manatees, is evidently related to the Proboscidea and hence presumably also originated in Africa. The same may be true of another order of aquatic mammals, the extinct Desmostylia, which also seems to be related to the elephants. The one snag in this interpretation is that desmostylian fossils are found only in the North Pacific, which seems rather a long way from Africa. Nonetheless, once they were waterborne, early desmostylians might have crossed the Atlantic, which was then only a narrow sea, navigated the Bolívar Trench and, rather like Cortes (but stouter), found themselves in the Pacific.

Early Mammals of Africa

Thus there are certainly four, and possibly six, mammalian orders for which an African origin can be postulated. Here it should be noted that Africa had an impressive array of primates in the Oligocene. This suggests that the order Primates had a comparatively long history in Africa before that time. Even though the order as such does not have its roots in Africa, it is possible that the higher primates—the Old World monkeys, the apes and the ancestors of man —may have originated there. Most of the fossil primates found in the Oligocene formations of Africa are primitive apes or monkeys, but there is at least one form (*Propliopithecus*) whose dentition looks like a miniature blueprint of a set of human teeth.

The Rest of Gondwanaland

We know little or nothing of the zoogeographic roles played by India and Antarctica in the early Tertiary. Mammalian fossils from the early Tertiary are also absent in Australia. It may be assumed, however, that the orders of mammals now limited to Australia probably originated there. These include two orders of marsupials: the Peramelina, comprised of several bandicoot genera, and the Diprotodonta, in which are found the kangaroos, wombats, phalangers and a number of extinct forms. In addition the order Monotremata, a very primitive group of mammals that includes the spiny anteater and the platypus, is likely to be of Australian origin. This gives us a total of three orders probably founded in Australia.

Summing up, we find that the three Laurasian continents produced a total of 16 orders of mammals, an average of five or six orders per continent. As for Gondwanaland, South America produced six orders, Africa four to six and Australia three. The fact that Australia is a small continent probably accounts for the lower number of orders founded there. Otherwise the distribution—the average of five or six orders per subdivision—is remarkably uniform for both the Laurasian and Gondwanaland supercontinents. The mammalian record should be compared with the data on Cretaceous reptiles, which show that the two supercontinents produced a total of 12 or 13 orders (or adaptively distinct suborders). A regularity is suggested, as if a single nucleus of radiation would tend in a given time to produce and support a given amount of basic zoological variation.

As the Tertiary period continued new land connections were gradually formed, replacing those sundered when the old supercontinents broke up. Africa made its landfall with Eurasia in the Oligocene and Miocene epochs. Laurasian orders of mammals spread into Africa and crowded out some of the local forms, but at the same time some African mammals (notably the mastodons and elephants) went forth to conquer almost the entire world. In the Western Hemisphere the draining and uplifting of the Bolívar Trench was followed by intense intermigration and competition among the mammals of the two Americas. In the process much of the typical South American mammal population was exterminated, but a few forms pressed successfully into North America to become part of the continent's spectacular ice-age wildlife.

India, a fragment of Gondwanaland that finally became part of Asia, must have made a contribution to the land fauna of that continent but just what it was cannot be said at present. Of all the drifting Noah's arks of mammalian evolution only two—Antarctica and Australia—persist in isolation to this day. The unknown mammals of Antarctica have long been extinct, killed by the ice that engulfed their world. Australia is therefore the only island continent that still retains much of its pristine mammalian fauna. [*see illustration on page 98*].

If the fragmentation of the continents at the beginning of the age of mammals promoted variety, the amalgamation in the latter half of the age of mammals has promoted efficiency by means of a large-scale test of the survival of the fittest. There is a concomitant loss of variety; 13 orders of land mammals have become extinct in the course of the Cenozoic. Most of the extinct orders are island-continent productions, which suggests that a system of semi-isolated provinces, such as the daughter continents of Laurasia, tends to produce a more efficient brood than the completely isolated nuclei of the Southern Hemisphere. Not all the Gondwanaland orders were inferior, however; the edentates were moderately successful and the proboscidians spectacularly so.

As far as land mammals are concerned, the world's major zoogeographic provinces are at present four in number: the Holarctic-Indian, which consists of North America and Eurasia and also northern Africa; the Neotropical, made up of Central America and South America; the Ethiopian, consisting of Africa south of the Sahara, and the Australian. This represents a reduction from seven provinces with about 30 orders of mammals to four provinces with about 18 orders. The reduction in variety is proportional to the reduction in the number of provinces.

In conclusion it is interesting to note that we ourselves, as a subgroup within the order Primates, probably owe our origin to a radiation within one of Gondwanaland's island continents. I have noted that an Oligocene primate of Africa may have been close to the line of human evolution. By Miocene times there were definite hominids in Africa, identified by various authorities as members of the genus *Ramapithecus* or the genus *Kenyapithecus*. Apparently these early hominids spread into Asia and Europe toward the end of the Miocene. The cycle of continental fragmentation and amalgamation thus seems to have played an important part in the origin of man as well as of the other land mammals.

III

THE GROWTH AND INTERACTION OF POPULATIONS

III

THE GROWTH
AND INTERACTION
OF POPULATIONS

The laws of ecology are written in the equations of population growth. The capacity of prey to feed their predators, the effectiveness of predators in controlling the numbers of prey, and the outcome of contests between competing species are familiar examples of ecological relationships that depend primarily on the growth of populations. For this reason ecologists place *demography* at the heart of their discipline. Like actuaries plotting insurance rates, they pore over schedules of birth and death as a necessary first step in many of the more basic studies.

An ironclad axiom of population ecology states that, in the long run, the death rate of all but the shortest-lived species equals their birth rate, and the overall population growth rate is zero. Common sense tells us that no species can increase indefinitely. The trend must eventually be stopped or reversed; if it continues too long, the populations will crash and approach extinction. The history of species usually consists of endlessly alternating periods of expansion and decline. It is the causes of these fluctuations that interest ecologists the most. Another central problem of ecology is what determines the "carrying capacity of the environment"—the average population size around which the fluctuations occur.

The analysis of both problems begins with a study of the factors controlling the birth and death schedules. The schedules can be altered, as Edward S. Deevey explains in the first article of this section, by an amelioration of the environment. Death is postponed in fruit flies when they are starved in the laboratory but otherwise protected from the usual perils of the natural environment. Death is being increasingly postponed in the human populations of the advanced industrial nations. But the reprieve lasts only until internal physiological senescence begins. At that time the organism breaks down no matter how protective its environment. The result is a survivorship curve that slopes gently to the age of senescence and then plummets to the zero line. Under the most favorable environments, survivorship tends to assume this form, while the birth rate simultaneously approaches its maximum within each age group. The result is the greatest possible rate of overall population growth.

But to repeat the axiom, maximum population growth cannot last. As population density increases, either survivorship declines, organisms emigrate more, the birth rate falls, or various combinations of these events occur, until the population growth is stopped or reversed. The specific biological changes that underlie population regulation are referred to as *density-dependent effects*. In order to be truly regulatory, they must intensify as the population grows up toward the stable limit and relax as the population comes down from some point above that level. An example of a density-dependent effect is death from predators. If predators multiply disproportionately with an increase in the population density of their prey, the growth rate of the prey will decelerate until it is halted. In his article on social pathology of rats, John B. Calhoun describes a series of other kinds of density-dependent controls that seem rather horrible from the human point of view. In his now famous experiment, Calhoun took away two of the principal density-dependent controls that regulate populations of rodents in nature. He fed the animals ad libitum, and then prevented the population surplus from emigrating. Contrary to what might have been expected, the rats did not continue to multiply until they were standing on top of each others' shoulders. They were halted instead by new density-dependent controls that emerged for the first time in the new, artificial conditions. Groups of males were turned into nonterritorial wanderers; females grossly neglected their young; and other pathological responses cropped up frequently. It is generally true that, when one density-dependent effect is blocked, another takes its place. When enough of the natural controls are circumvented, pathological effects take their place. Each species has its own set of such controls that appear in a more or less predictable sequence.

One of the most effective and highly organized modes of natural population control is emigration. As C. G. Johnson explains in the third article of this series, he and his coworkers discovered that many kinds of insects disperse in a programmed, orderly manner. Much of the ordinary flight of these organisms observed on a typical summer day is not directed toward searching for food or mates, but is simply a random departure from the area. In groups as diverse as locusts, aphids, and lemmings, the rate of dispersal is markedly density-dependent and serves as a principal mode of population regulation.

Not all forms of regulation are so clear-cut. In "Population Control in Animals," Wynne-Edwards presents his controversial theory that much of the regulation is altruistic in nature. Wynne-Edwards argues that animals use special kinds of displays to inform other members of their species of their presence. When the mutual advertisement indicates that population densities are approaching the danger level, the organisms sacrifice their own fitness in one or more ways to avert the crisis. For example, they may emigrate, decrease their birth rates, or even succumb more readily to stress diseases. In Wynne-Edwards' view, these responses are in effect voluntary: the individual sacrifices itself or its offspring for the good of the population. Most ecologists interpret the observed phenomena differently. They believe that density-dependent effects, far from entailing altruism, represent the best bargain individual organisms can make out of a bad situation. Animals emigrate, for example, not to help out the population left behind, but because there is at least an equally good chance of surviving and reproducing by taking a random journey. This "selfish" theory explains death by stress in overcrowded populations: the animal's system finally crumbles under the strain and not as a voluntary act performed for the good of the population. The principal difficulty of the Wynne-Edwards model, aside from its weak plausibility in particular cases, is its assumption of a high level of group selection. The only known way for altruistic genes to be fixed (as suggested in the Introduction to Part I) is for groups such as populations to be competing in some way. In the Wynne-Edwards case, populations must be suffering extinction or decimation at a high rate. Yet many of the cases where population-assessment displays are considered to be most advanced are the ones most noted for population stability. The reader is invited to consider this matter with some caution and to use it to reflect on the possible connections between natural selection and population regulation. Considerable controversy still exists on the evolution of density-dependent controls, with Wynne-Edwards' article advocating one extreme position.

An organism dwells in both a living and a nonliving environment. Its interaction with other organisms—the living part—is at once the more intense and subtle. Species that have influenced one another's birth and death schedules over periods of evolutionary time develop intimate forms of communication and exploitation that biologists have only begun to explore. In turning, then, from population ecology to physiological ecology, it is logical to begin with the special but crucial case of predation. Predators evolve so as to consume more prey; prey evolve to escape. The result, compounded over millions of years, is a balance of extraordinarily elaborate systems of offense and defense. The principle is nowhere better exemplified than in the defensive mechanisms of plants, as Paul R. Ehrlich and Peter H. Raven suggest in their article. We all know from casual observations that herbivores are efficient predators of plants. What is less well known, the authors point out, is that the plants "have not taken the onslaught of the herbivores lying down." In addition to physical defenses such as spines and horny leaf coatings, plants are saturated with chemical defenses that range from merely repellent to deadly substances. Many plant products used by man, such as spices and alkaloid drugs, are chemicals which are effective against the main enemies of the plant species; they are quite accidentally useful in one way or another to man.

The phrase *balance of nature* refers in large part to this standoff between prey and their predators. When species of plants or animals are introduced by man into new countries, they leave most of their natural enemies behind and the balance in the adoptive countries is disturbed. The result is sometimes a population explosion, with the alien form becoming a pest by sheer numbers alone. The catalog of such ecological accidents is long and painfully familiar: the Hessian fly from Europe into the wheat fields of North America, the Colorado potato beetle from America into Europe, the common rabbit from Europe into Australia, and many others. The ecologically safest method of control of such aliens is not the use of poison sprays and baits but the introduction into the new country of the organism's natural predators and diseases from its home environment. This method, known as *biological control*, has met with irregular but often spectacular success. One happy example, involving the destructive Klamath weed, is described by James K. Holloway in his article "Weed Control by Insect."

Species also compete with each other for the resources that limit their population growth: plants compete for space in the sunlight and for nutrients; herbivores compete for plants; predators for prey; and so on. A basic idea in ecology is called the *principle of competitive exclusion* or "Gause's Law," after G. F. Gause, the Russian biologist who illustrated its application in experiments on microorganisms. This idea is often presented as the simple axiom that no two species which are ecologically identical can coexist for very long. The principle is more precisely and realistically formulated in the following rule: two species can coexist only if their personal density-dependent controls prevent them from extinguishing each other. For example, if one has the potential to out-eat the other but is constrained from doing so by the presence of a predator, the two competitors can coexist. Ecologists routinely look for critical differences in the niches of coexisting species that provide the adequate degree of self-limitation. An elegant example of this procedure is provided by George A. Bartholomew and Jack W. Hudson in their article on desert ground squirrels.

Other possibilities exist for the mutual exploitation and coexistence of organisms. One especially elaborate case is described by Lincoln P. Brower in "Ecological Chemistry." The monarch butterfly has overcome the poisonous chemical defenses of the milkweed plants on which it feeds as a caterpillar. In so doing it has reaped a second benefit: the adult incorporates the poisonous cardiac glycosides into its own body, which then protect it from insect-eating birds and other vertebrates. In learning to avoid monarchs and other poisonous butterflies, which have easily recognizable color patterns, these predators also pass up other edible species that resemble the poisonous ones. This is *Batesian mimicry*, in which harmless species receive a free ride with their dangerous models. Sometimes the mimicry is *Müllerian*, meaning that dangerous species resemble each other, reinforcing the protection their distinctive appearance provides. The evidence is strong, as Brower concludes, that whole complexes of mimics have evolved as an adaptation for thwarting predators.

By far the most intricate associations of species, however, and in many ways the most esthetically appealing, are those that live in symbiosis. Two of the extreme cases of mutually beneficial symbiosis are presented in articles in this section. Conrad Limbaugh, a pioneering marine biologist who lost his life in a diving accident while his contribution was being prepared, describes the remarkable behavior of certain marine shrimp and fishes that are specialized to feed on edible debris and parasites which they clean from larger fish. In some cases their hosts regularly come to "cleaning stations" to obtain this service. Suzanne and Lekh Batra review the equally bizarre associations between insects and fungi. Some kinds of ants and beetles go so far as to culture their fungi in special nest chambers, planting and pruning the organisms like expert gardeners. In the last article of the section, Lynn Margulis develops the theory of the symbiotic origin of the eucaryotic cell—the critical prelude for the evolution of multicellular organisms. Persuasive evidence exists that the eucaryotic cell arose by the mutualistic symbiosis of single-celled organisms. Mitochondria, chloroplasts, and even cilia might have begun their existence not as outgrowths of existing cells but as initially independent organisms that penetrated larger cells as symbionts and were gradually reduced in structure and function to their present status as organelles.

These paradigms of mimicry and symbiosis reveal the tightness with which ecosystems have been drawn together during the long course of evolution. In the fourth and final section of this collection, we will enlarge the view still further in order to consider the major features of ecosystems. The evidence reviewed so far gives no reason to doubt that the integrity of ecosystems as units is sufficient to justify a continuation of the search for general laws.

SUGGESTED

FURTHER READING

The books recommended below are listed in ascending order of difficulty. All, however, can be mastered with the background of an elementary course in biology or its equivalent.

Wickler, Wolfgang. *Mimicry in plants and animals.* London: Weidenfeld and Nicolson, 1968. 255 pp. Simply written and beautifully illustrated, this short book can serve as a layman's introduction to one of the most complex forms of ecological relationships.

Schaller, George. *The Serengeti lion.* Chicago: University of Chicago Press, 1972. 480 pp. Winner of the National Book Award in Science in 1973, Schaller's monograph on the lion is especially strong on the subject of predation. The social behavior of the lion is given new meaning as an adaptation for preying on the large ungulate herds of the African plains.

Wilson, Edward O., and Bossert, William H. *A primer of population biology.* Stamford, Conn.: Sinauer Associates, 1971. 192 pp. A self-teaching manual that introduces population growth, competition, and other basic concepts of ecology by use of programmed problem solving.

Krebs, Charles J. *Ecology.* New York: Harper and Row, 1972. 694 pp. This introductory ecology textbook provides a balanced treatment of theoretical and empirical studies of population growth and interactions.

Connell, J. H.; Mertz, D. B.; and Murdoch, W. W., eds. *Readings in ecology and ecological genetics.* New York: Harper and Row, 1970. 397 pp. For the reader who wishes to examine some of the original source materials, this is an excellent collection of research articles with an organization similar to that of the present collection.

Henry, S. Mark, ed. *Symbiosis. Vols. I and II.* New York: Academic Press, 1966, 1967. 478 pp. and 443 pp. A thorough scholarly review of the subject, useful as a source book but also fascinating for browsing.

11

THE PROBABILITY OF DEATH

EDWARD S. DEEVEY, JR.
April 1950

It varies considerably with age and species. Man, however, has manipulated his curve of survival so it rather resembles that of the starved fruit fly

IN a world where the only certainties are death and taxes, and where even taxes can sometimes be avoided, how certain is death? There can be no doubt that this question has been asked since earliest times, when men painted the bodies of their dead kinsmen or provided them with goods for the journey to the hereafter. From poets and philosophers we have had melodious answers to the question—defiant, anguished, acquiescent or exultant according to the authors' personality and culture. From science, as we have come to expect, we get a statistical expression, not of certainty but of probability.

How probable, then, is death? At birth the probability of death at the end of the life span is of course 1, but this is not exactly helpful. To know the probability of death at any given age, one needs to observe the mortality of a population, substituting the universality of averages for the chancy behavior of individuals.

Actuaries, on whose skill depends the whole ingenious procedure by which insurance companies convert the probability of death to the certainty of making a profit, have devised a handy scheme for expressing the facts of mortality. Their "life tables" become rather complicated, but the principles on which they are constructed are not difficult to understand if we deal with a population of experimental animals instead of a human population whose members were born at various times.

A group of fruit flies is allowed to be born in the usual half-pint milk bottle, and a daily census is taken until the last survivor is dead. The "raw data" then give the number of deaths, d, at any age, x—which is written d_x. We convert this figure to a percentage of the total original population. At any given time the percentage of deaths, subtracted from 100 per cent, gives the percentage of survivors, l_x. When the survivorship column of the life table is graphed, we can see at a glance the pattern of fruit-fly mortality. Thus if we assume that the initial population had 100 members,

those dying in their first day of life leave $100 - d_1 = l_1$ survivors, those dying in their second day leave $l_1 - d_2 = l_2$ survivors, and so on until on the nth day the last survivor dies and $l_{n-1} - d_n = 0$. The mortality rate at any age (q_x) is the ratio of those dying during the given day to those alive at the beginning of that day: $q_x = d_x / l_x$. Instead of taking a day as the time unit, we can of course use any interval, such as a year or a decade, but for accurate results the age intervals must be short in relation to the total life span.

If survivorship is graphed on a logarithmic instead of an arithmetic scale, so that a straight line represents equal rates rather than equal amounts of decreasing survivorship, q_x can be read directly from the graph. Other columns of the conventional life table are derived almost as simply from one or another of these values. In particular, if one were to sell insurance policies to fruit flies, one would need to know the expectation of life (e_x), better described as the mean subsequent life span.

It is easy enough to perform this kind of manipulation on data from any laboratory population, and the comparative mortality of lower organisms is full of interest for the student of man, as comparative studies usually are. The rate at which organisms die expresses the balance between the tendency of their cells and tissues to maintain their organization and the relentless hostility of the world in which they exist. In other words, the survivorship curve of a population is a mathematical life line, recording in its sinuosities the contest between physiology and environment which we call life—and which Herbert Spencer defined as "the continuous adjustment of internal relations to external relations."

A famous essay by Raymond Pearl and John R. Miner pointed to three distinct types of life curve: 1) Some animals, such as the mildly organized *Hydra,* appear to die without regard to age; no one age is more exposed to risk of death than another, and the l_x curve is a straight line. 2) Under special circum-

stances, as when adult fruit flies are given no food but are granted a barely sporting chance to show their tenacity of life, they live their few allotted hours together and die almost simultaneously. 3) More usually an organism, typified at the extreme limit by so insecure a creature as an oyster or a dandelion, runs a heavy risk of death in infancy, but the few survivors to advanced age die at low and comparatively constant rates.

WHAT of man's mortality? Is it like that of *Hydra* or of an oyster, or is it completely flexible, varying from type to type according to circumstances? How far can man control his own survival? To appreciate the answer it is important to realize that the evidence is not so easily gathered as it would be if men were born all at once at the will of some supreme experimenter. Under the conditions in which men live and reproduce, the facts of death relate to individuals born at various times and places in the past. To calculate a rate of mortality it is necessary to know not only the ages of those dying but the number alive at any age and exposed to the risk of death. Thus the basic datum of the human life table is not d_x but q_x.

Such data are obtained from censuses and from bureaus of vital statistics. When they are cast up, they do not describe the mortality of a defunct population, as in our experiment with fruit flies, but instead predict the future mortality of a hypothetical group. The members of this group are imagined as born within the year of the census and exposed throughout their lives to death risks at particular ages equal to those observed for those ages in the year of the census. Insurance companies have not failed to note that any general improvement in health as time goes on is a guarantee of profit, for the longer the average policyholder lives beyond the age at which he was expected to die, the more premiums he pays—at least in the case of "ordinary life" insurance. Customarily such profits are shared with the policyholders, but it is a fact that until

1948 all American insurance premiums were calculated on a life table worked out in 1868.

The human survivorship curve displays a remarkable sinuosity, corresponding to real variations in the chances of death according to age. Mortality is relatively heavy in the first years of life, especially so in the first week and month. Beyond age 4 the modern American child has an excellent chance of living to maturity. Throughout middle life survival ratios are high and rather constant. As old age approaches the rates of mortality begin to increase more sharply, but in extreme age, beyond age 90, it appears that one has almost as good a chance of living an additional 10 years as at age 80. This part of the curve is inevitably based on inadequate information, but assuming that its form is correct, it recalls that of an oyster from maturity onward, when the period of most excruciating hazard is over and a tiny fraction of survivors live to become literally superannuated.

The curve as a whole shows a kind of oscillating compromise among the theoretical types of Pearl and Miner: In infancy man is a little like the oyster or the mackerel; in childhood, when mortality rates are decreasing, a temporary approach is made to the "rectangular" curve of starved fruit flies; in the middle years the constant risk of death resembles that of *Hydra;* in old age man comes once more to imitate the oyster. Probably other mammals in a state of nature have life curves much like man's. Of the few for which data are at hand the one that most resembles man's is that of the bighorn sheep of Mount McKinley, which in extreme youth and in old age appear to be especially likely to fall prey to wolves.

It must not be forgotten that this human survivorship curve represents a hypothetical modern population. To judge the extent to which the life span may be modified, it is necessary to consider other groups of other times. Though we cannot easily look far forward, we can look backward. We see then a remarkable thing: in the so-called Western countries in general, and the U. S. in particular, the average length of life has increased in spectacular fashion. Between 1838 and 1844 the expectation of life at birth of a male born in England was 40.19 years; a century later, in 1937, it was 60.18 years. The life span of the men of Massachusetts rose from 38.3 years in 1850 to 63.3 in 1939-41. Since 1900 in the U. S. as a whole the average life span has risen from about 48 to about 63 years. In short, the average length of life has nearly doubled in a century. But it is important to remember that this gain has come only in the average, which is dependent on the general level of public health, i.e., on the physical and social environment. There is no evidence that the oldest people are living to greater ages than before; the maximum length of human life appears to be fixed at about 115 or 120 years.

IF the upper limit of age is determined by man's genetic constitution, obviously the elimination of all environmental causes of death, such as disease and accidents, would yield a population whose every member lived to about the same age. The survivorship curve would become a rectangle even sharper than that of starving fruit flies; birthdays would no longer warrant congratulation, and at age n−1 (114 years?) people would start to dispose of their belongings. But you and I will probably not enjoy the dubious pleasures of that day. The recent improvement of man's allotted term of years is almost entirely the result of a concerted attack on deaths in infancy and childhood; the ills attending old age have scarcely begun to attract medical attention.

"Death from old age" is a legal fiction, not a medical fact, but it is deeply ingrained in our thinking, even among physicians. Geriatrics has a long way to go to match the triumphs of pediatrics. That the infant science of aging is due for a boom is certain, if only as a matter of social justice. Partly because of declining birth rates, and partly as a result of the greatly increased mean life span, the proportion of U. S. people over 65 rose from 2.6 per cent in 1850 to 6.8 per cent in 1940; by the year 2000 it should approximate 13 per cent. Thus the U. S. as a whole is fast approaching the peculiar situation of southern California, where political and moral pressure is strong to "do something for the aged."

Whether anything can actually be done for the oldsters beyond providing them with more elderly companions is a question that cannot be answered, for it hinges on the unsolved problem of the

TOMBSTONES provide accurate data on the life span of man in Roman times. Birth dates were carefully preserved for astrological purposes.

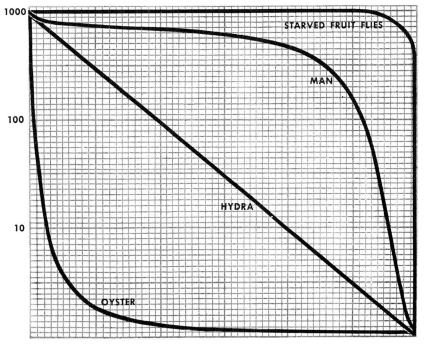

CURVES of survival for several organisms are plotted on the basis of survivors per thousand (*vertical coordinate*) and age in relative units of mean life span (*horizontal coordinate*). Most oysters die in infancy; most starved fruit flies in old age. Death rate of *Hydra* appears to be the same at all ages.

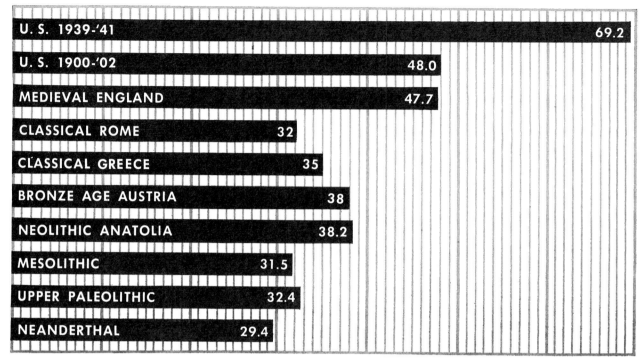

U. S. 1939-'41	69.2
U. S. 1900-'02	48.0
MEDIEVAL ENGLAND	47.7
CLASSICAL ROME	32
CLASSICAL GREECE	35
BRONZE AGE AUSTRIA	38
NEOLITHIC ANATOLIA	38.2
MESOLITHIC	31.5
UPPER PALEOLITHIC	32.4
NEANDERTHAL	29.4

AVERAGE LIFE SPAN of man has varied greatly through history and prehistory. The average life span in Greek and Roman times was shorter than that of certain prehistoric peoples whose remains have been found in fair numbers. Greatest increase has come in the past 50 years. Maximum life span appears unchanged.

relative importance of heredity and environment in governing length of life. There is evidence that exceptional longevity runs in families, but studies of lower organisms suggest that when the *rate* of living is taken into account, the total living that individuals can pack into their natural lives is about constant. In other words, if we live longer for genetic reasons we probably do so at a feebler rate, and may not enjoy life so much.

QUESTIONS about longevity might be more easily answered if man were not among the least convenient of organisms for breeding experiments. For some light on the matter we may look to history. As it happens, historians and archaeologists have lately begun to take an interest in population problems and to collect their scattered data.

It is not absolutely necessary to start with mortality rates in constructing a human life table. If the assumption can reasonably be made that the total population is neither growing nor declining, the distribution of ages among its members can be taken as constant in time, and a life table can be computed directly from records of the age at death, as in our fruit-fly study. Such an assumption would be grossly erroneous for populations in the Western world today, but it may not always have been so. At worst, the historian who is forced to make this assumption in order to use his data is in the same position as the animal ecologist attempting to study mortality outside the laboratory. The life table for the bighorn sheep, for example, was computed in

this way from skulls picked up on the range and apportioned to age groups by the growth rings on the horns.

So it was not altogether improper when the Scottish investigator W. R. Macdonell, following a suggestion of the great English statistician Karl Pearson, studied mortality in ancient Rome and some of its provinces by making use of ages at death obtained from tombstones. Such information is more accurate than might be supposed, for the astrology-minded ancients paid attention to precise birth dates. Other sources of data are court records, especially those having to do with inheritance of property; records of burial-insurance societies and other agencies granting annuities, which existed even in Roman times; genealogical tables; and ages determined on skeletons by the surprisingly accurate methods of physical anthropology. Much more remains to be learned, but a few inferences can be made now without much fear of contradiction.

FOR one thing, human survival has seldom or never been so successful as it is today in the U. S. and western Europe. No ancient or medieval population boasted a mean longevity greater than about 35 years, whereas the white male born in the U. S. in 1945 can expect to live 65.8 years. Primitive man appears to have had a negligible chance of surviving even to age 60. Longevity appears to be related to culture; however, "civilized" men as such live only a little longer than tribal huntsmen, for urbanization has unfavorable consequences which

have been circumvented only in modern times.

For another thing, there is a stubborn suggestion in some of the data that the well-known enhanced survival of females over males is a relatively modern phenomenon—primitive societies seem to have worked their women to death at earlier ages. But perhaps the most interesting finding from all these data is that despite the recent dramatic gain in average life span, there has been no appreciable gain in maximum longevity. People of great age were undoubtedly less numerous in ancient populations than they are now, but there is no reason to think men and women of that time could not live to 115 or 120 if they were lucky enough. There are several authentic-sounding centenarians among the Romans studied by Macdonell, including one of 120, and there may even have been some among the 14th-century British group whose vital statistics are preserved in the *Inquisitiones Post-Mortem.*

It would be ironic if all the "progress" implicit in modern life tables, and in the medical science that has so changed them, were to come to this: that we have been saved from measles to die of cancer or heart disease. That, however, is the outlook, as well as we can judge it, and the best recipe for longevity would still appear to be the nonoperational one: "choose long-lived parents."

12

POPULATION DENSITY AND SOCIAL PATHOLOGY

JOHN B. CALHOUN

February 1962

When a population of laboratory rats is allowed to increase in a confined space, the rats develop acutely abnormal patterns of behavior that can even lead to the extinction of the population

In the celebrated thesis of Thomas Malthus, vice and misery impose the ultimate natural limit on the growth of populations. Students of the subject have given most of their attention to misery, that is, to predation, disease and food supply as forces that operate to adjust the size of a population to its environment. But what of vice? Setting aside the moral burden of this word, what are the effects of the social behavior of a species on population growth—and of population density on social behavior?

Some years ago I attempted to submit this question to experimental inquiry. I confined a population of wild Norway rats in a quarter-acre enclosure. With an abundance of food and places to live and with predation and disease eliminated or minimized, only the animals' behavior with respect to one another remained as a factor that might affect the increase in their number. There could be no escape from the behavioral consequences of rising population density. By the end of 27 months the population had become stabilized at 150 adults. Yet adult mortality was so low that 5,000 adults might have been expected from the observed reproductive rate. The reason this larger population did not materialize was that infant mortality was extremely high. Even with only 150 adults in the enclosure, stress from social interaction led to such disruption of maternal behavior that few young survived.

With this background in mind I turned to observation of a domesticated albino strain of the Norway rat under more controlled circumstances indoors. The data for the present discussion come from the histories of six different populations. Each was permitted to increase to approximately twice the number that my experience had indicated could occupy the available space with only moderate stress from social interaction. In each

case my associates and I maintained close surveillance of the colonies for 16 months in order to obtain detailed records of the modifications of behavior induced by population density.

The consequences of the behavioral pathology we observed were most apparent among the females. Many were unable to carry pregnancy to full term or to survive delivery of their litters if they did. An even greater number, after successfully giving birth, fell short in their maternal functions. Among the males the behavior disturbances ranged from sexual deviation to cannibalism and from frenetic overactivity to a pathological withdrawal from which individuals would emerge to eat, drink and move about only when other members of the community were asleep. The social organization of the animals showed equal disruption. Each of the experimental populations divided itself into several groups, in each of which the sex ratios were drastically modified. One group might consist of six or seven females and one male, whereas another would have 20 males and only 10 females.

The common source of these disturbances became most dramatically apparent in the populations of our first series of three experiments, in which we observed the development of what we called a behavioral sink. The animals would crowd together in greatest number in one of the four interconnecting pens in which the colony was maintained. As many as 60 of the 80 rats in each experimental population would assemble in one pen during periods of feeding. Individual rats would rarely eat except in the company of other rats. As a result extreme population densities developed in the pen adopted for eating, leaving the others with sparse populations.

Eating and other biological activities were thereby transformed into social ac-

tivities in which the principal satisfaction was interaction with other rats. In the case of eating, this transformation of behavior did not keep the animals from securing adequate nutrition. But the same pathological "togetherness" tended to disrupt the ordered sequences of activity involved in other vital modes of behavior such as the courting of sex partners, the building of nests and the nursing and care of the young. In the experiments in which the behavioral sink developed, infant mortality ran as high as 96 per cent among the most disoriented groups in the population. Even in the absence of the behavioral sink, in the second series of three experiments, infant mortality reached 80 per cent among the corresponding members of the experimental populations.

The design of the experiments was relatively simple. The three populations of the first series each began with 32 rats; each population of the second series began with 56 rats. In all cases the animals were just past weaning and were evenly divided between males and females. By the 12th month all the populations had multiplied and each comprised 80 adults. Thereafter removal of the infants that survived birth and weaning held the populations steady. Although the destructive effects of population density increased during the course of the experiments, and the mortality rate among the females and among the young was much higher in the 16th month than it was earlier, the number of young that survived to weaning was always large enough to offset the effects of adult mortality and actually to increase the population. The evidence indicates, however, that in time failures of reproductive function would have caused the colonies to die out. At the end of the first series of experiments eight rats—the four healthi-

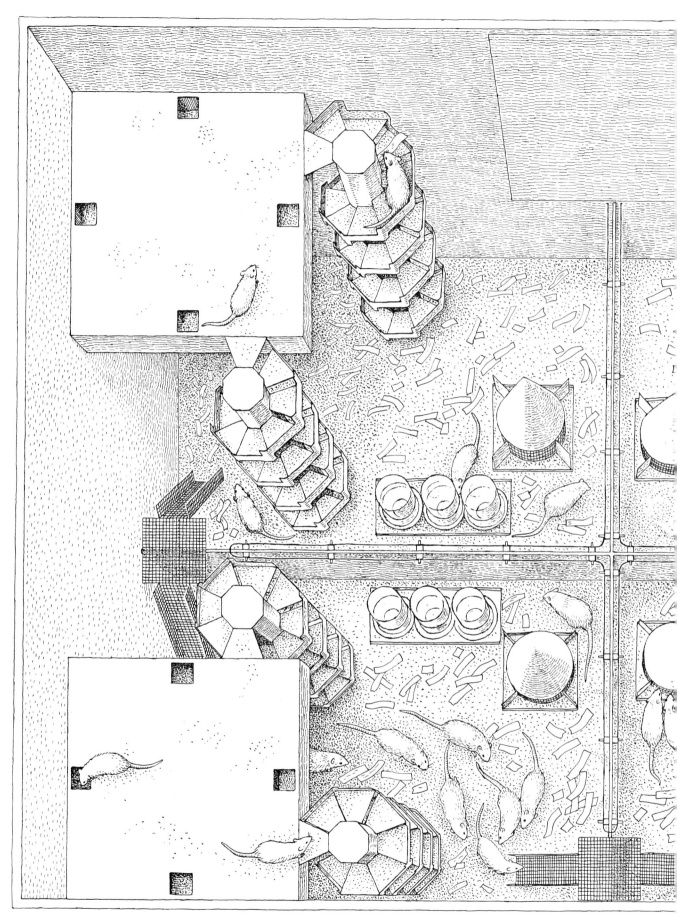

EFFECT OF POPULATION DENSITY on the behavior and social organization of rats was studied by confining groups of 80 animals in a 10-by-14-foot room divided into four pens by an electrified fence. All pens (numbered 1, 2, 3 and 4 clockwise from door) were complete dwelling units. Conical objects are food hoppers; trays with three bottles are drinking troughs. Elevated burrows, reached by winding staircases, each had five nest boxes, seen in pen 1, where top of burrow has been removed. Ramps connected all pens but 1 and 4. Rats therefore tended to concentrate in pens 2 and 3. Development of a "behavioral sink," which further increased population in one pen, is reflected in pen 2, where three rats are eating simultaneously. Rat approaching ramp in pen 3 is an estrous female

pursued by a pack of males. In pens 2 and 3, where population density was highest, males outnumbered females. In pens 1 and 4, a dominant male was usually able to expel all other males and possess a harem of females. Dominant males are sleeping at the base of the ramps in pens 1 and 4. They wake when other males approach, preventing incursions into their territories. The three rats peering down from a ramp are probers, one of the deviant behavioral types produced by the pressures of a high population density.

est males and the four healthiest females in each of two populations—were permitted to survive. These animals were six months old at the time, in the prime of life. Yet in spite of the fact that they no longer lived in overpopulated environments, they produced fewer litters in the next six months than would normally have been expected. Nor did any of the offspring that were born survive to maturity.

The males and females that initiated each experiment were placed, in groups of the same size and sex composition, in each of the four pens that partitioned a 10-by-14-foot observation room. The pens were complete dwelling units; each contained a drinking fountain, a food hopper and an elevated artificial burrow, reached by a winding staircase and holding five nest boxes. A window in the ceiling of the room permitted observation, and there was a door in one wall. With space for a colony of 12 adults in each pen—the size of the groups in which rats are normally found—this setup should have been able to support 48 rats comfortably. At the stabilized number of 80, an equal distribution of the animals would have found 20 adult rats in each pen. But the animals did not dispose themselves in this way.

Biasing factors were introduced in the physical design of the environment to encourage differential use of the four pens. The partitions separating the pens were electrified so that the rats could not climb them. Ramps across three of the partitions enabled the animals to get from one pen to another and so traverse the entire room. With no ramps to permit crossing of the fourth partition, however, the pens on each side of it became the end pens of what was topologically a row of four. The rats had to make a complete circuit of the room to go from the pen we designated 1 to the pen designated 4 on the other side of the partition separating the two. This arrangement of ramps immediately skewed the mathematical probabilities in favor of a higher population density in pens 2 and 3 than in pens 1 and 4. Pens 2 and 3 could be reached by two ramps, whereas pens 1 and 4 had only one each.

The use of pen 4 was further discouraged by the elevation of its burrow to a height greater than that of the burrow in the other end pen. The two middle pens were similarly distinguished from each other, the burrow in pen 3 being higher than that in pen 2. But here the differential appears to have played a smaller role, although pen 2 was used somewhat more often than pen 3.

With the distribution of the rats

biased by these physical arrangements, the sizes of the groups in each pen could have been expected to range from as few as 13 to as many as 27. With the passage of time, however, changes in behavior tended to skew the distribution of the rats among the pens even more. Of the 100 distinct sleeping groups counted in the 10th to 12th month of each experiment, only 37 fell within the expected size range. In 33 groups there were fewer than 13 rats, and in 30 groups the count exceeded 27. The sex ratio approximated equality only in those groups that fell within the expected size range. In the smaller groups, generally composed of eight adults, there were seldom more

than two males. In the larger groups, on the other hand, there were many more males than females. As might be expected, the smaller groups established themselves in the end pens, whereas the larger groups were usually observed to form in the middle pens. The female members of the population distributed themselves about equally in the four pens, but the male population was concentrated almost overwhelmingly in the middle pens.

One major factor in the creation of this state of affairs was the struggle for status that took place among the males. Shortly after male rats reach maturity, at about six months of age, they enter into

a round robin of fights that eventually fixes their position in the social hierarchy. In our experiments such fights took place among the males in all the pens, both middle and end. In the end pens, however, it became possible for a single dominant male to take over the area as his territory. During the period when the social hierarchy was being established, the subordinate males in all pens adopted the habit of arising early. This enabled them to eat and drink in peace. Since rats generally eat in the course of their normal wanderings, the subordinate residents of the end pens were likely to feed in one of the middle pens. When, after feeding, they wanted to

FOOD HOPPER used in first series of experiments is seen at the left in this drawing. Water tray is at the right. The hopper, covered with wire grating and holding hard pellets of food, made eating a lengthy activity during which one rat was likely to meet another.

Thus it fostered the development of a behavioral sink: the animals would eat only in the presence of others, and they preferred one of the four hoppers in the room to all the others. In time 75 per cent of the animals crowded into the pen containing this hopper to eat.

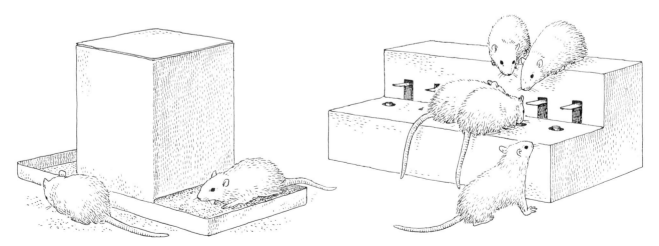

WATER FOUNTAIN used in second series of experiments is seen at the right in this drawing. Food hopper is at the left. The fountain was operated by pressing a lever. Thus it made drinking a lengthy activity, associated with the presence of others. But it

did not create a behavioral sink. Although the rats would drink only if other animals were present, they engaged in this activity in their home pens, immediately after awakening. The fountain therefore acted to produce an even distribution of the population.

return to their original quarters, they would find it very difficult. By this time the most dominant male in the pen would probably have awakened, and he would engage the subordinates in fights as they tried to come down the one ramp to the pen. For a while the subordinate would continue its efforts to return to what had been its home pen, but after a succession of defeats it would become so conditioned that it would not even make the attempt. In essence the dominant male established his territorial dominion and his control over a harem of females not by driving the other males out but by preventing their return.

Once a male had established his dominion over an end pen and the harem it contained, he was usually able to maintain it. Although he slept a good deal of the time, he made his sleeping quarters at the base of the ramp. He was, therefore, on perpetual guard. Awakening as soon as another male appeared at the head of the ramp, he had only to open his eyes for the invader to wheel around and return to the adjoining pen. On the other hand, he would sleep calmly through all the comings and goings of his harem; seemingly he did not even hear their clatterings up and down the wire ramp. His conduct during his waking hours reflected his dominant status. He would move about in a casual and deliberate fashion, occasionally inspecting the burrow and nests of his harem. But he would rarely enter a burrow, as some other males did, merely to ferret out the females.

A territorial male might tolerate other males in his domain provided they respected his status. Such subordinate males inhabited the end pens in several of the experiments. Phlegmatic animals, they spent most of their time hidden in the burrow with the adult females, and their excursions to the floor lasted only as long as it took them to obtain food and water. Although they never attempted to engage in sexual activity with any of the females, they were likely, on those rare occasions when they encountered the dominant male, to make repeated attempts to mount him. Generally the dominant male tolerated these advances.

In these end pens, where population density was lowest, the mortality rate among infants and females was also low. Of the various social environments that developed during the course of the experiments, the brood pens, as we called them, appeared to be the only healthy ones, at least in terms of the survival of the group. The harem females generally made good mothers. They nursed their young, built nests for them and protected them from harm. If any situation arose that a mother considered a danger to her pups, she would pick the infants up one at a time and carry them in her mouth to a safer place. Nothing would distract her from this task until the entire litter had been moved. Half the infants born in the brood pens survived.

The pregnancy rates recorded among the females in the middle pens were no lower than those recorded in the end pens. But a smaller percentage of these pregnancies terminated in live births. In the second series of experiments 80 per cent of the infants born in the middle pens died before weaning. In the first series 96 per cent perished before this time. The males in the middle pens were no less affected than the females by the pressures of population density. In both series of experiments the social pathology among the males was high. In the first series, however, it was more aggravated than it was in the second.

This increase in disturbance among the middle-pen occupants of the first series of experiments was directly related to the development of the phenomenon of the behavioral sink—the outcome of any behavioral process that collects animals together in unusually great numbers. The unhealthy connotations of the term are not accidental: a behavioral sink does act to aggravate all forms of pathology that can be found within a group.

The emergence of a behavioral sink was fostered by the arrangements that were made for feeding the animals. In these experiments the food consisted of small, hard pellets that were kept in a circular hopper formed by wire mesh. In consequence satisfaction of hunger required a continuous effort lasting several minutes. The chances therefore were good that while one rat was eating another would join it at the hopper. As was mentioned earlier, rats usually eat intermittently throughout their waking hours, whenever they are hungry and food is available. Since the arrangement of the ramps drew more rats into the middle pens than into the end ones, it was in these pens that individuals were most likely to find other individuals eating. As the population increased, the association of eating with the presence of other animals was further reinforced. Gradually the social aspect of the activity became determinant: the rats would rarely eat except at hoppers already in use by other animals.

At this point the process became a vicious circle. As more and more of the rats tended to collect at the hopper in one of the middle pens, the other hoppers became less desirable as eating places. The rats that were eating at these undesirable locations, finding themselves deserted by their groupmates, would transfer their feeding to the more crowded pen. By the time the three experiments in the first series drew to a close half or more of the populations were sleeping as well as eating in that pen. As a result there was a decided increase in the number of social adjustments each rat had to make every day. Regardless of which pen a rat slept in, it would go to one particular middle pen several times a day to eat. Therefore it was compelled daily to make some sort of adjustment to virtually every other rat in the experimental population.

No behavioral sinks developed in the second series of experiments, because we offered the rats their diet in a different way. A powdered food was set out in an open hopper. Since it took the animals only a little while to eat, the probability that two animals would be eating simultaneously was considerably reduced. In order to foster the emergence of a behavioral sink I supplied the pens with drinking fountains designed to prolong the drinking activity. The effect of this arrangement was unquestionably to make the animals social drinkers; they used the fountain mainly when other animals lined up at it. But the effect was also to discourage them from wandering and to prevent the development of a behavioral sink. Since rats generally drink immediately on arising, drinking and the social interaction it occasioned tended to keep them in the pens in which they slept. For this reason all social pathology in the second series of experiments, although severe, was less extreme than it was in the first series.

Females that lived in the densely populated middle pens became progressively less adept at building adequate nests and eventually stopped building nests at all. Normally rats of both sexes build nests, but females do so most vigorously around the time of parturition. It is an undertaking that involves repeated periods of sustained activity, searching out appropriate materials (in our experiments strips of paper supplied an abundance), transporting them bit by bit to the nest and there arranging them to form a cuplike depression, frequently sheltered by a hood. In a crowded middle pen, however, the ability of females to persist in this biologically essential activity became markedly impaired. The first sign of disruption was a failure to build the nest to normal specifications.

These females simply piled the strips of paper in a heap, sometimes trampling them into a pad that showed little sign of cup formation. Later in the experiment they would bring fewer and fewer strips to the nesting site. In the midst of transporting a bit of material they would drop it to engage in some other activity occasioned by contact and interaction with other individuals met on the way. In the extreme disruption of their behavior during the later months of the population's history they would build no nests at all but would bear their litters on the sawdust in the burrow box.

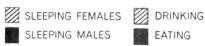

SLEEPING FEMALES   DRINKING
SLEEPING MALES   EATING

The middle-pen females similarly lost the ability to transport their litters from one place to another. They would move only part of their litters and would scatter them by depositing the infants in different places or simply dropping them on the floor of the pen. The infants thus abandoned throughout the pen were seldom nursed. They would die where they were dropped and were thereupon generally eaten by the adults.

The social stresses that brought about this disorganization in the behavior of the middle-pen females were imposed with special weight on them when they came into heat. An estrous female would be pursued relentlessly by a pack of males, unable to escape from their soon

unwanted attentions. Even when she retired to a burrow, some males would follow her. Among these females there was a correspondingly high rate of mortality from disorders in pregnancy and parturition. Nearly half of the first- and second-generation females that lived in the behavioral-sink situation had died of these causes by the end of the 16th month. Even in the absence of the extreme stresses of the behavioral sink, 25 per cent of the females died. In contrast, only 15 per cent of the adult males in both series of experiments died.

A female that lived in a brood pen was sheltered from these stresses even though during her periods of estrus she would leave her pen to mate with males

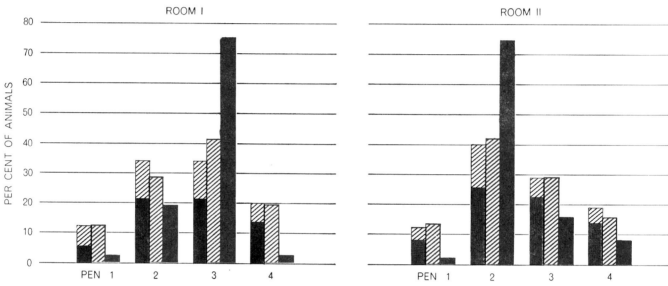

BEHAVIORAL SINK developed in the first series of three experiments, drawing half the rats either into pen 2 or pen 3 of each room to drink and sleep, and even more into that pen to eat. Chart

describes the situation in the 13th month of the experiment. By then the population distributions were fairly stable and many females in the densely populated pens had died. One male in room

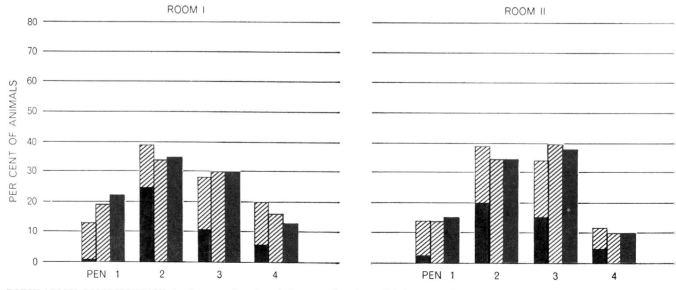

POPULATION DISTRIBUTIONS in the second series of three experiments, in which no behavioral sink developed, were more even than they were in the first series, and the death rate among

females and infants was lower. Chart shows the situation in the 13th month, when one male had established pens 3 and 4 of room III as his territory, and another was taking over pen 2, thus

in the other pens of the room. Once she was satiated, however, she could return to the brood pen. There she was protected from the excessive attention of other males by the territorial male.

For the effect of population density on the males there is no index as explicit and objective as the infant and maternal mortality rates. We have attempted a first approximation of such an index, however, by scoring the behavior of the males on two scales: that of dominance and that of physical activity. The first index proved particularly effective in the early period of the experiments, when the males were approaching adulthood and beginning the fights that eventually fixed their status in the social hierarchy.

ROOM III

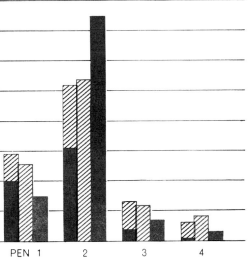

PEN 1   2   3   4

III had established pens 3 and 4 as his territory. Subsequently a male in room I took over pen 1, expelling all the other males.

ROOM III

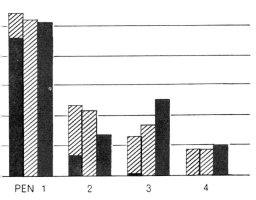

PEN 1   2   3   4

forcing most of the males into pen 1. Pen 1 in rooms I and II had also become territories; later pen 4 in room II became a territory.

The more fights a male initiated and the more fights he won, the more likely he was to establish a position of dominance. More than half the animals in each experiment gave up the struggle for status after a while, but among those that persisted a clear-cut hierarchy developed.

In the crowded middle pens no one individual occupied the top position in this hierarchy permanently. In every group of 12 or more males one was the most aggressive and most often the victor in fights. Nevertheless, this rat was periodically ousted from his position. At regular intervals during the course of their waking hours the top-ranking males engaged in free-for-alls that culminated in the transfer of dominance from one male to another. In between these tumultuous changings of the guard relative calm prevailed.

The aggressive, dominant animals were the most normal males in our populations. They seldom bothered either the females or the juveniles. Yet even they exhibited occasional signs of pathology, going berserk, attacking females, juveniles and the less active males, and showing a particular predilection —which rats do not normally display— for biting other animals on the tail.

Below the dominant males both on the status scale and in their level of activity were the homosexuals—a group perhaps better described as pansexual. These animals apparently could not discriminate between appropriate and inappropriate sex partners. They made sexual advances to males, juveniles and females that were not in estrus. The males, including the dominants as well as the others of the pansexuals' own group, usually accepted their attentions. The general level of activity of these animals was only moderate. They were frequently attacked by their dominant associates, but they very rarely contended for status.

Two other types of male emerged, both of which had resigned entirely from the struggle for dominance. They were, however, at exactly opposite poles as far as their levels of activity were concerned. The first were completely passive and moved through the community like somnambulists. They ignored all the other rats of both sexes, and all the other rats ignored them. Even when the females were in estrus, these passive animals made no advances to them. And only very rarely did other males attack them or approach them for any kind of play. To the casual observer the passive animals would have appeared to be the healthiest and most attractive

members of the community. They were fat and sleek, and their fur showed none of the breaks and bare spots left by the fighting in which males usually engage. But their social disorientation was nearly complete.

Perhaps the strangest of all the types that emerged among the males was the group I have called the probers. These animals, which always lived in the middle pens, took no part at all in the status struggle. Nevertheless, they were the most active of all the males in the experimental populations, and they persisted in their activity in spite of attacks by the dominant animals. In addition to being hyperactive, the probers were both hypersexual and homosexual, and in time many of them became cannibalistic. They were always on the alert for estrous females. If there were none in their own pens, they would lie in wait for long periods at the tops of the ramps that gave on the brood pens and peer down into them. They always turned and fled as soon as the territorial rat caught sight of them. Even if they did not manage to escape unhurt, they would soon return to their vantage point.

The probers conducted their pursuit of estrous females in an abnormal manner. Mating among rats usually involves a distinct courtship ritual. In the first phase of this ritual the male pursues the female. She thereupon retires for a while into the burrow, and the male lies quietly in wait outside, occasionally poking his head into the burrow for a moment but never entering it. (In the wild forms of the Norway rat this phase usually involves a courtship dance on the mound at the mouth of the burrow.) The female at last emerges from the burrow and accepts the male's advances. Even in the disordered community of the middle pens this pattern was observed by all the males who engaged in normal heterosexual behavior. But the probers would not tolerate even a short period of waiting at the burrows in the pens where accessible females lived. As soon as a female retired to a burrow, a prober would follow her inside. On these expeditions the probers often found dead young lying in the nests; as a result they tended to become cannibalistic in the later months of a population's history.

Although the behavioral sink did not develop in the second series of experiments, the pathology exhibited by the populations in both sets of experiments, and in all pens, was severe. Even

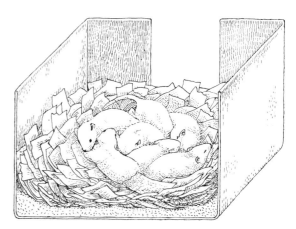

NORMAL MATERNAL BEHAVIOR among rats includes building a fluffy, well-shaped nest for the young. The drawing at the left shows such a nest, holding a recently born litter. The drawing at the right shows this same nest about two weeks later. It has been flattened by the weight of the animals' bodies but it still offers ample protection and warmth, and the remaining pups can still rest comfortably. In these experiments half the offspring of normal mothers survived infancy and were successfully weaned.

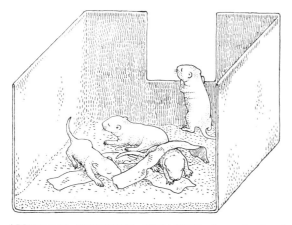

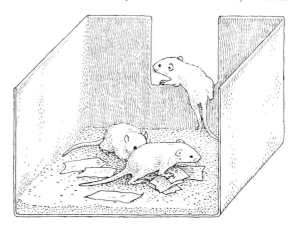

ABNORMAL MATERNAL BEHAVIOR, shown by females exposed to the pressures of population density, includes failure to build adequate nests. The drawing at the left shows the recently born young of a disturbed female. She started to make a nest but never finished it. The drawing at the right shows her young about two weeks later. One pup has already left and another is leaving. Neither can survive alone. In these experiments the mortality rate among infants of disturbed mothers was as high as 96 per cent.

in the brood pens females could raise only half their young to weaning. Nor does the difference in infant mortality between the middle pens of the first and second series—96 per cent in the first as opposed to 80 per cent in the second—represent a biologically significant improvement. It is obvious that the behavioral repertory with which the Norway rat has emerged from the trials of evolution and domestication must break down under the social pressures generated by population density. In time, refinement of experimental procedures and of the interpretation of these studies may advance our understanding to the point where they may contribute to the making of value judgments about analogous problems confronting the human species.

13

THE AERIAL MIGRATION OF INSECTS

C. G. JOHNSON
December 1963

A few insects migrate seasonally over great distances rather like birds. Recently it has been learned that most other species also migrate by simply beating their wings while the wind carries them

The literature of entomology, beginning with the Bible, records many astonishing accounts of the migration behavior of insects. Locusts in the desert, mosquitoes in the Arctic and the Tropics and butterflies, moths, beetles, bugs and dragonflies almost everywhere have been seen in sudden mass flights, often involving millions of insects all traveling in the same general direction at the same time. Particularly in the case of the desert locust of Africa and the monarch butterfly of North America—insects that can make seasonal flights of more than 2,000 miles—this behavior has been likened to that of migratory birds. The spectacular character of these flights has invited explanation in terms of a migration instinct that would cause the individual insects to congregate in response to overcrowding or to some other unfavorable change in the environment, and has inspired speculation about sensory mechanisms that would enable the individuals to orient themselves in space, navigate and hold course toward distant destinations. Migratory flight thus more or less elaborately defined became one hallmark of a few species and much controversy has flamed from efforts to distinguish "true" migrators from mere drifters whose populations were dispersed by the wind.

It was closer acquaintance with the desert locust—established with the aid of photographic film interpreted by R. C. Rainey and Z. V. Waloff of the Anti-Locust Research Centre in London—that helped to set modern studies of insect migration on an entirely new and more fruitful course. Locusts are insect migrants par excellence. Vigorous fliers, they give an observer the strong subjective impression of concerted, purposeful progress in a direction under their own control. The camera too will show whole groups of insects headed in one direction. In successive images registered on the same film, however, individuals headed in one direction are seen to be carried in another direction by the wind. Within a swarm there will be many groups of similarly oriented insects flying in different directions, but the swarm as a whole will move with the wind, albeit more slowly.

The discovery that locust swarms are wind-borne eliminated the need to postulate mechanisms of orientation and navigation as essential features of insect migration. What is common to all migrants, as J. D. Kennedy of the Agricultural Research Council in Cambridge, England, has insisted, is an intense "locomotory drive" that sets the insect off on a relatively prolonged and undistracted flight compared with other kinds of flight associated with egg-laying or feeding. The drive arises from the internal physiology of the individual in a way not yet understood, but it is associated somehow, at least in females, with sexual immaturity. With the behavior of individuals synchronized by the simultaneity of their development, the migratory flight seems to have evolved as an adaptation designed primarily to relinquish habitats destined to become unsuitable and to secure new ones. This often leads to dispersal of the species. In this view migratory behavior appears as a key phase in the life history not of merely a few species of insects but of a large proportion of winged species. To the universal cycle of birth, reproduction and death must be added the process of migration or dispersal, with the winged adult as the essential, mobile element in the system.

For an understanding of migratory behavior in a generalized form, the lowly plant-sucking aphid provides a most typical and instructive example. Aphids move on the wind. In spring and summer some species called the migratory aphids feed and deposit their larvae on herbs (these aphids are viviparous, delivering small larvae rather than eggs), and in fall and winter they transfer their activities to woody shrubs. These insects have been under intensive study by our group at the Rothamsted Experimental Station and by other workers at the Agricultural Research Council in Cambridge.

At the end of the larval stage the aphid molts into either a wingless or a winged adult [*see top illustration on page 119*]. The wingless form stays where it is, but every new winged adult, after waiting for some hours until its cuticle hardens, takes off on a strong vertical flight, attracted by the blue light of the sky. It is caught by the wind and, still flying actively, may be carried hundreds or thousands of feet aloft and often many miles overland. Typically the locomotory drive begins to fail within an hour or two and the aphid starts its fortuitous descent. If the plant on which it lands is one to which it is adapted, the insect feeds for the first time since leaving its birthplace. Then it may begin to deposit larvae. If the flight has been short or if the plant is unsuitable, the aphid may take off again. It may make several flights and cover many miles in the few days before it is finally grounded by the dissolution of its wing muscles. The migratory flight thus spreads the species to new habitats and effects the seasonal transfer of the population from green herbs to woody shrubs, even though the direction and distance of travel depend in part on the wind.

All other migrants share some elements of this behavioral routine with the aphid. Characteristically, most insects make their migratory flight soon after completion of their metamorphosis and

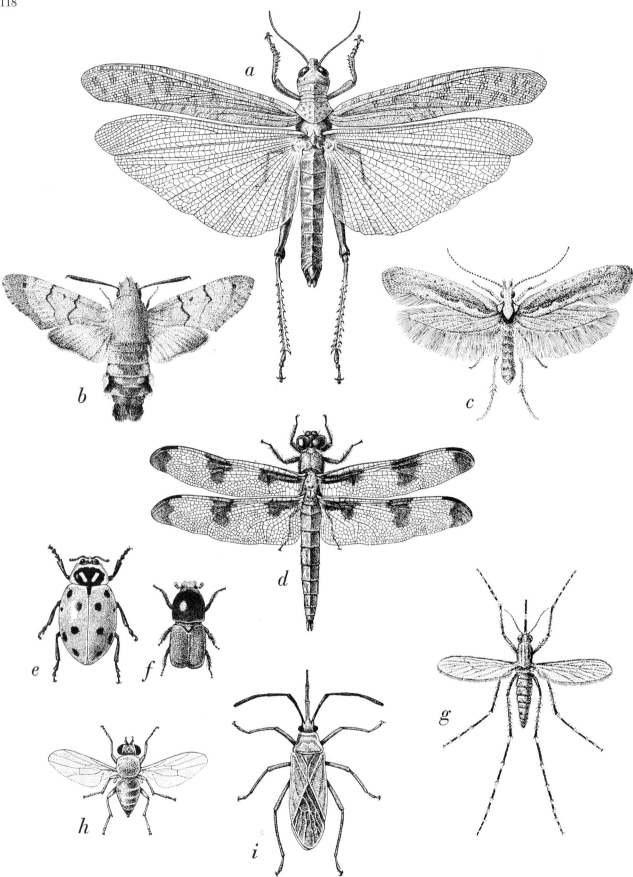

MIGRATORY INSECTS include (a) desert locust, *Schistocerca gregaria*, (b) hummingbird hawk moth, *Macroglossa stellatarum*, (c) diamondback moth, *Plutella maculipennis*, (d) dragonfly, *Libellula pulchella*, (e) ladybird beetle, *Hippodamia convergens*, (f) elm bark beetle, *Scolytus multistriatus*, (g) mosquito, *Aëdes taeniorhynchus*, (h) frit fly, *Oscinella frit*, and (i) tropical cotton stainer, *Dysdercus suturellus*. Although these insects are not drawn to exact scale, they are shown in their approximate relative sizes.

before they enter the reproductive phase of their life history. The mosquito *Aëdes taeniorhynchus*, studied in Florida by Maurice W. Provost, E. T. Nielsen and James S. Haeger, begins its migration with its first flight after emergence and may travel up to 20 miles in a direction strongly influenced by the wind. The butterfly *Ascia monuste*, also observed in Florida, makes a few preliminary feeding flights, but these gradually lengthen into a prolonged migratory flight along the coast in the shelter of the dunes. Although the individual insect normally migrates only during the first 24 hours of adult life, it may travel nearly 100 miles. Thereafter it settles down and makes many short local feeding and egg-depositing flights. The literature contains numerous reports of early migratory flights in other orders, including dragonflies and beetles. Of equal importance, species not usually regarded as migrants have been observed to do the same thing. Winged ants and termites make an intense first flight in the adult form. Although short in duration, these flights enable them to establish new colonies at some distance from their natal habitat.

Other insects, such as some scolytid beetles, hibernate after they emerge and, still sexually immature, migrate months later. Many insects, including some moths, thrips and beetles, migrate first to sites where they hibernate and then migrate again at the end of hibernation. Most adult insects live for less than a year, some for only a few days, but certain ladybird beetles live up to two or three years. They are believed to undertake several migratory or dispersal flights during their lifetime and not simply one flight after emergence. These are some of the insects that have attracted attention by their habit of migrating simultaneously and massing together during hibernation and therefore prior to re-migration.

In their migratory flight aphids do not excite as much wonder as the same behavior does in the case of larger insects. They appear against the sky as tiny elements in the aerial plankton, part of the busy swarm of "gnats" that may lend visual discomfort to the heat of a summer's day. At Rothamsted we have developed suction traps to plot the diurnal rise and fall of the aphid population in the air. Suspended at measured heights from steel towers or from barrage balloons, these traps suck in the air and collect the insects in a tube. Disks are dropped into the collecting tube at preset intervals in order to divide the catch

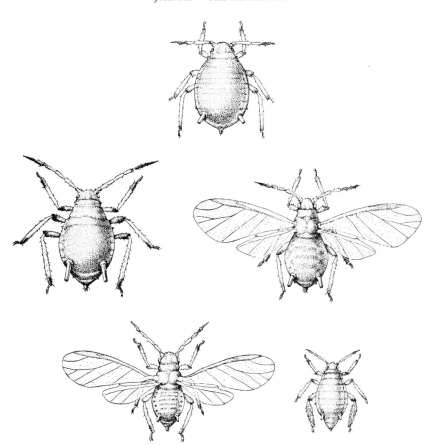

APHIS FABAE, a migratory species of aphid, occurs in many forms during a year. The five shown here are the fundatrix (*top*), which hatches in spring from an overwintering egg and founds a new line; a wingless female that gives live birth to new larvae (*center left*); a winged female that migrates and gives live birth (*center right*); a male (*bottom left*) that mates with an egg-laying female (*bottom right*). Species changes host plants with season.

DESERT LOCUSTS in this swarm covered 400 square miles of Ethiopia in October, 1958. Locusts are a form of grasshopper. They travel in swarms and decimate vegetation as they go.

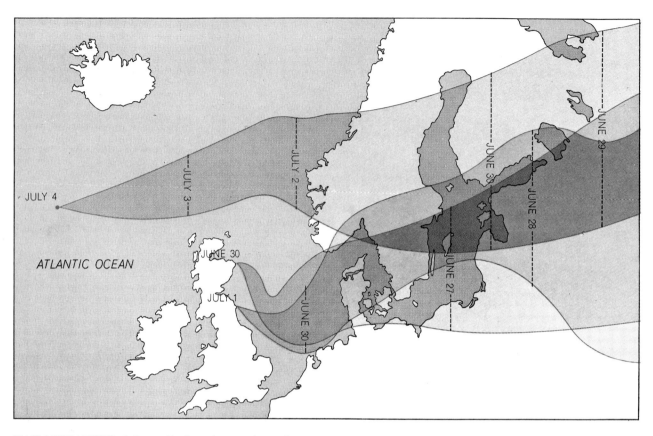

MASS MIGRATIONS of diamondback moth were observed June 30 and July 1, 1958, at two points on the northern coast of Britain, and on July 4, 1958, by a weather ship at sea, when thousands of tiny moths appeared on the bridge. The colored shading marks the air masses that carried the migrating moths. Dates indicate approxi-

mate positions of these air masses on days before observations of migrations. Presumably the moths came from the region where the three air masses overlap. Moths observed at sea had evidently traveled 1,000 miles from the coast of Norway, beating their wings all the time. If they reached America, they flew for two more days.

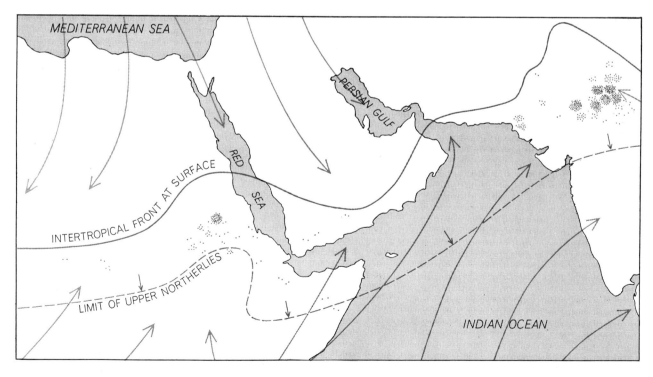

INTERTROPICAL CONVERGENCE ZONE, where winds from north meet those from south (colored arrows), producing rain, provides moisture that enables locusts to breed. The rain also brings

growth of vegetation, on which locust larvae can feed. Thus, travel with the wind serves ecological needs. Each colored dot denotes a report of a locust swarm between July 12 and July 31, 1950.

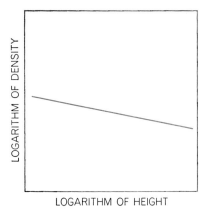

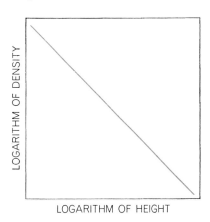

INSECT DENSITY varies with height according to turbulence of air. Rising currents carry insects up and slope of graph of logarithm of density plotted against logarithm of height is small (*left*). Still air produces a steep slope (*right*) because the insects remain near the ground. The colored dots in the accompanying panels represent insects and illustrate the density associated with each graph.

into fractions over periods of time. A count of the insects on each disk reveals the shifts and changes in the concentration of the air-borne population of aphids (and other insects) throughout the day.

By this technique we have found that aphid flights have a daily rhythm that frequently shows two peaks. We have also established the underlying mechanism of this cycle and thereby the explanation of the massing of the aphids in their migratory flight. The aphids that molt from the larval stage during the night are inhibited from flying by the cold and darkness. When the light and temperature rise above flight thresholds in the morning, the new adults that have accumulated all take off at the same time. Their exodus is recorded by our suction traps as a midmorning peak. Meanwhile the individuals whose maturation has been slowed by the low temperatures of the last hours before dawn mature more quickly as the day grows warmer. Their simultaneous departure yields another peak of migration in the early afternoon. By evening the fall in temperature and intensity of light from the sky brings a corresponding drop in the number of air-borne aphids. Since the temperature threshold for maturation is lower than that for flight, however, the next morning's crop of aphids now begins to accumulate. Trevor Lewis of Rothamsted has found that the mass migrations of another insect, the thrip, also occur in the warmup after a period of low temperature. Thus many mass insect flights must be regarded as gushes of newly emerged and waiting winged adults, released by a rise in temperature.

These observations can be matched to the recorded behavior of many classical and well-recognized migrants. As long ago as 1880 S. B. J. Skertchly noted an early-morning emergence of thousands of painted butterflies (*Vanessa cardui*); within an hour they all flew off together in the same direction. It is now known that such migrants as locusts, monarch butterflies, *Aëdes* and *Ascia* similarly emerge together at their breeding sites and then depart on the simultaneous flight that is featured in the literature on insect migration. The analogy so often drawn with bird migration in these cases fails to take into account the fact that all the individuals are of the same age; in contrast, flocks of birds may contain adults of all ages, and they may have congregated, unlike insects, from different places.

The strength and direction of the wind play an important but not necessarily crucial role in determining how far wind-borne migrants will go. The contribution of the insect—the duration of its locomotory drive—constitutes an equally important variable, for most insects must beat their wings if they are not to fall out of the air. The desert locust, geared to travel great distances, refueling as it goes, spends most of its adult life migrating, after which it lays eggs and dies. In contrast, termites migrate for only a few minutes but spend months reproducing. The travel of aphids (at least of those with temporary wing muscles) is limited by their initial fuel (fat) supply; they cannot refuel during migration.

In laboratory studies of flight capacity some insects turn in extraordinary performances. For example, although aphids are weak fliers, A. J. Cockburn of Rothamsted has shown that some can continue to beat their wings for 16 hours nonstop, until all their fuel is exhausted. These intrinsic performances, however, bear little relation to distances traveled in nature. An analysis of daily flight rhythms of aphids at different altitudes at Cardington in England shows that the average flight lasts for only one to three hours. In elegant flight-chamber experiments by J. S. Kennedy, aphids permitted to fly freely stay up for about the same length of time. Height-density studies of aphids and other insects reveal that the general aerial population, at least over Britain, resembles a daily explosion, with millions of insects thrown up, often to great heights, followed by an almost complete settling-out by nightfall.

In contrast with the short, daylight-only flights of the insects in the aerial plankton over Britain, desert locusts have been known to travel across the sea for 24 to 60 hours, going as many as 1,400 miles in one hop. This greatly exceeds their records for tethered flights in the laboratory. R. A. French and J. H. White have reported an observation by a ship 1,000 miles at sea of millions of tiny diamondback moths. Apparently they had been going for at least two days nonstop [*see top illustration on preceding page*], carried irresistibly by the wind at 20 miles per hour, beating their wings all the time in order to stay up.

The distance traveled overland does not necessarily reflect the duration of the insects' flight for another reason: the air currents may carry them upward as well as horizontally. In vigorous convection currents locusts form towering cumuliform swarms thousands of feet high. When convection is low, the swarms become flat and remain near the ground. As would be expected, smaller insects are even more sensitive to air currents. In still, stable air crowds concentrate near the ground; this accounts for dense swarms observed at eye level on quiet summer evenings. In rising currents they go up for thousands of feet. There is an approximately linear inverse relation between the logarithms of the density of the air-borne population and altitude, as would be expected in plotting the turbulent diffusion of small particles. The slope of the curve, when density is plotted against height, correlates well with the degree of atmospheric stability [*see* preceding page] and makes it possible to calculate from measurements of air currents the density of insects in particular altitude zones. These calculations show, for example, that in Britain in the middle of a typical summer day half of the population of frit flies (*Oscinella frit,* a cereal pest hitherto thought to fly only near the crop) is above 1,300 feet!

Travel in air currents is haphazard and many insects are lost in unfavorable places. Perhaps only a few reach a good site, but these are enough to perpetuate the species. Even this seemingly fortuitous system of movement can be highly adapted for survival, as Rainey has shown for the desert locust. Their migrations are associated with the movement of the convective air currents of the intertropical convergence zone, a region in which winds from the north and from the south converge, tend to ascend and so produce rain. As this zone moves across Africa and the Middle East with the change of seasons, the winds coming into it from the desert carry locusts from dry areas into wet areas [*see bottom illustration on page 120*]. Locust eggs must have moisture to survive and the larvae need vegetation when they hatch. Thus the apparent haphazard movements of the swarms are geared to their basic ecological requirements.

In all other species it can be anticipated that migratory behavior will prove to be correspondingly adapted to placing them in the right habitat at the right time in their life cycles. Some insects, such as the monarch butterfly, migrate long distances to overwintering sites and so escape adverse seasonal changes in climate and food. The migratory aphid, by moving a short distance from herbs to woody plants as the season changes, is doing the same thing. Adults of other species merely scatter in successive generations, without a regular change of host or complete change of habitat. In every case, however, the species engages in migration or adaptive dispersal (sometimes in both, since some classical migrants disperse en route) in order to relinquish a habitat that would eventually become untenable. T. R. E. Southwood of the Imperial College of Science

and Technology in London has recently shown that species occurring in relatively temporary habitats produce more migrant adults than species living in more permanent situations. Many migratory dragonflies, for example, live in ponds that dry up periodically, whereas nonmigratory species tend to inhabit rivers. Agricultural pests are wide-ranging and mobile because nearly all crops are temporary, annual plants. Hence pests are here today, gone tomorrow and where they come from often seems to be a mystery. It is not so mysterious, however, when one realizes that millions of individual insects of the aerial plankton rain down almost everywhere on the earth day after day.

Whereas adaptive advantages of migration are found in study of the eco-

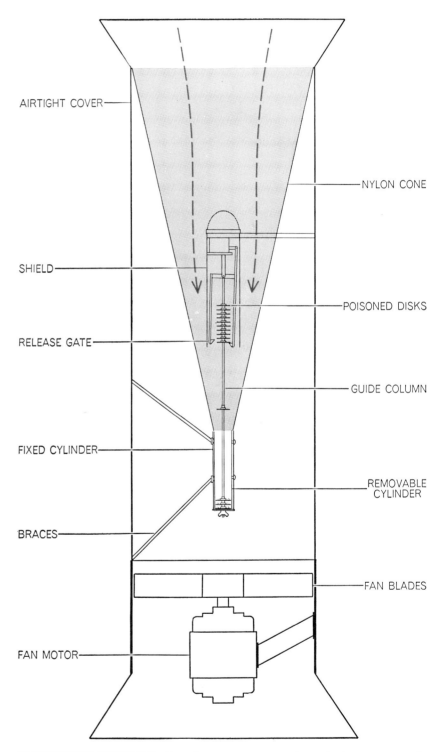

AIRTIGHT COVER

NYLON CONE

SHIELD

POISONED DISKS

RELEASE GATE

GUIDE COLUMN

FIXED CYLINDER

REMOVABLE CYLINDER

BRACES

FAN BLADES

FAN MOTOR

SEGREGATING SUCTION TRAP pulls in air and insects (*arrows*). At preset intervals, poisoned disks drop, dividing catch. This gives a direct measure of aerial density of insects at a given time. Various types of trap are suspended from posts, towers and balloons.

logical relations of each species, the cause of the behavior must be sought in the individual insects. In some cases a currently unfavorable environment induces the insects to leave; froghoppers have been known to move from cut vegetation and locusts have been thought to respond to dryness. Nevertheless, most mass migrations do not seem to be in direct response to any current adversity. Monarch butterflies, ladybird beetles, hover flies, noctuid moths and other species that go into winter quarters begin to migrate long before cold weather sets in. Neither food shortage nor "intolerable overcrowding" are evident to the human observer at the time of departure of aphids, *Ascia* and many others. The migration, therefore, usually comes in advance of any obvious change for the worse in living conditions.

The recognition that many mass migrations are made by fresh adults soon after emergence suggests that the cause be sought in the physiology and developmental history of the individual. It is well known that many insects are polymorphic: the adults of the same species differ in appearance either because of difference in sex (sexual polymorphism) or in structure, as in the various castes in a colony of termites or ants. Locusts reared in crowds produce adults of the phase *gregaria*, which are migrants and differ structurally to some extent from individuals reared in isolation, the phase *solitaria*. In migratory aphids the polymorphism takes the form of winged or wingless adults (alary polymorphism).

It has been observed that a small aphid population produces few winged adults, but as the population becomes large and dense the proportion with wings increases. This may be caused in some unknown manner by the increase in amount of direct contact between in-

dividuals or by other factors. Perhaps change in the quantity or quality of food influences development one way or the other. Be this as it may, winged aphids all migrate; as far as is known, none stay behind. Migration is obligatory once the winged form appears.

Many insects, however, produce only winged adults; then it is the proportion that migrates that varies from year to year, and some generations may have no migrants. This has been another mystery of migration. Yet perhaps the mystery is no deeper than that associated with aphid migrations. It is certainly not unreasonable to assume that if aphids produced winged individuals in response to the environmental pressures that induce migration, the insects that always produce winged adults can generate some individuals with a "behavioral polymorphism" that endows them with the locomotory drive necessary to migration. These polymorphs would appear when the ecological situation of the species demanded it, just as the winged aphids appear.

The principal physiological clue to the triggering of the locomotory drive is the finding that it is associated with delay in the development of ovaries and of the endocrines that control ovary development. Most migratory flights are made by sexually immature females. Among migratory insects it is always the females that engage in migration, because it is they that spread the species. Males present different and distinct problems since even in some migratory species the males never migrate.

It is known that several factors, such as crowding, a short day or poor food (particularly protein deficiency) all delay development of the ovaries. It is also known that many insects cease migrating when ovaries mature. It should be possible, therefore, to make experimental tests of whether or not changes in such

factors as length of day, food and temperature produce the postulated behavioral polymorphism. If they do, this would bring us back to the old idea that migration and adaptive dispersal are induced by overcrowding, changing seasons or poor food, but that the mechanism is in the biochemical rather than the sensory responses of the individual insect.

Still awaiting investigation by entomologists are some of the real puzzles of nature that surround such highly specialized migrants as the monarch butterfly. How, for example, do vast numbers of different species make their way seasonally along well-defined routes, often in mountain passes? What are the factors that determine the orientation of migrants that fly at a certain height when it is relatively calm and so control their own direction?

It will be difficult to find the means of attacking such problems. On the other hand, recent progress in the study of migratory behavior in insects has opened up equally interesting new questions to investigation. It remains to be determined, for example, if there is any general connection between the length of the period before egg-laying begins and the tendency to undistracted migration in different species. We must study the effect of length of day, larval crowding and quantity and quality of food on the length of the migratory period and also find out how these factors relate to the attraction of the sky that takes the migrating insect into the windy air. Finally, we should like to know how many species are in the aerial plankton by accident and how many by adaptation. I suspect that far more are there by adaptation than is commonly believed.

14

POPULATION CONTROL IN ANIMALS

V. C. WYNNE-EDWARDS
August 1964

*Unlike man, most animals maintain fairly constant
population levels. A new hypothesis suggests that they do so
by forms of social behavior that limit reproduction to avoid
overexploitation of food resources*

In population growth the human species is conspicuously out of line with the rest of the animal kingdom. Man is almost alone in showing a long-term upward trend in numbers; most other animals maintain their population size at a fairly constant level. To be sure, many of them fluctuate in number from season to season, from year to year or from decade to decade; notable examples are arctic lemmings, migratory locusts living in the subtropical dry belt, many northern game birds and certain fur-bearing animals. Such fluctuations, however, tend to swing erratically around a constant average value. More commonly animal populations maintain a steady state year after year and even century after century. If and when the population does rise or fall permanently, because of some change in the environment, it generally stabilizes again at a new level.

This well-established fact of population dynamics deserves to be studied with close attention, because the growth of human populations has become in recent years a matter of increasing concern. What sort of mechanism is responsible for such strict control of the size of populations? Each animal population, apart from man's, seems to be regulated in a homeostatic manner by some system that tends to keep it within not too wide limits of a set average density. Ecologists have been seeking to discover the nature of this system for many years. I shall outline here a new hypothesis that I set forth in full detail in a recently published book, *Animal Dispersion in Relation to Social Behaviour*.

The prevailing hypothesis has been that population is regulated by a set of negative natural controls. It is assumed that animals will produce young as fast as they efficiently can, and that the main factors that keep population density within fixed limits are predators, starvation, accidents and parasites causing disease. On the face of it this assumption seems entirely reasonable; overcrowding should increase the death toll from most of these factors and thus act to cut back the population when it rises to a high density. On close examination, however, these ideas do not stand up.

The notions that predators or disease are essential controllers of population density can be dismissed at once. There are animals that effectively have no predators and are not readily subject to disease and yet are limited to a stable level of population; among notable examples are the lion, the eagle and the skua [see "The Antarctic Skua," by Carl R. Eklund; SCIENTIFIC AMERICAN, February]. Disease per se does not act on a large scale to control population growth in the animal world. This leaves starvation as the possible control. The question of whether starvation itself acts directly to remove a population surplus calls for careful analysis.

Even a casual examination makes it clear that in most animal communities starvation is rare. Normally all the individuals in the habitat get enough food to survive. Occasionally a period of drought or severe cold may starve out a population, but that is an accident of weather—a disaster that does not arise from the density of population. We must therefore conclude that death from hunger is not an important density-dependent factor in controlling population size except in certain unusual cases.

Yet the density of population in the majority of habitats does depend directly on the size of the food supply; the close relation of one to the other is clear in representative situations where both variables have been measured [see *illustration on page 127*]. We have, then, the situation that no individual starves but the population does not outgrow the food supply available in its habitat under normal conditions.

For many of the higher animals one can see therefore that neither predators, disease nor starvation can account for the regulation of numbers. There is of course accidental mortality, but it strikes in unpredictable and haphazard ways, independently of population density, and so must be ruled out as a stabilizer of population. All these considerations point to the possibility that the animals themselves must exercise the necessary restraint!

Man's own history provides some vivid examples of what is entailed here. By overgrazing he has converted once rich pastures into deserts; by overhunting he has exterminated the passenger pigeon and all but eliminated animals such as the right whale, the southern fur seal and, in many of their former breeding places, sea turtles; he is now threatening to exterminate all five species of rhinoceros inhabiting tropical Africa and Asia because the horns of those animals are valued for their alleged aphrodisiac powers. Exploiting the riches of today can exhaust and destroy the resources of tomorrow. The point is that animals face precisely this danger with respect to their food supply, and they generally handle it more prudently than man does.

Birds feeding on seeds and berries in the fall or chickadees living on hibernating insects in winter are in such a situation. The stock of food to begin with is so abundant that it could feed an enormous population. Then, however, it would be gone in hours or days, and the birds must depend on this food supply for weeks or months. To make it

UNEMPLOYED BIRDS are visible at a gannetry on Cape St. Mary in Newfoundland. They are the ones on the slope at left; the main colony is on the large adjacent slope. The unemployed gannets are excluded from breeding, apparently as part of the colony's automatic mechanisms for controlling the population level. These birds do, however, constitute a reserve for raising the population level.

MASSED MANEUVERS by starling flocks occur frequently on fine evenings, particularly in the fall. The maneuvers are an example of communal activity that appears to have the purpose of providing the flock with an indication of population density. If the density is too high or too low in relation to the food supply, the flock automatically increases the activities that will improve the balance.

last through the season the birds must restrict the size of their population in advance. The same necessity holds in situations where unlimited feeding would wipe out the sources that replenish the food supply. Thus the threat of starvation tomorrow, not hunger itself today, seems to be the factor that decides what the density of a population ought to be. Long before starvation would otherwise occur, the population must limit its growth in order to avoid disastrous overexploitation of its food resources.

All this implies that animals restrict their population density by some artificial device that is closely correlated with the food supply. What is required

is some sort of automatic restrictive mechanism analogous to the deliberate conventions or agreements by which nations limit the exploitation of fishing grounds.

One does not need to look far to realize that animals do indeed possess conventions of this kind. The best-known is the territorial system of birds. The practice of staking out a territory for nesting and rearing a family is common among many species of birds. In the breeding season each male lays claim to an area of not less than a certain minimum size and keeps out all other males of the species; in this way a group of males will parcel out the available ground as individual territories

and put a limit on crowding. It is a perfect example of an artificial mechanism geared to adjusting the density of population to the food resources. Instead of competing directly for the food itself the members compete furiously for pieces of ground, each of which then becomes the exclusive food preserve of its owner. If the standard territory is large enough to feed a family, the entire group is safe from the danger of overtaxing the food supply.

The territorial convention is just one example of a convention that takes many other forms, some of them much more sophisticated or abstract. Seabirds, for instance, being unable to stake out a territory or nest on the sea itself,

PLACE IN HIERARCHY is at stake in this contest between male black bucks in India. Many mammal and bird groups have a hierarchical system or a system of defended territories. Successful individuals acquire food and breeding rights; the others leave, or perhaps stay as a reserve available for breeding if needed. By such means the group correlates its population with food resources.

adopt instead a token nesting place on the shore that represents their fishing rights. Each nesting site occupies only a few square feet, but the birds' behavior also limits the overall size of their colony, thereby restricting the number that will fish in the vicinity. Any adults that have not succeeded in winning a site within the perimeter of the colony are usually inhibited from nesting or starting another colony nearby.

Other restrictive conventions practiced by animals are still more abstract. Often the animals compete not for actual property, such as a nesting site, but merely for membership in the group, and only a certain number are accepted. In all cases the effect is to limit the density of the group living in the given habitat and unload any surplus population to a safe distance.

Not the least interesting fact is that the competition itself tends to take an abstract or conventional form. In their contest for a territory birds seldom actually draw blood or kill each other. Instead they merely threaten with aggressive postures, vigorous singing or displays of plumage. The forms of intimidation of rivals by birds range all the way from the naked display of weapons to the triumph of splendor revealed in the peacock's train.

This hypothesis about the mechanism of population control in animals leads to a generalization of broader scope, namely that this was the origin or root of all social behavior in animals, including man. Surprisingly there has been no generally acceptable theory of how the first social organizations arose. One can now argue logically, however, that the kind of competition under conventional rules that is typified by the territorial system of birds was the earliest form of social organization. Indeed, a society can be defined as a group of individuals competing for conventional prizes by conventional methods. To put it another way, it is a brotherhood tempered by rivalry. One does not need to ponder very deeply to see how closely this cap fits even human societies.

A group of birds occupying an area divided into individual territories is plainly a social organization, and it exhibits a considerable range of characteristically social behavior. This is well illustrated by the red grouse of Scotland—a bird that is being studied intensively in a long-term research project near Aberdeen.

The grouse population on a heather moor consists of individuals known to one another and differing among them-

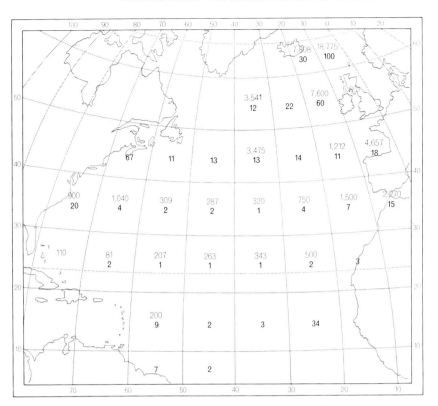

POPULATION AND FOOD SUPPLY show a correlation in the North Atlantic Ocean. The figures in light type give the average volume of plankton found per cubic centimeter of water; the darker figures show the average daily count of ocean birds that feed on plankton.

selves in social standing. The dominant males hold territories almost all year round, the most aggressive claiming on the average the largest territories. Their individual domains cover the moor like a mosaic]see *top illustration on page 129*]. The community admits as members some socially subordinate males and unmated hens that have no territories of their own, but with the onset of winter, or with a decline in the food supply for some other reason, these supernumeraries at the bottom of the social ladder get squeezed out. Only as many as can be supported by the lowered food level are allowed to stay. Thus the social hierarchy of the red grouse works as a safety valve or overflow mechanism, getting rid of any excess that would overtax the food resources. The existence of the peck-order system among birds has been known for some time, but its functional reason for being has been unclear; it now appears that the lowest members of the order serve as a dispensable reserve that can fill in as replacements for casualties among the established members or be dropped as circumstances require.

Certain definite rules mark the competition of the red grouse males for territory and status. One is that, at least in the fall, they crow and threaten only on fine mornings between first light

and two or three hours later. So aggressive is this struggle that the stress forces some of the losers to make a break away from the moor; on unfamiliar ground and without their usual food they soon weaken and are killed by predators or disease. Once the early-morning contest is over, however, those birds that remain in the habitat flock together amicably and feed side by side for the rest of the day.

The convention of competing at dawn or at dusk and leaving the rest of the day free for feeding and other peaceable activities is exceedingly common among animals of various kinds. The changes of light at dawn and dusk are, of course, the most conspicuous recurrent events of the day, and this no doubt explains why they serve so often as a signal for joint or communal activities. There are many familiar manifestations of this timing: the dawn chorus of songbirds and crowing cocks, the flight of ducks at dusk, the massed maneuvers of starlings and blackbirds at their roosts as darkness falls; the evening choruses of almost innumerable other birds, various tropical bats, frogs, cicadas and fishes such as the croaker, and the morning concerts of howler monkeys.

All these synchronized outbursts give an indication of the numbers present in the respective populations. They provide an index of the population density in the habitat from day to day, and so feed to the group information that causes it, not deliberately but automatically, to step up those activities that may be necessary to restore the balance between the density and the food supply.

The daily community display puts a changing pressure on the members taking part. If the stress is great enough, a reduction in the population can be triggered off; if it is felt lightly or not at all, there is room for new recruits. Overcrowding will lead to expulsion of the population surplus, as in the case of the red grouse. In the breeding season the density index, in the form of the daily display, can influence the proportion of adults that mate and breed; likewise the number of young can be restricted in a variety of other ways to the quota that the habitat will allow.

In the light of this hypothesis one would expect these "epideictic" displays (that is, population-pressure demonstrations) to be particularly prominent at the outset of the breeding season. That is actually the case. In birds the demonstrators are usually the males; they can be called the epideictic sex. They may swarm and dance in the air (as many flying insects do) or engage in ritual tournaments, gymnastics or parades (characteristic of sage grouse, prairie chickens, tropical hummingbirds, manakins and birds-of-paradise). The intensity of these activities depends on the density of the population: the more males there are, the keener the competition. The new hypothesis suggests that this will result in greater stress among the males and sharper restriction of the size of the population.

In many animals the males have vocal abilities the females lack; this is true of songbirds, cicadas, most crickets and katydids, frogs, drumfishes, howler monkeys and others. Contrary to what was once thought, these males use their voices primarily not to woo females but in the contest with their fellow males for real estate and status. The same ap-

plies to many of the males' adornments and scent glands, as well as to their weapons. This newly recognized fact calls for some rethinking of the whole vexed subject of sexual selection.

Epideictic displays rise to a height not only as a prelude to the breeding season but also at the time of animal migrations. They show the scale of the impending change in the population density of the habitat and, during the migration, give an indication of the size of the flocks that have gathered at the stopping places, thereby enabling the migrants to avoid dangerous congestion at any one place. Locusts build up for a great flight with spectacular massed maneuvers, and comparable excitement marks the nightly roosting of migratory chimney swifts and other big gatherings of birds, fruit bats and insects.

Altogether the hypothesis that animal populations regulate themselves through the agency of social conventions of this kind seems to answer satisfactorily several of the major questions that have concerned ecologists. Basically the average population level is set by the long-term food resources of the habitat. A system of behavioral conventions acts as homeostatic machinery that prevents the growth of the population from departing too far from the optimal density. Fluctuations from this average can be explained as being due partly to temporary accidents (such as climatic extremes) and partly to the working of the homeostatic machinery itself, which allows the population density to build up when the food yields are good and thins it down when the yields fall below average. At any particular time the availability of food in relation to the number of mouths to be fed—in other words, the standard of living at the moment—determines the response of the regulating mechanism. The mechanism acts by controlling the rate of recruitment, by creating a pressure to emigrate or sometimes by producing stresses that result in large-scale mortality.

It has been particularly gratifying to find that the hypothesis offers explanations of several social enigmas on which there has been no good theory, such as the biological origin of social behavior; the function of the social hierarchy, or peck-order system, among birds; the chorus of birds and similar social events synchronized at dawn and dusk.

The theory has wide ramifications which I have discussed at length in my book. The one that interests us most

POPULATION-CONTROL DEVICES include the territory, of which the four basic types are depicted. Birds or mammals with territories have an established right to the available food; they also are the ones that breed. The others are in effect squeezed out. At top are two types of territory occupied by single males and their mates. At bottom are the types occupied by animals that live in colonies. One is virtually exclusive. The other is overlapping; shown here are islands from which five seabird colonies fan out within a maximum radius.

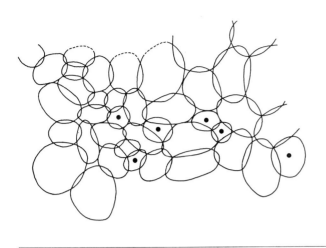

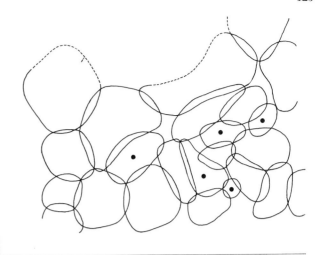

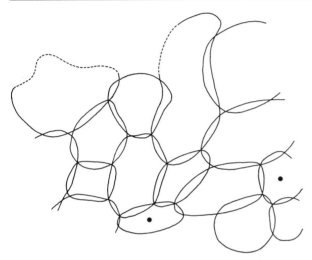

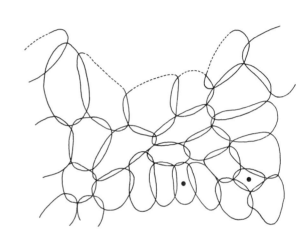

TERRITORIAL VARIATIONS of Scottish red grouse males reflect a form of population control. The drawings show the territorial holdings of individual cocks in four successive springs (1958–1961) on the same 140 acres of moorland. Some of the smaller territories, marked by dots, were held by males who remained unmated. Average territory size varies from year to year, thus affecting the density of breeding; in these four years the number of territories ranged between 40 in 1958 (*top left*) and 16 in 1960 (*bottom left*). The density of breeding is correlated with the food supply, which is to say with the quantity and quality of the heather.

BLACK GROUSE MALES are depicted in an "epideictic display," or ceremonial demonstration, that appears to be a form of population control. It evidently provides a measure of the population density within the area, because many males participate simultaneously on a communal strutting ground. It also serves as a means of excluding some less prominent males, who seldom display and often are chased away by the dominant birds. Epideictic displays also occur among many other bird and mammal species.

of course, is its bearing on the problem of the unchecked growth of the human population. The hypothesis opens up to clearer view the differences between man's demographic history and that of other animals.

There are two outstanding differences. In the first place, the homeostatic control of animal populations is strictly automatic: even the social conventions of behavior are innate rather than deliberately arrived at. In part the density-dependent control in many animals, including some of the mammals, is exercised by means of a biological reaction—either reduction of the rate of ovulation through a change in the output of hormones, or resorption of the embryos in the uterus as a result of stress (as occurs in rabbits, foxes and deer). Man's fertility and population growth, on the other hand, are subject only to his conscious and deliberate behavior. The second important difference is that modern man has progressively and enormously increased the food productivity of his habitat.

Primitive man, limited to the food he could get by hunting, had evolved a system for restricting his numbers by tribal traditions and taboos, such as prohibiting sexual intercourse for mothers while they were still nursing a baby, practicing compulsory abortion and infanticide, offering human sacrifices, conducting headhunting expeditions against rival tribes and so forth. These customs, consciously or not, kept the population density nicely balanced against the feeding capacity of the hunting range. Then, some 8,000 to 10,000 years ago, the agricultural revolution removed that limitation. There was no longer any reason to hold down the size of the tribe; on the contrary, power and wealth accrued to those tribes that allowed their populations to multiply, to develop farms, villages and even towns. The old checks on population growth were gradually discarded and forgotten. The rate of reproduction became a matter of individual choice rather than of tribal or community control. It has remained so ever since.

Given opportunity for procreation and a low death rate, the human population, whether well fed or hungry, now shows a tendency to expand without limit. Lacking the built-in homeostatic system that regulates the density of animal populations, man cannot look to any natural process to restrain his rapid growth. If the growth is to be slowed down, it must be by his own deliberate and socially applied efforts.

15

BUTTERFLIES AND PLANTS

PAUL R. EHRLICH AND PETER H. RAVEN

June 1967

*The hungry larvae of butterflies are selective in choosing
the plants they eat. This reflects the fact that the evolution
of both plants and the animals that feed on them is a
counterpoint of attack and defense*

Anyone who has been close to nature or has wandered about in the nonurban areas of the earth is aware that animal life sometimes raises havoc with plant life. Familiar examples are the sudden defoliation of forests by hordes of caterpillars or swarms of locusts and the less abrupt but nonetheless thorough denudation of large areas by grazing animals. A visitor to the Wankie National Park of Rhodesia can see a particularly spectacular scene of herbivore devastation. There herds of elephants have thinned the forest over hundreds of square miles and left a litter of fallen trees as if a hurricane had passed through.

Raids such as these are rare, and the fertile regions of the earth manage to remain rather green. This leads most people, including many biologists, to underestimate the importance of the perennial onslaught of animals on plants. Detailed studies of the matter in recent years have shown that herbivores are a major factor in determining the evolution and distribution of plants, and the plants in turn play an important part in shaping the behavior and evolution of herbivores.

The influence of herbivores on plants is usually far from obvious, even when it is most profound. In Australia huge areas in Queensland used to be infested with the spiny prickly-pear cactus, which covered thousands of square miles of the area and made it unusable for grazing herds. Today the plant is rare in these areas. It was all but wiped out by the introduction of a cactus moth from South America, which interestingly enough is now hardly in evidence. When one searches scattered remaining clumps of the cactus, one usually fails to find any sign of the insect. The plant survives only as a fugitive species; as soon as a

clump of the cactus is discovered by the moth it is devoured, and the population of moths that has flourished on it then dies away. A similar situation is found in the Fiji Islands. There a plant pest of the genus *Clidemia* was largely destroyed by a species of thrips brought in from tropical America, and the parasitic insect, as well as the plant, has now become rare in Fiji.

The interplay of plant and animal populations takes many forms—some direct, some indirect, some obvious, some obscure. In California the live oak is disappearing from many areas because cattle graze on the young seedlings. In Australia a native pine that was decimated by rabbits has made a dramatic comeback since the rabbit population was brought under control by the myxomatosis virus. Australia also furnishes a striking example of how the evolution of a plant can be influenced by the presence or absence of certain animals. The plant involved is the well-known acacia. In Africa and tropical America, where grazing mammals abound, the acacia species are protected by thorns that are often fearsomely developed. Until recently there were comparatively few grazing mammals in Australia, and most of the acacia plants there are thornless, apparently having lost these weapons of their relatives on other continents.

By far the most important terrestrial herbivores are, of course, the insects. They have evolved remarkably efficient organs for eating plants: a great variety of mouthparts with which to pierce, suck or chew plant material. They eat leaves from the outside and the inside, bore through stems and roots and devour flowers, fruits and seeds. In view of the abundance, variety and appetites of the insects, one may well wonder how it

is that any plants are left on the earth. The answer, of course, is that the plants have not taken the onslaught of the herbivores lying down. Some of their defenses are quite obvious: the sharp spines of the cactus, the sharp-toothed leaves of the holly plant, the toxins of poison ivy and the oleander leaf, the odors and pungent tastes of spices. The effectiveness of these weapons against animal predators has been demonstrated by laboratory experiments. For example, it has been shown that certain leaf-edge-eating caterpillars normally do not feed on holly leaves but will devour the leaves when the sharp points are cut away.

The plant world's main line of defense consists in chemical weapons. Very widespread among the plants are certain chemicals that apparently perform no physiological function for the plants themselves but do act as potent insecticides or insect repellents. Among these are alkaloids, quinones, essential oils, glycosides, flavonoids and raphides (crystals of calcium oxalate). Long before man learned to synthesize insecticides he found that an extract from chrysanthemums, pyrethrin, which is harmless to mammals, is a powerful killer of insects.

Particularly interesting are the alkaloids, a heterogeneous group of nitrogenous compounds found mainly in flowering plants. They include nicotine, caffeine, quinine, marijuana, opium and peyote. Considering the hallucinogenic properties of the last three drugs, it is amusing to speculate that the plants bearing them may practice "chemopsychological warfare" against their enemies! Does an insect that has fed on a fungus containing lysergic acid diethylamide (LSD) mistake a spider for its mate? Does a zebra that has eaten a

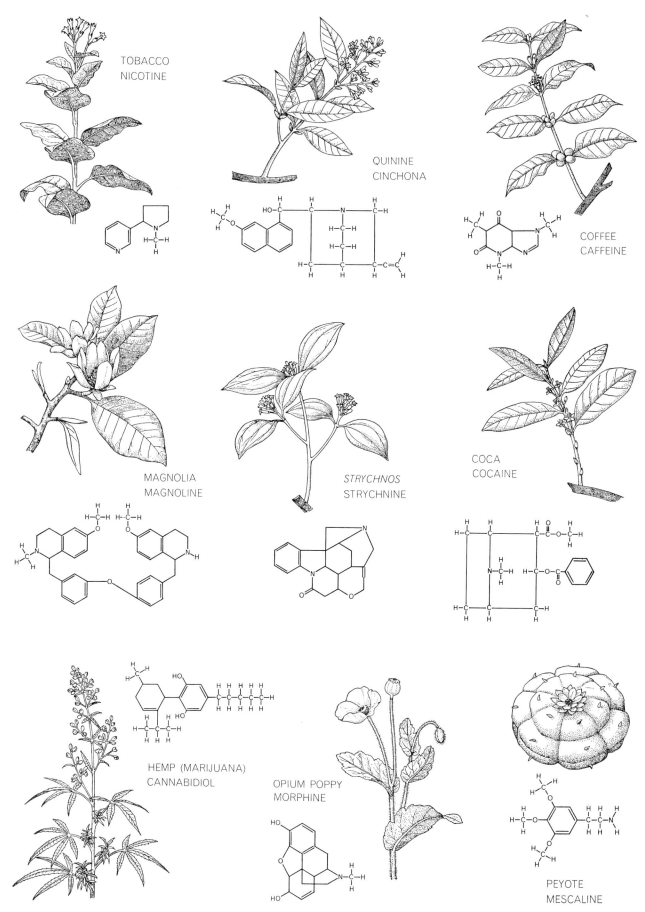

ALKALOIDS give the plants that contain them protection from predators; nine such plants are illustrated. The authors note that plant alkaloids can disturb a herbivore's physiology and that hallucinogenic alkaloids may be "chemopsychological" weapons.

plant rich in alkaloids become so intoxicated that it loses its fear of lions? At all events, there is good reason to believe eating plant alkaloids produces a profound disturbance of animals' physiology.

Of all the herbivores, the group whose eating habits have been studied most intensively is the butterflies—that is to say, butterflies in the larval, or caterpillar, stage, which constitutes the major part of a butterfly's lifetime. Around the world upward of 15,000 species of butterflies, divided taxonomically into five families, have been identified. The five families are the Nymphalidae (four-footed butterflies), the Lycaenidae (blues, metalmarks and others), the Pieridae (whites and yellows), the Papilionidae (including the swallowtails, the huge bird-wings of the Tropics and their relatives) and the Libytheidae (a tiny family of snout butterflies). The Nymphalidae and Lycaenidae account for most (three-fourths) of the known genera and species.

A caterpillar is a formidable eating machine: by the time it metamorphoses into a butterfly it has consumed up to 20 times its dry weight in plant material. The numerous species vary greatly in their choice of food. Some are highly selective, feeding only on a single plant family; others are much more catholic in their tastes, but none feeds on all plants indiscriminately. Let us examine the food preferences of various groups and then consider the evolutionary consequences.

One group that is far-ranging in its taste for plants is the Nymphalinae, a subfamily of the Nymphalidae that comprises at least 2,500 species and is widespread around the world. The plants that members of this group feed on include one or more genera of the figwort, sunflower, maple, pigweed, barberry, beech, borage, honeysuckle, stonecrop, oak, heather, mallow, melastome, myrtle, olive, buttercup, rose, willow and saxifrage families. Another group that eats a wide variety of plants is the Lycaeninae, a subfamily of the Lycaenidae that consists of thousands of species of usually tiny but often beautifully colored butterflies. The Lycaeninae in general are catholic in their tastes, and among their many food plants are members of the pineapple, borage, pea, buckwheat, rose, heather, mistletoe, mint, buckthorn, chickweed, goosefoot, morning glory, gentian, oxalis, pittosporum and zygophyllum families.

What determines the caterpillars'

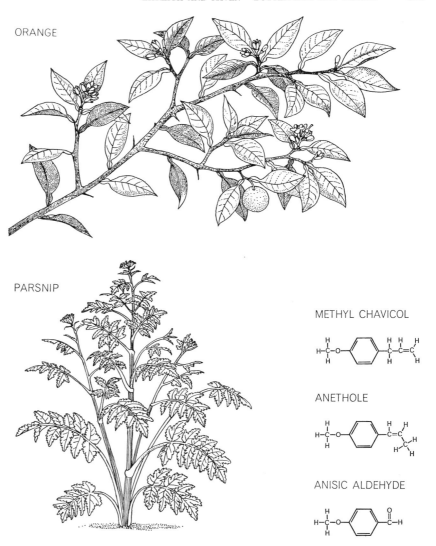

PLANTS OF TWO FAMILIES, citrus (*top*) and parsley (*bottom*), produce the same three essential oils attractive to the larvae of black swallowtail butterflies. The chemical kinship between these plant families suggests a closer ancestral tie than had been suspected.

food preferences? We learn a great deal about this subject by examining the diets of those butterfly species that are particularly selective in their choice of plants. One large group of swallowtails, for example, confines its diet mainly to plants of the Dutchman's-pipe family. Another feeds only on the "woody Ranales," a group of primitive angiosperms that includes the magnolias, the laurels and many tropical and subtropical plants. A third group of swallowtails is partial to plants of the citrus and parsley families; the striped caterpillars of these butterflies, which extrude two bright orange scent horns when they are disturbed, are familiar to gardeners, who often see them feeding on parsley, dill, fennel and celery plants. The caterpillars of the white butterfly group (a subfamily of the Pieridae) feed primarily on caper plants in the Tropics and on plants of the mustard family in temperate regions. Similarly, the monarch butterfly and its relatives (a subfamily of the Nymphalidae) confine their diet primarily to plants of the milkweed and dogbane families.

Analysis of the plant selections by the butterfly groups has made it clear that their choices have a chemical basis, just as parasitic fungi choose hosts that meet their chemical needs. Vincent G. Dethier, then at Johns Hopkins University, noted some years ago that plants of the citrus and parsley families, although apparently unrelated, have in common certain essential oils (such as methyl chavicol, anethole and anisic aldehyde) that presumably account for their attractiveness to the group of swallowtails that feeds on them. Dethier found that caterpillars of the black swallowtail would even attempt to feed on filter paper soaked in these substances. The

FIVE BUTTERFLIES protected by their unpalatability are illustrated with their preferred plants. They are *Thyridia themisto* and one of the nightshades (*a*), *Battus philenor* and Dutchman's-pipe (*b*), *Danaus plexippus* and milkweed (*c*), *Heliconius charitonius* and passion flower (*d*) and *Pardopsis punctatissima* and a representative of the violet family (*e*).

same caterpillars could also be induced to feed on plants of the sunflower family (for example goldenrod and cosmos), which contain these oils but are not normally eaten by the caterpillars in nature.

The chemical finding, incidentally, raises an interesting question about the evolutionary relationship of plants. The sunflower, citrus and parsley families have been considered to be very different from one another, but their common possession of the same group of substances suggests that there may be a chemical kinship after all, at least between the citrus and the parsley family. Chemistry may therefore become a basis for reconsideration of the present classification system for plants.

In the case of the cabbage white butterfly larva the attractive chemical has been shown to be mustard oil. The pungent mustard oils are characteristic of plants of the caper and mustard families (the latter family includes many familiar food plants, such as cabbages, Brussels sprouts, horseradish, radishes and watercress). The whites' larvae also feed occasionally on plants of other families that contain mustard oils, including the garden nasturtium. The Dutch botanist E. Verschaeffelt found early in this century that these larvae would eat flour, starch or even filter paper if it was smeared with juice from mustard plants. More recently the Canadian biologist A. J. Thorsteinson showed that the larvae would eat the leaves of plants on which they normally do not feed when the plants were treated with mustard oil glucosides.

In contrast to the attractive plants, there are plant families on which butterfly larvae do not feed (although other insects may). One of these is the coffee family. Although this family, with some 10,000 species, is probably the fourth largest family of flowering plants in the world and is found mainly in the Tropics, as the butterflies themselves are, butterfly larvae rarely, if ever, feed on these plants. A plausible explanation is that plants of the coffee family are rich in alkaloids. Quinine is one example. Other plant families that butterflies generally avoid eating are the cucurbits (rich in bitter terpenes), the grape family (containing raphides) and the spiny cactus family.

One of the most interesting findings is that butterflies that are distasteful to predators (and that are identified by conspicuous coloring) are generally narrow specialists in their choice of food. They tend to select plants on which other butterfly groups do not feed, notably plants that are rich in alkaloids. It seems highly probable that their use of these plants for food has a double basis: it provides them with a feeding niche in which they have relatively little competition, and it may supply them with the substances, or precursors of substances, that make them unpalatable to predators. The distasteful groups of butterflies apparently have evolved changes in physiology that render them immune to the toxic or repellent plant substances and thus enable them to turn the plants' chemical defenses to their own advantage. Curiously, the butterfly species that mimic the coloring of the distasteful ones are in general more catholic in their feeding habits; evidently their warning coloration alone is sufficient to protect them.

The fact that some butterflies' diets are indeed responsible for their unpalatability has been demonstrated recently by Lincoln P. Brower of Amherst College and his co-workers. They worked with the monarch butterfly, whose larvae normally feed on plants of the milkweed family. Such plants are rich in cardiac glycosides, powerful poisons that are used in minute quantities to treat heart disease in man. When adult butterflies of this species are offered to hand-reared birds (with no previous experience with butterflies), the butterflies are tasted and then promptly rejected, as are further offerings of either the monarch or its close mimic, the viceroy. Recently Brower succeeded in spite of great difficulties in rearing a generation of monarch butterflies on cabbage and found that the resulting adults were perfectly acceptable to the birds, although they were refused by birds that had had previous experience with milkweed-fed monarchs.

The concept of warfare between the plants and the butterflies leads to much enlightenment on the details of evolutionary development on both sides. On the plants' side, we can liken their problem to that of the farmer, who is obliged to defend his crops from attack by a variety of organisms. The plants must deploy their limited resources to protect themselves as best they can. They may confine their growing season to part of the year (limiting their availability to predators); they may be equipped with certain mechanical or chemical defenses; some develop a nutrient-poor sap or nutritional imbalances that make them an inefficient or inadequate source of food. The herbivorous insects, for their part, reply with specializations to cope with the special defenses, as a hunter uses a high-powered rifle to hit deer or bear, a shotgun to hit birds or a hook to catch fish. No butterfly larva (or other herbivore) possesses the varieties of physical equipment that would allow it to feed on all plants; in order to feed at all it must specialize to some degree. Some of the specializations are extremely narrow; certain sap-sucking insects, for example, have developed filtering mechanisms that trap the food elements in nutrient-poor sap, and some of the caterpillars possess detoxifying systems that enable them to feed on plants containing toxic substances.

By such devices herbivores of one kind or another have managed to breach the chemical defenses of nearly every group of plants. We have already noted several examples. The mustard oils of the mustard and caper plant families,

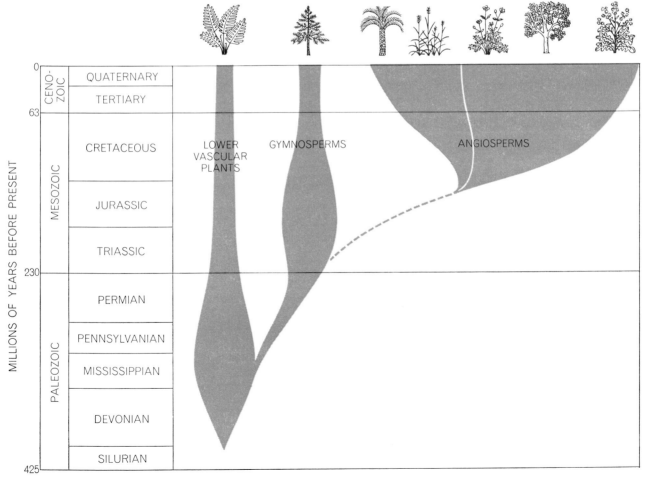

RECORD OF EVOLUTION within the plant kingdom shows that among the vascular plants the gymnosperms (*center*) declined as the angiosperms (*right*) became abundant. The authors attribute this to the acquisition of chemical defenses by the angiosperms.

BUTTERFLY EGGS (*top*) stand upright on a leaf of clover, the egg-laying site selected by the gravid female. Clover is the food plant preferred by this species: *Colias philodice*, the clouded sulphur. After hatching (*bottom*), growing clouded sulphur larvae feed on the plant preselected for them by the parent. When they metamorphose, they too will seek out clover as an egg-laying site.

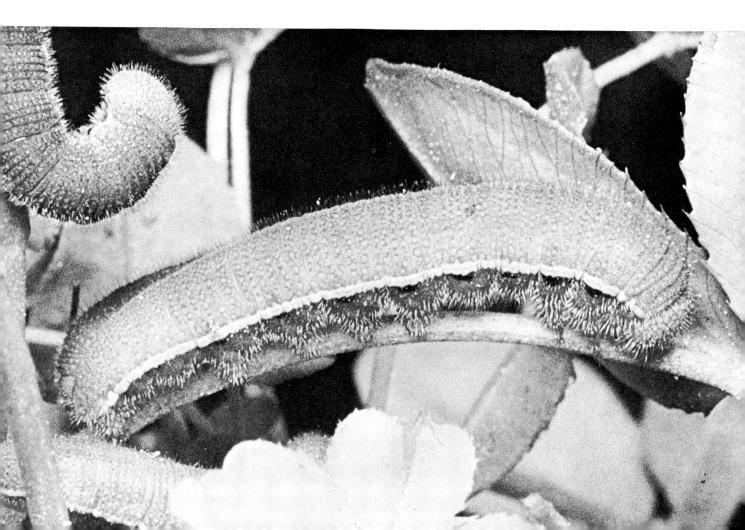

for instance, serve to make these plants unpalatable to most herbivores, but the white butterflies and certain other insects have become so adapted to this defense mechanism that the mustard oils actually are a feeding stimulus for them. O. L. Chambliss and C. M. Jones, then at Purdue University, showed that a bitter, toxic substance in fruits of the squash family that repels honeybees and yellow jackets is attractive to the spotted cucumber beetle. Incidentally, this substance has been bred out of the cultivated watermelon, as any picnicker who has had to wave yellow jackets away from the watermelon can testify. By selecting against this bitter taste man has destroyed one of the natural protective mechanisms of the plant and must contend with a much wider variety of predators on it than the watermelon had to in the wild.

An important aspect of the insects'
chemical adaptability is the recent finding that insects that feed on toxic plants are often immune to man-made insecticides. They evidently possess a generalized detoxifying mechanism. H. T. Gordon of the University of California at Berkeley has pointed out that this is commonly true of insects that are in the habit of feeding on a wide variety of plants. He suggests that through evolutionary selection such insects have evolved a high tolerance to biochemical stresses.

What can we deduce, in the light of the present mutual interrelations of butterflies and plants, about the evolutionary history of the insects and flowering plants? We have little information about their ancient history to guide us, but a few general points seem reasonably clear.

First, we can surmise that the great success of the angiosperm plants (plants
with enclosed seeds), which now dominate the plant world since most of the more primitive gymnosperm lines have disappeared, is probably due in large measure to the angiosperms' early acquisition of chemical defenses. One important group of protective secondary plant substances, the alkaloids, is found almost exclusively in this class of plants and is well represented in those groups of angiosperms that are considered most primitive. Whereas other plants were poorly equipped for chemical warfare, the angiosperms were able to diversify behind a biochemical shield that gave them considerable protection from herbivores.

As the flowering plants diversified, the insect world also underwent a tremendous diversification with them. The intimate present relation between butterflies and plants leaves no doubt that the two groups evolved together, each

MODEL   MIMETIC FORM   NONMIMETIC FORM

a   *b*   *c*

d   *e*

f   *g*   *h*

UNPALATABLE BUTTERFLIES, whose disagreeable taste originates with the plants they ate as larvae, are often boldly marked and predators soon learn to avoid them. The three "models," so called because unrelated species mimic them, are the monarch, *Danaus* (*a*), another Danaine, *D. chrysippus* (*d*) and a third Danaine, *Amauris* (*f*). Their imitators are the viceroy, *Limenitis* (*b*), one form of *Papilio dardanus* (*e*) and another form of *P. dardanus* (*g*). Mimicry is not a genus-wide phenomenon: *L. astyanax* (*c*), a relative of the viceroy, is nonmimetic. So is a third form of *P. dardanus* (*h*), whose cousins (*e, g*) mimic two of the Danaine models.

influencing the development of the other. In all probability the butterflies, which doubtless descended from the primarily nocturnal moths, owe their success largely to the decisive step of taking to daytime feeding. By virtue of their choice of food plants all butterflies are somewhat distasteful, and Charles L. Remington of Yale University has suggested that this is primarily what enabled them to establish themselves and flourish in the world of daylight. The butterflies and their larvae did not, of course, overwhelm the plant world; on the contrary, in company with the other herbivores they helped to accelerate the evolution of the plants into a great variety of new and more resistant forms.

From what little we know about the relationships between other herbivore groups and their associated plants, we can assume that the butterfly-plant association is typical of most herbivore-plant pairings. This information gives us an excellent starting point for understanding the phenomenon that we might call "communal evolution," or coevolution. It can help, for example, to account for the great diversity of plant and insect species in the Tropics compared with the much smaller number of species in the temperate zones. The abundance of plant-eating insects in the Tropics, interacting with the plants, unquestionably has been an important factor, perhaps the most important one, in promoting the species diversity of both plants and animals in those regions. Indeed, the interaction of plants and herbivores may be the primary mechanism responsible for generating the diversity of living forms in most of the earth's environ-

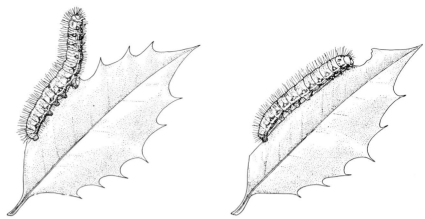

TOOTHED EDGE of the holly (*left*) normally protects it from leaf-edge eaters, such as the tent caterpillar. After the leaf's teeth are trimmed (*right*) the insect readily devours it.

ments.

Since the welfare, and even the survival, of mankind depend so heavily on the food supply and on finding ways to deal with insects without dangerous contamination of the environment with insecticides, great benefits might be derived from more intensive study of plant-herbivore associations. With detailed knowledge of these associations, plants can be bred for resistance to insects. Crop plants might be endowed with bred-in repellents, and strains of plants containing strong attractants for pests might be planted next to the crops to divert the insects and facilitate their destruction. New methods of eliminating insects without danger to man might be developed. Carroll M. Williams of Harvard University and his co-workers have discovered, for example, that substances analogous to the juvenile hormone of some insects are present in tissues of the American balsam fir. Since the juvenile

hormone acts to delay metamorphosis in insects, plants bred for such substances might be used to interfere with insect development. It is even possible that insects could be fought with tumor-inducing substances: at least one plant alkaloid, nicotine, is known to be a powerful carcinogen in vertebrates.

Such methods, together with techniques of biological control of insects already in use and under development, could greatly reduce the present reliance on hazardous insecticides. The insects have shown that they cannot be conquered permanently by the brand of chemical warfare we have been using up to now. After all, they had become battle-hardened from fighting the insecticide warfare of the plants for more than 100 million years. By learning from the plants and sharpening their natural weapons we should be able to find effective ways of poisoning our insect competitors without poisoning ourselves.

16

WEED CONTROL BY INSECT

JAMES K. HOLLOWAY
July 1957

For 30 years Klamath weed, a noxious plant imported from Europe, had infested the range lands of northern California. How it was brought under control by introducing its European insect enemies

For more than 400 years the mass migrations of man have been from east to west. In these migrations man has unintentionally brought with him many species of weeds, which may be defined as plants growing where they are not wanted. Such plants greatly increase the cost of crops and livestock by competing with useful plants, and their control has traditionally taxed human ingenuity. This is an account of how a troublesome alien plant was controlled by a novel device—the immigrant insect.

The plant *Hypericum perforatum* is a native of Europe, where it is commonly called St.-John's-wort because it blooms on or about June 24, the feast of Saint John the Baptist. St.-John's-wort is an erect, freely branching perennial herb with a stem one to five feet high. Its flowers are yellow and occur in clusters; its light green leaves are numerous and paired along the stem. Its root crown has many lateral runners which are capable of starting new plants; thus the spread of the plant is not entirely dependent on its seeds. These are produced in a pod which breaks into segments, releasing numerous small, cylindrical brown seeds which are spread by wind, water, man and animals.

St.-John's-wort was first reported in the U. S. in 1793 near Lancaster, Pa. By 1900 it had spread to California, where it was first reported in the northern part of the state around the Klamath River.

Thus the plant's common name—Klamath weed. (In some parts of the West it is referred to as goatweed.) In 1929 a survey showed that the pest had spread to some 19 counties in northern California and had occupied some 100,000 acres of previously useful range land. It was predicted that it might become one of the worst range-land weeds in the entire state.

By 1940 the infestation of the weed had increased: 27 counties reported it in an estimated 250,000 acres of range land. Wherever it grew land values depreciated. Improvement loans were no longer granted for ranches heavily infested; bankers felt that Klamath weed held the first mortgage.

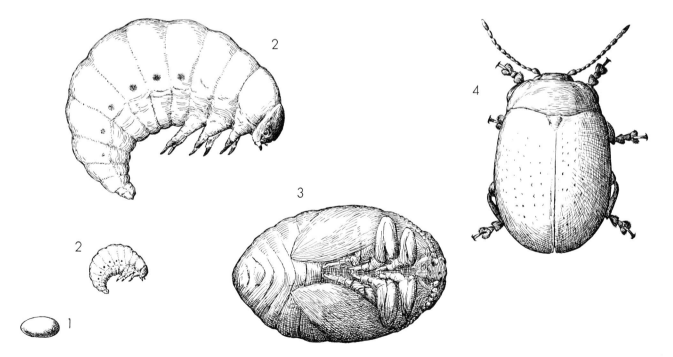

LEAF-EATING BEETLE *Chrysolina gemellata* was one of four insects introduced to control the Klamath weed. This drawing shows the four stages of its life cycle: egg (1), larva (2), pupa (3) and adult (4). The beetle was originally a native of France.

The weed not only competed with forage plants; it adversely affected the grazing animals which ate it. Cattle and sheep do not normally eat the plant, but in the late spring and early summer, when many of the food plants are dry or depleted, they will turn to Klamath weed. The plant has various effects on the animals, depending on the quantity they consume and the pigmentation of their skins. It contains an oil which, when it is ingested, sensitizes the white areas of the skin to light. The sensitized animal often suffers body sores, swollen ears and a sore muzzle. These afflictions do not kill the animal but reduce its weight and vigor, with obvious economic results for cattle- and sheepmen. The animals also become irritable, making them difficult to corral and transport.

How could the weed be controlled? Chemicals were out of the question: the range lands were too extensive and too inaccessible. For many years insects had been under consideration as a possible solution to the problem. As far back as 1920 the Commonwealth of Australia had begun to seek insect enemies of the weed. The search led to England and southern France, where it

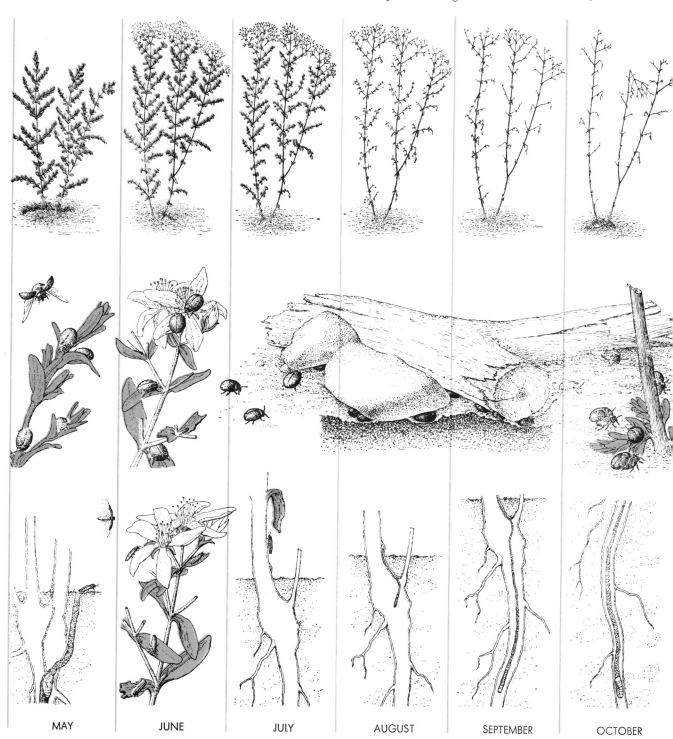

MAY   JUNE   JULY   AUGUST   SEPTEMBER   OCTOBER

LIFE CYCLES of Klamath weed (*top*), the leaf-eating beetle *C. gemellata* (*middle*) and the root borer *Agrilus hyperici* (*bottom*) are shown in this chart. In May and June the beetles, having emerged from their pupal cases in the ground, feed on the leaves of the weed. In July they go into their resting stage. In the fall they emerge again, mate and lay their eggs. When the larvae hatch from

was found that St.-John's-wort was attacked by two leaf-feeding beetles, a root borer and a gallfly. If these insects were established in Australia, would they also be destructive to useful plants? Before the step could be taken, a wide variety of plants were exposed to the insects under controlled conditions in both Europe and Australia. Finally the desirable insects were released in Australia,

and by 1944 encouraging results were reported.

When Harry S. Smith, then chairman of the Department of Biological Control at the University of California, heard of these results, he sought permission from the U. S. Department of Agriculture to introduce the beetles into California. The University was permitted to import two species of leaf-feeding beetles and

a root borer, with the proviso that it test six additional plants which had not been exposed to the insects in Europe or Australia. The University and the Department of Agriculture then set up a cooperative project to import, test and breed the insect species.

Because World War II was still in progress, the insects could not be obtained in Europe; they were thus im-

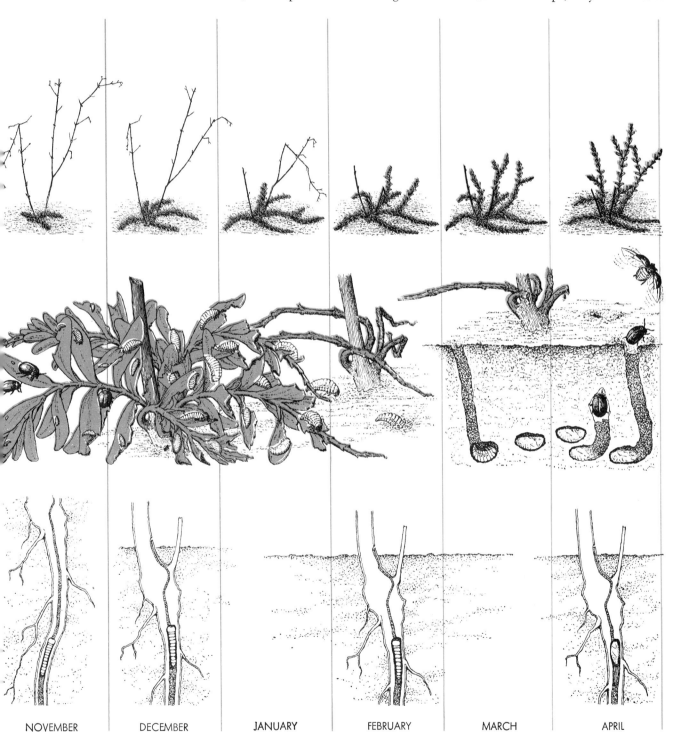

NOVEMBER   DECEMBER   JANUARY   FEBRUARY   MARCH   APRIL

the eggs, both they and the beetles feed on the low winter growth of the weed. Late in the winter the larvae burrow into the ground and metamorphose into pupae. The adult root borer emerges from the

taproot of the weed in May and feeds on its foliage. In July the adult lays its eggs. The larva which hatches out of the egg bores down through the root. Then it bores up and metamorphoses into a pupa.

KLAMATH WEED (*Hypericum perforatum*) is a perennial herb which grows one to five feet tall. Its flowers are yellow and edged with dots. In Europe it is known as St.-John's-wort.

ported from Australia. This created a curious problem: the life history of the insects was synchronized with the seasons of the Southern Hemisphere. The two species of leaf-feeding beetles arrived in November; they were then in their summer resting stage. For them to be in step with conditions in California required that they be in their egg-laying stage, which follows the resting stage. It was supposed that in their original habitat of France the beetles came out of the resting stage after fall and winter rains; on this theory they were sprayed with droplets of water. In a few hours they began to move about, to show interest in food and to mate. After they had been subjected to artificial rain twice a day for two weeks, the beetles began to produce fertile eggs. Their life histories were now synchronized with the seasons of the Northern Hemisphere.

The root borers were a more difficult problem. They were received as larvae in the taproots of St.-John's-wort, and they could not be induced to emerge. It was decided to curtail their further importation until after the war, when they could be sought in Europe.

Within a year after the beetles had been imported it was determined that they would feed and reproduce only on Klamath weed. The Department of Agriculture granted permission to release them in the field during 1945-46. This was the first attempt in North America to control a plant with plant-feeding insects. Both species established themselves readily, and by 1948 it was no longer necessary to import them. From two of the sites at which they had originally been released some 200,000 beetles were collected; these were transferred to locations in 16 counties.

The two beetle species are *Chrysolina hyperici* and *Chrysolina gemellata*. Both beetles are oval in shape and about a quarter of an inch in length; they have a metallic sheen and their color may be bronze, purple, blue or green. Within two years after they had been released it became apparent that, of the two, *C. gemellata* was multiplying much more rapidly. This species, a native of France, lays its eggs soon after the first fall rains. At that time the Klamath weed is at its most succulent; the larvae which hatch out of the eggs have time to complete their development while the plant is most suitable as food. Conditions are also favorable to prolonged egg-laying.

C. hyperici, a native of England, reacts more slowly to the fall rains. It does not start to lay eggs in abundance until

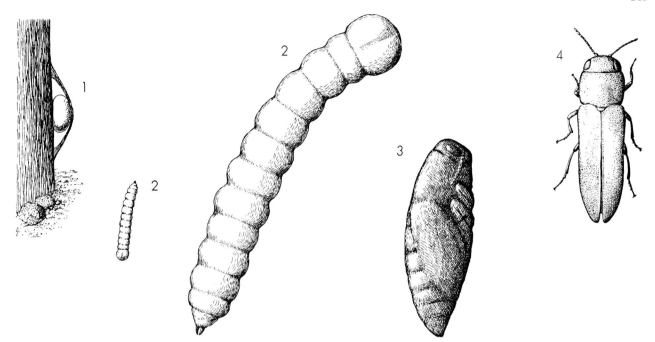

ROOT BORER *A. hyperici* is particularly useful because it bores in the roots of Klamath weed during the summer, when the leaf-eating beetles are in their resting stage. This drawing shows the four stages of the borer's life cycle: egg (1), larva (2), pupa (3) and adult (4).

there is too little time for a large proportion of its larvae to complete their development. The arrival of the dry season and its hard soils is unfavorable for the metamorphosis of the larvae into pupae.

The whole life history of *C. gemellata* is nicely synchronized with the growth phases of Klamath weed and climatic conditions in the important range areas of California. In April and early May the adult beetles issue from their pupal cells just beneath the surface of the soil. They feed voraciously on the foliage of the weeds, which are producing flower buds or are actually in flower. By the latter part of June and early July the beetles seclude themselves beneath stones, in debris or in crevices of the soil. When they find a comfortable refuge, they cease activity and go into a resting stage for the remainder of the summer. The plant, too, enters a dormant phase, dropping its leaves and becoming dry and woody.

When the fall rains begin, both weeds and beetles become active. The plants produce a low, trailing, leafy growth upon which the insects feed sparingly. Around mid-October the adults mate and begin to lay eggs; the eggs hatch into larvae. Because adults, eggs and larvae can survive relatively low temperatures, all three forms live together through the winter. By spring most of the eggs have hatched and the larvae are approaching maturity. The larvae completely destroy the trailing growth

of many plants. Early in the spring the plants which have escaped destruction develop upright shoots which are destined to become the flower-bearing stalks. At that time the larvae complete their feeding and enter the soil to a depth of about an inch, where they develop into pupae. This completes the one-year life cycle of the insect. The perennial plant has also gone through a complete growth cycle.

It was discovered that the adult beetles were very adept at finding new infestations of the weed. Their natural dispersion was greatly aided, however, by people who collected and distributed large quantities of them. The collecting program was organized with the cooperation of county agencies and the local press and radio. Ranchers and others interested in the destruction of Klamath weed met with the research staff on announced days in specified locations, and were given instructions on how to collect and pack the insects so that they could be moved to new localities.

The newly emerging beetles feed in voracious groups on the tops of the flowering stems. When they are disturbed, the beetles play dead and fall off the plant. The insects are easily collected by bending the heavily infested tops of the plants over a container. At first the collectors used containers of all kinds—automobile hubcaps, water buckets, paper cartons, hats. One woman was seen making her first catch in a tea strainer. Shortly after they are captured the beetles again become active and try to escape, but when the side of the container is given a sharp tap they again "drop dead." This makes it possible to collect large numbers of beetles before transferring them to a carton provided for transporting them to other locations. Fortunately the adult insects suffer no ill effects from being boxed in large masses; it is possible to transport them without much loss.

The containers most suitable for transferring the insects were round, half-gallon waterproofed paper cartons—the kind often used to pack ice cream. About one half to three quarters of a pint of beetles were placed in each carton; the remaining space was filled with Klamath weed. By providing this food supply every other day the beetles could be kept alive for two or three weeks. Beetles collected in the spring have not mated, and if they are distributed too thinly in their new location the probability that they will mate in the fall is decreased. The collectors were therefore advised to release 2,000 to 10,000 adult beetles in a circle not more than six feet in diameter. Where this recommendation was followed the beetles established themselves and produced flourishing populations. In the few instances where the advice was ignored and the beetles were spread thinly over a larger area, they became established, but their rate

SPHERICAL GALLS may be seen on the Klamath weed at the top. The gall develops when the larva of the gallfly enters the leaf bud of the weed. The photograph at the bottom shows two adult gallflies emerging from their pupal cases, which are held by the lips of the gall.

of increase was much slower; it took longer to control the weed.

Where the beetles wipe out the Klamath weed they must move on, because they will feed on nothing else. When they emerge in such an area in the spring, they take flight in search of food. They are capable of long, sustained flights. In the fall the beetles have not been seen to fly, but they disperse locally by crawling over the ground. They have remarkable ability to locate small and isolated patches of the weed. Individual beetles have been observed to travel more than a quarter of a mile in a month —visiting a plant, eating a little of it, depositing their eggs and moving on to the next plant. With man's help these natural modes of dispersion have spread the beetles to all areas in California where Klamath weed grows.

What about the root borer and the gallfly which the Australians had discovered would also attack the weed? They were not forgotten. At the end of World War II the root borer *Agrilus hyperici* and the gallfly *Zeuxidiplosis giardi* were imported to the U. S. from southern France.

The leaf-feeding beetle tends to avoid plants growing in the shade, but the root borer does not; thus the root borer may be used to supplement the work of the beetle. The root borer will efficiently attack Klamath weed found in feed lots, chicken yards and other locations where leaf-feeding larvae would be disturbed or eaten. It has proved to be effective in locating and destroying individual plants, as well as in completely reducing thick stands. The borer is a larva which gives rise to a beetle roughly the same size as the leaf feeders. This insect also has a metallic sheen but its color is mostly bronze.

Because the root borer attacks the roots and not the leaves of Klamath weed, it is not dependent on fall rains and the winter growth of the plant. Thus it is less important that the insect's life history be synchronized with the plant's growth phases. The root-borer beetles are active in June and July, when they feed on the leaves and flowers of Klamath weed. They place their eggs on the stem of the plant just above the surface of the ground. When the larvae hatch, they enter the plant immediately and burrow downward in either the main root or lateral roots. One or more larvae may be found in a root. In early fall they complete their downward feeding; then they move upward. By this time they are full grown. They remain all winter and spring in the taproot, from which they emerge as adults. The destruction of the root by the larvae kills the plant.

The natural spread of the root borer can be assisted by transplanting infested roots in the spring. This is best done after the spring rains have diminished, because the disturbed roots lose their capacity to repel water; when they are transplanted the unemerged insects may drown. Root-borer beetles may be collected by net, but this is difficult. The beetles are very active fliers; they are not found in bunches, and after they emerge they spread very rapidly.

The gallfly needs Klamath-weed foliage for most of the year, so it is less widely useful than the leaf feeder or root borer. Thus far gallflies have been most effective in localities which remain moist throughout the summer months. There the foliage of the weed remains luxuriant.

Depending upon the temperature and the availability of growing plants, the gallfly may give rise to several generations in a year. The adult fly deposits its eggs on the leaves and stems of the weed; the resulting larvae enter the leaf buds. There the larvae cause two opposite leaves to grow into a hollow spherical gall. The gall has two halves that meet in tightly compressed lips, which are exploited by the fly. When the pupa of the fly begins to emerge from its case within the gall, it wedges the case between the lips. The lips of the gall hold the case, permitting the adult to free itself completely. If the galls are injured in any way which keeps them from ap-

plying the proper pressure, the fly is not able to emerge successfully.

Because the adult gallfly is minute and fragile, it could not be successfully collected or transported in a container. The larvae, however, were successfully transported in the galls. The galls must not be allowed to dry out; the best way to prevent this is to transplant an infested plant. Another very successful way to distribute the insect is to place potted Klamath weeds among plants infested with galls; as soon as galls form on the potted plants, the pots are moved to new locations. Although it is difficult to spread the gallfly artificially, it has a very remarkable ability to migrate naturally. Gallflies released in one location have been found many miles away in a matter of two or three years.

The gallfly is most useful during the summer months, when the leaf-feeding beetles are inactive. It has a great capacity for rapidly increasing its numbers. The flies attack the weed by converting its leaf buds into galls; a heavy infestation of galls reduces the foliage, roots and vigor of the plant, impairing its ability to compete with other plants.

It is not necessary for insects to kill an entire stand of Klamath weed in order to control it. In most of the Western range lands the desirable forage plants are predominantly annuals. Klamath weed starts to grow in the fall, when the annual grasses germinate. It puts the annuals in the shade and competes with them for moisture and soil nutrients. Late in the spring, when the

upper six to 10 inches of soil tend to dry out, the growing plants must go deeper for water; often their roots go as deep as 36 inches. Here Klamath weed has the advantage because its roots can go deeper than those of the annual forage plants.

The competitive edge of Klamath weed is dulled by the leaf-eating beetles. By eating the leaves of the weed, the adult insects and larvae cut down the shade. When the larvae feed on the low winter leaves of the plant, they reduce the extent of its root system. Ultimately the root system goes no deeper than a foot, and the weed no longer has this advantage over the annual plants. Usually the weed cannot survive more than three years of such feeding by the beetles.

Thus the destruction of Klamath weed by the beetles has been attended by the return of desirable forage plants. In California many thousands of acres now have a markedly greater capacity for the support of livestock; land values have risen; expenditures for the control of the weed are negligible. Because stands of Klamath weed are no longer extensive and the infested areas are now widely separated, all of the immigrant insects, totally dependent on the weed for survival, have decreased in numbers. Fortunately their ability to locate new infestations and their high rate of reproduction have prevented any important resurgence of the weed. All indications are that this noxious range plant will be held in check and that its insect controls will perpetuate themselves.

EFFECT OF LEAF-EATING BEETLES is shown by this photograph of a field in northern California covered with Klamath weed. In the light area in the foreground the weed is in bloom; in the darker area in the background the beetles have killed the weed.

17

DESERT GROUND SQUIRRELS

GEORGE A. BARTHOLOMEW AND JACK W. HUDSON

November 1961

Two little animals of the Mohave Desert have evolved remarkable adaptations to heat and aridity. Each has adapted in its own way, which apparently enables them to live together without competing

Among the handful of animals that inhabit the hot, dry and sparsely vegetated Mohave Desert of California are two species of ground squirrel: the antelope ground squirrel and the mohave ground squirrel. Both species live in burrows, both are active and aboveground during the day and both feed on the small amount of plant life that is available.

This is an uncommon situation in nature. Species as closely related as these two, and as much alike in their food and habitat requirements, seldom live together even in more favorable environments. In his *Origin of Species* Charles Darwin suggested the reason. "As the species of the same genus usually have ...much similarity in habits and constitution, and always in structure," he wrote, "the struggle will generally be more severe between them, if they come into competition with each other, than between the species of distinct genera." Implicit in Darwin's statement is a concept now fundamental to biology. It is known as the principle of competitive exclusion and it says, in brief, that two noninterbreeding populations that stand in precisely the same relationship to their environment cannot occupy the same territory indefinitely. They cannot, in other words, live in "sympatry" forever. Sooner or later one will displace the other.

Such a displacement could be under way in the Mohave Desert right now. The mohave ground squirrel may well be a species in the process of extinction. Not only does it have a smaller total population and a narrower geographical distribution than the antelope ground squirrel (which is one of the commonest ground squirrels of the southwestern U.S.); it also appears to be less numerous in the small section of the Mohave Desert to which it is restricted. But since no historical information is available on the population trends of the two animals, there is no way of knowing exactly what the present difference in their number portends.

In any case the mohave ground squirrel is not as yet extinct. This raises a number of intriguing questions. Do the two species have the same way of life and the same relationship to their environment? If so, the competition between them must be severe. Or are there differences in their adaptation to their common environment? If there are, do these differences reduce competition between them sufficiently to permit them, at least temporarily, a period of peaceful coexistence?

These questions become more intriguing when one considers the nature of the desert environment. Aridity and heat make particularly severe demands on animals, and animals that live in deserts must be equipped with special physiological and behavioral adaptations to meet these demands. The camel, for example, withstands aridity because it can tolerate a high degree of dehydration, can restore its body fluids quickly and can travel long distances in search of water and succulent vegetation. It withstands heat through its tolerance of a wide range of body temperatures and

ANTELOPE GROUND SQUIRREL is found in the Mohave Desert and throughout the southwestern U.S. It is active during the day all year round, in spite of extremes of heat and aridity. Both of these photographs were made in the laboratory by Jack W. Hudson.

MOHAVE GROUND SQUIRREL is found only in one corner of the Mohave Desert. It is active during the day from March to August but remains in its burrow the rest of the year. Before retiring underground it becomes very fat, as this photograph shows.

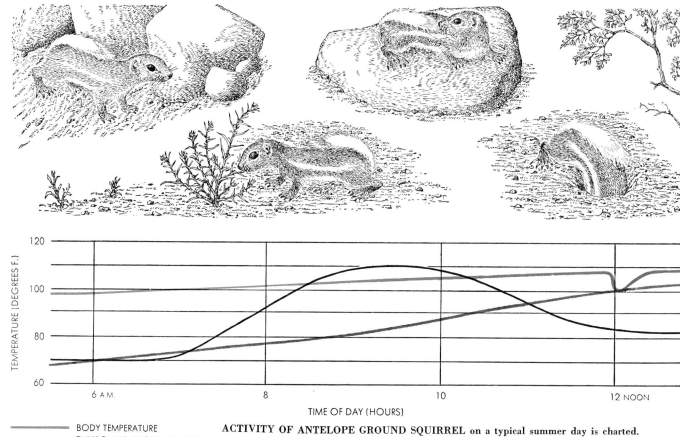

ACTIVITY OF ANTELOPE GROUND SQUIRREL on a typical summer day is charted. On emerging from its burrow animal runs to feeding area. Then it suns and grooms itself. When its body temperature rises too high, it goes to a special retreat burrow to cool

─────── BODY TEMPERATURE
▬▬▬▬▬ ENVIRONMENTAL TEMPERATURE
━━━━━━ LEVEL OF ACTIVITY

through the insulating qualities of its coat [see "The Physiology of the Camel," by Knut Schmidt-Nielsen; SCIENTIFIC AMERICAN Offprint 1096]. The desert rat of the U.S. Southwest has adapted equally well but in quite different ways. To combat aridity it conserves its body water; the desert rat's kidney is so efficient that it uses only about a fourth of the amount of water that the human kidney requires to excrete the same amount of urea. This adaptation enables the animal to meet a substantial fraction of

its water needs by the oxidation of foodstuff, as opposed to drinking. The desert rat deals with heat by avoiding it: the animal remains in its burrow during the daylight hours, emerging only at night, when the air and soil are cool [see "The Desert Rat," by Knut and Bodil Schmidt-Nielsen; SCIENTIFIC AMERICAN Offprint 1050].

Like the desert rat, most small, burrowing desert rodents are nocturnal. But both the mohave ground squirrel and the antelope ground squirrel are diurnal.

They emerge from their burrows near sunrise and forage outdoors throughout the day. They do so even in summer, when the air temperature may reach 110 degrees Fahrenheit or higher, and when the surface temperature of the soil may rise above 150 degrees F. Since the desert is as arid as it is hot, they must sustain their exposure to heat with a minimum loss of water for evaporative cooling.

In appearance and temperament the antelope ground squirrel resembles the

RETREAT BURROW OF ANTELOPE GROUND SQUIRREL is shown at right in this drawing. It is usually dug in soft soil close to desert vegetation and is about one foot deep and 12 to 15 feet long. The animal seems to use this burrow to unload body heat

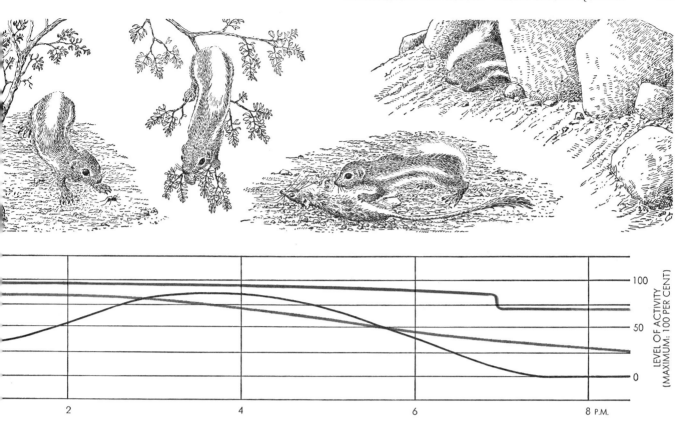

off. In early afternoon it stays in the shade. Before retiring to its home burrow it returns to feeding area, and at any time may catch insects or feed on dead animals. On the graph, dip in body tem-

perature is shown only at noon. But dips occur often, whenever animal goes underground to unload heat. At all other times its temperature is a few degrees above the environmental temperature.

chipmunk. Its body is about six inches long; its weight is about 90 grams. It has two white stripes down its grayish-brown back. It carries its tail high, exposing a white rump; this suggests the appearance of the pronghorn antelope, for which it is named. An extraordinarily active and high-strung animal, the antelope ground squirrel is constantly in motion, dashing from place to place, often traveling hundreds of feet from its home burrow. That it can maintain such hyperactivity even in soaring tempera-

tures is in itself evidence of unusual adaptive mechanisms.

For every animal the ability to adapt to external temperatures depends on two internal factors: the range of body temperatures in which it can function effectively and the rate at which it can produce body heat. Below a lower critical environmental temperature the body loses so much heat that internal temperature can be maintained only if the animal can step up its production of body heat sufficiently. Above an upper critical

environmental temperature the body retains so much metabolic heat that internal temperature can be held within the required range only if the animal can get rid of heat, in most cases by evaporative cooling; that is, by sweating or panting at a sufficient rate. Between the upper and lower critical temperatures—in the thermal neutral zone—an animal can maintain its optimum body temperature without having either to increase its metabolic rate or to lose body water. Such stratagems as contracting or dilat-

and to store food, but not as a living place; the dens in the burrow contain neither nests nor fecal matter. The antelope ground squir-

rel's living burrows have not been excavated. They are probably dug under rocky buttes, like that seen at left side of drawing.

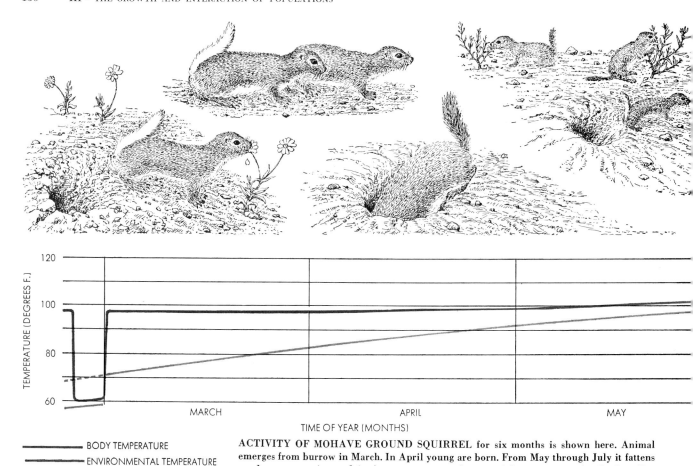

ACTIVITY OF MOHAVE GROUND SQUIRREL for six months is shown here. Animal emerges from burrow in March. In April young are born. From May through July it fattens on desert vegetation and in August returns underground for seven months. Broken line

ing cutaneous blood vessels and depressing or raising hair or feathers allow the animal to function at a minimum cost of energy for temperature maintenance.

In terms of this analysis of the adjustment of body temperature to environmental temperature, the adaptation of the antelope ground squirrel is admirable. It has a broad thermal neutral zone and one that accommodates to high environmental temperatures. Between environmental temperatures of 90 and 107 degrees F. its metabolic rate remains virtually constant. No other nonsweating mammal has a thermal neutral zone extending so high [see illustration on page 152].

Unlike man, the antelope ground squirrel can tolerate a high body temperature; in other words, it can "run a fever" without debility. It can therefore permit its temperature to rise with the temperature of the environment. Like the camel, it can store heat, and it does not have to dispose of heat until its body temperature reaches an extreme point. The antelope ground squirrel shows no serious discomfort even when its body temperature goes above 110 degrees. Throughout the thermal neutral zone it runs a temperature a few degrees above that of the environment [see top illustration on pages 148 and 149]. Instead of expending energy to cool itself and thereby adding to its heat load—as man must do—this animal actually disposes of a portion of its metabolic heat to the lower-temperature environment by

LIVING BURROW OF MOHAVE GROUND SQUIRREL is seen here at various stages and times of year. Burrow is dug in soft sand near the desert plants the animal eats. It is about 18 feet long and three feet deep. First panel shows burrow in early spring,

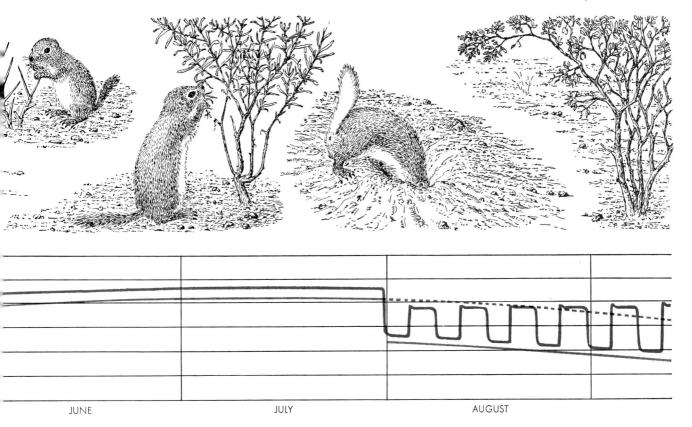

JUNE   JULY   AUGUST

on graph is desert air temperature when animal is in burrow. Gray line under it is burrow temperature then. Rise and fall of animal's temperature in August corresponds to its periods of wakefulness and torpor. Body temperature is always higher than environmental temperature, although when animal is active its temperature fluctuates sharply. A mean body temperature is shown here.

conduction, convection and radiation.

But environmental temperatures in the desert are commonly far higher than tissues can tolerate, and small animals heat up rapidly. The antelope ground squirrel must therefore unload some of its accumulated body heat at intervals during the day. It does this either by flattening itself against the soil in a shaded area or by retreating underground to its burrow. When its body temperature gets dangerously high, it has only to return to the relative coolness of its burrow and remain quiet for a few minutes until its fever has subsided. In our laboratory at the University of California at Los Angeles, antelope ground squirrels have lowered their body temperature from above 107 degrees to about 100 degrees within three minutes after being transferred from an environmental temperature of 104 degrees to one of 77 degrees.

The antelope ground squirrel contends with heat in still another way. Under protracted heat stress it will begin to drool. The animal then systematically spreads the saliva over its cheeks and head with its forepaws as though it were grooming itself. On very hot days, when it has had to tolerate air temperatures of 104 degrees or more for several hours, the antelope ground squirrel may be soaking wet around the head.

Drooling, with its high cost in water losses, is a last resort. But even when the temperature is not extreme, the antelope ground squirrel loses a considerable amount of body water. At 100

when animal emerges. Second shows animal digging new burrow. Third shows it closing burrow in August before retiring underground. In last panel it is winter and animal is torpid. Periods of torpor probably last longer in winter months than in summer.

degrees, long before it has begun to drool, this hyperactive animal gives up water equal to 10 per cent of its body weight in respiration and evaporation through its skin in the course of a day. This is 15 per cent of its total body water. Fortunately the animal withstands dehydration well. Although it gives up three times more water every day than it can extract from its food by oxidation, it can survive from three to five weeks on a completely dry diet. If the antelope ground squirrel is to maintain itself in a healthy state, however, it must find sources of preformed water. It is therefore hardly surprising that the animal is omnivorous, eating insects as well as desert vegetation. When it is seen on the highways, as it often is, it is probably feeding on the corpse of some animal, perhaps another of its species that has been hit by a car.

The antelope ground squirrel is able to stretch its scanty water supply because, like the desert rat, it loses a minimal amount of water in the excretion of nitrogenous wastes. On a dry diet this animal can produce urine with a mean concentration of 3,700 milliosmols (the

maximum concentration of human urine is about 1,300 milliosmols). The urine of the desert rat is somewhat more concentrated. But the antelope ground squirrel's urine is still 10 times more concentrated than its body fluids. Its ability to turn salty water to physiological use is even more impressive. The desert rat can maintain itself on sea water; the antelope ground squirrel can drink water approximately 1.4 times saltier than sea water and still remain in good health. No other mammal can process water of such high salinity. This capacity is important in the desert, where the little surface water that is available is usually highly mineralized.

The structure of the animal's kidney explains its efficient use of water. As in several other desert mammals, the renal papilla—that part of the kidney which contains the ascending and descending kidney tubules—of the antelope ground squirrel is extremely large, extending as far down as the ureter [see illustration on page 153]. In the formation of urine the kidney first extracts a filtrate containing all the constituents of blood except proteins and blood cells. This filtrate

is then converted to urine by the selective reabsorption of water and essential solutes in the kidney tubules. The longer the tubules, the greater the amount of water they can absorb and the greater the amount the body retains. As the antelope ground squirrel's tolerance for high body temperatures constitutes its major physiological adaptation to heat, so the efficiency of its kidney embodies its major adaptation to aridity.

Considering the success with which the antelope ground squirrel occupies its narrow desert niche, how does the mohave ground squirrel manage to find a place beside it? The question cannot be fully answered, because less is known about the life history of the mohave ground squirrel. This in itself is significant, because it appears that the mohave ground squirrel manages to persist largely by staying out of the way of the antelope ground squirrel.

Of the two animals the mohave ground squirrel is the bigger and fatter, and it has the temperament that goes with its more generous proportions. Its body length is about six and a half

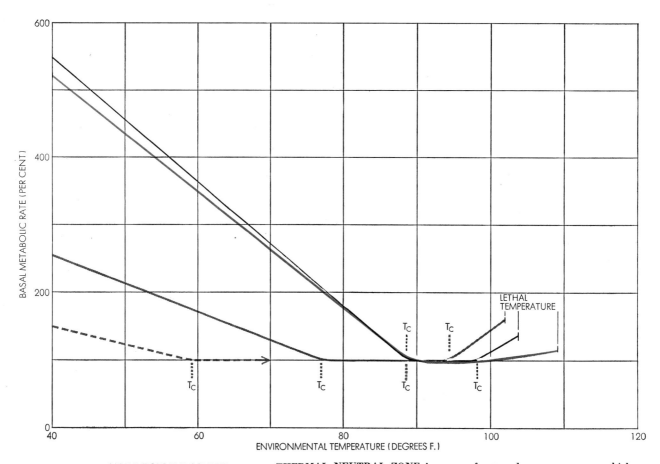

THERMAL NEUTRAL ZONE is range of external temperatures to which an animal is best adjusted. In it body temperature and metabolism can be held at optimum levels. At critical temperatures (T_C) metabolic rate begins to rise. Lemming is an arctic rodent. Kangaroo rat and ground squirrels are desert dwellers.

inches; its weight in its natural habitat, about 150 grams. In temperament it is placid, docile and sedentary. This little brown animal seldom wanders far from its home burrow, which it digs in loose sand, generally in the shade of the desert plants that provide it with its food. For more than half the year, from August to March, it remains in its burrow. During the spring months, when the desert vegetation is at its annual peak, the mohave ground squirrel emerges to reproduce and to fatten itself in preparation for its return underground.

The major proportion of the mohave ground squirrel's life is therefore normally concealed from observation. Fortunately it seems to show a comparable pattern of behavior in the laboratory. Here, as in its natural habitat, the animal is active throughout the day from March to August. During the remainder of the year, however, even at room temperature, and in spite of the continuous availability of food and water, it is intermittently torpid for periods lasting from several hours to several days. If food and water are at hand, it will eat and drink in its periods of wakefulness. If they are not, it does not seem to be disturbed. We do not know whether or not in its natural habitat it stores food in its burrow. We do know that it is usually thin in early spring, when it emerges from its burrow, and that it can add as much as 100 grams to its body weight in the period before its retirement underground. We also know that in the laboratory, where the animal becomes exceedingly fat, it loses an appreciable amount of weight during its period of dormancy only if no food and water have been made available to it.

Since this pattern of intermittent dormancy extends from late summer to early spring, it involves what would normally be considered two separate processes—hibernation and the summer dormancy called estivation. Our studies indicate, however, that in the mohave ground squirrel the two processes are merely aspects of the same physiological phenomenon. From early August to the end of February, whether the temperature in the laboratory is one that would normally be associated with estivation or whether it is one at which hibernation would be expected to occur, the same events take place. As the animal becomes torpid, its oxygen consumption and its body temperature drop sharply. Then both level off, and the body temperature stabilizes at the environmental temperature or very slightly above it. During the time the animal is dormant its torpor is more pronounced than

deep sleep, its breathing is suspended for long periods and its heart rate is profoundly reduced. On arousal it restores its body temperature to normal through increases in breathing movements, acceleration of heartbeat, shivering (which releases heat) and increased oxygen consumption. In the laboratory arousal may come about spontaneously or it may be induced by a touch or a sound. In either event it is extremely rapid. Although the animal can take as long as six hours to enter torpor, it can wake in less than one hour. Oxygen consumption can reach its peak in 15 to 20 minutes, and body temperature can rise from 68 to 86 degrees in 20 to 35 minutes.

Such rapid alterations in temperature do not occur during the five-month period in which the mohave ground squirrel is active. Even then, however, its body temperature is remarkably variable and fluctuates over a broad range. We have measured a deep-body temperature as low as 88 degrees in individual animals engaged in normal activity, and yet the animal does not seem to suffer any ill effects from body temperatures as high as 107 degrees. Its thermal neutral zone does not, however, extend as high as that of the antelope ground squirrel. The metabolism of the mohave ground squirrel begins to rise at an environmental temperature of about 98 degrees. Its tolerance for high body temperatures is of major adaptive value in June and July, when the desert is particularly hot.

Obviously the mohave ground squirrel's dormancy serves the function traditionally associated with hibernation: it conserves energy. At an environmental temperature of 68 degrees the oxygen consumption of a dormant mohave ground squirrel is only about a tenth that of the same animal active at the same temperature. Fat is undoubtedly the major energy source. Since the oxidation

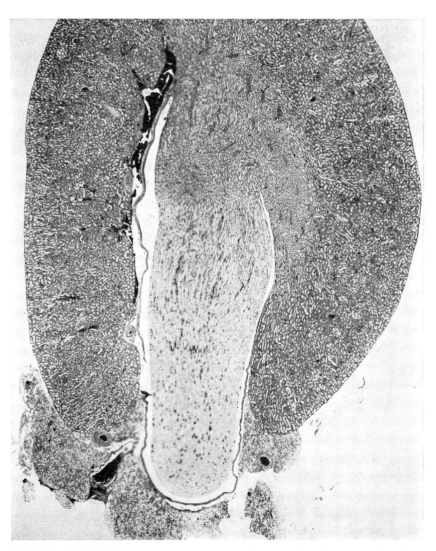

SECTION OF KIDNEY of antelope ground squirrel is magnified 20 times in this micrograph by Hudson. Mass outlined in white is papilla, containing renal tubules. In this species it is very large. This permits reabsorption of much water and production of concentrated urine.

of one gram of fat requires two liters of oxygen, a simple calculation shows that a torpid squirrel, weighing 300 grams and consuming oxygen at a rate of .08 cubic centimeter per gram per hour, will burn .29 gram of fat a day. Some 50 grams of fat would therefore supply it with all its energy requirements for 172 days; this is just half the fat supply it usually accumulates in the active months of the year. According to this calculation a mohave ground squirrel should be able to remain torpid for a whole year if it did not arouse at all. We do not know, of course, how much its energy requirements are increased by periods of arousal during the months of dormancy. Not being able to observe the animals in their burrows, we do not know how long these periods last. But from laboratory evidence we deduce that the cycles of torpor and wakefulness are repeated every week, with three to five days spent in torpor. The mohave ground squirrel should therefore be able to get along on its accumulated fat.

Energy conservation is not the only function that dormancy serves. Like the antelope ground squirrel, the mohave ground squirrel loses considerable body water in evaporative cooling and, like the antelope ground squirrel, it must have preformed water in its food. The sedentary mohave ground squirrel does not go in search of water; it gets its water almost entirely from the desert plants it eats. During the period the animal is underground this vegetation is in decline and the desert is at its driest. Thus dormancy is an important adaptation to seasonal aridity.

The mohave ground squirrel's seven months of estivation and hibernation serves still another function: it minimizes competition with the more active and abundant antelope ground squirrel. During the time the mohave ground squirrel is aboveground the food and water available are probably adequate to sustain both animals. But during its months of dormancy both food and water are in short supply.

The two animals have adapted well to desert life—the antelope ground squirrel by its tolerance for high body temperatures and the efficiency of its kidney, and the mohave ground squirrel by its avoidance underground of the most rigorous months of the year. One may conclude that these adaptations are sufficiently different to permit the two animals to live in sympatry in spite of Darwin's stern injunction.

18

ECOLOGICAL CHEMISTRY

LINCOLN PIERSON BROWER

February 1969

Certain insects feed on plants that make substances that are poisonous to vertebrates. Hence the insects are unpalatable to bird predators. These relations have surprising results

Many plants synthesize chemical compounds that apparently serve no purpose in the plant's metabolism. Some of these compounds are quite complex, and even if they were simple it would be puzzling that the plant should make them; the synthesis calls for a considerable expenditure of energy. Why, then, does the plant manufacture these substances? One reasonable explanation is that they promote the survival of the plant either by repressing the growth of competing plants and parasitic microorganisms or by repelling insects or other animals that would otherwise feed on it.

There is reason to believe this is only part of the story of the secondary substances made by plants. My colleagues and I (at Amherst College, the University of Oxford and the University of Basel) find evidence that such substances can play a much subtler role in a community of interacting plants and animals. For example, certain plants manufacture compounds that are poisonous to vertebrates, but certain insects are able to feed on the plants. An insect that feeds on such a plant ingests the poison and is therefore unpalatable to vertebrate predators. Moreover, an insect that does not feed on the plant can mimic the appearance of the insect that does, and is thus avoided by predators even though it is palatable. In the light of such relationships one begins to perceive that the study of secondary substances can be characterized as ecological chemistry.

A striking instance of the effectiveness of the secondary substances in repelling animals is provided in Costa Rica by the milkweed *Asclepias curassavica*. In the province of Guanacaste large herds of cattle completely avoid the plant even though it grows abundantly in the grass. The cattle do so with good

reason: this plant and others belonging to the large family Asclepiadaceae often cause sickness in livestock and occasionally death.

The poisons in the asclepiads have attracted much attention among pharmacologists and organic chemists because the substances are chemically similar to the drug digitalis; they share with it the remarkable property of having a highly specific effect on the vertebrate heart. These drugs, called cardiac glycosides or cardenolides, cause a weak and rapidly fluttering heart to beat more strongly and more slowly. Like most other drugs, cardiac glycosides produce side effects. One of profound importance is the activation of the nerve center in the brain that controls vomiting. Pharmacologists working with cats and pigeons have found that the dosage necessary to cause emesis is just about half the amount required to cause death. Hence an animal that eats a food containing cardiac glycosides will, provided that it is capable of vomiting, rid itself of the poisons before a lethal amount can be absorbed. In other words, although the animal suffers a very unpleasant gastronomic experience, vomiting protects it from being killed by the poisonous food.

In contrast to the animals that are made ill by eating milkweeds containing cardiac glycosides are the animals that eat the plants with no apparent adverse effects. For example, milkweeds are the exclusive food of the larvae of an entire group of tropical insects: the Danainae, which includes the familiar monarch and

queen butterflies. Naturalists have observed for more than a century that insect-eating vertebrates, particularly birds, avoid these butterflies. A widely accepted hypothesis has been that the predators avoid the butterflies because the larvae have assimilated the poisonous substances from the milkweeds. The implications of this hypothesis are most interesting: the Danaine butterflies not only must have developed the ability to feed on the poisonous milkweeds but also apparently are able to use the poisonous substances against their predators.

We undertook to test this hypothesis with a threefold approach. First, our group at Amherst reared a large number of monarchs on *Asclepias curassavica*, and John Parsons of Oxford subjected them to a series of pharmacological tests. Assaying extracts of the butterflies, he found that they contained cardiac glycosides similar to digitalis in their effects. Second, with new facilities at Amherst we were able to rear some two pounds of monarchs (1,540 butterflies) on *A. curassavica*, and Tadeus Reichstein of the University of Basel chemically analyzed both the butterflies and the plants. His results showed that the plant and the butterfly contain at least three cardiac glycosides that are identical. They are calactin, calotropin and calotoxin [see *bottom illustration on page 161*].

In the course of rearing the butterflies and plants for chemical analysis we had begun our third line of attack. By selec-

REACTION OF BLUE JAY to palatable and unpalatable monarch butterflies appears in the photographs on the following page. At top the jay attacks a palatable butterfly (1), eats it (2), and later eats another monarch (3). When the same jay is presented (4) with a monarch that is unpalatable because it fed on poisonous milkweed at the larval stage, the bird eats only part of it (5) and then reacts (6). Soon it vomits (7), and after drinking water it vomits again (8). It soon recovers (9) but rejects subsequent monarchs on sight.

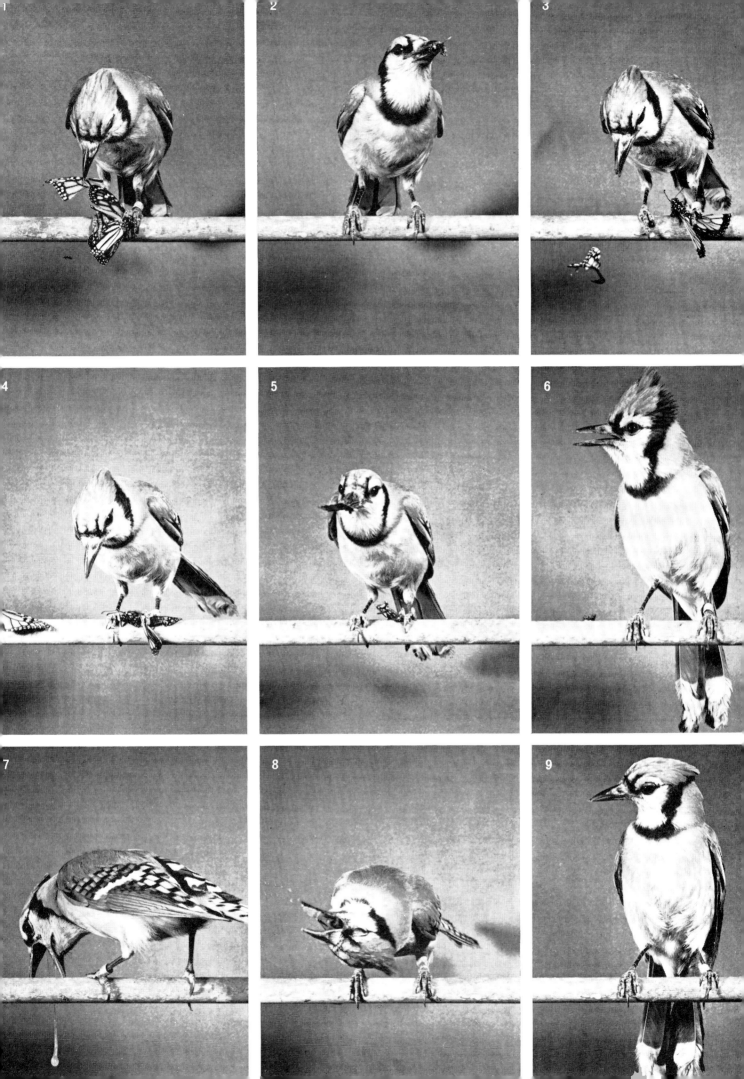

tive breeding we obtained a strain of monarch butterflies that could develop on cabbage, a plant known to lack cardiac glycosides. Our assumption was that cabbage-reared monarchs would prove acceptable to our test birds, which were blue jays captured locally. At first all our blue jays were extremely reluctant to attack the monarchs. We found, however, that if we deprived the jays of food for several hours, they would become hungry enough to attack and eat the butterflies. Once the jays had been induced to try the monarchs they would accept them readily whenever we offered them and would devour them with no signs of sickness.

Having broken down the initial reluctance of the blue jays, we then offered them monarchs reared on *A. curassavica*. Most of the birds promptly ate at least one butterfly. Within 12 minutes, on the average, every bird became violently ill, vomiting the ingested material and continuing to vomit as many as nine times over a half-hour period. All the birds recovered fully within about half an hour.

In preparation for our feeding experiments we had also cultivated several other milkweed plants in our greenhouse. Much to our surprise, one species from the tropical Western Hemisphere, *Gonolobus rostratus*, produced monarch adults that were as acceptable to birds as the cabbage-reared butterflies were. As the reader can readily imagine, we were delighted when Reichstein analyzed our *Gonolobus* plants and found that they completely lack cardiac glycosides. These findings showed clearly that the palatability of the monarch butterfly is directly related to the kind of plant eaten by the larvae: if the plant contains cardiac glycosides, the adult butterflies also contain them, and if the plant lacks the poisons, the butterflies also lack them.

The next question we asked was: Is there a spectrum of palatability in monarch butterflies that is dependent on the particular plants the larvae eat? To investigate the matter we first determined which species of milkweed produce emetic butterflies. Our technique was to induce the birds to eat the nonemetic butterflies reared on *Gonolobus* and then to offer them butterflies reared on a variety of other milkweeds. So far we have found that three species of *Asclepias* common in eastern North America produce palatable butterflies, whereas two milkweeds from the southeastern U.S. produce emetic ones. In addition we have discovered that monarchs

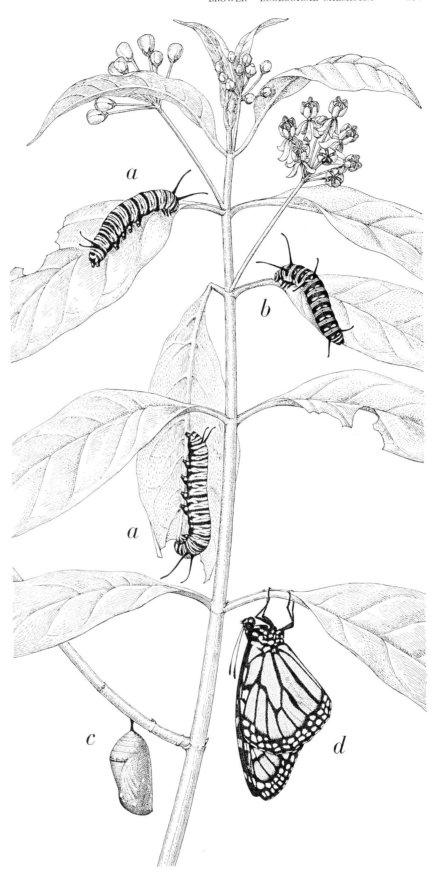

ECOLOGICAL SETTING of the plant-butterfly-bird relationship includes the milkweed *Asclepias curassavica* and the larval stage of such butterflies as the monarch (*a*) and the queen (*b*). The plant produces substances called cardiac glycosides, which have a strong effect on the vertebrate heart. Larvae assimilate the substances, which are retained by adults, so that an adult monarch (*d*) is unpalatable to birds. At *c* is a monarch butterfly chrysalis.

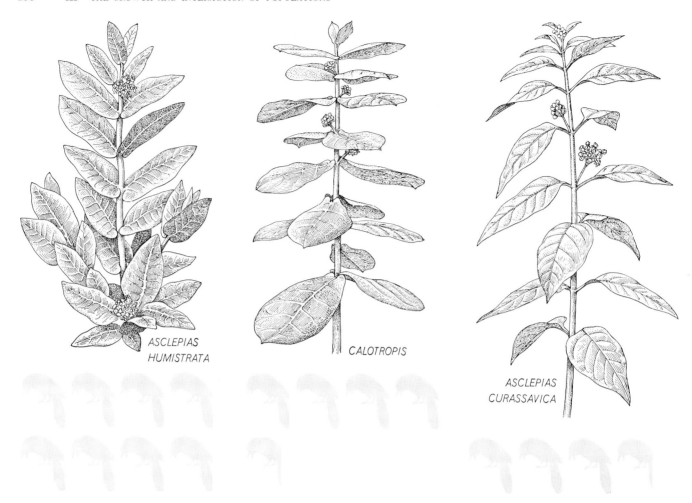

ASCLEPIAS
HUMISTRATA

CALOTROPIS

ASCLEPIAS
CURASSAVICA

RELATIVE TOXICITY of several milkweeds and of monarch butterflies raised on them is expressed in terms of blue jay emetic
units. The units represent the number of blue jays that will be
made ill by the poisons in one monarch butterfly raised on a given

reared on two African milkweeds belonging to the genera *Calotropis* and
Gomphocarpus are emetic.

Having established this emetic series,
William N. Ryerson (who is now at Yale
University) and I developed a new method for comparing the degree of toxicity
of the monarchs reared on the various
plants. The technique consists in drying
adult butterflies and grinding them to a
fine powder, which we load into gelatin

capsules that are force-fed to the birds.
In this way we could determine the precise dosage of butterfly needed to cause
emesis. Then, on the basis of the average
weight of both monarch butterflies and
blue jays, we calculated the number of
blue jay emetic units per monarch butterfly [*see top illustration on this page*].
The experiments showed that a monarch that has eaten *Asclepias humistrata*
contains enough poison to make approxi-

mately eight blue jays vomit; a butterfly
reared on *Calotropis procera* contains
4.8 blue jay emetic units; one that has
eaten *A. curassavica*, 3.8 units, and one
that has eaten *Gomphocarpus*, .8 unit.
In other words, there is a palatability
spectrum, and the most unpalatable butterfly is at least 10 times as emetic as the
most palatable one. Since the genus *Asclepias* consists of 108 known species in
North America alone, and there are

GOURMAND-GOURMET HYPOTHESIS put forward by the author holds that a bird can reject a poisonous insect at three physiological levels. To a naïve bird (*a*) flavor conveys no particular
information, so that the bird will eat any food it finds and is a
gourmand. When a bird is made ill by an insect, it associates the fla-

vor of the insect with the illness and thereafter can reject a similar
insect by tasting it (*b*), so that the bird becomes something of a
gourmet. At that level, however, the bird must still take the time
to catch the insect. Hence birds usually learn to reject such insects
on sight (*c*), which is the most efficient level of rejection.

GOMPHOCARPUS

GONOLOBUS

plant. For example, a single butterfly raised on milkweed *Asclepias humistrata* contains enough cardiac glycosides to cause emesis in eight blue jays (*left*). *Gonolobus* is nonemetic.

can it probably associate the taste of the food with the noxious effects. Initially a gourmand, the animal becomes by conditioning a gourmet, and for the rest of its life the taste signals in its food convey relevant information. Once conditioned in this way the animal will exercise judgment in assessing the taste of potential food items.

A plant-eating animal or a prey-catching one will always be confronted with a wide potential of food items in its natural environment. In terms of our blue jay–monarch butterfly system it is important to realize that the bird has three levels at which it can reject a poisonous butterfly. The most basic level is the automatic gastronomic rejection brought on by the emetic effect of the cardiac glycoside. Clearly this is the least efficient form of rejection, since the bird not only is made sick but also loses any food that was in its crop before it ate the poisonous insect. Once the bird has suffered this noxious primary experience and has learned to avoid food with the particular flavor, it can reject the same type of butterfly merely by tasting it. This is the second level of rejection. It too is rather inefficient, because if it is to operate, the bird must first catch the butterfly. The most efficient level of rejection is provided by the capacity to associate the visual characteristics of the food with its unpalatability, since the bird then need neither get sick nor even waste time catching the insect in order to determine its flavor.

The fact that many naturally occurring plant poisons, including alkaloids and cardiac glycosides, are bitter is highly relevant. The poison itself could very well be tasteless, provided that it was always associated with a flavor that could serve as a cue for conditioning predators. These considerations raise the possibility that certain plants and prey animals have flavors usually associated with particular poisons but actually lack the poisons. They would thus be exhibiting a form of mimicry.

Mimicry in insects usually refers, of course, to the imitation by one species of the distinctive coloration of another species. One can see how natural selection favored the evolution of distinctive coloring in unpalatable species, because the coloration operates as a cue that reminds the predator of its earlier unpleasant experience. The warning coloration is of advantage to both prey and predator: the prey is less frequently attacked, and the predator can hunt more efficiently because it does not need to waste time catching unpalatable insects.

several other genera of milkweed on the continent, it seems likely that the spectrum of palatability is very wide indeed.

Moreover, we have here an ecologically important criterion for measuring the palatability of food to wild animals. Clearly a butterfly is unsuitable food if it causes emesis, but if it carries less than an emetic dosage, it could serve as an emergency ration during periods of food shortage, provided that the birds ate successive individuals at a sufficiently slow rate. Measuring palatability by the criterion of emesis not only is more objective than many of the vague concepts of palatability that are so often discussed in the technical literature of biology but also provides insight into the kinds of problems that confront wild animals in their quest for food.

I have mentioned that most of the blue jays we trained to eat the nonemetic butterflies subsequently ate without hesitation the first highly emetic one we gave them. After recovering from their bout of vomiting the birds usually rejected all subsequent monarchs on sight

alone. By again depriving the jays of food, however, we were able to induce them to attack another nonemetic monarch. Now instead of swallowing the butterfly rapidly a bird would peck it apart, manipulate the mangled pieces in its bill and often regurgitate pieces several times before finally swallowing them.

This behavior has led us to propose a new way of looking at the biological significance of taste; we call it "the gourmand-gourmet hypothesis." According to this hypothesis items of food in the natural environment have a variety of flavors that in themselves convey no relevant information to a vertebrate animal eating the food for the first time. Hence the naïve animal will initially accept a wide range of food. If the animal eats the food and then vomits, however, it will associate the taste signals present in the food as it is expelled through the mouth with the noxious experience of the entire emesis syndrome. In other words, just as an animal can learn to associate an unpleasant experience with the color pattern of a food item and subsequently to reject the food on sight, so

160

LIMENITIS ARTHEMIS   LIMENITIS ARCHIPPUS   DANAUS PLEXIPPUS

BATESIAN MIMICRY, named for the 19th-century English naturalist Henry W. Bates, arises when a palatable insect comes to look like an unpalatable one, thereby sharing the unpalatable one's ca-

pacity to repel predators. An example is the North American butterfly *Limenitis.* From its original form (*left*) it has evolved a form (*center*) that mimics the monarch butterfly *Danaus* (*right*).

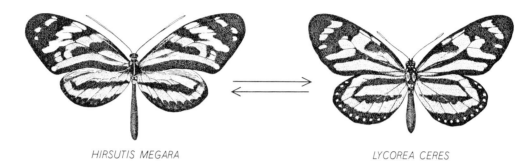

HIRSUTIS MEGARA   LYCOREA CERES

MÜLLERIAN MIMICRY, named for the 19th-century German zoologist Fritz Müller, appears when two species of unpalatable insects come to look alike. An example from Trinidad is the resem-

blance between butterflies *Hirsutis megara* from the family Ithomiidae (*left*) and *Lycorea ceres* from the family Danaidae (*right*). Similarity enables each species to gain protection from the other.

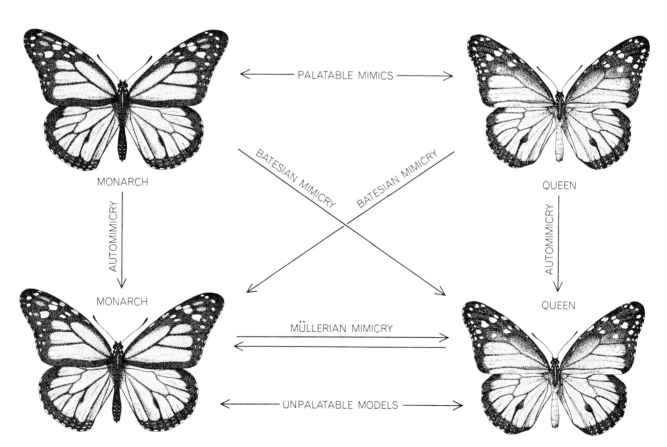

MULTIPLE MIMICRY found in Trinidad between monarch and queen butterflies is charted. Palatable monarchs resemble unpalatable queens in Batesian mimicry, as is the case with palatable queens resembling unpalatable monarchs. Unpalatable monarchs

and queens resemble each other in Müllerian mimicry. Automimicry describes recent discovery that not all monarchs and queens are unpalatable. The term refers to the fact that palatable butterflies gain protection from unpalatable ones of the same species.

Once unpalatable insects with a warning coloration evolved, the opportunity arose for natural selection to favor modifications in palatable species so that they came to look like unpalatable ones. This phenomenon, which is called Batesian mimicry after the 19th-century English naturalist Henry W. Bates, is widespread and involves many different groups of insects and other prey organisms. The mimic takes advantage of the fact that the predator has learned to avoid the model: the unpalatable prey with a warning coloration. Clearly the mimic must not become too common with respect to the model or the system would tend to break down because the predators would so frequently encounter palatable mimics.

Another form of mimicry is called Müllerian after Fritz Müller, a German zoologist of the late 19th century. It entails resemblances among unpalatable insects. Tropical regions abound with groups of unpalatable insects that have come to look alike because natural selection has favored the evolution of a few common warning colorations. This type of mimicry benefits predators by reducing the number of color patterns that need to be remembered. The prey benefit because the numbers of individuals that are killed in each group of Müllerian mimics are reduced: once predators learn to avoid one species on sight they will tend to reject them all.

If, as our experiments suggest, certain plants and prey insects have the flavors usually associated with particular poisons but do not contain the poisons, they would be flavor mimics and would gain the usual advantages of Batesian mimicry. Other foods could contain different poisons but have similar flavors. They would gain the mutualistic advantage of

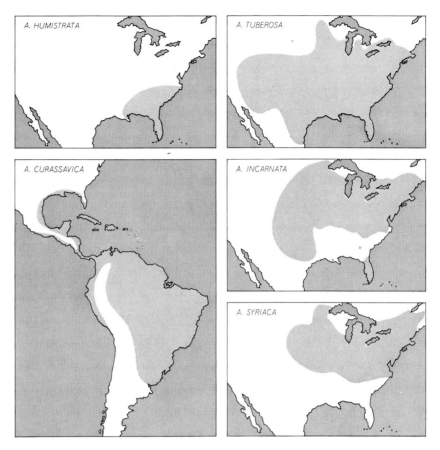

APPROXIMATE DISTRIBUTION of five species of milkweed of the genus *Asclepias* is indicated. The two species at left produce cardiac glycosides, so that butterflies feeding on the plants are unpalatable to birds. The three species at right lack the cardiac glycosides.

Müllerian mimicry.

The fact that monarch butterflies exhibit a spectrum of palatability from completely acceptable to totally unacceptable has led us to propose an extension of mimicry theory to include what we call automimicry. In our view butterflies that feed on poisonous plants can serve as unpalatable models and protect the individuals of their own species that have not fed on such plants. Since both butterflies are of the same species, the palatable individuals can be called automimics of the unpalatable ones. The advantage gained by an automimic is somewhat greater than the protection secured by a Batesian mimic; whereas the Batesian mimic has evolved a close re-

CALOTOXIN

CALOTROPIN

CALACTIN

CHEMICAL STRUCTURE of three cardiac glycosides found in both the milkweed *A. curassavica* and the monarch butterflies that feed on the plant is indicated. Assays of the plants and butterflies were made by Tadeus Reichstein of the University of Basel. It was he also who hypothesized the structures of calotropin and calactin on the basis of the known structure of calotoxin (*left*).

semblance to its model, the automimic is a perfect mimic because it is a member of the same species.

We have calculated that if birds continued eating monarchs until they encountered an emetic one, and they then stopped eating monarchs, the protection afforded a butterfly population in which only half of the individuals are unpalatable would be nearly as great as if the entire population were unpalatable. Let us assume, for example, that a bird can eat up to 16 butterflies but stops eating them as soon as it eats an unpalatable one. Under these circumstances a butterfly population with 50 percent unpalatable members would suffer only 7 percent more predation than a population with 100 percent unpalatable members. Indeed, at the same level of predation a population that was only 25 percent unpalatable would still gain an immunity of 75 percent. As the level of potential predation increases, the advantage of automimicry tends to stabilize [see illustration on this page].

It might seem ecologically strange for prey that can become unpalatable simply by eating poisonous plants to feed on nonpoisonous ones. Yet we have found thus far that only two out of eight species of North American milkweeds produce emetic butterflies. The two are Asclepias curassavica and A. humistrata. We were surprised to find that three very common eastern species—A. syriaca, A. tuberosa and A. incarnata—produce palatable butterflies. These species are widely fed on by monarch larvae. Evidently this is the key to understanding the selective advantage of automimicry: If the majority of milkweeds in a given area are nonpoisonous, the monarchs will be forced to lay eggs on those plants and will deposit eggs on poisonous milkweeds only when they can find them. Automimicry enables the species to more than double its numbers without losing much of its protection from predation.

Our studies have established that wild populations of monarchs do include both palatable and unpalatable individuals. Last fall we collected a number of wild monarchs in western Massachusetts during their southward migration and subsequently dried and force-fed one butterfly each to 50 blue jays. Twelve of the butterflies (24 percent) caused emesis; the other ones proved to be palatable automimics. This finding agrees well with the minimum proportion of unpalatable individuals needed to confer a substantial automimetic advantage as shown in the illustration at the right. It will be interesting to press further with the investigation to discover what milk-

weeds in the Northeast do produce emetic butterflies.

On the Caribbean island of Trinidad monarch butterflies live together with another species of the Danainae, the queen butterfly. In this part of their range both butterflies look very much alike in size and color pattern, and it has been assumed that they both are unpalatable species enjoying the mutualistic protection of Müllerian mimicry. In this area, as in North America, several species of asclepiad plants are available as food. The monarch lays its eggs almost exclusively on the common and poisonous A. curassavica but occasionally feeds on other asclepiads lacking cardiac glycosides. As one would expect, the majority (65 percent) of the monarchs from this area are emetic.

On the other hand, the queens are rarely found on A. curassavica, and only 15 percent of the adults captured are emetic. In the laboratory, however, the queens lay their eggs on the plant and freely feed on it. It seems likely that in this area of Trinidad the monarch somehow partly displaces the queen to the nonpoisonous milkweeds, which is why relatively few queens become emetic.

Yet the queens in Trinidad have evolved a great similarity to the monarchs in color pattern, which is not the case over most of the range where the two species live together. Hence the queens that are palatable gain the advantage of Batesian mimicry of the predominantly unpalatable monarch population, and the unpalatable queens share a Müllerian advantage with the unpalatable monarchs. At the same time the palatable monarchs are protected by the unpalatable monarchs and the palatable queens are protected by the unpalatable queens, so that automimicry is also involved. Thus in Trinidad the mimetic relations of the two species are complex and simultaneously involve Batesian mimicry, Müllerian mimicry and automimicry [see bottom illustration on page 160].

The discovery that certain insects can assimilate plant poisons they in turn employ as a defense against their predators provides a remarkable example of what George Gaylord Simpson has called the opportunistic aspect of evolution. Clearly ecological chemistry and its implications provide a fertile field for extending our understanding of the interrelations of ecology, sensory physiology and animal behavior.

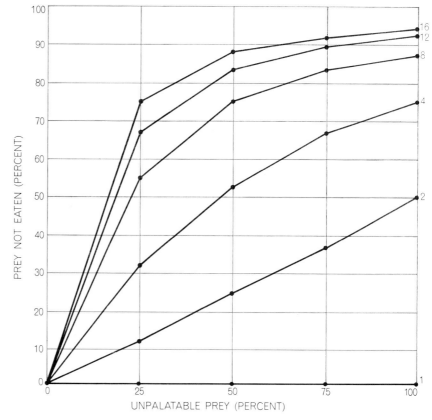

ADVANTAGES OF AUTOMIMICRY are charted for six levels of predation. Colored numbers refer to the maximum number of prey eaten by a single predator in a given time. A butterfly population in which only 25 to 50 percent of the individuals are unpalatable from having fed on poisonous plants is almost as well protected as if all individuals were emetic.

19

CLEANING SYMBIOSIS

CONRAD LIMBAUGH
August 1961

*The invasion of the oceans by skin-diving biologists has led
to the discovery that a surprisingly large number of marine
organisms either live by cleaning other marine organisms or
benefit by being cleaned*

While skin diving in the cool water off the coast of southern California in the spring of 1949, I observed a brief and seemingly casual meeting between a small golden kelp perch (*Brachyistius frenatus*) and a walleye surfperch (*Hyperprosopon argenteum*) twice its size. The walleye had separated itself from a milling school of its fellows several yards away and was holding itself rigid with fins extended, its body pointed at an unnatural angle to the surface of the water. The three-inch kelp perch spent several minutes picking at the silver sides of the walleye with its pointed snout. Then the kelp perch darted into the golden leaves of a nearby kelp plant, and the walleye returned to lose itself in the activity of the school. At the time I recorded this event in my notes only as an interesting incident.

Since then my studies and the observations of others have convinced me that this was not an isolated episode. On the contrary, it was an instance of a constant and vital activity that occurs throughout the marine world: cleaning symbiosis. Certain species of marine animal have come to specialize in cleaning parasites and necrotic tissue from fishes that visit them. This mutually beneficial behavior promotes the well-being of the host fishes and provides food for those that do the cleaning.

The relationship between the cleaner and the cleaned is frequently so casual as to seem accidental, as in the encounter that first caught my attention. On the other hand, one finds in the Bahamas the highly organized relationship between the Pederson shrimp (*Periclimenes pedersoni*) and its numerous clients. The transparent body of this tiny animal is striped with white and spotted with violet, and its conspicuous antennae are considerably longer than its body. It establishes its station in quiet water where fishes congregate or frequently pass, always in association with the sea anemone *Bartholomea annulata*, usually clinging to it or occupying the same hole. When a fish approaches, the shrimp will whip its long antennae and sway its body back and forth. If the fish is interested, it will swim directly to the shrimp and stop an inch or two away. The fish usually presents its head or a gill cover for cleaning, but if it is bothered by something out of the ordinary, such as an injury near its tail, it presents itself tail first. The shrimp swims or crawls forward, climbs aboard and walks rapidly over the fish, checking irregularities, tugging at parasites with its claws and cleaning injured areas. The fish remains almost motionless during this inspection and allows the shrimp to make minor incisions in order to get at subcutaneous parasites. As the shrimp approaches the gill covers, the fish opens each one in turn and allows the shrimp to enter and forage among the gills. The shrimp is even permitted to enter and leave the fish's mouth cavity. Local fishes quickly learn the location of these shrimp. They line up or crowd around for their turn and often wait to be cleaned when the shrimp has retired into the hole beside the anemone.

Such behavior has been considered a mere curiosity for many years. The literature contains scattered reports of cleaning symbiosis, including a few examples among land animals: the crocodile and the Egyptian plover, cattle and the egret, the rhinoceros and the tickbird. As early as 1892 the German biologist Franz von Wagner had suggested that the pseudoscorpion, a tiny relative of the spider that is frequently observed stealing a ride on larger insects, is actually engaged in removing parasitic mites from these insects. The U.S. biologist William Beebe in 1924 saw red crabs remove red ticks from sunbathing marine iguanas of the Galápagos Islands. While diving in the coral waters off Haiti four years later, Beebe also saw several small fishes of the wrasse family cleaning parrot fish. Mexican fishermen in the Gulf of California refer to a certain angelfish (*Holacanthus passer*) as *El Barbero*. They explain that this fish "grooms the other fishes" and so deserves its title as "The Barber."

Recognition of cleaning symbiosis and its implications has come only in recent years. The gear and the technique of skin diving have given marine biologists a new approach to the direct observation of undersea life. They have discovered numerous examples of cleaning behavior, enough to establish already that the behavior represents one of the primary relationships in the community of life in the sea. The known cleaners include some 26 species of fish, six species of shrimp and Beebe's crab. This number will undoubtedly increase when the many marine organisms now suspected of being cleaners have been studied more closely. It now seems that most other fishes seek out and depend on the service they render. The primary nature of the behavior is evident in the bright coloration and anatomical specialization that distinguish many cleaners. It appears that cleaning symbiosis may help to explain the range of species and the make-up of populations found in particular habitats, the patterns of local movement and migration and the natural control of disease in many fishes.

The importance of cleaning in the ecology of the waters off southern California became more and more apparent to me during the early 1950's as I accumulated observations of cleaners at work. My notes are particularly concerned with

FOUR CLEANING RELATIONSHIPS are depicted in this drawing by Rudolf Freund. In each the cleaner is in color. At top left a señorita (*Oxyjulis californica*) cleans a group of blacksmiths (*Chromis punctipinnis*). At top right are a butterfly fish (*Chaetodon nigrirostris*) and two Mexican goatfish (*Pseudupeneus dentatus*); in center, two neon gobies (*Elecatinus oceanops*) and a Nassau grouper (*Epinephelus striatus*); at bottom, a Spanish hogfish (*Bodianus rufus*) in the mouth of a barracuda (*Sphyraena barracuda*).

CALIFORNIA MORAY EEL (*Gymnothorax mordax*) has its external parasites removed by four California cleaning shrimps (*Hippolysmata californica*). At upper left is a fifth shrimp. This photograph and the one at right below were made by Ron Church.

SPANISH HOGFISH (*top*) in process of cleaning ocean surgeon (*Acanthurus bahianus*) was photographed by author in Bahamas.

LIONFISH (*Pterois volitans*) is host to a very much smaller cleaning wrasse (*purple fish in center*) of undetermined species.

the performance of the golden-brown wrasse (*Oxyjulis californica*), commonly called the señorita. This cigar-shaped fish is abundant in these waters and well known to fishermen as a bait-stealer.

Certain fishes, such as the opaleye (*Girella nigricans*), the topsmelt (*Atherinops affinis*) and the blacksmith (*Chromis punctipinnis*), crowd so densely about a señorita that it is impossible to see the cleaning activity. When I first saw these dense clouds, often with several hundred fish swarming around a single cleaner, I thought they were spawning aggregations. As the clouds dispersed at my approach, however, I repeatedly observed a señorita retreating into the cover of the rocks and seaweed nearby. Often the host fishes, unaware of my approach, would rush and stop in front of the retreating señorita, temporarily blocking its path. In less dense schools I was able to observe the señorita in the act of nibbling parasites from the flanks of a host fish. While being cleaned blacksmiths would remain motionless in the most awkward positions—on their sides, head up, head down or even upside down.

The material cleaned from fishes by the señorita and other cleaners has not been thoroughly studied. Among the organisms I have noted in the stomach contents of cleaners are copepods and isopods: minute parasitic crustaceans that attach themselves to the scales and integument of fishes. I have also found bacteria, and on several occasions I have seen señoritas in the act of nibbling away a white, fluffy growth that streamed as a milky cloud from the gills of infected fishes. Especially in the spring and summer months off California and farther south in the warmer waters off Mexico, many fishes display this infection; it ranges from an occasional dot of white to large ulcerated sores rimmed with white. Carl H. Oppenheimer, now at the University of Miami, has shown that this is a bacterial disease by infecting healthy individuals with material taken from diseased fishes.

Judging by the diversity of its clientele, the señorita is well known as a cleaner to many members of the marine community. Among the species that seek out its services I have counted pelagic (deep ocean) fishes as well as the numerous species that populate the kelp beds nearer shore. The black sea bass (*Stereolepis gigas*) and the even larger ocean sunfish (*Mola mola*) seem to come purposely to the outer edge of the kelp beds, where they attract large numbers of señoritas, which flock around them to pick off their parasites. I have also observed the señorita at work on the bat ray (*Holorhinus californicus*), showing that the symbiosis embraces the cartilaginous as well as the bony fishes.

Since first recognizing cleaning behavior in these southern California fishes, I have studied it in numerous places down the Pacific Coast of Mexico, in the Gulf of California, in the Bahamas and in the Virgin Islands. Observations such as mine have been paralleled in the literature by other skin-diving biologists and by underwater photographers. From 1952 to 1955 Vern and Harry Pederson made motion pictures in the Bahamas of cleaning behavior in a number of species of fish and in the violet-spotted shrimp that bears their name. In 1953 the German skin diver Hans Hass suggested that the pilot fish associated with manta rays ate the parasites of their hosts. Irenäus Eibl-Eibesfeldt, a German biologist, published notes in 1954 on cleaning behavior he had witnessed in fishes in Bahamian waters; he expressed the belief that it is common in the oceans of the world. In the Hawaiian and Society islands John E. Randall of the University of Miami identified as cleaners four fishes of the genus *Labroides*, two of which were new species.

A few generalizations about cleaning symbiosis may now be attempted. In the first place, the phenomenon appears to be more highly developed in clear tropical waters than in cooler regions of the seas. The tropical cleaner species are more numerous and include the young of the gray angelfish (*Pomacanthus aureus*), the butterfly fish (*Chaetodon*), gobies (*Elecatinus*) and several wrasses such as the Spanish hogfish (*Bodianus rufus*) and the members of the genus *Labroides*. Even distantly related species have analogous structures for cleaning, such as pointed snouts and tweezer-like teeth; this suggests convergent evolution toward specialization in the cleaning function. In the tropical seas the cleaning fish are generally brightly colored and patterned in sharp contrast to their backgrounds; it appears that most fishes that stand out in their environment are cleaners. Since cleaning fishes must be conspicuous, it is logical that they should have evolved toward maximum contrast with their surroundings. (The parasites on which they feed have evolved toward a maximum of protective coloration, matching the color of their hosts, and are usually invisible to the human observer of cleaning behavior.) In general these fishes are not gregarious and live solitarily or in pairs. In Temperate Zone waters, on the other hand, the cleaners are not so brightly colored or so contrastingly marked. They tend to be gregarious, to the point of living in schools, and are more numerous, though the number of species is smaller.

The cleaning behavior of the tropical forms is correspondingly more complex than that of the Temperate Zone species. Whereas the latter simply surround or follow a fish in order to clean it, the tropical cleaners put on displays not unlike those shown in courtship by some male fishes. They rush forward, turn sideways and then retreat, repeating the ritual until a fish is attracted into position to be cleaned. Frequently they sense the presence of a fish before a human observer can, and they hasten to take up their station before the fish arrives to be cleaned.

Some species clean only in their juvenile stage; none of them appears to depend exclusively on the habit for its food. Again, however, the tropical species come closer to being "full time" cleaners. One consequence of their higher degree of specialization is that they enjoy considerable immunity from predators. In an extensive investigation of the food habits of California kelp fishes I never found a señorita, a close cousin of the numerous cleaning wrasses of the tropics, in the stomach contents of other fishes. I have seen it safely enter the open mouth of the kelp bass, a fish that normally feeds on señorita-size fishes. On the other hand, the kelp perch, a more typical Temperate Zone cleaner, frequently turns up in the stomachs of fishes that it cleans. The immunity of certain cleaners is so well established that other fishes have come to mimic them in color and conformation and so share their immunity. Some mimics reverse the process and prey on the fish that mistake them for cleaners!

The same generalizations may be made in contrasting the cleaning shrimps of the Tropical and Temperate zones. Only one of the six known species occurs outside the tropics; this is the California cleaning shrimp (*Hippolysmata californica*). It is a highly gregarious and wandering animal, at the other pole of behavior from the tropical species as represented by the solitary and sedentary Pederson shrimp of the Bahamian waters. The California cleaning shrimp does not have the coloration and marking to make it stand out from its environment. So far as I have been able to determine, it does not display itself to attract fishes. These California shrimps wander abroad in troops numbering in the hundreds, feeding on the bottom at night and retiring to cover during the day. They act as cleaners when they come upon an animal, say a lobster, in need of cleaning or when a fish, perhaps a moray eel, swims into the crevice where they have found shelter. They will crawl rapidly over the entire outside surface of the animal, cleaning away everything removable, including decaying tissue. A lobster that has been worked over by a team of these shrimps comes out with a clean shell; a human diver's hand will receive the same treatment. Fishes do not seem to be bothered by these rough 'attentions, although the moray may occasionally jerk its head as if annoyed.

In some cases the shrimps may enter the mouth of the moray to get at parasites there, but not without risk; the stomachs of morays have yielded a considerable number of these shrimps. In

SPOTTED GOATFISH (*Pseudupeneus maculatus*) is host to the smaller Spanish hogfish. The hogfish is found in the tropical waters from Bermuda and Florida to Rio de Janeiro, in the Gulf of Mexico and around Ascension and St. Helena islands in the South Atlantic.

GARIBALDI (*Hypsypops rubicunda*) at top holds itself at an unnatural angle while being cleaned by a señorita. The latter, which is found in temperate waters from central California to central Lower California, cleans more than a dozen species of fish.

contrast, the tropical cleaning shrimps, all of them more exclusively specialized as cleaners, seem to have the same immunity from predation as the tropical cleaning fishes. With their bright colors, their fixed stations and their elaborate display behavior, they are plainly adver-tised to the community as cleaners and attract hosts rather than predators. It is easy to visualize the evolutionary path by which the more complex cleaning symbiosis may have developed from the imperfect cleaner-host relationships such as that of the California shrimp.

In the summer of 1955, in the Gulf of California near Guaymas, I noted that cleaning behavior appeared to be concentrated at rocky points: each point was manned by two butterfly fish and one angelfish. I assumed that the concentration of other fishes arose from the

JUVENILE GRAY ANGELFISH (*Pomacanthus aureus*) at right cleans external parasites from the tail of a bar jack (*Caranx ruber*). Below the jack is another cleaner, the Spanish hogfish. This photograph and those on the opposite page were made by the author.

"CLEANING STATION," consisting of a sponge (*light area with small, dark protuberances*) surrounded by turtle grass, is manned by a juvenile gray angelfish. The station, located off New Providence Island in the Bahamas, was photographed by the author's wife.

fact that these points constitute the intersection of the communities of fishes on each side. In 1958 Randall, reporting on his studies of the cleaning wrasses in the Society Islands, observed that fishes came from comparatively long distances to the sites occupied by the cleaners, not just from the immediate community. The Pederson brothers made the same observation in the Bahamas, reporting that the cleaners congregate in regular "cleaning stations" in the coral reefs and attract host fishes from large areas.

Subsequent studies have confirmed these observations. The various species of cleaning fish and shrimp tend to cluster in particular ecological situations: at coral heads, depressions in the bottom, ship wreckage or the edge of kelp beds. Their presence in these localities accounts in great part for the large assemblages of other fishes that are so frequently seen there. Even a small cleaning station in the tropics may process a large number of fish in the course of a day. I saw up to 300 fish cleaned at one station in the Bahamas during one six-hour daylight period. Some of the fishes pass from station to station and return many times during the day; those that could be identified by visible marks, such as infection spots, returned day after day at regular time intervals. Altogether it seemed that many of the fishes spent as much time at cleaning stations as they did in feeding.

At cleaning stations inhabited by thousands of cleaning organisms, cleaning symbiosis must assume great numerical significance in determining the distribution and concentration of marine populations. In my opinion, it is the presence of the señorita and the kelp perch that brings the deepwater coastal and pelagic fishes inshore to the edge of the kelp beds on the California coast. Most concentrations of reef fishes may similarly be understood to be cleaning stations. Cleaning symbiosis would therefore account for the existence of such well-known California sport-fishing grounds as the rocky points of Santa Catalina Island, the area around the sunken ship *Valiant* off the shore of Catalina, the La Jolla kelp beds and submarine

BLACKSMITHS IN GROUP waiting to be cleaned by a single señorita (*slender fish in nearly horizontal position at right center*) **assume various positions. This photograph was made by Charles H. Turner of the State of California Department of Fish and Game.**

PEDERSON CLEANING SHRIMP (*Periclimenes pedersoni*) attracts hosts by waving its antennae, which are longer than its body. Shell-like objects (*upper right*) are shrimp's uropods, or "flippers." Photograph was made by F. M. Bayer of Smithsonian Institution.

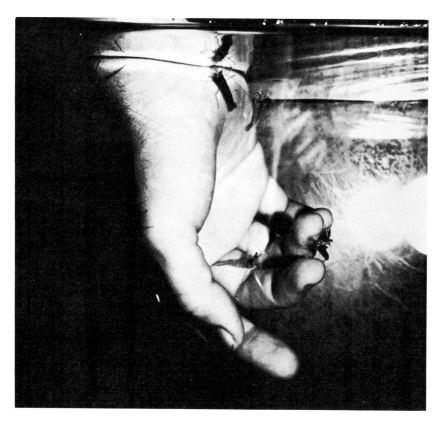

CALIFORNIA CLEANING SHRIMPS "clean" the author's hand, even to picking at his fingernails. These shrimps clean everything that is removable from the exterior of a host.

canyon and the Coronado Islands.

These generalizations of course call for further observation and perhaps experimental study. In a modest field experiment in the Bahamas I once removed all the known cleaning organisms from two small, isolated reefs where fish seemed particularly abundant. Within a few days the number of fish was drastically reduced; within two weeks almost all except the territorial fishes had disappeared.

This experiment also demonstrated the importance of cleaning symbiosis in maintaining the health of the marine population. Many of the fish remaining developed fuzzy white blotches, swelling, ulcerated sores and frayed fins. Admittedly the experiment was a gross one and not well controlled, but the observed contrast with the fish populations of the nearby coral heads was very striking. Certainly it appeared that the ailments occurred because of the absence of cleaning organisms. This impression was strengthened when a number of local fishes that had been maintained in an aquarium were found to be developing bacterial infections. I placed a cleaner shrimp in the aquarium, and it went to work at once to clean the infected fishes.

Symbiotic cleaning has some important biological implications. From the viewpoint of evolution it provides a remarkable instance of morphological and behavioral adaptation. Ecologically speaking, cleaners must be regarded as key organisms in the assembling of the species that compose the populations of various marine habitats. Cleaning raises a great many questions for students of animal behavior; it would be interesting to know what mechanism prevents ordinarily voracious fishes from devouring the little cleaners. In zoogeography the cleaning relationships may provide the limiting factor in the dispersal of various species. In parasitology the relationship between the cleaning activities on the one hand and host-parasite relations on the other needs investigation. The beneficial economic effect of cleaners on commercially important marine organisms must be considerable in some areas. The modern marine-fisheries biologist must now consider cleaners in any thorough work dealing with life history and fish population studies. From the standpoint of the philosophy of biology, the extent of cleaning behavior in the ocean emphasizes the role of co-operation in nature as opposed to the tooth-and-claw struggle for existence.

20

THE FUNGUS GARDENS OF INSECTS

SUZANNE W. T. BATRA AND LEKH R. BATRA
November 1967

Several kinds of insects live only in association with one kind of fungus, and vice versa. In some instances the insect actively cultivates the fungus, browsing on it and controlling its growth

Anyone with at least a passing interest in biology is aware that fungi, being plants that lack chlorophyll and cannot conduct photosynthesis, live on other organisms or on decaying organic matter. It is less well known that many insects are similarly dependent on fungi. Indeed, there are insects that tend elaborate gardens of a fungus, controlling the growth of the plant according to their own specialized needs.

Some insect species are always found in association with a certain fungus, and some fungi only with a certain insect. Such complete interdependence is called mutualism. The mutualistic partners of insects are not limited to fungi; they include other microbial forms such as bacteria and protozoa. In some cases the insect feeds on its partner or on the partner's own partly digested food. In others the partner lives in the insect's alimentary tract and digests food the insect cannot digest for itself; frequently the partner supplies an essential constituent that is deficient in the insect's diet, such as nitrogen or a vitamin. Some mutualistic partners serve more than one of these functions.

The insects that are mutualistic with microbial organisms are divided into two groups. In one group the fungus, bacterium or protozoon lives inside the insect, either in the alimentary tract or in specialized cells. In the other group a fungus lives in the insect's nest. Here we shall discuss the relations between fungi and insects in the latter group, leading up to those insects that actively cultivate fungus gardens. Such relations have been studied for more than a century, but they offer many new possibilities for investigation. One wants to know more about the physiology of the relations, about how the partners interact at the molecular level. A deeper knowledge of the physiological mechanisms would undoubtedly clarify how the mutualistic partnership came to be established in the course of evolution. It might also have important by-products. For example, much work has been done on the possibility of using fungi that are harmful to insects as a means of selectively controlling insect pests; such work might be advanced by knowing more about the relation between insects and beneficial fungi. As a second example, those insects that control the growth of fungi in gardens may do so by means of antibiotic substances that might well be useful to man.

The first kind of insect-fungus relation we shall take up centers on the tumor-like galls that sometimes appear on the bud, leaf or stem of a plant. These galls develop when certain insects deposit their eggs in the plant and somehow cause it to form an abnormal tissue which then nourishes the larva that emerges from the egg [see "Insects and Plant Galls," by William Hovanitz; SCIENTIFIC AMERICAN, November, 1959]. The galls caused by the mosquito-like midges of the family Itonididae also contain fungi. Growing parasitically on the gall tissue, these fungi usually form a thick layer on the inside of the gall. They appear at an early stage of the gall's development, and a single species of fungus is consistently found in association with larvae of each midge species. Many of these fungi, however, also grow independently of the insect. How fungus and insect come to be together in the gall is not known, but some workers believe the female midge deposits spores of fungus at the time she lays her eggs. Many of the fungus galls are caused by insects that feed by sucking plant sap, and except for a few cases it is unlikely that the fungus acts directly as a source of food. It may be that the fungus assists the insect indirectly by partly breaking down the gall tissue so that the insect can digest it.

Many plants bear insect-fungus galls but only a few of the fungi have been identified. Some galls we have studied in our laboratory at the University of Kansas are leaf-blister galls on several kinds of goldenrod and aster caused by at least nine species of the midge *Asteromyia* (all of them associated with the fungus *Sclerotium asteris* in the U.S.), and flower-bud galls of the broom (*Cytisus*) caused by the midge *Asphondylia cytisii* (associated with the fungus *Diplodia* in the U.S. and Europe).

In contrast to the casual association between insects and fungi in plant galls, several species of the fungus *Septobasidium* and various scale insects (family Coccidae) that inhabit the fungal tissue coexist in a manner that is clearly mutualistic. *Septobasidium* resembles a thick lichen: it clings tightly to the leaves or branches of trees. The scale insects that inhabit this fungus in some way modify its growth in their vicinity, giving it a different texture or color; as a result some colonies of *Septobasidium* have a mottled surface.

The relation between this fungus and the insects that colonize it has been described by John N. Couch of the University of North Carolina. The insect, which feeds on sap, is attached to the tree by its sucking tube. The mycelium of the fungus—its thick mat of fine threads—shelters the insect from the weather and shields it from birds and parasitic wasps. In turn a few of the insects are penetrated by specialized threads, called haustoria, that extract nourishment from the insects' blood. Scale insects characteristically ingest more sap than they need; the fungus may take advantage of this fact by uti-

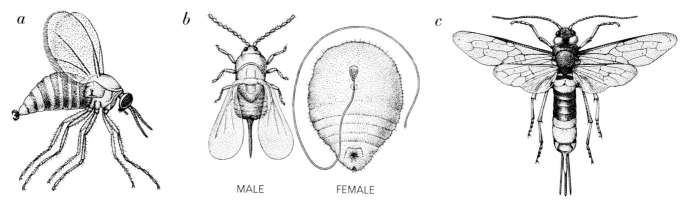

MALE   FEMALE

INSECT GARDENERS comprise unrelated species. Depicted here are representatives of six groups of insects that nest with a fungus. At left is a gall midge of the genus *Lasioptera*; its larvae probably feed on plant material that a fungus has partly digested. The scale insect *Aspidiotus osborni* (*b*) lives on trees under a protective canopy of fungus. The wood wasp *Sirex gigas* (*c*) deposits eggs cov-

lizing such nutrients while they are still circulating in the insect's body.

Septobasidium is distributed by scale insects as well as nourished by them; it does not live independently in nature. When the insects are young, some of them crawl on the surface of the fungus and become covered with spores. A few of the contaminated insects migrate to new areas on the tree, where they insert their sucking tube. Shielded by new mycelium, they survive. They are also invaded, however, by haustoria from the developing spores, and as a result they do not attain maturity and reproduce. The new mutualistic colony is nonetheless able to continue because uncontaminated insects now find shelter in the mycelium. In some species of *Septobasidium* the entire process has apparently been made more efficient by the development of hollow "insect houses" that attract and hold the migrating scale insects. Thus the fungus furnishes a shelter for the insects and the insects provide both a food supply and a means of dispersal for the fungus. Some insects are sacrificed for the benefit of the colony as a whole; both fungus and insect benefit at the expense of the tree.

A different kind of mutualism has been observed involving on the one hand the wood wasps of the genera *Sirex*, *Tremex* and *Urocerus* and on the other the fungi *Stereum* and *Daedalea*.

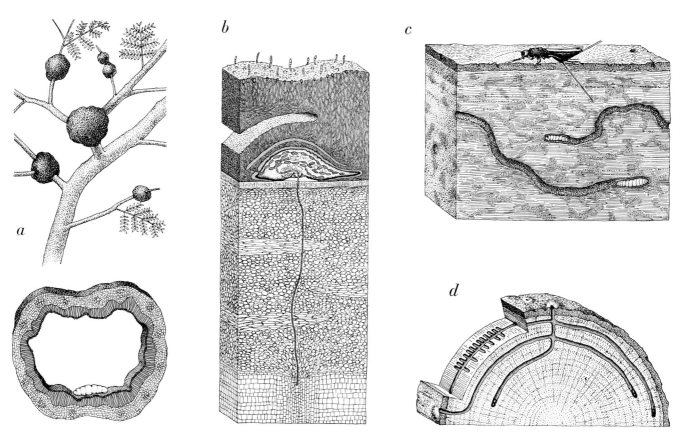

INSECT NESTS contain a fungus (*color*). The nests were made by the insects at the top of these two pages, or by an insect of the same group. The plant gall that encloses larvae of the midge is lined with a fungus parasitic on the plant (*a*). *Septobasidium* fungus sends threads into some of the insects it shelters and extracts nourishment from their blood (*b*). The burrows of wood

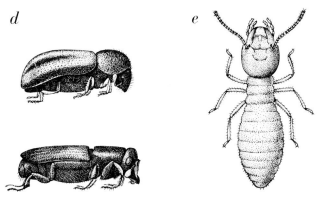

d

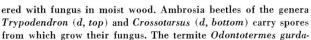

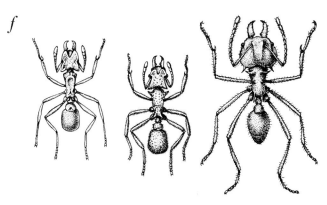

e

f

ered with fungus in moist wood. Ambrosia beetles of the genera *Trypodendron* (*d, top*) and *Crossotarsus* (*d, bottom*) carry spores from which grow their fungus. The termite *Odontotermes gurda-*

spurensis (*e*) fertilizes its fungus garden. Ants of the genera *Cyphomyrmex, Trachymyrmex* and *Atta* (*f, left to right*) actively cultivate fungus gardens. The insects are not drawn to the same scale.

These common fungi sometimes build a semicircular "bracket" out from a tree. The adult female wood wasp deposits her eggs in moist wood by means of a long, slender ovipositor, and at the base of this organ are tiny pouches that contain fungus cells called oidia. When the egg is deposited, oidia cling to it. Then the mycelium of the fungus grows into the wood, and when the wasp larva emerges from the egg it follows the path of the mycelium. The fungus partly di-

gests the wood before it is eaten by the larva. In the laboratory wood wasp larvae have been reared on a diet consisting only of *Stereum*, but whether the fungus is essential to the insect's nutrition is not known. Both in nature and in the laboratory the fungus grows well without the help of any insect.

The wood wasp nonetheless acts as an agent for the dissemination of *Stereum*. A larva that later develops into a female has organs that ensure the pres-

ervation of the fungus. These organs are tiny pits hidden in folds between the wasp's first and second abdominal segments; in them bits of fungus are trapped in a waxy material. Here an inoculum of fungus remains viable, whereas fungus in wood is inactivated when the wood eventually dries out. When the larva metamorphoses into a pupa, the organs that hold the fungus are discarded. Then, when the adult female wasp emerges from the pupal skin, tiny flakes

e

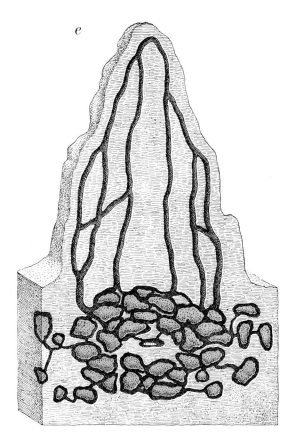

f

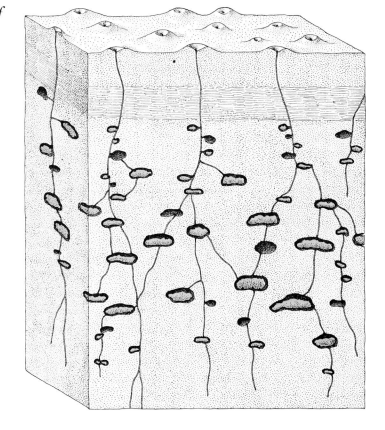

wasp larvae are made in wood infested with *Stereum* fungus, propagated by the insect (*c*). Fungus carried by an ambrosia beetle grows inside the insect's tunnels in timber (*d*). Mounds of earth

in which the termite nests contain fecal material permeated with fungus (*e*). *Atta texana* cultivates a garden of fungus in a huge underground nest (*f*). Here also the nests are not drawn to scale.

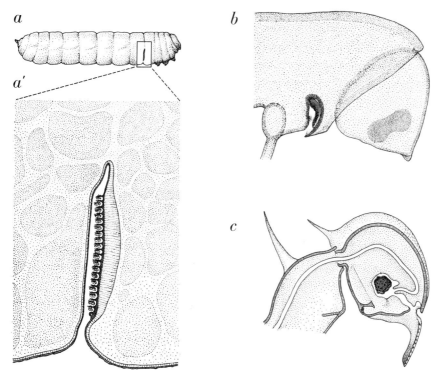

FUNGUS CONTAINERS of three insects are depicted with the fungus indicated in color. Larvae of wood wasps that develop into females carry an inoculum of fungus behind the thorax (*a*). A section through the first two abdominal segments of the larva shows one of the fungus-filled organs (*a'*). The ambrosia beetle, shown here in longitudinal section, conveys spores of fungus in pockets located at the base of its front legs (*b*). A longitudinal section of the head of a fungus-growing ant reveals the pouch in which it transports fungus (*c*).

of fungus-impregnated wax that have fallen from the organs become lodged in the moist pouch at the base of the ovipositor. The flakes now give rise to a fungal mycelium, which develops the oidia that will coat the eggs. The transfer of the fungus from generation to generation of wood wasps is thereby assured.

Ambrosia beetles also carry fungi within their bodies. The numerous species of these wood-boring insects (families Scolytidae, Platypodidae and Lymexylonidae) cannot survive without ambrosia fungi (several genera of Ascomycetes and "imperfect" fungi). In their external skeleton are small pockets called mycangia (literally "fungus containers"); these pockets always contain a supply of viable fungus spores. When an ambrosia beetle tunnels into wood, spores are dislodged from the mycangia, and soon a mass of velvety fungus lines the interior of the tunnel. On this "ambrosia," which concentrates in its cells nutrients that have been extracted from the wood, the beetles feed.

Ambrosia beetles have been the subject of considerable research because they destroy much timber all over the

world. Their tunnels, sometimes called "shot holes," extend deep into the sapwood of trees and are surrounded by streaks of a stain manufactured by the enzymatic action of the fungus. The beetles most often attack hardwoods, preferring trees that have been weakened by drought, disease or fire, or fallen timber that is moist and filled with sap. Attracted by the odor of fermenting sap, the beetles fly upwind, usually at dusk; it is easy to collect them in the evening around a newly felled log. They are similarly attracted by the yeasty smell of beer and beer drinkers, and it is also convenient to collect them at a beer picnic! Some kinds bore into beer and wine kegs, which is why in Europe they are called "beer beetles."

The tunnels of ambrosia beetles can be distinguished from those of other wood-boring insects by a black or brown discoloration of the wood around the neat circular tunnel opening. There is, moreover, no wood dust or fecal matter inside the tunnel. When the beetles are excavating, fine wood particles, sometimes mixed with the insect's brown feces, accumulate outside the tunnel entrance. The beetle does not as a rule eat wood, and it rids its nest of wood

borings. The males of some species assist the females with tunnel excavation. Inside the ambrosia beetle's tunnel system one finds, depending on the species, either separate niches, each enclosing a single glistening larva or a pearl-like egg, or several larvae sharing an enlargement of the tunnel. In many species the adult insect, on emerging from the pupal skin and proceeding to feed on the mass of ambrosia fungus lining the tunnel, rocks back and forth in a curious manner. What this does is force fungus spores into the mycangia before the insect flies away to found its own nest.

Each species of ambrosia beetle is normally associated with only one species of ambrosia fungus. Ambrosia fungi are pleomorphic: they can readily change, when their growth medium is changed, from a fluffy moldlike form to a dense yeastlike form. In the mycangia and the tunnels of the ambrosia beetles the yeastlike form prevails. Recently we have discovered that ambrosia beetles can also change the form of other fungi from the moldlike form to the yeastlike one. This is a significant phenomenon, and we shall be returning to it.

The most conspicuous and most destructive of the fungus-growing insects are termites. The termites that cultivate fungi are native to the Tropics of Africa and Asia. In West Africa it is estimated that the yearly cost of repairing the damage done by these insects to buildings is equal to 10 percent of the buildings' value. In addition to wood the insects eat growing and harvested crops and objects made of rubber, leather and paper; they destroy documents, works of art, clothing and even underground cables. The enormous mounds that some termite species build for nests interfere with farming and hinder road construction. If they are incompletely destroyed, the insects rebuild them.

Many species in the genera *Macrotermes* and *Odontotermes* make their nests in spectacular steeple-like mounds of hardened earth, which in Africa reach a height of as much as 30 feet. Other species, in the genus *Microtermes*, are completely subterranean, and if it were not for their mating flights and the damage they do, they would be quite inconspicuous. Each nest contains a white, sausage-like queen and a king, usually enclosed together in a protective cell of earth; the much smaller workers, soldiers and young termites (nymphs) of various ages and both sexes are found throughout the nest. At certain seasons winged male and female reproductives (future kings and queens) are also present. In each nest are one or several fungus gardens, the number and shape depending on the species of termite. Material collected by the workers is chewed and swallowed, and the partly digested fecal material is deposited on a fungus garden when the workers return to the nest. In the nests of some species there is a single large mass of fungus garden; in one of the nests of *Odontotermes obesus* that we studied in India the mass was two feet in diameter and weighed 60 pounds. In other nests many fungus gardens one or two inches long are scattered along burrows throughout the nest. Each fungus garden is enclosed in a close-fitting cavity lined with a mixture of saliva and dirt. The chambers of some species are ventilated by an elaborate system of vertical conduits ex-

tending to the surface of the nest [see "Air-conditioned Termite Nests," by Martin Lüscher; SCIENTIFIC AMERICAN, July, 1961].

The fungus gardens look like a gray or brownish sponge or may be convoluted like a walnut meat. They are moist but usually firm and brittle, and are permeated by threadlike mycelium. Scattered over the surface and inside the pores of the gardens are numerous minute, glistening, pearly white spherules composed of masses of rounded fungus cells.

The role of the fungi in the nutrition of the fungus-growing termites is not clear. It is well known that many common Temperate Zone termites cannot digest the cellulose in the wood they eat but rely on certain cellulose-digesting protozoa that live in their intestines to do it for them. No protozoa live in the gut of the fungus-growing

termites; therefore it seems likely that the fungi growing in the gardens break down cellulose and may provide vitamins also. In fact, these termites soon die on a diet restricted to wood. The termites continually eat away the fungus gardens as they add fresh fecal material. There is thus a communal interchange of food, the fecal material being partly broken down by fungi in the garden, then eaten again and redeposited in the garden for further digestion by the fungi.

The white spherules are frequently picked up by the workers and moved to other parts of the fungus garden or are sometimes eaten. The king, queen, young nymphs and soldiers are apparently fed saliva by the workers; no trace of fungus or plant material can be found in their digestive tract. Some winged reproductive termites contain material from the fungus gardens, with which

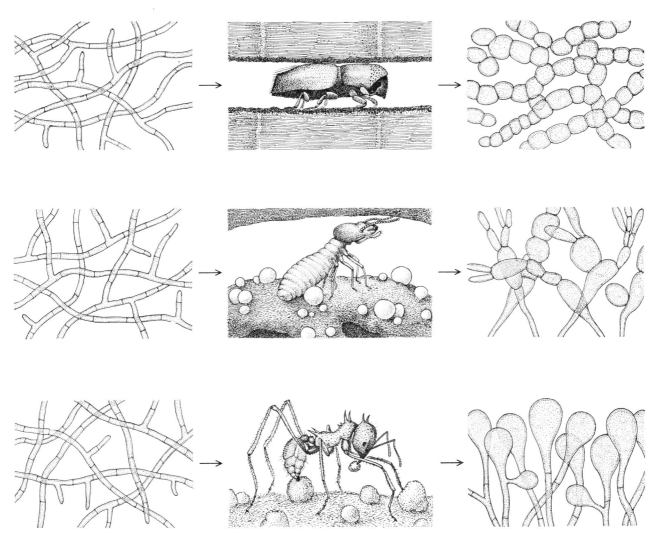

FUNGUS IS TRANSFORMED in being cultivated by insects. Under ordinary conditions in the laboratory fungus associated with the ambrosia beetle is threadlike (*top left*). In the beetle's tunnel, where it is continually grazed, the fungus is denser and more like a yeast (*top right*). The fungus-growing termites also modify their fungi (*middle*), which they fertilize, lick and enclose in mud. Under these conditions white spherules appear. The fungus of a fungus-growing ant (*bottom*) looks much like the others when grown in a culture; in association with the ant, which licks, manipulates and defecates on its garden, the fungus has thickened tips.

they may begin a new garden when they start a new nest.

Several genera of unrelated fungi grow in the fungus gardens of termites; the most abundant are species of the mushroom *Termitomyces*. The various species of *Termitomyces* are found only in nests of fungus-growing termites. Somehow the fruiting structure—the mushroom—of the fungi is not allowed to grow from fungus gardens while they are being actively tended by termites. If the termites are removed or die, however, some of the spherules grow into the mushrooms of *Termitomyces*.

In Africa and southern India termites in many nests simultaneously remove the outer layers of their fungus gardens and spread crumbs of them in a thin layer on the ground during the rainy season. Soon *Termitomyces* mushrooms appear, and after their spores have been disseminated by the wind the termites come to the surface to collect fungus that may have grown from a mixture of spores from many nests. It is believed that in this way the termites provide for the cross-fertilization of their fungi, as man does for corn and other crops.

Closely resembling the fungus-growing termites in behavior but only distantly related to them are the fungus-growing ants (tribe Attini). Here we have an example of convergent evolution, in which two nearly unrelated animals and their fungi occupy a very similar ecological niche. These ants are found only in the Western Hemisphere, and most of them are tropical. Some species are found in the deep South and the Southwest of the U.S.; a small species (*Trachymyrmex septentrionalis*) is found in sandy areas near the Atlantic coast as far north as Long Island.

Atta texana, which lives in eastern Texas and southern Louisiana, does considerable damage to citrus groves, gardens and plantations of young pine trees by cutting leaves from them for its fungus gardens. This ant is known locally as the "town ant," and it inhabits an ant metropolis that is sometimes 50 feet across and 20 feet deep. (One student of these ants, John C. Moser of the U.S. Forest Service, opens their nests with a bulldozer!) Other species of fungus-growing ants build smaller nests; some are so small that they are extremely difficult to find.

The fungus-growing ants probably represent the most advanced stage in the evolution of fungus gardening because they feed only on the fungus, and they actively cultivate it. The workers, depending on the species, collect cater-pillar excrement, fallen flower anthers and other soft plant debris as well as leaves cut from trees. Rather than eating the material the ant cuts it into pieces and adds them to a fungus garden in the nest. The ants' gardens look somewhat like those of the termites: they are gray, flocculent masses of finely divided moist plant material loosely held together by threads of mycelium. In the underground chambers of the nest the fungus garden often is suspended from the roots of plants. Scattered over the surface of the older parts of the garden are white specks just visible to the unaided eye. These specks, called kohlrabi bodies, are clusters of bromatia, the swollen tips of the filaments forming the mycelium. The kohlrabi bodies look much like the white spherules found in the gardens of termites. When the ants are not feeding on the bromatia, they lick them.

The flying, nest-founding ant queen carries a small pellet of fungus in a pouch below her mouthparts, much as the ambrosia beetle carries fungus in its mycangia. In starting a new nest the young queen grows a small fungus garden on her excreta; with this she feeds the first worker larvae. When the workers are mature, they leave the nest to gather the material with which the garden is enlarged. They feed bits of bromatia to the larvae that nestle in the mycelium of the gardens.

As long as the ants actively tend the garden the fungus does not develop fruiting structures, but mushrooms of four genera have been found growing from abandoned nests of some species or have been cultured from fungus gardens in the laboratory. We do not know how the ants control the growth of their fungi so that they produce bromatia and nothing else; perhaps it is by constantly "pruning" away excess growth of the mycelium. It is also possible that the excreta and the saliva of the ants, which are deposited on the fungus garden, contain some substance that influences the growth of the mutualistic fungus and inhibits the development of the many spores that accidentally enter the nest.

With the fungus-growing ants our brief survey of the mutualistic associations between insects and fungi ends. It can be seen that there are two distinct kinds of relation. In the gardens of wood wasps, ambrosia beetles, termites, ants and probably those of midge galls the fungus extracts nourishment from a substrate and the insect feeds either on the fungus, the substrate predigested by the fungus or both. The fun-

BEETLE TUNNELS are marked by the dark fungus that lines the interior surface. The photograph above shows a cross section of excavations made in wood by ambrosia beetles. Dark circles are niches at right angles to the tunnel that hold larvae. The beetles have penetrated through the bark into the sapwood; in this way they destroy felled timber.

FUNGUS-GARDENING ANT *Mycetosoritis hartmani* is shown in its underground nest feeding on a "kohlrabi body." These bodies are made up of bromatia, particles that consist of the swollen tips of the filaments of the fungus and that form only in the presence of the insect. Surrounding the ant are the filaments themselves. Photograph was provided by John C. Moser of the U.S. Forest Service.

gus is prevented from producing sexual fruiting structures but is supplied by an insect partner with a suitable habitat and a means of dispersal. In the colonies of the fungus *Septobasidium* and scale insects the situation is reversed: the insect feeds on the substrate and nourishes the fungus, and the fungus provides shelter for its castrated insect partner.

Insects are unique among animals in having developed mutualistic relations with fungi. This may have come about because so many insects and fungi share the same tiny habitats. Moreover, most insects are equipped to carry living spores of fungi, either in their gut, in folds between their joints that contain waxy secretions or among their bristles.

The fungus-gardening insects convey into their nest the spores of many fungi other than the one on which they depend. If the insects are removed, the alien fungi will grow and soon overrun the nest; they do not grow in the nest, however, when the insects live there. Apparently the fungus-gardening insects either secrete or excrete antibiotic substances that prevent the growth of alien fungi. The substances may also act to transform the mutualistic fungi, causing either ambrosia, spherules or bromatia to appear rather than sexual fruiting structures.

In the case of the termite, which licks the spherules of its fungus and encloses the fungus garden in saliva-moistened mud, the saliva may contain the substances in question. We have tested the effect of adding saliva taken from termites to a culture of their fungus, which under ordinary growing conditions in the laboratory does not produce spherules. After saliva was added to the culture spherules grew; the saliva also

FUNGUS-GARDENING TERMITE of the genus *Odontotermes* is photographed crawling on the surface of its garden. The round white objects are spherules of the fungus, which arise only in gardens that are tended and fertilized by termites. The insect in the picture is a soldier defending the nest; it produces a copious supply of pungent saliva for this purpose.

inhibited the growth of alien fungi. We have performed other tests on the excreta that ants deposit on their nest gardens. Although we have found that the excreta inhibit the growth of certain bacteria, much experimental work remains to be done. The saliva of the ant, which also licks its fungus, may help to form bromatia.

Spores of the ambrosia beetle's fungus remain in the yeastlike form while they are carried by the insect, and it is possible that the waxy secretion might also affect the form of fungi in the tunnel, where the beetle and the fungus are in close contact. On the other hand, it has been shown that the mutualistic fungi of some species of the beetle can be modified to the yeastlike form by certain physical conditions and in the absence of the beetle. These physical conditions duplicate conditions in the beetle's tunnel, where the feeding insect steadily mows the tips of the fungus as they grow.

In nature the presence of a living insect partner is necessary to maintain ambrosia, spherules or bromatia, but these forms can be produced in the laboratory on special mediums in the absence of the insects. When the mutualistic fungi are grown on ordinary carbohydrate-rich laboratory mediums, fluffy mycelium and sometimes sexual fruiting bodies appear. If the same fungi are grown on acid mediums that are rich in amino acids, and are exposed to more than .5 percent carbon dioxide, then bromatia, spherules or ambrosia are formed. These cultural conditions apparently resemble conditions in the nests of the insects. The fungi of some ambrosia beetles also become ambrosial if they are repeatedly scraped or are grown at low temperatures. Clearly the problem of how insects control the growth of a fungus partner remains an intriguing one.

21

SYMBIOSIS AND EVOLUTION

LYNN MARGULIS

August 1971

The cells of higher plants and animals have specialized organelles such as chloroplasts and mitochondria. There is increasing reason to believe that these organelles were once independent organisms

Every form of life on earth—oak tree and elephant, bird and bacterium—shares a common ancestry with every other form; this fact has been conclusively demonstrated by more than a century of evolutionary research. At the same time every living thing belongs primarily to one or another of two groups that are mutually exclusive: organisms with cells that have nuclei and organisms with cells that do not. (An exception is viruses and virus-like particles, but such organisms can reproduce only inside cells.) How can both of these facts be true? Why does so profound a biological schism exist? Ideas put forward and discarded some decades ago hinted at one explanation: Cells without nuclei were the first to evolve. Cells with nuclei, however, are not merely mutant descendants of the older kind of cell. They are the product of a different evolutionary process: a symbiotic union of several cells without nuclei.

The cells of the two classes of organisms are called prokaryotic ("prenuclear") and eukaryotic ("truly nucleated"). The two classes are not equally familiar to us. Most of the forms of life we see—ourselves, trees, pets and the plants and animals that provide our food—are eukaryotes. Each of their cells has a central organelle: a membrane-enclosed nucleus where genetic material is organized into chromosomes. Each has within its cytoplasm several other kinds of organelle. Prokaryotes are far less prominent organisms, although they exist in huge numbers. In the absence of a membrane-enclosed nucleus their genetic material is dispersed throughout their cytoplasm. Such primitive simplicity is characteristic of the blue-green algae and of all the myriad species of bacteria.

The relatedness of living things is fundamental. Organisms as apparently dissimilar as men and molds have almost identical nucleic acids and have similarly identical enzyme systems for utilizing the energy stored in foodstuffs. Their proteins are made up of the same 20 amino acid units. In spite of a bewildering diversity of forms, in these fundamental respects living things are the same. Yet we are left with the equally fundamental discontinuity represented by the two different classes of cells.

Varieties of Symbiosis

Symbiosis can be defined as the living together of two or more organisms in close association. To exclude the many kinds of parasitic relationships known in nature, the term is often restricted to associations that are of mutual advantage to the partners. One frequently cited instance of symbiosis is the partnership sometimes observed between the hermit crab and the sea anemone. The anemone attaches itself to the shell that shelters the crab; this provides its partner with camouflage, and stray bits of the crab's food nourish the anemone. An example that is more pertinent here is the relationship between the leguminous plants and certain free-living soil bacteria. Neither organism can by itself utilize the gaseous nitrogen of the atmosphere. The roots of the plants, however, develop projections known as infection threads that transport the soil bacteria into the root structure. Once present in the cytoplasm of the root cells, the bacteria (transformed into "bacteroids") combine with the host cells to form a specialized tissue: the root nodule. Inert atmospheric nitrogen is utilized by nodule cells as a nutrient. At the same time the nodules manufacture a substance—a pinkish protein known as leghemoglobin—that neither the plant nor the bacteria alone can produce. Because

the bacterial symbionts live within the tissue of the plant host the partnership is classified as "endosymbiosis."

Neither of these relationships is necessarily hereditary. The hermit crab will never give rise to the anemone, nor the anemone to the hermit crab. Nor in most instances does a pea or an alfalfa seed contain bacteria; each new generation of plants must establish its own association with a new generation of bacteria. On the other hand, there is one plant—*Psychotria bacteriophila*—that contains the bacterial symbiont in its seed. Thus its offspring inherit not only chromosomes and cytoplasm from the parent plants but bacteria as well. This constitutes hereditary endosymbiosis.

Hereditary symbiosis is surprisingly common. In many instances the host—plant or animal—cannot manufacture its own food and the guest belongs to the family of organisms that can synthesize nutrients by absorbing sunlight. Hosts of this kind are heterotrophs: "other-feeders." Among plants the fungi fit into this group; so do most forms of animal life. Their guests are autotrophs: "self-feeders." The process that nourishes them is the familiar one we call photosynthesis.

An instance of such a relationship is provided by lichens, the characteristically flat, crusty plants that can survive in harshly dry and cold environments. Microscopic study long ago demonstrated that a lichen is a symbiotic partnership between an alga (the autotroph) and a fungus (the heterotroph). Vernon Ahmadjian of Clark University has managed to dissociate the partners that form lichens of the genus *Cladonia*, and he has succeeded in raising the two components independently.

Endosymbiosis has been characterized as swallowing without digesting. One protozoan symbiont—*Paramecium bursaria*, commonly known as the green paramecium—provides an apt illustration. This protozoon has been studied intensively by Richard Siegel of the University of California at Los Angeles and Stephen Karakashian of the State University of New York at Old Westbury. It is green because numerous photosynthetic green algae inhabit its single cell. The photosynthetic guests, given adequate light, can keep the host alive under near-starvation conditions. When the host is deprived of its guests, it will survive only if extra nutrients are added to its medium. The guests (members of the genus *Chlorella*, a common green alga) will also survive when they are removed from the host.

When the organism is reconstituted in the laboratory by bringing the isolated paramecium and the algae together, an interesting thing happens. Once back inside the host, the algae multiply, but only until the normal, genetically regulated number of algae per paramecium is attained. The multiplication then stops. Should the protozoon encounter free-living *Chlorella*, they are promptly digested. Its own algal partners, however, are totally immune. Somehow the paramecium recognizes its symbiont, although even with the electron microscope it is not easy to see any morphological difference between the free-living *Chlorella* and the symbiotic one.

The relationships described thus far involve hosts whose guests all belong to a single species. Far more complex kinds of symbiosis are known. There is one protozoon, for example, that is itself a symbiont and at the same time is the host of three other symbionts. This is the flagellate *Myxotricha paradoxa*, a large, smooth-swimming single-celled organism that seems to be covered with hairlike flagella of various sizes. *Myxotricha* lives in the gut of certain Australian termites; it contributes to the insects' survival by helping them digest the pulverized wood that comprises their food.

When *Myxotricha* was first described, it was thought to be just another multiflagellate protozoon with an unusual mode of swimming.

A detailed study by A. V. Grimstone of the University of Cambridge and L. R. Cleveland of the University of Georgia revealed that *Myxotricha* actually had only a few normal flagella at one end. What were mistaken for flagella elsewhere on the organism were spirochetes—a kind of elongated motile bacterium—that were living symbiotically on the surface of the protozoan host. This was not all; each spirochete was associated with another kind of symbiotic bacterium that was also attached to the host's surface, and still a third kind of symbiotic bacterium lived inside *Myxotricha* [*see illustration on page 182*]. As Grimstone and Cleveland have noted, the protozoon "glides along uninterruptedly" through the gut of the termite "at constant speed and usually in a straight line," with its symbiotic spirochetes undulating vigorously.

Organelles of the Eukaryotic Cell

Having seen how many different kinds of independent organism can enter into symbiotic partnerships and how some of these partnerships can be perpetuated on a hereditary basis, we now turn to the eukaryotic cell. When we examine such a cell under the microscope, we see that it contains not only a nucleus but also other organelles. In the eukaryotic cells of a green leaf, for example, there are tiny green chloroplasts, where the chemical events of photosynthesis take place. In the cells of both plants and animals there are mitochondria, where foodstuffs are oxidized to produce ATP (adenosine triphosphate), the universal fuel of biochemical reactions. These are only two of several types of organelle.

Could these organelles have originated as independent organisms? One kind

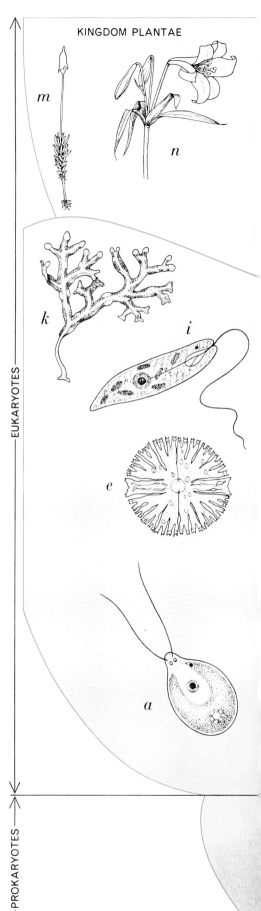

KINGDOM PLANTAE

EUKARYOTES

PROKARYOTES

"FIVE-KINGDOM" CLASSIFICATION of terrestrial life, proposed by R. H. Whittaker of Cornell University to solve the dilemma posed by the conventional classification of organisms as either plants or animals, is shown as modified by the author. The life forms comprise two unambiguous and mutually exclusive groups: prokaryotes, the organisms with cells that lack membrane-enclosed nuclei, all within the kingdom Monera, and the eukaryotes, the organisms with truly nucleated cells, which include the populations of the other four. Organisms representative of major phyla are illustrated. In the kingdom Monera these are various bacteria (*left*) and a blue-green alga, *Nostoc* (*right*). In the kingdom Protista are *Chlamydomonas*, one of the chlorophyta (*a*), diatoms (*b*), an amoeba (*c*), a dinoflagellate (*d*), a desmid (*e*), a foraminiferan (*f*), a trypanosome (*g*), a sun animalcule (*h*), a euglena (*i*), a paramecium (*j*), a brown seaweed (*k*) and a cellular slime mold (*l*). The two phyla in the kingdom Plantae, a group nourished by photosynthesis, are represented by a haircap moss (*m*) and a lily (*n*). In the kingdom Fungi, a group characterized by absorptive nutrition, are a bread mold (*o*) and a mushroom (*p*). In the kingdom Animalia, characterized by ingestive nutrition, the representatives are a mollusk (*q*), arthropod (*r*) and chordate (*s*).

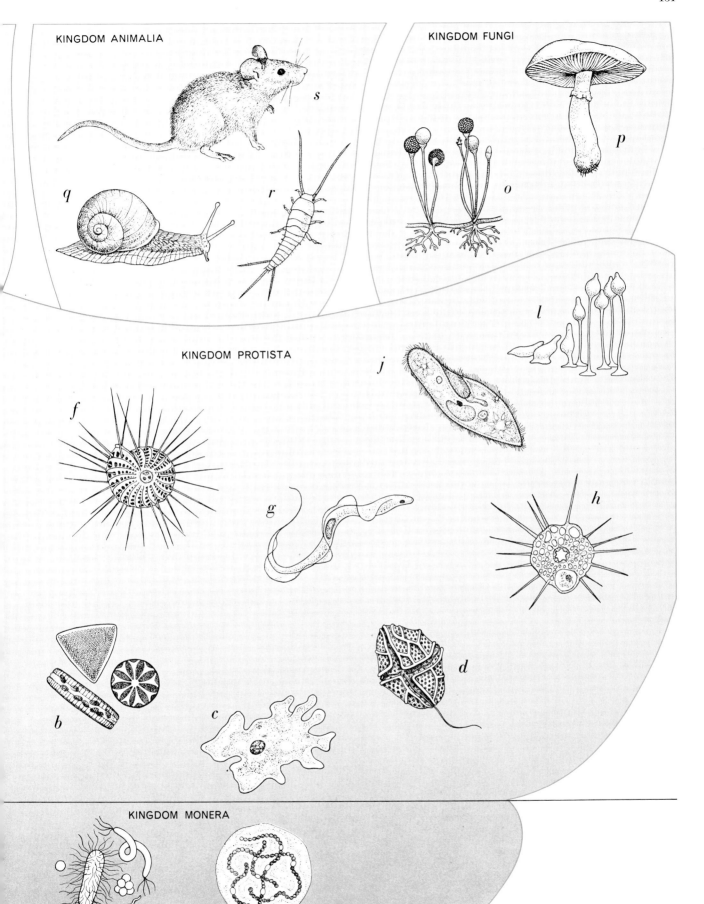

KINGDOM ANIMALIA

KINGDOM FUNGI

KINGDOM PROTISTA

KINGDOM MONERA

of evidence immediately suggests such an origin: the existence of what are known as cytoplasmic genes. When we speak of genes, we usually have in mind the hereditary material—the DNA—in the chromosomes of the cell nucleus. Yet genes are also found outside the nucleus in the cytoplasm, notably in association with chloroplasts and mitochondria.

Chloroplasts belong to a group of organelles collectively known as plastids. Plastids have their own unique DNA—a DNA unrelated to the DNA of the cell nucleus. As has been abundantly demonstrated over the past two decades, DNA is the replicative molecule of the cell. It encodes the synthesis of the proteins required for the doubling of the cell material before cell division. It has also been demonstrated that chloroplasts have their own ribosomes: the bodies where protein is synthesized. The present picture of cellular protein synthesis is that the hereditary information encoded in DNA is transcribed in "messenger" RNA, which then provides the ribosome with the information it needs to link amino acids into a particular protein. In the process each amino acid molecule temporarily combines with a specific molecule of another kind of RNA: "transfer" RNA. Chloroplasts also contain specific transfer RNA's and other components necessary for independent protein synthesis.

Mitochondria also contain DNA that is not related to the DNA of the cell nucleus. The mitochondria in animal cells apparently have only enough DNA and

the associated protein-synthesizing machinery to produce a fraction of the structural protein and enzymes needed by these organelles in order to function. Nonetheless, the machinery is there: DNA, messenger RNA, special mitochondrial ribosomes and so forth. The presence of DNA associated with protein synthesis implies that the mitochondria have a functional genetic system.

Here, then, are two organelles of eukaryotic cells that have their own genes and conduct protein synthesis. When one considers that almost all the protein synthesis in the eukaryotic cell is under the direction of nuclear DNA and that the synthesis is accomplished by ribosomes in the cytoplasm external to both the mitochondria and the plastids, it is natural to wonder why these organelles carry duplicate equipment. Does their ability to grow and divide within the cell and to make some of their own protein under the direction of their own genes imply that they were once free-living organisms? A number of investigators have thought so.

When the plastids of eukaryotic algae were studied under the microscope in the 19th century, it was remarked that they resembled certain free-living algae, and it was suggested that they had originated as such algae. A similar origin for mitochondria was proposed in the 1920's by an American physician, J. E. Wallin. On the basis of microscopic observations, of reactions to stains and of assertions (subsequently refuted) that he had grown isolated mitochondria in the laboratory, Wallin maintained that mito-

chondria were bacteria that had come to live symbiotically within animal cells. In his book *Symbioticism and the Origin of Species* he argued that new species arise as a result of this kind of symbiosis between distantly related organisms. As can happen to people obsessed by a novel concept, Wallin overstated his case and used doubtful data to defend it. His book fell into disrepute.

What is known today about the biochemical autonomy of mitochondria goes a long way toward rehabilitating Wallin's basic concept. It now seems certain that mitochondria were once free-living bacteria that over a long period of time established a hereditary symbiosis with ancestral hosts that ultimately evolved into animal cells, plant cells and cells that fit neither of these categories. The same history evidently holds true for plastids, which were originally free-living algae. I believe that still a third group of organelles, the flagella and cilia, became associated with the eukaryotic cell in much the same way.

Flagella and Cilia

Flagella and cilia are really the same. If these hairlike cell projections are long and few, they are called flagella; if they are short and many, they are called cilia. Their motion propels the cell through its medium or, if the cell is fixed in place, moves things past it. In the tissues of higher animals some flagella and cilia have been drastically modified to serve other functions. The light receptors in the eye of vertebrates are such structures. So are the smell receptors of vertebrates. Among prokaryotes the analogous structures are much simpler. They are small, single-stranded and consist of a protein called flagellin.

The flagella and cilia of eukaryotic cells are much larger than those of prokaryotes. Their basic structure is strikingly uniform, whether they come from the sperm of a fern or the nostril of a mouse. Seen in cross section, each consists of a circle of paired microtubules surrounding one centrally located pair. If the structure is motile, there are always two microtubules in the middle and always nine more pairs surrounding them; the pattern is known as the "9 + 2 array" [*see illustrations on page 184*]. Microtubules from any kind of eukaryotic flagella and cilia are composed of related proteins called tubulin.

At the base of every eukaryotic flagellum and cilium is a distinct microtubular structure: the basal body. The architecture of the basal body is identical with that of the centriole, a structure found

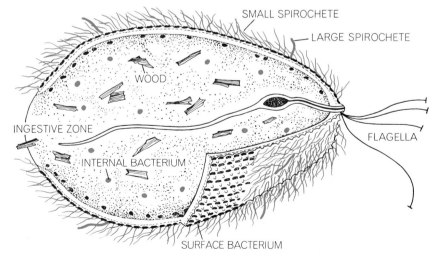

COMPLEX SYMBIONT, the protozoon *Myxotricha paradoxa*, lives as a guest in the gut of certain Australian termites and plays host to three symbionts of its own. These are surface bacteria of the spirochete group (*color*), which observers first mistook for flagella, other surface bacteria (*black*) and still other bacteria (*color*) that live inside the protozoon.

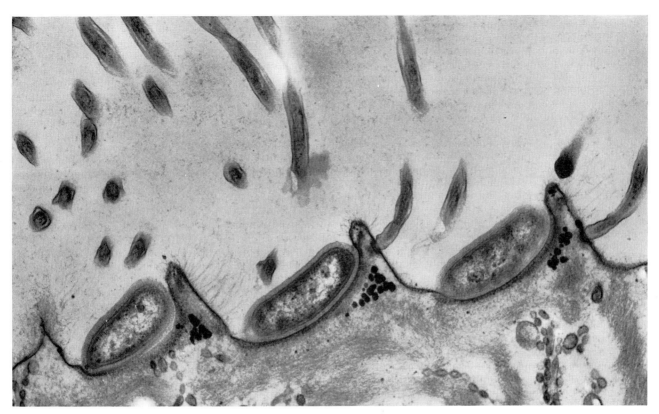

SURFACE OF *MYXOTRICHA* appears at the bottom in transverse section in this electron micrograph by A. V. Grimstone of the University of Cambridge. In the "hollow" to the left of each surface "peak" lies one of the bacterium guests of the protozoan host. Two symbiotic spirochetes are visible at right with their basal ends attached to the host membrane. Other spirochetes whose attachments are not in the plane of focus are partially visible elsewhere in the micrograph (*top*). The theory proposing that eukaryotic cells are the products of similar symbiotic relationships suggests that the first symbionts were free-living bacterium-like prokaryotes.

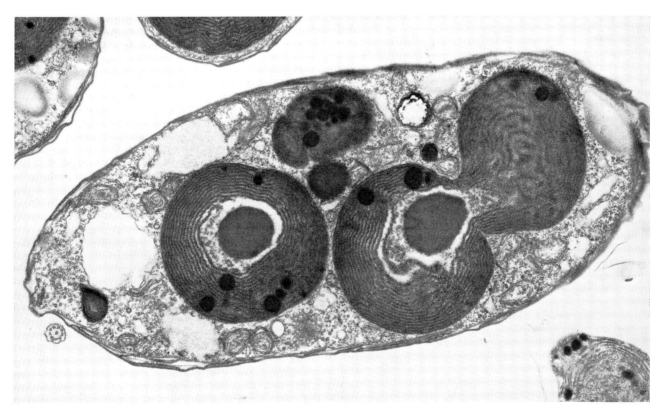

PROKARYOTIC GUESTS, identifiable by their array of concentric photosynthetic membranes as the blue-green alga *Cyanocyta*, are enlarged 15,000 times in this electron micrograph by William T. Hall of the National Institutes of Health. They are inside protozoan hosts of the species *Cyanophora paradoxa*. Similar hereditary symbioses between various photosynthetic alga-like prokaryotes and large, more advanced eukaryotic hosts from the kingdom Protista is suggested as the step leading to evolution of the plant kingdom.

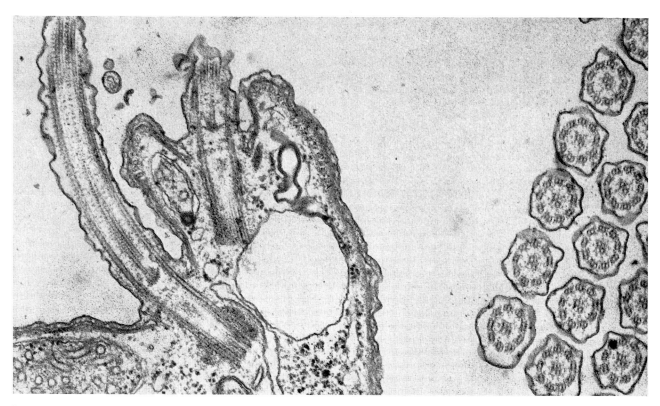

STRUCTURE OF FLAGELLA is shown in transverse section (*right*) and longitudinal section (*left*) in an electron micrograph by R. D. Allen of the University of Hawaii. In the part of the flagellum extending beyond the basal body a circle of paired micro-tubules surrounds a central pair in what is known as a "9 + 2 array." In the basal body the central pair of microtubules is absent and the array is "9 + 0." Such organelles are found only among the eukaryotes and may originally have been free-living cells.

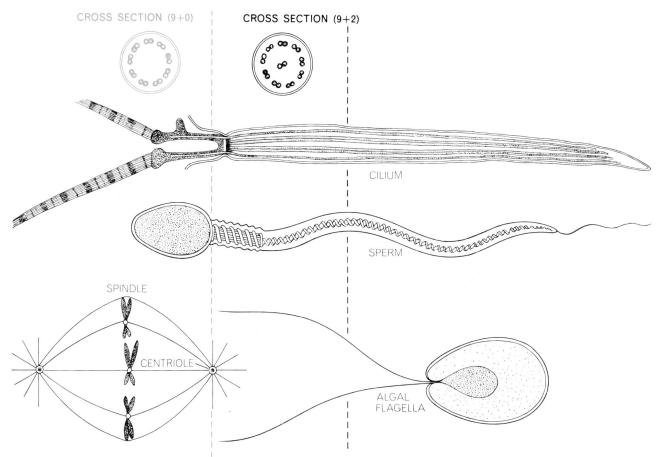

MICROTUBULES comprise a variety of structures, including the motile flagella of certain algae (*bottom right*) and of sperm, the cilia of tracheal membrane and the centrioles and the spindle structure that mediates halving of the nucleus in mitotic division.

at opposite poles of the eukaryotic cell nucleus. Centrioles come into particular prominence during mitosis, the process by which eukaryotic cells divide. (Centrioles are found in nearly all animal cells and in the cells of many eukaryotic algae but not in certain fungi and in most higher plants).

The structural array of the basal body and the centriole is "9 + 0": the central pair of microtubules is absent. In cells that possess mitotic centrioles the centrioles left over from earlier cell divisions often grow projections that become flagella or cilia as the new cell differentiates. Thus not only are basal bodies and centrioles identical in structural pattern but also centrioles can become basal bodies. Moreover, the mitotic spindle, the characteristic diamond-shaped structure that lies between the centrioles during cell division, is an array of microtubules composed of tubulin.

A further finding requires that we now ask two fundamental questions. When the plant alkaloid colchicine is added to tubulin, derived either from flagella or cilia or from spindles, the alkaloid is bound to the protein. The reaction is characteristic of tubulin from the cells of all animals and all eukaryotic plants, but it has never been observed with the flagellin from prokaryotic cells. Nor, for that matter, have microtubules ever been observed in either bacteria or blue-green algae.

The first question is this: What differentiates animals from plants? At the macroscopic level the differences are obvious; for example, most animals move around in order to feed themselves, whereas most plants stand still and nourish themselves by photosynthesis. At the microscopic level distinctions of this kind become meaningless. Many kinds of single-celled organism sometimes nourish themselves by photosynthesis and at other times swim about ingesting food particles. Some organisms crawl like an amoeba at one stage in their development but later stop, sprout stems and disperse a new generation in the form of spores. Further examples are almost innumerable.

Generations of biologists have been troubled by the need to force such organisms into the plant or animal kingdom. A far less ambiguous dichotomy is the division between prokaryotes and eukaryotes. Notable dissenters from the plant-animal classification are Herbert F. Copeland of Sacramento State College, G. Evelyn Hutchinson of Yale University and most recently R. H. Whittaker of Cornell University. In what follows I have modified Whittaker's "five-kingdom" classification, which takes the fundamental prokaryote-eukaryote dichotomy fully into account [see illustration on pages 180 and 181]. The answer to the first question, then, is that there are not just two basic kinds of organism but five.

This brings us to the second question: How did five kingdoms arise? I have already suggested that eukaryotic cells, which are characteristic of all higher forms of life, came into existence through an evolutionary advance of a kind fundamentally different from discrete mutation. Specific answers to the second question will appear in the following hypothetical reconstruction of the origin of eukaryotic cells. The reconstruction traces the rise of the more advanced four of Whittaker's five kingdoms from their origin in the least advanced one. That kingdom is the kingdom Monera: the prokaryotic single-celled organisms that were the first living things to evolve on the earth. The reader should be warned that my presentation of the theory here is necessarily brief and oversimplified.

The First Cells

All life on the earth is believed to have originated more than three billion years ago during Lower Precambrian times in the form of bacterium-like prokaryotic cells. At that time there was no free oxygen in the atmosphere. The cells that arose were fermenting cells; their food consisted of organic matter that had been produced earlier by the action of various abiotic processes. Under pressures of natural selection directly related to the depletion of this stock of abiotic nutrients, there arose among the first fermenting bacteria many metabolic traits that are still observable among bacteria living today. These traits include the ability to ferment many different carbohydrates, to incorporate atmospheric carbon dioxide directly into reduced metabolic compounds, to reduce sulfate to hydrogen sulfide as a by-product of fermentation, and so on.

As the ammonia available in some parts of the environment became depleted, certain bacteria evolved metabolic pathways that could "fix" atmospheric nitrogen into amino acids. Other fermenters developed into highly motile organisms that foreshadowed such highly mobile living bacteria as spirochetes. All these fermenting bacteria were "obligate anaerobes," that is, for them oxygen was a powerful poison. Through various detoxification mechanisms the fermenters were able to dispose of the small amount of this deadly element present in the environment as a result of abiotic processes. Finally, many if not all of the various fermenting bacteria were equipped with well-developed systems for the repair of DNA. Such systems were necessary to counteract the damage done by ultraviolet radiation, which at that time was intense because there was no ozone (O_3) in the atmosphere to filter it out.

All these bacteria were heterotrophs; they had not evolved the photosynthetic mechanisms that would have enabled them to nourish themselves in the absence of abiotic organic compounds. In time some of them developed metabolic pathways that led to the synthesis of the compounds known as porphyrins. It is a purely fortuitous property of porphyrins that they absorb radiation at the visible wavelengths; nonetheless, this property was eventually put to use by the evolution of bacterial photosynthesis. The process of photosynthesis requires a source of hydrogen. Bacteria can utilize such inorganic substances as hydrogen sulfide and gaseous hydrogen as well as various organic compounds of the kind that would have been present in the environment as by-products of fermentation. These first anaerobic photosynthesizers appeared in Lower Precambrian times.

When the new photosynthetic bacteria became well established, a process that may have taken millions of years, a second kind of photosynthesis was able to make its appearance. In the second process the uptake of hydrogen was accomplished by the splitting of water molecules; as a result increasing quantities of lethal free oxygen entered the atmosphere as a waste product. The evolution of this mode of photosynthesis led to the appearance of the blue-green algae, the first organisms on the earth that were adapted to the presence of free oxygen. Since they were active photosynthesizers of the newer type, they accelerated the increase in atmospheric oxygen.

The blue-green algae, whose Precambrian success is attested by the massive calcium-rich rock formations they left behind, presented a profound threat to all other forms of life. The other organisms were forced to adapt or perish. Some of the anaerobes adapted simply by retreating into the oxygen-free muds where their fellows are found today. Others developed new mechanisms of oxygen detoxification; still others, it is safe to assume, merely disappeared. In any case, one result of the success of the blue-green algae was the evolution of new kinds of bacteria that utilized free oxygen in their metabolic processes: aerobic respirers, oxidizers of sulfide and ammonia, and the like. As atmospheric oxygen continued to accumulate, the stage was set for the initial appearance of eukaryotic cells.

The First Eukaryote

The first advanced cell came into existence when some kind of host, perhaps a fermenting bacterium, acquired as symbiotic partners a number of smaller oxygen-respiring bacteria. As atmospheric oxygen continued to increase, selection pressure would have favored such a symbiosis. Eventually the small aerobic bacteria became the hereditary guests of their hosts; these were the first mitochondria. The host symbionts, in turn, evolved in the direction of amoebas, so that a new population of large aerobic cells evolved and faced the problem of finding nutrients.

In due course the partners were aided in their quest for food: a second group of symbionts, flagellum-like bacteria comparable to modern spirochetes, attached themselves to the host's surface and greatly increased its motility. If this

hypothetical triple partnership begins to resemble the termite symbiont *Myxotricha,* it is with good reason; I believe that just such a *Myxotricha*-like symbiotic association, formed in Precambrian times, was a universal ancestor to all eukaryotic organisms. With the appearance of this supercell the kingdom Monera gives rise, in a manner consistent with Whittaker's taxonomic system, to the kingdom Protista.

The internal guests, then, served as mitochondria and the external ones as flagella. The spirochete-like guests, however, slowly evolved another role. The specialized basal body of the flagellum and its associated microtubules came to serve the additional function of mediating the process of cell division. Respectively the centriole and the mitotic spindle, they were responsible for dividing the parent cell's genes evenly between daughter cells.

Mitotic cell division was the crucial genetic step toward further evolutionary advance. One would not expect it to have developed in a straight-line manner, starting with no mitosis and concluding with perfect mitosis. There must have been numerous dead ends, varia-

tions and byways. Evidence of just such uncertain gradualism is found today among the lower eukaryotes, for example the slime molds, the yellow-green and golden-yellow algae, the euglenids, the slime-net amoebas and others. Many of their mitotic arrangements are unconventional. The perfection of mitosis may have occupied as much as a billion years of Precambrian time.

Mitosis, however, was the key to the future. Without mitosis there could be no meiosis, the type of cell division that gives rise to eggs and sperm. There could be no complex multicellular organisms and no natural selection along Mendelian genetic lines. As mitosis was perfected the kingdom Protista gave rise to three other new kingdoms.

Plant-like protists probably appeared several times through symbiotic unions between free-living, autotrophic prokaryote blue-green algae and various heterotrophic eukaryote protists. After much modification the guest algae developed into those key organelles of the plant kingdom, the photosynthetic plastids. Some of the original symbiotic organisms are represented today by the eukaryotic algae that eventually evolved into the ancestors of the plant kingdom. Both algae with nucleated cells and higher plants have of course evolved a great deal since they first acquired photosynthetic guest plastids more than half a billion years ago. Their evolutionary progress, however, involves neither the origin nor any fundamental modification of the photosynthetic process. This heritage from their anaerobic prokaryote ancestors they received fully formed at the close of the Precambrian.

The group of organisms that we know as the fungi—molds, mushrooms, yeasts and the like—are also thought to derive directly from protists that relinquished flagellar motility in exchange for mitosis. This suggestion is consistent with Whittaker's classification. He splits the fungi from the plant kingdom and recognizes that these fundamentally different organisms deserve a domain of their own. The evolution of the animal kingdom, in turn, is considered a straight-line consequence of natural selection acting on the multicellular, sexually reproductive organisms that, like the fungi, did not happen to play host to plastids in Upper Precambrian times.

Testing the Hypothesis

Compared with what had gone before, however, all this seems to be virtually modern history. It is more pertinent at this juncture to see if the theory of

SYMBIOSIS THEORY is summarized in the three steps illustrated here. Union between two members of the kingdom Monera, a newly evolved aerobic bacterium (*bottom left*) and a larger host, possibly a fermenting bacterium (*bottom right*), brought into existence an amoeboid-like protist whose several guests became mitochondria. A second hereditary symbiosis, joining the amoeboid to a bacterium of the spirochete group (*center right*), brought into being an ancestral "amoeboflagellate" that was the direct forebear of two kingdoms: Fungi and Animalia. When the same amoeboflagellate went on to form another relationship, with algae that became plastids, the fifth kingdom, Plantae, was founded.

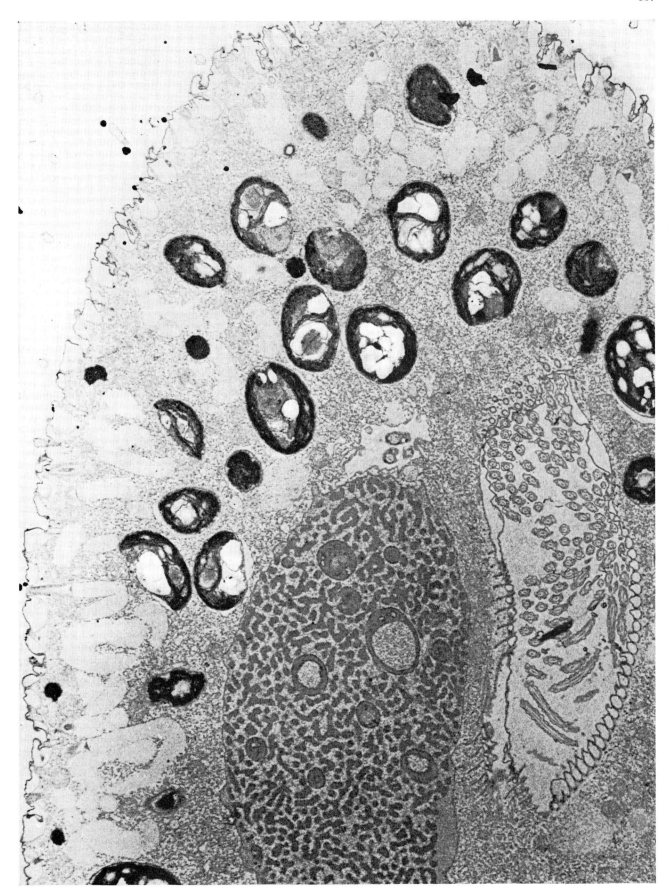

HEREDITARY SYMBIOSIS between photosynthetic green algae of the genus *Chlorella* (*scattered dark ovals*) and a single-celled animal host is characteristic of the species *Paramecium bursaria*, seen magnified 8,000 times in this electron micrograph. Even when the host is kept close to starvation, its guest symbionts satisfy its basic food requirements as long as sunlight is available. The chloroplasts in photosynthetic cells may once have been similar free-living alga-like organisms that eventually became guest symbionts.

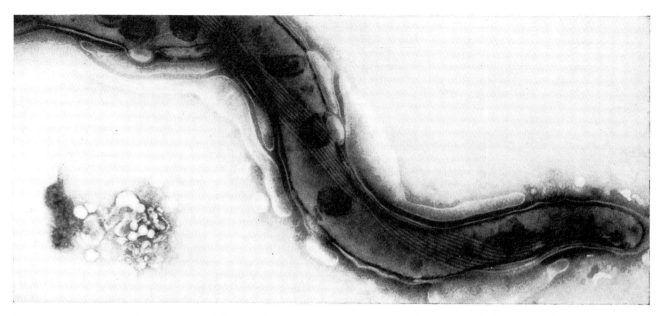

FREE-LIVING MONERAN, a bacterium of the spirochete group, is seen magnified 55,000 times in this electron micrograph. It is an anaerobic bacterium found in the human mouth. Organisms like this may have given rise to the eukaryotic flagella through symbiosis.

eukaryotic-cell origin through hereditary symbiosis offers useful answers to further outstanding questions.

Why are there genes outside cell nuclei? Some cytoplasmic genes may have arisen in other ways, but the symbiosis theory holds that the genes associated with chloroplasts and mitochondria demonstrate that these two kinds of organelle were once free-living organisms.

Why does evidence for photosynthesis appear in Middle Precambrian times, even though no higher plants appear in the fossil record until a mere 600 million years ago? The theory proposes that the higher plants are the result of a symbiosis between animal-like hosts and photosynthetic blue-green-alga-like guests whose partnership could not have evolved until relatively recent times, when mitosis had been perfected.

Why should there be any connection between, on the one hand, the basal body and the flagellum and, on the other, the centriole and the mitotic spindle? The proposal is that the original free-living organism that once accounted only for the function of motility was ancestral to the organelles that came to mediate the equal partition of genetic material between daughter cells during mitosis.

Obviously many other questions remain to be answered. Can the synthesis of DNA and of messenger RNA be detected in association with the reproduction of the basal body and the centriole? Can evidence be found of a unique protein-synthesis system associated with these bodies? Without such evidence the case for these organelles having once been free-living organisms is weak. How and when did meiosis evolve from mitosis? Which organisms were the initial hosts to the guest bacteria that became mitochondria? Were guest plastids of different kinds—red, brown, golden-yellow—acquired independently by the various kinds of eukaryotic algae? One related question is profoundly social. Can botanists, invertebrate zoologists and microbiologists, with their widely different backgrounds, agree on a single classification and a consistent evolutionary scheme for the lower organisms?

Conclusive proof that the symbiosis theory is correct demands experiment. The symbiotic partners will have to be separated, grown independently and then brought back into the same partnership. No organelle of a eukaryotic cell has yet been cultivated outside the cell. The function of a theory, however, is to make reasonable predictions that can be proved or disproved. The predictions of the symbiosis theory are clear.

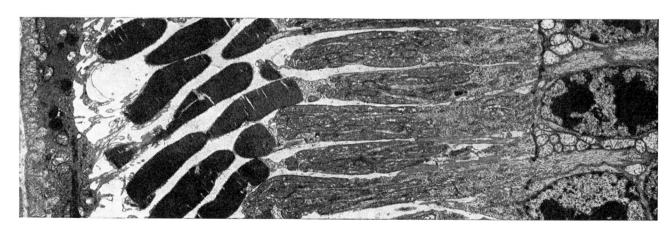

SPECIALIZED FLAGELLA, shown enlarged 3,900 times in an electron micrograph by Toichiro Kuwabara of the Harvard Medical School, are visual receptors in the retina of a rabbit. The darker structures at left are the outer segments of the visual receptors.

IV

ECOSYSTEMS

Life consists of a thin film, or more precisely a light dusting, over the surface of the earth. This biosphere, and the more or less separable divisions of it loosely referred to as *ecosystems*, are the subject of the articles to follow. G. Evelyn Hutchinson, George M. Woodwell, Bert Bolin, and C. C. Delwiche take a global view of the energy and mineral cycles in search of rules and laws that can increase our understanding of the workings of lesser units. These authors observe that although all life is powered by energy from the sun, it is relatively inefficient at harvesting and managing this resource. The photosynthesizing plants, including the microscopic algae that float in the sea, fix only about one-tenth of one percent of the solar energy reaching the surface of the earth. The great bulk of the captured energy is quickly leaked away by respiration; only about ten to twenty percent makes its way into plant-eating animals. Predatory animals that feed on the herbivores get ten to twenty percent of that reduced amount. Similar reductions occur at each step on up through the food chains. By the time we reach the top carnivores (three to five levels removed from the plants), the residue of energy is extremely small. This is why wolves, tigers, and killer whales must search far and wide for their prey and why no animals specialize on them—not because they are so dangerous to catch but because they yield too little energy to make the effort profitable. Man, as Edward S. Deevey points out in "The Human Crop," likes to live like a top carnivore, eating cattle and other big herbivorous mammals; but the continuing growth of his populations will force underdeveloped and affluent nations alike to turn increasingly to plants for enough energy to survive. Even the ocean fisheries have been exploited close to their limits. The most prized food fishes especially are at or close to the top of the marine food chains.

The materials of the earth, in contrast to its energy, cycle eternally. Many of the same carbon and nitrogen atoms that compose your body and the pages of this book circulated through the dinosaurs and tree ferns of the Mesozoic Era. Each element flows along a distinctive network of pathways into and out of organisms, water, the earth, and the atmosphere. The organisms incorporate their atoms into large molecules which are then quickly broken down again. While atoms are in the free ionic state or bonded into small molecules, they escape as excretion into the physical part of the environment; they are then picked up by the photosynthetic plants or entombed for varying periods of time within petroleum, rocks, and other geological deposits. An astonishing diversity of organisms have evolved to position themselves at strategic points along the material cycles. With specialized biochemical reactions, they extract energy denied to other kinds of organisms. Some bacteria, for example, profitably fix free nitrogen into ammonia. Others gain energy by decomposing amino acids to the ammonium ion (NH_4^+). Still others convert the ammonium ion to nitrite (NO_2^-), or nitrite to nitrate (NO_3^-), also with an energy gain. The food chains of an ecosystem, exemplified with particular lucidity in John D. Isaacs' "The Nature of Oceanic Life," are based entirely on such stepwise biochemical specializations.

Everyone is now aware to some extent that man's activities are disrupting the biosphere; but exactly what form does the disruption follow? Man does not halt the solar irradiation, nor does he even change the primary productivity of photosynthetic plants to any great extent. His major impact takes two forms. Agriculture has simplified the living environment over large parts of the earth by supplanting forests, grasslands, and other habitats once rich in species favorable to man's own survival. The price paid is in monotony, lessened ecological stability, and the loss of genetic reserves that future generations may judge to have been priceless. Man's second principal influence is in the alteration of the material cycles. The cycles cannot be stopped. They merely shift to new equilibria, but this transformation is usually maladaptive for both man and other organisms. The reason is ultimately genetic: our populations have been adapted by millions of years of evolution to the old cycles.

This principle of shifting the environment away from the genes is easily documented. The traumatic effect of deforestation on virtually every cycle was shown dramatically in the Hubbard Brook Forest experiment, described by F. Herbert Bormann and Gene E. Likens in "The Nutrient Cycles of an Ecosystem." When all the vegetation was cut in a small New Hampshire watershed and regrowth prevented by herbicides, the minerals and particulate organic matter began to wash out quickly, and the chemical content of the soil was altered. When such treatment is continued in any environment, either by experimental design or as a by-product of economic exploitation, few species can adjust; in the end the environment becomes unsuitable even for man's narrow purposes. As materials are redistributed, a few pockets occur where they are superabundant. The eutrophication of lakes and streams is a case in point. Microorganisms and algae thrive on excess nutrients from sewerage, agriculture, and industrial pollution. Such habitats teem with life, but the species are few and seldom useful to man; and their decomposition depletes the oxygen below the surface layer. The cycles have been altered and new ecosystems created, but they are not the ones to which man and the great majority of other species of animals and plants are adapted. Another harmful way of transforming the cycles is to manufacture plastics and other new kinds of compounds that cannot easily be decomposed by existing species of microorganisms. As a result, the larger molecules accumulate in the environment. When the man-made substances are also poisonous, the natural ecosystems are truly imperiled. Some of the worst examples of radioactive wastes and pesticides, including DDT in particular, are discussed authoritatively by George M. Woodwell in "Toxic Substances and Ecological Cycles."

It does not follow that everything man does to the environment is automatically harmful. In some parts of the world, large stretches of land are biological deserts because they are strongly deficient in such elements as zinc, copper, and molybdenum, small quantities of which are vital to life. By diagnosing these ecological ills, as A. J. Anderson and E. J. Underwood explain in their article "Trace-element Deserts," biologists are sometimes able to create rich new agricultural lands. But even here, care must be taken not to extinguish the special forms of plants and animals that were adapted to the mineral-deficient soil.

The forests and other complex, mature communities of organisms characterizing particular habitats do not spring up full blown. They are reached by a succession of other kinds of shorter-lived plants and animals. The process begins when bare space is occupied by peculiar constellations of pioneer species, which help to establish the conditions necessary for the establishment of other kinds of organisms. As species disappear, others take their place, sometimes by default and sometimes by competitive exclusion; and finally the climax communities assemble. But no climax community lives forever. Landslides, flooding, abnormal drought, and other drastic changes in the physical environment periodically kill the later successional stages and permit the earlier ones to return. As Edward S. Deevey and Charles F. Cooper show in their respective articles on bogs and the ecology of fire, every larger patch of the world's surface is in a dynamic equilibrium of successional stages. Each point on the earth's surface is in a stage determined partly by the period of time it has endured since the last significant physical change and partly by the speed with which ecological successions occur in the surrounding area.

The section closes with two articles, "The Life of a Sand Dune" by William H. Amos and "Life on the Human Skin" by Mary J. Marples. These articles remind the reader that ecosystems are not necessarily of great geographical range and complexity. Communities exist within communities, independent enough in their organization to be isolated in analysis and used to test and extend the basic ideas of ecology.

SUGGESTED

FURTHER READING

Kormondy, E. J. *Concepts of Ecology.* Englewood Cliffs, N. J.: Prentice-Hall, 1969. 209 pp. A short but substantial textbook that stresses the more descriptive aspects of ecosystem studies.

Smith, R. L. *Ecology and Field Biology.* New York: Harper and Row, 1966. 686 pp. A beautifully illustrated account of typical ecosystems. This is a serviceable elementary textbook for students with a strong interest in descriptive field work.

Ehrlich, P. R., and Ehrlich, Anne. *Population, resources, environment.* (2nd Ed.) San Francisco: W. H. Freeman and Company, 1972. 509 pp. Although a source book that stresses facts for practical use, this more scholarly successor to Paul Ehrlich's *Population Bomb* is written in a provocative and exciting manner and serves as a valuable companion for more general textbooks of ecology.

Ehrenfeld, D. W. *Biological conservation.* New York: Holt, Rinehart, and Winston, 1970. 226 pp. A brief and incisive introduction to some of the best practices of conservation insofar as they can be based on the general science of ecology.

Watt, K. E. F. *Ecology and resource management.* New York: McGraw-Hill, 1968. 450 pp. "Ecological engineering": an exposition of some of the possible methods of environmental management that can be developed from a knowledge of population and community ecology.

Whittaker, R. H. *Communities and ecosystems.* New York: Macmillan Company, 1970. 162 pp. A somewhat more advanced textbook on the organization of ecosystems, stressing theoretical aspects.

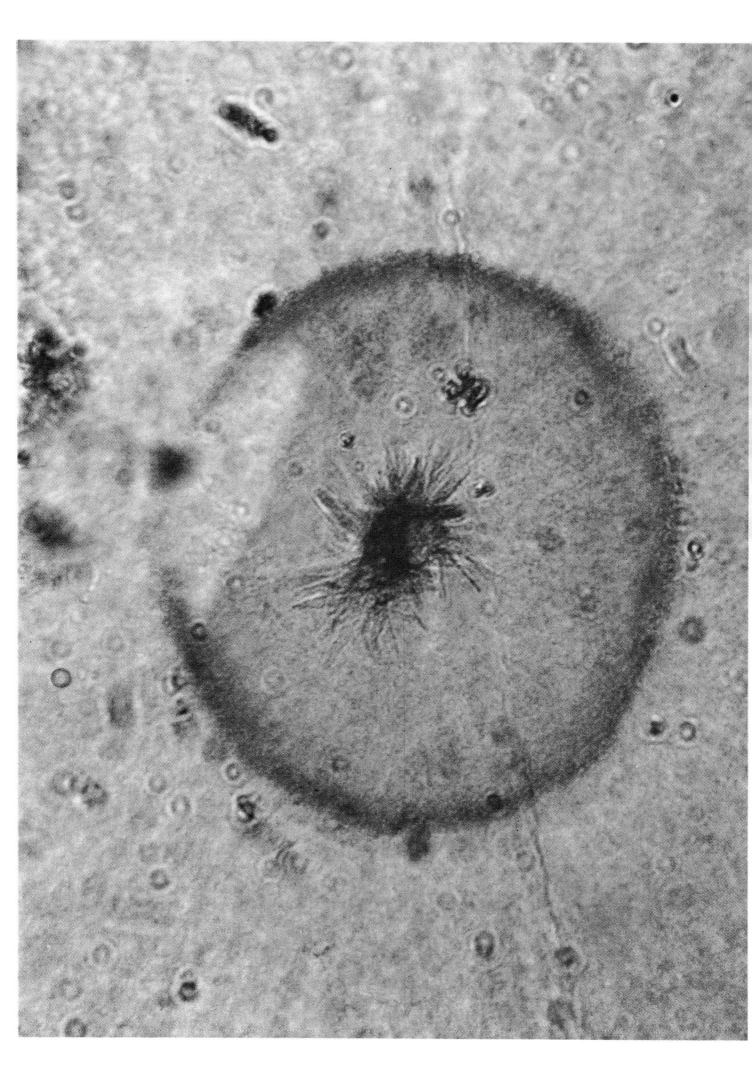

22

THE BIOSPHERE

G. EVELYN HUTCHINSON
September 1970

*How the earth's thin film of living matter is sustained
by grand-scale cycles of energy and chemical elements.
All of these cycles are presently affected by the
activities of man*

The idea of the biosphere was introduced into science rather casually almost a century ago by the Austrian geologist Eduard Suess, who first used the term in a discussion of the various envelopes of the earth in the last and most general chapter of a short book on the genesis of the Alps published in 1875. The concept played little part in scientific thought, however, until the publication, first in Russian in 1926 and later in French in 1929 (under the title *La Biosphère*), of two lectures by the Russian mineralogist Vladimir Ivanovitch Vernadsky. It is essentially Vernadsky's concept of the biosphere, developed about 50 years after Suess wrote, that we accept today. Vernadsky considered that the idea ultimately was derived from the French naturalist Jean Baptiste Lamarck, whose geochemistry, although archaically expressed, was often quite penetrating.

The biosphere is defined as that part of the earth in which life exists, but this definition immediately raises some problems and demands some qualifications. At considerable altitudes above the earth's surface the spores of bacteria and fungi can be obtained by passing air through filters. In general, however, such "aeroplankton" do not appear to be engaged in active metabolism. Even on the surface of the earth there are areas too dry, too cold or too hot to support metabolizing organisms (except technically equipped human explorers), but in such places also spores are commonly found. Thus as a terrestrial envelope the biosphere obviously has a somewhat irregular shape, inasmuch as it is surrounded by an indefinite "parabiospheric" region in which some dormant forms of life are present. Today, of course, life can exist in a space capsule or a space suit far outside the natural biosphere. Such artificial environments may best be regarded as small volumes of the biosphere nipped off and projected temporarily into space.

What is it that is so special about the biosphere as a terrestrial envelope? The answer seems to have three parts. First, it is a region in which liquid water can exist in substantial quantities. Second, it receives an ample supply of energy from an external source, ultimately from the sun. And third, within it there are interfaces between the liquid, the solid and the gaseous states of matter. All three of these apparent conditions for the existence of a biosphere need more detailed study and discussion.

All actively metabolizing organisms consist largely of elaborate systems of organic macromolecules dispersed in an aqueous medium. The adaptability of organisms is so great that even in some deserts or in the peripheral parts of the antarctic ice sheet there may be living beings that contain within themselves the only liquid water in the immediate neighborhood. Although such xerophytic (literally "dry plant") organisms may be able to conserve internal supplies of water for a long time, however, they still need some occasional dew or rain. (The hottest deserts appear to be formally outside the biosphere, although they may be parabiospheric in the sense explained above.) In the immediate past this kind of situation had a certain intellectual interest, since it seemed for a time that organisms might exist on Mars, in an almost waterless environment, by retaining water in their tissues. The most recent studies, however, seem to make any kind of biosphere on Mars quite unlikely.

The energy source on which all terrestrial life depends is the sun. At present the energy of solar radiation can enter the biological cycle only through the photosynthetic production of organic matter by chlorophyll-bearing orga-

REVOLUTION IN THE BIOSPHERE is symbolized by the fossilized blue-green alga in the photomicrograph on the opposite page. The cell, which is one of a variety of similar fossils found in the Gunflint geological formation in southern Ontario by Stanley A. Tyler and Elso S. Barghoorn of Harvard University, is estimated to be approximately two billion years old. The Gunflint algae are the oldest known photosynthetic and nitrogen-fixing organisms. As such they contributed to the original oxygenation of the earth's atmosphere and so prepared the way for all higher forms of plant and animal life in the biosphere.

YEARS BEFORE PRESENT	EVENT	GEOLOGICAL FORMATION	FOSSIL
0	OLDEST HOMINID	SIWALIK HILLS (INDIA)	*RAMAPITHECUS*
	OLDEST LAND PLANT	LUDLOVIAN SERIES, UPPER SILURIAN (BRITAIN)	*COOKSONIA*
	OLDEST METAZOAN ANIMAL	EDIACARA HILLS (AUSTRALIA)	*SPRIGGINA*
1 BILLION			
	OLDEST EUCARYOTIC CELLS	UPPER BECK SPRING DOLOMITE (CALIFORNIA)	UNNAMED
	FORMATION OF OXIDIZING ATMOSPHERE		
2 BILLION	OLDEST PHOTOSYNTHETIC AND NITROGEN-FIXING ORGANISM	GUNFLINT FORMATION (ONTARIO)	*GUNFLINTIA*
3 BILLION	OLDEST KNOWN ORGANISM	FIGTREE FORMATION (SOUTH AFRICA)	*EOBACTERIUM*
	FIRST ROCKS IN EARTH'S CRUST; FORMATION OF OCEAN		
4 BILLION	DIFFERENTIATION OF EARTH'S CRUST, MANTLE AND CORE; CRUST MELTED BY RADIOACTIVE HEATING		
4.5 BILLION	FORMATION OF EARTH		

ROUGH CHRONOLOGY OF THE BIOSPHERE as represented in the fossil record is given on this page, along with the geological formations in which the fossils were found and some other major events in the history of the earth. Data are from various sources.

nisms, namely green and purple bacteria, blue-green algae, phytoplankton and the vast population of higher plants. Such organisms are of course confined to the part of the biosphere that receives solar radiation by day. That includes the atmosphere, the surface of the land, the top few millimeters of soil and the upper waters of oceans, lakes and rivers. The euphotic, or illuminated, zone may be only a few centimeters deep in a very turbid river, or well over 100 meters deep in the clearest parts of the ocean. The biosphere does not end where the light gives out; gravity continues the energy flow downward, since fecal pellets, cast skins and organisms dead and alive are always falling from the illuminated regions into the depths.

The plant life of the open ocean, on which most of the animals of the sea depend for food, is planktonic, or drifting, in a special sense that is often misunderstood. Most of the cells composing a planktonic association are slightly denser than seawater, and under absolutely quiet conditions they would slowly sink to the bottom. That the upper layers are not depleted of plant cells and so of the capacity to generate food and oxygen is attributable entirely to turbulence. The plant cells sink at a speed determined by their size, shape and excess density; as they sink they divide and the population in the upper waters is continually replenished from below by turbulent upwelling water.

The sinking of the phytoplankton cells is in itself the simplest way by which a cell can move from a small parcel of water it has depleted of the available nutrients into a parcel still containing these substances. The mechanism can of course only operate when there is an adequate chance of a lift back to the surface for the cell and some of its descendants. The cellular properties that determine sinking rates, interacting with turbulence, are doubtless as important in the purely liquid part of the biosphere as skeletal and muscular structures, interacting with gravity, are to us as we walk about on the solid-gaseous interface we inhabit. Although this point of view was worked out some 20 years ago, largely through the efforts of the oceanographer Gordon A. Riley, it still seems hardly recognized by many biologists.

In addition to the extension of the biosphere downward, there is a more limited extension upward. On very high mountains the limit above which chlorophyll-bearing plants cannot live appears to be about 6,200 meters (in the Himalayas); it is partly set by a lack of liquid water, but a low carbon dioxide pressure, less than half the pressure at sea level, may also be involved. At still higher altitudes a few animals such as spiders may be found. These probably feed on springtails and perhaps mites that in turn subsist on pollen grains and other organic particles, blown up into what the high-altitude ecologist Lawrence W. Swan calls the aeolian zone.

The rather special circumstances that have just been recognized as needed for the life of simple organisms in the free liquid part of the biosphere emphasize how much easier it is to live at an interface, preferably when one side of the interface is solid, although quite a lot of microorganisms do well at the air-water interface in quiet pools and swamps. It is quite possible, as J. D. Bernal suggested many years ago, that the surface properties of solid materials in contact with water were of great importance in the origin and early development of life.

Studies of photosynthetic productivity show that often the plants that can produce the greatest organic yield under conditions of natural illumination are those that make the best of all three possible states, with their roots in sediments under water and their leaves in the air. Sugarcane and the ubiquitous reed *Phragmites communis* provide striking examples. The substances needed by such plants are (1) water, which is taken up by the roots but is maintained at a fairly constant pressure by the liquid layer over the sediments; (2) carbon dioxide, which is most easily taken up from the gaseous phase where the diffusion rate at the absorptive surface is maximal; (3) oxygen (by night), which is also more easily obtained from the air than from the water, and (4) a great number of other elements, which are most likely to be available in solution in the pore water of the sediment.

The present energetics of the biosphere depend on the photosynthetic reduction of carbon dioxide to form organic compounds and molecular oxygen. It is well known, however, that this process is only one of several of the form: $nCO_2 + 2nH_2A + energy \rightarrow (CH_2O)_n + nA_2 + nH_2O$. In this reaction the hydrogen donor H_2A may be hydrogen sulfide (H_2S), as in the case of the photosynthetic sulfur bacteria, water (H_2O), as in the case of the blue-green algae and higher green plants, or various other organic compounds, as in the case of the nonsulfur purple bacteria. (The last-mentioned case presents a paradox: Why be photosynthetic when there is plenty of metabolizable organic matter in the immediate neighborhood of the photosynthesizing cell?) The actual patterns of the possible reactions are extremely complicated, with several alternative routes in some parts of the process. For the purposes of this discussion, however, the important fact is probably that any set of coupled reactions so complex would take a good deal of mutation and selection to evolve.

The overall geochemical result of photosynthesis is to produce a more oxidized part of the biosphere, namely the atmosphere and most of the free water in which oxygen is dissolved, and a more reduced part, namely the bodies of organisms and their organic decomposition products in litter, soils and aquatic sediments. Some sediments become buried, producing dispersed organic carbon and fossil fuels, and there is a similar loss of oxygen by the oxidation of eroding primary rock. The quantitative relation of the fossilization of the organic (or reduced) carbon and the inorganic (or oxidized) carbon clearly bears on the history of the earth but so far involves too many uncertainties to produce unambiguous answers. From the standpoint of the day-to-day running of the biosphere what is important is the continual oxidation of the reduced part, living or dead, by atmospheric oxygen to produce carbon dioxide (which can be employed again in photosynthesis) and a certain amount of energy (which can be used for physical activity, growth and reproduction). The production of utilizable fossil fuels is essentially an accidental imperfection in this overall reversible cycle, one on which we have come to depend too confidently.

It is necessary to maintain a balance in our attitude by stressing the fragility and inefficiency of the entire process. If one considers a fairly productive lake, for example, it is usual to find about 2.5 milligrams of particulate organic matter under an average square centimeter of lake surface. Assuming that this organic matter is all phytoplankton, with a water content of 90 percent, there are about 25 cubic millimeters of photosynthetic organisms per 100 square millimeters of lake surface. If this were all brought to the surface, it would form a green film a quarter of a millimeter thick. Both assumptions undoubtedly exaggerate the thickness, which may well be no more than a tenth of a millimeter, or the thickness of a sheet of paper.

The total photosynthetic material of the open ocean can hardly be greater and

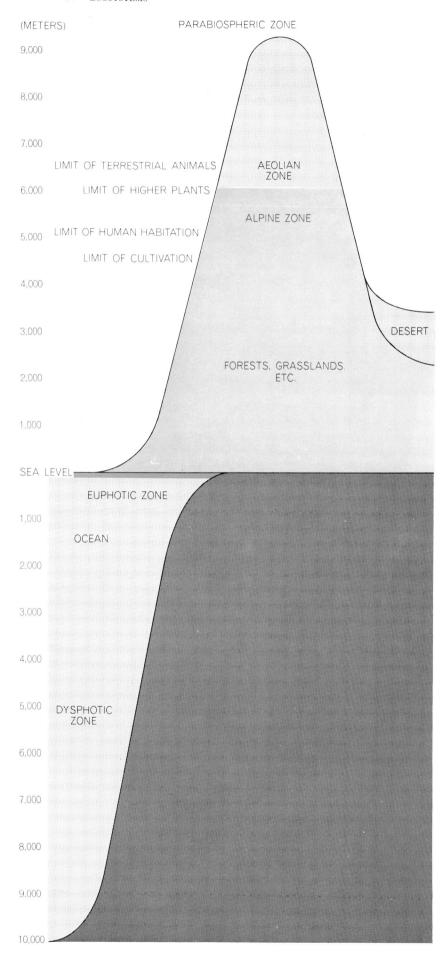

(METERS)

PARABIOSPHERIC ZONE

9,000

8,000

7,000

LIMIT OF TERRESTRIAL ANIMALS

AEOLIAN
ZONE

6,000   LIMIT OF HIGHER PLANTS

ALPINE ZONE

5,000   LIMIT OF HUMAN HABITATION

LIMIT OF CULTIVATION

4,000

3,000

DESERT

FORESTS, GRASSLANDS
ETC.

2,000

1,000

SEA LEVEL

EUPHOTIC ZONE

1,000

OCEAN

2,000

3,000

4,000

5,000   DYSPHOTIC
ZONE

6,000

7,000

8,000

9,000

10,000

may well be much less. Similarly, when one looks up from the floor of a broad-leaved forest, there is obviously some overlap of leaves, but five leaves, one above the other, would usually remove almost all the available energy. Moreover, in this case much of the organic material is in the form of skeletal cellulose, which provides support and control of evaporation; as a result there is an even less economical use of the volume of the plant than in the case of the phytoplankton. The machinery by which energy enters the living world is clearly quite tenuous.

Estimates of the efficiency of the photosynthetic process are quite variable and depend greatly on the circumstances. Under conditions of optimum cultivation an annual utilization of several percent of the incoming visible radiation is easily achieved on land, the limit probably being set by the carbon dioxide content of the air, but the overall efficiency of land surfaces as a whole seems to lie between .1 and .3 percent. In water, under special circumstances aimed at maximum yield, very high levels of production, apparently approaching the theoretical quantum efficiency of the photosynthetic process, seem possible, but again in nature as a whole efficiencies of the order of a few tenths of a percent are usual. On land much of the radiant energy falling on a tall plant is not wasted but is needed to maintain the stream of water being transpired from the leaves.

The movement of material through living organisms involves many more elements than those contained in water and carbon dioxide. In addition to carbon, oxygen and hydrogen, all organisms use nitrogen, phosphorus, sulfur, sodium, potassium, calcium, magnesium, iron, manganese, cobalt, copper, zinc and probably chlorine, and some certainly use for special functions aluminum, boron, bromine, iodine, selenium, chromium, molybdenum, vanadium, silicon,

VERTICAL EXTENT of the biosphere is depicted schematically in the illustration at the left. As a terrestrial envelope the biosphere has a somewhat irregular shape inasmuch as it is surrounded by an indefinite "parabiospheric" region in which some dormant forms of life, such as the spores of bacteria and fungi, are present. The euphotic, or illuminated, zone of aqueous bodies may be only a few centimeters deep in a very turbid river or well over 100 meters deep in the clearest parts of the ocean.

strontium, barium and possibly nickel. A few elements that occur fairly regularly in specific compounds or situations, such as cadmium in the vertebrate kidney or rare earths in the hickory leaf, are obviously of interest even if they are not functional. Some of the elements now known to be significant only in a particular group of organisms, such as boron in plants, iodine in many animals, chromium in veretebrates or selenium in some plants, birds and mammals, may ultimately prove to be universally essential. A few more functional elements, germanium perhaps being a good candidate, may remain to be discovered. Even the rarer trace elements, when they are unquestionably functional, are present in metabolically versatile tissues, such as those of the liver, in quantities on the order of a million atoms per cell. Very little substitution of one element by another is possible, although some bacteria and algae can use rubidium in place of potassium with no adverse effects other than a slowed growth rate. We all know that certain elements are highly toxic (lead, arsenic and mercury are obvious examples), whereas many of the functional elements are poisonous when high levels of intake are induced by local concentrations in the environment. This means that the detailed geochemistry of each element, particularly in the process of crossing the solid-liquid interface, is of enormous biological importance.

Often the possibility of an element's migrating from the solid state to an ionic form in an aqueous phase (from which an organism can obtain a supply of the element) depends on the state of oxidation at the solid-liquid boundary. Under reducing conditions iron and manganese are freely mobile as divalent (doubly ionized) ions, whereas under oxidizing conditions iron, except when it is complexed organically, is essentially insoluble, and manganese usually precipitates as manganese dioxide. Chromium, selenium and vanadium, all of which are required in minute quantities by some organisms, migrate most easily in an oxidized state as chromate, selenate and vanadate, and so behave in a way opposite from iron. The extreme insolubility of the sulfides of iron, copper, zinc and some other heavy metals may limit the availability of these elements when reduction is great enough to allow hydrogen sulfide to be formed in the decomposition of proteins or by other kinds of bacterial action. Phenomena of this kind mean that under different chemical conditions different materials determine how much living matter can be present.

Expanding this 19th-century agriculturist's idea of limiting factors a little, it is evident that in a terrestrial desert hydrogen and oxygen in the form of water determine the amount of life. In the blue waters of the open ocean the best results indicate that a deficiency of iron is usually limiting, the element probably being present only as dispersed ferric hydroxide, which can be used by phytoplankton cells if it becomes attached to their cell wall. In an intermediate situation, as in a natural terrestrial soil in a fairly humid region, or in a lake or coastal sea, phosphorus is probably the most usual limiting element.

The significance of phosphorus in controlling the quantity of living organisms in nature is due not only to its great biological importance but also to the fact that among the light elements it is relatively scarce. As an element of odd atomic number it is almost two orders of magnitude rarer in the universe than its neighbors in the periodic table, silicon and sulfur. Moreover, in iron meteorites

LIFE AT THE FRINGE of the biosphere is represented by this strange-looking creature photographed recently by an automatic camera lowered to a depth of 15,900 feet from the U.S. Naval oceanographic vessel *Kane*, which at the time was situated in the South Atlantic some 350 miles off the coast of Africa. The plantlike organism is actually an animal: a polyp of the family Umbellulidae. The stem on which its food-gathering tentacles are mounted is approximately three feet long and is leaning toward the camera at an angle of 30 degrees.

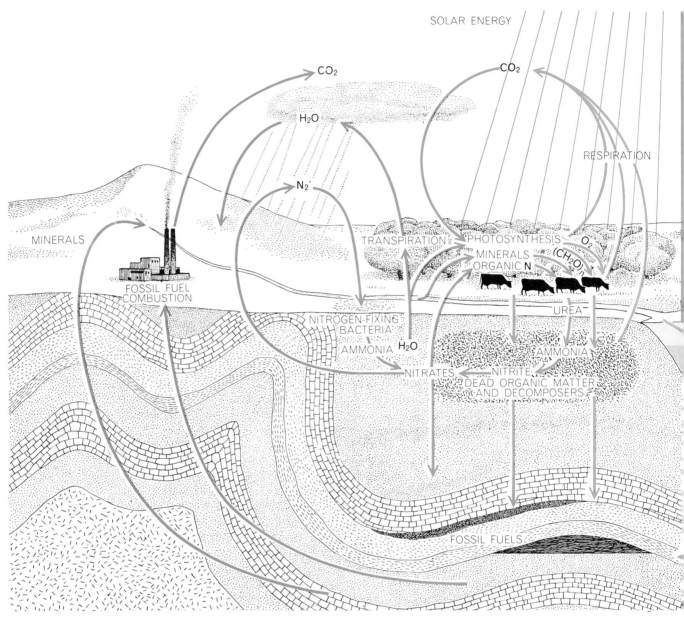

SOLAR ENERGY

CO₂   CO₂

H₂O

RESPIRATION

N₂

MINERALS

TRANSPIRATION   PHOTOSYNTHESIS   O₂
MINERALS   (CH₂O)
ORGANIC N

FOSSIL FUEL
COMBUSTION

UREA

NITROGEN-FIXING
BACTERIA

AMMONIA   H₂O   AMMONIA

NITRATES   NITRITE
DEAD ORGANIC MATTER
AND DECOMPOSERS

FOSSIL FUELS

MAJOR CYCLES OF THE BIOSPHERE are indicated in a general way in the illustration on these two pages; more detailed versions of specific cycles accompany the succeeding articles in this issue. In brief, the operation of the biosphere depends on the utili-

phosphorus is found to be enriched in the form of the iron-nickel phosphide schreibersite, so that it is not unlikely that a good part of the earth's initial supply of the element is locked up in the metallic core of our planet. The amount of phosphorus available is thus initially limited by cosmogenic and planetogenic processes. In the biosphere the element is freely mobile under reducing but not too alkaline conditions; since the supply of reduced iron is nearly always much in excess of the phosphorus, oxidation precipitates not only the iron but also the phosphorus as the very insoluble ferric phosphate.

In many richly productive localities where phosphorus is reasonably accessible the quantity of combined nitrogen evidently builds up by biological fixa-

tion, so that the ratio of the two elements in water or soil will tend to be about the same as it is in living organisms. In such circumstances both the phosphorus and the nitrogen are limiting; the addition of either one alone produces little or no increase in living matter in a bottle of water or in any other system isolated from the environment, whereas the addition of both often leads to a great increase. Where nitrogen alone is limiting it may be the result of a disturbance of the ecological balance between the nitrogen-fixing organisms (mainly blue-green algae in water and bacteria in soil) and the other members of the biological association. Limitation by nitrogen is never due to a dearth of the element as such, since it is the commonest gas in the atmosphere, but rather

depends on the level of activity of the special biological mechanisms, chemically related to photosynthesis but retained only by primitive organisms, for dissociating the two atoms of molecular nitrogen (N_2) and forming from them the amino ($-NH_2$) groups of proteins and other organic compounds.

If the biosphere is to continue in running order, the biologically important materials must undergo cyclical changes so that after utilization they are put back, at the expense of some solar energy, into a form in which they can be reused. The rate at which this happens is quite variable. The rate of circulation of the organic matter of terrestrial organisms, derived from the carbon dioxide of the atmosphere, is measured in decades. In

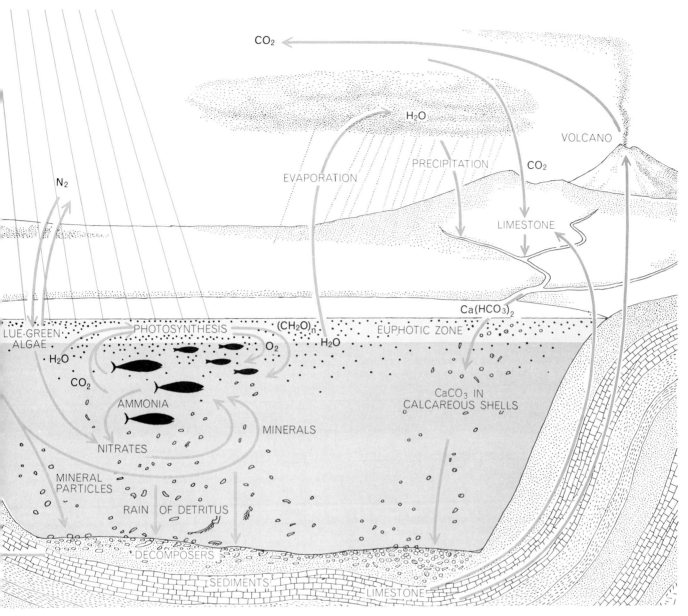

zation of solar energy for the photosynthetic reduction of carbon dioxide (CO_2) from the atmosphere to form organic compounds on .the one hand $(CH_2O)_n$ and molecular oxygen (O_2) on the other. The cycling of certain other vital elements is also indicated.

the case of calcium, which is carried from continental rocks in rivers as calcium bicarbonate ($Ca(HCO_3)_2$) and precipitated as calcium carbonate ($CaCO_3$) in the open ocean largely in the form of the tiny shells of foraminifera, most of the replacement must be due to the movement of the ocean floors toward coastal mountain-building belts; presumably the rate of cyclical replacement would be measured in hundreds of millions of years. Phosphorus would behave rather like calcium, nitrogen more like carbon, although the atmospheric reservoir of nitrogen is of course much larger and the biological fixation of the element is less widespread and energetically more expensive.

At present the artificial injection of some elements in a mobile form into the ocean and atmosphere is occurring much faster than it did in preindustrial days; new cycles have come into being that may distribute very widely and in toxic quantities elements such as lead and mercury, as well as fairly stable new compounds such as insecticides and defoliants. It should be obvious that the possible action of all such substances on the tenuous and geochemically inefficient green mantle of the earth demands intense study if life is to continue in the biosphere.

How did the system we have been examining come into being? There are now a few facts that seem clear and a few inferences that are reasonable. We know that the present supply of atmospheric oxygen is continually replenished by photosynthesis, and that if it were not, it would slowly be used up in the process of oxidation of ferrous to ferric iron and sulfides to sulfates in weathering. All the evidence points to the atmosphere of the earth's being secondary. The extreme rarity of the cosmically abundant but chemically inert gas neon compared with water vapor, which has almost the same molecular weight, shows (as Harrison Brown pointed out 25 years ago) that only gases that could be held in combination in the solid earth were available for the formation of the secondary atmosphere. The slow production of oxygen by the photolysis (literally "splitting by light") of water and by the thermal dissociation of water with the loss of hydrogen into space is possible even in the early atmosphere, but nearly everyone agrees that this would merely lead to a little local oxidation of material at or near the earth's crust.

Some mixture of water vapor, methane, carbon monoxide, carbon dioxide, ammonia and nitrogen presumably initiated the secondary atmosphere. We know from laboratory experiments that when an adequate energy source (such as ultraviolet light or an electric discharge) is available, many organic compounds, including practically all the building blocks of biological macromolecules, can be formed in such an atmosphere. We also know from studies of meteorites that such syntheses have occurred under extraterrestrial conditions, but that a good many substances not of biological significance were also formed. It is just possible that ultimately exploration of the asteroids may produce evidence of the kind of environment on a disrupted planet in which these kinds of prebiological organic syntheses took place.

However that may be, we can be reasonably confident that a great deal of prebiological organic synthesis occurred on the earth under reducing conditions at an early stage in our planet's history. The most reasonable energy source

would be solar ultraviolet radiation. Since some of the most important compounds are not only produced but also destroyed by the wavelengths available in the absence of an oxygen screen, it is probable that the processes leading to production of the first living matter took place under specific structural conditions. Syntheses may have occurred in the water vapor and gases above a primitive system of pools or a shallow ocean, while at the bottom of the latter, somewhat shielded by liquid water, polymerization of some of the products on clay particles or by other processes may have taken place.

The first hint that organisms had been produced is the presence of bacterialike structures in the Figtree geological formation of South Africa; these fossils are believed to be a little more than three billion years old. Carbon-containing cherts from Swaziland that are older than that have been examined by Preston Cloud of the University of California at Santa Barbara, who did not find any indication of biological objects. The oldest really dramatic microflora are those described by Stanley A. Tyler and

Elso S. Barghoorn of Harvard University from the Gunflint formation of Ontario, which is about two billion years old [see illustration on page 194]. Sedimentary rocks from that formation seem to contain genuine filamentous blue-green algae that were doubtless both photosynthetic and nitrogen-fixing. Cellular structures that were probably components of blue-green algal reefs certainly occurred a little earlier than two billion years ago. The most reasonable conclusion that can be drawn from the work of Barghoorn, Cloud and others, who are at last giving us a real Precambrian paleobiological record, is that somewhere around three billion years ago biochemical evolution had proceeded far enough for discrete heterotrophic organisms to appear.

These organisms (which, as their name implies, draw their nourishment from externally formed organic molecules) could utilize the downward-diffusing organic compounds in fermentative metabolism, but they lived at sufficient depths of water or sediment to be shielded from the destructive effect of the solar ultraviolet radiation. After somewhat less than another billion years procaryotic

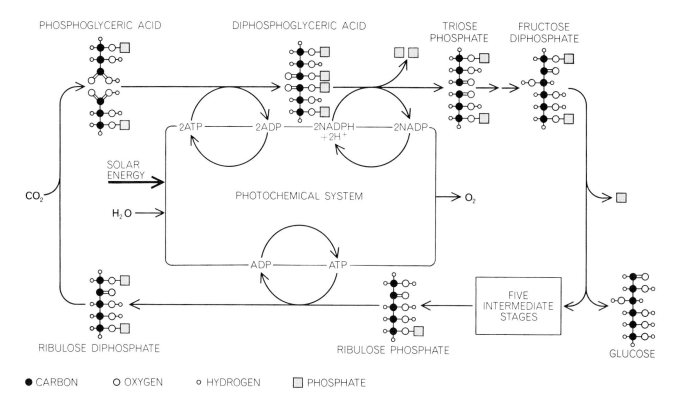

● CARBON   ○ OXYGEN   ∘ HYDROGEN   ☐ PHOSPHATE

PHOTOSYNTHESIS, the fundamental process for sustaining life on the earth, is accomplished by plants on land, by freshwater algae and by phytoplankton in the sea. Utilizing the energy contained in sunlight, they convert carbon dioxide and water into some form of carbohydrate (for example glucose), releasing oxygen as a waste product. This simplified diagram shows the cyclical process by which a molecule of carbon dioxide is attached to a five-carbon molecule, ribulose-1,5-diphosphate, previously assembled from five molecules of carbon dioxide. The photochemical system packages part of the incoming solar energy by converting adenosine diphosphate (ADP) to adenosine triphosphate (ATP) and by converting nicotinamide adenine dinucleotide phosphate (NADP) to its reduced form (NADPH). Two molecules of NADPH and three of ATP are required to fix one molecule of carbon dioxide. Carbon atoms from CO_2 can be incorporated into a variety of compounds and removed at various points in the cycle.

cells—cells without a fully developed mitotic mechanism for cell division and without mitochondria—had already started photosynthesis. The result of these developments would have ultimately been the complete transformation of the biosphere from the old heterotrophic fermentative regime to the new autotrophic (self-nourishing), respiratory and largely oxidized condition. How fast the change took place we do not know, but it was certainly the greatest biological revolution that has occurred on the earth. The net result of this revolution was no doubt the extermination of a great number of inefficient and primitive organisms that could not tolerate free oxygen and their replacement by more efficient respiring forms.

Cloud and his associates have recently found evidence of eucaryotic cells— cells with a fully developed mitotic mechanism and with mitochondria— some 1.2 to 1.4 billion years old. It is reasonable to regard the rise of the modern eucaryotic cell as a major consequence of the new conditions imposed by an oxygen-containing atmosphere. Moreover, Lynn Margulis of Boston University has assembled most convincingly the scattered but extensive evidence that this response was of a very special kind, involving a multiple symbiosis between a variety of procaryotic cells and so constituting an evolutionary advance quite unlike any other known to have occurred.

If the first eucaryotes arose 1.2 to 1.4 billion years ago, there would be about half of this time available for the evolution of soft-bodied multicellular organisms, since the first fossil animal skeletons were deposited around 600 million years ago at the beginning of the Cambrian period. Although most of the detailed history consists of a series of blanks, we do have a time scale that seems sensible.

Without taking too seriously any of the estimates that have been made of the expectation of the life of the sun and the solar system, it is evident that the biosphere could remain habitable for a very long time, many times the estimated length of the history of the genus *Homo,* which might be two million years old. As inhabitants of the biosphere, we should regard ourselves as being in our infancy, particularly when we throw destructive temper tantrums. Many people, however, are concluding on the basis of mounting and reasonably objective evidence that the length of life of the biosphere as an inhabitable region for organisms is to be measured in decades rather than in hundreds of mil-

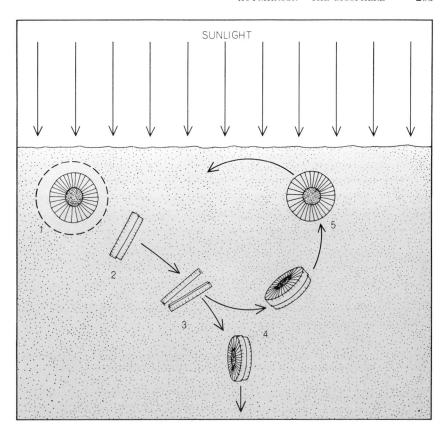

SUNLIGHT

PHYTOPLANKTON CELL is slightly denser than seawater and under absolutely quiet conditions would slowly sink to the bottom. In this way the cell can move from a small parcel of water (*broken circle*) from which it has removed all the available nutrients (*black dots*) into a parcel still containing these substances. As the cell sinks it divides, and losses from the population in the surface waters that constitute the euphotic zone are continually made good by upward turbulence, which returns some of the products of cell division to the surface layer. The particular phytoplankton shown is a diatom of the genus *Coscinodiscus.*

lions of years. This is entirely the fault of our own species. It would seem not unlikely that we are approaching a crisis that is comparable to the one that occurred when free oxygen began to accumulate in the atmosphere.

Admittedly there are differences. The first photosynthetic organisms that produced oxygen were probably already immune to the lethal effects of the new poison gas we now breathe. On the other hand, our machines may be immune to carbon monoxide, lead and DDT, but we are not. Apart from a slight rise in agricultural productivity caused by an increase in the amount of carbon dioxide in the atmosphere, it is difficult to see how the various contaminants with which we are polluting the biosphere could form the basis for a revolutionary step forward. Nonetheless, it is worth noting that when the eucaryotic cell evolved in the middle Precambrian period, the process very likely involved an unprecedented new kind of evolutionary development. Presumably if we want to continue living in the biosphere we must also introduce unprecedented processes.

Vernadsky, the founder of modern biogeochemistry, was a Russian liberal who grew up in the 19th century. Accepting the Russian Revolution, he did much of his work after 1917, although his numerous philosophic references were far from Marxist. Just before his death on January 6, 1945, he wrote his friend and former student Alexander Petrunkevitch: "I look forward with great optimism. I think that we undergo not only a historical, but a planetary change as well. We live in a transition to the noosphere." By noosphere Vernadsky meant the envelope of mind that was to supersede the biosphere, the envelope of life. Unfortunately the quarter-century since those words were written has shown how mindless most of the changes wrought by man on the biosphere have been. Nonetheless, Vernadsky's transition in its deepest sense is the only alternative to man's cutting his lifetime short by millions of years.

23

THE ENERGY CYCLE OF THE BIOSPHERE

GEORGE M. WOODWELL
September 1970

Life is maintained by the finite amount of solar energy that is fixed by green plants. An increasing fraction of that energy is being diverted to the direct support of one living species: man

The energy that sustains all living systems is solar energy, fixed in photosynthesis and held briefly in the biosphere before it is reradiated into space as heat. It is solar energy that moves the rabbit, the deer, the whale, the boy on the bicycle outside my window, my pencil as I write these words. The total amount of solar energy fixed on the earth sets one limit on the total amount of life; the patterns of flow of this energy through the earth's ecosystems set additional limits on the kinds of life on the earth. Expanding human activities are requiring a larger fraction of the total and are paradoxically making large segments of it less useful in support of man.

Solar energy has been fixed in one form or another on the earth throughout much of the earth's 4.5-billion-year history. The modern biosphere probably had its beginning about two billion years ago with the evolution of marine organisms that not only could fix solar energy in organic compounds but also did it by splitting the water molecule and releasing free oxygen.

The beginning was slow. Molecular oxygen released by marine plant cells accumulated for hundreds of millions of years, gradually building an atmosphere that screened out the most destructive of the sun's rays and opened the land to exploitation by living systems [see "The Oxygen Cycle," by Preston Cloud and Aharon Gibor; SCIENTIFIC AMERICAN Offprint 1192]. The colonization of the land began perhaps 400 million years ago. New species evolved that derived more energy from a more efficient respiration in air, accelerating the trend.

Evolution fitted the new species together in ways that not only conserved energy and the mineral nutrients utilized in life processes but also conserved the nutrients by recycling them, releasing more oxygen and making possible the fixation of more energy and the support of still more life. Gradually each landscape developed a flora and fauna particularly adapted to that place. These new arrays of plants and animals used solar energy, mineral nutrients, water and the resources of other living things to stabilize the environment, building the biosphere we know today.

The actual amount of solar energy diverted into living systems is small in relation to the earth's total energy budget [see "The Energy Cycle of the Earth," by Abraham H. Oort; SCIENTIFIC AMERICAN Offprint 1189]. Only about a tenth of 1 percent of the energy received from the sun by the earth is fixed in photosynthesis. This fraction, small as it is, may be represented locally by the manufacture of several thousand grams of dry organic matter per square meter per year. Worldwide it is equivalent to the annual production of between 150 and 200 billion tons of dry organic matter and includes both food for man and the energy that runs the life-support systems of the biosphere, namely the earth's major ecosystems: the forests, grasslands, oceans, marshes, estuaries, lakes, rivers, tundras and deserts.

The complexity of ecosystems is so great as to preclude any simple, single-factor analysis that is both accurate and satisfying. Because of the central role of energy in life, however, an examination of the fixation of energy and its flow through ecosystems yields understanding of the ecosystems themselves. It also reveals starkly some of the obscure but vital details of the crisis of environment.

More than half of the energy fixed in photosynthesis is used immediately in the plant's own respiration. Some of it is stored. In land plants it may be transferred from tissues where it is fixed, such as leaves, to other tissues where it is used immediately or stored. At any point it may enter consumer food chains.

There are two kinds of chain: the grazing, or browsing, food chains and the food chains of decay. Energy may be stored for considerable periods in both kinds of chain, building animal populations in the one case and accumulations of undecomposed dead organic matter and populations of decay organisms in the other. The fraction of the total energy fixed that flows into each of these chains is of considerable importance to the biosphere and to man. The worldwide increase in human numbers not only is shifting the distribution of energy within ecosystems but also requires that a growing fraction of the total energy fixed be diverted to the direct support of man. The implications of such diversions are still far from clear.

Before examining the fixation and flow of energy in ecosystems it is important to consider the broad pattern of their development throughout evolution. If one were to ascribe a single objective to evolution, it would be the perpetuation of life. The entire strategy of evolution is focused on that single end. In realizing it evolution divides the resources of any

GREEN PLANTS are the "primary producers" of the biosphere, converting solar energy into organic compounds that maintain the plants and other living things. Forests, which cover about a tenth of the earth's surface, fix almost half of the biosphere's total energy. The photograph on the opposite page, which was made in the Mazumbai forest in Tanzania, illustrates the rich diversity typical of a relatively mature ecosystem, with many species arranged in a structure that apportions the available solar energy as effectively as possible.

206

STRUCTURE OF FORESTS changes with disturbance according to well-defined patterns. The photographs show the loss of structure in an oak-pine forest at the Brookhaven National Laboratory as a result of continued exposure to gamma radiation. Exposure of the intact forest (*top left*) to radiation first destroys pine trees and then other trees, leaving tree sprouts, shrubs and ground cover (*top right*). Longer exposure kills shrubs (*bottom left*) and finally the sedge, grasses and herbs of the ground cover (*bottom right*).

location, including its input of energy, among an ever increasing number of different kinds of users, which we recognize as plant and animal species.

The arrangement of these species in today's ecosystems is a comparatively recent event, and the ecosystems continue to be developed by migration and continuing evolution. Changes accrue slowly through a conjoint evolution that is not only biological but also chemical and physical. The entire process appears to be open-ended, continuous, self-augmenting and endlessly versatile. It builds on itself, not merely preserving life but increasing the capacity of a site to support life. In so doing it stabilizes the site and the biota. Mineral nutrients are no longer leached rapidly into watercourses; they are conserved and recirculated, offering opportunities for more evolution. Interactions among ecosystems are exploited and stabilized, by living systems adapted to the purpose. The return of the salmon and other fishes from years at sea to the upper reaches of rivers is one example; impoverished upland streams are thus fertilized with nutrients harvested in the ocean, opening further possibilities for life.

The time scale for most of these developments, particularly in the later stages when many of the species have large bodies and long life cycles, is very long. Such systems are for all practical purposes stable. These are the living systems that have shaped the biosphere. They are self-regulating and remarkably resilient. Now human activities have become so pervasive as to affect these systems all over the world. What kinds of change can we expect? The answers depend on an understanding of the patterns of evolution and on a knowledge of the structure and function of ecosystems. And the fixation and flow of energy is at the core.

Much of our current understanding of ecosystems has been based on a paper published in *Ecology* in 1942 by Raymond L. Lindeman, a young colleague of G. Evelyn Hutchinson's at Yale University. (It was Lindeman's sixth and last paper; his death at the age of 26 deprived ecology of one of its most outstanding intellects.) Lindeman drew on work by earlier scholars, particularly Arthur G. Tansley and Charles S. Elton of England and Frederick E. Clements and Victor E. Shelford of the U.S., to examine what he called the "trophic-dynamic aspect" of ecology. He called attention to the fixation of energy by natural ecosystems and to the quantitative relations that must exist in nature be-

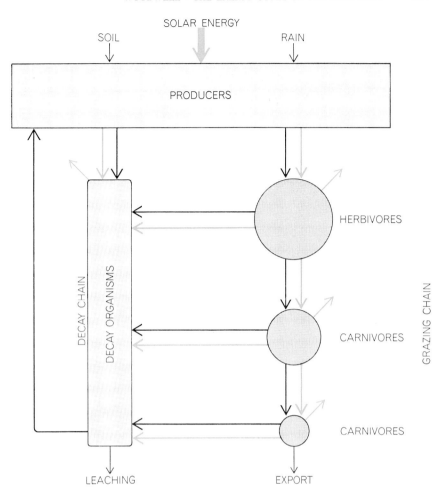

NET FLOW OF ENERGY (*colored arrows*) and nutrients (*black arrows*) through a natural community is diagrammed in simplified form. In a mature community all the energy fixed by the primary producers, the plants, is dissipated as heat in the respiration of the plants, the consumers (herbivores and successive echelons of carnivores) and decay organisms. Almost all nutrients are eventually recycled, however, to renew plant and animal populations.

tween the different users of this energy as it is divided progressively among the various populations of an ecosystem.

Lindeman's suggestions were provocative. They stimulated a series of field and laboratory studies, all of which strengthened his synthesis. One of the most useful generalizations of his approach, sometimes called "the 10 percent law," simply states that in nature some fraction of the energy entering any population is available for transfer to the populations that feed on it without serious disruption of either. The actual amount of energy transferred probably varies widely. It seems fair to assume that in the grazing chain perhaps 10 to 20 percent of the energy fixed by the plant community can be transferred to herbivores, 10 to 20 percent of the energy entering the herbivore community can be transferred to the first level of carnivores and so on. In this way what is called a mature community may support three or four levels of animal popu-

lations, each related to its food supply quantitatively on the basis of energy fixation.

No less important than the grazing food chains are the food chains of decay. On land these chains start with dead organic matter: leaves, bits of bark and branches. In water they originate in the remains of algae, fecal matter and other organic debris. The organic debris may be totally consumed by the bacteria, fungi and small animals of decay, releasing carbon dioxide, water and heat. It may enter far more complex food webs, potentially involving larger animals such as mullet, carp, crabs and ultimately higher carnivores, so that although it is convenient to think of the grazing and decay routes as being distinct, they usually overlap.

The decay food chain does not always function efficiently. Under certain circumstances it exhausts all the available oxygen. Decay is then incomplete; its products include methane, alcohols, amines, hydrogen sulfide and partially decomposed organic matter. Its connections to the grazing food chain are reduced or broken, with profound effects on living systems. Such shifts are occurring more frequently in an increasingly man-dominated world.

How much energy is fixed by the major ecosystems of the biosphere? The question is more demanding than it may appear because measuring energy fixation in such diverse vegetations as forests, fields and the oceans is most difficult. Rates of energy fixation vary from day to day—even from minute to minute—and from place to place. They are affected by many factors, including light and the concentration of carbon dioxide, water and nutrients.

In spite of the difficulties in obtaining unequivocal answers several attempts have been made to appraise the total amounts of energy fixed by the earth's ecosystems. Most recently Robert H.

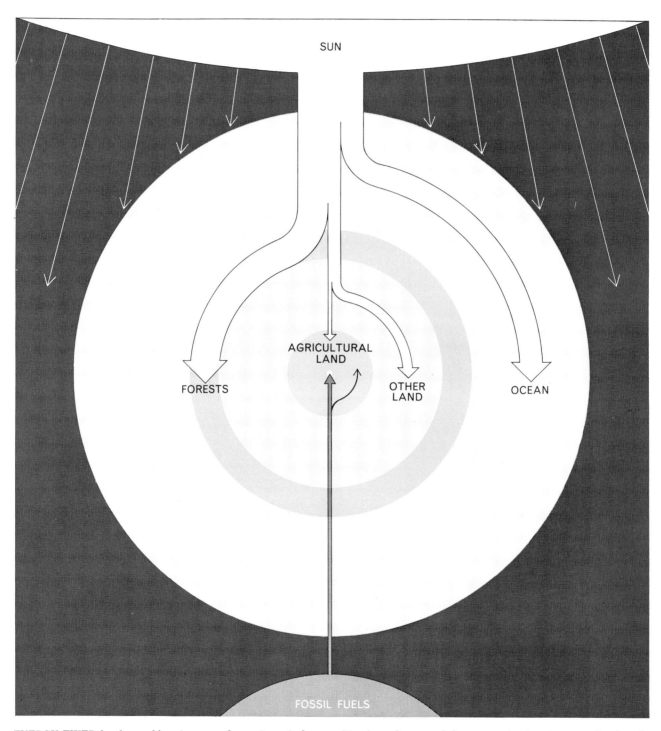

ENERGY FIXED by the earth's primary producers is equivalent to about 164 billion metric tons of dry organic matter a year, according to Robert H. Whittaker and Gene E. Likens of Cornell University. About 5 percent of the energy is fixed by agricultural ecosystems and is utilized directly by man, one species among millions. Man also draws annually on fossil fuel reserves for about the same amount of energy. In this anthropocentric view of the biosphere the area of the concentric rings is proportional to the major ecosystems' share of the surface area of the earth (indicated in millions of square kilometers). The width of the arrows is proportional to the amount of energy fixed in each ecosystem and contributed by fossil fuels (indicated in billions of metric tons of dry matter per year). The intensity of the color in each ring suggests the productivity (production per unit area) of each ecosystem.

Whittaker and Gene E. Likens of Cornell University have estimated that in all the earth's ecosystems, both terrestrial and marine, 164 billion metric tons of dry organic matter is produced annually, about a third of it in the oceans and two-thirds of it on land. This "net production" represents the excess of organic production over what is required to maintain the plants that fixed the energy; it is the energy potentially available for consumers.

Virtually all the net production of the earth is consumed annually in the respiration of organisms other than green plants, releasing carbon dioxide, water and the heat that is reradiated into space. The consumers are animals, including man, and the organisms of decay. The energy that is not consumed is either stored in the tissues of living organisms or in humus and organic sediments.

The relations between the producers and the consumers are clarified by two simple formulas. Consider the growth of a single green plant, an "autotroph" that is capable of fixing its own solar energy. Some of the energy it fixes is stored in organic matter that accumulates as new tissue. The amount of the new tissue, measured as dry weight, is the net production. This does not, however, represent all the energy fixed. Some energy is required just to support the living tissues of the plant. This is energy used in respiration.

The total energy fixed, then, is partitioned immediately within the plant according to the equation $GP - Rs_A = NP$. The total amount of energy fixed is gross production (GP); Rs_A is the energy used in the respiration of the autotrophic plant, and the amount of energy left over is net production (NP). The growth of a plant is measurable as net production, which can be expressed in any of several different ways, including energy stored and dry weight.

The same relations hold for an entire plant community and for the biosphere as a whole. If we consider not only the plants but also the consumers of plants and the entire food web, including the organisms of decay, we must add a new unit of respiration without adding any further producers. That is what happens as an ecosystem matures: consumer populations increase substantially, adding to the respiration of the plants the respiration (Rs_H) of the heterotrophs, the organisms that obtain their energy from the photosynthesizing plants. For an ecosystem (the total biota of any unit of the earth's surface) NEP equals GP − ($Rs_A + Rs_H$). NEP is the net ecosystem

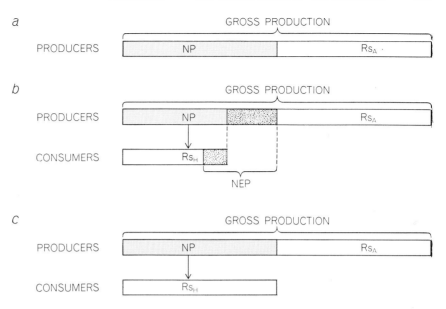

ENERGY IS UTILIZED by producers and consumers as shown here. In the case of a single green plant (a) some of the total energy fixed, or gross production, is expended in the plant's own respiration (Rs_A) and the rest goes into net production (NP), or new tissue. In a successional plant-and-animal community (b) some of the net production is stored as growth, contributing to net ecosystem production (NEP); the rest is used by consumers, which expend most of it in respiration (Rs_H) and store some as growth, adding to net ecosystem production. In a mature community (c) all the energy fixed is used in respiration.

production, the net increase in energy stored within the system. $Rs_A + Rs_H$ is the total respiration of the ecosystem.

This last equation establishes the important distinction between a "successional," or developmental, ecosystem and a "climax," or mature, one. In the successional system the total respiration is less than the gross production, leaving energy (NEP) that is built into structure and adds to the resources of the site. (A forest of large trees obviously has more space in it, more organic matter and probably a wider variety of microhabitats than a forest of small trees.) In a climax system, on the other hand, all the energy fixed is used in the combined respiration of the plants and the heterotrophs. NEP goes to zero: there is no energy left over and no net annual storage. Climax ecosystems probably represent a most efficient way of using the resources of a site to sustain life with minimum impact on other ecosystems. It is of course such ecosystems that have dominated the biosphere throughout recent millenniums.

These general relations are clarified if one asks, with regard to a specific ecosystem, how much energy is fixed and how it is used, and how efficient the ecosystem is in harvesting solar energy and supporting life. The answers are found by solving the simple production equations, but in order to solve them one must measure the metabolism of an en-

tire unit of landscape. Such studies are being attempted in many types of ecosystem under the aegis of the International Biological Program, a major research effort designed to examine the productivity of the biosphere. The example I shall give is drawn from research in an oak-pine forest at the Brookhaven National Laboratory.

The research has spanned most of a decade and has involved many contributors. A most important contribution was made by Whittaker, who collaborated with me in completing a detailed description of the structure of the forest, including the total amount of organic matter, the weight and area of leaves, the weight of roots and the amount of net production. The techniques developed in that work are now being used in many similar studies. Such data are necessary to relate other measurements, including measurements of the gas exchange between leaves and the atmosphere, to the entire forest and so provide an additional measurement of net production and respiration.

A major problem was measuring the forest's total respiration. We used two techniques. First, Winston R. Dykeman and I took advantage of the frequent inversions of temperature that occur in central Long Island and used the rate of accumulation of carbon dioxide during these inversions as a direct measurement of total respiration. The inversions are nocturnal; this eliminates the effect of photosynthesis, which of course proceeds only in daylight.

During an inversion the temperature of the air near the ground is (contrary to the usual daytime situation) lower than that of the air at higher elevations. Since the cooler air is denser, the air column remains vertically stable for as much as several hours; the carbon dioxide released by respiration accumulates, and its buildup at a given height is an index of the rate of respiration at that height. The calculation of the buildup during more than 40 inversions in the course of a year provided one measure of total respiration [*see top illustration on page 212*]. A second measurement came from a detailed study of the rates of respiration of various segments of the forest (including the branches and stems of trees) and the soil.

The estimates available from these studies and others are converging on the following solution of the production equations, all in terms of grams of dry organic matter per square meter per year: The gross production is 2,650 grams; the net production, 1,200 grams; the net ecosystem production, or net storage, 550 grams, and the total respiration, or energy loss, 2,100 grams, of which Rs_A is 1,450 and Rs_H is 650 [*see illustration on these two pages*]. The forest is obviously immature in the sense that it is still storing energy (NEP) in an increased plant population. The ratio of total respiration to gross production (2,100/2,650) suggests that the forest is at about 80 percent of climax and confirms other studies that show that the forest is "late successional."

The net production of the Brookhaven forest of 1,200 grams per square meter per year is in the low middle range for forests and is typical of the productivity of small-statured forests. The efficiency of this forest in using the annual input of solar energy effective in photosynthesis is about .9 percent. Large-statured forests (moist forests of the Temperate Zone, where nutrients are abundant, and certain tropical rain forests) have a net productivity ranging up to several thousand grams per square meter per year. They may have an efficiency approaching 3 percent of the usable energy available throughout the year at the surface of the ground, but usually not much more.

Sugarcane productivity in the Tropics has been reported as exceeding 9,000 grams per square meter per year. The new strains of rice that are contributing to the "green revolution" have a maximum yield under intensive triple-cropping regimes that may approach 2,000 grams of rice per square meter per year. Over large areas the yield is much lower, seldom exceeding 350 to 400 grams of milled rice per square meter per year. These yields are to be compared with corn yields in the U.S., which approach 500 grams. (The rice and corn yields are expressed as grain, not as total net production as we have been discussing it. Net production including the chaff, stems, leaves and roots is between three and five times the harvest of grain. Thus the net production of the most productive agriculture is 6,000 to 10,000 grams, probably the highest net production in the world. Most agriculture, however, has net production of 1,000 to 3,000 grams, the same range as most forests.)

The high productivities of agriculture are somewhat misleading in that they are bought with a contribution of energy from fossil fuels: energy that is applied to cultivate and harvest the crop, to manufacture and transport pesticides and fertilizers and to provide and control irrigation. The cost accounting is incomplete; these systems "leak" pesti-cides, fertilizers and often soil itself, injuring other ecosystems. It is clear, however, that the high yields of agriculture are dependent on a subsidy of energy that was fixed as fossil fuels in previous ages and is available now (and for some decades to come) to support large human populations. Without this subsidy or some other source of power, yields would drop. They may suffer in any case as it becomes increasingly necessary to reduce the interactions between agriculture and other ecosystems. One sign is the progressive restriction in the use of insecticides because of hazards far from where they are applied. Similar restraint may soon be necessary in the use of herbicides and fertilizers.

The oceans appear unproductive compared with terrestrial ecosystems. In separate detailed analyses of the fish production of the world's oceans William E. Ricker of the Fisheries Research Board of Canada and John H. Ryther of the Woods Hole Oceanographic Institution recently emphasized that the oceans are far from an unlimited resource. The net production of the open ocean is about

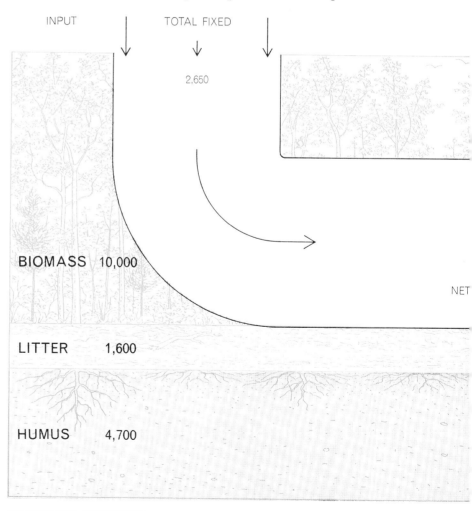

INPUT   TOTAL FIXED

2,650

BIOMASS   10,000

LITTER   1,600

HUMUS   4,700

NET

ENERGY RELATIONSHIPS were worked out for an oak-pine forest at the Brookhaven National Laboratory. Of the annual gross production of 2,650 grams of dry matter per

50 grams of fixed carbon per square meter per year. Areas of very high productivity, including coastal areas and areas of upwelling where nutrients are abundant, do not average more than 300 grams of carbon. The mean productivity of the oceans, according to this analysis, would be about 55 grams of carbon, equivalent to between 120 and 150 grams of dry organic matter.

Inasmuch as the highest productivity of enriched areas of the ocean barely approaches that of diminutive forests such as Brookhaven's, the oceans do not appear to represent a vast potential resource. On the contrary, Ryther suggests on the basis of an elaborate analysis of the complex trophic relations of the oceans that "it seems unlikely that the potential sustained yield of fish to man is appreciably greater than 100 million [metric] tons [wet weight]. The total world fish landings for 1967 were just over 60 million tons, and this figure has been increasing at an average rate of about 8 percent per year for the past 25 years.... At the present rate, the in-

dustry can expand for no more than a decade." Ricker comes to a similar conclusion. Neither he nor Ryther appraised the effects on the productivity of the oceans of the accumulation of toxic substances such as pesticides, of industrial and municipal wastes, of oil production on the continental shelves, of the current attempts at mining the sea bottom and of other exploitation of the seas that is inconsistent with continued harvesting of fish.

The available evidence suggests that, in spite of the much larger area of the oceans, by far the greater amount of energy is fixed on land. The oceans, even if their productivity can be preserved, do not represent a vast unexploited source of energy for support of larger human populations. They are currently being exploited at close to the maximum sustainable rate, and their continued use as a dump for wastes of all kinds makes it questionable whether that rate will be sustained.

A brief consideration of the utilization of the energy fixed in the Brookhaven forest will help to clarify this

point. The energy fixed by this late-successional forest is first divided between net production and immediate use in plant respiration, with about 55 percent being used immediately. (The ratio of 55 percent going directly into respiration appears consistent for the Temperate Zone forests examined so far; the ratio appears to rise in the Tropics and to decline in higher latitudes.) The net production is divided among herbivores, decay and storage. In the Brookhaven forest herbivore populations have been reduced by the exclusion of deer, leaving as the principal herbivores insects and limited populations of small mammals.

Our estimates indicate that only a few percent of the net production is consumed directly by herbivores (a low rate in comparison with other ecosystems). Practically all this quantity is consumed immediately in animal respiration, so that the animal population shows virtually no annual increase, or contribution to the net ecosystem production. The principal contribution to the net ecosystem production is the growth of the plant populations, which

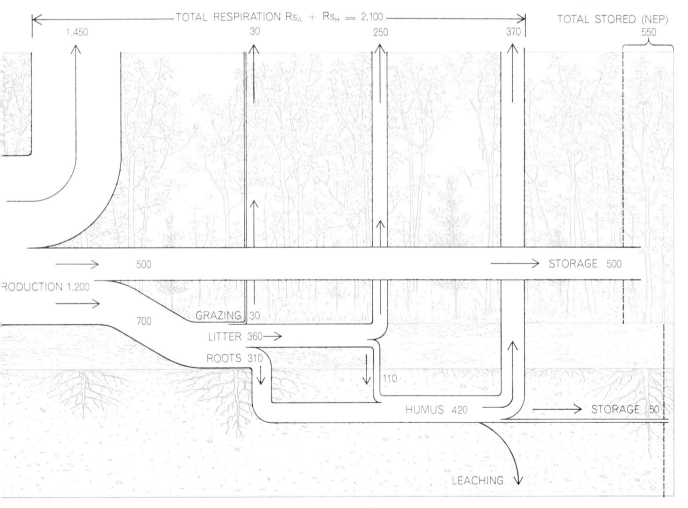

square meter, some 2,100 grams are lost in respiration, leaving 550 stored as new plant growth, litter and humus. The animal population is not increasing appreciably. This is a "late successional" forest in which 80 percent of the production is expended in respiration.

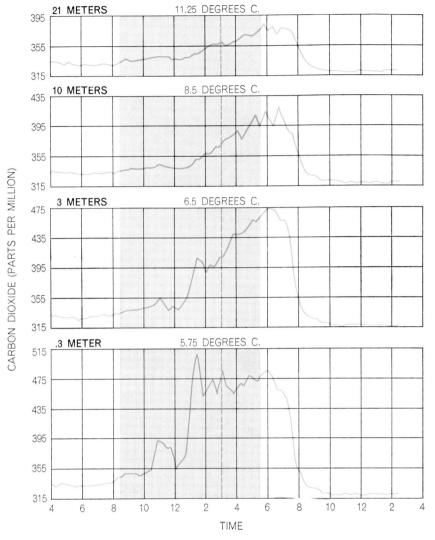

RATE OF RESPIRATION of the forest was determined by measuring the rate at which carbon dioxide, a product of respiration, accumulated during nights when the air was still because of a temperature inversion. The curves give the carbon dioxide concentration at four elevations in the course of one such night. (Note that the temperature, recorded at 3:00 A.M., was lower near the ground than at greater heights.) The hourly increase in carbon dioxide concentration, which was calculated from these curves, yielded rate of respiration.

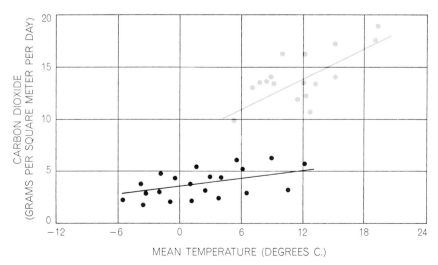

RESPIRATION of the forest, plotted against temperature, is seen to proceed at a higher rate in summer (colored curve) than in winter (black curve). Annual respiration was calculated in grams of carbon dioxide, then converted to yield the total respiration, 2,100 grams.

accounts for more than 40 percent of the net production. The remainder of the net production enters the food chains of decay, which are obviously well developed. Clearly the elimination of deer, combined with poorly developed herbivore and carnivore populations, has resulted in a diversion of energy from the grazing chain into the food chains of decay.

This is precisely what happens in aquatic systems as they are enriched with nutrients washed from the land; the shift to decay is also caused by the accumulation of any toxic substance, whether it affects plants or animals. Any reduction in populations of grazers shifts the flow of energy toward decay. Any effect on the plants shifts plant populations away from sensitive species toward resistant species that may not be food for the indigenous herbivores, thereby eliminating the normal food chains and also shifting the flow of energy into decay.

These observations simply show that the structure and function of major ecosystems are sensitive to many influences. Clearly the amount of living tissue that can be supported in any ecosystem depends on the amount of net production. Net production, however, is coupled to both photosynthesis and respiration, both of which can be affected by many factors. Photosynthesis is sensitive to light intensity and duration, to the availability of water and mineral nutrients and to temperature. It is also sensitive to the concentration of carbon dioxide; on a worldwide basis the amount of carbon dioxide in the atmosphere may exert a major control over rates of net production. Greenhouse men have recognized the sensitivity of photosynthesis to carbon dioxide concentration for many years and sometimes increase the concentration artificially to stimulate plant growth. Has the emission of carbon dioxide from the combustion of fossil fuels in the past 150 years caused a worldwide increase in net production, and if so, how much of an increase?

With equipment specially designed at Brookhaven, Robert Wright and I supplied air with enhanced levels of carbon dioxide to trees and determined the effect on net photosynthesis by measuring the uptake of the gas by leaves. The net amount of carbon dioxide that was fixed increased linearly with the increase in the carbon dioxide concentration in the air. Such small increases in carbon dioxide concentration have virtually no effect on rates of respiration. The data suggest that the increase of about 10 percent (30 parts per million) in the carbon dioxide concentration of the atmosphere since the middle of the 19th century caused by the industrial revolution may have increased net production by as much as 5 to 10 percent. This increase, if applicable worldwide and considered alone, would increase the total energy (and carbon) stored in natural ecosystems by an equivalent amount, and would result in an equivalent improvement in the yields of agriculture. The increase in net production also tends to stabilize the carbon dioxide content of the atmosphere by storing more carbon in living organic matter, particularly in forests, and in the nonliving organic matter of sediments and humus. Such changes have almost certainly occurred on a worldwide basis as an inadvertent result of human activities in the past 100 years or so.

Such simple single-factor analyses of environmental problems, however, are almost always misleading. As the carbon dioxide concentration in the atmosphere has been increasing, many other factors have changed. There was a period of rising temperature, possibly due to the increased carbon dioxide concentration. More recently, however, there has been a decline in world temperatures that continues. This can be expected to reduce net production worldwide by reducing the periods favorable for plant growth. Added to the effects of changing temperature—and indeed overriding it—is the accumulation of toxic wastes from human activities. The overall effect is to reduce the structure of ecosystems. This in turn shortens food chains and favors (1) populations of small hardy plants, (2) small-bodied herbivores that reproduce rapidly and (3) the food chains of decay. The loss of structure also implies a loss of "regulation"; the simplified communities are subject to rapid changes in the density of these smaller, more rapidly reproducing organisms that have been released from their normal controls.

Local increases in water temperature also give rise to predictable effects. There is talk, for example, of warming the waters of the New York region with waste heat from reactors to produce a rich "tropical" biota, but such manipulation would produce a degraded local biota supplemented by a few hardy species of more southerly ecosystems. Such circumstances again favor productivity not by complex, highly integrated arrays of specialized organisms but by simple arrays of generalized ones. Energy then is funneled not into intricate food webs capped by tuna, mackerel, petrels, dolphins and other highly specialized carni-

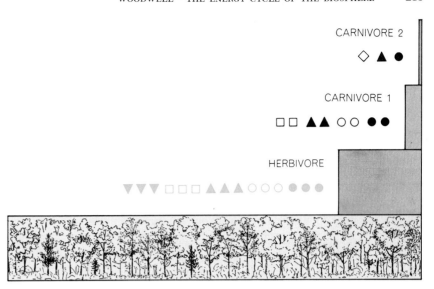

INTACT NATURAL ECOSYSTEM is exemplified by a mature oak-hickory forest that supports several stages of consumers in the grazing food chain, with from 10 to 20 percent of the energy in each trophic level being passed along to the next level. The symbols represent different herbivore and carnivore species. Complexity of structure regulates population sizes, maintaining the same pattern of energy distribution in the system from year to year.

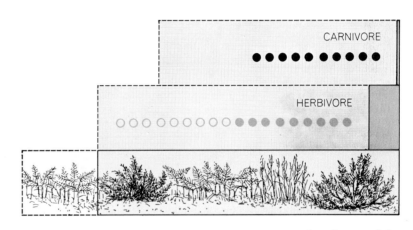

DEGRADED ECOSYSTEM has a truncated grazing chain. The annual production of the sparse grasses, herbs and shrubs fluctuates (*shaded area*). So do populations of herbivores and carnivores, which are characterized by large numbers of individuals but few different species. Under extreme conditions most of the net production may be consumed, leading to the starvation of herbivores and accentuating the characteristic fluctuation in populations.

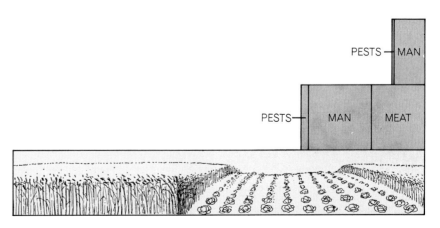

AGRICULTURAL ECOSYSTEM is a special case, yielding a larger than normal harvest of net production for herbivores, including man and animals that provide meat for man. Stability is maintained through inputs of energy in cultivation, pesticides and fertilizer.

NATURAL ECOSYSTEMS

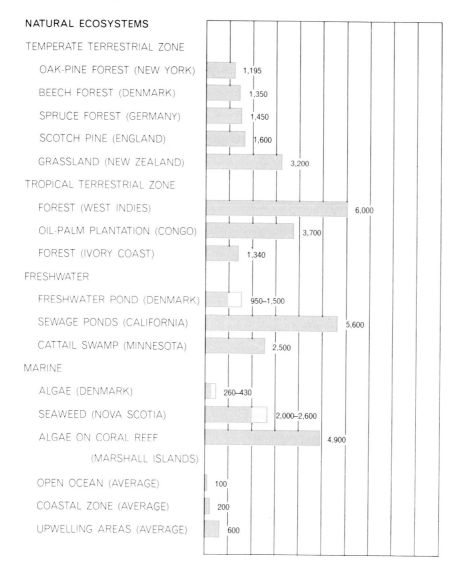

TEMPERATE TERRESTRIAL ZONE
- OAK-PINE FOREST (NEW YORK) — 1,195
- BEECH FOREST (DENMARK) — 1,350
- SPRUCE FOREST (GERMANY) — 1,450
- SCOTCH PINE (ENGLAND) — 1,600
- GRASSLAND (NEW ZEALAND) — 3,200

TROPICAL TERRESTRIAL ZONE
- FOREST (WEST INDIES) — 6,000
- OIL-PALM PLANTATION (CONGO) — 3,700
- FOREST (IVORY COAST) — 1,340

FRESHWATER
- FRESHWATER POND (DENMARK) — 950–1,500
- SEWAGE PONDS (CALIFORNIA) — 5,600
- CATTAIL SWAMP (MINNESOTA) — 2,500

MARINE
- ALGAE (DENMARK) — 260–430
- SEAWEED (NOVA SCOTIA) — 2,000–2,600
- ALGAE ON CORAL REEF (MARSHALL ISLANDS) — 4,900
- OPEN OCEAN (AVERAGE) — 100
- COASTAL ZONE (AVERAGE) — 200
- UPWELLING AREAS (AVERAGE) — 600

AGRICULTURAL ECOSYSTEMS

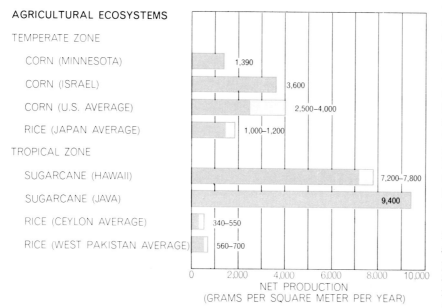

TEMPERATE ZONE
- CORN (MINNESOTA) — 1,390
- CORN (ISRAEL) — 3,600
- CORN (U.S. AVERAGE) — 2,500–4,000
- RICE (JAPAN AVERAGE) — 1,000–1,200

TROPICAL ZONE
- SUGARCANE (HAWAII) — 7,200–7,800
- SUGARCANE (JAVA) — 9,400
- RICE (CEYLON AVERAGE) — 340–550
- RICE (WEST PAKISTAN AVERAGE) — 560–700

0   2,000   4,000   6,000   8,000   10,000
NET PRODUCTION
(GRAMS PER SQUARE METER PER YEAR)

NET PRODUCTION LEVELS of a number of natural and agricultural ecosystems are compared. (The total net production of U.S. corn and of rice is calculated from grain yields.)

vores but into simple food webs dominated by hardy scavengers such as gulls and crabs and into the food webs of decay. As the annual contribution to decay increases, these webs in water become overloaded; the oxygen dissolved in the water is used up and metabolism shifts from the aerobic form where oxygen is freely available to the much less efficient anaerobic respiration; organic matter accumulates, releasing methane, hydrogen sulfide and other noxious gases that only reinforce the tendency.

The broad pattern of these changes is clear enough. On the one hand, an increasing fraction of the total energy fixed is being diverted to the direct support of man, replacing the earth's major ecosystems with cities and land devoted to agriculture—the simplified ecosystems of civilization that require continuing contributions of energy under human control for their regulation. On the other hand, the leakage of toxic substances from the man-dominated provinces of the earth is reducing the structure and self-regulation of the remaining natural ecosystems. The trend is progressive. The simplification of the earth's biota is breaking down the insulation of large units of the earth's surface, increasing the interactions between terrestrial and aquatic systems, between upland and lowland, between river and estuary. The long-term trend of evolution toward building complex, integral, stable ecosystems is being reversed. Although the changes are rapid, accelerating and important, they do not mean that the earth will face an oxygen crisis; photosynthesis will continue for a long time yet, perhaps at an accelerated rate in certain places, stimulated by increased carbon dioxide concentrations in air and the availability of nutrients in water. A smaller fraction of the earth's fixed energy is easily available to man, however. The energy flows increasingly through smaller organisms such as the hardy shrubs and herbs of the irradiated forest at Brookhaven, the scrub oaks that are replacing the smog-killed pines of the Los Angeles basin, the noxious algae of eutrophic lakes and estuaries, into short food chains, humus and anaerobic sediments.

These are major man-caused changes in the biosphere. Many aspects of them are irreversible; their implications are poorly known. Together they constitute a major series of interlocking objectives for science and society in the next decade focused on the question: "How much of the energy that runs the biosphere can be diverted to the support of a single species: man?"

24

THE HUMAN CROP

EDWARD S. DEEVEY, JR.

April 1956

All animals are ultimately nourished by plants. Therefore the abundance of plants regulates the quantity of animals. How many acres of vegetation does it take to raise a man?

History's only recorded crop of human beings is the one reaped from dragon's teeth by Cadmus, but it may not be farfetched to regard the human race literally as a crop derived from the land. Some students of population believe that the ever-increasing harvest of human substance threatens to overflow the earth, like the porridge secreted by the magic pot in the Scottish folktale. In discussing this problem it is helpful to look at the production of human beings in the context of what ecologists say about productivity in general.

The fundamental idea is a good deal older than ecology and its jargon. All life on the earth receives its energy from the sun, but animals cannot use this energy directly; they must get their energy secondhand from the green plants. Since the plants spend some of their energy for their own vegetable purposes, and since animals which feed on them spend an even larger proportion of their energy in activities other than body-building, it follows that no area can produce as much animal as plant substance. Moreover, carnivores spend still more energy in chasing other animals than herbivores spend in grazing, so even if pursuit of food were the only means of dissipating energy, a carnivore would be an uneconomical beast. It is no accident that all of the animals man has domesticated for food (with the sole exception of the Aztecs' edible dog) are herbivores.

The late Raymond Lindeman, of the University of Minnesota, made a notable attempt to compute the energy balance sheet of a whole community. His working model was a small lake near Minneapolis. He studied the rates of production and turnover of algae, pondweeds, copepods, fish and other plant and animal life in the lake, and estimated the chemical energy stored in their bodies. Lindeman found that the plants converted solar energy to organic matter with an efficiency of about one tenth of 1 per cent; the herbivorous animals utilized the available plant energy with about 10 per cent efficiency, and the carnivores were at least 10 per cent efficient in utilizing herbivores. Applied to a community consisting of man, domestic animals and plants, these figures are helpful as well as easy to remember. If the people eat nothing but meat, and keep out all inedible herbivores (such as beetles) and all competing carnivores (such as wolves and botflies), an area that would support 10 vegetarians will support just one meat eater.

The dependence of the human crop on plants as the ultimate source of bodily fuel can be compared to the life of a crowd of squatters along a railroad track whose only source of warming fuel is coal dropped by passing trains. Clearly, if the situation is to last indefinitely, the squatters must adjust their rate of coal consumption to the rate at which coal is lost from the tenders. The efficiency of squatting could be expressed in various ways, but none is quite so fundamental as the ratio of these two rates.

Eugene Rabinowitch, the eminent student of photosynthesis at the University of Illinois, has calculated the

IVORY CARVING from the Belgian Congo depicts the activities of a primitive culture which lived largely by hunting and fishing. The members of such a culture, by eating herbivorous and carnivorous animals, receive most of their plant nourishment indirectly.

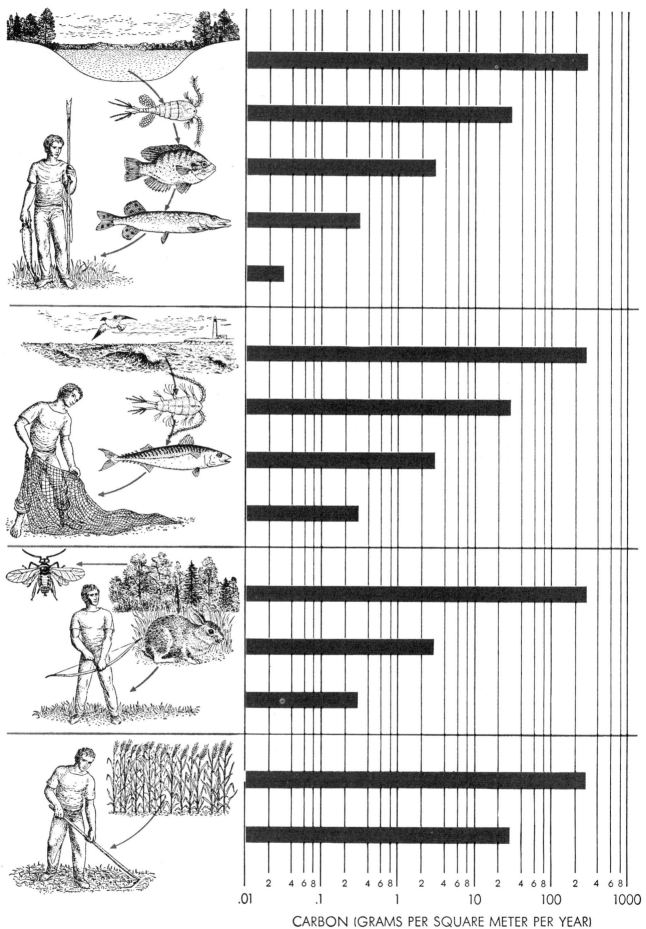

CARBON (GRAMS PER SQUARE METER PER YEAR)

efficiency of the human population's consumption of living matter as 1 per cent. He arrived at this figure by multiplying the world population (2.2×10^9 persons) by its total annual output of energy (at the average rate of 2,100 large calories per person per day) and dividing by the production of plant carbon on land in terms of its potential energy (1.9×10^{17} large calories per year).

The figure of 1 per cent for mankind's efficiency in utilizing the plant production of the earth is impressive. However, it is open to the objection that it is not actually a measure of the human crop's efficiency in producing human substance. It amounts to comparing the rate of loss of coal to the size of the squatters' fires.

A better way of stating the facts is to consider the net production of human

EFFICIENCY of four basic human economies is schematically presented in the chart on the opposite page. The logarithmic scale at the bottom of the page indicates the production of living matter by its carbon content. At the top of the chart is a primitive lake-fishing culture. The lake itself produces about 300 grams of plant carbon per square meter per year (*top horizontal bar*). Tiny animals such as copepods utilize about 10 per cent of the plant carbon, *i.e.*, 30 grams (*second bar*). Larger animals such as sunfish utilize 10 per cent of the carbon in the smaller ones, *i.e.*, 3 grams (*third bar*). Larger fishes such as pickerel utilize 10 per cent of the carbon in the smaller ones, *i.e.*, .3 grams (*fourth bar*). Fishermen utilize 10 per cent of the carbon in the larger fishes, *i.e.*, .03 grams (*fifth bar*). Second from the top in the chart is a more advanced oceanic fishing culture. The supply of plant carbon is the same, but because the chain of predation is more efficient, the fishermen represent .3 grams of carbon per square meter per year. Third from the top is a hunting culture. Here again the supply of plant carbon is the same, but it is eaten by insects as well as other animals. The supply of catchable animals such as rabbits therefore utilizes only about 1 per cent of the plant carbon, *i.e.*, 3 grams. Thus the over-all efficiency of the hunting culture is about the same as that of the advanced fishing culture. At the bottom of the chart is an agricultural society. Here the plant production (including stems and leaves) is about the same as before, *i.e.*, 300 grams of carbon per square meter per year. Because the plants are directly utilized by the society, its human crop can amount to about 10 per cent of this, or 30 grams per square meter per year. Thus the agricultural society comprises 1,000 times more living matter than the primitive lake-fishing culture.

substance and the total metabolic cost of maintaining that net. Since human beings are warm-blooded, active and expensive to keep, only about one sixth of the energy they spend appears in the form of net production of bodily substance (which to maintain the size of the crop must be replaced at the rate of one 25th per year—taking 25 years as the generation interval). That is, the human race spends 5.18×10^{13} large calories per year in stoking itself (respiration) and only 1.09×10^{13} calories in creating the replacement crop. The two figures, added together, give the gross productivity of the human population—*i.e.*, 6.27×10^{13} calories. The gross productivity of the plant world comes to $19,000 \times 10^{13}$ calories. On this basis, dividing the former by the latter, we get only .03 per cent as the efficiency of human production.

There are theoretical objections to this figure, too, and it seems to be too small, as Rabinowitch's is too large. In the calculation of the gross total productivity of the land plants it was assumed, for averaging purposes, that all the carbon produced is in the form of glucose, whereas actually it is mainly cellulose—a compound which most animals can digest only after bacteria have broken it down. To be fair to human efficiency we should allow for the fact that a large fraction of the world's vegetation is inedible. What that fraction may be is hard to say. If it is larger than our assumption implies, the efficiency of human production must be reckoned higher than .03 per cent. A second objection is that the calculation of the efficiency is based on plant growth on all land areas of the earth, but it may not be fair to include such regions as the Arctic, where there is a fair amount of plant production but the people live on walrus, supplemented by canned goods shipped from Moscow and New York.

Allowing for such objections, it seems reasonable to raise the estimate of .03 per cent efficiency to about one tenth of 1 per cent. If this guess is correct, it is a startling figure. It would mean, supposing that man were exclusively carnivorous, that he would account for one tenth of all the meat eaten by all the carnivores of the earth. Even allowing for the fact that the diet of most human beings is at least partly vegetable, the future looks ominous. Granting that the men of the future will consume less meat (though they certainly will want more), when the world's population grows to 10 times its present size (which it will do in 230 years at the present rate) it

will be consuming about a tenth of all the *plant* food that is produced. In such a community no competing carnivores, even as inoffensive as a robin or a perch, will be tolerable, and the existence of a single pickerel (a second-degree carnivore) will threaten the whole balance of nature.

Fortunately the future is not so black as this implies. Farms will replace the forest primeval, and when agriculture has done all it can on land, we may be able to farm the sea in earnest. Besides, we may expect other utilizations of energy (solar and atomic) to emancipate us all some day from our bondage to chlorophyll.

Still, the thought of 10 times as many mouths to feed is rather appalling, and romantics may prefer to look back nostalgically at the productivity of past ages. Through most of human history man lived off land in the "wild" state—either forests or steppes. His tribal groups were small. How many people can an acre of wilderness support? Anthropologists dislike to attempt a general answer to such questions, because human efficiency depends so heavily on skills, *i.e.*, on culture. We know that the aboriginal American Indians averaged about four persons per 100 square kilometers, and the aboriginal Australians about three per 100 square kilometers. Most authorities would guess that the size of hunting-and-gathering populations was related to the size of the catchable food supply. Certain rough calculations show, however, that food supply cannot have been the whole story, for the population did not approach the numbers that the wilderness might have supported.

R. G. Green and C. A. Evans carefully studied the population of snowshoe hares, certainly an eligible Indian food, in Minnesota. The average density of these animals was 255 per square mile. On the basis of an average lifetime of just under one year and an average weight per animal of 1.9 kilograms, of which 35 per cent is protein with an energy content of 5,650 small calories per gram, we calculate that the net productivity of the hares was about 410 calories per square meter. By the same kind of arithmetic the productivity of wood mice (as studied in Michigan) is estimated at 271 calories per square meter. Deer, according to a census in Wisconsin, yield 24.5 calories per square meter. If we add forest birds, we get another 31.6 calories. So we have 737 calories per square meter as the total net production of catchable animals. Several kinds of checks show that this figure is conservative, and that the best forest can produce many times that amount of animal food, particularly if insects are counted. Grassland is no less productive than forest, so it is safe to consider prairie and woodland Indians together.

To calculate how many Indians could live on the catchable animals, we assume they could utilize these animals with 10 per cent efficiency: say 700 calories of animal food would support 70 calories of Indian per square meter. The mean Indian longevity would have been about 25 years, so the potential standing crop of hunters was 1,750 calories or 310 milligrams of protein or 885 milligrams of wet weight or 1.45×10^{-5} persons per square meter, $i.e.$, 1,450 Indians per 100 square kilometers. This is about 400 times the estimate of the actual population. Not even in James Fenimore Cooper's novels were the woods so full of Indians.

A possible flaw in the calculations is that they are based on averages. Indians cannot eat statistics: they require living rabbits. The size of the rabbit population fluctuates by twenty- or fiftyfold from year to year, and it may be objected that the human population would be adjusted to the poorest rabbit crop rather than to the average. However, we may answer that other animals would not be likely to fluctuate exactly in phase with the rabbits. In years when rabbits were scarce, the people could lean more heavily on wood mice.

Assuming there is nothing seriously wrong with the arithmetic on food supply, the trouble must be with the Indians. If food did not limit their numbers, what did? The answer, probably, is "social forces"—vague as that may sound. No doubt there was a lot of no-man's-land, bordering the ranges of all the tribes, where the Indians did not dare hunt regularly for fear their enemies, or perhaps an evil spirit, would catch them at it. Fear of evil spirits is a social force, and taboos on certain kinds of food would have the same effect. Whatever the reason, it seems that the primitive crop of men was adjusted to its means of subsistence with a wide margin of safety. Populations had ample room to fluctuate without danger of destroying the whole economy.

It would be comforting, but decidedly naive, to think that the same conditions hold today. The margin of safety is rapidly narrowing, and at its present rate the expansion of the human crop may soon force mankind to face up to the logic of the ecologist's arithmetic.

25

THE CARBON CYCLE

BERT BOLIN
September 1970

*The main cycle is from carbon dioxide to living matter and
back to carbon dioxide. Some of the carbon, however, is
removed by a slow epicycle that stores huge inventories in
sedimentary rocks*

The biosphere contains a complex mixture of carbon compounds in a continuous state of creation, transformation and decomposition. This dynamic state is maintained through the ability of phytoplankton in the sea and plants on land to capture the energy of sunlight and utilize it to transform carbon dioxide (and water) into organic molecules of precise architecture and rich diversity. Chemists and molecular biologists have unraveled many of the intricate processes needed to create the microworld of the living cell. Equally fundamental and no less interesting is the effort to grasp the overall balance and flow of material in the worldwide community of plants and animals that has developed in the few billion years since life began. This is ecology in the broadest sense of the word: the complex interplay between, on the one hand, communities of plants and animals and, on the other, both kinds of community and their nonliving environment.

We now know that the biosphere has not developed in a static inorganic environment. Rather the living world has profoundly altered the primitive lifeless earth, gradually changing the composition of the atmosphere, the sea and the top layers of the solid crust, both on land and under the ocean. Thus a study of the carbon cycle in the biosphere is fundamentally a study of the overall global interactions of living organisms and their physical and chemical environment. To bring order into this world of complex interactions biologists must combine their knowledge with the information available to students of geology, oceanography and meteorology.

The engine for the organic processes that reconstructed the primitive earth is photosynthesis. Regardless of whether it takes place on land or in the sea, it can be summarized by a single reaction: $CO_2 + 2H_2A + light \rightarrow CH_2O + H_2O + 2A + energy$. The formaldehyde molecule CH_2O symbolizes the simplest organic compound; the term "energy" indicates that the reaction stores energy in chemical form. H_2A is commonly water (H_2O), in which case 2A symbolizes the release of free oxygen (O_2). There are, however, bacteria that can use compounds in which A stands for sulfur, for some organic radical or for nothing at all.

Organisms that are able to use carbon dioxide as their sole source of carbon are known as autotrophs. Those that use light energy for reducing carbon dioxide are called phototrophic, and those that use the energy stored in inorganic chemical bonds (for example the bonds of nitrates and sulfates) are called chemolithotrophic. Most organisms, however, require preformed organic molecules for growth; hence they are known as heterotrophs. The nonsulfur bacteria are an unusual group that is both photosynthetic and heterotrophic. Chemoheterotrophic organisms, for example animals, obtain their energy from organic compounds without need for light. An organism may be either aerobic or anaerobic regardless of its source of carbon or energy. Thus some anaerobic chemoheterotrophs can survive in the deep ocean and deep lakes in the total absence of light or free oxygen.

There is more to plant life than the creation of organic compounds by photosynthesis. Plant growth involves a series of chemical processes and transformations that require energy. This energy is obtained by reactions that use the oxygen in the surrounding water and air to unlock the energy that has been stored by photosynthesis. The process, which releases carbon dioxide, is termed respiration. It is a continuous process and is therefore dominant at night, when photosynthesis is shut down.

If one measures the carbon dioxide at various levels above the ground in a forest, one can observe pronounced changes in concentration over a 24-hour period [*see top illustration on page 222*]. The average concentration of carbon dioxide in the atmosphere is about 320 parts per million. When the sun rises, photosynthesis begins and leads to a rapid decrease in the carbon dioxide concentration as leaves (and the needles of conifers) convert carbon dioxide into organic compounds. Toward noon, as the temperature increases and the humidity decreases, the rate of respiration rises and the net consumption of carbon dioxide slowly declines. Minimum values of carbon dioxide 10 to 15 parts per million below the daily average are reached around noon at treetop level. At sunset photosynthesis ceases while respiration continues, with the result that the car-

CARBON LOCKED IN COAL and oil exceeds by a factor of about 50 the amount of carbon in all living organisms. The estimated world reserves of coal alone are on the order of 7,500 billion tons. The photograph on the following page shows a sequence of lignite coal seams being strip-mined in Stanton, N.D., by the Western Division of the Consolidation Coal Company. The seam, about two feet thick, is of low quality and is discarded. The second seam from the top, about three feet thick, is marketable, as is the third seam, 10 feet farther down. This seam is really two seams separated by about 10 inches of gray clay. The upper is some 3 1/2 feet thick; the lower is about two feet thick. Twenty-four feet below the bottom of this seam is still another seam (*not shown*) eight feet thick, which is also mined.

bon dioxide concentration close to the ground may exceed 400 parts per million. This high value reflects partly the release of carbon dioxide from the decomposition of organic matter in the soil and partly the tendency of air to stagnate near the ground at night, when there is no solar heating to produce convection currents.

The net productivity, or net rate of fixation, of carbon dioxide varies greatly from one type of vegetation to another. Rapidly growing tropical rain forests annually fix between one kilogram and two kilograms of carbon (in the form of carbon dioxide) per square meter of land surface, which is roughly equal to the amount of carbon dioxide in a column of air extending from the same area of the earth's surface to the top of the atmosphere. The arctic tundra and the nearly barren regions of the desert may fix as little as 1 percent of that amount. The forests and cultivated fields of the middle latitudes assimilate between .2 and .4 kilogram per square meter. For the earth as a whole the areas of high productivity are small. A fair estimate is that the land areas of the earth fix into organic compounds 20 to 30 billion net metric tons of carbon per year. There is considerable uncertainty in this figure; published estimates range from 10 to 100 billion tons.

The amount of carbon in the form of carbon dioxide consumed annually by phytoplankton in the oceans is perhaps 40 billion tons, or roughly the same as the gross assimilation of carbon dioxide by land vegetation. Both the carbon dioxide consumed and the oxygen released are largely in the form of gas dissolved near the ocean surface. Therefore most of the carbon cycle in the sea is self-contained: the released oxygen is consumed by sea animals, and their ultimate decomposition releases carbon dioxide back into solution. As we shall see, however, there is a dynamic exchange of carbon dioxide (and oxygen) between the atmosphere and the sea, brought about by the action of the wind and waves. At any given moment the amount of carbon dioxide dissolved in the surface layers of the sea is in close equilibrium with the concentration of carbon dioxide in the atmosphere as a whole.

The carbon fixed by photosynthesis on land is sooner or later returned to the atmosphere by the decomposition of dead organic matter. Leaves and litter fall to the ground and are oxidized by a series of complicated processes in the soil. We can get an approximate idea of the rate

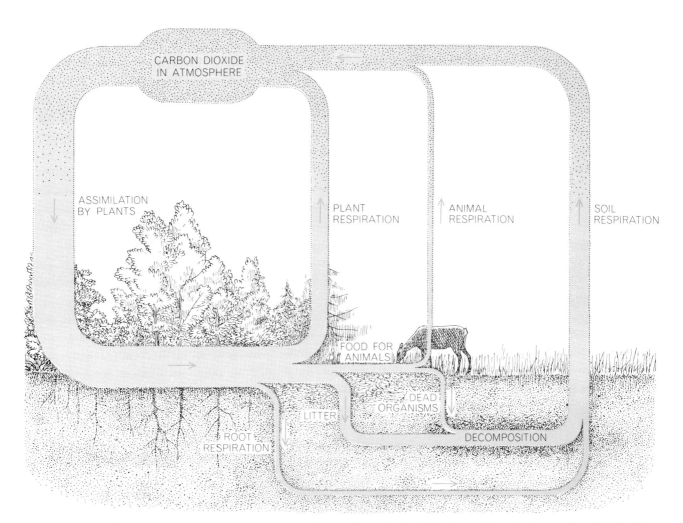

CARBON CYCLE begins with the fixation of atmospheric carbon dioxide by the process of photosynthesis, conducted by plants and certain microorganisms. In this process carbon dioxide and water react to form carbohydrates, with the simultaneous release of free oxygen, which enters the atmosphere. Some of the carbohydrate is directly consumed to supply the plant with energy; the carbon dioxide so generated is released either through the plant's leaves or through its roots. Part of the carbon fixed by plants is consumed by animals, which also respire and release carbon dioxide. Plants and animals die and are ultimately decomposed by microorganisms in the soil; the carbon in their tissues is oxidized to carbon dioxide and returns to the atmosphere. The widths of the pathways are roughly proportional to the quantities involved. A similar carbon cycle takes place within the sea. There is still no general agreement as to which of the two cycles is larger. The author's estimates of the quantities involved appear in the flow chart on page 226.

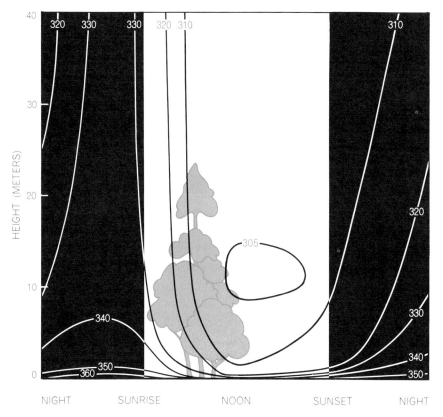

VERTICAL DISTRIBUTION OF CARBON DIOXIDE in the air around a forest varies with time of day. At night, when photosynthesis is shut off, respiration from the soil can raise the carbon dioxide at ground level to as much as 400 parts per million (ppm). By noon, owing to photosynthetic uptake, the concentration at treetop level can drop to 305 ppm.

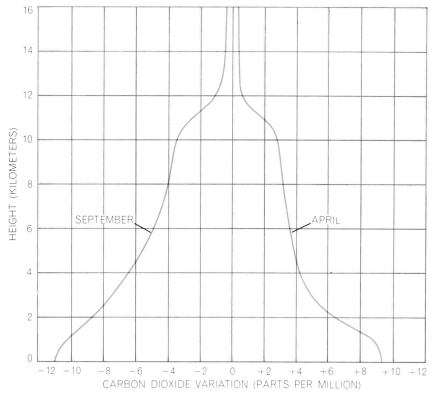

SEASONAL VARIATIONS in the carbon dioxide content of the atmosphere reach a maximum in September and April for the region north of 30 degrees north latitude. The departure from a mean value of about 320 ppm varies with altitude as shown by these two curves.

at which organic matter in the soil is being transformed by measuring its content of the radioactive isotope carbon 14. At the time carbon is fixed by photosynthesis its ratio of carbon 14 to the nonradioactive isotope carbon 12 is the same as the ratio in the atmosphere (except for a constant fractionation factor), but thereafter the carbon 14 decays and becomes less abundant with respect to the carbon 12. Measurements of this ratio yield rates for the oxidation of organic matter in the soil ranging from decades in tropical soils to several hundred years in boreal forests.

In addition to the daily variations of carbon dioxide in the air there is a marked annual variation, at least in the Northern Hemisphere. As spring comes to northern regions the consumption of carbon dioxide by plants greatly exceeds the return from the soil. The increased withdrawal of carbon dioxide can be measured all the way up to the lower stratosphere. A marked decrease in the atmospheric content of carbon dioxide occurs during the spring. From April to September the atmosphere north of 30 degrees north latitude loses nearly 3 percent of its carbon dioxide content, which is equivalent to about four billion tons of carbon [*see bottom illustration at left*]. Since the decay processes in the soil go on simultaneously, the net withdrawal of four billion tons implies an annual gross fixation of carbon in these latitudes of at least five or six billion tons. This amounts to about a fourth of the annual terrestrial productivity referred to above (20 to 30 billion tons), which was based on a survey of carbon fixation. In this global survey the estimated contribution from the Northern Hemisphere, where plant growth shows a marked seasonal variation, constituted about 25 percent of the total tonnage. Thus two independent estimates of worldwide carbon fixation on land show a quite satisfactory agreement.

The forests of the world not only are the main carbon dioxide consumers on land; they also represent the main reservoir of biologically fixed carbon (except for fossil fuels, which have been largely removed from the carbon cycle save for the amount reintroduced by man's burning of it). The forests contain between 400 and 500 billion tons of carbon, or roughly two-thirds of the amount present as carbon dioxide in the atmosphere (700 billion tons). The figure for forests can be estimated only approximately. The average age of a tree can be assumed to be about 30 years, which implies that about 15 billion tons of carbon in the form of carbon dioxide is annually transformed into wood, which seems reasonable in comparison with a total annual assimilation of 20 to 30 billion tons.

The pattern of carbon circulation in the sea is quite different from the pattern on land. The productivity of the soil is mostly limited by the availability of fresh water and phosphorus, and only to a degree by the availability of other nutrients in the soil. In the oceans the overriding limitation is the availability of inorganic substances. The phytoplankton require not only plentiful supplies of phosphorus and nitrogen but also trace amounts of various metals, notably iron.

The competition for food in the sea is so keen that organisms have gradually developed the ability to absorb essential minerals even when these nutrients are available only in very low concentration. As a result high concentrations of nutrients are rarely found in surface waters, where solar radiation makes it possible for photosynthetic organisms to exist. If an ocean area is uncommonly productive, one can be sure that nutrients are supplied from deeper layers. (In limited areas they are supplied by the wastes of human activities.) The most productive waters in the world are therefore near the Antarctic continent, where the deep waters of the surrounding oceans well up and mix with the surface layers. There are similar upwellings along the coast of Chile, in the vicinity of Japan and in the Gulf Stream. In such regions fish are abundant and the maximum annual fixation of carbon approaches .3 kilogram per square meter. In the "desert" areas of the oceans, such

as the open seas of subtropical latitudes, the fixation rate may be less than a tenth of that value. In the Tropics warm surface layers are usually effective in blocking the vertical water exchange needed to carry nutrients up from below.

Phytoplankton, the primary fixers of carbon dioxide in the sea, are eaten by the zooplankton and other tiny animals. These organisms in turn provide food for the larger animals. The major part of the oceanic biomass, however, consists of microorganisms. Since the lifetime of such organisms is measured in weeks, or at most in months, their total mass can never accumulate appreciably. When microorganisms die, they quickly disintegrate as they sink to deeper layers. Soon most of what was once living tissue has become dissolved organic matter.

A small fraction of the organic particulate matter escapes oxidation and settles into the ocean depths. There it profoundly influences the abundance of chemical substances because (except in special regions) the deep layers exchange water with the surface layers very slowly. The enrichment of the deep layers goes hand in hand with a depletion of oxygen. There also appears to be an increase in carbon dioxide (in the form of carbonate and bicarbonate ions) in the ocean depths. The overall distribution of carbon dioxide, oxygen and various minor constituents in the sea reflects a balance between the marine life and its chemical milieu in the surface layers and the slow transport of substances by the general circulation of the ocean. The net effect is to prevent the ocean from becoming saturated with oxygen and to enrich the deeper strata with carbonate and bicarbonate ions.

The particular state in which we find the oceans today could well be quite different if the mechanisms for the exchange of water between the surface layers and the deep ones were either more intense or less so. The present state is determined primarily by the sinking of cold water in the polar regions, particularly the Antarctic. In these regions the water is also slightly saltier, and therefore still denser, because some of it has been frozen out in floating ice. If the climate of the earth were different, the distribution of carbon dioxide, oxygen and minerals might also be quite different. If the difference were large enough, oxygen might completely vanish from the ocean depths, leaving them to be populated only by chemibarotrophic bacteria. (This is now the case in the depths of the Black Sea.)

The time required to establish a new equilibrium in the ocean is determined by the slowest link in the chain of processes that has been described. This link is the oceanic circulation; it seems to take at least 1,000 years for the water in the deepest basins to be completely replaced. One can imagine other conditions of circulation in which the oceans would interact differently with sediments and rocks, producing a balance of substances that one can only guess at.

So far we have been concerned only with the basic biological and ecological processes that provide the mechanisms for circulating carbon through living organisms. Plants on land, with lifetimes measured in years, and phytoplankton in the sea, with lifetimes measured in weeks, are merely the innermost wheels in a biogeochemical machine that embraces the entire earth and that retains important characteristics over much longer time periods. In order to understand such interactions we shall need some rough estimates of the size of the various carbon reservoirs involved and the nature of their contents [*see illustration on page 226*]. In the context of the present argument the large uncertainties in such estimates are of little significance.

Only a few tenths of a percent of the immense mass of carbon at or near the surface of the earth (on the order of 20×10^{15} tons) is in rapid circulation in the biosphere, which includes the atmosphere, the hydrosphere, the upper portions of the earth's crust and the biomass itself. The overwhelming bulk of near-surface carbon consists of inorganic deposits (chiefly carbonates) and organic fossil deposits (chiefly oil shale, coal and petroleum) that required hundreds of

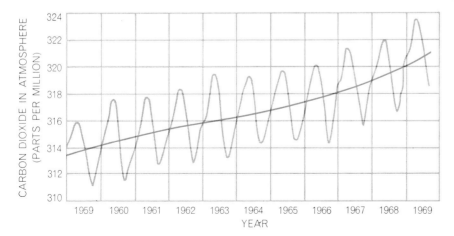

LONG-TERM VARIATIONS in the carbon dioxide content of the atmosphere have been followed at the Mauna Loa Observatory in Hawaii by the Scripps Institution of Oceanography. The sawtooth curve indicates the month-to-month change in concentration since January, 1959. The oscillations reflect seasonal variations in the rate of photosynthesis, as depicted in the bottom illustration on the preceding page. The smooth curve shows the trend.

OIL SHALE is one of the principal sedimentary forms in which carbon has been deposited over geologic time. This photograph, taken at Anvil Points, Colo., shows a section of the Green River Formation, which extends through Colorado, Utah and Wyoming. The formation is estimated to contain the equivalent of more than a trillion barrels of oil in seams containing more than 10 barrels of oil per ton of rock. Of this some 80 billion barrels is considered recoverable. The shale seams are up to 130 feet thick.

WHITE CLIFFS OF DOVER consist of almost pure calcium carbonate, representing the skeletons of phytoplankton that settled to the bottom of the sea over a period of millions of years more than 70 million years ago. The worldwide deposits of limestone, oil shale and other carbon-containing sediments are by far the largest repository of carbon: an estimated 20 quadrillion (10^{15}) tons.

millions of years to reach their present magnitude. Over time intervals as brief as those of which we have been speaking—up to 1,000 years for the deep-ocean circulation—the accretion of such deposits is negligible. We may therefore consider the life processes on land and in the sea as the inner wheels that spin at comparatively high velocity in the carbon-circulating machine. They are coupled by a very low gear to more majestic processes that account for the overall circulation of carbon in its various geologic and oceanic forms.

We now know that the two great systems, the atmosphere and the ocean, are closely coupled to each other through the transfer of carbon dioxide across the surface of the oceans. The rate of exchange has recently been estimated by measuring the rate at which the radioactive isotope carbon 14 produced by the testing of nuclear weapons has disappeared from the atmosphere. The neutrons released in such tests form carbon 14 by reacting with the nitrogen 14 of the atmosphere. In this reaction a nitrogen atom ($_7N^{14}$) captures a neutron and subsequently releases a proton, yielding $_6C^{14}$. (The subscript before the letter represents the number of protons in the nucleus; the superscript after the letter indicates the sum of protons and neutrons.)

The last major atmospheric tests were conducted in 1963. Sampling at various altitudes and latitudes shows that the constituents of the atmosphere became rather well mixed over a period of a few years. The decline of carbon 14, however, was found to be rapid; it can be explained only by assuming an exchange of atmospheric carbon dioxide, enriched in carbon 14, with the reservoir of much less radioactive carbon dioxide in the sea. The measurements indicate that the characteristic time for the residence of carbon dioxide in the atmosphere before the gas is dissolved in the sea is between five and 10 years. In other words, every year something like 100 billion tons of atmospheric carbon dioxide dissolves in the sea and is replaced by a nearly equivalent amount of oceanic carbon dioxide.

Since around 1850 man has inadvertently been conducting a global geochemical experiment by burning large amounts of fossil fuel and thereby returning to the atmosphere carbon that was fixed by photosynthesis millions of years ago. Currently between five and six billion tons of fossil carbon per year are being released into the atmosphere. This would be enough to increase the amount of carbon dioxide in the air by 2.3 parts per million per year if the carbon dioxide were uniformly distributed and not removed. Within the past century the carbon dioxide content of the atmosphere has risen from some 290 parts per million to 320, with more than a fifth of the rise occurring in just the past decade [see illustration on page 223]. The total increase accounts for only slightly more than a third of the carbon dioxide (some 200 billion tons in all) released from fossil fuels. Although most of the remaining two-thirds has presumably gone into the oceans, a significant fraction may well have increased the total amount of vegetation on land. Laboratory studies show that plants grow faster when the surrounding air is enriched in carbon dioxide. Thus it is possible that man is fertilizing fields and forests by burning coal, oil and natural gas. The biomass on land may have increased by as much as 15 billion tons in the past century. There is, however, little concrete evidence for such an increase.

Man has of course been changing his environment in other ways. Over the past century large areas covered with forest have been cleared and turned to agriculture. In such areas the character of soil respiration has undoubtedly changed, producing effects that might have been detectable in the atmospheric content of carbon dioxide if it had not been for the simultaneous increase in the burning of fossil fuels. In any case the dynamic equilibrium among the major carbon dioxide reservoirs in the biomass, the atmosphere, the hydrosphere and the soil has been disturbed, and it can be said that they are in a period of transition. Since even the most rapid processes of adjustment among the reservoirs take decades, new equilibriums are far from being established. Gradually the deep oceans become involved; their turnover time of about 1,000 years and their rate of exchange with bottom sediments control the ultimate partitioning of carbon.

Meanwhile human activities continue to change explosively. The acceleration in the consumption of fossil fuels implies that the amount of carbon dioxide in the atmosphere will keep climbing from its present value of 320 parts per million to between 375 and 400 parts per million by the year 2000, in spite of anticipated large removals of carbon dioxide by land vegetation and the ocean reservoir [see illustrations on page 227]. A fundamental question is: What will happen over the next 100 or 1,000 years? Clearly the exponential changes cannot continue.

If we extend the time scale with which we are viewing the carbon cycle by several orders of magnitude, to hundreds of thousands or millions of years, we can anticipate large-scale exchanges between organic carbon on land and carbonates of biological origin in the sea. We know that there have been massive exchanges in the remote past. Any discussion of these past events and their implications for the future, however, must necessarily be qualitative and uncertain.

Although the plants on land have probably played an important role in the deposition of organic compounds in the soil, the oceans have undoubtedly acted as the main regulator. The amount of carbon dioxide in the atmosphere is essentially determined by the partial pressure of carbon dioxide dissolved in the

GIANT FERN of the genus *Pecopteris*, which fixed atmospheric carbon dioxide 300 million years ago, left the imprint of this frond in a thin layer of shale just above a coal seam in Illinois. The specimen is in the collection of the Smithsonian Institution.

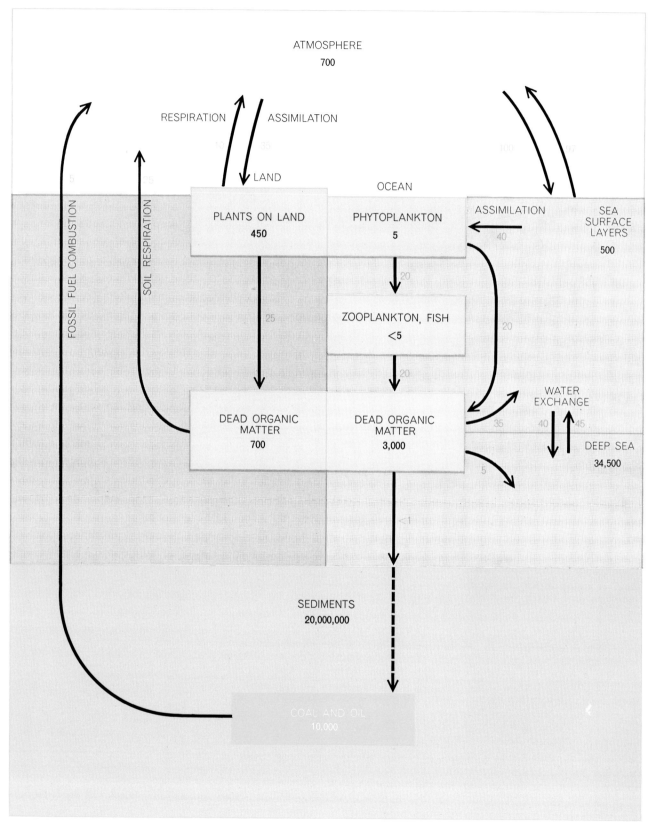

CARBON CIRCULATION IN BIOSPHERE involves two quite distinct cycles, one on land and one in the sea, that are dynamically connected at the interface between the ocean and the atmosphere. The carbon cycle in the sea is essentially self-contained in that phytoplankton assimilate the carbon dioxide dissolved in seawater and release oxygen back into solution. Zooplankton and fish consume the carbon fixed by the phytoplankton, using the dissolved oxygen for respiration. Eventually the decomposition of organic matter replaces the carbon dioxide assimilated by the phytoplank- ton. All quantities are in billions of metric tons. It will be seen that the combustion of fossil fuels at the rate of about five billion tons per year is sufficient to increase the carbon dioxide in the atmosphere by about .7 percent, equivalent to adding some two parts per million to the existing 320 ppm. Since the observed an- nual increase is only about .7 ppm, it appears that two-thirds of the carbon dioxide released from fossil fuels is quickly removed from the atmosphere, going either into the oceans or adding to the total mass of terrestrial plants. The estimated tonnages are the author's.

sea. Over a period of, say, 100,000 years the leaching of calcium carbonates from land areas tends to increase the amount of carbon dioxide in the sea, but at the same time a converse mechanism—the precipitation and deposition of oceanic carbonates—tends to reduce the amount of carbon dioxide in solution. Thus the two mechanisms tend to cancel each other.

Over still longer periods of time—millions or tens of millions of years—the concentrations of carbonate and bicarbonate ions in the sea are probably buffered still further by reactions involving potassium, silicon and aluminum, which are slowly weathered from rocks and carried into the sea. The net effect is to stabilize the carbon dioxide content of the oceans and hence the carbon dioxide content of the atmosphere. Therefore .it appears that the carbon dioxide environment, on which the biosphere fundamentally depends, may have been fairly constant right up to the time, barely a moment ago geologically speaking, when man's consumption of fossil fuels began to change the carbon dioxide content of the atmosphere.

The illustration on page 226 represents an attempt to synthesize into a single picture the circulation of carbon in nature, particularly in the biosphere. In addition to the values for inventories and transfers already mentioned, the flow chart contains other quantities for which the evidence is still meager. They have been included not only to balance the books but also to suggest where further investigation might be profitable. This may be the principal value of such an exercise. Such a flow chart also provides a semiquantitative model that enables one to begin to discuss how the global carbon system reacts to disturbances. A good model should of course include inventories and pathways for all the elements that play a significant role in biological processes.

The greatest disturbances of which we are aware are those now being introduced by man himself. Since his tampering with the biological and geochemical balances may ultimately prove injurious —even fatal—to himself, he must understand them much better than he does today. The story of the circulation of carbon in nature teaches us that we cannot control the global balances. Therefore we had better leave them close to the natural state that existed until the beginning of the Industrial Revolution. Out of a simple realization of this necessity may come a new industrial revolution.

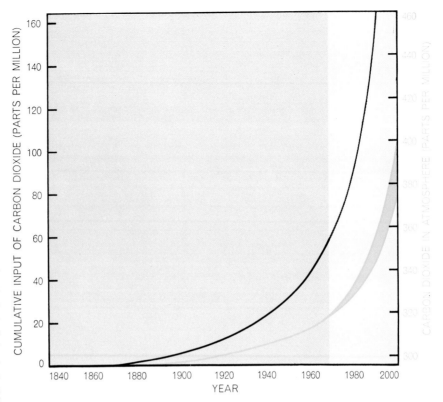

INCREASE IN ATMOSPHERIC CARBON DIOXIDE since 1860 is shown by the lower curve, with a projection to the year 2000. The upper curve shows the cumulative input of carbon dioxide. The difference between the two curves represents the amount of carbon dioxide removed by the ocean or by additions to the total biomass of vegetation on land.

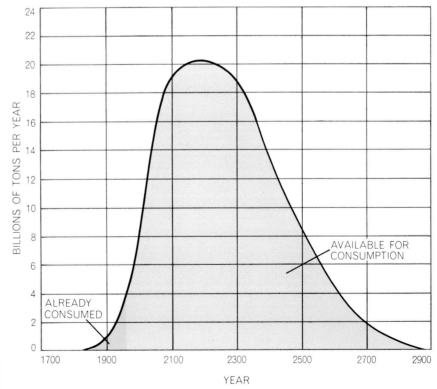

POSSIBLE CONSUMPTION PATTERN OF FOSSIL FUELS was projected by Harrison Brown in the mid-1950's. Here the fuel consumed is updated to 1960. If a third of the carbon dioxide produced by burning it all were to remain in the atmosphere, the carbon dioxide level would rise from 320 ppm today to about 1,500 ppm over the next several centuries.

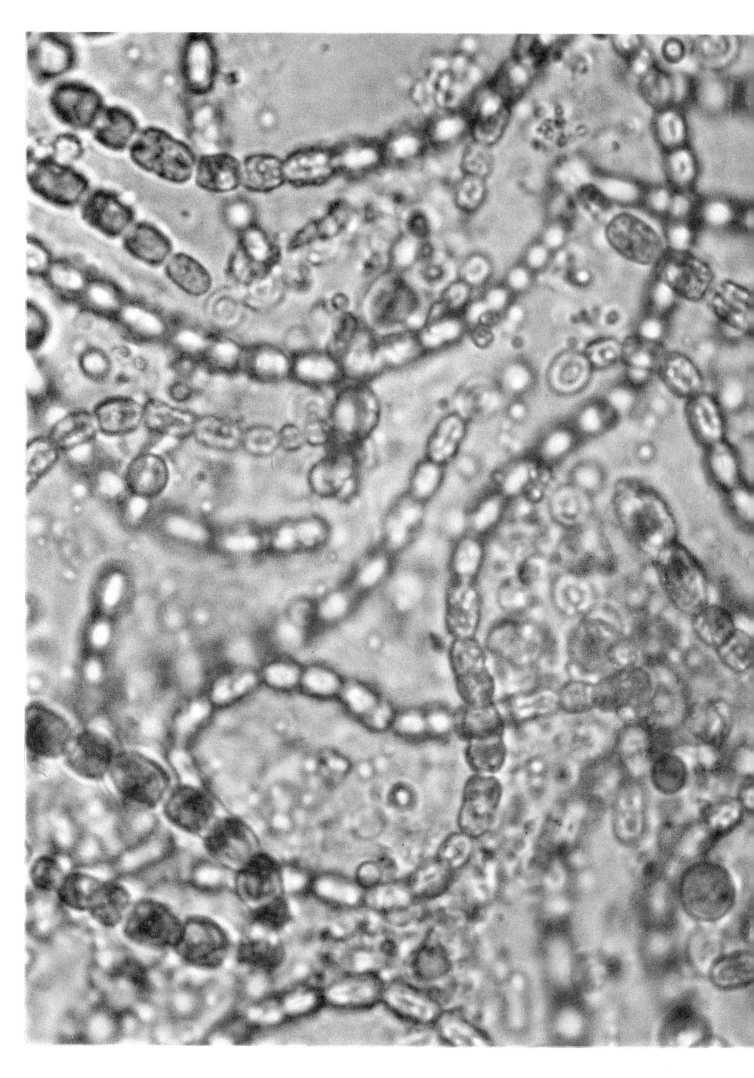

26

THE NITROGEN CYCLE

C. C. DELWICHE
September 1970

Nitrogen is 79 percent of the atmosphere, but it cannot be used directly by the large majority of living things. It must first be "fixed" by specialized organisms or by industrial processes

Although men and other land animals live in an ocean of air that is 79 percent nitrogen, their supply of food is limited more by the availability of fixed nitrogen than by that of any other plant nutrient. By "fixed" is meant nitrogen incorporated in a chemical compound that can be utilized by plants and animals. As it exists in the atmosphere nitrogen is an inert gas except to the comparatively few organisms that have the ability to convert the element to a combined form. A smaller but still significant amount of atmospheric nitrogen is fixed by ionizing phenomena such as cosmic radiation, meteor trails and lightning, which momentarily provide the high energy needed for nitrogen to react with oxygen or the hydrogen of water. Nitrogen is also fixed by marine organisms, but the largest single natural source of fixed nitrogen is probably terrestrial microorganisms and associations between such microorganisms and plants.

Of all man's recent interventions in the cycles of nature the industrial fixation of nitrogen far exceeds all the others in magnitude. Since 1950 the amount of nitrogen annually fixed for the production of fertilizer has increased approximately fivefold, until it now equals the amount that was fixed by all terrestrial ecosystems before the advent of modern agriculture. In 1968 the world's annual output of industrially fixed nitrogen amounted to about 30 million tons of ni-

trogen; by the year 2000 the industrial fixation of nitrogen may well exceed 100 million tons.

Before the large-scale manufacture of synthetic fertilizers and the wide cultivation of the nitrogen-fixing legumes one could say with some confidence that the amount of nitrogen removed from the atmosphere by natural fixation processes was closely balanced by the amount returned to the atmosphere by organisms that convert organic nitrates to gaseous nitrogen. Now one cannot be sure that the denitrifying processes are keeping pace with the fixation processes. Nor can one predict all the consequences if nitrogen fixation were to exceed denitrification over an extended period. We do know that excessive runoff of nitrogen compounds in streams and rivers can result in "blooms" of algae and intensified biological activity that deplete the available oxygen and destroy fish and other oxygen-dependent organisms. The rapid eutrophication of Lake Erie is perhaps the most familiar example.

To appreciate the intricate web of nitrogen flow in the biosphere let us trace the course of nitrogen atoms from the atmosphere into the cells of microorganisms, and then into the soil as fixed nitrogen, where it is available to higher plants and ultimately to animals. Plants and animals die and return the fixed nitrogen to the soil, at which point the nitrogen may simply be recycled through a new generation of plants and animals

or it may be broken down into elemental nitrogen and returned to the atmosphere [*see illustration on next two pages*].

Because much of the terminology used to describe steps in the nitrogen cycle evolved in previous centuries it has an archaic quality. Antoine Laurent Lavoisier, who clarified the composition of air, gave nitrogen the name azote, meaning without life. The term is still found in the family name of an important nitrogen-fixing bacterium: the Azotobacteraceae. One might think that fixation would merely be termed nitrification, to indicate the addition of nitrogen to some other substance, but nitrification is reserved for a specialized series of reactions in which a few species of microorganisms oxidize the ammonium ion (NH_4^+) to nitrite (NO_2^-) or nitrite to nitrate (NO_3^-). When nitrites or nitrates are reduced to gaseous compounds such as molecular nitrogen (N_2) or nitrous oxide (N_2O), the process is termed denitrification. "Ammonification" describes the process by which the nitrogen of organic compounds (chiefly amino acids) is converted to ammonium ion. The process operates when microorganisms decompose the remains of dead plants and animals. Finally, a word should be said about the terms oxidation and reduction, which have come to mean more than just the addition of oxygen or its removal. Oxidation is any process that removes electrons from a substance. Reduction is the reverse process: the addition of electrons. Since electrons can neither be created nor destroyed in a chemical reaction, the oxidation of one substance always implies the reduction of another.

One may wonder how it is that some organisms find it profitable to oxidize

BLUE-GREEN ALGAE, magnified 4,200 diameters on the opposite page, are among the few free-living organisms capable of combining nitrogen with hydrogen. Until this primary fixation process is accomplished, the nitrogen in the air (or dissolved in water) cannot be assimilated by the overwhelming majority of plants or by any animal. A few bacteria are also free-living nitrogen fixers. The remaining nitrogen-fixing microorganisms live symbiotically with higher plants. This micrograph, which shows blue-green algae of the genus *Nostoc*, was made by Herman S. Forest of the State University of New York at Geneseo.

nitrogen compounds whereas other organisms—even organisms in the same environment—owe their survival to their ability to reduce nitrogen compounds. Apart from photosynthetic organisms, which obtain their energy from radiation, all living forms depend for their energy on chemical transformations.

These transformations normally involve the oxidation of one compound and the reduction of another, although in some cases the compound being oxidized and the compound being reduced are different molecules of the same substance, and in other cases the reactants are fragments of a single molecular species. Ni-

trogen can be cycled because the reduced inorganic compounds of nitrogen can be oxidized by atmospheric oxygen with a yield of useful energy. Under anaerobic conditions the oxidized compounds of nitrogen can act as oxidizing agents for the burning of organic compounds (and a few inorganic com-

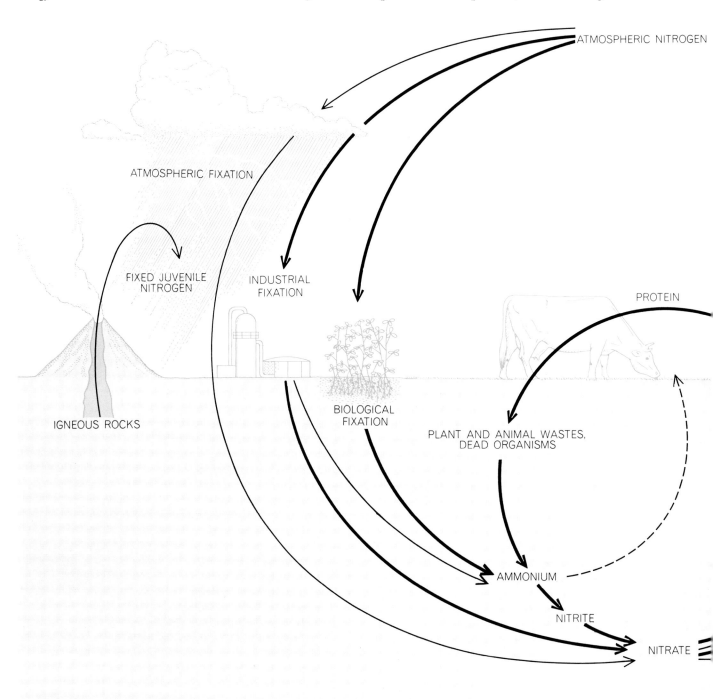

NITROGEN CYCLE, like the water, oxygen and carbon cycles, involves all regions of the biosphere. Although the supply of nitrogen in the atmosphere is virtually inexhaustible, it must be combined with hydrogen or oxygen before it can be assimilated by higher plants, which in turn are consumed by animals. Man has intervened in the historical nitrogen cycle by the large-scale cultivation of nitrogen-fixing legumes and by the industrial fixation of nitrogen. The amount of nitrogen fixed annually by these two expedients now exceeds by perhaps 10 percent the amount of nitrogen fixed by terrestrial ecosystems before the advent of agriculture.

pounds), again with a yield of useful energy.

Nitrogen is able to play its complicated role in life processes because it has an unusual number of oxidation levels, or valences [*see illustration on page 233*]. An oxidation level indicates the number of electrons that an atom in a

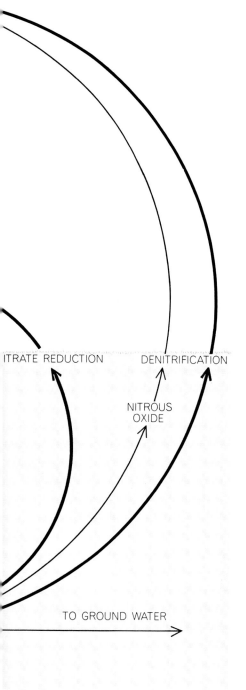

ITRATE REDUCTION   DENITRIFICATION

NITROUS
OXIDE

TO GROUND WATER

A cycle similar to the one illustrated also operates in the ocean, but its characteristics and transfer rates are less well understood. A global nitrogen flow chart, using the author's estimates, appears on the next page.

particular compound has "accepted" or "donated." In plants and animals most nitrogen exists either in the form of the ammonium ion or of amino ($-NH_2$) compounds. In either case it is highly reduced; it has acquired three electrons by its association with three other atoms and thus is said to have a valence of minus 3. At the other extreme, when nitrogen is in the highly oxidized form of the nitrate ion (the principal form it takes in the soil), it shares five of its electrons with oxygen atoms and so has a valence of plus 5. To convert nitrogen as it is found in the ammonium ion or amino acids to nitrogen as it exists in soil nitrates involves a total valence change of eight, or the removal of eight electrons. Conversely, to convert nitrate nitrogen into amino nitrogen requires the addition of eight electrons.

By and large the soil reactions that reduce nitrogen, or add electrons to it, release considerably more energy than the reactions that oxidize nitrogen, or remove electrons from it. The illustration on page 234 lists some of the principal reactions involved in the nitrogen cycle, together with the energy released (or required) by each. As a generalization one can say that for almost every reaction in nature where the conversion of one compound to another yields an energy of at least 15 kilocalories per mole (the equivalent in grams of a compound's molecular weight), some organism or group of organisms has arisen that can exploit this energy to survive.

The fixation of nitrogen requires an investment of energy. Before nitrogen can be fixed it must be "activated," which means that molecular nitrogen must be split into two atoms of free nitrogen. This step requires at least 160 kilocalories for each mole of nitrogen (equivalent to 28 grams). The actual fixation step, in which two atoms of nitrogen combine with three molecules of hydrogen to form two molecules of ammonia (NH_3), releases about 13 kilocalories. Thus the two steps together require a net input of at least 147 kilocalories. Whether nitrogen-fixing organisms actually invest this much energy, however, is not known. Reactions catalyzed by enzymes involve the penetration of activation barriers and not a simple change in energy between a set of initial reactants and their end products.

Once ammonia or the ammonium ion has appeared in the soil, it can be absorbed by the roots of plants and the nitrogen can be incorporated into amino acids and then into proteins. If the plant is subsequently eaten by an animal, the

nitrogen may be incorporated into a new protein. In either case the protein ultimately returns to the soil, where it is decomposed (usually with bacterial help) into its component amino acids. Assuming that conditions are aerobic, meaning that an adequate supply of oxygen is present, the soil will contain many microorganisms capable of oxidizing amino acids to carbon dioxide, water and ammonia. If the amino acid happens to be glycine, the reaction will yield 176 kilocalories per mole.

A few microorganisms represented by the genus *Nitrosomonas* employ nitrification of the ammonium ion as their sole source of energy. In the presence of oxygen, ammonia is converted to nitrite ion ($NO_2{}^-$) plus water, with an energy yield of about 65 kilocalories per mole, which is quite adequate for a comfortable existence. *Nitrosomonas* belongs to the group of microorganisms termed autotrophs, which get along without an organic source of energy. Photoautotrophs obtain their energy from light; chemoautotrophs (such as *Nitrosomonas*) obtain energy from inorganic compounds.

There is another specialized group of microorganisms, represented by *Nitrobacter,* that are capable of extracting additional energy from the nitrite generated by *Nitrosomonas*. The result is the oxidation of a nitrite ion to a nitrate ion with the release of about 17 kilocalories per mole, which is just enough to support the existence of *Nitrobacter*.

In the soil there are numerous kinds of denitrifying bacteria (for example *Pseudomonas denitrificans*) that, if obliged to exist in the absence of oxygen, are able to use the nitrate or nitrite ion as electron acceptors for the oxidation of organic compounds. In these reactions the energy yield is nearly as large as it would be if pure oxygen were the oxidizing agent. When glucose reacts with oxygen, the energy yield is 686 kilocalories per mole of glucose. In microorganisms living under anaerobic conditions the reaction of glucose with nitrate ion yields about 545 kilocalories per mole of glucose if the nitrogen is reduced to nitrous oxide, and 570 kilocalories if the nitrogen is reduced all the way to its elemental gaseous state.

The comparative value of ammonium and nitrate ions as a source of nitrogen for plants has been the subject of a number of investigations. One might think that the question would be readily resolved in favor of the ammonium ion: its valence is minus 3, the same as the valence of nitrogen in amino acids, whereas the valence of the nitrate ion is plus 5.

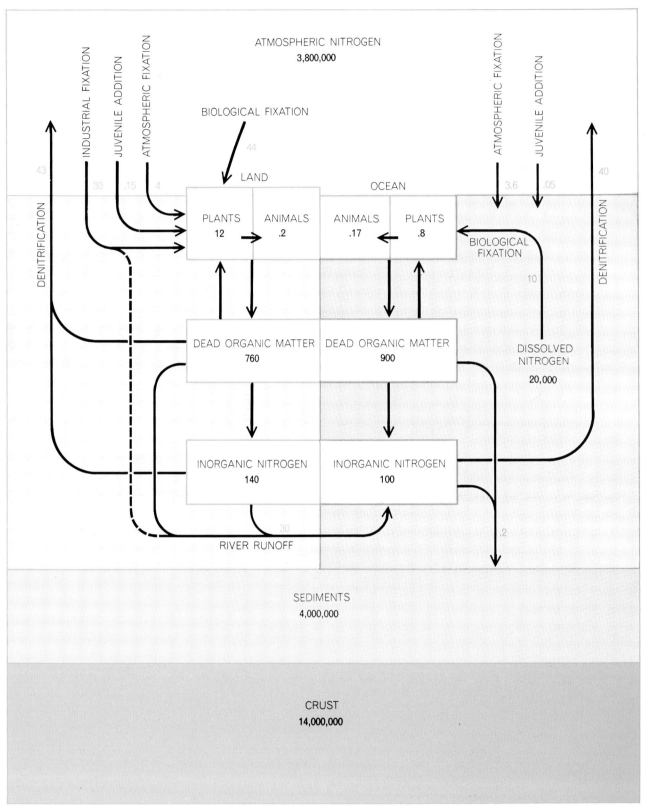

DISTRIBUTION OF NITROGEN in the biosphere and annual transfer rates can be estimated only within broad limits. The two quantities known with high confidence are the amount of nitrogen in the atmosphere and the rate of industrial fixation. The apparent precision in the other figures shown here reflects chiefly an effort to preserve indicated or probable ratios among different inventories. Thus the figures for atmospheric fixation and biological fixation in the oceans could well be off by a factor of 10. The figures for inventories are given in billions of metric tons; the figures for transfer rates (*color*) are given in millions of metric tons. Because of the extensive use of industrially fixed nitrogen the amount of nitrogen available to land plants may significantly exceed the nitrogen returned to the atmosphere by denitrifying bacteria in the soil. A portion of this excess fixed nitrogen is ultimately washed into the sea but it is not included in the figure shown for river runoff. Similarly, the value for oceanic denitrification is no more than a rough estimate that is based on the assumption that the nitrogen cycle was in overall balance before man's intervention.

On this basis plants must expend energy to reduce nitrogen from a valence of plus 5 to one of minus 3. The fact is, however, that there are complicating factors; the preferred form of nitrogen depends on other variables. Because the ammonium ion has a positive charge it tends to be trapped on clay particles near the point where it is formed (or where it is introduced artificially) until it has been oxidized. The nitrate ion, being negatively charged, moves freely through the soil and thus is more readily carried downward into the root zone. Although the demand for fertilizer in solid form (such as ammonium nitrate and urea) remains high, anhydrous ammonia and liquid ammoniacal fertilizers are now widely applied. The quantity of nitrogen per unit weight of ammonia is much greater than it is per unit of nitrate; moreover, liquids are easier to handle than solids.

Until the end of the 19th century little was known about the soil organisms that fix nitrogen. In fact, at that time there was some concern among scientists that the denitrifying bacteria, which had just been discovered, would eventually deplete the reserve of fixed nitrogen in the soil and cripple farm productivity. In an address before the Royal Society of London, Sir William Crookes painted a bleak picture for world food production unless artificial means of fixing nitrogen were soon developed. This was a period when Chilean nitrate reserves were the main source of fixed nitrogen for both fertilizer and explosives. As it turned out, the demand for explosives provided the chief incentive for the invention of the catalytic fixation process by Fritz Haber and Karl Bosch of Germany in 1914. In this process atmospheric nitrogen and hydrogen are passed over a catalyst (usually nickel) at a temperature of about 500 degrees Celsius and a pressure of several hundred atmospheres. In a French version of the process, developed by Georges Claude, nitrogen was obtained by the fractional liquefaction of air. In current versions of the Haber process the source of hydrogen is often the methane in natural gas [see illustration on page 235].

As the biological fixation of nitrogen and the entire nitrogen cycle became better understood, the role of the denitrifying bacteria fell into place. Without such bacteria to return nitrogen to the atmosphere most of the atmospheric nitrogen would now be in the oceans or locked up in sediments. Actually, of course, there is not enough oxygen in the

VALENCE	COMPOUND	FORMULA	VALENCE ELECTRONS
+ 5	NITRATE ION	NO_3^-	
+ 3	NITRITE ION	NO_2^-	
+ 1	NITROXYL	[HNO]	
0	NITROGEN GAS	N_2	
− 1	HYDROXYLAMINE	$HONH_2$	
− 3	AMMONIA	NH_3	

NITROGEN'S VARIETY OF OXIDATION LEVELS, or valence states, explains its ability to combine with hydrogen, oxygen and other atoms to form a great variety of biological compounds. Six of its valence states are listed with schematic diagrams (right) showing the disposition of electrons in the atom's outer (valence) shell. The ions are shown combined with potassium (K). In the oxidized (+) states nitrogen's outer electrons complete the outer shells of other atoms. In the reduced (−) states the two electrons needed to complete the outer shell of nitrogen are supplied by other atoms. Actually the outer electrons of two bound atoms spend some time in the shells of both atoms, contributing to the electrostatic attraction between them. Electrons of nitrogen (N) are in color; those of other atoms are black dots or open circles. The nitroxyl radical, HNO, is placed in brackets because it is not stable. It can exist in its dimeric form, hyponitrous acid (HONNOH).

atmosphere today to convert all the free nitrogen into nitrates. One can imagine, however, that if a one-way process were to develop in the absence of denitrifying bacteria, the addition of nitrates to the ocean would make seawater slightly more acidic and start the release of carbon dioxide from carbonate rocks. Eventually the carbon dioxide would be taken up by plants, and if the carbon were then deposited as coal or other hydrocarbons, the remaining oxygen would be available in the atmosphere to be combined with nitrogen. Because of the large number of variables involved it is difficult to predict how the world would look without the denitrification reaction, but it would certainly not be the world we know.

The full story of the biological fixation of nitrogen has not yet been written. One would like to know how the activating enzyme (nitrogenase) used by nitrogen-fixing bacteria can accomplish at ordinary temperatures and pressures what takes hundreds of degrees and thousands of pounds of pressure in a synthetic-ammonia reactor. The total amount of nitrogenase in the world is probably no more than a few kilograms.

The nitrogen-fixing microorganisms are divided into two broad classes: those that are "free-living" and those that live in symbiotic association with higher plants. This distinction, however, is not as sharp as it was once thought to be, because the interaction of plants and microorganisms has varying degrees of intimacy. The symbionts depend directly on the plants for their energy supply and probably for special nutrients as well. The free-living nitrogen fixers are indirectly dependent on plants for their energy or, as in the case of the blue-green algae and photosynthetic bacteria, obtain energy directly from sunlight.

Although the nitrogen-fixation reaction is associated with only a few dozen species of higher plants, these species are widely distributed in the plant kingdom. Among the more primitive plants whose symbionts can fix nitrogen are the cycads and the ginkgos, which can be traced back to the Carboniferous period of some 300 million years ago [see bottom illustration on page 237]. It is probable that the primitive atmosphere of the earth contained ammonia, in which case the necessity for nitrogen fixation did not arise for hundreds of millions of years.

Various kinds of bacteria, particularly the Azotobacteraceae, are evidently the chief suppliers of fixed nitrogen in grasslands and other ecosystems where plants with nitrogen-fixing symbionts are absent. Good quantitative information on the rate of nitrogen fixation in such ecosystems is hard to obtain. Most investigations indicate a nitrogen-fixation rate of only two or three kilograms per hectare per year, with a maximum of perhaps five or six kilograms. Blue-green algae seem to be an important source of fixed nitrogen under conditions that favor their development [see illustration on page 228]. They may be a significant source in rice paddies and other environments favoring their growth. In natural ecosystems with mixed vegetation the symbiotic associations involving such plant genera as Alnus (the alders) and Ceanothus (the buckthorns) are important suppliers of fixed nitrogen.

For the earth as a whole, however, the greatest natural source of fixed nitrogen is probably the legumes. They are certainly the most important from an agronomic standpoint and have therefore been the most closely studied. The input of nitrogen from the microbial symbionts of alfalfa and other leguminous crops can easily amount to 350 kilograms per hectare, or roughly 100 times the annual rate of fixation attainable by nonsymbiotic organisms in a natural ecosystem.

Recommendations for increasing the world's food supply usually emphasize increasing the cultivation of legumes not only to enrich the soil in nitrogen but also because legumes (for example peas and beans) are themselves a food crop containing a good nutritional balance of amino acids. There are, however, several obstacles to carrying out such recommendations. The first is custom and taste. Many societies with no tradition of growing and eating legumes are reluctant to adopt them as a basic food.

For the farmer legumes can create a more immediate problem: the increased yields made possible by the extra nitrogen lead to the increased consumption of other essential elements, notably potassium and phosphorus. As a consequence farmers often say that legumes are "hard on the soil." What this really means is that the large yield of such crops places

REACTION	ENERGY YIELD (KILOCALORIES)
DENITRIFICATION	
1 $C_6H_{12}O_6 + 6KNO_3 \longrightarrow 6CO_2 + 3H_2O + 6KOH + 3N_2O$ GLUCOSE POTASSIUM POTASSIUM NITROUS NITRATE HYDROXIDE OXIDE	545
2 $5C_6H_{12}O_6 + 24KNO_3 \longrightarrow 30CO_2 + 18H_2O + 24KOH + 12N_2$ NITROGEN	570 (PER MOLE OF GLUCOSE)
3 $5S + 6KNO_3 + 2CaCO_3 \longrightarrow 3K_2SO_4 + 2CaSO_4 + 2CO_2 + 3N_2$ SULFUR POTASSIUM CALCIUM SULFATE SULFATE	132 (PER MOLE OF SULFUR)
RESPIRATION	
4 $C_6H_{12}O_6 + 6O_2 \longrightarrow 6CO_2 + 6H_2O$ CARBON WATER DIOXIDE	686
AMMONIFICATION	
5 $CH_2NH_2COOH + 1\frac{1}{2}O_2 \longrightarrow 2CO_2 + H_2O + NH_3$ GLYCINE OXYGEN AMMONIA	176
NITRIFICATION	
6 $NH_3 + 1\frac{1}{2}O_2 \longrightarrow HNO_2 + H_2O$ NITROUS ACID	66
7 $KNO_2 + \frac{1}{2}O_2 \longrightarrow KNO_3$ POTASSIUM NITRITE	17.5
NITROGEN FIXATION	
8 $N_2 \longrightarrow 2N$ "ACTIVATION" OF NITROGEN	− 160
9 $2N + 3H_2 \longrightarrow 2NH_3$	12.8

ENERGY YIELDS OF REACTIONS important in the nitrogen cycle show the various means by which organisms can obtain energy and thereby keep the cycle going. The most profitable are the denitrification reactions, which add electrons to nitrate nitrogen, whose valence is plus 5, and shift it either to plus 1 (as in N_2O) or zero (as in N_2). In the process glucose (or sulfur) is oxidized. Reactions No. 1 and No. 2 release nearly as much energy as conventional respiration (No. 4), in which the agent for oxidizing glucose is oxygen itself. The ammonification reaction (No. 5) is one of many that release ammonium for nitrification. The least energy of all, but still enough to provide the sole energetic support for certain bacteria, is released by the nitrification reactions (No. 6 and No. 7), which oxidize nitrogen. Only nitrogen fixation, which is accomplished in two steps, calls for an input of energy. The true energy cost of nitrogen fixation to an organism is unknown, however.

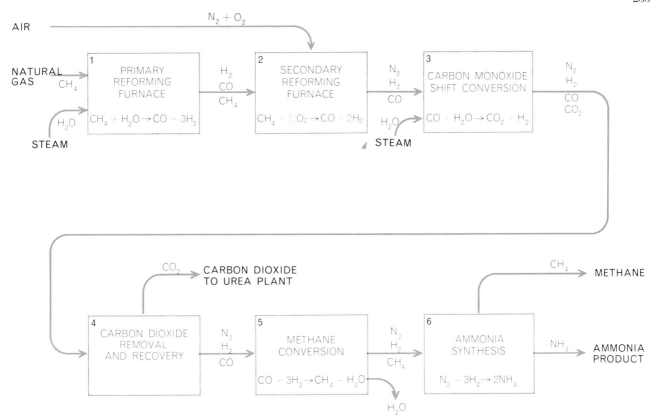

AIR —————————— $N_2 + O_2$

NATURAL GAS CH_4

H_2O

STEAM

1 PRIMARY REFORMING FURNACE
$CH_4 + H_2O \rightarrow CO + 3H_2$

H_2 CO CH_4

2 SECONDARY REFORMING FURNACE
$CH_4 + \tfrac{1}{2}O_2 \rightarrow CO + 2H_2$

H_2O

STEAM

N_2 H_2 CO

3 CARBON MONOXIDE SHIFT CONVERSION
$CO + H_2O \rightarrow CO_2 + H_2$

N_2 H_2 CO CO_2

CO_2 → CARBON DIOXIDE TO UREA PLANT

CH_4 → METHANE

4 CARBON DIOXIDE REMOVAL AND RECOVERY

N_2 H_2 CO

5 METHANE CONVERSION
$CO + 3H_2 \rightarrow CH_4 + H_2O$

N_2 H_2 CH_4

6 AMMONIA SYNTHESIS
$N_2 + 3H_2 \rightarrow 2NH_3$

NH_3 → AMMONIA PRODUCT

H_2O

INDUSTRIAL AMMONIA PROCESS is based on the high-pressure catalytic fixation method invented in 1914 by Fritz Haber and Karl Bosch, which supplied Germany with nitrates for explosives in World War I. This flow diagram is based on the process developed by the M. W. Kellogg Company. As in most modern plants, the hydrogen for the basic reaction is obtained from methane, the chief constituent of natural gas, but any hydrocarbon source will do. In Step 1 methane and steam react to produce a gas rich in hydrogen. In Step 2 atmospheric nitrogen is introduced; the oxygen accompanying it is converted to carbon monoxide by partial combustion with methane. The carbon monoxide reacts with steam in Step 3. The carbon dioxide is removed in Step 4 and can be used elsewhere to convert some of the ammonia to urea, which has the formula $CO(NH_2)_2$. The last traces of carbon monoxide are converted to methane in Step 5. In Step 6 nitrogen and hydrogen combine at elevated temperature and pressure, in the presence of a catalyst, to form ammonia. A portion of the ammonia product can readily be converted to nitric acid by reacting it with oxygen. Nitric acid and ammonia can then be combined to produce ammonium nitrate, which, like urea, is another widely used fertilizer.

a high demand on all minerals, and unless the minerals are supplied the full benefit of the crop is not realized.

Symbiotic nitrogen fixers have a greater need for some micronutrients (for example molybdenum) than most plants do. It is now known that molybdenum is directly incorporated in the nitrogen-fixing enzyme nitrogenase. In Australia there were large areas where legumes refused to grow at all until it was discovered that the land could be made fertile by the addition of as little as two ounces of molybdenum per acre. Cobalt turns out to be another essential micronutrient for the fixation of nitrogen. The addition of only 10 parts per trillion of cobalt in a culture solution can make the difference between plants that are stunted and obviously in need of nitrogen and plants that are healthy and growing vigorously.

Although legumes and their symbionts are energetic fixers of nitrogen, there are indications that the yield of a legume crop can be increased still further by direct application of fertilizer instead of depending on the plant to supply all its own needs for fixed nitrogen. Additional experiments are needed to determine just how much the yield can be increased and how this increase compares with the industrial fixation of nitrogen in terms of energy investment. Industrial processes call for some 6,000 kilocalories per kilogram of nitrogen fixed, which is very little more than the theoretical minimum. The few controlled studies with which I am familiar suggest that the increase in crop yield achieved by the addition of a kilogram of nitrogen amounts to about the same number of calories. This comparison suggests that one can exchange the calories put into industrial fixation of nitrogen for the calories contained in food. In actuality this trade-off applies to the entire agricultural enterprise. The energy required for preparing, tilling and harvesting a field and for processing and distributing the product is only slightly less than the energy contained in the harvested crop.

Having examined the principal reactions that propel the nitrogen cycle, we are now in a position to view the process as a whole and to interpret some of its broad implications. One must be cautious in trying to present a worldwide inventory of a particular element in the biosphere and in indicating annual flows from one part of a cycle to another. The balance sheet for nitrogen [see top illustration on page 237] is particularly crude because we do not have enough information to assign accurate estimates to the amounts of nitrogen that are fixed and subsequently returned to the atmosphere by biological processes.

Another source of uncertainty involves the amount of nitrogen fixed by ionizing phenomena in the atmosphere. Although one can measure the amount of fixed nitrogen in rainfall, one is forced to guess how much is produced by ionization and how much represents nitrogen that has

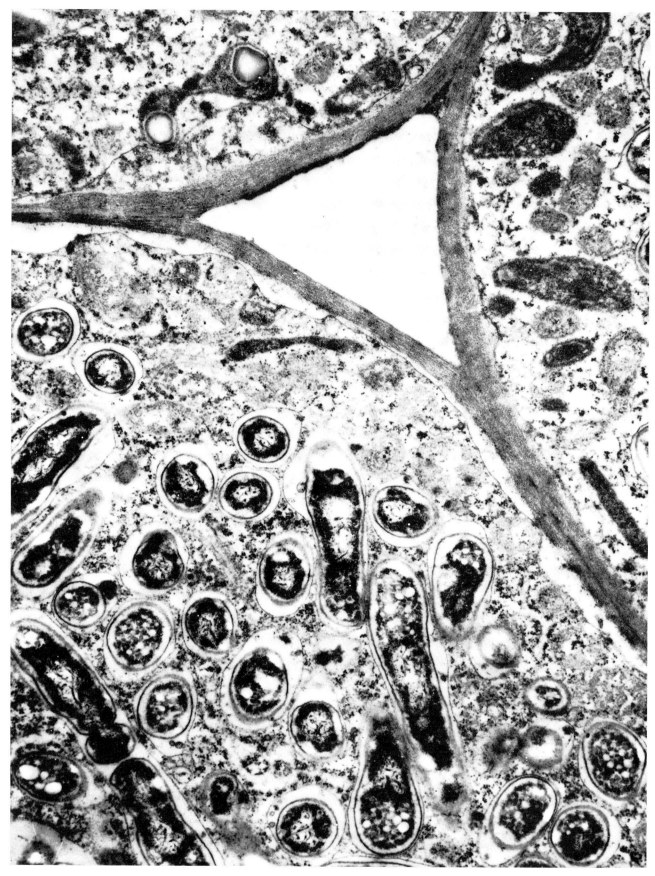

CROSS SECTION OF SOYBEAN ROOT NODULE, enlarged 22,-000 diameters, shows portions of three cells that have been infected by the nitrogen-fixing bacterium *Rhizobium japonicum*. More than two dozen bacteria are visible, each surrounded by a membrane. After the bacteria have divided, within a few days, each membrane will contain four to six "bacteroids." This electron micrograph was made by D. J. Goodchild and F. J. Bergersen of the Commonwealth Scientific and Industrial Research Organization in Australia.

entered the atmosphere from the land or the sea, either as ammonia or as oxides of nitrogen. Because the ocean is slightly alkaline it could release ammonia at a low rate, but that rate is almost impossible to estimate. Land areas are a more likely source of nitrogen oxides, and some reasonable estimates of the rate of loss are possible. One can say that the total amount of fixed nitrogen delivered to the earth by rainfall is of the order of 25 million metric tons per year. My own estimate is that 70 percent of this total is previously fixed nitrogen cycling through the biosphere, and that only 30 percent is freshly fixed by lightning and other atmospheric phenomena.

Another factor that is difficult to estimate is the small but steady loss of nitrogen from the biosphere to sedimentary rocks. Conversely, there is a continuous delivery of new nitrogen to the system by the weathering of igneous rocks in the crust of the earth. The average nitrogen content of igneous rocks, however, is considerably lower than that of sedimentary rocks, and since the quantities of the two kinds of rock are roughly equal, one would expect a net loss of nitrogen from the biosphere through geologic time. Conceivably this loss is just about balanced by the delivery of "juvenile" nitrogen to the atmosphere by volcanic action. The amount of fixed nitrogen reintroduced in this way probably does not exceed two or three million tons per year.

Whereas late-19th-century scientists worried that denitrifying bacteria were exhausting the nitrogen in the soil, we must be concerned today that denitrification may not be keeping pace with nitrogen fixation, considering the large amounts of fixed nitrogen that are being introduced in the biosphere by industrial fixation and the cultivation of legumes. It has become urgent to learn much more about exactly where and under what circumstances denitrification takes place.

We know first of all that denitrification does not normally proceed to any great extent under aerobic conditions. Whenever free oxygen is available, it is energetically advantageous for an organism to use it to oxidize organic compounds rather than to use the oxygen bound in nitrate salts. One can conclude that there must be large areas in the biosphere where conditions are sufficiently anaerobic to strongly favor the denitrification reaction. Such conditions exist wherever the input of organic materials exceeds the input of oxygen for their degradation. Typical areas where the deni-

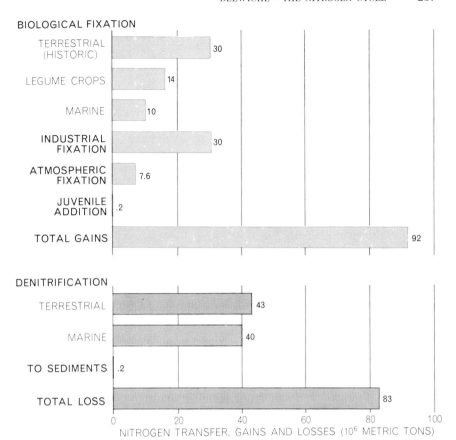

BALANCE SHEET FOR NITROGEN CYCLE, based on the author's estimates, indicates that nitrogen is now being introduced into the biosphere in fixed form at the rate of some 92 million metric tons per year (*colored bars*), whereas the total amount being denitrified and returned to the atmosphere is only about 83 million tons per year. The difference of some nine million tons may represent the rate at which fixed nitrogen is building up in the biosphere: in the soil, in ground-water reservoirs, in rivers and lakes and in the ocean.

ASSOCIATIONS OF TREES AND BACTERIA are important fixers of nitrogen in natural ecosystems. The ginkgo tree (*left*), a gymnosperm, has shown little outward change in millions of years. The alder (*right*), an angiosperm, is common in many parts of the world.

trification process operates close to the surface are the arctic tundra, swamps and similar places where oxygen input is limited. In many other areas where the input of organic material is sizable, however, denitrification is likely to be proceeding at some point below the surface, probably close to the level of the water table.

There are even greater uncertainties regarding the nitrogen cycle in the ocean. It is known that some marine organisms do fix nitrogen, but quantitative information is scanty. A minimum rate of denitrification can be deduced by estimating the amount of nitrate carried into the ocean by rivers. A reasonable estimate is 10 million metric tons per year in the form of nitrates and perhaps twice that amount in the form of organic material, a total of about 30 million tons. Since the transfer of nitrogen into sediments is slight, one can conclude that, at least before man's intervention in the nitrogen cycle, the ocean was probably capable of denitrifying that amount of fixed nitrogen.

The many blanks in our knowledge of the nitrogen cycle are disturbing when one considers that the amount of nitrogen fixed industrially has been doubling about every six years. If we add to this extra nitrogen the amounts fixed by the cultivation of legumes, it already exceeds (by perhaps 10 percent) the amount of nitrogen fixed in nature. Unless fertilizers and nitrogenous wastes are carefully managed, rivers and lakes can become loaded with the nitrogen carried in runoff waters. In such waterways and in neighboring ground-water systems the nitrogen concentration could, and in some cases already does, exceed the levels acceptable for human consumption. Under some circumstances bacterial denitrification can be exploited to control the buildup of fixed nitrogen, but much work has to be done to develop successful management techniques.

The problem of nitrogen disposal is aggravated by the nitrogen contained in the organic wastes of a steadily increasing human and domestic-animal population. Ideally this waste nitrogen should be recycled back to the soil, but efficient and acceptable means for doing so remain to be developed. At present it is economically sounder for the farmer to keep adding industrial fertilizers to his crops. The ingenuity that has been used to feed a growing world population will have to be matched quickly by an effort to keep the nitrogen cycle in reasonable balance.

27

THE NATURE OF OCEANIC LIFE

JOHN D. ISAACS

September 1969

*The conditions of the marine environment have given rise
to a food web in which the dominant primary production of
organic matter is carried out by microscopic plants*

I plan to take the reader on a brief tour of marine life from the surface layers of the open sea, down through the intermediate layers to the deep-sea floor, and from there to the living communities on continental shelves and coral reefs. Like Dante, I shall be able to record only a scattered sampling of the races and inhabitants of each region and to point out only the general dominant factors that typify each domain; in particular I shall review some of the conditions, principles and interactions that appear to have molded the forms of life in the sea and to have established their range and compass.

The organisms of the sea are born, live, breathe, feed, excrete, move, grow, mate, reproduce and die within a single interconnected medium. Thus interactions among the marine organisms and interactions of the organisms with the chemical and physical processes of the sea range across the entire spectrum from simple, adamant constraints to complex effects of many subtle interactions.

Far more, of course, is known about the life of the sea than I shall be able even to suggest, and there are yet to be achieved great steps in our knowledge of the living entities of the sea. I shall mention some of these possibilities in my concluding remarks.

A general discussion of a living system should consider the ways in which plants elaborate basic organic material from inorganic substances and the successive and often highly intricate steps by which organisms then return this material to the inorganic reservoir. The discussion should also show the forms of life by which such processes are conducted. I shall briefly trace these processes through the regions I have indicated, returning later to a more detailed discussion of the living forms and their constraints.

Some organic material is carried to the sea by rivers, and some is manufactured in shallow water by attached plants. More than 90 percent of the basic organic material that fuels and builds the life in the sea, however, is synthesized within the lighted surface layers of open water by the many varieties of phytoplankton. These sunny pastures of plant cells are grazed by the herbivorous zooplankton (small planktonic animals) and by some small fishes. These in turn are prey to various carnivorous creatures, large and small, who have their predators also.

The debris from the activities in the surface layers settles into the dimly lighted and unlighted midlayers of the sea, the twilight mesopelagic zone and the midnight bathypelagic zone, to serve as one source of food for their strange inhabitants. This process depletes the surface layers of some food and particularly of the vital plant nutrients, or fertilizers, that become trapped below the surface layers, where they are unavailable to the plants. Food and nutrients are also actively carried downward from the surface by vertically migrating animals.

The depleted remnants of this constant "rain" of detritus continue to the sea floor and support those animals that live just above the bottom (epibenthic animals), on the bottom (benthic animals) and burrowed into the bottom. Here filter-feeding and burrowing (deposit-feeding) animals and bacteria rework the remaining refractory particles. The more active animals also find repast in mid-water creatures and in the occasional falls of carcasses and other larger debris. Except in unusual small areas there is an abundance of oxygen in the deep water, and the solid bottom presents advantages that allow the support of a denser population of larger creatures than can exist in deep mid-water.

In shallower water such as banks, atolls, continental shelves and shallow seas conditions associated with a solid bottom and other regional modifications of the general regime enable rich populations to develop. Such areas constitute about 7 percent of the total area of the ocean. In some of these regions added food results from the growth of larger fixed plants and from land drainage.

With the above bare recitation for general orientation, I shall now discuss these matters in more detail.

The cycle of life in the sea, like that on land, is fueled by the sun's visible light acting on green plants. Of every million photons of sunlight reaching the earth's surface, some 90 enter into the net production of basic food. Perhaps 50 of the 90 contribute to the growth of land plants and about 40 to the growth of the single-celled green plants of the sea, the phytoplankton [*see illustration, page 242*]. It is this minute fraction of the sun's radiant energy that supplies the living organisms of this planet not only with their food but also with a breathable atmosphere.

The terrestrial and marine plants and animals arose from the same sources, through similar evolutionary sequences and by the action of the same natural laws. Yet these two living systems differ greatly at the stage in which we now view them. Were we to imagine a terrestrial food web that had developed in a form limited to that of the open sea, we would envision the land populated predominantly by short-lived simple plant cells grazed by small insects, worms and snails, which in turn would support a sparse predaceous population of larger insects, birds, frogs and lizards. The population of still larger carnivores would be a small fraction of the populations of

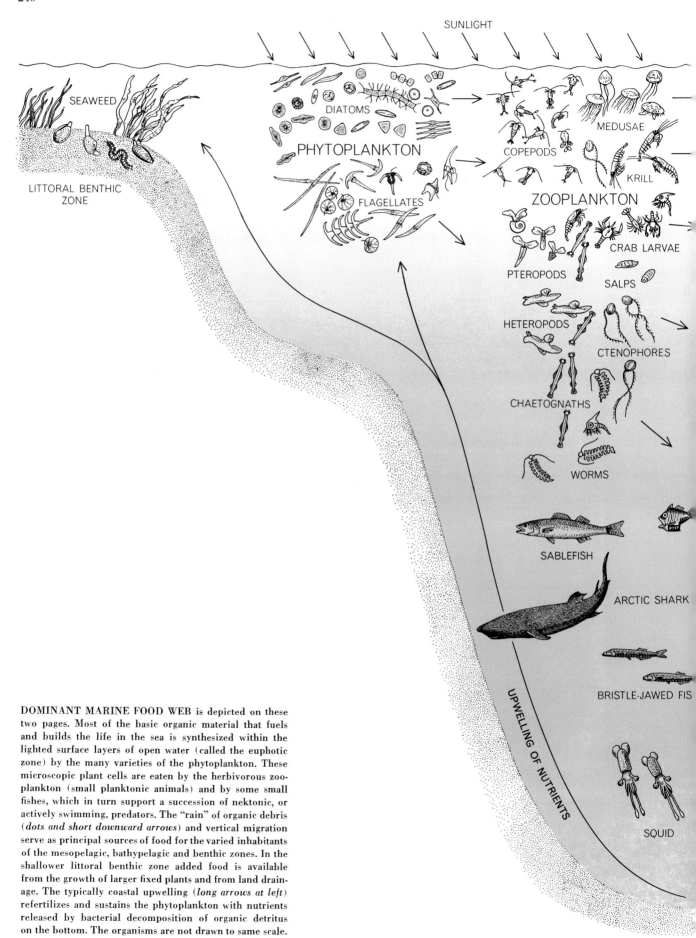

SUNLIGHT

SEAWEED

LITTORAL BENTHIC ZONE

PHYTOPLANKTON

DIATOMS

FLAGELLATES

MEDUSAE

COPEPODS

KRILL

ZOOPLANKTON

CRAB LARVAE

PTEROPODS

SALPS

HETEROPODS

CTENOPHORES

CHAETOGNATHS

WORMS

SABLEFISH

ARCTIC SHARK

BRISTLE-JAWED FIS

UPWELLING OF NUTRIENTS

SQUID

DOMINANT MARINE FOOD WEB is depicted on these two pages. Most of the basic organic material that fuels and builds the life in the sea is synthesized within the lighted surface layers of open water (called the euphotic zone) by the many varieties of the phytoplankton. These microscopic plant cells are eaten by the herbivorous zooplankton (small planktonic animals) and by some small fishes, which in turn support a succession of nektonic, or actively swimming, predators. The "rain" of organic debris (*dots and short downward arrows*) and vertical migration serve as principal sources of food for the varied inhabitants of the mesopelagic, bathypelagic and benthic zones. In the shallower littoral benthic zone added food is available from the growth of larger fixed plants and from land drainage. The typically coastal upwelling (*long arrows at left*) refertilizes and sustains the phytoplankton with nutrients released by bacterial decomposition of organic detritus on the bottom. The organisms are not drawn to same scale.

241

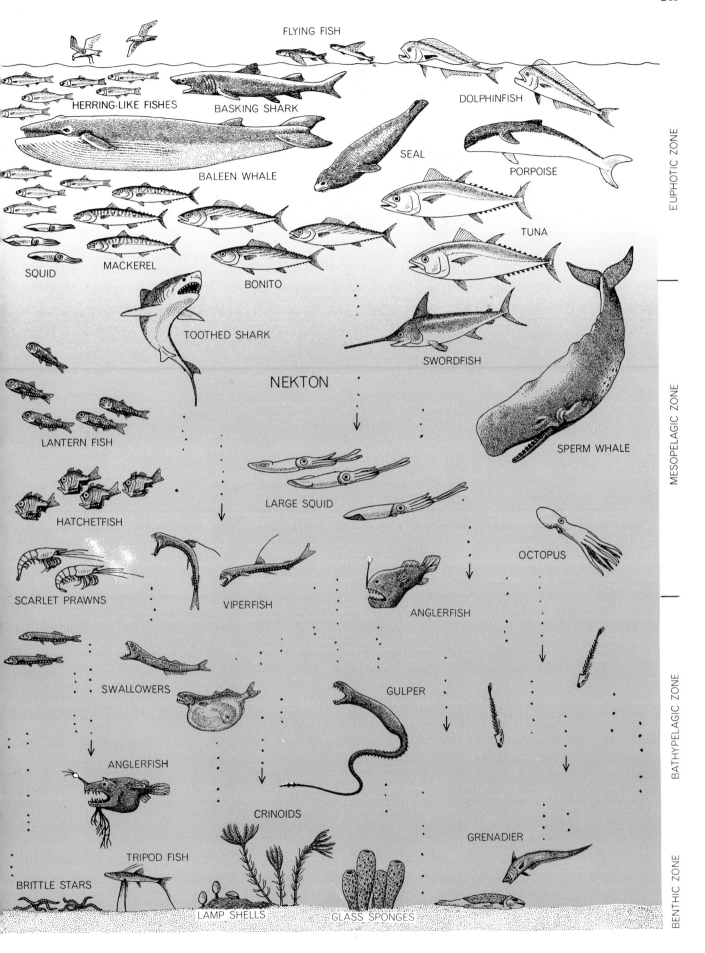

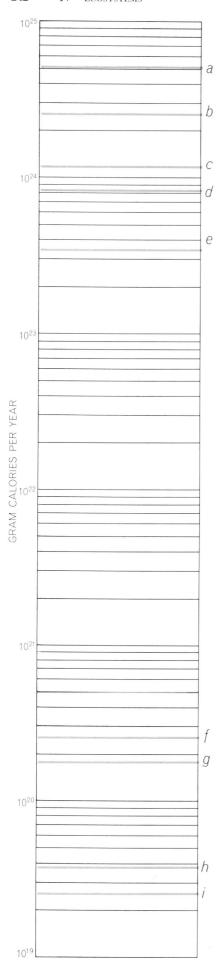

large creatures that the existing land food web can nurture, because organisms in each of these steps pass on not more than 15 percent of the organic substance.

In some important respects this imaginary condition is not unlike that of the dominant food web of the sea, where almost all marine life is sustained by microscopic plants and near-microscopic herbivores and carnivores, which pass on only a greatly diminished supply of food to sustain the larger, more active and more complex creatures. In other respects the analogy is substantially inaccurate, because the primary marine food production is carried out by cells dispersed widely in a dense fluid medium.

This fact of an initial dispersal imposes a set of profound general conditions on all forms of life in the sea. For comparison, the concentration of plant food in a moderately rich grassland is of the order of a thousandth of the volume of the gross space it occupies and of the order of half of the mass of the air in which it is immersed. In moderately rich areas of the sea, on the other hand, food is hundreds of times more dilute in volume and hundreds of thousands of times more dilute in relative mass. To crop this meager broth a blind herbivore or a simple pore in a filtering structure would need to process a weight of water hundreds of thousands of times the weight of the cell it eventually captures. In even the densest concentrations the factor exceeds several thousands, and with each further step in the food web dilution increases. Thus from the beginnings of the marine food web we see many adaptations accommodating to this dilution: eyes in microscopic herbivorous animals, filters of exquisite design, mechanisms and behavior for discovering local concentrations, complex search gear and, on the bottom, attachments to elicit the aid of moving water in carrying out the task of filtration. All these adaptations stem from the conditions that limit plant life in the open sea to microscopic dimensions.

It is in the sunlit near-surface of the open sea that the unique nature of the dominant system of marine life is irrevocably molded. The near-surface, or mixed, layer of the sea varies in thickness from tens of feet to hundreds depending on the nature of the general circulation, mixing by winds and heating [see "The Atmosphere and the Ocean," by R. W. Stewart; SCIENTIFIC AMERICAN Offprint 881]. Here the basic food production of the sea is accomplished by single-celled plants. One common group of small phytoplankton are the coccolithophores, with calcareous plates, a swimming ability and often an oil droplet for food storage and buoyancy. The larger microscopic phytoplankton are composed of many species belonging to several groups: naked algal cells, diatoms with complex shells of silica and actively swimming and rotating flagellates. Very small forms of many groups are also abundant and collectively are called nannoplankton.

The species composition of the phytoplankton is everywhere complex and varies from place to place, season to season and year to year. The various regions of the ocean are typified, however, by dominant major groups and particular species. Seasonal effects are often strong, with dense blooms of phytoplankton occurring when high levels of plant nutrients suddenly become usable or available, such as in high latitudes in spring or along coasts at the onset of upwelling. The concentration of phytoplankton varies on all dimensional scales, even down to small patches.

It is not immediately obvious why the dominant primary production of organic matter in the sea is carried out by microscopic single-celled plants instead of free-floating higher plants or other intermediate plant forms. The question arises: Why are there no pelagic "trees" in the ocean? One can easily compute the advantages such a tree would enjoy, with its canopy near the surface in the lighted levels and its trunk and roots extending down to the nutrient-rich waters under the mixed layer. The answer to this fundamental question probably has several parts. The evolution of plants in

PRODUCTIVITY of the land and the sea are compared in terms of the net amount of energy that is converted from sunlight to organic matter by the green cells of land and sea plants. Colored lines denote total energy reaching the earth's upper atmosphere (*a*), total energy reaching earth's surface (*b*), total energy usable for photosynthesis (*c*), total energy usable for photosynthesis at sea (*d*), total energy usable for photosynthesis on land (*e*), net energy used for photosynthesis on land (*f*), net energy used for photosynthesis at sea (*g*), net energy used by land herbivores (*h*) and net energy used by sea herbivores (*i*). Although more sunlight falls on the sea than on the land (by virtue of the sea's larger surface area), the total land area is estimated to outproduce the total sea area by 25 to 50 percent. This is primarily due to low nutrient concentrations in the euphotic zone and high metabolism in marine plants. The data are from Walter R. Schmitt of Scripps Institution of Oceanography.

the pelagic realm favored smallness rather than expansion because the mixed layer in which these plants live is quite homogeneous; hence small incremental extensions from a plant cell cannot aid it in bridging to richer sources in order to satisfy its several needs.

On land, light is immediately above the soil and nutrients are immediately below; thus any extension is of immediate benefit, and the development of single cells into higher erect plants is able to follow in a stepwise evolutionary sequence. At sea the same richer sources exist but are so far apart that only a very large ready-made plant could act as a bridge between them. Although such plants could develop in some other environment and then adapt to the pelagic conditions, this has not come about. It is difficult to see how such a plant would propagate anyway; certainly it could not propagate in the open sea, because the young plants there would be at a severe disadvantage. In the sea small-scale differential motions of water are rapidly damped out, and any free-floating plant must often depend on molecular diffusion in the water for the uptake of nutrients and excretion of wastes. Smallness and self-motion are then advantageous, and a gross structure of cells cannot exchange nutrients or wastes as well as the same cells can separately or in open aggregations.

In addition the large-scale circulation of the ocean continuously sweeps the pelagic plants out of the region to which they are best adapted. It is essential that some individuals be returned to renew the populations. More mechanisms for this essential return exist for single-celled plants than exist for large plants, or even for any conventional spores, seeds or juveniles. Any of these can be carried by oceanic gyres or diffused by large-scale motions of surface eddies and periodic counterflow, but single-celled plants can also ride submerged countercurrents while temporarily feeding on food particles or perhaps on dissolved organic material. Other mechanisms of distribution undoubtedly are also occasionally important. For example, living marine plant cells are carried by storm-borne spray, in bird feathers and by well-fed fish and birds in their undigested food.

No large plant has solved the many problems of development, dispersal and reproduction. There *are* no pelagic trees, and these several factors in concert therefore restrict the open sea in a profound way. They confine it to an initial food web composed of microscopic forms, whereas larger plants live at-

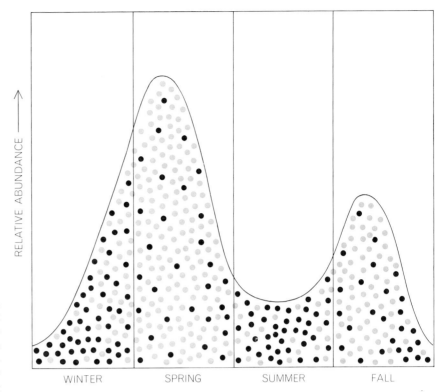

SPECIES COMPOSITION AND ABUNDANCE of the phytoplankton varies from season to season, particularly at high latitudes. During the winter the turbulence caused by storms replenishes the supply of nutrients in the surface layers. During this period flagellates (*black dots*) tend to dominate. In early spring the increase in the amount of sunlight reaching the surface stimulates plant growth, and diatoms (*colored dots*) are stimulated to grow. Later in spring grazing by zooplankton and a decrease in the supply of nutrients caused by calmer weather result in a general reduction in the phytoplankton population, which reaches a secondary minimum in midsummer, during which time flagellates again dominate. The increased mixing caused by early autumn storms causes a rise in the supply of nutrients and a corresponding minor surge in the population of diatoms. The decreasing sunlight of late fall and grazing by zooplankton again reduce the general level of the plant population.

tached only to shallow bottoms (which comprise some 2 percent of the ocean area). Attached plants, unlike free-floating plants, are not subject to the aforementioned limitations. For attached plants all degrees of water motion enhance the exchange of nutrients and wastes. Moreover, their normal population does not drift, much of their reproduction is by budding, and their spores are adapted for rapid development and settlement. Larger plants too are sometimes found in nonreproducing terminal accumulations of drifting shore plants in a few special convergent deep-sea areas such as the Sargasso Sea.

Although species of phytoplankton will populate only regions with conditions to which they are adapted, factors other than temperature, nutrients and light levels undoubtedly are important in determining the species composition of phytoplankton populations. Little is understood of the mechanisms that give rise to an abundance of particular species under certain conditions. Grazing

herbivores may consume only a part of the size range of cells, allowing certain sizes and types to dominate temporarily. Little is understood of the mechanisms that give rise to an abundance of particular species under certain conditions. Chemical by-products of certain species probably exclude certain other species. Often details of individual cell behavior are probably also important in the introduction and success of a species in a particular area. In some cases we can glimpse what these mechanisms are.

For example, both the larger diatoms and the larger flagellates can move at appreciable velocities through the water. The diatoms commonly sink downward, whereas the flagellates actively swim upward toward light. These are probably patterns of behavior primarily for increasing exchange, but the interaction of such unidirectional motions with random turbulence or systematic convective motion is not simple, as it is with an inactive particle. Rather, we would expect diatoms to be statistically abundant in upward-moving water and to sink out of the near-surface layers when turbulence or upward convection is low.

Conversely, flagellates should be statistically more abundant in downwelling water and should concentrate near the surface in low turbulence and slow downward water motions. These effects seem to exist. Off some continental coasts in summer flagellates may eventually collect in high concentrations. As they begin to shade one another from the light, each individual struggles closer to the lighted surface, producing such a high density that large areas of the water are turned red or brown by their pigments. The concentration of flagellates in these "red tides" sometimes becomes too great for their own survival. Several species of flagellates also become highly toxic as they grow older. Thus they sometimes both produce and participate in a mass death of fish and invertebrates that has been known to give rise to such a high yield of hydrogen sulfide as to blacken the white houses of coastal cities.

Large diatom cells, on the other hand, spend a disproportionately greater time in upward-moving regions of the water and an unlimited time in any region where the upward motion about equals their own downward motion. (The support of unidirectionally moving objects by contrary environmental motion is observed in other phenomena, such as the production of rain and hail.) Diatom cells are thus statistically abundant in upwelling water, and the distribution of diatoms probably is often a reflection of the turbulent-convective regime of the water. Sinking and the dependence of the larger diatoms on upward convection and turbulence for support aids them in reaching upwelling regions, where nutrients are high; it helps to explain their dominance in such regions and such other features of their distribution as their high proportion in rich ocean regions and their frequent inverse occurrence with flagellates. Differences in adaptations to the physical and chemical conditions, and the release of chemical products, probably reinforce such relations.

In some areas, such as parts of the equatorial current system and shallow seas, where lateral and vertical circulation is rapid, the species composition of phytoplankton is perhaps more simply a result of the inherent ability of the species to grow, survive and reproduce under the local conditions of temperature, light, nutrients, competitors and herbivores. Elsewhere second-order effects of the detailed cell behavior often dominate. Those details of behavior that give rise to concentrations on any dimensional scale are particularly important to all subsequent steps in the food chain.

All phytoplankton cells eventually settle from the surface layers. The depletion of nutrients and food from the surface layers takes place continuously through the loss of organic material, plant cells, molts, bodies of animals, fecal pellets and so forth, which release their content of chemical nutrients at various depths through the action of bacteria and other organisms. The periodic downward migration of zooplankton further contributes to this loss.

These nutrients are "trapped" below the level of light adequate to sustain photosynthesis, and therefore the water in which plants must grow generally contains very low concentrations of such vital substances. It is this condition that is principally responsible for the comparatively low total net productivity of the sea compared with that of the land. The regions where trapping is broken down or does not exist—where there is upwelling of nutrient-rich water along coasts, in parts of the equatorial regions, in the wakes of islands and banks and in high latitudes, and where there is rapid recirculation of nutrients over shallow shelves and seas—locally bear the sea's richest fund of life.

The initial factors discussed so far have placed an inescapable stamp on the form of all life in the open sea, as irrevocably no doubt as the properties and

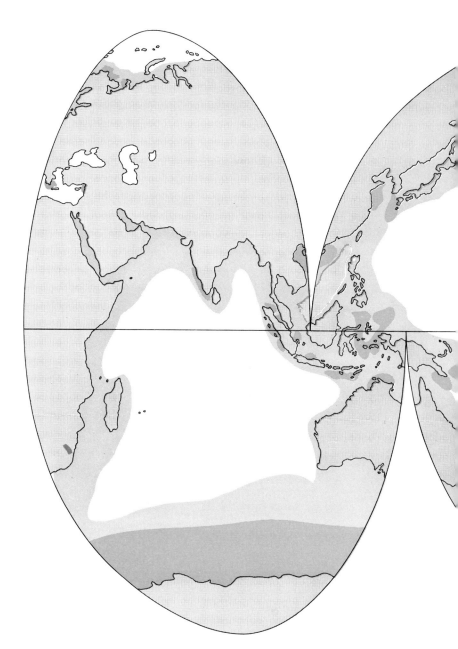

FAVORABLE CONDITIONS for the growth of phytoplankton occur wherever upwelling or mixing tends to bring subsurface nutrients up to the euphotic layer of the ocean. This map,

distribution of hydrogen have dictated the form of the universe. These factors have limited the dominant form of life in the sea to an initial microscopic sequence that is relatively unproductive, is stimulated by upwelling and mixing and is otherwise altered in species composition and distribution by physical, chemical and biological processes on all dimensional scales. The same factors also limit the populations of higher animals and have led to unexpectedly simple adaptations, such as the sinking of the larger diatoms as a tactic to solve the manifold problems of enhancing nutrient and waste exchange, finding nutrients, remaining in the surface waters and repopulating.

The grazing of the phytoplankton is principally conducted by the herbivorous members of the zooplankton, a heterogeneous group of small animals that carry out several steps in the food web as herbivores, carnivores and detrital (debris-eating) feeders. Among the important members of the zooplankton are the arthropods, animals with external skeletons that belong to the same broad group as insects, crabs and shrimps. The planktonic arthropods include the abundant copepods, which are in a sense the marine equivalent of insects. Copepods are represented in the sea by some 10,000 or more species that act not only as herbivores, carnivores or detrital feeders but also as external or even internal

parasites! Two or three thousand of these species live in the open sea. Other important arthropods are the shrimplike euphausiids, the strongest vertical migrators of the zooplankton. They compose the vast shoals of krill that occur in high latitudes and that constitute one of the principal foods of the baleen whales. The zooplankton also include the strange bristle-jawed chaetognaths, or arrowworms, carnivores of mysterious origin and affinities known only in the marine environment. Widely distributed and abundant, the chaetognaths are represented by a surprisingly small number of species, perhaps fewer than 50. Larvae of many types, worms, medusae (jellyfish), ctenophores (comb jellies), gastro-

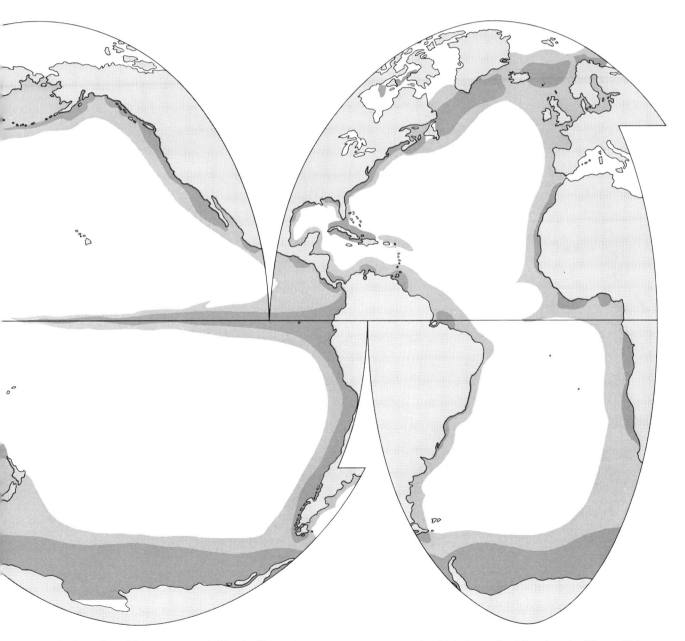

which is adapted from one compiled by the Norwegian oceanographer Harald U. Sverdrup, shows the global distribution of such waters, in which the productivity of marine life would be expected to be very high (*dark color*) and moderately high (*light color*).

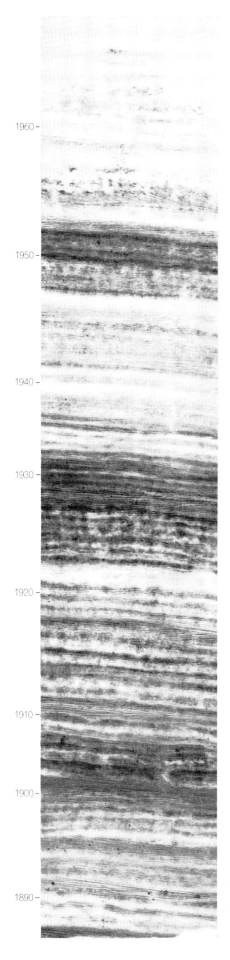

1960 —

1950 —

1940 —

1930 —

1920 —

1910 —

1900 —

1890 —

pods (snails), pteropods and heteropods (other pelagic mollusks), salps, unpigmented flagellates and many others are also important components of this milieu, each with its own remarkably complex and often bizarre life history, behavior and form.

The larger zooplankton are mainly carnivores, and those of herbivorous habit are restricted to feeding on the larger plant cells. Much of the food supply, however, exists in the form of very small particles such as the nannoplankton, and these appear to be available almost solely to microscopic creatures. The immense distances between plant cells, many thousands of times their diameter, place a great premium on the development of feeding mechanisms that avoid the simple filtering of water through fine pores. The power necessary to maintain a certain rate of flow through pores or nets increases inversely at an exponential rate with respect to the pore or mesh diameter, and the small planktonic herbivores, detrital feeders and carnivores show many adaptations to avoid this energy loss. Eyesight has developed in many minute animals to make possible selective capture. A variety of webs, bristles, rakes, combs, cilia and other structures are found, and they are often sticky. Stickiness allows the capture of food that is finer than the interspaces in the filtering structures, and it greatly reduces the expenditure of energy.

A few groups have developed extremely fine and apparently quite effective nets. One group that has accomplished this is the Larvacea. A larvacian produces and inhabits a complex external "house," much larger than its owner, that contains a system of very finely constructed nets through which the creature maintains a gentle flow [*see illustration on page 248*]. The Larvacea have appar-

RARE SEDIMENTARY RECORD of the recent annual oceanographic, meteorological and biological history of part of a major oceanic system is revealed in this radiograph of a section of an ocean-bottom core obtained by Andrew Soutar of the Scripps Institution of Oceanography in the Santa Barbara Basin off the California coast. In some near-shore basins such as this one the absence of oxygen causes refractory parts of the organic debris to be left undecomposed and the sediment to remain undisturbed in the annual layers called varves. The dark layers are the densest and represent winter sedimentation. The lighter and less dense layers are composed mostly of diatoms and represent spring and summer sedimentation.

ently solved the problem of energy loss in filtering by having proportionately large nets, fine strong threads and a low rate of flow.

The composition of the zooplankton differs from place to place, day to night, season to season and year to year, yet most species are limited in distribution, and the members of the planktonic communities commonly show a rather stable representation of the modes of life.

The zooplankton are, of course, faced with the necessity of maintaining breeding assemblages and, like the phytoplankton, with the necessity of establishing a reinoculation of parent waters. In addition, their behavior must lead to a correspondence with their food and to the pattern of large-scale and small-scale spottiness already imposed on the marine realm by the phytoplankton. The swimming powers of the larger zooplankton are quite adequate for finding local small-scale patches of food. That this task is accomplished on a large scale is indirectly demonstrated by the observed correspondence between the quantities of zooplankton and the plant nutrients in the surface waters. How this large-scale task is accomplished is understood for some groups. For example, some zooplankton species have been shown to descend near the end of suitable conditions at the surface and to take temporary residence in a submerged countercurrent that returns them upstream.

There are many large and small puzzles in the distribution of zooplankton. As an example, dense concentrations of phytoplankton are often associated with low populations of zooplankton. These are probably rapidly growing blooms that zooplankton have not yet invaded and grazed on, but it is not completely clear that this is so. Chemical repulsion may be involved.

The concentration of larger zooplankton and small fish in the surface layers is much greater at night than during the day, because of a group of strongly swimming members that share their time between the surface and the mesopelagic region. This behavior is probably primarily a tactic to enjoy the best of two worlds: to crop the richer food developing in the surface layers and to minimize mortality from predation by remaining always in the dark, like timid rabbits emerging from the thicket to graze the nighttime fields, although still in the presence of foxes and ferrets. Many small zooplankton organisms also make a daily migration of some vertical extent.

In addition to its primary purpose

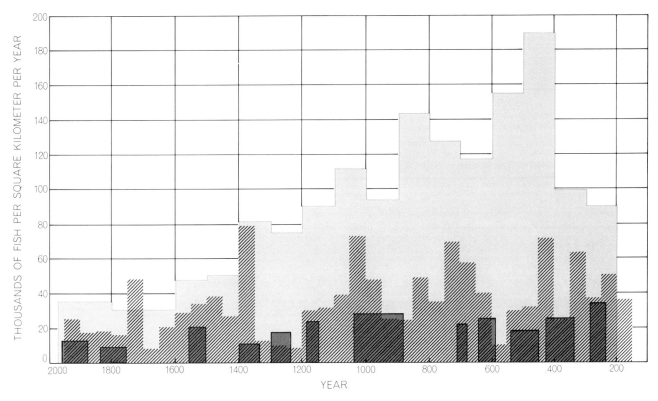

ESTIMATED FISH POPULATIONS in the Santa Barbara Basin over the past 1,800 years were obtained for three species by counting the average number of scales of each species in the varves of the core shown on the opposite page. Minimum population estimates for fish one year old and older are given for Pacific sardines (gray), northern sardines (colored areas) and Pacific hake (hatched).

daily vertical migration undoubtedly serves the migrating organisms in a number of other ways. It enables the creatures to adjust their mean temperature, so that by spending the days in cooler water the amount of food used during rest is reduced. Perhaps such processes as the rate of egg development are also controlled by these tactics. Many land animals employ hiding behavior for similar kinds of adjustment. Convincing arguments have also been presented to show that vertical migration serves to maintain a wide range of tolerance in the migrating species, so that they will be more successful under many more conditions than if they lived solely in the surface layers. This migration must also play an important part in the distribution of many species. Interaction of the daily migrants with the water motion produced by daily land-sea breeze alternation can hold the migrants offshore by a kind of "rectification" of the oscillating water motion. More generally, descent into the lower layers increases the influence of submerged countercurrents, thereby enhancing the opportunity to return upstream, to enter upwelling regions and hence to find high nutrient levels and associated high phytoplankton productivity.

Even minor details of behavior may strongly contribute to success. Migrants spend the day at a depth corresponding to relatively constant low light levels, where the movement of the water commonly is different from that at the surface. Most of the members rise somewhat even at the passage of a cloud shadow. Should they be carried under the shadow of an area rich in phytoplankton, they migrate to shallower depths, thereby often decreasing or even halting their drift with respect to this rich region to which they will ascend at night. Conversely, when the surface waters are clear and lean, they will migrate deeper and most often drift relatively faster.

We might simplistically view the distribution of zooplankton, and phytoplankton for that matter, as the consequence of a broad inoculation of the oceans with a spectrum of species, each with a certain adaptive range of tolerances and a certain variable range of feeding, reproducing and migrating behavior. At some places and at some times the behavior of a species, interacting even in detailed secondary ways with the variable conditions of the ocean and its other inhabitants, results in temporary, seasonal or persistent success.

There are a few exceptions to the microscopic dimensions of the herbivores in the pelagic food web. Among these the herrings and herring-like fishes are able to consume phytoplankton as a substantial component of their diet. Such an adaptation gives these fishes access to many times the food supply of the more carnivorous groups. It is therefore no surprise that the partly herbivorous fishes comprise the bulk of the world's fisheries [see "The Food Resources of the Ocean," by S. J. Holt; SCIENTIFIC AMERICAN Offprint 886].

The principal food supplies of the pelagic populations are passed on in incremental steps and rapidly depleted quantity to the larger carnivorous zooplankton, then to small fishes and squids, and ultimately to the wide range of larger carnivores of the pelagic realm. In this region without refuge, either powerful static defenses, such as the stinging cells of the medusae and men-o'-war, or increasing size, acuity, alertness, speed and strength are the requirements for survival at each step. Streamlining of form here reaches a high point of development, and in tropical waters it is conspicuous even in small fishes, since the lower viscosity of the warmer waters will enable a highly streamlined small prey to escape a poorly streamlined predator, an effect that exists only for fishes of twice the length in cold, viscous, arctic or deep waters.

The pelagic region contains some of the largest and most superbly designed creatures ever to inhabit this earth: the exquisitely constructed pelagic tunas; the multicolored dolphinfishes, capturers of flying fishes; the conversational porpoises; the shallow- and deep-feeding swordfishes and toothed whales, and the greatest carnivores of all, the baleen whales and some plankton-eating sharks, whose prey are entire schools of krill or small fishes. Seals and sea lions feed far into the pelagic realm. In concert with these great predators, large carnivorous sharks await injured prey. Marine birds, some adapted to almost continuous pelagic life, consume surprising quantities of ocean food, diving, plunging, skimming and gulping in pursuit. Creatures of this region have developed such faculties as advanced sonar, unexplained senses of orientation and homing, and extreme olfactory sensitivity.

These larger creatures of the sea commonly move in schools, shoals and herds. In addition to meeting the needs of mating such grouping is advantageous in both defensive and predatory strategy, much like the cargo-ship convoy and submarine "wolf pack" of World War II. Both defensive and predatory assemblages are often complex. Small fishes of several species commonly school together. Diverse predators also form loosely cooperative groups, and many species of marine birds depend almost wholly on prey driven to the surface by submerged predators.

At night, schools of prey and predators are almost always spectacularly illuminated by bioluminescence produced by the microscopic and larger plankton. The reason for the ubiquitous production of light by the microorganisms of the sea remains obscure, and suggested explanations are controversial. It has been suggested that light is a kind of inadvertent by-product of life in transparent organisms. It has also been hypothesized that the emission of light on disturbance is advantageous to the plankton in making the predators of the plankton conspicuous to *their* predators! Unquestionably it does act this way. Indeed, some fisheries base the detection of their prey on the bioluminescence that the fish excite. It is difficult, however, to defend the thesis that this effect was the direct factor in the original development of bioluminescence, since the effect was of no advantage to the individual microorganism that first developed it. Perhaps the luminescence of a microorganism also discourages attack by the light-avoiding zooplankton and is of initial survival benefit to the individual. As it then became general in the population, the effect of revealing plankton predators to their predators would also become important.

The fallout of organic material into the deep, dimly lighted mid-water supports a sparse population of fishes and invertebrates. Within the mesopelagic and bathypelagic zones are found some of the most curious and bizarre creatures of this earth. These range from the highly developed and powerfully predaceous intruders, toothed whales and swordfishes, at the climax of the food chain, to the remarkable squids, octopuses, eu-phausiids, lantern fishes, gulpers and anglerfishes that inhabit the bathypelagic region.

In the mesopelagic region, where some sunlight penetrates, fishes are often countershaded, that is, they are darker above and lighter below, as are surface fishes. Many of the creatures of this dimly lighted region participate in the daily migration, swimming to the upper layers at evening like bats emerging from their caves. At greater depths, over a half-mile or so, the common inhabitants are often darkly pigmented, weak-bodied and frequently adapted to unusual feeding techniques. Attraction of prey by luminescent lures or by mimicry of small prey, greatly extensible jaws and expansible abdomens are common. It is, however, a region of Lilliputian monsters, usually not more than six inches in length, with most larger fishes greatly reduced in musculature and weakly constructed.

There are some much larger, stronger and more active fishes and squids in this region, although they are not taken in trawls or seen from submersibles. Knowledge of their existence comes mainly from specimens found in the stomach of sperm whales and swordfish. They must be rare, however, since the slow, conservative creatures that are taken in trawls could hardly coexist with large numbers of active predators. Nevertheless, populations must be sufficiently large to attract the sperm whales and swordfish. There is evidence that the sperm whales possess highly developed long-range hunting sonar. They may locate their prey over relatively great distances, perhaps miles, from just such an extremely sparse population of active bathypelagic animals.

Although many near-surface organisms are luminescent, it is in the bathypelagic region that bioluminescence has reached a surprising level of development, with at least two-thirds of the species producing light. Were we truly marine-oriented, we would perhaps be more surprised by the almost complete absence of biological light in the land environment, with its few rare cases of fireflies, glowworms and luminous bacteria. Clearly bioluminescence can be valuable to higher organisms, and the creatures of the bathypelagic realm have developed light-producing organs and structures to a high degree. In many cases the organs have obvious functions. Some fishes, squids and euphausiids possess searchlights with reflector, lens and iris almost as complex as the eye. Others have complex patterns of small lights that may serve the functions of recogni-

FOOD NET · MOUTH · STOMACH · INTAKE FILTER · WATER OUTLET · TAIL · ANUS · GILL SLIT · NERVOUS SYSTEM · EMERGENCY EXIT

LARVACIAN is representative of a group of small planktonic herbivores that has solved the problem of energy loss in filtering, apparently without utilizing "stickiness," by having proportionately large nets, strong fine threads and a low rate of water flow. The larvacian (black) produces and inhabits a complex external "house" (color), much larger than its owner, which contains a system of nets through which the organism maintains a gentle flow. In almost all other groups simple filters are employed only to exclude large particles.

tion, schooling control and even mimicry of a small group of luminous plankton. Strong flashes may confuse predators by "target alteration" effects, or by producing residual images in the predators' vision. Some squids and shrimps are more direct and discharge luminous clouds to cover their escape. The luminous organs are arranged on some fishes so that they can be used to countershade their silhouettes against faint light coming from the surface. Luminous baits are well developed. Lights may also be used for locating a mate, a problem of this vast, sparsely populated domain that has been solved by some anglerfishes by the development of tiny males that live parasitically attached to their relatively huge mates.

It has been shown that the vertebrate eye has been adapted to detect objects in the lowest light level on the earth's surface—a moonless, overcast night under a dense forest canopy—but not lower. Light levels in the bathypelagic region can be much lower. This is most probably the primary difference that accounts for the absence of bioluminescence in

higher land animals and the richness of its development in the ocean forms.

The densest populations of bathypelagic creatures lie below the most productive surface regions, except at high latitudes, where the dearth of winter food probably would exhaust the meager reserves of these creatures. All the bathypelagic populations are sparse, and in this region living creatures are less than one hundred-millionth of the water volume. Nevertheless, the zone is of immense dimensions and the total populations may be large. Some genera, such as the feeble, tiny bristle-jawed fishes, are probably the most numerous fishes in the world and constitute a gigantic total biomass. There are some 2,000 species of fishes and as many species of the larger invertebrates known to inhabit the bathypelagic zone, but only a few of these species appear to be widespread. The barriers to distribution in this widely interconnected mid-water region are not obvious.

The floor of the deep sea constitutes an environment quite unlike the mid-

water and surface environments. Here are sites for the attachment of the larger invertebrates that filter detritus from the water. Among these animals are representatives of some of the earliest multicelled creatures to exist on the earth, glass sponges, sea lilies (crinoids)—once thought to have been long extinct—and lamp shells (brachiopods).

At one time it was also thought that the abyssal floor was sparsely inhabited and that the populations of the deep-ocean floor were supplied with food only by the slow, meager rain of terminal detrital food material that has passed through the surface and bathypelagic populations. Such refractory material requires further passage into filter feeders or through slow bacterial action in the sediment, followed by consumption by larger burrowing organisms, before it becomes available to active free-living animals. This remnant portion of the food web could support only a very small active population.

Recent exploration of the abyssal realm with a baited camera throws doubt on the view that this is the exclusive

CHAMPION FILTER FEEDER of the world ocean in terms of volume is the blue whale, a mature specimen of which lies freshly butchered on the deck of a whaling vessel in this photograph. The whale's stomach has been cut open with a flensing knife to reveal its last meal: an immense quantity of euphausiids, or krill, each measuring about three inches in length. The baleen whales are not plankton-filterers in the ordinary sense but rather are great carnivores that seek out and engulf entire schools of small fish or invertebrates. The photograph was made by Robert Clarke of the National Institute of Oceanography in Wormley, England.

mechanism of food transfer to the deep bottom. Large numbers of active fishes and other creatures are attracted to the bait almost immediately [see illustration on page 251]. It is probably true that several rather independent branches of the food web coexist in support of the deep-bottom creatures: one the familiar rain of fine detritus, and the other the rare, widely separated falls of large food particles that are in excess of the local feeding capacity of the broadly diffuse bathypelagic population. Such falls would include dead whales, large sharks or other large fishes and fragments of these, the multitude of remnants that are left when predators attack a school of surface fish and now, undoubtedly, garbage from ships and kills from underwater explosions. These sources result in an influx of high-grade food to the sea floor, and we would expect to find a population of active creatures adapted to its prompt discovery and utilization. The baited cameras have demonstrated that this is so.

Other sources of food materials are braided into these two extremes of the abyssal food web. There is the rather subtle downward diffusion of living and dead food that results initially from the daily vertical migration of small fish and zooplankton near the surface. This migration appears to impress a sympathetic daily migration on the mid-water populations down to great depths, far below the levels that light penetrates. Not only may such vertical migration bring feeble bathypelagic creatures near the bottom but also it accelerates in itself the flux of dead food material to the bottom of the deep sea.

There must also be some unassignable flux of food to the abyssal population resulting from the return of juveniles to their habitat. The larvae and young of many abyssal creatures develop at much shallower levels. To the extent that the biomass of juveniles returning to the deep regions exceeds the biomass of spawn released from it, this process, which might be called "Faginism," constitutes an input of food.

Benthic animals are much more abundant in the shallower waters off continents, particularly offshore from large rivers. Here there is often not only a richer near-surface production and a less hazardous journey of food to the sea floor but also a considerable input of food conveyed by rivers to the bottom. The deep slopes of river sediment wedges are typified by a comparatively rich population of burrowing and filtering animals that utilize this fine organic material. All the great rivers of the world save one, the Congo, have built sedimentary wedges along broad reaches of their coast, and in many instances these wedges extend into deep water. The shallow regions of such wedges are highly productive of active and often valuable marine organisms. At all depths the wedges bear larger populations than are common at similar depths elsewhere. Thus one wonders what inhabits the fan of the Congo. That great river, because of a strange invasion of a submarine canyon into its mouth, has built no wedge but rather is depositing a vast alluvial fan in the two-mile depths of the Angola Basin. This great deep region of the sea floor may harbor an unexplored population that is wholly unique.

In itself the pressure of the water at great depths appears to constitute no insurmountable barrier to water-breathing animal life. The depth limitations of many creatures are the associated conditions of low temperature, darkness, sparse food and so on. It should perhaps come as no surprise, therefore, that some of the fishes of high latitudes, which are of course adapted to cold dark waters, extend far into the deep cold waters in much more southern latitudes. Off the coast of Lower California, in water 1,200 to 6,000 feet deep, baited cameras have found an abundance of several species of fishes that are known at the near surface only far to the north. These include giant arctic sharks, sablefish and others. It appears that some of the fishes that have been called arctic species are actually fishes of the dark cold waters of the seas, which only "outcrop" in the Arctic, where cold water is at the surface.

I have discussed several of the benthic and epibenthic environments without pointing out some of the unique features the presence of a solid interface entails. The bottom is much more variable than the mid-water zone is. There are as a result more environmental niches for an organism to occupy, and hence we see organisms that are of a wider range of form and habit. Adaptations develop for hiding and ambuscade, for mimicry and controlled patterns. Nests and burrows can be built, lairs occupied and defended and booby traps set.

Aside from the wide range of form and function the benthic environment elicits from its inhabitants, there are more fundamental conditions that influence the nature and form of life there. For example, the dispersed food material settling from the upper layers becomes much concentrated against the sea floor. Indeed, it may become further concentrated by lateral currents moving it into depressions or the troughs of ripples.

In the mid-water environment most creatures must move by their own energies to seek food, using their own food stores for this motion. On the bottom, however, substantial water currents are present at all depths, and creatures can await the passage of their food. Although this saving only amounts to an added effectiveness for predators, it is of critical importance to those organisms that filter water for the fine food material it contains, and it is against the bottom interface that a major bypass to the microscopic steps of the dominant food web is achieved. Here large organisms can grow by consuming microscopic or even submicroscopic food particles. Clams, scallops, mussels, tube worms, barnacles and a host of other creatures that inhabit this zone have developed a wide range of extremely effective filtering mechanisms. In one step, aided by their attachment, the constant currents and the concentration of detritus against the interface, they perform the feat, most unusual in the sea, of growing large organisms directly from microscopic food.

Although the benthic environment enables the creatures of the sea to develop a major branch of the food web that is emancipated from successive microscopic steps, this makes little difference to the food economy of the sea. The sea is quite content with a large population of tiny organisms. From man's standpoint, however, the shallow benthic environment is an unusually effective producer of larger creatures for his

NEW EVIDENCE that an abundance of large active fishes inhabit the deep-sea floor was obtained recently by the author and his colleagues in the form of photographs such as the one on the opposite page. The photograph was made by a camera hovering over a five-gallon bait can at a depth of 1,400 meters off Lower California. The diagonal of the bait can measures a foot. The larger fish are mostly rat-tailed grenadiers and sablefish. The fact that large numbers of such fish are attracted almost immediately to the bait suggests that two rather independent branches of the marine food web coexist in support of the deep-bottom creatures by dead material: the rain of fine detritus, which supports a variety of attached filter-feeding and burrowing organisms, and rare, widely separated falls of large food fragments, which support active creatures adapted to the discovery and utilization of such food.

food, and he widely utilizes these resources.

Man may not have created an ideal environment for himself, but of all the environments of the sea it is difficult to conceive of one better for its inhabitants than the one marine creatures have created almost exclusively for themselves: the coral islands and coral reefs. In these exquisite, immense and well-nigh unbelievable structures form and adaptation reach a zenith.

An adequate description of the coral reef and coral atoll structure, environments and living communities is beyond the scope of this article. The general history and structure of atolls is well known, not only because of an inherent fascination with the magic and beauty of coral islands but also because of the wide admiration and publicity given to the prescient deductions on the origin of atolls by Charles Darwin, who foresaw much of what modern exploration has affirmed.

From their slowly sinking foundations of ancient volcanic mountains, the creatures of the coral shoals have erected the greatest organic structures that exist. Even the smallest atoll far surpasses any of man's greatest building feats, and a large atoll structure in actual mass approaches the total of all man's building that now exists.

These are living monuments to the success of an extremely intricate but balanced society of fish, invertebrates and plants, capitalizing on the basic advantages of benthic populations already discussed. Here, however, each of the reef structures acts almost like a single great isolated and complex benthic organism that has extended itself from the deep poor waters to the sunlit richer surface. The trapping of the advected food from the surface currents enriches the entire community. Attached plants further add to the economy, and there is considerable direct consumption of plant life by large invertebrates and fish. Some of the creatures and relationships that have developed in this environment are among the most highly adapted found on the earth. For example, a number of the important reef-building animals, the corals, the great tridacna clams and others not only feed but also harbor within their tissues dense populations of single-celled green plants. These plants photosynthesize food that is then directly available within the bodies of the animals; the plants in turn depend on the animal waste products within the body fluids, with which they are bathed, to derive their basic nutrients. Thus within the small environment of these plant-animal composites both the entire laborious nutrient cycle and the microscopic food web of the sea appear to be substantially bypassed.

There is much unknown and much to be discovered in the structure and ecology of coral atolls. Besides the task of unraveling the complex relationships of its inhabitants there are many questions such as: Why have many potential atolls never initiated effective growth and remained submerged almost a mile below the surface? Why have others lost the race with submergence in recent times and now become shallowly submerged, dying banks? Can the nature of the circulation of the ancient ocean be deduced from the distribution of successful and unsuccessful atolls? Is there circulation within the coral limestone structure that adds to the nutrient supply, and is this related to the curious development of coral knolls, or coral heads, within the lagoons? Finally, what is the potential of cultivation within these vast, shallow-water bodies of the deep open sea?

There is, of course, much to learn about all marine life: the basic processes of the food web, productivity, populations, distributions and the mechanisms of reinoculation, and the effects of intervention into these processes, such as pollution, artificial upwelling, transplantation, cultivation and fisheries. To learn of these processes and effects we must understand the nature not only of strong simple actions but also of weak complex interactions, since the forms of life or the success of a species may be determined by extremely small second- and third-order effects. In natural affairs, unlike human codes, *de minimis curat lex*— the law *is* concerned with trivia!

Little is understood of the manner in which speciation (that is, the evolution of new species) occurs in the broadly intercommunicating pelagic environment with so few obvious barriers. Important yet unexpected environmental niches may exist in which temporary isolation may enable a new pelagic species to evolve. For example, the top few millimeters of the open sea have recently been shown to constitute a demanding environment with unique inhabitants. Further knowledge of such microcosms may well yield insight into speciation.

As it has in the past, further exploration of the abyssal realm will undoubtedly reveal undescribed creatures including members of groups thought long extinct, as well as commercially valuable populations. As we learn more of the conditions that control the distribution of species of pelagic organisms, we shall become increasingly competent to read the pages of the earth's marine-biological, oceanographic and meteorological history that are recorded in the sediments by organic remains. We shall know more of primordial history, the early production of a breathable atmosphere and petroleum production. Some of these deposits of sediment cover even the period of man's recorded history with a fine time resolution. From such great records we should eventually be able to increase greatly our understanding of the range and interrelations of weather, ocean conditions and biology for sophisticated and enlightened guidance of a broad spectrum of man's activities extending from meteorology and hydrology to oceanography and fisheries.

Learning and guidance of a more specific nature can also be of great practical importance. The diving physiology of marine mammals throws much light on the same physiological processes in land animals in oxygen stress (during birth, for example). The higher flowering plants that inhabit the marine salt marshes are able to tolerate salt at high concentration, desalinating seawater with the sun's energy. Perhaps the tiny molecule of DNA that commands this process is the most precious of marine-life resources for man's uses. Bred into existing crop plants, it may bring salt-water agriculture to reality and nullify the creeping scourge of salinization of agricultural soils.

Routine upstream reinoculation of preferred species of phytoplankton and zooplankton might stabilize some pelagic marine populations at high effectiveness. Transplanted marine plants and animals may also animate the dead saline lakes of continental interiors, as they have the Salton Sea of California.

The possible benefits of broad marine-biological understanding are endless. Man's aesthetic, adventurous, recreational and practical proclivities can be richly served. Most important, undoubtedly, is the intellectual promise: to learn how to approach and understand a complex system of strongly interacting biological, physical and chemical entities that is vastly more than the sum of its parts, and thus how better to understand complex man and his interactions with his complex planet, and to explore with intelligence and open eyes a huge portion of this earth, which continuously teaches that when understanding and insight are sought for their own sake, the rewards are more substantial and enduring than when they are sought for more limited goals.

28

TRACE-ELEMENT DESERTS

A. J. ANDERSON AND E. J. UNDERWOOD

January 1959

Throughout the world potential farmland goes to waste for the lack of elements required in traces by plants and animals. By rectifying such deficiencies, Australia hopes to reclaim some 300 million acres

Until recently South Australia's Ninety Mile Desert was a scrubby wasteland of heath and eucalyptus thickets. Today its six million once worthless acres are being swiftly transformed into bounteous pastureland. The "Desert," which formerly supported one sheep per 20 acres, can now sustain 40 times that number. Indeed, the Desert—in name, at any rate—is no more: its prosperous new residents have rechristened it Coonalpyn Downs.

The new fertility of Coonalpyn Downs was not obtained by expensive irrigation or clearance projects. Like much of the world's unproductive land, it suffered from an ailment subtler than lack of water. Recent investigations have made it possible to diagnose a large group of deficiencies of soil, plants and animals. The infertility of the soil at Coonalpyn Downs was found to arise from the absence of an almost infinitesimal sprinkling of zinc and copper.

In the context of biology, zinc and copper are numbered among the "trace elements," that is, elements that com-

RECLAIMED DESERT in eastern Australia was once infertile from lack of molybdenum, which plants require in order to fix nitrogen from the air. Shown here are sheep being mustered for shearing on the reclaimed Southern Tablelands near Canberra.

RECLAMATION of Australia's Southern Tablelands is illustrated in this series of photographs. At left is shown a still-infertile portion of the Tablelands, which the reader may compare to the reclaimed area illustrated on the preceding page. The middle photograph shows

prise so small a part of the substance of an animal or plant that chemists of an earlier time, unable to measure them exactly, could state only that they had found a trace of them. Trace amounts of 20 to 30 elements occur in living matter. Some of the elements may be present by accident. Others—we cannot yet be sure how many—are indispensable to higher organisms. Most of them apparently contribute to the catalytic activity of particular enzymes in the chains of molecular events that constitute the processes of life. The trace elements, along with the vitamins, are often called "micronutrients."

The study of trace elements promises rich rewards for the agriculture of the future. The world's food-producing capacity is already sorely taxed by the explosive multiplication of the human species. Yet it seems likely that hundreds of millions of acres are now kept from productivity by nothing more than the easily remedied lack of trace elements. The reclamation of Coonalpyn Downs is today being repeated in many parts of Australia; tomorrow the same methods may be ameliorating trace-element deficiencies in other underdeveloped regions of our planet.

The trace elements now recognized as essential to plant life are seven in number: iron, manganese, copper, zinc, molybdenum, boron and chlorine. High-

er forms of animal life also need seven: the first five listed above plus cobalt and iodine. As research proceeds, these lists will doubtless grow. There is already suggestive, if not conclusive, evidence that plants need cobalt, sodium and vanadium, and that animals require selenium, bromine, barium and strontium.

The need of the human body for certain trace elements has been known for some 100 years. Nineteenth-century French physicians found that iron therapy remedied the "green sickness" (anemia) of adolescent girls; the French investigator Eusebe Gris ascertained that plants grown in a medium free of iron were yellow and stunted. The careful observations of A. Chatin, another French worker, disclosed the connection between goiter and lack of environmental iodine. Thus iron and iodine were the first trace elements to be identified. Many years passed, however, before investigators traced these elements to the metabolic system: oxidative enzymes in the case of iron, and the thyroid hormone thyroxine in the case of iodine.

Not until this century was it known that organisms require trace elements other than iron and iodine. As early as 1860 the German workers W. Knop and J. von Sachs were able to raise green plants in artificial media without soil or organic matter of any kind. By supply-

ing measured amounts of apparently pure mineral salts and water, they and their successors sought to determine the exact chemical requirements of plant life. The need for trace elements went unnoticed, because they were unwittingly supplied in the form of unobserved contaminants of the salts.

Experiments of this kind were conducted for more than half a century before the "pure" mineral salts were observed to contain trace elements. Without these hidden elements the plants could not have lived. While the trace elements had escaped detection by chemists, they were easily found and utilized by the plants growing in culture solution.

Animal experiments similarly overlooked the trace elements, which contaminated not only the mineral content of "pure" diets, but were also present in the crude vitamin supplements which the animals needed for growth. After it was recognized that trace elements might be essential to life, new techniques were developed which made it possible to control their content in both plant and animal nutrients. The present list of vital elements is the work of the past 35 years. New methods of purifying the diet of experimental animals, developed particularly at the University of Wisconsin, showed that mammals require copper, manganese and zinc. The

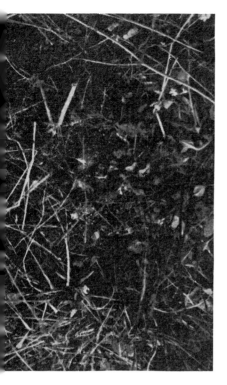

the continuing infertility of this land when sown to clover and treated with fertilizers (but no trace elements). At right the same land has received molybdenum as well as fertilizers. An ounce of molybdenum per acre amply insures the clover's health and nitrogen-fixing ability.

latest addition to the list of elements needed by plants is chlorine, which is acquired largely from the air—a discovery made possible by a new technique, developed at the University of California, for eliminating trace elements from experimental atmospheres.

In our country—Australia—more than 400 million acres of adequately watered land lie undeveloped, much of it for lack of the trace elements required by farm crops and animals. To appreciate the significance of this fact for Australia, one must compare the enormous figure of 400 million acres with our 22 million acres of cropland, 27 million acres of forest and 28 million acres of improved pasture. Suppose that we eliminate 25 per cent of the 400 million acres as unsuitable for agriculture or needed for urban development. That still leaves 300 million acres of potentially useful land—more than four times the present acreage! This area may ultimately be of enormous importance not only to Australia but to a world hard-pressed for food. Of course most of the land needs the benefit of routine agricultural measures, such as treatment with superphosphate and the planting of nitrogen-accumulating legumes. But the fact remains that much of it would have to remain forever in the category of "inherently infertile" land unless it is treated with a tiny but vital dose of trace elements.

Copper, zinc and molybdenum are the elements that cropland and pasture most often lack. Copper and cobalt are those most generally needed for the health and productivity of sheep and cattle. At Coonalpyn Downs the sowing of seven pounds per acre of zinc sulfate and seven pounds of copper sulfate made the difference between infertility and fertility. More recently workers of the Western Australia Department of Agriculture have found that traces of zinc and copper, together with superphosphate, provide the key to the development of the three-million-acre Esperance Plain, near the southwest corner of the continent. This area now bears nothing but harsh native scrub; agriculturists have always thought it worthless despite its adequate rainfall. Very likely the entire region will soon contribute to Australia's food-producing capacity.

While copper and zinc deficiencies occur in southern and western Australia, the eastern part of the continent suffers mostly from a lack of molybdenum. About a third of the so-called podsolic soils in eastern Australia is more or less deficient in the metal. The podsolic soils stretch for 1,000 miles along the east coast, reaching more than 150 miles inland into Victoria, New South Wales and Queensland. They also cover much of the island of Tasmania. The whole of the podsolic belt receives more than 20 inches of rainfall per year, and most of it can be sown to pasture if treated with a molybdenum-superphosphate fertilizer. This is rapidly being done.

The lack of molybdenum in Australian soils was discovered only in 1942. It works in an unusual way on the affected plants. Symptoms of molybdenum deficiency were observed in plants in the laboratory before any attempt was made to diagnose the infertility of podsolic soils. But the laboratory symptoms were quite unlike those observed in the plants of podsolic pastures. The first clue to what was wrong with the pastures was gained when they were found to respond well to treatment with wood-ash, lime or other alkaline matter. At first it was thought that the lime aided pasture growth by counteracting phosphate fixation in the soil. Experiments disproved this theory, however, and the search continued. Finally it was observed that clover grown on the podsolic soils responded spectacularly to molybdenum. Now it has been discovered that plants of many species all over the world grow faster in soils to which molybdenum has been added.

But why did the molybdenum-deficient pasture plants not resemble those grown in the laboratory? The reason is that the lack of molybdenum in the soil interfered with the ability of the pasture plants to fix nitrogen from the air, but was not severe enough to induce the symptoms obtained in the laboratory. The laboratory plants, on the other hand, received nitrogen in their well-balanced diet, and did not exhibit the symptoms of nitrogen deficiency. Thus the pasture plants were stunted by lack of nitrogen, and did not show the other symptoms of molybdenum deficiency. The laboratory plants were afflicted only with the other symptoms. To appreciate the importance of this fact, one must realize that clover is especially valued for its capacity to enrich the soil with nitrogen. A small dose of molybdenum restored its dark-green color and normal growth, just as if the pasture had been heavily dressed with a nitrogen fertilizer.

Remarkably little molybdenum is needed to correct its deficiency in the soil. On some soils even one sixteenth of an ounce per acre is sufficient to effect a

COMMONWEALTH OF AUSTRALIA has been scene of pioneer efforts to amend trace-element deficiencies, which occur in the areas hatched in color. Areas A and B (*black hatching*) are, re-spectively, the zinc- and copper-deficient Ninety Mile Desert (now Coonalpyn Downs) and a similar area, the Esperance Plain. The broken colored lines define areas of equal average rainfall per

clear-cut response in clover plants. The normal commercial application for pasture is of the order of one ounce per acre. This homeopathic dose, by far the smallest in trace-element therapy, is known to be effective for at least 10 years.

Some trace-element deficiencies affect plants, some affect animals and some

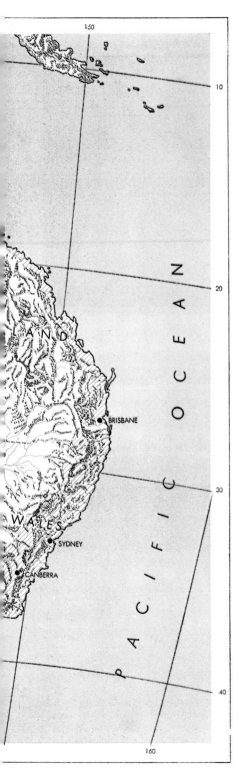

year. Deficient areas total about 400 million acres, three fourths of which (three times the now productive area) may be reclaimed.

affect both. Even where pasture growth is poor from lack of zinc or manganese, the sparse herbage will contain enough of these elements to meet the needs of livestock grazing on it. Naturally the livestock will benefit greatly from treatment of their pasturage with zinc and manganese. But the benefit to them will lie in the increase of herbage, not in the increase of zinc and manganese. It is otherwise in the case of cobalt or copper. Pasture plants can apparently thrive with no cobalt at all, yet a lack of this element is deadly to sheep and cattle. Both plants and animals require copper.

When sheep suffer a deficiency of copper, their wool often loses its crimp and takes on a stringy or steely appearance. Such sheep are poor wool producers, and their product brings much less in the market than normal wool. Extensive areas exist where wool production and quality are thus affected. Fortunately the condition is easily remedied, either by feeding the land five pounds per acre of copper (in the form of "copperized" superphosphate) or by providing the stock with copper-treated salt licks.

In some parts of Australia, notably the south and west, the copper deficiency is more serious. Here the breeding performance of ewes as well as the quality of wool is likely to suffer. Lambs may be stillborn, or they may be born with a curious wobbly gait and die soon afterward. It has been found that lambs which are dropped by copper-deficient ewes have malformed brains and spinal cords. The condition is completely prevented by the addition of copper to the pasturage, by salt licks or by drenching the pregnant ewes with a solution of a copper salt.

Calves born on such land rarely suffer from symptoms as severe as those observed in lambs. But cows often have a strange malady, locally known as "falling disease" because the afflicted animals suddenly drop dead in the fields. These cows have died of heart failure. Prolonged copper deficiency has so weakened their heart muscles that any momentary stress can kill them. This disease, too, can be prevented. We should add that in all cases the copper not only prevents the specific ailment but markedly improves the over-all health and productivity of the flock or herd.

Some parts of southern Australia have suffered from a deficiency of both copper and cobalt so severe that sheep and cattle could not survive unless they were regularly transferred to a healthier area. This problem has also been solved, with the result that several hundred thousand acres of well-nigh valueless land have

been transformed into thriving communities. It has recently been found that the cobalt requirements of a ruminant stem from a unique symbiosis of the animal and the vitamin-producing microorganisms in its gut. For this reason the cobalt deficiency and its cure merit special attention.

The fact that cobalt is essential to life was first discovered in 1935 by Australian workers. Their observation emerged from the study of a peculiar and highly localized disease. In some parts of southern and western Australia, animals from seemingly healthy pastures weakened and died, apparently of starvation. New Zealand also suffered from this disease: workers there attributed it to deficiency of iron, having observed that the malady did not affect animals dosed with crude iron compounds.

This explanation did not satisfy students of the problem in western Australia. The effect of various iron compounds seemed unrelated to their iron content; moreover, the doses needed were suspiciously large. Perhaps, these workers thought, the effectiveness of the compounds was due not to iron but to some other element. Accordingly they fractionated one of the compounds and tested its constituent elements separately. It at once became clear that cobalt was the effective substance. Soil from the sick pastures and from the livers of diseased animals were found to be abnormally low in cobalt. An exceedingly small amount of cobalt is needed by ruminants: less than a tenth of their copper requirement. A sheep needs only a tenth of a milligram of cobalt per day; cattle must have five to 10 times as much. A single ounce of cobalt will sustain nearly 800 sheep or 80 cattle for a year!

While this investigation was proceeding, investigators in southern Australia, working on a similar disease of sheep, arrived independently at the same discovery. These workers found that cobalt is ineffective if injected with a needle; it must be taken by mouth. To obviate the need for repeated oral doses, they invented an ingenious cobalt "bullet"—four to five grams of cobalt oxide mixed with clay and baked into a small, heavy slug. Placed in the sheep's throat with a special gun, the bullet lodges in the upper alimentary canal, where it yields a steady supply of cobalt. One bullet lasts for months, and sometimes for years. It is possible that this novel technique can be used with other trace elements.

New interest in cobalt was aroused 10 years ago by the discovery in England

COBALT-DEFICIENT SHEEP (*number 38*) is compared to healthy sheep (*number 37*) in an experiment performed by H. A. Keener at the University of New Hampshire. Cobalt deficiency, identified in the U. S., Britain and Australia, can be remedied by dosage (for sheep) of one tenth of a milligram per day. The cobalt is needed for synthesis of vitamin B-12 by microorganisms in gut.

and the U. S. that the element appears in the molecule of vitamin B-12. Within three years workers at Cornell University and in Australia had demonstrated that vitamin B-12 injections swiftly secured the remission of cobalt deficiency symptoms. Ruminants, they found, derive their natural supply of the vitamin entirely from the microorganisms in their gut. The microorganisms must have a steady supply of cobalt for their synthesis of the vitamin. It would be more accurate to call cobalt deficiency a nutritional disease of the microorganisms, rather than of their animal host.

Many chemical reactions in plants and animals are now known to require the presence of a trace element. But it is difficult to connect these reactions in cells and tissues with the outward symptoms of trace-element deficiency. Boron deficiency, for example, profoundly inhibits the growth of plants. Yet we know next to nothing of the biochemical role of boron. It is possible the element takes part in the transport of sugars by forming ionizable sugar-borate complexes, but evidence for this is meager.

Encouraging progress is being made in the study of trace elements as components of enzymes. Within the past few years several enzymes containing molybdenum have been isolated from living tissues. One of these is nitrate reductase, a plant enzyme which abets the synthesis of proteins by converting nitrate nitrogen from the soil into nitrite nitrogen. When this enzyme is deprived of its molybdenum, it ceases to function; when the molybdenum is restored, the enzyme is reactivated. In the nitrate reductase molecule the molybdenum serves as an electron carrier, alternately undergoing oxidation and reduction. It is not surprising that some plants lacking in molybdenum contain high levels of raw nitrate nitrogen. Of course this does not apply to clover, which fixes nitrogen from the air, or to plants that obtain their nitrogen from the soil as ammonia.

Zinc also plays a part in enzymes, notably the carbonic anhydrase of animals, which breaks down carbonic acid into carbon dioxide and water. Carbonic anhydrase must play an important role in respiration, for it helps convert carbon dioxide flushed from body tissues into blood-borne bicarbonate, and to convert bicarbonate back into carbon

dioxide in the lungs. Though the role of this and several other zinc-containing enzymes has been well established, no one so far has been able to connect any deficiency-disease symptom to a reduction of their activity, even in gravely zinc-deficient animals. The symptoms of zinc deficiency—failure of growth and appetite, skin lesions and, in birds, poorly formed bones and feathers—remain unexplained.

More is known about the complex role of copper in enzymes. Recently investigators at the University of Utah and the University of London have traced certain of the signs caused by copper starvation in rats and pigs to a lack of the enzyme cytochrome oxidase, which is essential for the respiration of cells. While there is no copper in cytochrome oxidase, this enzyme has an iron component, called heme *a*, the synthesis of which is catalyzed by copper. Without heme *a*, cytochrome oxidase cannot be formed. It has been known for some time that copper deficiency plays a similar role in anemia; copper-starved bone marrow fails to mobilize the available iron and incorporate it in the red blood cells which the marrow manufactures. In addition it now seems that the red blood cells themselves utilize copper. Radioactive-tracer studies conducted at the University of Utah suggest that the cells require copper in order to complete their normal life span.

Investigators at the University of London have established a suggestive connection between lack of copper and ataxia, or poor coordination, in newborn lambs. The ataxia of the lambs is caused by underdevelopment of the myelin, or fatty outer coating of the nerve fibers, in their brains and spinal cords, and this in turn is due to a lack of the phospholipids of which myelin is largely composed. The lambs' tissues require copper to catalyze a crucial stage in the synthesis of the phospholipids.

Many recent studies suggest that trace-element disorders tend to involve pairs or triads of elements. A striking instance is the interplay of copper, molybdenum and inorganic sulfate in a disorder afflicting some Australian sheep. This disease develops on pastures rich in copper but poor in molybdenum. Sheep on such land will succumb to copper poisoning unless their molybdenum intake is increased. But molybdenum will not counteract the effect of copper except in the presence of a third substance: inorganic sulfate. The chemical reactions involved are not simple, and there are indications that still other substances are involved.

What of trace elements in man's own diet? The indications are that civilized man is not likely to suffer trace-element deficiencies. Unlike range-fed cattle or sheep, modern man derives his diet from many localities and soil types. The inadequacies of one food source are made up from another. After 100 years of study, iron and iodine are still the only trace elements that human populations are known to lack. While iodine deficiency is a genuinely regional disease, iron deficiency stems from loss of blood or poor choice of foods rather than from a local lack of iron in the soil.

So trace-element deficiencies have little direct effect upon man. Their indirect effects, on the other hand, are profoundly important. How we husband the chemical health of our crops, our stock and our land may have immense import for the future of man. As population pressure mounts, we will have to evolve ever faster-growing and higher-yielding strains of domestic plants and animals. Will the quality of our food keep pace with its quantity? That may well depend upon how carefully we monitor its content of the trace elements.

29

THE NUTRIENT CYCLES OF AN ECOSYSTEM

F. HERBERT BORMANN AND GENE E. LIKENS
October 1970

When all vegetation was cut in a 38-acre watershed in an experimental forest in New Hampshire, the output of water and nutrients increased. The experiment illustrates ecological principles of forest management

An ecological system has a richly detailed budget of inputs and outputs. One of the reasons it is difficult to assess the impact of human activities on the biosphere is the lack of precise information about these inputs and outputs and about the delicate adjustments that maintain a balance. As a result the people planning a project such as the logging of a forest or the building of a power plant often cannot take into account or even foresee the full range of consequences the project will have. Even if they could, the traditional practice in the management of land resources has been to emphasize strategies that maximize the output of some product or service and give little or no thought to the secondary effects of the strategies. As a result one sees such ecological maladjustments as the export of food surpluses while natural food chains become increasingly contaminated with pesticides and runoff waters carry increasing burdens of pollutants from fertilizers and farm wastes; the cutting of forests with inadequate perception of the effects on regional water supplies, wildlife, recreation and aesthetic values, and the conversion of wetlands to commercial use with little concern over important hydrologic, biological, aesthetic and commercial values lost in the conversion.

It seems evident that a new conceptual approach to the management of resources would be desirable. One approach that has been suggested is to consider entire ecological systems. In an experimental forest in New Hampshire we and the U.S. Forest Service have been conducting a large-scale investigation aimed at supplying the kind of information that is usually lacking about ecosystems. The investigation represents a multidisciplinary collaboration between workers at a number of universities and in several government agencies.

The investigation has involved two major operations. First we attempted to determine the inputs and outputs affecting the forest under normal circumstances. Then we inflicted a serious disruption on an ecosystem by cutting down an entire section of the forest. Over a period of years we have been measuring the results of that drastic action on the ecosystem's budget of nutrients. We believe our findings help to show how a natural ecosystem works and what happens when man perturbs it. Moreover, our data provide a conceptual basis for taking into account the ecological factors that in the long run determine whether or not a new technology or a particular economic policy is wise.

An ecosystem, as we use the term, is a basic functional unit of nature comprising both organisms and their nonliving environment, intimately linked by a variety of biological, chemical and physical processes. The living and nonliving components interact among themselves and with each other; they influence each other's properties, and both are essential for the maintenance and development of the system. An ecosystem, then, can be visualized as a grouping of components—living organisms, organic debris, available nutrients, primary and secondary minerals and atmospheric gases—linked by food webs, flows of nutrients and flows of energy.

A typical forest ecosystem might be visualized as a 1,000-hectare stand of mature deciduous forest. (A hectare is 2.47 acres.) The lateral boundaries of the system can be either an edge of the stand or an arbitrarily determined line. The upper boundary is the treetop level, and the lower one is the deepest level of soil where significant biological activity takes place.

Our ecosystem is in the Hubbard Brook Experimental Forest, which is maintained in the White Mountain National Forest by the Forest Service. We have focused on the movement of nutrients across the boundary of the system (both in and out) and their circulation within it. Nutrients are found in four basic compartments of the ecosystem that are intimately linked by an array of natural processes. The organic compartment consists of the living organisms and their debris. (There are probably more than 2,500 species of plants and animals in a 1,000-hectare system.) The available-nutrient compartment is composed of nutrients held on the surface of particles of the clay-humus complex of the soil or in solution in the soil. Roots as they grow produce positively charged hydrogen ions that exchange with the nutrient ions (of calcium, magnesium and so on) held on the negatively charged particles, and the nutrients are then taken up by the roots. The third compartment consists of soil and rocks containing nutrients in forms temporarily unavailable to living organisms. The atmospheric compartment is made up of gases, which can be found not only in the air but also in the ground.

Nutrients can flow between these compartments along a variety of pathways. In most cases the flow is powered directly or indirectly by solar energy. Available nutrients are taken up and assimilated by vegetation and microor-

DRAINAGE OF WATERSHED is measured by means of a weir at the base of the cutover watershed in the White Mountain National Forest. The chemical content of the water in the stream feeding into the weir shown in the photograph on the opposite page is also ascertained by means of water samples taken from the stream periodically.

ganisms. They also circulate in complex food webs within the organic compartment, subsequently being made available again through decomposition or leaching. Minerals in soil and rock are decomposed by weathering, so that nutrients are made available to organisms. Sometimes available nutrients are returned to the soil-and-rock compartment through the formation of new minerals such as clay. Nutrients tend to cycle between the organic, available-nutrient and soil-and-rock compartments, forming an intrasystem cycle. Nutrients in gaseous form are continually being transferred to and from other compartments by inorganic chemical reactions such as oxidation and reduction and by organic reactions related to such processes as photosynthesis, respiration and the fixation and volatilization of nitrogen.

An ecosystem is connected to the surrounding biosphere by its system of inputs and outputs. They arrive or leave in such forms as radiant energy, gases, inorganic chemicals and organic substances. Inputs and outputs can be transported across ecosystem boundaries by meteorological forces such as precipitation and wind, geological forces such as running water and gravity and biological vectors involving the movement of animals in and out of the system.

Ordinarily it is difficult to measure the input-output relations of an ecosystem, particularly those involving nutrients. The nutrient cycle is closely connected to the water cycle: precipitation brings nutrients in, water leaches them from rocks and soil and stream flow carries them away. Hence one cannot measure the input and output of nutrients

without simultaneously measuring the input and output of water. The problem usually is that subsurface flows of water, which can be a significant fraction of the hydrologic cycle, are almost impossible to measure.

Several years ago it occurred to us that under certain circumstances the interaction of the nutrient cycle and the hydrologic cycle could be turned to good advantage in the study of an ecosystem. The requirements are that the ecosystem be a watershed underlain by tight bedrock or some other impermeable base. In that case the only inputs would be meteorological and biological; geological input need not be considered because there would be no transfer between adjacent watersheds. In humid areas where surface wind is a minor factor losses from the system would be only

SCENE OF EXPERIMENT is the Hubbard Brook Experimental Forest in the White Mountain National Forest. After the normal inputs and outputs of precipitation and nutrients had been ascer-   tained in six contiguous watersheds in the forest, all vegetation in one of the watersheds was cut and dropped in place, and regrowth was inhibited by herbicide. The purpose of the treatment was to

geological and biological. Given an impermeable base, all the geological output would inevitably turn up in the streams draining the watershed. If the watershed is part of a larger and fairly homogeneous biotic unit, the biological output tends to balance the biological input because animals move randomly in and out of the watershed, randomly acquiring or discharging nutrients. Thus one need measure only the meteorological input and the geological output of nutrients in order to arrive at the net gain or loss of a given nutrient in the ecosystem.

This is the approach we use at Hubbard Brook, where we have been studying six contiguous watersheds ranging in size from 12 to 43 hectares [see top illustration on next page]. They are

ascertain the effect on the outputs of the ecological system. The drainage of the cutover watershed is to south, which is at right.

all tributary to Hubbard Brook and forested with a well-developed, second-growth stand of sugar maple, beech and yellow birch. The forest has been undisturbed by cutting or fire since 1919, when much of the first growth was removed in lumbering operations.

We measure the meteorological inputs to these watersheds by means of a network of gauging stations. We measure the geological outputs by means of a weir built at the foot of each watershed, that is, at the point where the principal stream leaves the watershed [see illustration on page 271]. With the weir, which also includes a ponding basin, one can both measure the water that is leaving the watershed and, by combining these data with frequent chemical measurements, ascertain the quantities of chemical substances that are leaving the watershed.

Inasmuch as the impermeable base prohibits deep seepage in these watersheds, the loss of water by evaporation and by transpiration through leaves is calculated by subtracting the hydrologic output from the hydrologic input. Water budgets for the six watersheds from 1955 to 1968 indicate an average annual precipitation of 123 centimeters and a runoff of 72 centimeters, with evapotranspiration therefore averaging 51 centimeters. Precipitation is distributed rather evenly throughout the year, but runoff is uneven. Most of the runoff (57 percent) occurs during the snowmelt period of March, April and May; indeed, 35 percent of the total runoff occurs in April. In contrast, only .7 percent of the yearly runoff takes place in August.

We accomplish chemical measurements by taking weekly samples of the water output (stream water at the weir) and collecting the total weekly water input (rain and snow) and analyzing them for calcium, magnesium, potassium, sodium, aluminum, ammonium, nitrate, sulfate, chloride, bicarbonate, hydrogen ion and silicate. The concentrations of these elements in precipitation and in stream water are entered in a computing system, where weekly concentrations are multiplied by the weekly volume of water entering and leaving the ecosystem. In this way the input and output of chemicals is computed in terms of kilograms of an element per hectare of watershed.

Knowing the input and output of chemicals, we have made nutrient budgets for nine elements. Considering four of the major ones, we find the following annual averages in kilograms per

hectare entering the system and being flushed out of it: calcium, 2.6 and 11.8; sodium, 1.5 and 6.9; magnesium, .7 and 2.9, and potassium, 1.1 and 1.7. These inputs and outputs represent connections of the undisturbed forest ecosystem with worldwide biogeochemical systems. The data also provide a comparative basis for judging the effects of managerial practices on biogeochemical cycles.

Net losses of calcium, sodium and magnesium were recorded each year even though the period of measurement included wet and dry years as well as years of average precipitation. Potassium, a major component of the bedrock, showed net gains in two years and a smaller average net loss than was recorded for the other elements. Evidently potassium is accumulating in the ecosystem with respect to other elements. One reason may be that it is retained in the structure of illitic clays developing in the ecosystem. Perhaps also potassium is retained in proportionately larger amounts than other elements are in the slowly increasing biomass of the system.

Highly predictable relations appear between the concentrations of dissolved chemicals in stream water and the discharge rates of the stream. For example, the concentrations of sodium and silica are inversely related to discharge rates, whereas the concentrations of aluminum, hydrogen ion and nitrate increase as discharge rates increase. Magnesium, calcium, sulfate, chloride and potassium are relatively independent of discharge rate.

The magnitudes of change of concentration, however, are fairly small. The concentrations of potassium, calcium and magnesium hardly change at all, and the concentration of sodium decreases by only three times as the discharge rate increases by four orders of magnitude. These results were unexpected: we had thought that during the spring melt period there would be considerable dilution, making the concentrations of elements in stream water relatively low. All these relations show how strongly stream-water chemistry is under the control of processes inherent in the forest ecosystem.

Because of the comparative constancy of chemical concentrations, the total output of elements is strongly dependent on the volume of stream flow. Hence it is now possible, knowing only the hydrologic output, to predict with fair accuracy both the output and the concentration of chemicals in the stream water draining from our mature, forested eco-

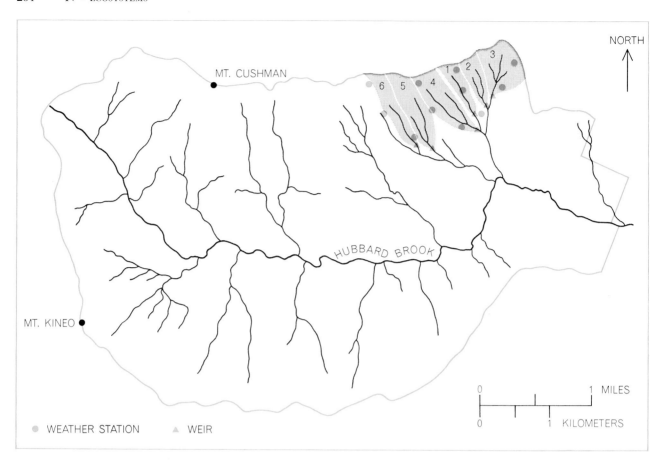

NORTH

MT. CUSHMAN

6   5   4   1   2   3

MT. KINEO

HUBBARD BROOK

0   1   MILES

0   1   KILOMETERS

● WEATHER STATION   ▲ WEIR

HUBBARD BROOK EXPERIMENTAL FOREST is in central New Hampshire, about 30 miles north of Laconia. The six watersheds figuring in experiment are in the northeast corner (*color*). Vegetation was cut and regrowth repressed in Watershed No. 2.

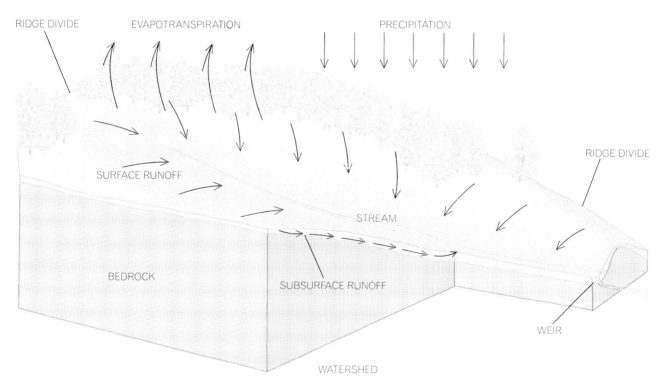

RIDGE DIVIDE   EVAPOTRANSPIRATION   PRECIPITATION

RIDGE DIVIDE

SURFACE RUNOFF

STREAM

BEDROCK

SUBSURFACE RUNOFF

WEIR

WATERSHED

UNDISTURBED WATERSHED receives inputs from precipitation and discharges outputs through its principal stream. In many watersheds there also would be outputs arising from deep seepage, which is almost impossible to measure, but watersheds of Hubbard Brook ecosystem are underlain by impermeable bedrock, so that all liquid output is by stream. Another aspect of the ecosystem is the intrasystem cycle, involving the release of nutrients into the soil by weathering of rocks, the uptake of nutrients by vegetation and their return to the soil by decomposition and leaching. Destruction of vegetation blocks a major pathway, nutrient uptake.

system. This relation would seem to have considerable value for regional planners concerned with water quality.

A particularly interesting finding is that almost the entire loss of cations (positively charged nutrient ions) from the undisturbed forest ecosystem is balanced by the input of positively charged hydrogen ions in precipitation. The proportion of hydrogen ions is related to the amount of sulfate in precipitation. It is estimated that 50 percent of the sulfate in precipitation results from industrial activities that put sulfur dioxide and other sulfur products into the air. These sulfur compounds may ultimately form ionized sulfuric acid, which consists of hydrogen ions and sulfate ions. When the precipitation enters the ecosystem, the hydrogen ions replace the nutrient cations on the negatively charged exchange sites in the soil, and the cations are washed out of the system in stream water. Thus air pollution is directly related to a small but continuous loss of fertility from the land area of the ecosystem and a small but continuous chemical enrichment of streams and lakes. The relation appears to represent an important hidden cost of air pollution, made apparent through the analysis of ecosystems.

So far we have mentioned only chemical losses appearing as dissolved substances. Losses also arise when chemicals locked up in particulate matter such as rock or soil particles and in organic matter such as leaves and twigs are washed out of the ecosystem by the stream. We have measured these outputs and developed equations expressing the loss of particulate matter as a function of the discharge rate of the stream. The loss is highly dependent on the discharge rate.

Losses of dissolved substances account for the great bulk of the chemical loss from our undisturbed ecosystem. Whereas they are largely independent of the discharge rate, losses of particulate matter are highly dependent on it. This point is of particular interest since forest-management practices can either increase or decrease stream-discharge rates and thereby shift the balance between the loss of dissolved substances and the loss of particulate matter.

Weathering, or the release of elements bound in primary minerals, is another factor that must be considered in an ecosystem, since the elements thus released are made available as nutrients to the vegetation and animals. Based on net losses of elements from our ecosystem, a relatively uniform geology in the region

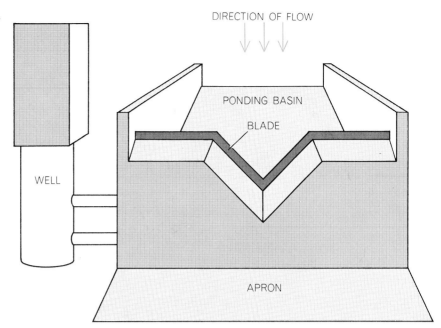

STRUCTURE OF WEIR is designed to collect all the water draining from a watershed and to release it in a measurable way over the *V*-shaped blade. Well is used to gauge water level, which is continuously recorded in well house. Each Hubbard Brook watershed has one weir.

and a knowledge of the bulk chemistry of the rock and soil, we estimate that the nutrients contained in some 800 kilograms per hectare of rock and soil are made available each year by weathering.

We now have for the undisturbed Northern hardwood ecosystem of Hubbard Brook estimates of chemical input in precipitation and output in stream water and the rates of generation of ions by the weathering of minerals within the system. To complete the picture of nutrient cycling it is necessary to measure the nutrient content of the four compartments and the flow rates among them arising from uptake, decomposition and leaching and the formation of new minerals. A typical set of relations, using calcium as an example, is shown in the illustration on page 277.

The annual net loss of calcium from the ecosystem is 9.2 kilograms per hectare. This loss represents only about .3 percent of the calcium in the available-nutrient and organic compartments of the system and only 1.3 percent of what is in the available-nutrient compartment alone. The data suggest that Northern hardwood forests have a remarkable ability to hold and circulate nutrients.

It was against this background that we and the Forest Service embarked on the experiment of cutting down everything that was growing in one watershed. One of the objectives of this severe treatment was to block a major pathway of the ecosystem—the uptake of nutrients

by higher plants—while the pathway of ultimate decomposition continued to function. We questioned whether or not the ecosystem had the capacity under these circumstances to hold the nutrients accumulating in the available-nutrient compartment. We also wanted to determine the effect of deforestation on stream flow, to examine some of the fundamental chemical relations of the forest ecosystem and to evaluate the effects of forest manipulation on nutrient relations and the eutrophication of stream water.

The experiment was begun in the winter of 1965–1966 when the forest of Watershed No. 2, covering 15.6 hectares, was completely leveled by the Forest Service. All trees, saplings and shrubs were cut and dropped in place; their limbs were removed so that no slash was more than 1.5 meters above the ground. No products were removed from the forest, and great care was taken to prevent disturbance of the surface of the soil that might promote erosion. The following summer regrowth of vegetation was inhibited by an aerial application of the herbicide Bromacil at a rate of 28 kilograms per hectare.

Deforestation had a pronounced effect on runoff. Beginning in May, 1966, runoff from the cut watershed began to increase over the levels that would have been expected if there had been no cutting. The cumulative runoff for 1966 exceeded the expected amount by 40 percent. The largest difference was re-

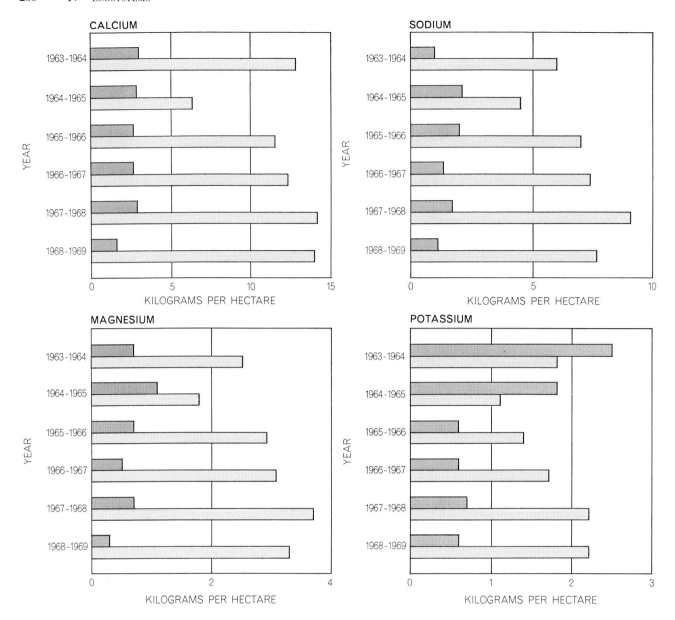

INPUT AND OUTPUT of four major nutrients were recorded for the undisturbed watersheds at Hubbard Brook. Input (*gray*) was in precipitation; output (*color*) was in stream flow, and the difference represents the net loss or gain from the ecosystem in a given year.

corded during the four months from June through September, when the runoff was 418 percent higher than the expected amount. This difference is directly attributable to changes in the hydrologic cycle resulting from the removal of the transpiring surface. Accelerated runoff has continued through the succeeding summers.

Our treatment also resulted in a fundamental alteration of the nitrogen cycle, which in turn caused extraordinary losses of soil fertility. In an undisturbed ecosystem nitrogen incorporated in organic compounds is ultimately decomposed in a number of steps to ammonium nitrogen (NH_4^+), a positively charged ion that can be held fairly tightly in the soil on the negatively charged exchange

sites. Ammonium ions can be taken up directly by green plants and used in the fabrication of nitrogen-containing organic compounds. Ammonium ions can also be used as the substrate for the process of nitrification. In this process two genera of soil bacteria, *Nitrosomonas* and *Nitrobacter,* oxidize ammonium to nitrate (NO_3^-). Two hydrogen ions are produced for every ion of ammonium oxidized to nitrate. As we have already mentioned, hydrogen ions can play a key role in the release of nutrient cations from the soil. Nitrate, being negatively charged, is highly leachable. If it is not taken up by higher plants, it can easily be removed from the ecosystem in drainage water.

The available evidence indicates that

nitrification is of minor importance in undisturbed forests such as ours, underlain by acid podzol soil. The nitrate drained by our streams (invariably in low concentration) can be largely accounted for by its input in precipitation. In fact, our budgetary analyses show that undisturbed ecosystems are accumulating nitrogen at a rate of about two kilograms per hectare per year.

The concentration of nitrate in stream water from undisturbed forests shows a seasonal cycle, being higher from November through April than it is from May through October. The decline in May and the low concentration in the summer are correlated with heavy demand for nutrients by the vegetation and generally increased biological activity associated with warming of the soil.

Beginning in June, 1966, the concentration of nitrate in the deforested watershed rose sharply. At the same time the undisturbed ecosystem showed the normal spring decline [*see illustration on next page*]. The high concentration has continued in the deforested watershed during the succeeding years. Average net losses of nitrate nitrogen were 120 kilograms per hectare per year from 1966 through 1968. We estimate that the annual turnover of nitrogen in our undisturbed forests is about 60 kilograms per hectare. Therefore an amount of elemental nitrogen equivalent to double the amount normally taken up by the forest has been lost from the deforested watershed each year since cutting. The magnitude of nitrate loss is a clear indication of the acceleration of nitrification in the watershed. There is no doubt that the cutting drastically altered the conditions controlling the nitrification process.

Another factor of interest about nitrification is the body of evidence from other regions that certain types of vegetation can inhibit nitrification chemically. Presumably the effect is to inhibit production of the highly leachable nitrate ion. At the same time the positively charged ammonium ions may be held within the system on the negatively charged exchange sites in the soil. If this inhibition process goes on at Hubbard Brook, cutting the vegetation would promote nitrification. The effect may account for much of the nitrate loss from the deforested ecosystem.

The export of nitrate to the small stream draining the cut watershed has resulted in nitrate concentrations exceeding the levels established by the U.S. Public Health Service for drinking water. In general the deforestation has led to eutrophication of the stream and to the development of algal "blooms." This finding indicates that in some circumstances forest-management practices can contribute significantly to the eutrophication of streams.

Since nitrification produces hydrogen ions that replace metallic cations on the exchange surfaces in the soil, one would expect a loss of metallic nutrients from the deforested watershed. We have recorded substantial losses of this kind. The concentrations of calcium, magnesium, sodium and potassium in the stream water increased almost simultaneously with the increase in nitrate. About a month later the concentration of aluminum rose sharply.

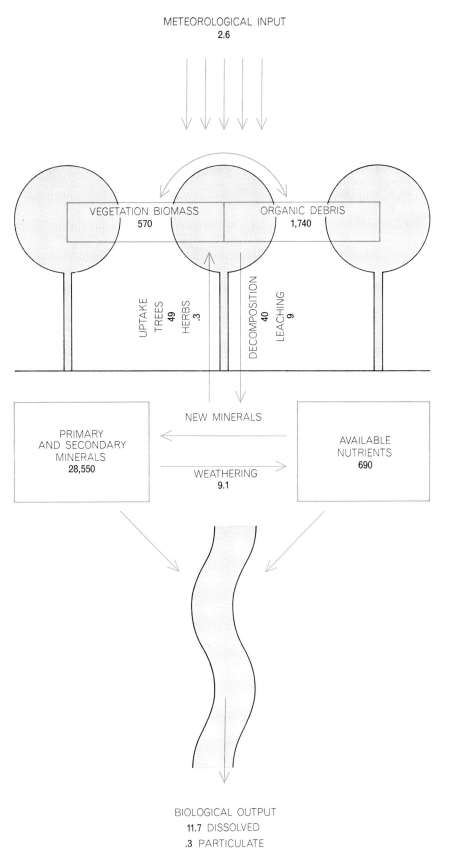

CALCIUM CYCLE is depicted for an undisturbed forest ecosystem. Numerals represent the average number of kilograms per hectare per year. Thus the meteorological input to the ecosystem in precipitation and dust is 2.6 kilograms per hectare annually. A substantial amount of calcium is in soil and rock; 9.1 kilograms is released annually by weathering. Vegetation takes up 49.3 kilograms; 49 kilograms is returned to the soil by decomposition and leaching. Gross loss in stream drainage is 12 kilograms, so the net loss is 9.4 kilograms.

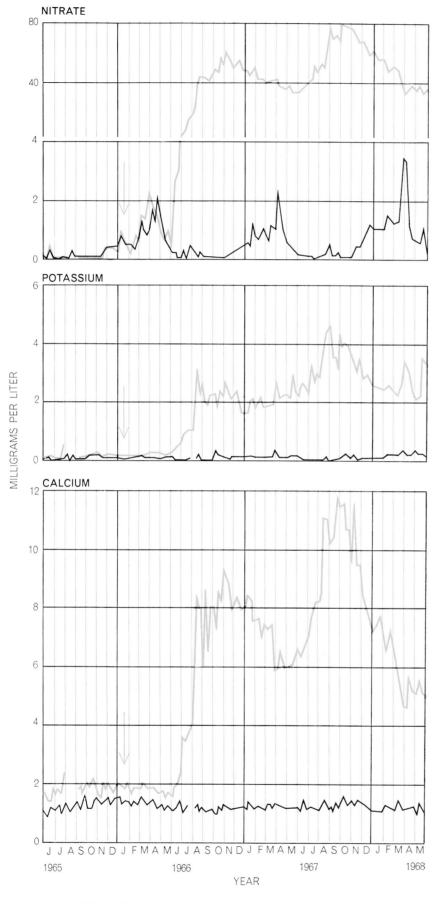

MILLIGRAMS PER LITER

NITRATE

POTASSIUM

CALCIUM

J J A S O N D J F M A M J J A S O N D J F M A M J J A S O N D J F M A M
1965   1966   1967   1968

YEAR

RESULTS OF DEFORESTATION shown by the output of three nutrients in stream water appear in a comparison of Watershed No. 6 (*black*), which was undisturbed, with Watershed No. 2 (*color*), which was deforested. The arrows indicate the time of the deforestation.

Net losses of potassium were 21 times higher than those in an undisturbed watershed; of calcium, 10 times; of aluminum, nine; of magnesium, seven, and of sodium, three. These figures represent a substantial loss of nutrients from the ecosystem. The finding suggests that commercial forestry should focus more on the effect of harvesting practices on the loss of nutrients, giving more consideration to such corrective procedures as selective cutting and the promotion of regrowth on cut areas.

Our results indicate that the capacity of the ecosystem to retain nutrients is dependent on the maintenance of nutrient cycling within the system. When the cycle is broken, as by the destruction of vegetation, the loss of nutrients is greatly accelerated. This effect is related both to the cessation of nutrient uptake by plants and to the larger quantities of drainage water passing through the system. The loss may also be related to increased rates of decomposition resulting from such changes in the physical environment as higher soil temperature and moister soil.

We also found a basic change in the pattern of loss of particulate matter in the deforested watershed. The data for three years indicate an increase of some ninefold over a comparable undisturbed ecosystem. After an initial surge the loss of particulate organic matter has declined as a result of the virtual elimination of the production of primary organic matter in the ecosystem. In contrast the loss of inorganic material from the stream bed has accelerated because of the greater erosive capacity of the augmented stream flow and also because several biological barriers to the erosion of surface soil and stream banks have been greatly diminished. The continuous layer of litter that once protected the soil surface is now discontinuous. The extensive network of fine roots that tended to stabilize the stream bank is now dead, and the dead leaves that tended to plaster over exposed banks are gone. The erosive trend can be expected to rise exponentially as long as regrowth of vegetation is inhibited in the watershed.

Our study clearly shows that the stability of an ecosystem is linked to the orderly flow of nutrients between the living and the nonliving components of the system and the production and decomposition of biomass. These processes, integrated with the seasonal changes in climate, result in relatively tight nutrient cycles within the system, a minimum output of nutrients and water and good resistance to erosion. Destruction of the vegetation sets off a chain of interactions. Their net effect is an increase in the amount and flow rate of water and the breakdown of biological barriers to erosion and transportation, coupled with an increase in the export of nutrient capital and inorganic particulate matter.

Three points, which are inherent in the ecosystem concept and are emphasized by the Hubbard Brook study, should be recognized as being basic to any wise scheme for managing the use of land. First, the ecosystem is a highly complex natural unit composed of or-

ganisms (plants and animals, including man) and their inorganic environment (air, water, soil and rock). Second, all parts of an ecosystem are intimately linked by natural processes that are part of the ecosystem, such as the uptake of nutrients, the fixation of energy, the movement of nutrients and energy through food webs, the release of nutrients by the decomposition of organic matter, the weathering of rock and soil minerals to release nutrients and the formation of new minerals. Third, individual ecosystems are linked to surrounding land and water ecosystems and to the biosphere in general by connections with

food webs and the worldwide circulation of air and water.

Failures in environmental management often result from such factors as failure to appreciate the complexity of nature, the assumption that it is possible to manage one part of nature alone and the belief that somehow nature will absorb all types of manipulation. Good management of the use of land—good from the viewpoint of society at large—requires that managerial practices be imposed only after a careful analysis and evaluation of all the ramifications. A focus for this type of analysis and evaluation is the ecosystem concept.

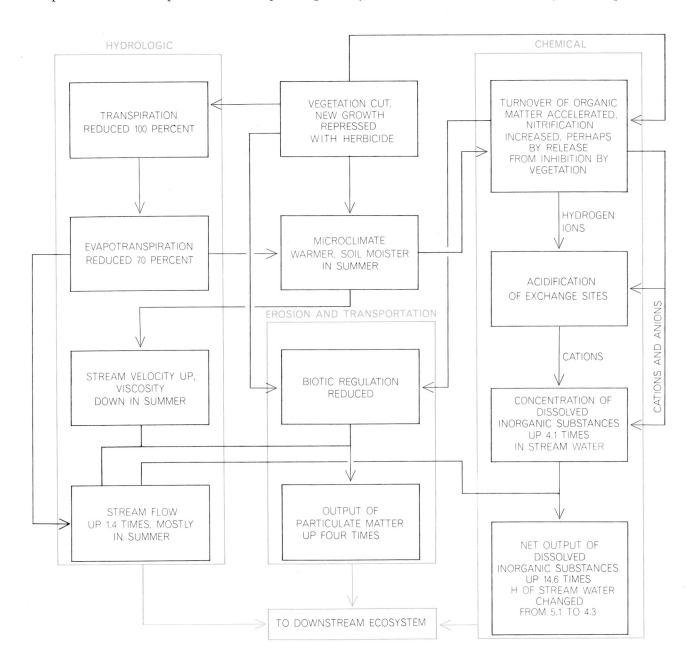

IMPACT OF DEFORESTATION on the ecosystem relations of Watershed No. 2 is portrayed in terms of three types of effect (*color*). Cations are positively charged nutrient ions; anions are negatively charged. Normally cations are held fairly tightly within the ecosystem, but with deforestation they tended to leak away. The accelerated loss was related to the intensified nitrification.

30

TOXIC SUBSTANCES AND ECOLOGICAL CYCLES

GEORGE M. WOODWELL
March 1967

Radioactive elements or pesticides such as DDT that are released in the environment may enter meteorological and biological cycles that distribute them and can concentrate them to dangerous levels

The vastness of the earth has fostered a tradition of unconcern about the release of toxic wastes into the environment. Billowing clouds of smoke are diluted to apparent nothingness; discarded chemicals are flushed away in rivers; insecticides "disappear" after they have done their job; even the massive quantities of radioactive debris of nuclear explosions are diluted in the apparently infinite volume of the environment. Such pollutants are indeed diluted to traces—to levels infinitesimal by ordinary standards, measured as parts per billion or less in air, soil and water. Some pollutants do disappear; they are immobilized or decay to harmless substances. Others last, sometimes in toxic form, for long periods. We have learned in recent years that dilution of persistent pollutants even to trace levels detectable only by refined techniques is no guarantee of safety. Nature has ways of concentrating substances that are frequently surprising and occasionally disastrous.

We have had dramatic examples of one of the hazards in the dense smogs that blanket our cities with increasing frequency. What is less widely realized is that there are global, long-term ecological processes that concentrate toxic substances, sometimes hundreds of thousands of times above levels in the environment. These processes include not only patterns of air and water circulation but also a complex series of biological mechanisms. Over the past decade detailed studies of the distribution of both radioactive debris and pesticides have revealed patterns that have surprised even biologists long familiar with the unpredictability of nature.

Major contributions to knowledge of these patterns have come from studies of radioactive fallout. The incident that triggered worldwide interest in large-scale radioactive pollution was the hydrogen-bomb test at Bikini in 1954 known as "Project Bravo." This was the test that inadvertently dropped radioactive fallout on several Pacific islands and on the Japanese fishing vessel *Lucky Dragon*. Several thousand square miles of the Pacific were contaminated with fallout radiation that would have been lethal to man. Japanese and U.S. oceanographic vessels surveying the region found that the radioactive debris had been spread by wind and water, and, more disturbing, it was being passed rapidly along food chains from small plants to small marine organisms that ate them to larger animals (including the tuna, a staple of the Japanese diet).

The U.S. Atomic Energy Commission and agencies of other nations, particularly Britain and the U.S.S.R., mounted a large international research program, costing many millions of dollars, to learn the details of the movement of such debris over the earth and to explore its hazards. Although these studies have been focused primarily on radioactive materials, they have produced a great deal of basic information about pollutants in general. The radioactive substances serve as tracers to show the transport and concentration of materials by wind and water and the biological mechanisms that are characteristic of natural communities.

One series of investigations traced the worldwide movement of particles in the air. The tracer in this case was strontium 90, a fission product released into the earth's atmosphere in large quantities by nuclear-bomb tests. Two reports in 1962 —one by S. Laurence Kulp and Arthur R. Schulert of Columbia University and the other by a United Nations committee—furnished a detailed picture of the travels of strontium 90. The isotope was concentrated on the ground between the latitudes of 30 and 60 degrees in both hemispheres, but concentrations were five to 10 times greater in the Northern Hemisphere, where most of the bomb tests were conducted.

It is apparently in the middle latitudes

FOREST COMMUNITY is an integrated array of plants and animals that accumulates and reuses nutrients in stable cycles, as indicated schematically in black. DDT participates in parallel cycles (*color*). The author measured DDT residues in a New Brunswick forest in which four pounds per acre of DDT had been applied over seven years. (Studies have shown about half of this landed in the forest, the remainder dispersing in the atmosphere.) Three years after the spraying, residues of DDT were as shown (in pounds per acre).

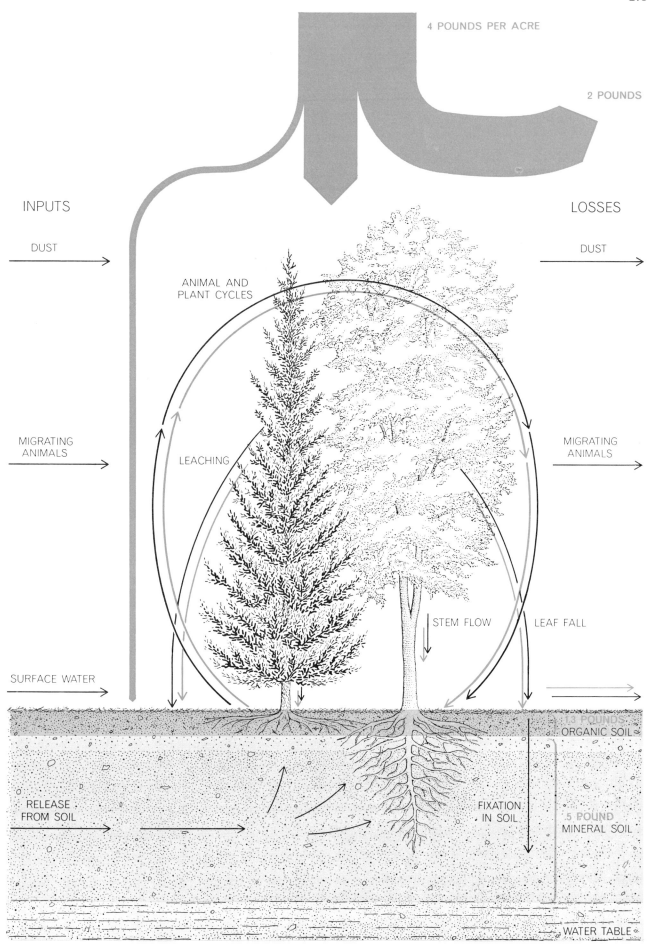

4 POUNDS PER ACRE

2 POUNDS

INPUTS

DUST

ANIMAL AND
PLANT CYCLES

LEACHING

MIGRATING
ANIMALS

SURFACE WATER

RELEASE
FROM SOIL

LOSSES

DUST

MIGRATING
ANIMALS

STEM FLOW

LEAF FALL

1.3 POUNDS
ORGANIC SOIL

.5 POUND
MINERAL SOIL

FIXATION
IN SOIL

WATER TABLE

that exchanges occur between the air of upper elevations (the stratosphere) and that of lower elevations (the troposphere). The larger tests have injected debris into the stratosphere; there it remains for relatively long periods, being carried back into the troposphere and to the ground in the middle latitudes in late winter or spring. The mean "half-time" of the particles' residence in the stratosphere (that is, the time for half of a given injection to fall out) is from three months to five years, depending on many factors, including the height of the injection, the size of the particles, the latitude of injection and the time of year. Debris injected into the troposphere has a mean half-time of residence ranging from a few days to about a month. Once airborne, the particles may travel rapidly and far. The time for one circuit around the earth in the middle latitudes varies from 25 days to less than 15. (Following two recent bomb tests in China fallout was detected at the Brookhaven National Laboratory on Long Island respectively nine and 14 days after the tests.)

Numerous studies have shown further that precipitation (rain and snowfall) plays an important role in determining where fallout will be deposited. Lyle T. Alexander of the Soil Conservation Service and Edward P. Hardy, Jr., of the AEC found in an extensive study in Clallam County, Washington, that the amount of fallout was directly proportional to the total annual rainfall.

It is reasonable to assume that the findings about the movement and fallout of radioactive debris also apply to other particles of similar size in the air. This conclusion is supported by a recent report by Donald F. Gatz and A. Nelson Dingle of the University of Michigan, who showed that the concentration of pollen in precipitation follows the same pattern as that of radioactive fallout. This observation is particularly meaningful because pollen is not injected into the troposphere by a nuclear explosion; it is picked up in air currents from plants close to the ground. There is little question that dust and other particles, including small crystals of pesticides, also follow these patterns.

From these and other studies it is clear that various substances released into the air are carried widely around the world and may be deposited in concentrated form far from the original source. Similarly, most bodies of water—especially the oceans—have surface currents that may move materials five to 10 miles a day. Much higher rates, of course, are found in such major oceanic currents as

the Gulf Stream. These currents are one more physical mechanism that can distribute pollutants widely over the earth.

The research programs of the AEC and other organizations have explored not only the pathways of air and water transport but also the pathways along which pollutants are distributed in plant and animal communities. In this connection we must examine what we mean by a "community."

Biologists define communities broadly to include all species, not just man. A natural community is an aggregation of a great many different kinds of organisms, all mutually interdependent. The basic conditions for the integration of a community are determined by physical characteristics of the environment such as climate and soil. Thus a sand dune supports one kind of community, a freshwater lake another, a high mountain still another. Within each type of environment there develops a complex of organisms that in the course of evolution becomes a balanced, self-sustaining biological system.

Such a system has a structure of interrelations that endows the entire community with a predictable developmental pattern, called "succession," that leads toward stability and enables the community to make the best use of its physical environment. This entails the development of cycles through which the community as a whole shares certain resources, such as mineral nutrients and energy. For example, there are a number of different inputs of nutrient elements into such a system. The principal input is from the decay of primary minerals in the soil. There are also certain losses, mainly through the leaching of substances into the underlying water table. Ecologists view the cycles in the system as mechanisms that have evolved to conserve the elements essential for the survival of the organisms making up the community.

One of the most important of these cycles is the movement of nutrients and energy from one organism to another along the pathways that are sometimes called food chains. Such chains start with plants, which use the sun's energy to synthesize organic matter; animals eat the plants; other animals eat these herbivores, and carnivores in turn may constitute additional levels feeding on the herbivores and on one another. If the lower orders in the chain are to survive and endure, there must be a feedback of nutrients. This is provided by decay organisms (mainly microorganisms) that break down organic debris

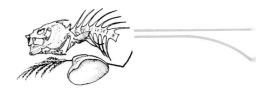

ORGANIC DEBRIS
MARSH 13 POUNDS PER ACRE
BOTTOM .3 POUND PER ACRE

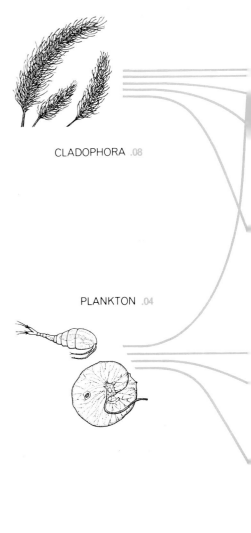

CLADOPHORA .08

PLANKTON .04

MARSH PLANTS
SHOOTS .33
ROOTS 2.80

FOOD WEB is a complex network through which energy passes from plants to herbivores and on to carnivores within a biologi-

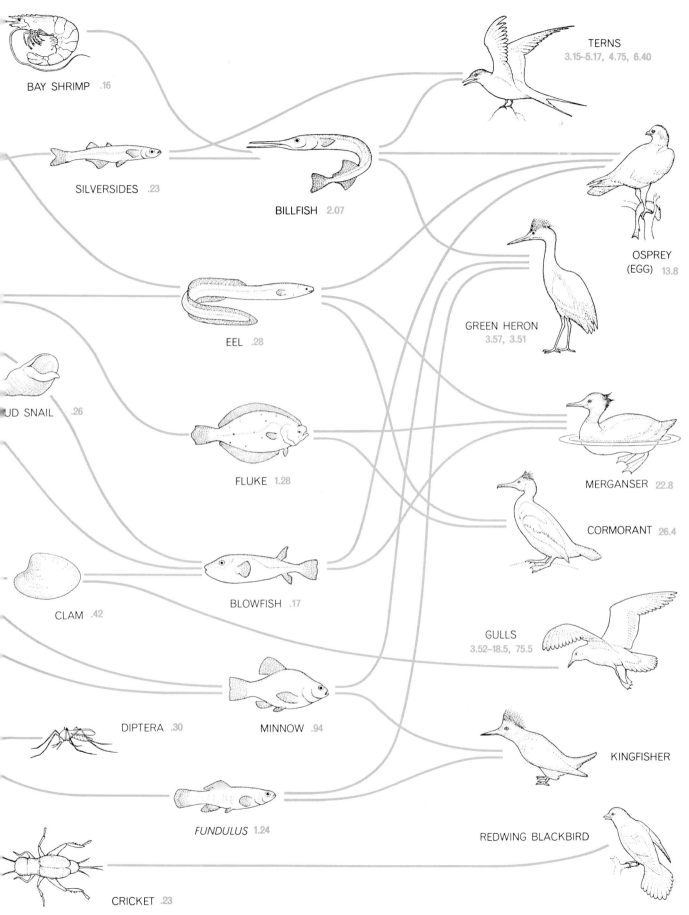

BAY SHRIMP .16

SILVERSIDES .23

BILLFISH 2.07

TERNS
3.15–5.17, 4.75, 6.40

OSPREY
(EGG) 13.8

EEL .28

GREEN HERON
3.57, 3.51

UD SNAIL .26

FLUKE 1.28

MERGANSER 22.8

CORMORANT 26.4

CLAM .42

BLOWFISH .17

GULLS
3.52–18.5, 75.5

DIPTERA .30

MINNOW .94

KINGFISHER

FUNDULUS 1.24

REDWING BLACKBIRD

CRICKET .23

cal community. This web showing some of the plants and animals in a Long Island estuary and along the nearby shore was developed by Dennis Puleston of the Brookhaven National Laboratory. Numbers indicate residues of DDT and its derivatives (in parts per million, wet weight, whole-body basis) found in the course of a study made by the author with Charles F. Wurster, Jr., and Peter A. Isaacson.

into the substances used by plants. It is also obvious that the community will not survive if essential links in the chain are eliminated; therefore the preying of one level on another must be limited.

Ecologists estimate that such a food chain allows the transmission of roughly 10 percent of the energy entering one level to the next level above it, that is, each level can pass on 10 percent of the energy it receives from below without suffering a loss of population that would imperil its survival. The simplest version of a system of this kind takes the form of a pyramid, each successively higher population receiving about a tenth of the energy received at the level below it.

Actually nature seldom builds communities with so simple a structure. Almost invariably the energy is not passed along in a neatly ordered chain but is spread about to a great variety of organisms through a sprawling, complex web of pathways [see illustration on preceding two pages]. The more mature the community, the more diverse its makeup and the more complicated its web. In a natural ecosystem the network may consist of thousands of pathways.

This complexity is one of the principal factors we must consider in investigating how toxic substances may be distributed and concentrated in living communities. Other important basic factors lie in the nature of the metabolic process. For example, of the energy a population of organisms receives as food, usually less than 50 percent goes into the construction of new tissue, the rest being spent for respiration. This circumstance acts as a concentrating mechanism: a substance not involved in respiration and not excreted efficiently may be concentrated in the tissues twofold or more when passed from one population to another.

Let us consider three types of pathway for toxic substances that involve man as the ultimate consumer. The three examples, based on studies of radioactive substances, illustrate the complexity and variety of pollution problems.

The first and simplest case is that of strontium 90. Similar to calcium in chemical behavior, this element is concentrated in bone. It is a long-lived radioactive isotope and is a hazard because its energetic beta radiation can damage the mechanisms involved in the manufacture of blood cells in the bone marrow. In the long run the irradiation may produce certain types of cancer. The route of strontium 90 from air to man is rather direct: we ingest it in leafy vegetables, which absorbed it from the soil or received it as fallout from the air, or in milk and other dairy products from cows that have fed on contaminated vegetation. Fortunately strontium is not usually concentrated in man's food by an extensive food chain. Since it lodges chiefly in bone, it is not concentrated in passing from animal to animal in the same ways other radioactive substances may be (unless the predator eats bones!).

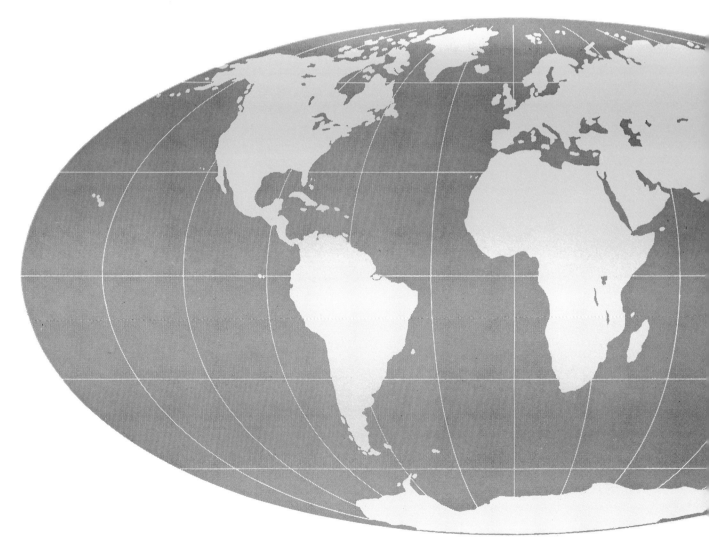

FALLOUT is distributed around the earth by meteorological processes. Deposits of strontium 90, for instance, are concentrated between 30 and 60 degrees north, as shown by depth of color on the map and by the curve (right). Points on the chart represent individual samples. The data are from a study made in 1963 and 1964 by Robert J. List and colleagues in several U.S. agencies. Such

Quite different is the case of the radioactive isotope cesium 137. This isotope, also a fission product, has a long-lived radioactivity (its half-life is about 30 years) and emits penetrating gamma rays. Because it behaves chemically like potassium, an essential constituent of all cells, it becomes widely distributed once it enters the body. Consequently it is passed along to meat-eating animals, and under certain circumstances it can accumulate in a chain of carnivores.

A study in Alaska by Wayne C. Hanson, H. E. Palmer and B. I. Griffin of the AEC's Pacific-Northwest Laboratory showed that the concentration factor for cesium 137 may be two or three for one step in a food chain. The first link of the chain in this case was lichens growing in the Alaskan forest and tundra. The lichens collected cesium 137 from fallout in rain. Certain caribou in Alaska live mainly on lichens during the winter, and caribou meat in turn is the principal diet of Eskimos in the same areas. The investigators found that caribou had accumulated about 15 micromicrocuries of cesium radioactivity per gram of tissue in their bodies. The Eskimos who fed on these caribou had a concentration twice as high (about 30 micromicrocuries per gram of tissue) after eating many pounds of caribou meat in the course of a season. Wolves and foxes that ate caribou sometimes contained three times the concentration in the flesh of the caribou. It is easy to see that in a longer chain, involving not just two animals but several, the concentration of a substance that was not excreted or metabolized could be increased to high levels.

A third case is that of iodine 131, another gamma ray emitter. Again the chain to man is short and simple: The contaminant (from fallout) comes to man mainly through cows' milk, and thus the chain involves only grass, cattle, milk and man. The danger of iodine 131 lies in the fact that iodine is concentrated in the thyroid gland. Although iodine 131 is short-lived (its half-life is only about eight days), its quick and localized concentration in the thyroid can cause damage. For instance, a research team from the Brookhaven National Laboratory headed by Robert Conard has discovered that children on Rongelap Atoll who were exposed to fallout from the 1954 bomb test later developed thyroid nodules.

The investigations of the iodine 131 hazard yielded two lessons that have an important bearing on the problem of pesticides and other toxic substances released in the environment. In the first place we have had a demonstration that the hazard of the toxic substance itself often tends to be underestimated. This was shown to be true of the exposure of the thyroid to radiation. Thyroid tumors were found in children who had been treated years before for enlarged thymus glands with doses of X rays that had been considered safe. As a result of this discovery and studies of the effects of iodine 131, the Federal Radiation Council in 1961 issued a new guide reducing the permissible limit of exposure to ionizing radiation to less than a tenth of what had previously been accepted. Not the least significant aspect of this lesson is the fact that the toxic effects of such a hazard may not appear until long after the exposure; on Rongelap Atoll 10 years passed before the thyroid abnormalities showed up in the children who had been exposed.

The second lesson is that, even when the pathways are well understood, it is almost impossible to predict just where toxic substances released into the environment will reach dangerous levels. Even in the case of the simple pathway followed by iodine 131 the eventual destination of the substance and its effects on people are complicated by a great many variables: the area of the cow's pasture (the smaller the area, the less fallout the cow will pick up); the amount and timing of rains on the pasture (which on the one hand may bring down fallout but on the other may wash it off the forage); the extent to which the cow is given stored, uncontaminated feed; the amount of iodine the cow secretes in its milk; the amount of milk in the diet of the individual consumer, and so on.

If it is difficult to estimate the nature and extent of the hazards from radioactive fallout, which have been investigated in great detail for more than a decade by an international research program, it must be said that we are in a poor position indeed to estimate the hazards from pesticides. So far the

studies have not been made for pesticides but it appears that DDT may also be carried in air and deposited in precipitation.

STRONTIUM 90 (MILLICURIES PER SQUARE MILE)

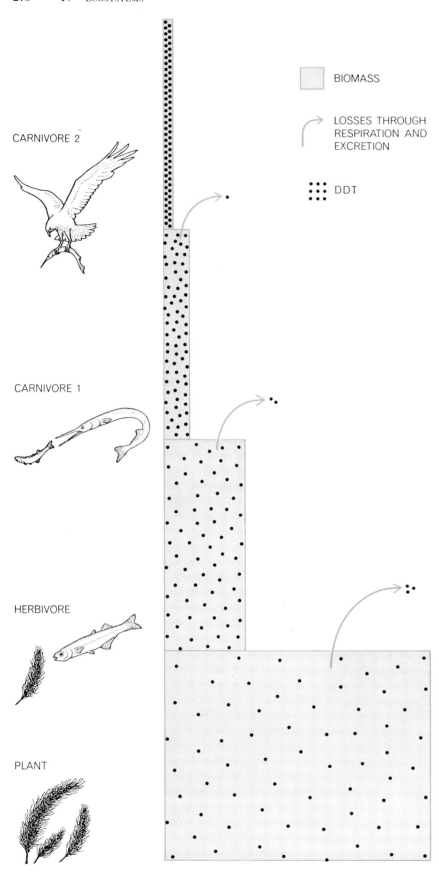

CARNIVORE 2

CARNIVORE 1

HERBIVORE

PLANT

BIOMASS

LOSSES THROUGH
RESPIRATION AND
EXCRETION

DDT

CONCENTRATION of DDT residues being passed along a simple food chain is indicated schematically in this diagram. As "biomass," or living material, is transferred from one link to another along such a chain, usually more than half of it is consumed in respiration or is excreted (*arrows*); the remainder forms new biomass. The losses of DDT residues along the chain, on the other hand, are small in proportion to the amount that is transferred from one link to the next. For this reason high concentrations occur in the carnivores.

amount of research effort given to the ecological effects of these poisons has been comparatively small, although it is increasing rapidly. Much has been learned, however, about the movement and distribution of pesticides in the environment, thanks in part to the clues supplied by the studies of radioactive fallout.

Our chief tool in the pesticide inquiry is DDT. There are many reasons for focusing on DDT: it is long-lasting, it is now comparatively easy to detect, it is by far the most widely used pesticide and it is toxic to a broad spectrum of animals, including man. Introduced only a quarter-century ago and spectacularly successful during World War II in controlling body lice and therefore typhus, DDT quickly became a universal weapon in agriculture and in public health campaigns against disease-carriers. Not surprisingly, by this time DDT has thoroughly permeated our environment. It is found in the air of cities, in wildlife all over North America and in remote corners of the earth, even in Adélie penguins and skua gulls (both carnivores) in the Antarctic. It is also found the world over in the fatty tissue of man. It is fair to say that there are probably few populations in the world that are not contaminated to some extent with DDT.

We now have a considerable amount of evidence that DDT is spread over the earth by wind and water in much the same patterns as radioactive fallout. This seems to be true in spite of the fact that DDT is not injected high into the atmosphere by an explosion. When DDT is sprayed in the air, some fraction of it is picked up by air currents as pollen is, circulated through the lower troposphere and deposited on the ground by rainfall. I found in tests in Maine and New Brunswick, where DDT has been sprayed from airplanes to control the spruce budworm in forests, that even in the open, away from trees, about 50 percent of the DDT does not fall to the ground. Instead it is probably dispersed as small crystals in the air. This is true even on days when the air is still and when the low-flying planes release the spray only 50 to 100 feet above treetop level. Other mechanisms besides air movement can carry DDT for great distances around the world. Migrating fish and birds can transport it thousands of miles. So also do oceanic currents. DDT has only a low solubility in water (the upper limit is about one part per billion), but as algae and other organisms in the water absorb the substance in fats, where it is highly soluble, they make room for more DDT to be dissolved into the water. Accordingly water that never contains more than a trace of DDT can continuously transfer it from deposits on the bottom to organisms.

DDT is an extremely stable compound that breaks down very slowly in the environment. Hence with repeated spraying the residues in the soil or water basins accumulate. Working with Frederic T. Martin of the University of Maine, I found that in a New Brunswick forest where spraying had been discontinued in 1958 the DDT content of the soil increased from half a pound per acre to 1.8 pounds per acre in the three years between 1958 and 1961. Apparently the DDT residues were carried to the ground very slowly on foliage and decayed very little. The conclusion is that DDT has a long half-life in the trees and soil of a forest, certainly in the range of tens of years.

Doubtless there are many places in the world where reservoirs of DDT are accumulating. With my colleagues Charles F. Wurster, Jr., and Peter A. Isaacson of the State University of New York at Stony Brook, I recently sampled a marsh along the south shore of Long Island that had been sprayed with DDT for 20 years to control mosquitoes. We found that the DDT residues in the upper layer of mud in this marsh ranged up to 32 pounds per acre!

We learned further that plant and animal life in the area constituted a chain that concentrated the DDT in spectacular fashion. At the lowest level the plankton in the water contained .04 part per million of DDT; minnows contained one part per million, and a carnivorous scavenging bird (a ring-billed gull) contained about 75 parts per million in its tissues (on a whole-body, wet-weight basis). Some of the carnivorous animals in this community had concentrated DDT by a factor of more than 1,000 over the organisms at the base of the ladder.

A further tenfold increase in the concentrations along this food web would in all likelihood result in the death of many of the organisms in it. It would then be impossible to discover why they had disappeared. The damage from DDT concentration is particularly serious in the higher carnivores. The mere fact that conspicuous mortality is not observed is no assurance of safety. Comparatively low concentrations may inhibit reproduction and thus cause the species to fade away.

That DDT is a serious ecological hazard was recognized from the beginning of its use. In 1946 Clarence Cottam and

LOCATION	ORGANISM	TISSUE	CONCENTRATION (PARTS PER MILLION)
U.S. (AVERAGE)	MAN	FAT	11
ALASKA (ESKIMO)			2.8
ENGLAND			2.2
WEST GERMANY			2.3
FRANCE			5.2
CANADA			5.3
HUNGARY			12.4
ISRAEL			19.2
INDIA			12.8-31.0
U.S. — CALIFORNIA	PLANKTON		5.3
CALIFORNIA	BASS	EDIBLE FLESH	4-138
CALIFORNIA	GREBES	VISCERAL FAT	UP TO 1,600
MONTANA	ROBIN	WHOLE BODY	6.8-13.9
WISCONSIN	CRUSTACEA		.41
WISCONSIN	CHUB	WHOLE BODY	4.52
WISCONSIN	GULL	BRAIN	20.8
MISSOURI	BALD EAGLE	EGGS	1.1-5.6
CONNECTICUT	OSPREY	EGGS	6.5
FLORIDA	DOLPHIN	BLUBBER	ABOUT 220
CANADA	WOODCOCK	WHOLE BODY	1.7
ANTARCTICA	PENGUIN	FAT	.015-.18
ANTARCTICA	SEAL	FAT	.042-.12
SCOTLAND	EAGLE	EGGS	1.18
NEW ZEALAND	TROUT	WHOLE BODY	.6-.8

DDT RESIDUES, which include the derivatives DDD and DDE as well as DDT itself, have apparently entered most food webs. These data were selected from hundreds of reports that show DDT has a worldwide distribution, with the highest concentrations in carnivorous birds.

Elmer Higgins of the U.S. Fish and Wildlife Service warned in the *Journal of Economic Entomology* that the pesticide was a potential menace to mammals, birds, fishes and other wildlife and that special care should be taken to avoid its application to streams, lakes and coastal bays because of the sensitivity of fishes and crabs. Because of the wide distribution of DDT the effects of the substance on a species of animal can be more damaging than hunting or the elimination of a habitat (through an operation such as dredging marshes). DDT affects the entire species rather than a single population and may well wipe out the species by eliminating reproduction.

Within the past five years, with the development of improved techniques for detecting the presence of pesticide residues in animals and the environment, ecologists have been able to measure the extent of the hazards presented by DDT and other persistent general poisons. The picture that is emerging is not a comforting one. Pesticide residues have now accumulated to levels that are catastrophic for certain animal populations, particularly carnivorous birds. Furthermore, it has been clear for many years that because of their shotgun effect these weapons not only attack the pests but also destroy predators and competitors that normally tend to limit proliferation of the pests. Under exposure to pesti-

cides the pests tend to develop new strains that are resistant to the chemicals. The result is an escalating chemical warfare that is self-defeating and has secondary effects whose costs are only beginning to be measured. One of the costs is wildlife, notably carnivorous and scavenging birds such as hawks and eagles. There are others: destruction of food webs aggravates pollution problems, particularly in bodies of water that receive mineral nutrients in sewage or in water draining from heavily fertilized agricultural lands. The plant populations, no longer consumed by animals, fall to the bottom to decay anaerobically, producing hydrogen sulfide and other noxious gases, further degrading the environment.

The accumulation of persistent toxic substances in the ecological cycles of the earth is a problem to which mankind will have to pay increasing attention. It affects many elements of society, not only in the necessity for concern about the disposal of wastes but also in the need for a revolution in pest control. We must learn to use pesticides that have a short half-life in the environment—better yet, to use pest-control techniques that do not require applications of general poisons. What has been learned about the dangers in polluting ecological cycles is ample proof that there is no longer safety in the vastness of the earth.

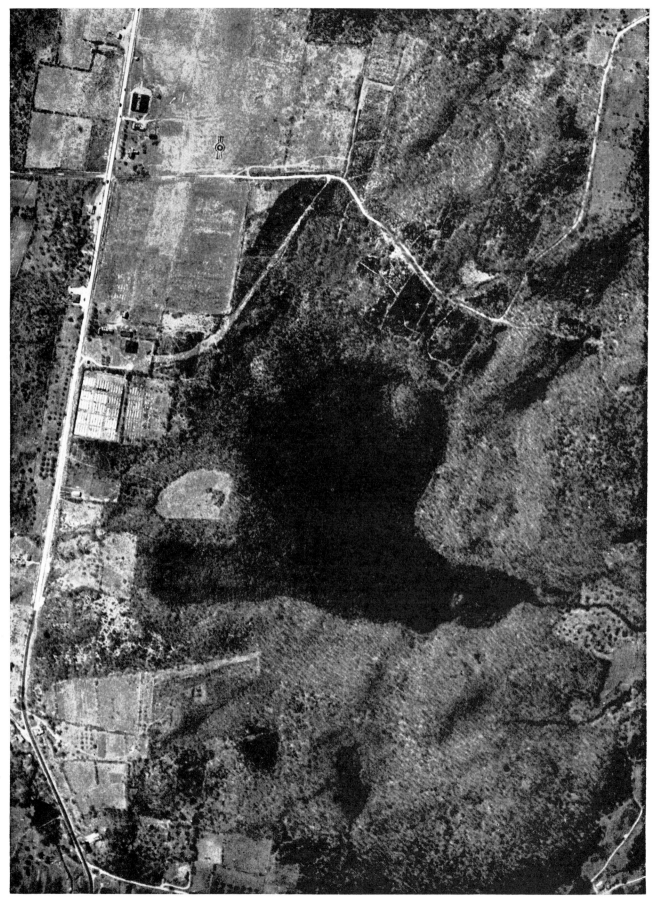

BOG near Bethany, Conn., is represented by the large dark patch in this aerial photograph. The area, once a lake, now has only one pool of open water (*tiny dark spot near center of bog*). Evergreen trees such as spruce and cedar grow around periphery of the bog.

31

BOGS

EDWARD S. DEEVEY, JR.

October 1958

When a lake is filled with silt and organic debris, it gives
way to a unique system of living things and their remains.
These wet spots on the land may have a significant effect on
world climate

Matthew Arnold could never have expressed his feeling for Dover Beach with such words as: "The heath is calm tonight,/ The swamp is full, the moon lies fair/ Upon the peat." For the poetic geographer a bog is Gothic when it is not downright menacing, a "ghoul-haunted woodland" or a trysting place for witches. Myths of bogland are very old, and may be based on a well-founded dread of savage woodsmen; Western civilization, originating near the Mediterranean shores, has fought the forest and its denizens at every step, and has successively driven the Goth, the Pict, the Caledonian and the Seminole into dank morasses of oblivion. Today the connection between Picts and pixies, bogs and bogeys is generally forgotten. By odd coincidence, however, the bog itself offers a historical record of changing landscape and climate that leads back into those murky mists of memory. Close study suggests also that the boglands of the Northern Hemisphere may be cast to play an ominous role in changes of the earth's climate that are yet to come.

The true bog must be distinguished from the reedy marsh. Marshes form near salt water and contain mainly grasses; few trees other than mangroves can stand much salt around their roots. Bogs are found in the drier interiors of continents as well as near the ocean, but they require some rainfall—deserts have few bogs. If the rainfall is great enough and the summers are cool enough for trees to grow on the uplands of a region, bogs may be expected in the lowlands. Bogs in rainy areas may be more sodden than a tropical rain forest, but the rain water they soak up contains few salts and other nutrients. Only plants that partake sparingly of nutrients, like the shrubs and perennials of arctic bar-rens and cold steppes, can survive in a bog.

Upland and lowland are relative terms, and refer to the flow of water through the ground. Whenever a barrier lies athwart the flow, water is interrupted in its steady descent to the sea and may rise above the surface of the ground behind the dam. So lowlands can occur near the tops of hills. A lake of clear water formed in this way will not last long. An entering stream dumps silt into the lake, and plants growing along the water's edge add their debris. More organic material may be deposited by runoff from land above the lake, especially from swampy flats. Eventually the lake is obliterated and the mud becomes

PLANT ZONES are clearly visible in this photograph of a bog outside Bemidji, Minn.
The kinds of plants found in such zones are shown in detail in the illustration on next page.

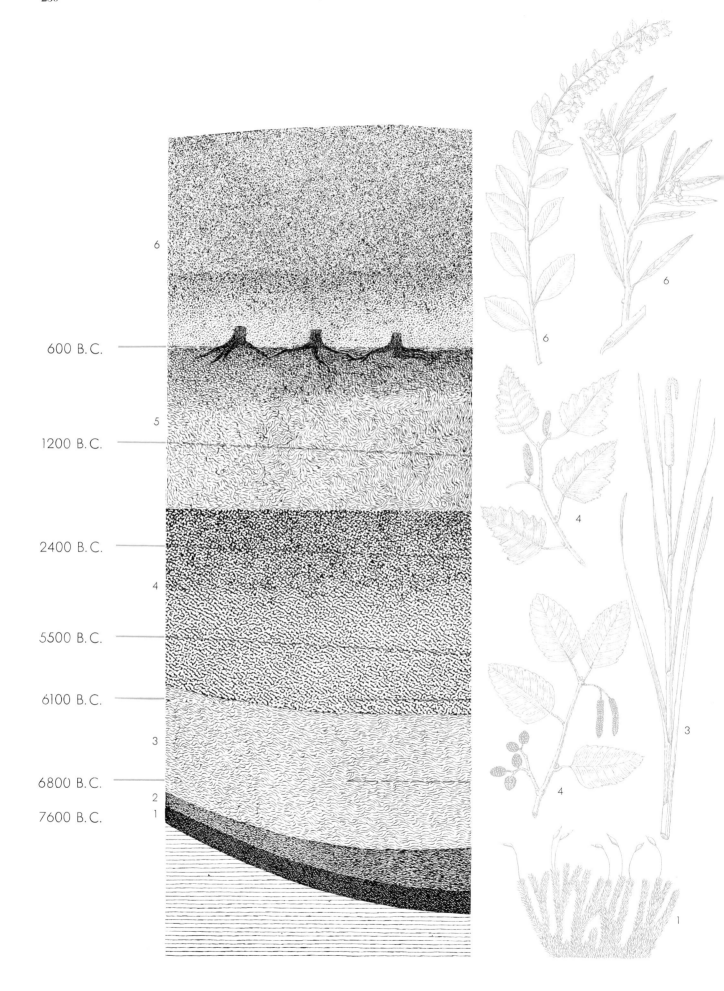

600 B.C.

1200 B.C.

2400 B.C.

5500 B.C.

6100 B.C.

6800 B.C.

7600 B.C.

firm enough to support shrubs and then trees. Pools left in the center of the lake may be bridged by plants like the sedge or swamp loosestrife. With their aid other plants form a floating mat on which trees can grow while the water below is yet unfilled. Most bogs are probably made in this way.

The raised bog (the German *Hoch-moor*) does not have to start in a lake but can form in any wet meadow. It depends on the presence of sphagnum, commonly known as peat moss. When dry, this remarkable substance resembles a sponge in its ability to take up great quantities of water by capillary action. It holds more water than absorbent cotton and so is useful as a plant mulch or even as a surgical dressing. The accumulation of dead sphagnum in a meadow forms a layer of half-decayed material, or peat, which draws ground water upward, thus permitting still more of the moss to grow on top. Where sphagnum grows in large masses, it actually raises the water table. When thoroughly wet, however, peat is as impervious to more water as dry rock. Rainwater then cannot percolate downward and runs off horizontally. The extra water eventually reaches the edge of the dome-shaped mass of sphagnum, where the peat is thinner. Thus watered at its margins, the bog grows upward and outward, and can even grow uphill. Plants other than sphagnum grow on the surface, and their remains are added to the peat. So long as the bog is growing, this debris, being water-soaked, accumulates almost unchanged. Eventually the bog reaches a size at which evaporation from the surface balances the rainfall and upward flow of ground water, and growth on the bog halts. Plant debris on the surface then decays about as fast as it accumulates, and little or no new peat forms. Material below the outer skin of the bog does not decay because oxygen cannot reach it, and plant remains—even corpses of men—do not decompose for centuries. Heather or other shrubs of the same family may grow on the stabilized surface, but few trees are to be seen. A

growth of forest on a raised bog probably implies a recent change toward a drier climate.

All bogs are stores of peat with sluggish circulation. The water at the surface is poor in salts and bases, partly because much of it is rain water, and partly also because the peat absorbs dissolved matter like a chemist's Amberlite resin. In most boggy districts there is a third reason: The local rock is usually granite, which contributes almost no minerals to the ground water flowing through it. The result is that bog plants are starved for lime, phosphorus and nitrogen. The deeper the peat, the more this is true. In consequence bogs are enclaves of subarctic life; they abound in plants like black spruce, cotton grass and Labrador tea. The bogs of Cape Cod support cranberries; those of New Jersey, blueberries. Both these plants are heaths of northern lands. Even subarctic animals like the bog lemming and the olive-backed thrush may be found far south of their regular ranges, giving bogs in temperate regions a northern flavor. In a sense they were left behind as the last continental ice sheet retreated northward, taking with it the belts of tundra and taiga (spruce forest) that lay beyond its margin when it covered the present locations of New York and Chicago. Probably no area has been continuously boggy since those days, but any partly closed-in bog in the northern U. S. can be thought of, from a lemming's point of view, as tundra enclosed by taiga.

Amid the plants of the muskeg, however, are others reminiscent of the tropics. Sogginess and nitrogen deficiency are common to rain forests as well as to bogs. So a few of the hardier orchids have ventured northward to meet the Labrador tea. Insectivorous plants, mainly tropical, are also successful in bogs, since their unorthodox behavior solves the problem of nitrogen deficiency; sundews, butterwort and pitcher plants grow in bogs. The pitcher plants, in fact, go north almost to the arctic tree-line, and their rain-filled leaves serve not only as traps for unwary insects but, being enriched in nitrogen and

HISTORY OF A RAISED BOG is recorded in the layers of peat (*left*), dated by pollen and radiocarbon content. This section is taken from left center of the bog diagrammed on next page. The oldest layers contain the remains of forest mosses (1), followed by diatoms (2) that once grew in a nutrient-poor pond. Between 6800 B.C. and 6100 B.C. the pond was dry enough to permit the growth of cattails, cotton grass and sedge (3, *left to right*), and on their remains grew birch (4, *upper*) and alder (4, *lower*). The fifth layer, formed during a moist period, is rich in moss such as *Sphagnum cuspidatum* (5). The tree stumps overlying this layer mark a cold, dry period about 600 B.C. When the climate again grew cooler and moister, bog plants returned; leatherleaf, bog rosemary, butterwort and *Sphagnum rubellum* (6, *left to right*) may be represented in the layer of peat at top of bog.

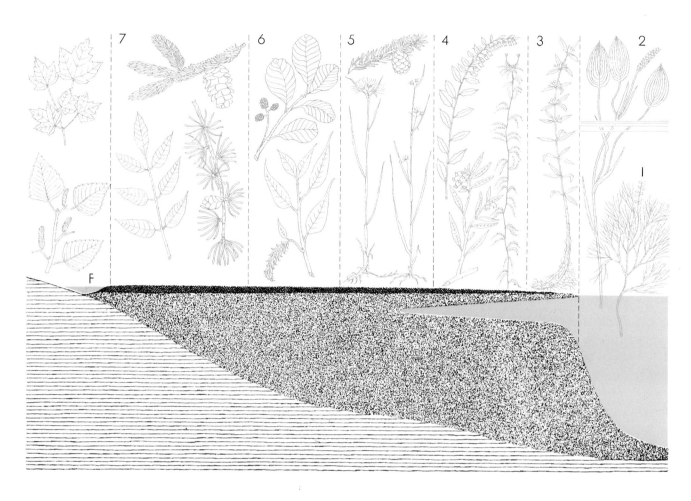

ECOLOGICAL ZONES mark the conversion of a lake to a bog, both in space and in time. Pondweed (1) grows in deeper water; pondweeds with floating leaves (2), in shallows. Loosestrife (3) invades the water by means of a creeping stem and gradually forms a floating mat which permits the spread of leatherleaf, bog rosemary and sphagnum (4, *left to right*). Where the fill is drier (5) black spruce, cottongrass and sedge prosper; they are followed by tall shrubs such as smooth alder and shining willow (6, *top and bottom*). At the edge of the bog is a forest of red spruce, mountain ash or larch (7). A shallow ditch or "fossa" of water (F) marks the original shoreline, and separates the bog forest from dryland trees such as red maple (*top*) and white birch (*bottom*).

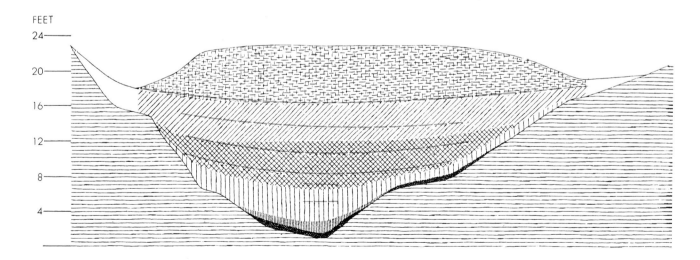

SECTION OF A RAISED BOG (the German *Hochmoor*) is diagrammed to show the depth of the various layers. The original ground level is indicated by the horizontally hatched area. The broken lines correspond to the dated levels in the diagram on the preceding two pages, where the layers are described in detail. The clear areas on either side are ditches of water around the bog.

phosphorus, form an aquatic habitat for the larvae of other insects (particularly those of midges, blowflies and mosquitoes) which can withstand the digestive enzymes in the leaves. The pitcher plant mosquito (*Wyeomyia smithii*) has followed its host northward.

Although cool, cloudy summers are essential for the existence of a raised bog, a few hot days will not destroy it, but will merely dry out its surface. A bog can then be crossed dry-shod. In damp or cooler weather it squishes underfoot like the arctic muskeg. A change in temperature or rainfall over a long period of time, however, upsets the stability of a bog. Raised bogs especially are sensitive indicators of climate. If the climate becomes moister or cooler, the bogs renew their growth both upward and outward. In drier or warmer conditions the surface will stabilize, but air will penetrate deeper into the drying peat and the zone of decay will thicken downward. If the drought is long-continued, the peat will be deeply weathered, the decay zone extending even into the older peat, and the bog will dwindle away in the sun like an ice cube.

Sensitive indicators of weather are nowhere hard to find. In tune with the variable march of the seasons, some insects emerge, some birds arrive or depart, some flowers bloom. The term of such an indicator, however, is short. Bogs exist for such long periods and respond to weather so slowly that they integrate weather into climate. Best of all, they also record it. When we cut into a bog for fuel and garden mulch, it resembles a cake of three, four, five or more layers, each marking a change in climate. At each boundary the dark, well-oxidized peat which formed, or rather weathered, when that layer was at the surface is topped by a brighter, fresher (and less combustible) peat representing renewed growth.

The episodes of rejuvenation indicated by the layers in any one bog may not mean anything important. The local water table could rise and fall for many reasons. But when all the bogs for miles around have layers formed at the same time, the implication can only be that the climate has changed repeatedly. Bright-colored layers composed of raw sphagnum peat, rich in the remains of such water plants as cotton grass, record a stage of flooding which lasted for years: the climate was cooler, and rainfall was more effective. Dark-colored, humus-rich peat—poor in recognizable fossils because of oxidation, but sometimes containing the remains of heather,

birch, or alder—records a stage of stability or destruction during a run of drier, warmer summers.

This matchless record of past climates needs only a time scale to be read with assurance. The climatic chronology determined by the pollen method—according to ratios of fossilized pollen grains from different plants—is relatively coarse [see "Living Records of the Ice Age," by Edward S. Deevey, Jr.; SCIENTIFIC AMERICAN Offprint 834]. Pollen is plentiful in the peat, but a pollen period is thousands of years long, covering the span of two or three bog layers. Nevertheless one point of equivalence with the pollen chronology became obvious early in the science of bogs. Before 1916, when the pollen method was founded by the great Swedish geologist Lennart von Post, C. A. Weber had noticed that one of the episodes of bog rejuvenation in northern Germany was especially well-

marked and widespread. Von Post soon realized that Weber's *Grenzhorizont* coincided with the beginning of his own last pollen period, the "sub-Atlantic climatic deterioration" when northern countries such as Germany and Sweden became cold and rainy. Refinements such as radiocarbon dating confirm von Post's deduction that Europe's climate took a turn for the worse about 600 B.C. The upland vegetation responded to the new conditions slowly—some plants thriving, others dying out—and the pollen count reflects this. But the bogs record a finer embroidery of moisture changes superimposed on the longer swings of temperature.

Human history has not been unrelated to these events. The decline of Greece and the rise of Rome clearly correlate with climatic change shortly after 600 B.C. The climate was somewhat

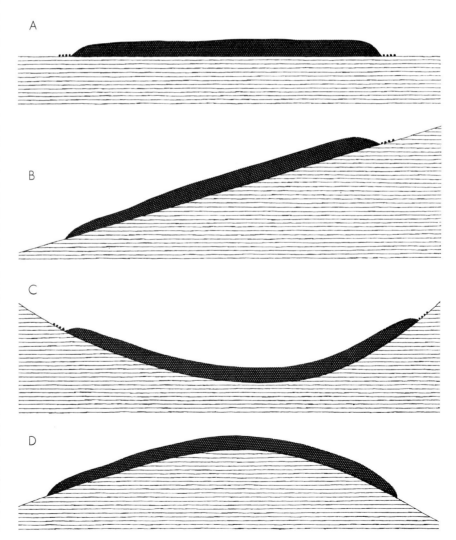

CREEPING BOGS rich in sphagnum can spread on flat land (A), uphill (B), in valleys (C) and on hills (D). The rows of dots indicate the ditch of water which bounds most bogs.

better when Rome's power was at its height, but Rome's conquest of Britain was given up, in part for climatic reasons, at the time of another change, about 400 A.D. As Gibbon put it, "The masters of the fairest and most wealthy climates on the globe turned with contempt . . . from the cold and lonely heaths over which the deer of the forest were chased by a troop of naked barbarians." Since that time, or at most since 600 B.C., the extraordinary blanket-bog has crept like a glacier down the slopes of the Irish and Scottish mountains, and down the Pennines in England, overwhelming pine forests and cropland alike. Today the British Isles are very different from the sunny, forested land the Neolithic farmers knew in the third millennium B.C. Already in the Middle Bronze Age (about 1200 B.C.) the bogs were getting out of hand. Wooden tracks were laid over the increasingly squishy countryside, in an effort to keep trade routes open. Such tracks, datable by pollen, by artifacts and by radiocarbon, often turn up when British bogs are dug.

Most of Europe's forests were cut down long ago. Peat is not so good a fuel as wood, but it will burn, and the heat can be used for distilling. Fortified with peat-smoke-flavored alcohol, a man can tolerate the sight of a treeless landscape and can even come to prefer a heath to a forest. The raised bogs have been drained and dug extensively in Ireland, Scotland, Denmark, western Scandinavia, northern Germany, and to a smaller extent in Maine and New Brunswick, where wood is more plentiful. As a fuel resource the peat bogs of the world are not to be despised. George Kazakov, a Russian peat expert now living in this country, computes that there are 223 billion dry tons of peat available on earth, more than half of it in the U.S.S.R.

So large a supply of combustible carbohydrate, delicately poised between growth and destruction, can seriously affect the earth's carbon balance. The carbon-dioxide content of air has increased by 11 per cent since about 1870 and apparently is still increasing. Radiocarbon assays by Hans Suess, now of the Scripps Institution of Oceanography prove that most of the added carbon dioxide is compounded of modern carbon. It is much too young, judging by its high radiocarbon content, to have all come from the burning of fossil fuels by industry. Fossil fuels can account for only a small portion of the increase. The rest of the new carbon dioxide must be modern, and a finger of suspicion points to bogs as the source.

The warming of the world's climate since the last century may well have set a slow fire to the peat, simply by favoring surface oxidation by soil bacteria. If the world's climate should become so warm and dry that all the peat is oxidized, about 366 billion tons of carbon dioxide would be released. This is a sixth of the amount now present in the atmosphere, and the whole reserve of carbon in land plants and animals is only 15 times as much. The estimate does not include the carbon of humus in ordinary soils which would also be oxidized if the climate changed. So it is not impossible that the carbon dioxide added to the earth's atmosphere may have come mainly from peat and humus.

Though the changes of climate and of the amount of carbon dioxide have run parallel, we cannot yet be sure which is cause and which effect. Carbon dioxide added to air causes it to absorb more heat from the sun, and it may be that the climate has become warmer because of the extra 11 per cent of "dephlogisticated air." If so, we may be in for trouble. A doubling in the carbon dioxide content of the air would almost certainly warm the climate enough to cause the glaciers to melt. The added water would raise the sea level perhaps by 100 feet, drowning the largest cities of the world. It may be that before such a calamity happens, a new balance will be struck; the carbon dioxide should be dissolved in the oceans, and it is a major mystery why the extra 11 per cent has not been dissolved already. But if the added carbon dioxide does not go into the oceans, New York and London will simply have to move, and the pixies too will need new haunts, for the bogs will be thin air.

32

THE LIFE OF A SAND DUNE

WILLIAM H. AMOS
July 1959

The region near the surface of these wind-driven hills can be an almost intolerably hot and arid environment, yet an entire community of plants and animals have become adapted to it

Few environments on earth are as hostile to life as a sand dune. The surface of a dune, heated by the midday sun, can reach a temperature of more than 150 degrees Fahrenheit. The same surface, baked by the sun and drained by the porosity of the sand, is almost perfectly arid. The very stuff of the surface is constantly shifted by the wind that both builds and destroys the dune. Yet wherever sand dunes occur, certain plants and animals take up residence and survive by remarkable evolutionary adaptations.

To people who live in the temperate zones the most familiar kind of dune is the foredune, a ridge of sand that rises behind an ocean beach. Sometimes a section of foredune will be blown inland, giving rise to the dramatic traveling dune. Such a dune can attain an im-

CROSS SECTION OF A DUNE is shown on this and the next three pages. The sand is hotter in a hollow because of the "condensing effect" (1). The bembecid wasp (10) repeatedly rises into the air to keep cool. Also shown are bayberry (2), American holly (3), wild black cherry (4), poison ivy (5), woodbine (6), meadow vole (7), cottontail rabbit (8), stork's-bill (9) and wire grass (11).

pressive rate of progress. The dunes of Cape Henlopen in southern Delaware once traveled 60 feet a year, overwhelming a historic lighthouse and its service buildings and then moving inland to inundate a forest. (The smaller buildings reappeared in a good state of preservation 50 years later.) It is on the life of the Cape Henlopen dunes that this article is largely based.

The fate of dunes and the fate of plants are inexorably drawn together. Certain plants (*e.g.,* marram grass, beach heather and sand cherry) flourish in sand. Once established on a dune, they are barriers to the wind; by slowing the wind and causing it to drop its freight of sand grains they hasten the growth of the dune. But as the dune grows the plants, if they are to survive, must grow with it. As a result certain shrubs often develop elongated stems. When the dune moves on, the plants left behind may have peculiar topknots of

foliage, if they can stand erect. More often their stems, no longer supported by the sand, simply topple over.

As a dune travels, it overwhelms the plants in its path. If a tree can keep enough of its foliage above the sand, it will survive. What appears to be a small pitch pine on the crest of a dune may actually be the upper branches of a 30-foot tree. Even if their growth is accelerated, however, most trees cannot keep pace with the rising sand; they are inundated and die. Years later their bare, gaunt forms reappear on the windward side of the dune. Meanwhile the buried trees may have provided a curious oasis for large numbers of minute organisms. When such trees have been located and excavated in the dunes of Cape Henlopen, they have been found to be thoroughly saturated with water. In the dead, wet tissues of the wood dwell roundworms, protozoa and bacteria. Usually a few larvae of wood-

boring beetles, and sometimes colonies of termites, can be found deep in the buried tree. Occasionally the wood feeds the mycelium of a fungus, and mushrooms erupt on the dune.

The plants of the dunes are marvelously adapted to their rigorous environment. Marram grass and other sand grasses appear to be modest surface dwellers, but their roots reach down several feet for water. Other plants with extensive water-seeking root systems are poison ivy, grape, stork's-bill and woodbine. Many successful dune plants, both annual and perennial, have a long taproot; some species (*e.g.,* wild lupine) which do not have a taproot in good soils will grow one when they settle on a dune. Usually these roots are not very sturdy; they descend like a string for 10 or 15 feet until they encounter a supply of water, and then they branch profusely. Because water is so scarce on the

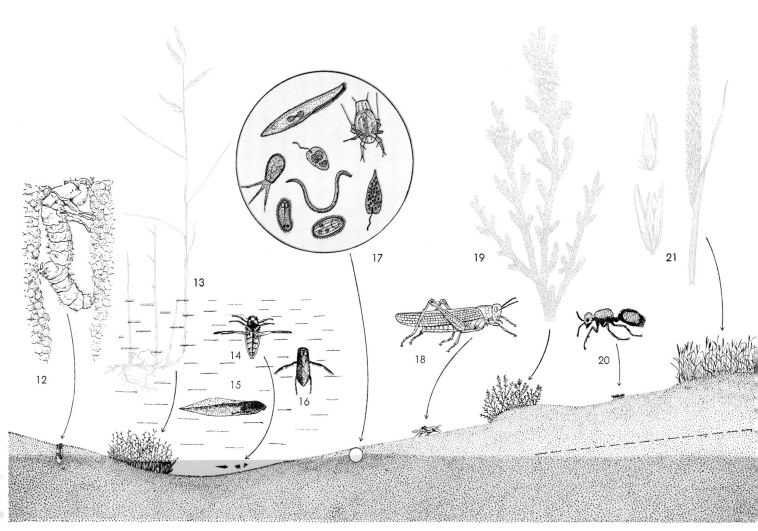

SECTION CONTINUED on these two pages contains a pool (*dark color*) where the level of the ground water (*light color*) is above the sand surface. The life near and in the water includes cord grass (13), back swimmer (14), the tadpole of Fowler's toad (15), water boatman (16). In pool or sand water are microscopic forms such as roundworms, copepods, protozoa and bacteria (17, 22).

dunes, such plants are seldom crowded: competition for water would jeopardize the survival of their species.

Plants that spread their foliage close to the dune surface usually have specialized leaves that minimize the effects of intense light and heat, either direct or reflected and radiated from the sand. Even when they are not related, such plants may have similar leaf structures because they share the common hazard of losing water by the evaporative process of transpiration. Dusty miller exemplifies those plants that have leaves densely covered with matted white fibers, which provide an effective insulation against light and heat. In other dune plants the waxy cuticle that covers a leaf is thickened. The leaves of beach heather are heavy and scalelike; those of western burroweed have relatively few stomate pores, thus reducing transpiration. In the common wire grass found in most sandy regions the expo-

sure of surface area is lessened by thick, heavy leaves with tightly folded blades. Some dune plants moderate the effects of heat and light with leaves that are held vertically rather than horizontally. Such leaves have symmetrical internal structures, so that both of their sides have the same capacity for photosynthesis.

There are plants such as the western white primrose that lose most of their leaves during a drought and grow new ones when the drought is over. Some plants have lost their leaves permanently. Of these leafless succulent plants one of the best known is the prickly-pear cactus, found throughout the coastal and southern regions of the U. S. This species has the remarkable ability to grow at a temperature as high as 136 degrees F.

Many dune plants are adapted to their environment not only by their anatomy and physiology but also by their life cycles. Dramatic examples of such

adaptation are provided by desert plants, the environment of which closely resembles that of dune plants. Seeds alone demonstrate the resistance of desert plants to heat and drought. E. B. Kurtz, Jr., of the University of Arizona found that seeds of the saguaro cactus, a plant common to the deserts of the U. S. Southwest, would still germinate after they had been subjected for seven days to a temperature of 181 degrees F. The seeds of many plants in deserts throughout the world germinate in winter and early spring when there is a sufficiency of water followed immediately by temperature conditions that favor growth. If seedlings are to survive, they must take advantage of these intervals and produce both roots that quickly arrive at a permanently moist stratum and hardy foliage that resists heat and light long enough to permit the plant to bloom and go to seed.

There are times in late winter and

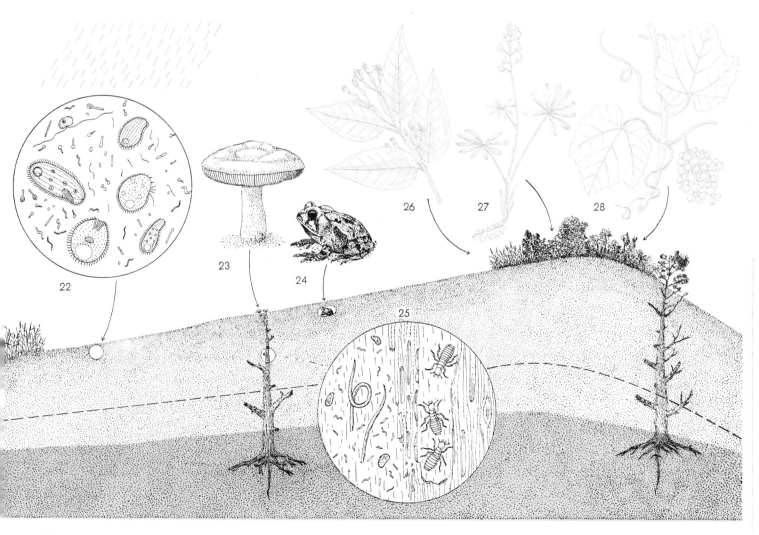

Wet wood of buried trees may also support the growth of mushrooms (23) and termites (25). Other animals of the dune are tiger beetle larva (12), grasshopper (18), Fowler's toad (24) and velvet ant (20). Plants include beach heather (19) and marram grass (21) on the windward slope; honeysuckle (26), wild lupine (27), grape (28), and the unburied tops of trees on the crest.

early spring when both deserts and dunes suddenly erupt with blossoms and foliage. In our western deserts, plants respond to an almost infinitesimal amount of rain, either by the germination of seed or the resuscitation of dying plants. Lloyd Tevis, Jr., of the California Institute of Technology recently reported that minimum conditions of rain and precipitation dramatically revived sand verbena, white primrose and desert gold. In the dunes of the eastern U. S. the common beach heather *Hudsonia* may seem to become entirely brittle and dry, yet will be restored to a brilliant green by a brief shower.

When we consider the distribution of plant species over an entire dune area, we see that the plant communities are divided into more or less distinct zones. In one zone there will be only a few grasses; in another there will be thicker cover vegetation; in another,

trees will predominate. This zonation, as the ecologist terms it, can be understood as a sequence of events at a particular spot. First the raw, new dune is invaded by sand-loving grasses. Later, as the dune is stabilized by plants, it passes through various stages of cover vegetation. Finally a permanent "climax" community develops on the sand, which now can no longer be called a dune.

Dunes are also characterized by another kind of zonation. This is evident in the distribution and growth of both plants and animals, and is due chiefly to the vertical stratification of temperature. At noon on a summer day the temperature stratification, from top to bottom, is roughly as follows: warm air, hot air, exceedingly hot surface, hot sand, warm sand, cool sand. The highest surface temperature on the dunes of Cape Henlopen is about 125 degrees F.; in French Equatorial Africa a surface temperature of 183 degrees has been recorded. Natu-

rally the temperature varies considerably with the season, the time of day, the wind, the humidity, the clarity of the atmosphere, the color of the sand and the configuration of the dune. A hollow in the sand, for example, will concentrate the sun's rays, and considerably raise the temperature. It is not simply due to the absence of wind that a hollow in a dune feels hot.

Each of the stratified temperature zones can be a favored environment for a specific animal, at least during part of the animal's life. The animal population of the dunes is almost entirely limited to joint-footed arthropods such as insects, and vertebrates such as mice. Notably absent are animals with moist skins, such as worms and amphibians. The dune vertebrates generally come out of their burrows only at night, so it is the insects that are most evident by day.

Only a few of the insects dwell directly on the hot surface. Of these the

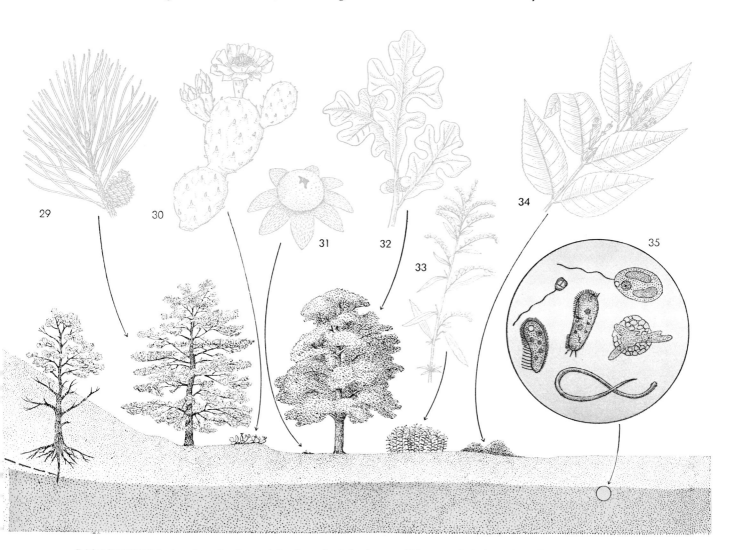

LAST SECTION is the advancing front of the dune. A pitch pine (29) lies in the path; another is already partly buried. In this region, which is quite sandy, grow prickly-pear cactus (30), earth stars (31), post oak (32), goldenrod (33) and honeysuckle (34). Here the sand water again contains roundworms and protozoa (35). Nighthawks, owls, mice, rabbits and opossum also live in this region.

most conspicuous is the so-called velvet ant, which is actually a species of wasp in which the females are wingless. Velvet ants are covered with dense, colored hair which protects them against light and heat. They can be found coursing about the sand on extremely hot days, but as the surface temperature approaches 120 degrees they seek shelter in the shade of plants. This horizontal migration to a tolerable microclimate is also used by a number of other dune animals.

Certain beetles seek a comfortable environment by vertical migration, moving up and down the stems of plants as the heat increases and decreases. A sand-dwelling grasshopper can solve the heat problem temporarily by extending its long legs, thus raising its body into a perceptibly cooler stratum of air. From time to time it flies a few feet, and is further cooled while it is aloft. Predatory tiger beetles, bee flies and robber flies alight briefly on the hot sand; they are cooled as they range about above the dunes in search of food.

Of all the insects that spend part of their lives on the surface and rise into the air to cool off, none is more easily observed (or has been more thoroughly studied) than the bembecid, or digger wasp. The problem of the bembecid is this: Because it hunts other insects by sight, it must dig its small burrow and provision it during the hottest hours of the day. But the bembecid is not insulated with hair like the velvet ant; it is quite susceptible to overheating. If a bembecid is experimentally restrained at the hot surface, it will rapidly succumb to heat stupor. Accordingly it solves the heat problem by behavior.

A bembecid will hover in the air, descend almost vertically to the site of its burrow and dig like a terrier with its curved front feet. It does so only for a moment, leaving a small depression and an apron of sand. It now rises a foot or more in the air, where the temperature is at least 10 degrees lower. It hovers briefly, then drops down to resume its excavation. This happens repeatedly, until the hole is deep enough for the wasp to enter. When the burrow extends below the high-temperature zone of the surface, the bembecid remains in the relative coolness of the burrow to complete its digging and lay its eggs. Some burrows collapse before they are finished and must be redug or abandoned; when they are successfully made they extend several inches into the side of the

ADVANCING FRONT OF DUNE on Cape Henlopen in southern Delaware has covered all but the tops of these trees. If enough foliage remains above the sand, a tree can survive.

BACK OF THE DUNE on Cape Henlopen the dead remains of trees reappear as the sand which covered them moves on. This dune at one time traveled at the rate of 60 feet a year.

TRACK OF A SNAKE found in the early morning is evidence of the night-life on the sand. Many dune animals, particularly vertebrates, are only active during nocturnal hours.

dune and retain their shape in spite of the looseness of the sand.

Many insects spend a part of their lives not on the surface but immediately below it. The voracious larva of the tiger beetle dwells in a vertical burrow and seizes insects that blunder across the entrance. Another larva that lives in the subsurface zone is the ant lion, which faces away from the sun at the bottom of a conical pit. When an insect tumbles into the pit, the larva backs deeper into the sand and tosses up a shower of sand grains with its head. The sand falls about the rim of the pit and cascades down, carrying the scrambling insect with it. The prey is seized with large, sickle-shaped jaws, dragged beneath the surface, paralyzed by means of a fluid that also liquefies the inner tissues, and is sucked dry. Despite the formidable behavior of its larva, the adult form of the ant lion is a weak, graceful insect. After it has developed and emerged from its pit, it survives only long enough to mate and (in the case of the female) deposit its eggs in the loose sand under a shrub.

If the dry surface sand of a dune is examined under the microscope, there are a few indications of life; but when the sand is saturated with rain, even for a brief period, a bustling population of tiny organisms appears and pursues a short, vigorous existence. One-celled protozoans, some of them resembling the familiar Paramecium, emerge from an encysted state. They feed upon bacteria that have been similarly activated from resistant spores. Round worms may also hatch from eggs. The ability to remain dormant is well developed in these small creatures of the dune surface; water may be absent for extended periods, but when it is present they emerge, feed, grow and reproduce—veritable Rip van Winkles of the dune world.

The specializations of dune animals vary in detail, but all are directed toward enabling the animal to resist heat and desiccation. Consider desiccation alone: If the water content of an animal is to remain constant, the water gain must equal the water loss—a delicate balance not easy to maintain in the arid environment of the dunes. Fortunately animals have the capacity to obtain water not only by drinking but also by oxidizing foodstuff. In the insects and rodents that feed upon the grasses of the dunes this capacity is developed to a high degree; they obtain some moisture from the grasses but fill a substantial fraction of their water need by metabolic processes. Some rodents of the desert, such as the kangaroo rat and the pocket mouse, eat seeds that have no appreciable moisture content, and obtain virtually all of their water from their metabolism [see "The Desert Rat," by Knut and Bodil Schmidt-Nielsen; SCIENTIFIC AMERICAN Offprint 1050].

Most dune animals are obliged not only to conserve or manufacture water but also to lose it by evaporation in order to cool themselves. In this way a dune insect can actually reduce its temperature below that of the surrounding air. It achieves this remarkable result by energetic ventilation of its tracheal breathing system. An increase in the temperature of the air can paradoxically decrease the relative temperature of the insect, because the insect's metabolism will be accelerated by the temperature increase. But the two factors—heat and evaporation—eventually work against each other; if the insect evaporates too much water, and cannot replenish its supply, its activity decreases until it falls into heat stupor and dies.

Many animals of the dunes are light in color, a phenomenon which has given rise to certain speculations. Light coloration is due to the lack of melanin, the dark pigment found in most animals. Melanin is formed in the presence of oxygen by an enzyme acting upon a colorless substance, the chromogen; its synthesis is enhanced at relatively low temperatures and suppressed in hot environments. This phenomenon has been demonstrated in the wasp *Habrobracon* and the bug *Perillus*; it is a matter of significance to the dune ecologist, although neither insect is a resident of dunes. There are a number of other factors that influence such coloration: A moist environment, for example, causes certain butterflies and grasshoppers to become darker, and an arid environment has the opposite effect. So some light-colored insects seem to be affected by the environment, while others remain pale for generations regardless of external conditions, resembling in this respect the colorless animals of caves. Coloration in insects and higher animals is not a simple affair; it may not only be dependent on external and internal factors, but also involves pigments other than melanin. The fact remains that the significant conditions of the dune environment—heat and aridity—produce pale insects in the laboratory, and may have the same effect on other animals.

Light colors that blend with sand are seen in a great many (but not all) grass-

LARVA OF THE TIGER BEETLE waits in the bottom of its vertical burrow (*seen here in a cutaway view*) to seize and eat any insects that blunder across the mouth of its lair.

ANT LION, another insect-eating larva that lives in the subsurface zone, seizes its prey with its large sickle-shaped jaws. The adult of this larva is a weak, short-lived insect.

hoppers, tiger beetles, spiders, reptiles, birds and mammals in dunes and deserts the world over. This characteristic presumably favors the survival of the animals by making them hard to see in daylight. It is an odd fact that light colors are also found in many nocturnal dune animals, which would not seem to need this protective device. It may be that the production of melanin in these animals that do not emerge in daylight is affected by the conduction of heat from the surface of the sand. (Aridity should not have an important role, since burrows that descend even a few inches are comparatively humid.)

On the other hand, light coloration may protect the nocturnal animal more than we think. In moonlight, or even on moonless nights, predators might be able to see a dark-colored animal against the sand more clearly than they could perceive a light-colored one. There is another possibility, though it is probably rather remote. Cold-blooded animals that are light in color do not absorb heat from the sand as readily as do similar animals that are dark. It is known that rattlesnakes can locate their prey with sensory organs that are extraordinarily sensitive to heat radiation. Could other predators hunt in the same way? It is probable that there is no single explanation for the pale coloration of animals in dunes and deserts; rather, a number of unrelated influences seem to lead to the same result.

The burrows of the animals that emerge at night or during the twilight hours usually extend deep below the surface of the dune. Most of the burrows are inhabited by the animals that excavated them, but some have been taken over by new occupants not capable of extensive digging. During the day the dune mice remain in their cool, humid tunnels; large predatory spiders rest quietly at the bottom of burrows that go down two feet or more; ants cluster and work in their galleries.

Although the dune ants may emerge only for brief periods at twilight, they are among the most successful residents of dunes. This success is due to the ease with which they excavate tunnels deep in the sand (some ants have special sand-carrying structures on their heads) and to the fact that they limit their activities to times when the surface temperature is moderate. The twilight activity of the dune is perhaps greater than either the nocturnal or the diurnal. Early in the morning the sand is etched with the tracks and trails, the signs of pursuit and capture, left by animals abroad in the gray hours before dawn. It is only from this record, soon to be erased by the wind, that one can gain full realization of the intense animal activity of the dunes.

What is it that induces nocturnal and crepuscular animals to migrate up and down at the appropriate time? One species of carabid beetle is as abundant on the surface of the dunes at night as the bembecid wasp is during the day. Other beetles, not necessarily residents of dunes, have been observed to remain head-up in the soil until twilight, at which time they emerge and fly away. In a recent issue of the journal *Ecology* George G. Gyrisco and W. G. Evans of Cornell University report their observations of how light triggers the twilight emergence of the European chafer, a member of the beetle family. It is a certain intensity of light that stimulates the chafer—an intensity characteristic of the twilight hours. Such environmental stimuli may also account for the vertical migration of dune animals. Many animals, however, are known to have inborn rhythms of behavior, and these "biological clocks" may provide an alternative explanation.

There is one dune population that never comes to the surface—the so-called sand-water organisms. That sand-water is an environment in itself was recognized some years ago by Robert W. Pennak of the University of Colorado and the late C. B. Wilson of the Massachusetts State Normal School, who found a considerable assortment of tiny organisms in the saturated upper levels of beaches adjacent to both salt and fresh water. Some species of this fauna appeared to be migrants from open waters, but others were adapted and restricted to wet sands. Investigations at Cape Henlopen and elsewhere indicate that the sand-water fauna is even more abundant than heretofore believed.

One of the most curious animals found in the sand-water environment is an elongated crustacean, related to the planktonic shrimp found swimming in surface waters all over the world. Such relatively large sand-water animals are most abundant in sand near visible surface water. But whenever we have sent cores into the Cape Henlopen dunes and collected water we have found an abundant smaller fauna: roundworms, ciliated protozoa, bacteria. And among them are occasional representatives of larger organisms such as rotifers, gastrotrichs, tartigrades and insect larvae.

The extent of the sand-water environment may even now be underestimated; though the surface of a dune is arid, its interior can contain large quantities of water. Because sand is porous, water circulates freely through it and does not stagnate. This movement can be due to surface evaporation, which causes a slow upward capillary flow; to rainfall, which causes a more rapid downward flow; or to the slope of the water table, which causes a lateral flow. Under a dune the water table bulges upward; it is this copious reservoir that supplies water to the deeper plant roots and constitutes the principal habitat of the sand-water organisms.

Despite their abundance, the sand-water animals probably play only a small role in the biological economy of a dune. This is because they are isolated from predators that dwell in the intermediate or surface levels. The surface layers of a dune are above all a world of predation. In most other environments the pyramid of life is based upon great numbers of plants, which are eaten by herbivores, which in turn are eaten by relatively few carnivores. In the dunes plant life is relatively scarce, so the carnivores must prey largely on one another.

The bembecid wasp is a case in point. Bembecids prey upon weak or weakened insects, but the bembecids themselves are prey. In her rapid, gyrating travels across the surface of the dune, the female velvet ant descends into the burrows containing bembecid larvae and lays her eggs. When the eggs hatch, the velvet-ant larvae feed upon the immature bembecids. Certain bee flies parasitize velvet ants, and robber flies have been observed to capture bee flies. When they are dead, any of these insects may be taken off by bembecids. Thus the bembecids, though they are predators themselves, provide the basis for the existence of a variety of predators. Of course such a pyramid must ultimately rest upon herbivores and plants, but in the dunes the pyramid has a narrow base, and the animal population is sharply limited.

The harsh environment of a dune is a transitory thing. The dune must drift on, and when it is finally anchored by vegetation it gradually fades into gray, humus-laden sand. It exists through successive populations of animals and covering grasses, shrubs, pines and climax hardwoods until only its vague contour is left. But elsewhere other dunes arise and creep across the land. Changing and changeless, the dunes provide an environment in which the almost infinite adaptability of living organisms is dramatically demonstrated.

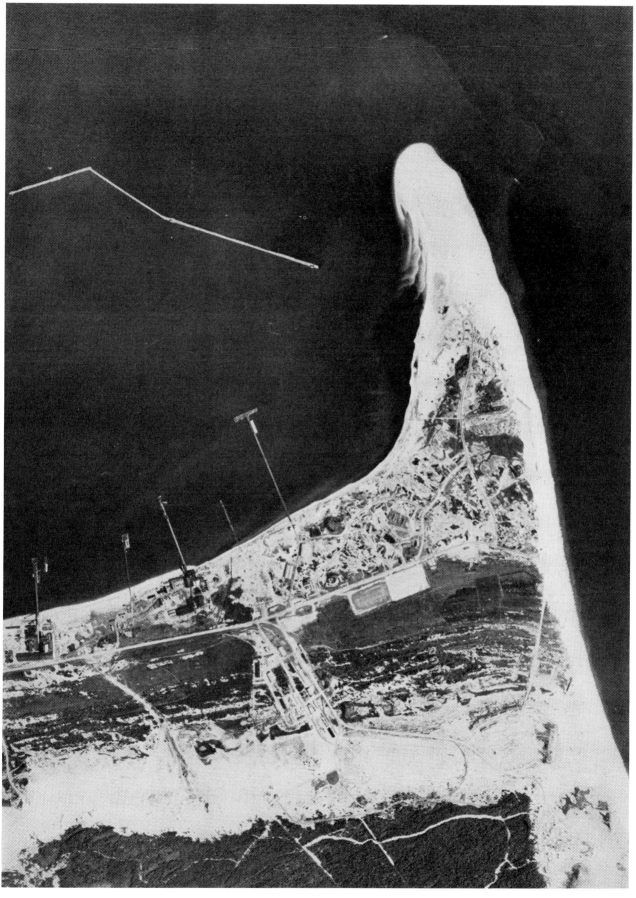

CAPE HENLOPEN is backed by a great sand dune (*light strip in the lower part of this aerial photograph*). The moving sand has started to cover a forest (*at the bottom of the photograph*), and vegetation has grown up in the region left behind (*dark strip above dune*). The body of water to the left of the promontory is Delaware Bay; to the right is the Atlantic Ocean.

33

THE ECOLOGY OF FIRE

CHARLES F. COOPER
April 1961

Fire has played a major role in shaping the world's grasslands and forests. Attempts to eliminate it have introduced problems fully as serious as those created by accidental conflagrations

Before Europeans came to North America, fires periodically swept over virtually every acre on the continent that had anything to burn. Along with climate, soil, topography and animal life, these conflagrations helped shape the pattern of vegetation that covered the land.

Civilization brought a tendency to regard fire as pure disaster, together with massive efforts to exclude fire completely from forest and grassland. The attempts frequently succeeded all too well. Over wide regions the pattern of plant life has changed, but not always in a way that users of the land could wish. Paradoxically, in some forest areas fire prevention has greatly increased the destructiveness of subsequent fires.

There is evidence that natural fires have occurred over most of the earth for thousands of years. Buried layers of charcoal testify to prehistoric fires. Historical writings mention great conflagrations witnessed by men. In the narratives of the explorers of North America are numerous accounts of traveling for days through smoke from distant fires, and of passing through burned-over prairies and woodlands.

Tree trunks in forested areas contain a record of past fires. A moderately intense fire often kills an area on one side of a tree, leaving the rest of the tree unharmed. As new layers of tissue grow over the dead spot, they count off the years since the fire. Examining freshly cut stumps of large redwoods, the California forester Emanuel Fritz found evidence of about four fires a century during the 1,100-year history of the stand. The figure is probably conservative, because there must have been many fires not severe enough to leave scars. In the ponderosa pine forests of California and Arizona, fire scars indicate an average of one burning every eight years.

Many forest fires are started by lightning; on the prairies rain immediately extinguishes lightning-set grass fires. Most prehistoric fires were undoubtedly the work of man.

Notwithstanding the popular conception, American Indians were not cautious in using fire. They did not conscientiously put out camp fires nor, unless their villages were threatened, did they try to keep fires from spreading. Often they burned intentionally—to drive game in hunting, as an offensive or defensive measure in warfare, or merely to keep the forest open to travel. A contemporary history of the Massachusetts Bay Colony, dated 1632, relates that "the Salvages are accustomed to set fire of the country in all places where they come; and to burn it twize a year, vixe, at the Spring, and at the fall of the leafe. The reason that moves them to do so, is because it would be otherwise so overgrown with underweedes that it would all be a copice wood, and the people could not be able in any wise to passe through the country out of a beaten path."

In open country fire favors grass over shrubs. Grasses are better adapted to withstand fire than are woody plants. The growing point of dormant grasses,

FIRE MAINTAINS GRASSLAND by holding back spread of mesquite (*shown here*) and other shrubs, which originally constitute small part of vegetation (*a*) but which soon proliferate and reduce areas available to grass (*b*). Fire (*c*) reduces grasses and shrubs alike, but

from which issues the following year's growth, lies near or beneath the ground, protected from all but the severest heat. A grass fire removes only one year's growth, and usually much of this is dried and dead. The living tissue of shrubs, on the other hand, stands well above the ground, fully exposed to fire. When it is burned, the growth of several years is destroyed. Even though many shrubs sprout vigorously after burning, repeated loss of their top growth keeps them small. Perennial grasses, moreover, produce seeds in abundance one or two years after germination; most woody plants require several years to reach seed-bearing age. Fires that are frequent enough to inhibit seed production in woody plants usually restrict the shrubs to a relatively minor part of the grassland area.

Most ecologists believe that a substantial portion of North American grasslands owe their origin and maintenance to fire. Some disagree, arguing that climate is the deciding factor and fire has had little influence. To be sure, some areas, such as the Great Plains of North America, are too dry for most woody plants, and grasses persist there without fire. In other places, for example the grass-covered Palouse Hills of the southeastern part of the state of Washington, the soil is apparently unsuited to shrub growth, although the climate is favorable. But elsewhere—in the desert grasslands of the Southwest and the prairies of the Midwest—periodic fires must have tipped the vegetation equilibrium toward grasses.

Large parts of these grasslands are now being usurped by such shrubs as mesquite, juniper, sagebrush and scrub oak. Mesquite alone has spread from its former place along stream channels and on a few upland areas until now it occupies about 70 million acres of former grassland. Many ecologists and land managers blame the shrub invasion entirely on domestic livestock; they argue that overgrazing has selectively weakened the grasses and allowed the less palatable shrubs to increase. These explanations do not suffice; even on plots fenced off from animals shrubs continue to increase. A decrease in the frequency of fires is almost surely an essential part of the answer.

Fire has played an equally decisive role in many forests. A good example is found in the forests of jack pine that now spread in a broad band across Michigan, Wisconsin and Minnesota. When lumbermen first entered this region, they found little jack pine; the forests consisted chiefly of hardwood trees and white pines that towered above the general forest canopy. The loggers singled out the white pines for cutting, considering the other species worthless. Their activities were usually followed by fires, accidental or intentional. Supported by the dry debris of logging, the fires became holocausts that killed practically all the remaining vegetation. The mixed forest had little chance to regenerate; even the seeds of most trees were destroyed. But those of the jack pine survived. Unlike most pine cones, which drop off and release their seeds in the fall, jack pine cones stay closed and remain attached to the tree, sometimes so firmly that branches grow right around them. Inside the cones the seeds remain viable for years. When the cones are heated, as in a forest fire, they slowly open and release their seeds. Thus the fires simultaneously eliminated the seeds of competing species and provided an abundant supply of jack pine seed together with a bed of ash that is ideal for germination. The result of the process is a pure stand of jack pine.

The valuable Douglas fir forests of the Pacific Northwest also owe their origin to fire. This species requires full sunlight; it cannot grow in the dense shade cast by a mature fir forest. When old Douglas firs die, their place is taken not by new Douglas firs but by cedars and hemlocks, more tolerant of shade, which therefore constitute the "climax" vegetation of the region. Forest fires, however, arrest the succession by creating openings in the forest into which the light, winged seeds of Douglas firs can fly from adjacent stands. The seedlings

while growing point of grass lies near or beneath ground (*root system at right in "c"*) and is left unharmed, buds and growing tissue of shrub stand fully exposed and are destroyed. Balance is further tipped toward grasses (*d*) because they produce abundant seed a year or two after germination; as a result they lose only one or two years' growth in fire. Shrubs lose several years' growth.

ORIGINAL FORESTS of Great Lakes region were of mixed hard-woods, some jack pines (*at right in* "*a*") and white pines (*middle distance and background*). Early loggers cut white pines and left other species standing (*jack pine cone is in foreground of*

take advantage of the sunlight in the openings: they flourish and top competing vegetation; ultimately they grow into pure stands of uniform age.

Jack pine and Douglas fir are dependent on fire for their establishment but cannot endure frequent burning thereafter. In other forests fire is a normal part of the environment during the whole life of the stand. The longleaf pine of the southeastern U. S. is a striking example. This species is almost ideally adapted to recurring fires.

Unlike most pines, the young longleaf does not grow uniformly after germination. The seedling reaches a height of a few inches in a few weeks. Then it stops growing upward and sprouts a grasslike ring of long drooping needles that surrounds the stem and terminal bud. During this so-called grass stage, which usually lasts from three to seven years, the plant's growth processes are concentrated in forming a deep and extensive root system and in storing food reserves.

Longleaf pine is easily shaded out by

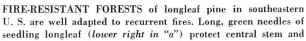

FIRE-RESISTANT FORESTS of longleaf pine in southeastern U. S. are well adapted to recurrent fires. Long, green needles of seedling longleaf (*lower right in* "*a*") protect central stem and bud against surface fires that burn out forest debris and saplings of competing hardwoods (*middle distance and background in* "*b*"). Rapid vertical growth of tree after seedling stage carries

"b"). Debris of logging supported holocausts that consumed remaining vegetation. Although jack pines were destroyed, their cones survived and released seeds (c). Seedling jack pines (d) grew in fertile ashes, giving rise to pure jack pine stands today (e).

competing hardwoods and is susceptible to a serious blight known as brown spot. The brown spot fungus multiplies during the dry summer, and the autumn rains splash its spores onto the needles of the low seedlings. Unless overtopping vegetation is cleared away and brown spot is controlled, the young pines may remain in the grass stage indefinitely.

One of America's first professional foresters, H. H. Chapman of Yale University, perceived in the early 1920's that periodic fires were essential to the life of longleaf pine. Protected by its canopy of needles, the longleaf seedling can withstand heat that kills the above-ground portions of competing hardwoods and grasses. At the same time the

flames consume dry needles infected with brown spot, destroying the principal source of fungus spores. After the young pine emerges from the grass stage, its phenomenal growth—often four to six feet a year for the first two or three years—quickly carries the buds beyond the reach of surface fires. The thick, corky bark of the sapling protects its

vulnerable bud beyond reach of bigger fires (c); thickening bark affords increasing insulation for delicate cambium against hotter fires. At the same time the tree drops more needles, supporting hotter fires that clear out larger saplings (d). Self-governing mechanism keeps forest open (e). Illustrations follow single tree from seedling ("a" and "b") to sapling ("c" and "d") to maturity (e).

sensitive growing tissue. As the tree grows and the bark thickens, it becomes resistant to any but the most intense fires.

Largely at Chapman's urging, prescribed fire has become an accepted management tool in the southeastern longleaf pine forests. Before a stand is harvested a fire is run through during the dry summer, when it will burn fairly hot. This clears out most of the undergrowth without killing the trees and prepares a good seedbed. The old trees are cut during the following winter, after the seeds have fallen. About three winters later, when burning conditions permit only a relatively cool fire and the seedlings have entered the grass stage, the area is burned again. Fires at regular three-year intervals thereafter keep down the worthless scrub oaks and help control brown spot. They hold back the normal succession, which would lead to a climax oak-hickory forest. Moreover, a regime of periodic fires reduces the accumulation of dry fuel on the ground that might otherwise lead to an uncontrollable holocaust.

My own work has dealt with the ponderosa pine forests of the Southwest. As

PRIMEVAL DOUGLAS FIR FORESTS of western U. S. have origin in fires of previous centuries. Young Douglas firs, which are intolerant of shade, cannot grow beneath mature Douglas fir forest (a), yield to cedars and hemlocks, which make up the climax

REPLACEMENT OF DOUGLAS FIRS by hardwoods is in part attributable to exclusion of fire. Cedar and hemlock saplings (a), unlike young Douglas firs, grow well in shade of mature Douglas fir forest, take over as older firs die (b). As cedar and hemlock

19th-century chronicles attest, they used to be open, parklike forests arranged in a mosaic of discrete groups, each containing 10 to 30 trees of a common age. Small numbers of saplings were dispersed among the mature pines, and luxuriant grasses carpeted the forest floor. Fires, when they occurred, were easily controlled and seldom killed a whole stand. Foresters in other regions envied the men assigned to the "asbestos forests" of the Southwest.

Today dense thickets of young trees have sprung up everywhere in the forests. The grass has been reduced, and dry branches and needles have accumulated to such an extent that any fire is likely to blow up into an inferno that will destroy everything in its path. Foresters have generally blamed the overproduction of trees on a period of unusually favorable weather conditions, or on removal of competing grasses and exposure of bare soil through past trampling and grazing by domestic animals. But it is becoming increasingly apparent that a vigorous policy of fire exclusion, too long followed, is at least partly responsible.

vegetation of the region. Succession was interrupted by frequent small fires that burned out cedar and hemlock trees (b). Douglas fir seeds from adjacent stands blew into new openings (c), grew well in seedbed of ashes and became pure stands of Douglas fir (d).

trees grow (c), they diminish remaining opportunities for Douglas fir seedlings to survive. Climax vegetation that results is composed of cedar and hemlock (d). These illustrations, like those on preceding and following pages, are drawn from same point of view.

Lightning is frequent in the ponderosa pine region, and the Indians set many fires there. Tree rings show that the forests used to burn regularly at intervals of three to 10 years. The mosaic pattern of the forest has developed under the influence of recurrent light fires. Each even-aged group springs up in an opening left by the death of a predecessor.

(After remaining intact for 300 years or more, groups break up quite suddenly— often in less than 20 years.) The first fire that passes through consumes the dead trees, and leaves a good seedbed of ash and mineral soil, into which seed drifts from surrounding trees. Young ponderosa seedlings cannot withstand even a light surface fire, but in the new-

ly seeded opening they are protected by the lack of dry pine needles to fuel such fires. Consequently the young stand escapes burning for the first few years. Eventually the saplings drop enough needles to support a light surface fire, which kills many smaller saplings but leaves most of the larger ones alive. The roots of the survivors quickly appropri-

PARKLIKE PONDEROSA PINE FORESTS of Southwest were typically a mosaic of even-aged groups (*mature stand in middle distance of "a"; young stand in background*). Frequent fires kept forest debris from accumulating (*b*); thus the fires were mild and created openings for seedlings (*c*), which cannot grow in shade. As new trees matured, they dropped more needles, providing more fuel for hotter fires, which killed new seedlings (*d*). Mosaic and parklike character of the forest was thereby maintained.

ate the soil made vacant, and their growth is stimulated.

The degree of thinning accomplished by a fire depends upon the quantity of fuel on the ground. The denser the sapling stand, the more needles it drops and the hotter the fire it will support. The process is thus a sort of self-regulating feedback mechanism governed by the density of the stand. Thinning by fire is less efficient than the forester might wish, but it does help to prevent the stagnation resulting from extreme over-crowding.

As a group of trees grows toward maturity, new seedlings germinate beneath it. The volume of dry fuel dropped by the older trees, however, supports fires hot enough to eradicate the seedlings entirely. Fire and shade together prevent younger trees from developing; the even-aged character of the group is maintained throughout its life.

Wild-land managers have historically, and properly, concentrated on suppressing accidental fires in forests and grasslands and on discouraging deliber-

CLUTTERED PONDEROSA PINE FORESTS (a), in contrast to those illustrated on page 8, result from the elimination of the periodic fires that occurred naturally. Saplings that would have been thinned out by fire now vie for space in the formerly open avenues between trees, the grass cover is reduced and forest debris and undergrowth have accumulated to the point (b) that fires that formerly would have been mild and easily controlled often explode into holocausts (c) that destroy the entire stand of trees (d).

ate overburning by man. While fire may favor the establishment of jack pine forests, the annual burning long practiced in the South will prevent the growth of any forest at all. By the same token, occasional fires may be needed to maintain African grasslands, but deliberately set- ting fire to the country every few months has unquestionably damaged them seriously. In many cases the time has come to relax the ingrained prejudices against fire and to utilize it, judiciously, as a tool in the management of both forests and grasslands.

SEROTINOUS JACK PINE CONES resist fire (*top*). Unlike other pine cones, which open and release their seeds in the fall, jack pine cones open after being heated (*bottom*).

34

LIFE ON THE HUMAN SKIN

MARY J. MARPLES
January 1969

The skin is an ecosystem, with a microscopic flora and fauna and diverse ecological niches: the desert of the forearm, the cool woods of the scalp and the tropical forest of the armpit.

When someone is told that his skin supports a large population of microorganisms, he may look a bit uneasy and respond that he takes a shower every morning. His unease will scarcely be lessened by the information that showering or bathing, which washes away some of the skin, exposes microorganisms hidden in its crevices and therefore increases the total population on the skin surface. The mere thought may well induce involuntary scratching.

If, on the other hand, one considers the skin from the standpoint of its natural inhabitants rather than in terms of the appearance, comfort and defense mechanisms of the human host, a fascinating world comes into view. The skin is then seen as a kind of soil with attributes that are beneficial or harmful for the organisms it supports. This environment and the populations that live in it form an ecosystem, a discrete world whose living and nonliving components, all interacting with one another, exist in equilibrium.

Strictly speaking there is only one ecosystem, the ecosystem of the entire earth, but in ecology (which studies the mutual relations between organisms and their environment) localized areas such as a desert, a forest, a pond or a stream are treated as being independent. The skin of course differs from the inorganic substrate of terrestrial ecosystems. Whereas the earth's crust is composed of solid minerals, the nonliving surface of the skin is constantly renewed from below and is supplied with glandular secretions. The skin is nonetheless uniquely qualified to serve as an ecosystem. An enormous amount of information has been gathered concerning its structure and function; indeed, the characteristics of the human skin are probably better

understood than those of any other naturally inhabited area. Furthermore, the cutaneous fauna and flora are readily accessible. Repeated sampling does not lead to any permanent change in their population structure, and most of the cutaneous species can be grown in the laboratory.

In spite of these obvious advantages investigations into cutaneous ecology have been sporadic and have been mainly concerned with the pathogenic, or disease-causing, species. Only recently have studies been undertaken of the natural cutaneous organisms, microbes that are harmless or even beneficial and that live in large numbers on the skin of most human beings. Some of these organisms are potential pathogens; although they are harmless on the skin surface, they may cause disease if they penetrate the deeper cutaneous layers. The study of skin ecology is thus essential to the control of skin and wound infections, and it may also help to elucidate problems that classical ecology has failed to solve. In what follows I shall outline the information about the natural cutaneous world that is currently available by considering the questions: What is this world like? What lives there? What happens when a newcomer arrives?

The surface of the skin is a distinctly unstable environment for the organisms that live on it. The most superficial cutaneous layer, the stratum corneum (horny layer), consists of flat, scalelike "squames" made up of the fibrous protein keratin. The squames are continuously replaced from below by epidermal cells that die in the process of manufacturing keratin, and during the host's various activities the squames are always being shed. From the viewpoint of a microorganism on the skin the

squames are enormous flat boulders of inert material, boulders that suddenly curl up and float away, bearing with them any organism that happens to be aboard.

The uneven surface of the cutaneous world is pierced at intervals by two types of orifice. One is the duct of the eccrine sweat gland, a spring from which oozes a weak saline solution containing a small quantity of nitrogenous substances and other nutrients. The flow from the gland varies and the solution evaporates, so that in some ways the conditions resemble those of a pool at the edge of the sea, with its frequent changes of water level and salinity.

The other cutaneous opening is the hair follicle, a cylindrical infolding of the skin from which projects the hair, a tall tree trunk of hard keratin. The hair follicle exudes sebum, which is manufactured by the sebaceous glands. Sebum is a complex secretion containing a high proportion of lipids, or fatty substances. It mixes with sweat and spreads over the epidermal surface adjacent to the hair follicle. Sweat glands and hair follicles are not evenly distributed over the body but vary in size and density. These variations, together with other factors, confer a special character on certain areas of the skin. For example, the axilla, or armpit, is provided with coarse hairs that receive secretions from specialized structures, the apocrine sweat glands. The external canal of the ear has glands that produce ear wax, and the palm of the hand and the sole of the foot have many sweat glands but are without hair follicles.

The glandular secretions and the byproducts of the process that forms keratin provide free amino acids as nutrients for the inhabitants of the skin. Carbohydrates in a readily available state and

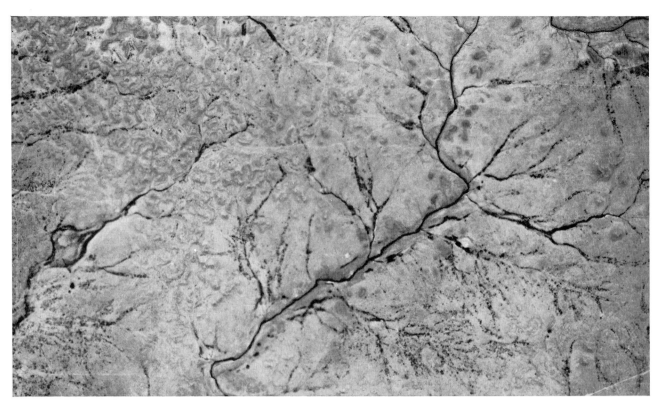

TERRAIN OF AN ARID GRASSLAND, a typical ecosystem on the surface of the earth, appears in this aerial photograph of an area in northwestern Texas. The principal feature of the terrain is the stream valleys, which support a somewhat denser vegetation.

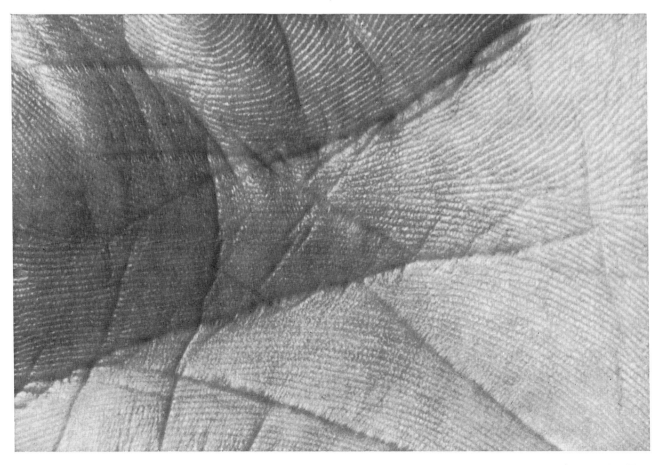

TERRAIN OF THE HUMAN SKIN is seen in this photograph of part of the palm of the hand. The palm and the sole of the foot differ from other areas of the skin in that they have no hair follicles. Thus they support a somewhat different population of microorganisms.

certain of the vitamins appear to be less abundant, but there is no direct evidence that they are in inadequate supply. The climate of the skin is pleasantly warm and is subject to little variation, except on the feet. The temperature and the water supply are favorable for microbial growth, although for many species the slight acidity of the skin is something of a handicap.

Let us now consider the species that are likely to be found on healthy, undamaged skin. The ecologist Eugene P. Odum divided the living members of a classical ecosystem into three main groups: the producers (chiefly green plants that utilize solar energy to manufacture organic substances out of inorganic ones), the consumers (animals that derive their energy directly or indirectly from plants) and the decomposers (mainly fungi and bacteria that break down dead plants and animals and thus return the essential elements to the soil substrate). To what extent are these physiological groups represented on the skin? There are no true producers; the host himself is the great producer. The microorganisms live, as Adam and Eve did, in a paradise where all their needs are supplied. There is only one animal consumer, the follicle mite *Demodex folliculorum.* This microscopic creature lives, mates and breeds in and around the eyelashes, the hair follicles of the outer nose folds and the chin and a few other restricted areas. *Demodex* inhabits the skin of most adult humans. The remaining cutaneous organisms are yeasts, bacteria and perhaps viruses. It is not easy to fit host-supported communities into Odum's metabolic groups, but the inhabitants of the skin can be regarded either as consumers that utilize cutaneous secretions or as decomposers of the by-products of keratin manufacture.

Among the residents of the healthy skin are several pathogenic species that live in an uneasy balance with the host. After a long period during which they remain harmless, a change of the internal or external cutaneous environment can upset the equilibrium; then these species multiply and penetrate the horny layer. A good example is the fungi that give rise to "athlete's foot." These fungi often inhabit the sole of the foot and the spaces between the toes without causing more than minimal changes in the skin. Then a change in the host environment—a move to the Tropics, a temporary failure of hygiene, a change in immunological status—will lead to proliferation of the fungi and the appearance of disease.

Only a few yeasts are represented in the normal skin flora. Some of them are partially or entirely dependent on lipids and grow most abundantly on the scalp and in greasy areas of the face, such as the folds of the nose and the ear. Less prevalent than these forms are a group of yeasts that grow between the toes but are never harmful.

The dominant members of the cutaneous community are bacteria. The types that are present can be divided into Gram-positive and Gram-negative organisms, according to their reaction to the Gram stain. This simple staining method, named for the Danish bacteriologist Hans Christian Joachim Gram, is most useful in bacteriology in that the two groups it distinguishes differ not only in chemical characteristics but also in physiology and in pathogenic properties. On healthy skin the Gram-positive bacteria predominate and are represented by two groups. One is the aerobic (oxygen-utilizing) cocci, whose cells are spherical; the other is the diphtheroids, whose rodlike shape varies among individual bacteria. Almost all the cocci are harmless, except in very special circumstances, but one species, *Staphylococcus aureus,* is the cause of pimples, boils and more serious infections (among them infections of the newborn and hospital wound infections).

Staphylococcus aureus has received much attention in recent years, primarily because of its capacity to acquire resistance to antibiotics. The chief domicile of this species is the nostrils. In many infants it is also found in the umbilicus and the abdominal skin; in the adults it colonizes the perineum (the region between the genitalia and the anus). Normally it does not cause pathological changes in the skin.

The diphtheroids can be divided into three ecological groups. One consists of the species *Corynebacterium acnes,* the "acne bacillus," which is anaerobic and lives in the depths of the hair follicle. The other diphtheroids are aerobic; they separate into two types, one requiring lipid nutrients and the other not requiring them.

On the skin of most people the Gram-negative strains of bacteria are also found. One group, the *Mimeae,* which includes potential pathogens, appears to be common on the feet of children and adult males but is seldom found on adult females.

It is impossible to say to what extent viruses inhabit the healthy skin, since their presence is difficult to recognize in the absence of damage to the host. Inasmuch as viruses are parasites on living cells and there are no living cells in the upper layer of skin, any cutaneous viruses would have to be living in deeper levels. On the other hand, the viruses that parasitize bacteria (bacteriophages) are present on the skin in significant numbers. For example, many strains of *Staphylococcus aureus* are known to be lysogenic, which is to say that they carry a virus partner whose genetic material is linked to their own. Recently Leopoldo F. Montes of the University of Alabama Medical Center has demonstrated that all stages of the bacteriophage life cycle are represented in one of the cutaneous diphtheroids. It is likely that bacteriophages also infect other species of cutaneous bacteria.

How densely populated is the human skin? The determination of the number of individuals of each kind per unit of area or volume is a major preoccupation of the classical ecologist, and this is perhaps the best-documented aspect of cutaneous ecology, at least so far as bacteria are concerned. As in other branches of ecology, however, it is difficult to secure consistent and reproducible observations, not least because several sampling methods are employed at the present time. In spite of the great variation in measurements, it is clear that people differ significantly in the density of the populations they support. These differences are maintained over considerable time intervals, so that some people consistently have a high bacterial count and others a low one. Such differences can also be demonstrated between the sparsely inhabited desert of the forearm, the more heavily populated tropical forest of the axilla and the cool dark woods of the scalp. It is generally agreed that the densest bacterial populations are found on the face and the neck and in the axilla and the groin; the trunk and the upper arms have much sparser populations. The microbial community on the sole of the foot and between the toes is large and diverse.

One of the most reliable sampling techniques has been perfected by workers at the University of Pennsylvania. Peter Williamson of this group has reported that in adult males the axilla is the most densely inhabited area, with a mean population of 2.41 million bacteria per square centimeter of epidermis. The mean counts for the scalp and the forehead were also high (respectively 1.46 million and 200,000 per square centimeter). In contrast, the counts taken

a

b

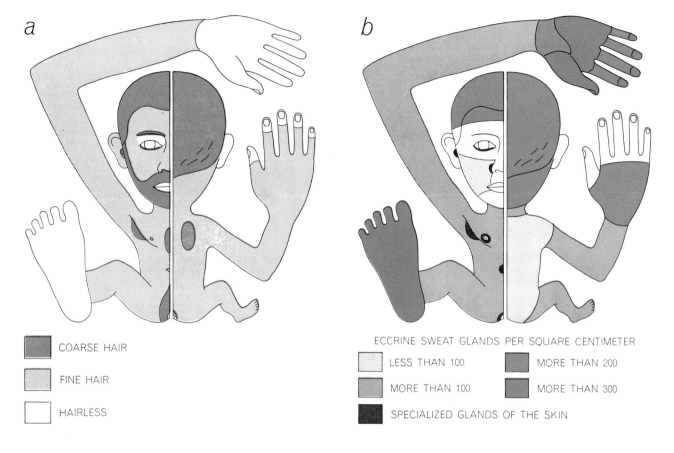

COARSE HAIR

FINE HAIR

HAIRLESS

ECCRINE SWEAT GLANDS PER SQUARE CENTIMETER

LESS THAN 100

MORE THAN 100

MORE THAN 200

MORE THAN 300

SPECIALIZED GLANDS OF THE SKIN

from the back averaged only 314 bacteria per square centimeter. The forearm counts divided into two groups, one with an average of 4,500 bacteria per square centimeter, the other with only 105 bacteria per square centimeter. These figures refer only to aerobic bacteria. There is evidence that in the areas of the skin supplied with large sebaceous glands anaerobic organisms may outnumber the aerobic ones 10 to one.

One cannot readily determine if these figures indicate that the skin is densely populated compared with other habitats. Should the cutaneous populations be compared with the microbial community of a small terrestrial area or with the medium-sized or larger organisms of bigger areas? Kitty Paviour-Smith of the University of Oxford has sampled the population of animal organisms other than protozoans in a salt meadow in New Zealand. She obtained a maximum figure of 7.6 million metazoans per square meter. The lowest count obtained by Williamson (for the forearm) works out to 1.05 million bacteria per square meter, making the forearm more sparsely populated than a salt meadow. On the other hand, the populations of the forehead and axilla are much larger (respectively two billion and 24.1 billion per square meter). It seems that there are many more aerobic bacteria on the salt

meadow of the skin than there are metazoans in a salt meadow in New Zealand.

The best terrestrial ecosystem for purposes of comparison with the skin is probably an ordinary soil. Both the soil and the skin lack producer organisms and obtain their organic material from without: the soil from above (in the form of dead plant material) and the skin from below. In both soil and skin there is an extensive nonliving matrix that is permeated by solutions, and the living organisms in both are grouped around structures that penetrate the surface to deeper layers. In the soil the densest populations of microorganisms are in the rhizosphere, the region that surrounds plant roots. The comparable region in the skin is the hair follicle.

There are many estimates of the number of bacteria and fungi in the soil; the figures fall (according to soil type) in the range of 10 million to 10 billion individual organisms per gram. There are few figures for bacteria per unit weight of skin, but the University of Pennsylvania workers report an average of 530,000 bacteria per milligram of scurf (the surface of the epidermis). This would indicate a count around 530 million per gram of scurf, a figure within the range for fertile soil. It would appear that at least some areas of the skin are as densely

populated with microorganisms as natural soils.

Numerous efforts have been made to determine how pathogenic staphylococci spread from one host to another. These investigations have been directed toward the control of cross infection in hospitals but have brought to light much that is relevant to the transfer of members of the normal flora. The acquisition of a cutaneous flora begins very early in life. An infant delivered by Cesarian section has no cutaneous inhabitants, but Imrich Sarkany of the Royal Free Hospital in London has shown that the skin of a baby born by the normal route carries a sparse population of cocci and diphtheroids derived from the mother's birth canal. The community is augmented soon after birth both directly by contact with adults and indirectly by aerial transmission.

This flora has distinctive characteristics. There is apparently a greater variety of potential pathogens on the skin of infants than there is on the skin of older individuals. Several harmless species not found in adults inhabit the skin of older children. This may be due, at least in part, to the fact that children come in contact with the soil more often than adults do. Many of the soil organisms, however, cannot survive in a cutaneous habitat, so that the juvenile skin flora

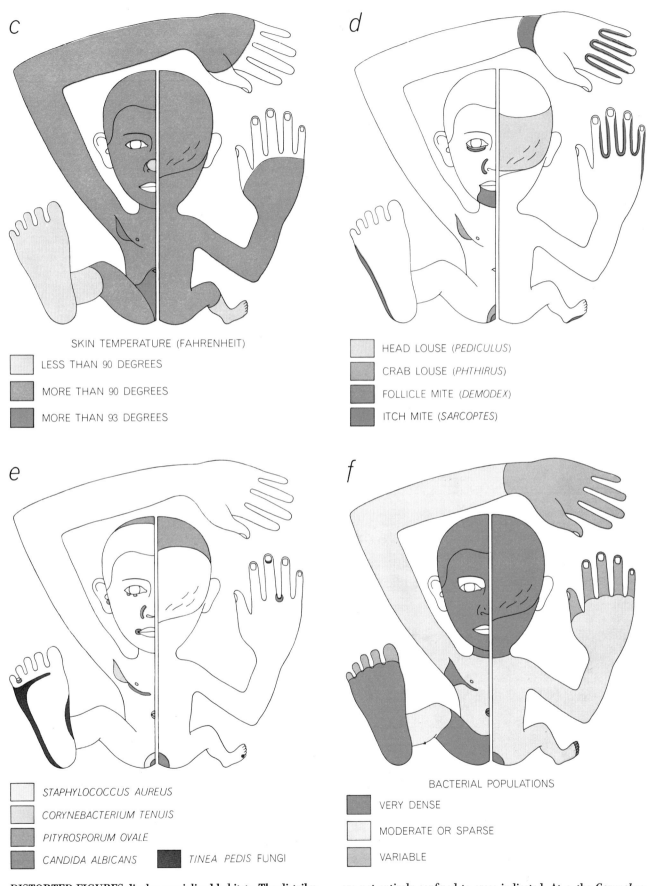

c

SKIN TEMPERATURE (FAHRENHEIT)

LESS THAN 90 DEGREES

MORE THAN 90 DEGREES

MORE THAN 93 DEGREES

d

HEAD LOUSE (*PEDICULUS*)

CRAB LOUSE (*PHTHIRUS*)

FOLLICLE MITE (*DEMODEX*)

ITCH MITE (*SARCOPTES*)

e

STAPHYLOCOCCUS AUREUS

CORYNEBACTERIUM TENUIS

PITYROSPORUM OVALE

CANDIDA ALBICANS

TINEA PEDIS FUNGI

f

BACTERIAL POPULATIONS

VERY DENSE

MODERATE OR SPARSE

VARIABLE

DISTORTED FIGURES display specialized habitats. The distribution of hair (*a*) is that of an adult male. Skin temperatures (*c*) are those of an adult at rest in an environment of 73 degrees Fahrenheit. Except for the follicle mite, the fauna (*d*) are pathogens; they are not entirely confined to areas indicated. At *e*, the *Corynebacterium tenuis* group forms nodules on hair; the yeast *Pityrosporum ovale* increases when dandruff is present; fungus *Candida albicans* causes infections. At *f*, only oxygen-utilizing bacteria are included.

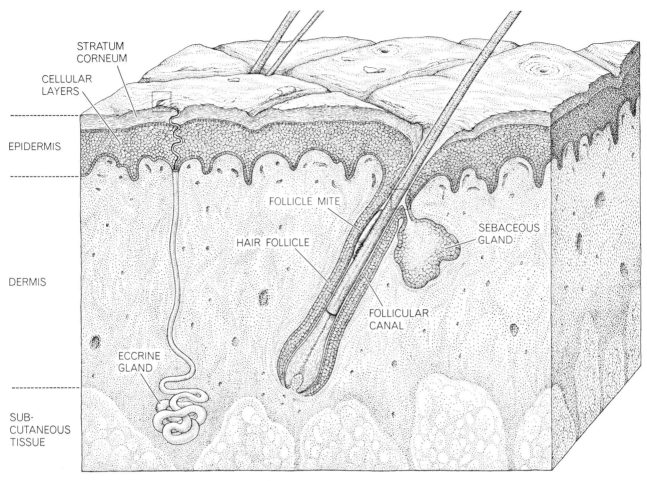

HABITAT OF NORMAL MICROORGANISMS is displayed in an idealized section. *Demodex folliculorum*, the follicle mite, is the only faunal form that resides in healthy, undamaged skin. Scarcely visible to the unaided eye, it is 400 times larger than an average bacterium. The squares indicate regions of the skin that appear below in an enlarged view. *Demodex* inhabits the skin of most adults.

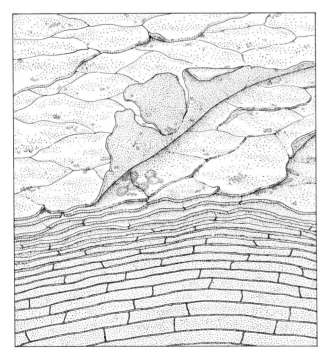

UPPER LAYER of the skin, the stratum corneum, consists of flat, scalelike "squames" that curl up and flake off. Lodged under and around the squames are bacteria and yeastlike cells of fungi (*color*).

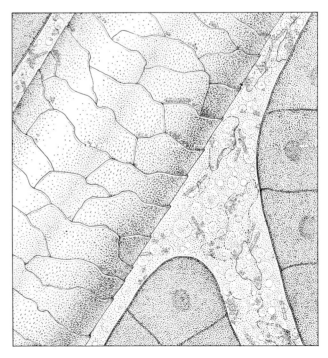

HAIR FOLLICLE houses many bacteria. The illustration at top of this page shows the skin enlarged 50 diameters. In this drawing and the one at left the skin is enlarged about 1,000 diameters.

does not mirror the flora of the larger environment. By the same token, most cutaneous organisms do not multiply in soil or dust, although some can survive for an appreciable time. It is for this reason that contact with other humans (and to a lesser extent with other mammals) is far more important in the transfer of cutaneous microorganisms than contact with an inanimate object, however dirty it is.

One might think that once the characteristic adult cutaneous community was established there would be no further exchange of inhabitants between individuals. It is here that our analogy of each individual as a discrete world breaks down. In man, if the pattern of staphylococcus can be regarded as a model, there is a constant transfer of microorganisms from one carrier to another, even when stringent preventive measures are taken.

R. R. Davies and W. C. Noble of St. John's Hospital for Diseases of the Skin in London have shown that staphylococci are transmitted on tiny "rafts" of skin shed from the body. The most satisfactory raft from the point of view of the coccus has a size somewhere in the range of 14 microns (.014 millimeter). Each raft can carry perhaps four viable microbial units. As the host moves about these fragments of skin are shed, and there is every reason to think that the flora is also shed and presumably is available to a new host. Thus the dispersal of microorganisms goes on almost constantly; even the gentle exercise involved in dressing and undressing is accompanied by the shedding of an appreciable number of bacteria-bearing rafts.

The term "raft" suggests a comparison with the way geographically isolated islands become populated. It is believed the atypical animal and plant populations of remote islands are partly the result of fortuitous transfer on natural rafts (a dead tree, say) that carry organisms across the water. A well-documented example of such transfer is provided by Krakatoa, the island in the East Indies that was sterilized by a huge volcanic explosion in 1883. Charles S. Elton of the University of Oxford states that in 1933, 50 years later, Krakatoa had been reclothed in jungle, and that at least 720 species of insects and more than 30 species of vertebrates (including nonflying forms) had managed to cross the 25 miles of water that separates the island from its nearest neighbor.

One might compare Krakatoa with a newborn infant, and indeed the success

| | | SKIN | | | | |
| | | EPIDERMIS | | | | |
	SKIN SURFACE	CORNIFIED LAYERS	CELLULAR LAYERS	DERMIS	HAIR FOLLICLE	ECCRINE SWEAT GLAND
RESIDENTS — USUALLY HARMLESS						
FOLLICLE MITE (*DEMODEX*)	●				●	
LIPOPHILIC YEASTS		●			●	
NONLIPOPHILIC YEASTS		●				
GRAM-POSITIVE COCCI		●				
AEROBIC DIPHTHEROIDS		●				
ACNE BACILLUS		●			●	
RESIDENTS — POTENTIAL PATHOGENS						
STAPHYLOCOCCUS AUREUS		●				
MIMA (HERELLEA)		●				
"COLD SORE" VIRUS			●			
FREQUENT VISITORS — USUALLY HARMLESS						
SOIL ORGANISMS	●					
GRAM-NEGATIVE BACILLI		●				
GRAM-POSITIVE COCCI						●
FREQUENT VISITORS — POTENTIAL PATHOGENS						
HUMAN LICE	●					
ITCH MITE (SCABIES)		●				
RINGWORM FUNGI		●			●	
PATHOGENIC YEASTS		●	●			
STAPHYLOCOCCUS AUREUS					●	●
STREPTOCOCCI		●	●	●		
WART VIRUS			●			

SKIN INHABITANTS that are relatively plentiful in the upper cornified (horny) layers of the epidermis diminish in number in the deeper layers. Pathogenic streptococci and yeasts may pass through a breach in the skin to reach the dermis and the deeper tissues.

of some pathogens in establishing themselves in an infant host may be the result of their being the first to arrive. The infant, however, is exposed to many organisms other than the ones carried on aerial rafts; sooner or later he makes direct contact with well-colonized relatives and friends. Since it is now possible to rear germ-free animals from birth in special chambers, it would be interesting to expose such an animal to aerial inoculation only and then observe what kind of skin flora it develops. So far as I am aware this experiment has not been undertaken.

Microorganisms depart from the host, then, by air and by contact. What happens when such an organism arrives at a fully colonized individual? Elton has shown that the newcomer is most successful where there is an ecological niche that is not exploited by an indigenous inhabitant, and that invasion into an established and complex community is very difficult. An example is afforded by the surprising number of birds that have succeeded in colonizing New Zealand during the past 100 years. There seems to be no doubt that this has been made possible by catastrophic changes in the ecosystem of the region that have resulted from its invasion by Europeans. New niches have been opened up for the colonizers, perhaps including niches vacated by the former fauna.

In considering the ecological niches of the skin we are again obliged to speak in terms of pathogens, since so little is known about the activities of the harmless species. There is evidence that, as in the classic ecological situation, the invader can establish itself less readily when there is competition with a resident flora. Thus attempts to control staphylococcus cross infection by treating carriers with antibiotics have not been very successful because a resistant strain is likely to replace the original inhabitants of the nostrils. On the other hand, Henry R. Shinefield and his colleagues at the University of California School of Medicine have had considerable success in controlling infection in maternity wards. The infants and those with whom they had contact were inoculated with a staphylococcus of low virulence, so that strains of greater virulence would have to compete with a resident for the habitat.

The nostril habitat of staphylococci is a rather special one, but the situation probably is much the same on the "outer" surface of the skin. Although pathogenic organisms constantly alight on the skin, they find it a most unfavorable environment and in the absence of injury have great difficulty colonizing it. This "self-sterilizing" capacity of the skin does not, as the term suggests, seem to be an attribute of the skin itself. Rather it is the characteristic displayed by all well-developed ecosystems, namely that all influences tend to maintain the status quo.

This homeostasis is clearly evident in the ecosystem of the skin, and we know something—albeit not a great deal—about the processes involved. The skin is an unfavorable habitat for the vast majority of microorganisms because it is extremely rare for species whose headquarters are in the soil, the water and elsewhere in our surroundings to multiply on the skin surface. Provided that it is undamaged, the skin is also unfavorable for exploitation by most human pathogens. There are a variety of reasons for this. The skin is too acid for some species. (This "acid mantle" was once regarded as a major protective feature, but there is now good evidence that many pathogens that fail to establish themselves are not inhibited by it.) There seems to be little doubt that much of the skin is too arid for colonization by some species. The constant shedding of the surface skin layers is another process that hinders the establishment of invaders. From the ecological standpoint, however, the most interesting defense mechanism is one that results from the metabolic activities of the resident flora. It has been known for some years that unsaturated fatty acids are an important component of sebum collected from the skin surface, and that they inhibit the growth of several bacterial and fungal cutaneous pathogens. More recently it has been shown that these substances are a metabolic product of the Gram-positive members of the cutaneous community, which break down (by means of specific enzymes) the more complex lipids in freshly secreted sebum.

This activity of the Gram-positive species helps to protect the skin from invasion by potential pathogens. The Gram-positive species also (but not necessarily by the same means) exert a restrictive effect on the population growth of Gram-negative organisms. In the healthy axilla Gram-positive species predominate but small numbers of Gram-negative organisms are also present. If a deodorant that contains an antibiotic with a selective action against the Gram-positive species is regularly applied, the cutaneous population gradually changes to a Gram-negative one of approximately the original density. Withdrawal of the deodorant is followed by a return to a predominantly Gram-positive flora. It would seem that some attribute of the cocci and diphtheroids in the axilla is a limiting factor for Gram-negative organisms. The fact that the axillary odor is absent while the Gram-negative bacteria are dominant also indicates that it is the metabolic by-products of the Gram-positive species that confer this odor on us.

It is clear that a complex and fascinating community maintains itself on the surface of each one of us. Perhaps it is not amiss to suggest that we might profit from considering our own importance to the inhabitants of that ecosystem. When one feels about to be overwhelmed by the "acts of God" and man-inspired catastrophes that threaten and afflict us, one might take comfort in the thought that some action of which one is scarcely aware is a cataclysm in the cutaneous world.

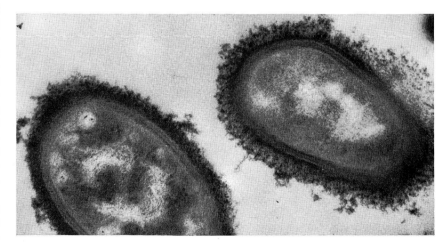

TWO SKIN BACTERIA are diphtheroids, a group common on healthy skin. This electron micrograph of *Corynebacterium minutissimum* was made by Leopoldo F. Montes of the University of Alabama Medical Center. The magnification is about 40,000 diameters.

BIBLIOGRAPHIES

I THE EVOLUTIONARY PROCESS

1. Genetic Load

OUR LOAD OF MUTATION. H. J. Muller in *The American Journal of Human Genetics*, Vol. 2, No. 2, pages 111–176; June, 1950.

A MOLECULAR APPROACH TO THE STUDY OF GENIC HETEROZYGOSITY IN NATURAL POPULATIONS. J. L. Hubby and R. C. Lewontin in *Genetics*, Vol. 54, No. 2, pages 577–609; August, 1966.

THE FATE OF X-RAY INDUCED CHROMOSOMAL REARRANGEMENTS INTRODUCED INTO LABORATORY POPULATIONS OF *Drosophila melanogaster*. Edwin Vann in *The American Naturalist*, Vol. 100, No. 914, pages 425–449; September–October, 1966.

THREE KINDS OF GENETIC VARIABILITY IN YEAST POPULATIONS. Christopher Wills in *Proceedings of the National Academy of Sciences of the United States of America*, Vol. 61, No. 3, pages 937–944; November, 1968.

2. Sickle Cells and Evolution

SICKLE-CELL ANEMIA. George W. Gray in *Scientific American*, Vol. 185, No. 2, pages 56–59; August, 1951.

PROTECTION AFFORDED BY SICKLE-CELL TRAITS AGAINST SUBTERTIAN MALARIAL INFECTION. A. C. Allison in *British Medical Journal*, Vol. 1, pages 290–301; February 1954.

3. 'Genetic Drift' in an Italian Population

FREQUENCIES OF PEDIGREES OF CONSANGUINEOUS MARRIAGES AND MATING STRUCTURE OF THE POPULATION. I. Barrai, L. L. Cavalli-Sforza and A. Moroni in *Annals of Human Genetics*, Vol. 25, Part 4, pages 347–377; May, 1962.

THE PROBABILITY OF CONSANGUINEOUS MARRIAGES. L. L. Cavalli-Sforza, M. Kimura and I. Barrai in *Genetics*, Vol. 54, No. 1, Part 1, pages 37–60; July, 1966.

EXPERIMENTS WITH AN ARTIFICIAL POPULATION. L. L. Cavalli-Sforza and G. Zei in *Proceedings of the International Congress of Human Genetics*, edited by James F. Crow and James V. Neel. The Johns Hopkins Press, 1967.

4. The Structure and History of an Ancient Protein

THE STRUCTURE AND ACTION OF PROTEINS. Richard E. Dickerson and Irving Geis. Harper & Row, Publishers, 1969.

THE STRUCTURE OF CYTOCHROME c AND THE RATES OF MOLECULAR EVOLUTION. Richard E. Dickerson in *Journal of Molecular Evolution*, Vol. 1, No. 1, pages 26–45; 1971.

FERRICYTOCHROME c: I, GENERAL FEATURES OF THE HORSE AND BONITO PROTEINS AT 2.8 Å RESOLUTION. Richard E. Dickerson, Tsunehiro Takano, David Eisenberg, Olga B. Kallai, Lalli Samson, Angela Cooper and E. Margoliash in *The Journal of Biological Chemistry*, Vol. 246, No. 5, pages 1511–1535; March 10, 1971.

CONFORMATIONAL CHANGES UPON REDUCTION OF CYTOCHROME c. T. Takano, R. Swanson, O. B. Kallai and R. E. Dickerson in *Cold Spring Harbor Symposium on Quantitative Biology*, in press.

5. The Social Order of Turkeys

THE GENETICAL EVOLUTION OF SOCIAL BEHAVIOUR: I. W. D. Hamilton in *Journal of Theoretical Biology*, Vol. 7, No. 1, pages 1–16; July, 1964.

THE ADAPTIVE SIGNIFICANCE OF AVIAN SOCIAL ORGANIZATIONS. John Hurrell Crook in *Symposia of the Zoological Society of London, No. 14: Social Organization of Animal Communities*. Zoological Society of London, April, 1965.

ECOLOGICAL ADAPTATIONS FOR BREEDING IN BIRDS. David Lack. Barnes & Noble, 1968.

II THE MULTIPLICATION AND DISPERSAL OF SPECIES

6. Darwin's Finches

DARWIN'S FINCHES. David Lack. Cambridge University Press, 1947.

SYSTEMATICS AND THE ORIGIN OF SPECIES. Ernst Mayr. Columbia University Press, 1942.

7. The Desert Pupfish

THE CYPRINODONT FISHES OF THE DEATH VALLEY SYSTEM OF EASTERN CALIFORNIA AND SOUTHWESTERN NEVADA. R. R. Miller. Museum of Zoology, University of Michigan, 1948.

SPECIATION IN FISHES OF THE GENERA Cyprinodon AND Empetrichthys, INHABITING THE DEATH VALLEY REGION. Robert Rush Miller in Evolution, Vol. 4, No. 2, pages 155–163; June, 1950.

EVOLUTION IN CONSTANT AND FLUCTUATING ENVIRONMENTS: THERMAL TOLERANCES OF DESERT PUPFISH (Cyprinodon). James H. Brown and C. Robert Feldmeth in Evolution, Vol. 25, No. 2, pages 390–398; June, 1971.

8. The Geography of Birds

THE GEOGRAPHIC DISTRIBUTION OF ANIMALS. A. R. Wallace. Macmillan and Co., 1876.

SYSTEMATICS AND THE ORIGINS OF SPECIES. Ernst Mayr. Columbia University Press, 1942.

9. Continental Drift and the Fossil Record

THE ORIGIN OF CONTINENTS AND OCEANS. Alfred L. Wegener. Methuen, 1966.

THE BEARING OF CERTAIN PALAEOZOOGEOGRAPHIC DATA OF CONTINENTAL DRIFT. Anthony Hallam in Palaeogeography Palaeoclimatology Palaeoecology, Vol. 3, pages 201–241; 1967.

CONTINENTAL DRIFT AND THE EVOLUTION OF THE BIOTA ON SOUTHERN CONTINENTS. Allen Keast in The Quarterly Review of Biology, Vol. 46, No. 4, pages 335–378; December, 1971.

ATLAS OF PALAEOBIOGEOGRAPHY. Edited by Anthony Hallam. American Elsevier Publishing Co., in press.

10. Continental Drift and Evolution

VERTEBRATE PALEONTOLOGY. Alfred Sherwood Romer. The University of Chicago Press, 1966.

THE AGE OF THE DINOSAURS. Björn Kurtén. World University Library, 1968.

III THE GROWTH AND INTERACTION OF POPULATIONS

11. The Probability of Death

LENGTH OF LIFE. Louis I. Dublin, Alfred J. Lotka and Mortimer Spiegelman. The Ronald Press Company, 1949.

LIFE TABLES FOR NATURAL POPULATIONS OF ANIMALS. Edward S. Deevey, Jr., in Quarterly Review of Biology, Vol. 22, pages 283–314; 1947.

12. Population Density and Social Pathology

THE HUMAN POPULATION. Edward S. Deevey, Jr., in Scientific American, Vol. 203, No. 3, pages 194–204; September, 1960.

A METHOD FOR SELF-CONTROL OF POPULATION GROWTH AMONG MAMMALS LIVING IN THE WILD. John B. Calhoun in Science, Vol. 109, No. 2831, pages 333–335; April 1, 1949.

POPULATIONS OF HOUSE MICE. Robert L. Strecker in Scientific American, Vol. 193, No. 6, pages 92–100; December, 1955.

THE SOCIAL ASPECTS OF POPULATION DYNAMICS. John B. Calhoun in Journal of Mammalogy, Vol. 33, No. 2, pages 139–159; May, 1952.

SOCIAL WELFARE AS A VARIABLE IN POPULATION DYNAMICS. John B. Calhoun in Cold Spring Harbor Symposia on Quantitative Biology, Vol. 22, pages 339–356; 1957.

13. The Aerial Migration of Insects

THE DISTRIBUTION OF INSECTS IN THE AIR AND THE EMPIRICAL RELATION OF DENSITY TO HEIGHT. C. G. Johnson in The Journal of Animal Ecology, Vol. 26, pages 479–494; 1957.

INSECT MIGRATION. C. B. Williams. N. N. Collins, 1958.

PHYSIOLOGICAL FACTORS IN INSECT MIGRATION BY FLIGHT. C. G. Johnson in Nature, Vol. 198, No. 4879, pages 423–427; May 4, 1963.

WEATHER AND THE MOVEMENTS OF LOCUST SWARMS: A NEW HYPOTHESIS. R. C. Rainey in Nature, Vol. 168, No. 4286, pages 1057–1060; December 22, 1951.

14. Population Control in Animals

ANIMAL DISPERSION IN RELATION TO SOCIAL BEHAVIOUR. V. C. Wynne-Edwards. Hafner Publishing Company, 1962.

THE LIFE OF VERTEBRATES. John Z. Young. Oxford University Press, 1950.

THE NATURAL REGULATION OF ANIMAL NUMBERS. David Lack. Oxford University Press, 1954.

15. Butterflies and Plants

BIRDS, BUTTERFLIES, AND PLANT POISONS: A STUDY IN ECOLOGICAL CHEMISTRY. Lincoln Pierson Brower and Jane Van Zandt Brower in *Zoologica*, Vol. 49, No. 3, pages 137–159; 1964.

BUTTERFLIES AND PLANTS: A STUDY IN COEVOLUTION. Paul R. Ehrlich and Peter H. Raven in *Evolution*, Vol. 18, No. 4, pages 586–608; January 28, 1965.

COEVOLUTION OF MUTUALISM BETWEEN ANTS AND ACACIAS IN CENTRAL AMERICA. Daniel H. Janzen in *Evolution*, Vol. 20, No. 3, pages 249–275; 1966.

16. Weed Control by Insect

ESTABLISHMENT OF A ROOT BORER AND A GALL FLY FOR CONTROL OF KLAMATH WEED. J. K. Holloway and C. B. Huffaker in *Journal of Economic Entomology*, Vol. 46, No. 1, pages 65–67; February, 1953.

INSECTS TO CONTROL A WEED. James K. Holloway, C. B. Huffaker in *Insects: The Yearbook of Agriculture, 1952*. United States Department of Agriculture, 1952.

THE ROLE OF CHRYSOLINA GEMELLATA IN THE BIOLOGICAL CONTROL OF KLAMATH WEED. J. K. Holloway and C. B. Huffaker in *Journal of Economic Entomology*, Vol. 44, No. 2, pages 244–247; April, 1951.

17. Desert Ground Squirrels

THE COMPETITIVE EXCLUSION PRINCIPLE. Garrett Hardin in *Science*, Vol. 131, No. 3409, pages 1292–1297; April 29, 1960.

EFFECTS OF SODIUM CHLORIDE ON WEIGHT AND DRINKING IN THE ANTELOPE GROUND SQUIRREL. George A. Bartholomew and Jack W. Hudson in *Journal of Mammalogy*, Vol. 40, No. 3, pages 354–360; August 20, 1959.

HEAT REGULATION IN SOME ARCTIC AND TROPICAL MAMMALS AND BIRDS. P. F. Scholander, Raymond Hock, Vladimir Walters, Fred Johnson and Laurence Irving in *The Biological Bulletin*, Vol. 99, No. 2, pages 237–258; October, 1950.

HIBERNATION. Charles P. Lyman and Paul O. Chatfield in *Scientific American*, Vol. 183, No. 6, pages 18–21; December, 1950.

WATER METABOLISM OF DESERT MAMMALS. Knut Schmidt-Nielsen and Bodil Schmidt-Nielsen in *Physiological Reviews*, Vol. 32, No. 2, pages 135–166; April, 1952.

18. Ecological Chemistry

PLANT POISONS IN A TERRESTRIAL FOOD CHAIN. Lincoln P. Brower, Jane Van Zandt Brower and Joseph M. Corvino in *Proceedings of the National Academy of Sciences*, Vol. 57, No. 4, pages 893–898; April 15, 1967.

ECOLOGICAL CHEMISTRY AND THE PALATABILITY SPECTRUM. Lincoln P. Brower, William N. Ryerson, Lorna L. Coppinger and Susan C. Glazier in *Science*, Vol. 161, No. 3848, pages 1349–1350; September 27, 1968.

19. Cleaning Symbiosis

ECOLOGICAL ANIMAL GEOGRAPHY. Richard Hesse, W. C. Allee and Karl P. Schmidt. John Wiley & Sons, Inc., 1951. Page 84.

EXAMPLES OF MIMICRY AND PROTECTIVE RESEMBLANCE IN TROPICAL MARINE FISHES. John E. Randall and Helen A. Randall in *Bulletin of Marine Science of the Gulf and Caribbean*, Vol. 10, No. 4, pages 444–480; December, 1960.

FISH LIFE IN THE KELP BEDS AND THE EFFECTS OF KELP HARVESTING ON FISH. Conrad Limbaugh. University of California Institute of Marine Resources, Report 55–9, pages 1–158; September, 1955.

GALÁPAGOS: WORLD'S END. William Beebe, G. P. Putnam's Sons, 1924. Pages 121–122.

A REVIEW OF THE LABRID FISH GENUS LABROIDES, WITH DESCRIPTIONS OF TWO NEW SPECIES AND NOTES ON ECOLOGY. John E. Randall in *Pacific Science*, Vol. 12, No. 4, pages 327–347; October, 1958.

SYSTEMATIC CATALOGUE OF THE FISHES OF TORTUGAS, FLORIDA. William H. Longley and Samuel E. Hildebrand. Carnegie Institute of Washington, Publication 535; 1941.

20. The Fungus Gardens of Insects

AMBROSIA FUNGI: EXTENT OF SPECIFICITY TO AMBROSIA BEETLES. Lekh R. Batra in *Science*, Vol. 153, No. 3732, pages 193–195; July 8, 1966.

FUNGUS-GROWING ANTS. Neal A. Weber in *Science*, Vol. 153, No. 3736, pages 587–604; August 5, 1966.

SYMBIOSIS AND SIRICID WOODWASPS. E. A. Parkin in *Annals of Applied Biology*, Vol. 29, No. 4, pages 268–274; August, 1942.

TERMITES: THEIR RECOGNITION AND CONTROL. W. Victor Harris. Longmans, Green and Co. Ltd., 1961.

TRAILS OF THE LEAFCUTTERS. John C. Moser in *Natural History*, Vol. 76, No. 1, pages 32–35; January, 1967.

21. Symbiosis and Evolution

THE PLASTIDS: THEIR CHEMISTRY, STRUCTURE, GROWTH AND INHERITANCE. John T. O. Kirk and Richard A. E. Tilney-Bassett. W. H. Freeman and Company, 1967.

THE BIOGENESIS OF MITOCHONDRIA. D. B. Roodyn and D. Wilkie. Methuen & Co. Ltd, 1968.

THE MICROBAL WORLD. Roger Y. Stanier, Michael Doudoroff and Edward A. Adelberg. Prentice-Hall, Inc., 1970.

ORIGIN OF EUKARYOTIC CELLS. Lynn Margulis. Yale University Press, 1970.

THE OLDEST FOSSILS. Elso S. Barghoorn in *Scientific American*, Vol. 224, No. 5, pages 30–42; May, 1971.

IV ECOSYSTEMS

22. The Biosphere

LA BIOSPHÈRE. W. Vernadsky. Libraire Fèlix Alcan, 1929.

THE ECOLOGICAL THEORY AND THE EVOLUTIONARY PLAY. G. Evelyn Hutchinson. Yale University Press, 1965.

ORIGIN OF EUKARYOTUC CELLS: EVIDENCE AND REASEARCH IMPLICATIONS FOR A THEORY OF THE ORIGIN AND EVOLUTION OF MICROBIAL, PLANT, AND ANIMAL CELLS ON THE PRECAMBRIAN EARTH. Lynn Margulis. Yale University Press, in press.

23. The Energy Cycle of the Biosphere

FUNDAMENTALS OF ECOLOGY. Eugene P. Odum and Howard T. Odum. W. B. Saunders Company, 1959.

ECOLOGICAL ENERGETICS. John Phillipson. St. Martin's Press, 1966.

TRACE ELEMENTS IN BIOCHEMISTRY. H. J. M. Bowen. Academic Press, 1966.

PRIMARY PRODUCTION IN TERRESTRIAL ECOSYSTEMS. George M. Woodwell and Robert H. Whittaker in American Zoologist, Vol. 8, No. 1, pages 19–30; February, 1968.

COMMUNITIES AND ECOSYSTEMS. R. H. Whittaker. The Macmillan Company, 1970.

24. The Human Crop

FUNDAMENTALS OF ECOLOGY. Eugene Odum. W. B. Saunders Company, 1955.

A HISTORY OF TECHNOLOGY: FROM EARLY TIMES TO THE FALL OF ANCIENT EMPIRES. Edited by Charles Singer, E. J. Holmyard and A. R. Hall. Oxford University Press, 1954.

PRIMITIVE SOCIETY AND ITS VITAL STATISTICS. L. Krzywicki. Macmillan & Co., Ltd., 1934.

25. The Carbon Cycle

GEOGRAPHIC VARIATIONS IN PRODUCTIVITY. J. H. Ryther in The Sea: Ideas and Observations on Progress in the Study of the Seas. Vol. II: The Composition of Sea-Water—Comparative and Descriptive Oceanography, edited by M. N. Hill. Interscience Publishers, 1963.

THE INFLUENCE OF ORGANISMS ON THE COMPOSITION OF SEA-WATER. A. C. Redfield, B. H. Ketchum and F. A. Richards in The Sea: Ideas and Observations on Progress in the Study of the Seas. Vol. II: The Composition of Sea-Water—Comparative and Descriptive Oceanography, edited by M. N. Hill. Interscience Publishers, 1963.

THE ROLE OF VEGETATION IN THE CARBON DIOXIDE CONTENT OF THE ATMOSPHERE. Helmut Lieth in Journal of Geophysical Research, Vol. 68, No. 13, pages 3887–3898; July 1, 1963.

GROSS-ATMOSPHERIC CIRCULATION AS DEDUCED FROM RADIOACTIVE TRACERS. Bert Bolin in Research in Geophysics, Vol. II: Solid Earth and Interface Phenomena, edited by Hugh Odishaw. The M.I.T. Press, 1964.

IS CARBON DIOXIDE FROM FOSSIL FUEL CHANGING MAN'S ENVIRONMENT? Charles D. Keeling in Proceedings of the American Philosophical Society, Vol. 114, No. 1, pages 10–17; February 16, 1970.

PHOTOSYNTHESIS. E. Rabinowitch and Govindjee. John Wiley & Sons, Inc., 1969.

26. The Nitrogen Cycle

AUTOTROPHIC MICRO-ORGANISMS: FOURTH SYMPOSIUM OF THE SOCIETY FOR GENERAL MICROBIOLOGY HELD AT THE INSTITUTION OF ELECTRICAL ENGINEERS, LONDON, APRIL, 1954. Cambridge University Press, 1954.

DENITRIFICATION. C. C. Delwiche in A Symposium on Inorganic Nitrogen Metabolism: Function of Metallo-Flavoproteins, edited by William D. McElroy and Bentley Glass. The Johns Hopkins Press, 1956.

NITROGEN FIXATION IN PLANTS. W. D. P. Stewart. Athlone Press, 1966.

SYMBIOSIS: ITS PHYSIOLOGICAL AND BIOCHEMICAL SIGNIFICANCE. Edited by S. Mark Henry. Academic Press, 1966.

FIXATION OF NITROGEN BY HIGHER PLANTS OTHER THAN LEGUMES. G. Bond in Annual Review of Plant Physiology: Vol. XXVIII, edited by Leonard Machlis, Winslow R. Briggs and Roderic B. Park. Annual Reviews, Inc., 1967.

27. The Nature of Oceanic Life

THE OPEN SEA: THE WORLD OF PLANKTON. Alister C. Hardy. Houghton Mifflin Company, 1957.

THE OPEN SEA: FISH AND FISHERIES. Alister C. Hardy. Houghton Mifflin Company, 1959.

OCEANS: AN ATLAS-HISTORY OF MAN'S EXPLORATION OF THE DEEP. Edited by G. E. R. Deacon. Paul Hamlyn, 1962.

BIOLOGY OF SUSPENSION FEEDING. C. B. Jorgensen. Pergamon Press, 1966.

28. Trace-Element Deserts

THE DIAGNOSIS OF MINERAL DEFICIENCIES IN PLANTS BY VISUAL SYMPTOMS. T. Wallace. Chemical Publishing Company, 1953.

MECHANISM OF ACTION OF MICRONUTRIENT ELEMENTS IN ENZYME SYSTEMS. W. D. McElroy and A. Nason in Annual Review of Plant Physiology, Vol. 5, pages 1–30; 1954.

MICRONUTRIENTS IN CROP VIGOR. Perry R. Stout in Journal of Agricultural and Food Chemistry, Vol. 4, No. 12, pages 1,000–1,006; December, 1956.

TRACE ELEMENTS IN HUMAN AND ANIMAL NUTRITION. E. J. Underwood. Academic Press, Inc., 1956.

29. The Nutrient Cycles of an Ecosystem

NUTRIENT CYCLING. F. H. Bormann and G. E. Likens in Science, Vol. 155, No. 3761, pages 424–429; January 27, 1967.

FOREST TRANSPIRATION REDUCTION BY CLEARCUTTING AND CHEMICAL TREATMENT. Robert S. Pierce in *Proceedings of the Northeastern Weed Control Conference*, Vol. 23, pages 344–349; 1969.

EFFECTS OF FOREST CUTTING AND HERBICIDE TREATMENT ON NUTRIENT BUDGETS IN THE HUBBARD BROOK WATERSHED-ECOSYSTEM. Gene E. Likens, F. Herbert Bormann, Noye M. Johnson, D. W. Fisher and Robert S. Pierce in *Ecological Monographs*, Vol. 40, No. 1, pages 23–47; Winter, 1970.

30. Toxic Substances and Ecological Cycles

ENVIRONMENTAL RADIOACTIVITY. Merril Eisenbud. McGraw-Hill Book Company, Inc., 1963.

PESTICIDES AND THE LIVING LANDSCAPE. Robert L. Rudd. University of Wisconsin Press, 1964.

REPORT OF THE UNITED NATIONS SCIENTIFIC COMMITTEE ON THE EFFECTS OF ATOMIC RADIATION. Official Records of the General Assembly, 13th Session, Supplement No. 17, 1958; 17th Session, Supplement No. 16, 1962; 19th Session, Supplement No. 14, 1964.

31. Bogs

CARBON DIOXIDE EXCHANGE BETWEEN ATMOSPHERE AND OCEAN AND THE QUESTION OF AN INCREASE OF ATMOSPHERIC CO_2 DURING THE PAST DECADES. R. Revelle and H. E. Suess in *Tellus*, Vol. 9, No. 1, pages 18–27; February, 1957.

MOUTAINS AND MOORLANDS. W. H. Pearsall. Collins, 1950.

RADIOCARBON DATING AND POST-GLACIAL VEGETATIONAL HISTORY. H. Godwin, D. Walker and E. H. Willis in *Proceedings of the Royal Society*, Vol. 147, No. 928, pages 352–366; December 3, 1957.

32. The Ecology of Fire

CHANGES IN VEGETATION, STRUCTURE AND GROWTH OF SOUTHWESTERN PINE FORESTS SINCE WHITE SETTLEMENT. Charles F. Cooper in *Ecological Monographs*, Vol. 30, No. 2, pages 129–164; April, 1960.

THE DESERT GRASSLAND: A HISTORY OF VEGETATIONAL CHANGE AND AN ANALYSIS OF CAUSES. Robert R. Humphrey in *The Botanical Review*, Vol. 24, No. 4, pages 193–252; April, 1958.

FIRE AS THE FIRST GREAT FORCE EMPLOYED BY MAN. Omer C. Stewart in *Man's Role in Changing the Face of the Earth*, edited by William L. Thomas, Jr., pages 115–133. University of Chicago Press, 1956.

33. The Life of a Sand Dune

ANIMAL LIFE IN DESERTS. Patrick A. Buxton. St. Martin's Press, 1955.

DEMONS OF THE DUST. William Morton Wheeler. W. W. Norton & Company, Inc., 1930.

THE PHYSICS OF BLOWN SAND AND DESERT DUNES. R. A. Bagnold. Methuen & Co. Ltd., 1941.

34. Life on the Human Skin

THE ECOLOGY OF INVASIONS BY ANIMALS AND PLANTS. Charles S. Elton. John Wiley & Sons, Inc., 1958.

THE ECOLOGY OF THE HUMAN SKIN. Mary J. Marples. Charles C. Thomas Publisher, 1965.

SKIN BACTERIA AND THEIR ROLE IN INFECTION. Edited by Howard I. Maibach and Gavin Hildick-Smith. McGraw-Hill Book Company, 1965.

INDEX

Italicized page numbers indicate figures.